I0868588

Achieving the Arbitration Dream

Achieving the Arbitration Dream

Liber Amicorum for Professor Julian D.M. Lew KC

Edited by

Stavros Brekoulakis
Romesh Weeramantry
Lilit Nagapetyan

Wolters Kluwer

Published by:
Kluwer Law International B.V.
PO Box 316
2400 AH Alphen aan den Rijn
The Netherlands
E-mail: lrs-sales@wolterskluwer.com
Website: www.wolterskluwer.com/en/solutions/kluwerlawinternational

Sold and distributed by:
Wolters Kluwer Legal & Regulatory U.S.
920 Links Avenue
Landisville, PA 17538
United States of America
E-mail: customer.service@wolterskluwer.com

ISBN 978-94-035-4906-4

e-Book: ISBN 978-94-035-4916-3
web-PDF: ISBN 978-94-035-4926-2

© 2023 Kluwer Law International BV, The Netherlands

All rights reserved. No part of this publication may be reproduced, stored in a retrieval system, or transmitted in any form or by any means, electronic, mechanical, photocopying, recording, or otherwise, without written permission from the publisher.

Permission to use this content must be obtained from the copyright owner. More information can be found at: www.wolterskluwer.com/en/solutions/legal-regulatory/permissions-reprints-and-licensing

Editors

Prof. Stavros Brekoulakis is a Professor of International Arbitration at Queen Mary University of London; Brekoulakis also practises as an arbitrator at a leading commercial Chambers 3 Verulam Buildings (Gray's Inn) having been appointed as arbitrator in more than 80 commercial and investment arbitrations. Stavros is widely recognized as a leading authority in the field of international law and arbitration and has been invited to give the prestigious *Summer Course on Private International Law* at the Hague Academy of International Law in 2026. He is the author of eight monographs, books and edited volumes and more than 30 articles in leading peer-reviewed law journals. Stavros has led important policy projects and advised governmental, intergovernmental, and non-governmental organizations, Co-Chair of the International Council of Commercial Arbitration Task Force on Third Party Funding, he co-authored the leading report on Third Party Funding in International Arbitration which has informed the regulatory policy of several international arbitration institutions and national legislation, including as a member of the London Bar Reform Committee, a member of the Steering Committee of the UNCITRAL Academic Forum on Investor-State Dispute Settlement, a member of the *Investment Expert Trade Advisory Group of the UK Department for International Trade*. He holding several public positions including being a member of the Governing body of the *International Council of Commercial Arbitration*, Court of the *LCIA Arbitration* and ICC *Commission on Arbitration*. He is the Editor-in-Chief of the *International Journal of Arbitration, Mediation and Dispute Management*; the General Editor of the *Journal of International Dispute Settlement*; the Co-editor of Kluwer's *International Arbitration Law Library Series*; a member of the Editorial Board of the *Arbitration International*; the *International Chamber of Commerce Bulletin on International Arbitration*; and the *Arab Yearbook of Public & Private International Law*.

Dr Romesh Weeramantry is Special Counsel at Clifford Chance, specializing in investment treaty disputes and international commercial arbitrations. He is currently a Senior Fellow at the University of Melbourne Law School and a Global Fellow at the Centre for International Law (CIL), National University of Singapore (NUS). While at

Clifford Chance, he was also the Head of International Dispute Resolution team at CIL (2018-2022) and a full Adjunct Professor at NUS Faculty of Law. Prior to that he was an Associate Professor of Law at the City University of Hong Kong, an Associate Adjunct Professor at the Faculty of Law, University of Hong Kong, a Legal Officer at the United Nations Compensation Commission (Geneva) and a Legal Advisor to the President of the Iran-United States Claims Tribunal (The Hague). He is the author of two books, over 35 articles and is the general editor of three major arbitration publications.

Lilit Nagapetyan ACA CFE is a dispute resolution lawyer and a doctoral student of prof. Julian Lew KC and prof. Stavros Brekoulakis. In her practice she focuses on international commercial arbitration, as well as complex cross-border disputes and enforcement proceedings. She is also a Teaching Fellow at Queen Mary University of London (School of International Arbitration) where she pursues her PhD. She has previously practised in London as a forensic accountant with a top-10 accounting firm where she has been involved in a wide range of litigation and arbitration disputes, as well as EC and CMA Monitoring Trustee mandates.

Contributors

Prof. Mohamed S. Abdel Wahab, Professor of International Arbitration, Private International Law and English Contract Law at Cairo University; founding partner and Head of International Arbitration, Construction and Energy Groups at Zulficar & Partners Law Firm (Egypt); ICCA Treasurer & Member of the Governing Board; Dean of the Africa Arbitration Academy; Chair of the International Expert Committee of the Permanent Forum for China Construction Law; Vice-Chair of the ICC Governing Body for Dispute Resolution Services; Co-Chair, IBA Arab Regional Forum; Vice-Chair of the Advisory Committee of the CRCICA; Member of the CIMAC Court of Arbitration; Member of the Advisory Board of the MIAC; Member of the LACIAC Court of Arbitration; Member of the Board of Trustees of the CIArb; Member of the ITA Academic Council; Member of the Advisory Board, Indonesian Arbitration Centre; Member of the Court, PCA; Member of ICODR's Governing Board; Member of the International Academy for Construction Lawyers; Former Vice-President of the ICC International Court of Arbitration (2015 – 2021); and Former Court Member of the LCIA (2014-2019).

Dr Gloria Alvarez, is an international academic on international dispute resolution, energy and investment law. She acts as legal expert and independent arbitrator (ICC, ICSID and LCIA experience).Her work spans in the areas of international economic law, climate and social justice. She has held prestigious academic posts at the Shanghai University of Finance, Queen Mary University of London, Max Planck Institute (Luxemburg), Lauterpacht Centre (University of Cambridge) and a Research Associate at UKERC (EPSRC Grant).Gloria has published numerous leading books and is the founder of 'Hydrogen Talks' and co-founder of 'Arbitration Links', initiatives to learn about the use of hydrogen in the energy transition and promote international arbitration from a Mexican perspective, respectively. Gloria sits in the Editorial Board of ICSID Review, Journal of International Arbitration and European Investment Law and Arbitration Review. She is currently working in: Arbitration in Mexico (Wolters Kluwer) and International Investment Arbitration and Energy Disputes (Hart). She is also a visiting lecturer at the University of Eastern Finland and Osgoode Hall Law School in Canada.

Dr Crina Baltag is Associate Professor (Docent) in International Arbitration at Stockholm University and qualified attorney-at-law, with twenty years of extensive practice in various aspects on international dispute resolution, private and public international law. Crina is the Academic Director of the Master in International Commercial Arbitration Law at Stockholm University and member of the Board of the Arbitration Institute of the Stockholm Chamber of Commerce. Crina is the managing editor of Kluwer Arbitration Blog, co-managing editor of ITA Arbitration Report and member of editorial boards of prestigious journals and book series in the field, including of the Journal of International Arbitration. Crina has been appointed as arbitrator in numerous arbitrations under the rules of the ICC, LCIA, SIAC, SCC, FAI, VIAC, etc., and has acted as expert in various international commercial and investment arbitrations. Crina holds a PhD degree in International Arbitration from Queen Mary University of London (UK), LLM in International Commercial Arbitration Law from Stockholm University (Sweden), MSc in International Business from Academy of Economic Studies (Romania), LLB from University of Bucharest (Romania). Crina publishes extensively on commercial and investment arbitration topics.

John Beechey, the founding partner of Clifford Chance's international arbitration practice until his retirement in 2008, President of the ICC International Court of Arbitration between 2009 and 2015 and a well-known arbitrator of commercial and investment disputes around the world. A member of the ICCA Governing Board.

Prof. George A. Bermann is professor of law and Director of the Center for International Commercial and Investment Arbitration at Columbia Law School, as well as member of the faculty of the Ecole de droit, Sciences Po (Paris) and the Geneva LLM in International Dispute Settlement (MIDS). He has been arbitrator in scores of international commercial and investment cases since 1985 under the aegis of most leading international arbitral institutions. He is head of the global advisory board of the New York International Arbitration Center (NYIAC), fellow of Chartered Institute of Arbitrators, founding member of the Governing Board of the ICC International Court of Arbitration (Paris), and head of the advisory board of the Thai Arbitration Center (Bangkok) and Center for International Investment and Commercial Arbitration (Lahore, Pakistan). Professor Bermann is Chief Reporter of the ALI Restatement of the US Law of International Commercial Arbitration, co-editor-in-chief American Review of International Arbitration and member of Board of Editors of Revue de l'Arbitrage. He co-authored (with E. Gaillard) the UNCITRAL Guide to the New York Convention and author of many books, book chapters and articles on international dispute resolution, notably international arbitration.

Viraj Bhide is an Indian advocate and formerly an attorney at the Paris Bar. His principal practice areas include advice on international arbitration and on matters of private and public international law. He also teaches international commercial and investment treaty arbitration on QMUL's LLM in international dispute resolution.

Lawrence Collins was a partner in Herbert Smith & Co (1971-2000). He was one of the first two solicitors to be appointed Queen's Counsel (1997). He was the first solicitor to be appointed direct to the High Court bench (2000). He served as a judge in the Chancery Division and Commercial Court (2000-2007), in the Court of Appeal (2007-2009) and the House of Lords/UK Supreme Court (2009-2011). Since 1987 he has been the general editor of what is now Dicey, Morris & Collins on the Conflict of Laws. Since 2011 he has been a full-time international arbitrator. He is also Professor, University College, London and a member of the Institut de droit international.

Prof. Dr Nayla Comair-Obeid is the founding partner of Obeid & Partners and heads the firm's dispute resolution practice since 1987. She is an Associate Member at 3VB Barristers Chambers in London, a member of the Beirut Bar and the Paris Bar, and Professor of international commercial arbitration. Prof Comair-Obeid has been actively involved in more than 170 domestic and international investment and complex commercial arbitrations and has been identified amongst the world's foremost arbitrator practitioners by internationally renowned legal publications. Professor Comair-Obeid has held and continues to hold pre-eminent positions in many of the major institutions. She is currently the Vice-Chair of the International Chamber of Commerce (ICC), member of the ICC Executive Board since 2019, Trustee of the Cairo Regional Center for International Commercial Arbitration (CRCICA), Vice-Chair of the Arbitration Committee in the International Bar Association (IBA), member of the International Council for Commercial Arbitration (ICCA) Governing Board, amongst others. Professor Comair-Obeid is the author of Law of Business Contracts in the Middle East and numerous other publications in Arabic, French and English covering a range of legal fields.

Caroline Croft is an associate in the International Dispute Resolution group of Squire Patton Boggs and an Associate Lecturer at the School of International Arbitration at Queen Mary University of London where she teaches international arbitration to lawyers from around the world. She is currently Co-Chair of the Equal Representation in Arbitration Pledge's Young Practitioners branch. An alumna of the School and former student of Professor Julian D M Lew KC, she worked as his arbitral assistant in numerous arbitrations in 2018-2019 before returning to private practice.

Justin D'Agostino MH is the global Chief Executive Officer at Herbert Smith Freehills, overseeing its client, people, practices and growth strategy. A thought leader and skilled practitioner in international arbitration and dispute resolution, Justin has appeared before tribunals around the world and regularly sits as arbitrator. He also plays an active role in the global legal community as a member of the Executive Board of the International Chamber of Commerce. He is Co-Chair of the Equal Representation in Arbitration Pledge global steering committee and is a strong advocate for diversity and inclusion in the legal profession and the wider community.

Dr Alix de Zitter, is an associate in the Paris office of Clifford Chance. She is a qualified lawyer in France and holds a Master's degree from Paris I Panthéon Sorbonne as well as a LLM (MJur) and a PhD (DPhil) from the University of Oxford. Her practice focuses on international commercial arbitration, investor-State arbitration and EU law, with a focus on complex large-scale disputes. Before joining Clifford Chance, Dr de Zitter worked with leading arbitration practices in France and Switzerland.

Domenico Di Pietro, Partner at GST LLP focusing on international commercial and investment arbitration. QMUL School of International Arbitration alumnus.

Dr Stuart Dutson, Partner and head of International Arbitration, Simmons & Simmons LLP, London. Stuart first met and worked with Julian in 1996 at Herbert Smith after Stuart finished his PhD in private international law and public international law at Gonville and Caius College, Cambridge. Stuart joined Julian's arbitration and conflict of laws group at Herbert Smith the glorious 'group 2 litigation'. Stuart worked with Julian again at the CCLS QMW before Stuart re-entered private practice at Linklaters. Stuart has appeared before Julian as counsel in numerous arbitrations, from investment treaty arbitrations defending States and representing investors, to commercial arbitrations under the ICC, LCIA and CIETAC rules.

Prof. Susan Franck is a Professor at American University, Washington College of Law. Before joining the academy, she practiced in Washington, DC (Wilmer Hale) and London (Allen & Overy), serving as counsel in ICC, LCIA, ICSID, and UNCITRAL arbitrations, and acting as tribunal secretary in Lauder v. Czech Republic. She has written over forty articles and the book Arbitration Costs: Myths and Realities of Investment Treaty Arbitration. She currently serves as an arbitrator and mediator in commercial disputes.

Dr Alice Fremuth-Wolf is Market Head for Austria & CEE region. Before joining Nivalion, Alice was Secretary General of the Vienna International Arbitral Centre (VIAC) for 10 years. She is a lecturer for arbitration at the Institute of Civil Procedure Law at the Law Faculty of Vienna University, and frequently acts as guest lecturer. She has authored numerous articles and books on arbitration and ADR. In addition to her academic career, she worked as an associate for the leading law firms Wolf Theiss and Baker McKenzie in Vienna where she passed the Austrian bar exam, acting as counsel and arbitrator in international arbitration and mediation cases. Alice graduated in law from Vienna University (Mag. iur.), holds a PhD in law (Dr iur.) and an LLM degree (London School of Economics). She is also a trained mediator and mediation advocate. Alice speaks German and English.

Norah Gallagher is a public international lawyer specialized in dispute resolution for over twenty years. She has advised on a range of issues on international commercial and investment cases and sits regularly as arbitrator. Norah is Director of the School of International Arbitration and Academic Director of the Energy & Climate Change Law Institute at the Centre for Commercial Law Studies. She teaches Energy Law & Climate Change, Investment and Commercial Arbitration on the LLM in London, Paris and Distance Learning programmes.

Dr Rémy Gerbay is a partner in Hughes Hubbard & Reed's Arbitration Group in Washington, D.C. office. Prior to joining Hughes Hubbard, Remy practised with leading litigation law firms in the US and UK. A former Deputy Registrar of the LCIA and Registrar of DIFC-LCIA, Remy has been appointed as arbitrator in over 25 international cases. Remy also holds a permanent academic appointment at Queen Mary University of London, where he is the Co-Director of an LLM programme in arbitration. Remy is a Vice-President of AFSA's International Court, a Co-Chair of the American Society of International Law's Dispute Resolution Group, and a member of the editorial board of the Journal of International Arbitration.

Elizabeth Gloster was a Lady Justice of the Court of Appeal from 2013, and Vice-President of the Civil Division from 2016, until she retired from the court in May 2018 to return to practise as an international commercial arbitrator at One Essex Court, Temple. She was the first woman to be appointed as a Commercial Court judge in 2004 and as Judge in Charge of the Commercial Court from 2010-2012. She presided over numerous important commercial and financial markets cases, including JP Morgan Chase Bank v Springwell Navigation Corporation and the notable Berezovsky v Abramovitch trial.

Dr Alfonso Gómez-Acebo, Lawyer, Doctor in Law and partner at Cuatrecasas. He has acted as counsel in over 70 international arbitrations involving private parties, States and State-owned entities with interests in Europe, Latin America, North America, Africa and Western Asia. He has particular experience in cases related to cross-border acquisitions, construction, energy, oil & gas, telecommunications, financial services, insurance and sports. He also serves as arbitrator. He is a member of the Madrid Bar Association, a Fellow of the Chartered Institute of Arbitrators (FCIArb), a member of the International Council for Commercial Arbitration (ICCA) and a member of the ICC Commission on Arbitration and ADR.

Prof. Sir Roy Goode KC is Emeritus Professor of Law in the University of Oxford and Emeritus Fellow of St John's College, Oxford. He holds the degrees of DSc(Econ) from the University of London and DCL from the University of Oxford as well as honorary doctorates from the Universities of London and East Anglia and the University of Law, England. Author of several textbooks on commercial law, corporate insolvency law and secured transactions widely used by students, practitioners and the courts he was a solicitor for many years before moving to the Bar and is an Honorary Bencher of the Inner Temple. He founded the Centre for Commercial Law Studies at Queen Mary, University of London, in 1980 and is its Honorary President. He has served as a member of the Committee on Consumer Credit and the Departmental Committee on Arbitration and was Chairman of the Pension Law Review Committee, the reports of all three committees being implemented by legislation.

Simon Greenberg is a partner in the Paris office of Clifford Chance and a member of the firm's international arbitration group. Simon acts as both counsel and arbitrator and has extensive experience of both ad hoc arbitrations and those under the rules of most major international arbitral institutions, notably the ICC. His experience covers numerous governing laws and seats of arbitration and encompasses a range of dispute types and business sectors such as telecoms, technology, IP, aviation, construction and infrastructure, energy and resources, shareholders, post-acquisition, and general commercial disputes. Before joining Clifford Chance in early 2012, Simon spent four years as Deputy Secretary General of the ICC International Court of Arbitration (Paris), having previously practised with leading international dispute resolution teams in Paris and Australia. He remains close to the ICC as a Court Member (Australia) of the ICC International Court of Arbitration. Simon is a lecturer at the Institute of Political Science of Paris (Sciences Po) since 2008 (formerly of international commercial contracts; arbitration since 2014), a visiting professor of international commercial arbitration at Hong Kong University since 2011 and a regular speaker at arbitration conferences. He has published more than 30 journal articles and two books on subjects of international arbitration. Simon is also a part time judge of the Commercial Division of the Supreme Court of Bahrain.

Prof. Bernard Hanotiau is member of the Brussels and Paris bars and a partner in the boutique law firm Hanotiau & van den Berg (Brussels & Singapore). He is professor emeritus of the universities of Louvain and Namur (Belgium) and a visiting professor at NUS University (Singapore). Since 1978, he has been involved in more than 600 international arbitrations, in all parts of the world, according to the rules of most arbitral institutions. He is the author of numerous articles on international arbitration and of a treatise on 'Complex Arbitrations: Multi-party, Multi-contract and Multi-issue' (2nd edition, Kluwer, 2020).

Paula Hodges KC heads Herbert Smith Freehills' Global Arbitration Practice with over 30 years' experience advising multinational clients on international disputes under the auspices of the major arbitral institutions, particularly in the energy/natural resources, telecommunications and technology sectors. Paula was appointed Queen's Counsel (now King's Counsel) in 2014 and President of the LCIA Court in May 2019.

Dr Ole Jensen practices international arbitration at Wilmer Cutler Pickering Hale and Dorr LLP in Berlin and London. He has represented clients and assisted tribunals in arbitrations conducted under most major rules, including those of the ICC, LCIA, DIS, SCC and UNCITRAL. Apart from his practice, Ole is engaged in academia. He is an award-winning author, holds academic visiting positions at universities in Europe and Latin America, and is an Assistant Editor for the Journal of International Arbitration.

Prof. Doug Jones, AO, RFD is an independent international commercial and investor-State arbitrator based in London, Sydney and Toronto, with over 40 years' prior experience as an international transactional and disputes project lawyer. He is a door tenant at Atkin Chambers, London, a member of Sydney Arbitration Chambers, and a member of Toronto Arbitration Chambers in Toronto, Canada. He serves as an International Judge of the Singapore International Commercial Court. Doug has published and presented extensively and holds professorial appointments at Queen Mary College, University of London and Melbourne University Law School. In addition, Doug has held appointments at several international professional associations, including serving as the President of the Chartered Institute of Arbitrators (CIArb) and the Australian Centre for International Commercial Arbitration (ACICA).

Neil Kaplan CBE KC has been an international arbitrator for 35 years. He was the Judge in charge of the Arbitration List in Hong Kong, was President of the Chartered Institute of Arbitrators, Chair of the Hong Kong International Arbitration Centre, has been a Court member of the ICC, is President of the Court of MARC (Mauritius), is Chair of Delos Committee of Experts and is a member of the Bahrain Court of Cassation.

Prof. Dr Stefan Kröll, LLM is Professor for International Dispute Resolution at Bucerius Law School. Germany and one of the directors of the Vis Moot Court. He is the Chairman of the German Arbitration Institute, on the international advisory board of several other arbitration institutions and has published widely in the field of international arbitration.

Founder of Studio Legale Landi, **Niccolo Landi** has served and serves variously as presiding arbitrator, sole arbitrator and counsel in arbitrations administered by the Milan Chamber of Arbitration (CAM), the International Chamber of Commerce (ICC), the Vienna International Arbitral Centre (VIAC) and in ad hoc domestic Italian and international arbitration proceedings. He also acts as administrative secretary to tribunals before the ICC and the International Centre for Settlement of Investment Disputes (ICSID). Niccolò is President of the Supervisory Body established under the Legislative Decree No. 231/2001of several multinationals, overseeing their compliance with all applicable corporate governance and ethical rules. He lectures on arbitration-related topics at the University of Roma Tre and at the University of Turin.

Lauren Levin, Daughter of Julian Lew.

Ariella Lew, Daughter of Julian Lew.

Mohamed Mahayni is a dual-qualified solicitor (England & Wales) and avocat (Paris Bar). His work mainly consists of advising lead counsel on issues arising out of international arbitration theory and practice. In parallel, he teaches international commercial and investment treaty arbitration on QMUL's LLM in international dispute resolution.

Isabelle Michou is a Partner at Quinn Emanuel Urquhart & Sullivan. She is based in Paris. She is dual national, French and Canadian, and dual qualified as a Paris Avocat and a Solicitor of England & Wales. Isabelle's practice focuses on international arbitration and international law. She has substantial experience in both commercial and investor-State arbitration, in a range of industries, including in telecoms, energy, mining, aerospace, large-scale infrastructure projects, hospitality and media. She has appeared before numerous high-profile arbitral tribunals, under the auspices of the major institutional rules including ICC, ICSID, LCIA, Stockholm Chamber of Commerce, as well as ad hoc arbitrations under the UNCITRAL Rules. Isabelle also appears in arbitration-related proceedings before the French courts, in cases involving issues of sovereign immunities, interlocutory, interim or conservatory relief, enforcement and challenges of arbitral awards. She is regularly appointed arbitrator under the ICC, LCIA or other rules.

Wendy Miles KC is a specialist in international arbitration and dispute resolution with a focus on private and public international law. With over 25 years of experience, Wendy has advised on international law matters and conducted arbitrations under all the major institutions and ad hoc. In the field of climate change and finance, Wendy acts as global coordinating counsel to various major corporates in relation to climate change transition, disclosure, reporting, compliance and investment. She regularly advises investors and States in respect of climate-related physical, transition and litigation risk.

Prof. Loukas Mistelis is the Clive M Schmitthoff Professor of Transnational Commercial Law and Arbitration at Queen Mary University of London. He has served as Director of the School of International Arbitration from 2002 to 2019 and is currently the Director of the QMUL-UNIDROIT Institute of Transnational Commercial Law and Partner in the International Arbitration Group of Clyde & Co. He is a widely acknowledged authority in international arbitration.

Dr Mary Mitsi is Lecturer in Commercial Law specializing in International Arbitration at Queen Mary University of London. She teaches in the LLM programme in London and Paris. She is the Director of Executive Education at CCLS contributing to the training of industry professionals. Mary's publications include the monograph on 'The decision-making process of Investor-State Arbitration Tribunals' (Kluwer Law International 2019).

Prof. Emilia Onyema is an independent arbitrator and Professor of International Commercial Law at SOAS University of London where she teaches International Commercial Arbitration, International Investment Law, cross-border Commercial Law and contributes to the law and development in Africa course. She is qualified to practise law in Nigeria, as a Solicitor in England & Wales, Fellow of the Chartered Institute of Arbitrators. She convenes the SOAS Arbitration in Africa conference series and leads the SOAS Arbitration in Africa biennial survey research project. Her research interests focus on the development of international arbitration in Africa and the engagement of Africans in international arbitration.

Prof. William W. Park is Professor of Law at Boston University, US, where he teaches in the areas of tax, finance and conflict of laws. After studies at Yale (US) and Columbia (US), Park practised in Paris and Geneva. Park served for 17 years as General Editor of Arbitration International. He is former President of the London Court of International Arbitration. Park is an Honorary Fellow of Selwyn College, Cambridge.

Dr Stefan Riegler heads the firm-wide arbitration team of Wolf Theiss. He specializes in advising on disputes in the energy, construction and infrastructure sectors; he is also experienced in handling corporate, post-M&A and banking disputes. Stefan serves as President of the Board of the Austrian Arbitration Association (ArbAut) and is a member of the Board of the Vienna International Arbitral Centre (VIAC); he is also an active member of the ICC Commission on Arbitration and ADR. Stefan is an alumnus of the School of International Arbitration (2003).

Sir Bernard Rix retired in 2013 from the Court of Appeal after 20 years as first a High Court Judge and then a Lord Justice of Appeal. He now practises as an arbitrator and accredited mediator. Since his retirement, he has been appointed to positions as a member of the Cayman Islands Court of Appeal and of the Singapore International Commercial Court and as a Professor of International Commercial Law at Queen Mary, University of London. He was educated at New College Oxford, of which he is an honorary fellow, and at Harvard Law School, where he was a Kennedy Scholar. He is a past President of the Harvard Law School Alumni Association of the UK. He has lectured abroad or spoken at international conferences or debates in St Petersburg, Moscow, Paris, Doha, Oslo, Florence, Padua, Venice, New York, Washington, Singapore, Hong Kong, Barcelona, Malmo, Jerusalem, Tokyo, and Warsaw, as well as in London. Other positions held have been or are: Treasurer of the Inner Temple, Chairman of Coexist House, President of the British Insurance Law Association, Trustee and honorary fellow of the British Institute of International and Comparative Law, Chairman of the Advisory Council of the Centre for Commercial Law Studies at Queen Mary, University of London, Chairman of the Razumovsky Trust, and a Director of the London Philharmonic Orchestra. He has also participated in a performance of Der Rosenkavalier at the ENO.

Prof. Catherine A. Rogers is a scholar of international arbitration and professional ethics at Bocconi University. Prof. Rogers co-chaired the ICCA-Queen Mary Task Force on Third-Party Funding in International Arbitration, and is the Founder and CEO of Arbitrator Intelligence, a global information aggregator and legal tech start-up that aims at improving arbitrator selection. She regularly engages in capacity-building activities to promote international dispute resolution and the rule of law in developing and emerging economies. She is a Reporter for the American Law Institute's Restatement of the U.S. Law of International Commercial and Investor-State Arbitration and sits on the Board of Directors of the Lagos Court of Arbitration, the International Advisory Board of the Vienna International Arbitration Centre, the Geneva Center for International Dispute Settlement (CIDS) Academic Forum on ISDS, and the Oxford University Press Investment Claims Advisory Board.

Prof. Eduardo Silva Romero, Professor Emeritus, Rosario University, Bogota; lecturer on international contracts and arbitration at Sciences Po, Paris; lecturer on arbitration at Pantheon-Assas, MIDS and Paris-Dauphine Universities; Chairman of the ICC Institute of World Business Law; International Arbitration Partner at Dechert LLP.

Noah Rubins KC is a partner at Freshfields in Paris. Originally qualified in the US, he is admitted to practice in France and is a barrister of England & Wales. His experience spans more than 20 years, with a focus on the former USSR, Central and Eastern Europe, Israel and North Africa. In additional to his work as counsel in commercial and investment treaty arbitration, Noah serves frequently as arbitrator.

Dr Monique Sasson is Of Counsel at D|R Litigation & Arbitration in Milan and a member of Arbitra. Her practice includes serving as counsel, as arbitrator and as mediator, and she has also appeared as an expert witness on investment law in an

ICSID case (CEAC v Montenegro). The second edition of her book, Substantive Law in Investment Arbitration, was published in 2017 (Kluwer Law). Monique graduated in law from LUISS - Rome (with honours); she holds a PhD in public international law from Cambridge University and an LLM from Queen Mary University, London. Monique previously worked in London at Herbert Smith and in Rome at Studio Legale Chiomenti.

Dr Silja Schaffstein is counsel at Lévy Kaufmann-Kohler, a leading arbitration firm based in Geneva, Switzerland. She frequently serves as arbitrator and acts as counsel or co-counsel, or secretary of the tribunal, in international and domestic ad hoc and institutional arbitration proceedings. Silja also provides legal advice and represents clients in arbitration-related court proceedings in Switzerland. She speaks regularly and has published extensively on arbitration, including her book titled The Doctrine of Res Judicata Before International Commercial Arbitral Tribunals. A German national, Silja has a dual common law and civil law background, being admitted to the Geneva and New York Bars. She holds a PhD from Queen Mary, University of London and the University of Geneva, and an LLM from Columbia University.

Prof. Dr Maxi Scherer, LLM is a Special Counsel at Wilmer Cutler Pickering Hale and Dorr LLP in London and a Professor of Law at Queen Mary University of London, where she holds the Chair for International Arbitration, Dispute Resolution and Energy Law. She has practised international arbitration for more than 20 years and represented clients, served as arbitrator or legal expert in more than 120 commercial and investor-State arbitrations. She is Vice-President of the London Court of International Arbitration (LCIA), a member of the Governing Body of International Council for Commercial Arbitration (ICCA), a Co-Chair of the IBA Investment Arbitration Subcommittee and holds many other public appointments and commissions of trust, including being a member of the panel of arbitrators (The International Centre for Settlement of Investment Disputes (ICSID)). Maxi is regularly ranked by Who's Who Legal, Chambers, The Legal 500, BestLawyer, etc. as leading arbitration practitioner and, since 2019, included in the selective highest category of 'Global Elite Thought Leaders' in the field.

Dr Patricia Shaughnessy, Associate Professor at Stockholm University, specializes in international disputes and commercial law. She acts as an arbitrator, expert, and consultant in legal development projects in many countries. She is a member of the ICC Court of Arbitration and the international boards of the Georgian International Arbitration Centre and the Tehran Regional Arbitration Centre. Until 2019, she was the Vice-Chair of the Board of the SCC Arbitration Institute, having been a Board member since 2006. Prior to her academic career, she practised law in Hawaii for ten years specialized in commercial law and litigation.

Audley Sheppard KC is Co-Head of the International Arbitration Group at Clifford Chance LLP. His current professional activities include: Governing Body, International Council for Commercial Arbitration (ICCA); Chair of the Advisory Council, School of

International Arbitration, Queen Mary, University of London; Advisory Board, Lauterpacht Centre for International Law, Cambridge; and Board Chair of Sport Resolutions. He is a former: Board Chair of the LCIA; Member of the ICC Court; Co-Chair of the IBA Arbitration Committee; and Rapporteur of the ILA Arbitration Committee. He graduated with LLB (Hons) and BCom (Victoria Univ. of Wellington, NZ) and LLM (Cambridge, England).

Dr Laurence Shore is Of Counsel at BonelliErede-Milan. He previously practised international arbitration at Herbert Smith and Gibson Dunn, and he began his career in the law as an associate at Williams & Connolly. Laurence's law degree is from Emory University, US, where he was editor-in-chief of the Emory Law Journal. He earned a PhD in American History from Johns Hopkins University.

Eleanor Taylor, Acquisition Manager (Arbitration), Wolters Kluwer Law & Regulatory, International Group US.

Prof. Pierre Tercier is an Emeritus Professor of the University of Fribourg. He is the Honorary Chairman of the ICC International Court of Arbitration, after having been the President of the Court between 2006 and 2008, and an international arbitrator with extensive international arbitration and dispute resolution experience both in commercial and investment treaty cases. He is a visiting professor of law at numerous universities around the world. He graduated from the University of Fribourg summa cum laude and was admitted to the bar in 1969. He is also Doctor honoris causa of the University of Paris II Panthéon-Assas. He recently joined Peter & Kim as Senior Counsel.

Prof. John Uff CBE KC, Emeritus Professor, Centre of Construction Law, Kings College London. Member of the Departmental Advisory Committee on Arbitration Law which drafted the Arbitration Act.

Simona Valkova is an independent tribunal secretary specializing in international commercial and investment arbitration. She has been working in the international arbitration field for over five years and has experience with arbitrations under a variety of institutional and ad hoc rules (including the ICC, HKIAC, LCIA, SIAC, SCC, ICSID and UNCITRAL Rules). Ms Valkova is also a Teaching Fellow at the School of International Arbitration, Queen Mary University of London.

Dr Jacomijn J. van Haersolte-van Hof has been the Director General of the LCIA since 1 July 2014. She regularly sits as arbitrator and has handled cases under the ICC, LCIA, UNCITRAL Rules, as well as those of the Netherlands Arbitration Institute (NAI) and UNUM. She is on the ICSID roster of arbitrators and was and is a member of several ICSID Annulment Committees, including as president. She is a professor of civil law, in particular arbitration law, at Leiden University, Netherlands and a member of GAR's editorial board. Previously, she practised as counsel and arbitrator in The Hague at her GAR 100 boutique HaersolteHof which she set up in 2008 after three years as counsel in the international arbitration group at Freshfields Bruckhaus Deringer in Amsterdam. Before that she was at De Brauw Blackstone Westbroek and Loeff Claeys Verbeke.

Prof. Hans van Houtte (hans.vanhoutte@arbitration.be) is Professor at KULeuven and independent arbitrator. He was President of the Iran-United States Claims Tribunal (2011-2017) and of the Eritrea-Ethiopia Claims Commission (2001-2009), Judge at the Dormant Accounts Tribunal (1998-2002), Member of the United Nations Compensation Commission (1998-2001) and Commissioner for Real Property Claims in Bosnia (1996- 2005). In 2016, he was bestowed the title of Baron by H.M. the King of the Belgians for his contribution to the settlement of international disputes.

Dr Claus von Wobeser is the founding partner of Von Wobeser y Sierra. He has acted in over 200 international arbitration proceedings and has served as Vice-President of the International Court of Arbitration of the ICC, Co-Chair of the IBA Arbitration Committee, President of the Arbitration Commission of ICC Mexico, Member of the Panel of Arbitrators of ICSID, Member of the London Court of International Arbitration, Member of the Board of Directors of the AAA and as a Member of the ICC Court. In 1994 he founded and since teaches on the diploma course on arbitration co-organized by the Escuela Libre de Derecho and ICC México. Currently, he serves as President of ALARB and ICC Mexico and as a member of the ICCA Governing Board. He studied law at Escuela Libre de Derecho in Mexico City and a PhD at Université de Paris 2, Sorbonne.

Prof. Janet Walker CM CD is an independent arbitrator at Atkin Chambers in London, Toronto Arbitration Chambers, and Sydney Arbitration Chambers. For more than 20 years, she has served as sole arbitrator, co-arbitrator and chair in ad hoc arbitrations and arbitrations administered by the major institutions in a variety of seats. She is a Distinguished Research Professor (past Associate Dean) at Osgoode Hall Law School, a member of the Ontario Bar, and a licensed legal consultant of the New York State Bar. She authors Canada's main text on the conflict of laws, cited in more than 400 judgments. Janet is a member of the Order of Canada.

Matthew Weiniger KC specializes in international arbitration and public international law. He also advises on non-contentious matters involving the protection of investments under public international law. He has particular expertise in investment treaty arbitrations. Matthew is a co-author of *International Investment Arbitration: Substantive Principles* (OUP 2nd Ed 2017).

Dr Stephan Wilske studied at the Universities of Tübingen, Aix-en-Provence (Maîtrise en Droit 1986) and Chicago (LL.M.; Casper Platt Award 1996). He was admitted to the New York bar and the German bar in 1997 and has been a partner at Gleiss Lutz since 2002. He is a Fellow of the Chartered Institute of Arbitrators (FCIArb) and of the Asian Institute of Alternative Dispute Resolution (AIADR), and a member of the American Law Institute (ALI), the ICC Task Force 'Addressing Issues of Corruption in International Arbitration', and the International Arbitration Committee (IAC) of the KCAB International. Since 2019, he is a Vice-President of the CAAI Court of Arbitration. He also serves as a lecturer at the Universities of Jena and Heidelberg.

Prof. Ali Yeşilırmak is a professor at Ibn Haldun University School of Law, Turkey. He acts as arbitrator in various institutional and ad hoc arbitrations. He is a member of the Permanent Court of Arbitration and of the Court of Arbitration at the Istanbul Chamber of Commerce Arbitration Court (ITOTAM). He was an Of Counsel to Esin Attorney Partnership an affiliate of Baker & McKenzie Istanbul (2011-2014); and was seconded to Herbert Smith London (2000-2001). Ali holds an LLB from Dokuz Eylul University, an LL.M. from the University of Texas at Austin and a PhD from CCLS, Queen Mary, University of London.

Dr Noam Zamir is an international arbitrator, lawyer and Associate Professor of Law at Lyon Catholic University, France, where he teaches public international law, international investment law and dispute settlement. Dr Zamir has written various articles in the field of public international law, notably international arbitration, international humanitarian law and human rights law. His articles were published in top journals such as the American Journal of International Law (CUP) and Arbitration International (OUP) and his book on international humanitarian law was published by Edward Elgar (2017)

Summary of Contents

Introduction

Stavros Brekoulakis, Romesh Weeramantry & Lilit Nagapetyan

We are deeply honoured to be the editors of this Liber Amicorum dedicated to Professor Julian Lew KC on his 75th birthday. In the great tradition of a Liber Amicorum (or 'book of friends'), the following pages comprise a work in which the contributions of Julian's friends and colleagues have led to a collection of personal notes and world-class essays. It is a worthy tribute to his remarkable service as a leading legal practitioner, arbitrator, scholar, teacher and beloved mentor to several generations of arbitration practitioners and academics.

We have set out a detailed CV of Julian's monumental career at the end of this book. However, by way of introduction, we wanted to highlight three of Julian's main achievements: first, Julian has made a profound contribution to the development of arbitration practice. When Julian started his career as a lawyer in leading UK law firms (including in the legacy law firm Herbert Smith, now Herbert Smith Freehills), no specialised arbitration groups operated within law firms; international arbitration was considered part of the remit of litigation groups. Julian was one of the first (together with three other pioneers of the field, namely John Beechy at Clifford Chance, and Alan Hunter and Martin Hunter at Freshfields) to develop and lead a team within a law firm dedicated exclusively to the practice of international arbitration. Today, almost all major law firms in the UK and abroad have an arbitration group, including arbitration lawyers working exclusively in arbitration sub-fields, such as construction arbitration or energy arbitration. By developing a specialised group, Julian contributed to the realisation that the legal knowledge and advocacy skills required for the practice of international arbitration must necessarily be different from those required for the practice of domestic litigation.

Second, and perhaps relatedly, Julian's work had a major influence on the understanding of arbitration as an autonomous and international legal field. While originally the doctrine of arbitration was mainly influenced by an old-fashion version of positivism focusing on national legal concepts and state legal rules, Julian's scholarly work, notably with his essay on *Achieving the Dream: Autonomous Arbitration*,[1] set out an exciting vision of arbitration as an autonomous system with the capacity to produce non-state legal norms and be practised without reference to domestic laws.

Third, Julian has made a remarkable contribution to academia by single-handedly introducing the subject of international commercial arbitration in the curricula of law schools in England. Effectively, he created a new academic field. Indeed, Julian wrote the first doctoral thesis in English on the subject of international arbitration. His monograph on the *Law Applicable in International Commercial Arbitration* was published in 1978. This work, together with Philippe Fouchard's *L' Arbitrage Commercial International* (1965), Pierre Lalive's Hague Course on *Problèmes Relatifs a l'arbitrage International Commercial* (1967), Albert Jan van Den Berg's exposition on the New York Convention (1981), Craig, Park and Paulsson book on *International Chamber of Commercial Arbitration* (1984) and Redfern and Hunter's *Law and Practice of International Commercial Arbitration* (1986) are widely considered the theoretical foundations of arbitration as a distinct international legal field.

Not only did Julian produce one of the first scholarly works in international arbitration; he established the first academic institution dedicated to the teaching of international arbitration. When Julian started to practise law in 1981, he soon realised that there was no law school where students or young lawyers could study international arbitration. At the time, arbitration was not considered a subject of academic importance, not least because of its close relevance to legal practice, and therefore arbitration was not taught by any law school in the world. As was generally accepted then, if one wanted to *learn* about arbitration, they should do so by *practising* arbitration in a *law firm*. However, Julian understood arbitration as a legal field which had important academic significance and required the development of specialised academic courses. Thus, in 1985, he approached Professor Sir Roy Goode, who, at the time, was the Director of Queen Mary University of London's Centre for Commercial Law Studies, and proposed to develop and teach the first ever postgraduate course on international arbitration. Over the next forty years, the course on international arbitration which originally attracted no more than 15 students became one of the flagship courses of the Queen Mary's master's in law programme. It has since attracted more than 2,500 master's students from all over the world. During this time, Julian has mentored many students and young professionals interested in international arbitration. Importantly, while there was no other law school in the UK or worldwide offering a course on international arbitration, the growing success of Queen Mary's course has prompted more than 30 law schools in the UK and abroad to introduce similar courses. More than 300 students come to the UK annually to study international arbitration now; drawn by Julian's outstanding reputation, more than 100 of them come to Queen Mary University of London where Julian still teaches. Today, the School of International Arbitration, which Julian founded in 1985 is widely considered one of the leading places to study international arbitration.

1. Julian D.M. Lew, *Achieving the Dream: Autonomous Arbitration*, 22-2 ARB. INT'L 179, 186 (2006).

There is a saying that teaching is the greatest act of optimism. Prof. Lew has been and remains an optimist of an unfathomable scale. An irreplaceable Head of the School of International Arbitration since 1985, he has always been well ahead of the curve with his vision of arbitration as a discipline and his innovative teaching methods. For example, Alice Fremuth-Wolf, among several others, makes specific note in her contribution in Chapter 35 to Prof. Lew's practice of posing questions to students without looking for one 'right' answer and of teaching critical, innovative, outside the box thinking. Decades later, that intellectual rigour remains at the core of his teaching and supervision method, of which we are the lucky attestants as his PhD students.

Julian's remarkable vision to develop and teach a course on international arbitration and found a school dedicated to international arbitration, as well as his tireless teaching and writing for more than 40 years has led to the creation of a thriving academic subject. Julian's contribution to academia was duly recognised by Lord Neuberger, the UK Supreme Court President, who at the dinner of the Queen Mary School of International Arbitration 30th Anniversary in April 2015, noted that the School which Julian founded has 'contributed enormously to the rule of law and a thriving economy, globally and more in the UK in particular. We have a great deal to thank you for'.

In a field which has become increasingly busier (arguably to a point of saturation) in terms of events and publications, the high number of contributors to this volume is a testament of the great esteem that Julian enjoys among his peers. We were touched that in their responses to our request, many contributors described how Julian had deeply impacted their lives – personally and professionally, others acknowledged how much Julian's professional achievements deserved a commemorative volume in his honour, and a large number offered personal comments, for example, by expressing their genuine admiration for Julian as a dear friend.

The high regard the contributors have for Julian is easily identifiable in many places in this volume where contributors variously describe him as 'charismatic', 'inspirational', 'amazing', 'brilliant', 'a visionary', 'stellar', 'hugely impressive', 'extraordinary', 'graceful, thoroughly researched and thought-provoking', and 'truly innovative'. Some contributions contain personal notes in which authors have indicated that they are 'forever grateful for the generosity he showed me', that 'I owe my whole career in arbitration to Professor Julian Lew' and that 'I can say without hesitation that Julian influenced my life in multiple ways'. On his work and professional achievements, authors have indicated that Julian has made 'iconic contributions' to the teaching of arbitration, he is a 'world-leading arbitrator', that 'his written work has the virtue of aging well', that he is 'a pivotal figure in international arbitration', and that he has 'incomparable skills' and 'the highest ethical standards'. One contributor writes that 'I am an academic because I want to display the same love and commitment that [Julian] shows to everyone in the classroom'. Another has emphasised the importance Julian places on inclusiveness, observing that Julian welcomes 'all those to the arbitration field, broadly defined, who wish to be a part of an international community of practitioners and scholars' and that he lobbies 'for bringing people from every jurisdiction into the field, paying particular attention to creating opportunities that are gender, race and age neutral'. That same contributor also admiringly refers to Julian's view that 'international arbitration does not … preclude – indeed, it must not preclude – devotion to family and community'.

As to Julian's family, we are fortunate to have a contribution from his two daughters, who endearingly observe:

> *'it is clear to us that the professor who taught so many, the partner you looked up to, the arbitrator who ruled on your case, the author whose book you have on your shelf and the dad who raised us are really no different. At the heart of all his personal and professional dealings, seems to be the biblical injunction of 'justice, justice, you shall pursue'. Similarly, the dedication he shows to his work is the dedication he shows to our family. His generosity of time for colleagues and students is palpable in the special relationships he has with his children and each of his grandchildren.'*

We are extremely grateful to the contributors who kindly agreed at relatively short notice to take time out of their busy schedules and write their essays or a personal note. A special note of thanks is owed to Eleanor Taylor who enthusiastically accepted our proposal to produce a Liber Amicorum for Julian and, indeed, volunteered to write one of the essays to celebrate Julian's role as editor of the seminal series of Kluwer's International Arbitration Law Library Series.

Stavros, Romesh and Lilit
February 2023

Editors' Personal Notes

Stavros Brekoulakis:

I have known Julian for more than 20 years now as my teacher and supervisor, a mentor and colleague, and above all a good friend. I have learned from Julian all these years and admired him for many reasons, including his unwavering dedication to international law and arbitration. But I have mostly admired him because of three powerful ideals which Julian used as his guiding principles in his professional work and personal life: simplicity, humility and generosity.

Julian is a simple man. In a world which has become increasingly (and often unnecessarily) complex, simplicity is sometimes mistaken as a lack of sophistication. But I refer to simplicity as the quality to navigate through ostentation and arrive at what really matters. In this sense, Julian's doctrine of simplicity is the antidote to superficiality. For Julian, a lawyer or a scholar must speak and write simple to be understood by clients and students of different ethnic, cultural and class backgrounds. Including Latin terms in a legal text (as is the tradition of many legal scholars in continental Europe) was considered as a pretentious anathema to Julian and was banned from his manuscripts. Using his famous Socratic method to teach arbitration by asking several questions in the class was an effective technique to take students to consider the basic but important questions about arbitration. Equally, his conception of international arbitration as an autonomous system of resolving disputes was simple but powerful. While some scholars have attempted to ground arbitration's autonomy on complicated (if not grandiose) 'representations' of transnational law, Julian's thesis of arbitration's autonomy was simply grounded on reality.[2] Julian has been taking a simple but meaningful approach to his life too: what has always really mattered for Julian was to spend time (preferably under the sun) with his loving wife, Margot, in South Africa or lately in Jerusalem, and with his children and grandchildren in London or Australia.

Julian's principle of simplicity essentially derives from a deep-rooted sense of humility, namely the realisation that we live, speak and write in simple terms not because we seek to validate ourselves; but because we want to be helpful to others. While other 'megastars' of the field measure their success by the number of their books and cases, Julian (despite being – by any standard – *the* leading figure of our field) measures his achievements by the number of individuals who worked with Julian as junior associates or lecturers and have now, with Julian's help, become distinguished partners, arbitrators and professors.

It is this sense of humility that has equipped Julian with generosity. Many contributors in this Liber Amicorum emphasise Julian's generosity, and I have greatly benefitted from it. Julian has been generous with the time he has dedicated to advise and encourage me in my career; and he has been equally generous with his feelings not only to celebrate my achievements but also support me through challenges. Co-editing this volume is a small token of my gratitude to him.

Romesh Weeramantry:

A transformative event in my life took place on the day I sat in on an arbitration lecture delivered by Julian Lew. It was during my LLM at the University of London. I decided to go to the lecture after hearing from other LLM students about a brilliant arbitration professor at Queen Mary College (I was enrolled at King's College). I clearly recall sitting close to the front of the lecture room, listening in awe to the questions Julian posed, the passion he displayed for his topic, his captivating descriptions as to the nature and function of arbitration, and his mastery of the subject (both practical and academic). Clearly palpable was his desire that the class questioned but at the same time valued (or at least, respected) the subject matter he was teaching.

Unfortunately, I was not registered in this arbitration course and was unable to continue attending it. However, the experience of that lecture has never left me. Years later, this experience was a reason why I approached Julian to be one of my PhD supervisors. In my first meeting with him, he straight away asked in his avuncular manner: 'Why do you want to enrol for a PhD? Can't you simply write a book on your topic without undertaking a PhD?' My immediate response to that question was embarrassingly rudimentary. As the years passed as a PhD candidate under him, thinking more deeply through the answers to those two questions helped me traverse the darkest valleys I encountered on my PhD journey.

Throughout my PhD, I was privileged to have Julian as a beacon of reason, which guided me around difficult intellectual roadblocks. His guidance was not to make suggestions as to what my conclusions should be, but what questions I should ask

2. This was how Julian put it in his famous SIA-Freshfields Lecture *Achieving the dream: Autonomous Arbitration*: 'It is essential to recognise the reality of when, how and why arbitration is chosen.'

before any conclusions were reached. Even after my PhD was completed, Julian was proactive in maintaining contact no matter where I was located, with coffees in London, breakfasts in Singapore and Hong Kong, and an extremely fortuitous 'bump' into him at the Four Seasons hotel in Seoul.

To highlight the excellence that Julian embodies, I would like to go back in time and refer to his own PhD. The published form of his ground-breaking 1978 thesis *Applicable Law in International Commercial Arbitration* (cited many times in chapters in this book) includes a preface by his supervisor, the late Professor François Rigaux. Among the glowing terms Professor Rigaux showers on Julian, he mentions that Julian spent several years at the Centre Charles de Visscher pour le Droit International at Louvain University and that the members of the Centre 'have been the privileged witnesses of Julian Lew's qualities as a lawyer. The publication of his [PhD] will enable many others to obtain the same conviction.'

Over 40 years later, I can say unreservedly that I have obtained that same conviction and have been a privileged witnesses of Julian's qualities, not just as a lawyer, but also as a scholar, mentor and friend. I am forever indebted to Julian for his support during my academic and legal career. Editing this Liber Amicorum is a small repayment on that debt.

Lilit Nagapetyan:

'Do you know why I am still doing this?' – Prof. Lew asked me at one of the very first PhD supervision meetings we had a few years ago. He then followed on to explain how he himself was very fortunate to have had the chance to learn from the most extraordinary legal minds (both practitioners and academics) who were very generous with him with their time, and how it has significantly impacted his own career path and development. 'This is my way of giving it back', – he said, adding then 'if only I can be of any help'. The halftones of humble irony transpiring from that last comment coming from such a grandiose figure sitting in front of me turned out, what I realised with time, to be an epitome of Prof Lew's personality: extraordinary intelligence, elegant sense of humour, and boundless generosity.

That memory of my first encounter with Prof. Lew came back to me again very recently. Last year I was given a chance to present at the XXVth ICCA Congress 2022 in Edinburgh, which was my first public speaking experience of such scale especially among significantly more qualified and distinguished panel members. A few moments before going on stage, Prof. Lew met me and said some very important words of encouragement, and then I spotted him and Prof. Stavros Brekoulakis, who himself was fortunate to have worked with and guided by Prof. Lew throughout his career, sitting together in the audience, having left all their engagements behind simply to showcase their joint support to their PhD student. It all suddenly made sense once again: behind every greatness stands humanity. Prof. Lew is a model example of the highest commitment to preserve the link between different generations of arbitration scholarship, to share knowledge, and to elevate others, the testament of which are the contributions in this book which also illustrate vividly the overarching success of that commitment.

Editing this book was a real honour and also an immense excitement as a chance to learn of the multiple ways that Prof. Lew personally and through his work inspired, guided, and developed so many prominent academics and practitioners from various jurisdictions, but also influenced and forecasted the development of arbitration itself. It can be argued (at least I do in my doctoral research) that Prof. Lew's dream of 'autonomous arbitration' has now come closer to reality than ever, all while various implications of that dream are still at the heart of the current debate, which only proves the visionary and topical nature of Prof. Lew's ideas. His writings on a large variety of issues in international arbitration explain the diverse nature of the contribution topics in this book which all relate to his scholarship in one way or another.

This is also my own way of giving it back to Prof. Lew on behalf of so many inspired by his legacy to develop, in words of Monique Sasson, the 'art' of international arbitral process. And to keep dreaming.

Part I Scholarly Contributions in Honour of Julian Lew

A Arbitration and Dispute Resolution Generally

CHAPTER 1

Autonomous Arbitration: Were We Dreaming?

Noah Rubins KC

In November 2005 I was a mid-level associate at Freshfields in Paris, having joined the year before after a few years' practice in the United States. The intellectual foment in that environment was intoxicating, and now I was to experience for the first time the apex of the arbitration community – the Freshfields Lecture. And what a lecture it was to be – delivered by Professor Julian Lew QC, one of those at the origin of the lecture as an institution in London, one of the world's leading arbitrators and an accomplished educator and advocate. Professor Lew delivered the lecture in his unmistakable style: graceful, thoroughly researched, and thought-provoking without a trace of overwrought seriousness. It is these qualities that I would discover in Professor Lew in the years to follow as he offered me mentorship and even friendship. I am forever grateful for the generosity he showed me in that early stage of my career.

Also reflected in that lecture of seventeen years ago was Professor Lew's optimism and excitement. Underlying his thesis was the idea that arbitration is a positive force that is gradually overcoming resistance around the world. Who else would open a discussion of the law with the words: 'Do you dream?' The message was that the dream of internationalized, autonomous arbitration was one worth pursuing, and that after centuries its realization was at hand. I do not propose to challenge the conclusions that Professor Lew shared with us in London that day. But I would like to revisit them nearly a generation later to consider whether his dream is closer to reality today than it was then.[1]

1. The question of the autonomy of arbitration was one that prompted me to write my first publication in the field, a short commentary in which I concluded that 'at its present stage of development, arbitration would not be served by a divorce from geography and State-based jurisprudence'. Noah Rubins, 'The Arbitral Seat Is No Fiction', 16(1) *Mealey's International Arbitration Report* 23, 24-26 (2001).

The direction of travel was described concisely at the outset:

> The ideal and expectation is for international arbitration to be established and conducted according to internationally accepted practices, free from the controls of parochial national laws, and without the interference or review of national courts. Arbitration agreements and awards should be recognized and given effect, with little or no complication or review, by national courts.[2]

The 'nightmare scenario' alternative was legal cacophony, with particular national interests and procedures restricting access to private dispute resolution processes, undermining business expectations, and offering opportunities for tactical play to those bent on evading contractual obligations.

In 2005 the world seemed set on a solid course of integration and convergence. The European Union had just expanded to include for the first time countries of the former Communist bloc. Relations between the United States and Russia were relatively strong and cooperative. And the competition that today characterizes the relationship with China and the West had not yet begun in earnest. Professor Lew's lecture traced a similarly positive evolution of international arbitration. In particular, the New York Convention of 1958 had transformed the legal landscape by providing a single framework for the recognition and enforcement of foreign arbitral awards. While the Convention did not deal with annulment at the arbitral seat, it served as a model for legislators in many countries who would consider the limited list of grounds for refusing enforcement when devising domestic provisions on annulment.

Where has international arbitration moved since 2005? Has the dream of autonomous arbitration moved closer or further away? Below I offer illustration in three distinct areas that Professor Lew highlighted in his Freshfields lecture, and which can serve as a barometer for the autonomy of arbitration: arbitrability, set aside proceedings at the arbitral seat, and international arbitration procedure. In each of these key areas, Professor Lew noted significant changes in the direction of self-contained and homogeneous arbitration around the world. But with respect to each of these elements, the subsequent years have seen reversals, and diversity remains.

§1.01 ARBITRABILITY

In many ways municipal laws on arbitrability form the cornerstone of arbitration.[3] It is by the grace of governments that parties are free to resolve their disputes privately in binding fashion. In the absence of that permission, national courts generally enjoy unlimited subject-matter jurisdiction – no one can be compelled to arbitrate, and resulting awards will be set aside if they transgress the exclusive jurisdiction of the courts. But the impact of limitations on arbitrability is broader than this. First, the New York Convention specifically allows enforcing courts in Member States to refuse

2. Julian Lew QC, 'Achieving the Dream: Autonomous Arbitration', 22(2) *Arbitration International* 179 (2006).
3. *See* generally Loukas Mistelis & Stavros Brekoulakis, *Arbitrability: International and Comparative Perspectives* (Kluwer 2009).

recognition and enforcement of foreign arbitral awards where the subject matter of the award to be enforced is not capable of being resolved by arbitration at the place where it was issued.[4] Moreover, arbitral tribunals faced with objections on the ground of arbitrability frequently look beyond the law at the arbitral seat. Jurisdiction may also be declined if the dispute is non-arbitrable under the proper law of the contract or the law at the place of likely enforcement.[5] As a result, the broadening of subject matter that can be submitted to arbitration has long been seen as a key measure of arbitral autonomy.

The 1980s and 1990s saw a marked expansion of arbitrability around the world, as Professor Lew convincingly documented in his Freshfields Lecture.[6] However, there remains a great deal of variety in the approaches of national laws with respect to arbitrability. None of the international conventions on arbitration touch the issue of arbitrability, other than to reserve the right of Member States to refuse enforcement where local law limits it.[7] Many countries continue to reserve to State courts exclusive jurisdiction with respect to competition, real estate, insolvency, and family law. These are areas that lie at the intersection of core State functions, public policy, and third-party rights, and the reluctance of governments to cede judicial control is therefore understandable. But there are other areas where arbitrability has remained restricted, or even retreated, that are harder to reconcile with an inexorable march towards autonomous arbitration.

Most notable in this regard is the Russian Federation. The Russian Law on International Commercial Arbitration declares that all matters are arbitrable unless legislation otherwise indicates.[8] But the Code of Civil Procedure and the Arbitrazh (Commercial Court) Procedure Code introduces extensive lists of non-arbitrable subject matter.[9] These include insolvency, labour relations, inheritance, environmental damage, and public procurement.[10] Moreover, a wide range of corporate disputes are relegated to national courts while others - including post-M&A and shareholder disputes - can only be arbitrated if the seat is in Russia and the chosen arbitral institution has received a licence from the Russian government to operate.[11] The

4. New York Convention 1958, Article V(2)(a). For a detailed discussion of the perceived shortcomings of the New York Convention in relation to arbitrability and proposed solutions, *see* Homayoon Arfazadeh, 'Arbitrability under the New York Convention: The *Lex Fori* Revisited', 17(1) *Arbitration International* 73 (2001).
5. Bernard Hanotiau, 'What Law Governs the Issue of Arbitrability?', 12(4) *Arbitration International* 391 (1996). *See also* Nigel Blackaby, Constantine Partasides, Alan Redfern & Martin Hunter, *Redfern and Hunter on International Arbitration* (Oxford University Press, 2015) at para. 2.128.
6. In the United States, the seminal case on arbitrability that signalled a course towards broad autonomy in this area was *Mitsubishi Motors Corp. v. Soler Chrysler-Plymouth, Inc.*, 105 S. Ct. 3346 (1985), in which the US Supreme Court held that competition (antitrust) matters can be decided by international arbitration tribunals.
7. There is nothing particularly surprising about this lacuna, which is similar in nature and scope to the absence of guidance in international conventions on the definition of public policy.
8. Law on International Commercial Arbitration of the Russian Federation, Article 1(3).
9. Civil Procedure Code of the Russian Federation, Article 22(1); Arbitrazh Procedural Code of the Russian Federation, Article 33.
10. For a detailed review of court decisions surrounding the arbitration of public procurement disputes, *see* Egor Kosarev, 'ВС РФ взял курс на арбитрабельность', Zakon.ru, 9 August 2018.
11. Civil Procedure Code of the Russian Federation, Article 22.1(3)-(4).

restriction on arbitrating purely commercial corporate disputes is unusual,[12] and has been maintained despite substantial legislative changes in 2017.

More surprising still were changes introduced to the Arbitrazh Procedure Code in 2020, ostensibly in response to sanctions imposed by the European Union and United States after the 2014 annexation of Crimea.[13] The amendment accords exclusive jurisdiction to the Russian commercial courts over disputes involving sanctioned Russian individuals or companies who are targeted by Western sanctions, to the extent that the sanctions could deprive the Russian party of 'access to justice' abroad.[14] Also rendered non-arbitrable are disputes concerning the application of foreign sanctions against Russian nationals or companies. The impact of the 2020 changes was negligible until the war in Ukraine brought new international sanctions against Russian individuals and companies of unprecedented breadth and intensity. Today a wide swathe of disputes with Russian companies are effectively non-arbitrable under Russian law, with parallel international arbitration and litigation in the Russian courts very likely.

Such an extreme example should not overshadow remaining pockets of non-arbitrability for run-of-the-mill commercial disputes in more conventional jurisdictions. For example, in Belgium the list of non-arbitrable matters is long. Among the subjects relegated to exclusive court competence are typical areas of public policy such as family law and labour relations.[15] But the Belgian legislator appears to have maintained a relatively interventionist stance in commercial relations, putting into practice an assumption that a presumed weaker party must be protected from presumed coercion into an arbitration process that is presumed to be unable to ensure a fair application of the law. This is certainly the case with respect to insurance contracts. The Law on Insurance (2014) stipulates that 'a clause by which the parties to an insurance contract commit in advance to submit to arbitrators their disputes arising from the contract is deemed a nullity'.[16] Where the insured is an individual and the policy covers personal risks (health, home, etc) one might argue that the relationship with the insurer is akin to a consumer contract – excluded from arbitrability in

12. Many jurisdictions prohibit the arbitration of certain disputes internal to the workings of corporations, which potentially affect a wide range of shareholders. For example, in Italy disputes relating to the validity of financial statements can only be arbitrated if an arbitration clause is included in the company's deed of incorporation or bylaws.
13. Federal Law No. 171-FZ of 2020 'On amendments to the Arbitrazh Procedure Code to protect persons and legal entities from foreign sanctions', creating Article 248(1) and 248(2) of the Arbitrazh Procedural Code.
14. The Russian courts have set the threshold of proving a limitation on 'access to justice' due to sanctions extremely low. In *Ural Transport Machinery Company LLC*, the Russian Supreme Court overturned a first-instance court decision refusing to recognize an international commercial dispute as non-arbitrable on the basis that the Russian respondent was subject to international sanctions. The lower court had reasoned that the Russian party was subject to financial difficulties but could not show any particular obstacle to participating in arbitration in Stockholm. The Supreme Court held that a Russian party need only demonstrate that it is subject to sanctions, and that the existence of sanctions was in itself presumed to hinder its access to justice in foreign-seated international arbitration. It decreed that the dispute was non-arbitrable pursuant to the Arbitrazh Procedural Code. Supreme Court of the Russian Federation, Decision No. 309-ЭС21-6955 of 9 December 2021.
15. Civil Procedure Code of Belgium, Article 1678(2).
16. Belgian Law on Insurance (2014), Article 90(1).

many jurisdictions in the interest of avoiding uninformed consent and inequality of arms. But this is not the case with a wide range of insurance contracts covered by the Belgian ban against arbitration (political risk, aviation, business interruption, property coverage, etc).

Until recently, Belgian law also had an unusual aversion to the arbitration of distributorship agreements. For some time, the law in Belgium dealing with such contracts stipulated that disputes arising out of a distribution relationship must be submitted to the Belgian courts and governed by Belgian law.[17] Any arbitration clause calling for the application of foreign law was therefore null.[18] The rationale behind this rule was that the relevant legislation offers a minimum level of compensation to Belgian distributors whose contracts with the manufacturer are terminated early, and that this safety net was a mandatory provision of law.[19] This is despite the fact that Belgium's Advocate General opined as early as 1979 that protecting distributors was not a matter of public policy for the country, particularly in cases not involving an individual potentially subject to undue pressure.[20] Throughout the 2000s, Belgium's highest court repeatedly declared arbitration agreements in distribution contracts to be null and void.[21] A reform of the Arbitration Act in 2013 was in part intended to bring arbitrability in Belgium into line with the UNCITRAL Model Law - and EU law.[22] Arbitrability was ostensibly expanded to cover '[a]ny pecuniary claim' and '[n]on-pecuniary claims with regard to which a settlement agreement may be made'.[23] Recent lower court decisions have interpreted this broad scope to prevent the nullification of arbitration clauses in distributorship agreements.[24] But the Court of Cassation has yet to pronounce on the issue, and disputes still arise in Belgium as to whether a disgruntled distributor may ignore the choice of law and forum in its contract and turn to the protective courts at home for favourable compensation.

A discussion of the shifting arbitrability landscape cannot avoid mention of the fierce battle that has raged since 2016 in Europe as to whether EU Member States can agree in bilateral and multilateral treaties to arbitrate investment claims advanced by EU nationals. When Professor Lew gave his lecture, investment treaties had reached a high mark in Europe, both in terms of the number of treaties signed and the frequency of arbitrated disputes under their auspices. EU countries were at the forefront of investment protection, having signed in some cases over 100 bilateral investment

17. Belgian Code of Economic Law, Article X.39.
18. *Audi-NSU v. Adelin Petit*, Belgian Court of Cassation, 28 June 1979, 5 YBK Comm Arb 257-259 (1980).
19. Belgian Code of Economic Law, Article X.37.
20. Opinion of Advocate General E. Krings, 1979(I) Pasicrisie 1260, 1268.
21. *See, e.g.*, *Van Hopplynus Instruments v. Coherent Inc.*, Belgian Court of Cassation, decision of 16 November 2006; 31 Yearbook of Commercial Arbitration 587-588 (2006); *Sebastian International Inc. v. Common Market Cosmetics S.A.*, Belgian Court of Cassation, decision of 14 January 2010, 2010 Pasicrisie 119-126.
22. *Corman-Collins SA v. La Maison du Whisky SA*, European Court of Justice, Case C-9/12, decision of 19 December 2013.
23. Belgian Civil Procedure Code, section 1676(1).
24. Alexander Hansebout, 'Belgium: The Arbitrability of Distributorship Law Disputes', *IBA Arbitration Newsletter* 45-46 (June 2017).

treaties (BITs). but the attitude began to change after the accession of eight former Eastern bloc countries in 2004. As early as January 2006 the Commission began systematically to intervene in investment disputes involving its members and their investors, insisting that BITs between EU members were invalid.[25]

This issue, which came to a head in the European Court of Justice's (ECJ) *Achmea* decision,[26] has rarely been discussed in terms of arbitrability. Whether in public statements or positions in litigation and arbitration, the European Commission and EU Member States have tended to explain their hostility to intra-EU BITs and the Energy Charter Treaty as a matter of treaty interpretation and the hierarchy of international norms as between the EU treaties and investment agreements. But the reasoning of the Commission – and later most Member States – is directly analogous to that underlying limitations on arbitrability in municipal law systems. In particular, EU law establishes exclusive jurisdiction of the ECJ for the determination of EU law issues.[27] According to the Commission and the ECJ, these issues include the protection of investments made by EU nationals. Allowing arbitral tribunals to decide these questions, so goes the argument, would undermine the autonomy and integrity of EU law. Effectively the Commission and ECJ have come to the view that arbitral tribunals operating under investment protection treaties cannot be trusted to apply EU law correctly, or at all. It is for this reason (among others) that the EU insists on the invalidity of arbitration clauses found in intra-EU treaties (including the multilateral Energy Charter Treaty (***ECT***)). This is an odd position, given that EU law gives extensive deference to *commercial arbitration* tribunals, although they are also frequently faced with issues of EU law.[28] Like investment treaty panels, commercial arbitrators are unable to seek definitive rulings on EU law questions from the ECJ, ostensibly one of the central concerns that led to the *Achmea* and *Komstroy* decisions.

This brief discussion is not intended to explore the merits of the EU position on intra-EU investment treaties, but rather to illustrate once again that the scope of arbitrability has not proceeded in a single direction in recent years. Even in the pro-arbitration space of the European Union, State willingness to allow arbitrators to operate autonomously has waned in at least one important area of economic activity.

§1.02 SETTING ASIDE ARBITRAL AWARDS AT THE SEAT

As already noted, the New York Convention was of seminal importance in the increasing autonomy of arbitration. With nearly 170 countries now members of the Convention, uniform standards for the enforcement of arbitral awards outside the

25. Letter of the European Commission to the Czech Ministry of Finance, 6 January 2006, reproduced in full in *Eastern Sugar v. Czech Republic*, SCC Case 088/2004, Partial Award of 27 March 2007, para. 119.
26. *Slovak Republic v. Achmea BV*, Case C-284/16, Judgement of 6 March 2018.
27. *Energoalians LLC v. Republic of Moldova*, Judgement of the Grand Chamber of the CJEU, 2 September 2021 (the 'Komstroy' judgement), paras 42 et seq. *See also* Treaty on the Functioning of the European Union, Articles 267 and 354; Treaty on European Union, Article 19.
28. *See* Georgios Zekos, 'The Treatment of Arbitration under EU Law', 54 *Dispute Resolution* 9 (1999).

arbitral situs have become nearly universal. And despite the leeway left to Member States with respect to the content of arbitrability and public policy (discussed earlier), the grounds for refusing enforcement of arbitral awards are tightly circumscribed.[29]

However, the New York Convention says nothing about the grounds for setting aside an arbitration award in the courts at the seat of arbitration. This was no doubt one of the reasons for its success, since Member States retain control of the set-aside process and need not relinquish judicial supervision over the way in which arbitrators conduct themselves, interpret arbitration agreements, and respect public policy within their borders. While a number of important amendments have been proposed to amend the New York Convention to bring it into line with the UNCITRAL Model Law and current international practice (for example with respect to the definition of public policy), there has been little serious discussion of a new Convention that would harmonize grounds or procedure for the annulment of arbitration awards.[30] The one international instrument dealing with the topic, the European Convention on International Commercial Arbitration, sought only to harmonize the extraterritorial effect of an award that has been set aside at the place of arbitration, leaving States free to nullify awards on the grounds of their choice.[31] Given that the New York Convention allows for the refusal of enforcement where an award has been set aside at the place of arbitration, the effectiveness of awards - and therefore the autonomy of arbitration - remains potentially hostage to national legislation on vacatur and its application.[32]

One of the major goals of the UNCITRAL Model Law was to address this lacuna. It provides for a limited set of defects justifying the setting-aside of arbitral awards at the seat of arbitration, which tracks almost verbatim the grounds for rejecting recognition and enforcement under the New York Convention.[33] Several dozen countries have implemented the Model Law at least in part, and most major jurisdictions that have not adopted it have nevertheless followed the same general lines in terms of set-aside grounds. Nevertheless, a good deal of legislative variety remains in this area. Still more variation is found in the application of the law, naturally given the general nature of the most common grounds for vacatur such as public policy and violations of due process.

A recent example of the potential for parochial application of the grounds for setting aside can be found in relation to the English Arbitration Act 1996, which is not

29. New York Convention (1958), Article V.
30. Albert Jan van den Berg, 'A Closer Look at the New York Convention', 3(3) *Global Arbitration Review* 14 (2008).
31. European Convention on International Commercial Arbitration (1961), Article IX. For a detailed discussion on the Convention's interaction with the New York Convention and the harmonization of set-aside grounds more generally, *see* Albert Jan van den Berg, 'Should the Setting Aside of the Arbitral Award be Abolished?', 2014 *ICSID Review*, 1, 12-13 (2014).
32. The extraterritorial effect of set-aside at the place of arbitration is in turn potentially muted to the extent that enforcing jurisdictions disregard such set-aside. Much attention has been given to the variety of approaches in various countries to the effect of vacatur at the arbitral seat. *See, e.g.*, Rashda Rana, 'The Enforceability of Awards Set Aside at the Seat: An Asian And European Perspective', 40(3) *Fordham Law Journal* 813 (2017). Suffice it to say for present purposes that there is no uniform solution internationally that would definitively mitigate the risk of parochial decisions to set aside an award.
33. UNCITRAL Model Law on International Commercial Arbitration (2006), Article 34(2).

based on the UNCITRAL Model Law, and which includes a number of nullification bases not mentioned in the Model Law or the New York Convention. In *P v D*, the High Court examined a petition to set aside an international arbitration award issued by a London-seated tribunal based on section 68 of the Arbitration Act, which empowers the court to set aside an arbitral award for serious procedural irregularities if 'substantial injustice' has been caused to the applicant.[34] There, the tribunal had decided a central issue of fact against the losing party without the point having been covered by the prevailing side's counsel in cross-examination of the losing side's key witness. This was said to run afoul of the English law rule in *Brown v Dunn*, a nineteenth-century House of Lords decision outside the arbitration context requiring that witnesses be given the opportunity to address contrary evidence suggesting that they are not telling the truth.[35] The High Court accepted the argument that the rule applies in international arbitration and found that the failure to give the witness a chance to explain evidentiary discrepancies violated 'natural justice'.[36] It set aside the award. The idea that failing to address particular issues in cross-examination constitutes a fundamental injustice so infecting an award as to merit its nullification appears far-fetched in the international context. Indeed, the IBA Rules on the Taking of Evidence appear to envisage precisely the opposite – that parties may refrain from examining a witness at all, and still maintain the position that his or her testimony is false.[37] The High Court's position was clearly grounded in the particular English experience of commercial litigation, where exhaustive cross-examination is common and circumscribed by many customs and rules both written and unwritten.

P v D illustrates the persistent local element that can suffuse the adjudication of petitions to set aside arbitral awards. Optimists would say that the significance of this lack of international autonomy is limited, because very few awards are actually set aside at the seat. They would further suggest that autonomy is effectively being achieved *ad hoc*, as judges around the world converge upon a reluctance to annul international arbitral awards in the absence of defects that rise to the level of an 'international' defect. Whether that is right is a question of empirical data and the subjective assessment as to what is 'very few'. Recent research indicates that across all jurisdictions set-aside petitions are successful 23 % of the time.[38] That level has been characterized as a 'low chance of success',[39] but that is a matter of opinion. The fact

34. *P v. D and Ors* [2019] EWHC 1277 (Comm).
35. *Browne v. Dunn* (1893) 6 R. 67, H.L.
36. *P v. D and Ors* [2019] EWHC 1277 (Comm), para 37 (citing *The Vimeira* [1984] 2 Lloyd's Law Rep 66, in which Ackner LJ said, 'Where there is a breach of natural justice, as a general proposition it is not for the Courts to speculate what would have been the result if the principles of fairness had been applied').
37. IBA Rules on the Taking of Evidence in International Arbitration (2021), Article 4(8) ('If the appearance of a witness has not been requested ... none of the other Parties shall be deemed to have agreed to the correctness of the content of the Witness Statement').
38. Roger P. Alford, Crina Baltag & Matthew E.K. Hall, Monique Sasson, 'Empirical Analysis of National Courts Vacatur and Enforcement of International Commercial Arbitration Awards', 39(3) *Journal of International* Arbitration 299-330 (2022).
39. Monique Sasson, 'Empirical Analysis of National Court Judgements in Commercial Arbitration: What Do the Data Tell Us?', Kluwer Arbitration Blog, 13 June 2022.

remains that nearly one in four of the cases surveyed resulted in vacatur, and even accounting for inevitable self-selection (awards that are obviously valid will rarely be challenged, and those resulting in vacatur may be more likely to be published), that figure is material by any measure. It suggests either that arbitrators are making grave mistakes with surprising frequency, or that national courts are exercising discretion in the application of national arbitration laws more often than necessary. At the very least, the numbers confirm that there has been no substantial reduction of the set-aside rate in recent decades.[40]

It should also be said that the procedures in place for challenging arbitral awards in national courts remain diverse. Very few jurisdictions have established specialized tribunals to review arbitration-related matters.[41] Some systems, as in France, Switzerland and Sweden, concentrate arbitration-related matters at the second instance or highest court, to ensure better expertise of judges and to reduce the possibilities of endless appeals. But in most countries, regardless of which court is seized of the matter an action to set aside an arbitral award follows the standard procedures established for domestic civil litigation. This can pose a material obstacle to predictability in the enforcement of international arbitration awards. In France, for example, this has led to annulment proceedings (particularly in investor-State cases) that have lasted several years, with repeated examinations of arbitral awards by the Court of Appeal and the Court of Cassation.[42]

In short, national courts continue to exert significant influence over international arbitration in their application of local laws on setting aside awards. It is difficult to see any particular trend over recent years in this regard in the direction of increased autonomy of international arbitration.

§1.03 ARBITRATION PROCEDURE

It appeared in the early 2000s that arbitration procedures were becoming more uniform. Key to that development was the adoption of the IBA Rules on the Taking of Evidence in 1999. The speed with which those rules spread and gained acceptance reflected the real demand for predictability in the area of witness and documentary evidence.[43] Over the course of the decade that followed, a more or less 'standard'

40. National studies suggest that there may be a substantially lower rate of set-aside in some jurisdictions. *See, e.g.*, Marie Labno, 'How Often Are Arbitration Awards Set Aside? Analysis of Polish Case Law Shows That They Rarely Are', ArbitrationLinks, 24 May 2022 ('The statistical data made available by the Polish Ministry of Justice shows that between 2016 and 2020, only c. 7.24 % proceedings ended in the arbitral award being set aside').
41. These include Australia and India.
42. In *Serafim Garcia v. Venezuela*, for example, a decision of an arbitral tribunal seated in Paris upholding jurisdiction was challenged in the Paris Court of Appeal in January 2015. The Court of Appeal partially annulled the decision, and this judgement was reversed by the Court of Cassation. Subsequent repeated challenges to the decision in the Court of Appeal and appeals to the Court of Cassation followed, with proceedings pending today, more than seven years later.
43. Jeffrey Waincymer, *Procedure and Evidence in International Arbitration* 757-758 (Kluwer, 2012) ('Even where no agreement is present, a significant number of tribunals will utilize the rules simply because of their status. Over time, broad use will constitute a consistent body of arbitral

approach emerged in relation to the collection and presentation of evidence in commercial arbitration. This involves two sequential rounds of 'memorial'-style pleading accompanied by full documentary support, witness statements and expert reports. The two rounds are separated by a document production phase involving requests, objections and replies laid out in a 'Redfern Schedule' and referring to the requirements of the IBA Rules. Direct examination at hearing practically disappeared from international disputes, although in some places (such as Sweden) this had previously been quite common. Hearings involve extensive cross-examination of witnesses, with counsel having relatively free rein to explore relevant topics within the witnesses' knowledge or expertise.[44]

The process of procedural harmonization - and separation from national legal traditions - remained far from complete. In particular, a substantial proportion of London-seated arbitrations continued to mirror English court practice. Using a 'pleading style' of submissions, the parties exchange written arguments and some supporting documentation at the outset of the case, often on a relatively expedited basis. After these initial exchanges comes the document production phase, followed by simultaneous exchanges of witness statements and expert reports. This material is then linked to the pleadings in a pre-hearing 'skeleton' submission in writing, and through oral argument at the hearing itself.

The distinction between pleading and memorial submissions is more than formal - it can determine tactics and strategy for the entire case and reflects deep-seated views about how evidence should be presented in the United Kingdom and in Europe. It bears note that procedural norms such as these are rarely derived from national laws on arbitration or even from arbitration rules,[45] but rather from the diverse legal cultures and resulting expectations of parties and arbitrators.

This persistent split in approach was compounded by a debate that intensified in the 2010s regarding the need to distance arbitration procedure from the common law tradition that was perceived to have infiltrated 'standard' arbitral practice.[46] This was first because of a posited conflict between the emphasis on document production and oral testimony found in the IBA Rules and expectations of many parties and counsel

practice that can only be self-supportive. Counsel in arbitrations will also naturally look to the IBA Rules as part of their evidentiary submissions ...').

44. *See generally* Roman Khodykin and Siobhan Abraham, 'But at the Length Truth Will Out: Witness Evidence in International Arbitration: Developments and Future Trends', in Greg Fullelove, Laila Hamzi, Daniel Harrison (eds), *International Arbitration in England: Perspectives in Times of Change* 299 (Kluwer 2022).
45. The LCIA Rules include a default procedure which can apply absent contrary agreement of the parties or order of the tribunal. This procedure suggests that witness and expert testimony is to be served after an initial exchange of argument and documents, but it could also accommodate memorial-style submissions. LCIA Rules (2021), Article 15. In practice the default procedure is rarely used.
46. This is despite the IBA's stated purpose to create rules that combine common law and civil law elements. In 2017, the Russian Arbitration Association's annual conference included a session dedicated to demonstrating the tilt of standard arbitration practice towards the common law tradition, entitled 'Creeping Americanization of international arbitration: is it the right time to develop inquisitorial rules of evidence?' This session was one of the catalysts for the development of the Prague Rules.

from civil law jurisdictions, and second because of the substantial time and cost associated with these ostensibly common law imports. The result was the publication in 2018 of the Prague Rules on the Efficient Conduct of Proceedings in International Arbitration. The Prague Rules purported to reflect the civil law tradition's inquisitorial approach, limiting document production and witness testimony and placing the collection and presentation of evidence squarely under the supervision of the arbitral tribunal.[47] Although empirical evidence is scarce as to the adoption of the Prague rules in international arbitration, they appear to have achieved a sufficient level of acceptance to undermine the dominance of the IBA Rules.

The continuing diversity of arbitration procedure appears to be the result of resistance by practitioners and end users entirely to discard their national legal traditions. A purely international, autonomous form of dispute resolution procedure is in this sense less real than it was in 2005. Although many parochial practices specific to a single jurisdiction have become less common (at least in international disputes), the distinction between common-law and civil-law approaches would seem to be more pronounced than before.

§1.04 CONCLUSION

So where does this leave the dream that Professor Lew articulated in his Freshfields Lecture? Is autonomous arbitration closer or further away today than it was then? I had no intention here of undertaking the empirical analysis that would be required to offer a definitive answer to that question. It does seem on an anecdotal level that the dream of arbitral autonomy was probably further away than it seemed in the auditorium that Thursday evening in London seventeen years ago. The international arbitration infrastructure that was in place then remains largely unchanged, and the same lacunae remain today. Arbitrability is constantly shifting in various countries, and while many countries move towards the UNCITRAL Model Law standard of sweeping authorization, some important jurisdictions have reserved more space in commercial disputes for their national courts. Set-aside procedures still vary, both in terms of the standards and grounds for review and the procedures involved. And despite some broadly common features, arbitration procedure is no more harmonized today than it was then. If anything, the differences between civil and common law arbitration have crystallized, particularly in relation to the taking of evidence.

But is this really a nightmare? Or is it simply a reflection of the reality of the international system and cross-border commerce? Countries are not the same, and each State has its own priorities, traditions and sensitivities. By retaining some control over arbitration, they can be reassured that arbitration will not transgress their most important values. This escape valve, using both targeted arbitrability restrictions and judicial review of awards on limited grounds, gives States the confidence necessary to lend their police powers to the arbitral process, which otherwise entirely lacks enforcement authority. Moreover, the persistence of national influence allows a

47. Gonzalo Stampa, 'The Prague Rules', 35(2) *Arbitration International* 221 (2019).

continuing competition of ideas, with institutions, arbitrators, counsel and end users of arbitration borrowing and discarding elements of municipal law systems in a constant search for improvement. After all, increased autonomy can bring with it the risk of sterility and stagnation.

If we do accept Prof Lew's normative assessment that autonomous arbitration is a dream that the nations of the world should aspire to achieve, then we must also accept that there remains a great deal to be done before the dream becomes reality. It may well be that we have reached the limit of international harmonization in relation to international arbitration. Cultural and political divisions appear more durable and pervasive than they did at the beginning of the twenty-first century. Consolidation of autonomy may be a more productive endeavour than expansion in light of this reality. I also submit that there are a range of scenarios between dream and nightmare. The world remains a diverse place, and the legal effect of that reality offers advantages as well as obstacles to the international business community.

CHAPTER 2

Stateless Law as a Psycho-Social Phenomenon: A Short Contribution to International Arbitration Theory

Rémy Gerbay, Viraj Bhide & Mohamed Mahayni

Professor Lew's impact on international arbitration has been rich and multifaceted – much like his own career. A scholar, counsel, and arbitrator, Professor Lew helped shape every aspect of our discipline. On a personal level, Professor Lew's visionary idea for a 'School of International Arbitration' made it possible for legions of lawyers (like us) to cut their 'academic teeth', and take their first steps on their own journeys as legal scholars. This chapter offers a small repayment for the personal debt each of this chapter's authors owe Professor Lew.

One of Professor Lew's most salient contributions to our discipline is in the field of legal theory and, in particular, on the so-called autonomous theory of arbitration, of which he is a partisan.[1] *In reality, the word 'partisan' does not do justice to Professor Lew's open-mindedness and intellectual curiosity. Indeed, those who worked with him know that Professor Lew always welcomes a salutary debate.*[2] *The present chapter offers a small contribution to the body of academic work discussing the autonomous theory of arbitration.*

1. *See* for example 'Chapter 5 Juridical Nature of Arbitration', in Julian D.M. Lew et al., Comparative International Commercial Arbitration, Kluwer Law International, 2003, 71-97: Julian Lew, 'Chapter 20: Achieving the Dream: Autonomous Arbitration?', in Julian D.M. Lew & Loukas A. Mistelis (eds), Arbitration Insights: Twenty Years of the Annual Lecture of the School of International Arbitration, Kluwer Law International, 2007, 455-485.
2. *See* for example the invitation extended to Lord Mance to speak at the 2015 Freshfields – Queen Mary Lecture where he defended his own State-centred view of arbitration theory: Lord Mance, 'Arbitration – A Law unto Itself? 30th Annual Lecture organised by the School of International Arbitration and Freshfields Bruckhaus Deringer' (2015), available at https://www.supremecourt.uk/docs/speech-151104.pdf.

§2.01 INTRODUCTION

International arbitration practice has evolved tremendously in the past few decades, becoming ever more sophisticated.[3] That evolution has been characterized by a measure of convergence towards certain common procedural rules or practices, borrowed largely from the common law and civil law. In the words of John Barkett and Jan Paulsson, '[i]nternational commercial arbitration is conducted today with a broad consensus as to many important features'.[4] Some of these procedural rules or practices appear to be obvious and are now rarely questioned.

To list only a few examples:

- The merits of a case should not be discussed during a prospective arbitrator's pre-appointment interview.
- Neither party must communicate with the tribunal ex-parte after it has been constituted.
- During the proceedings, it is for the party introducing into evidence a document that is not in the arbitration's language to provide a translation.
- Anybody (including an employee of a party or party herself) can be a factual witness.
- If there is to be a document production phase, a party may be ordered to produce evidence that is relevant to the case and material to its outcome.
- Witnesses cannot attend hearings until after they have testified.
- Arbitrators cannot render default awards without putting to test the arguments which the defaulting party would reasonably invoke were it to participate.
- Arbitrators must disclose if they have been appointed three times or more in the past three years by the same law firm.

In the absence of party agreement to the contrary in a given case, few arbitration practitioners would contend that these are 'optional'. Yet, one does not always find an applicable rule requiring them. This raises fascinating questions. Can these generally complied-with practices constitute legal norms, even though they do not have any

3. Stavros Brekoulakis, 'Chapter 1: Introduction: The Evolution and Future of International Arbitration', in Stavros Brekoulakis et al. (eds), The Evolution and Future of International Arbitration, International Arbitration Law Library, Volume 37, Kluwer Law International, 2016, 1-20; V.V. Veeder, 'Strategic Management in Commencing an Arbitration', in Albert Jan Van den Berg (ed.), Arbitration Advocacy in Changing Times, ICCA Congress Series, Volume 15, Kluwer Law International; ICCA & Kluwer Law International, 2011 27-34; Leon Trakman & Hugh Montgomery, 'The "Judicialization" of International Commercial Arbitration: Pitfall or Virtue?', 30(2) Leiden Journal of International Law (2017); Remy Gerbay, 'Is the End Nigh Again? An Empirical Assessment of the "Judicialization" of International Arbitration'. 25(4) American Journal of International Arbitration (2014), available at SSRN: https://ssrn.com/abstract=2656624. On the increasing sophistication of international arbitration's governance mechanism, *see* Alec Stone Sweet & Florian Grisel, *The Evolution of International Arbitration: Judicialization, Governance, Legitimacy*, Oxford University Press, 2017.
4. John M. Barkett and Jan Paulsson, 'The Myth of Culture Clash in International Commercial Arbitration', 5 FIU Law Review (2009), 1-11, at 1.

basis in State-based legal orders? Why are these autonomous, non-statal, norms obeyed?

On the first question, the autonomous theory of arbitration posits that some such practices are indeed legal norms, which form part of a primitive, transnational legal order - the arbitral order. The second question has, to date, largely been left unanswered by the various theories of arbitration. In this article, we posit that compliance with international arbitration norms like the ones identified above is best explained by psycho-social factors; and that such psycho-social factors form the foundation of the arbitral order's juridicity.[5]

This article is structured in four sections. In §2.02, we discuss how legal orders can emanate from outside the State. In §2.03, we provide an overview of the different theories of arbitration. Focusing on the autonomous theory, we explain how a set of non-statal norms can become an autonomous legal order. In §2.04, we explore how psycho-social factors may explain compliance with the autonomous norms of international arbitration. In §2.05, we conclude that international arbitration community's shared beliefs and practices can be described as a source of juridicity,[6] regardless of differences of opinion as to whether it should.

§2.02 NON-STATAL LEGAL ORDERS AND THE LIMITS OF THE CONVENTIONAL STATIST MODEL

The fact that non-national legal orders exist, and have existed in the past, should not be controversial.

Historically, as Rudolf Sacco explains, up until 2,000 years ago, the law existed and operated efficiently in the absence of 'law-givers', much less a 'legislative power'.[7] In effect, Sacco found that 'prior to 3500 B.C. there was no centralized power and yet there was - and flourished - law.'[8]

Recent history offers other real-life examples of national legal systems.[9] When settlers occupied lands in the North American 'far west' before they were opened for sale by the federal government, '[i]n law they were trespassers; in fact they were

5. Our topic lends itself to a closely related question which we briefly touch upon, but surely merits further commentary: how do these autonomous norms develop and establish themselves in the absence of a central authority?
6. By 'juridicity', a term borrowed from Professor Emmanuel Gaillard, we mean the legal character of a norm or set of norms. That term is used to distinguish legal norms (i.e., law) from other non-legal norms and systems (e.g., morals, socials norms).
7. Rudolf Sacco, 'Mute Law', 43(3) The American Journal of Comparative Law (Summer, 1995), pp. 455-467.
8. *Ibid.*, at 458.
9. *See* for example Terry L. Anderson & Peter J. Hill, *The Not So Wild, Wild West: Property Rights on the Frontier*, Stanford University Press, 2004; Eugene W. Hollon, *Frontier Violence: Another Look*, Oxford University Press, 1974.

honest farmers'.[10] These settlers formed land clubs, with their own constitutions, bylaws and elected officers for adjudicating disputes among themselves relating to their purported property rights.[11] These were purely 'extra-statal' organizations, without any backing by the government. Similar associations were formed by cattlemen for the protection of grazing rights.[12] Other instances of State-less law were observed during the gold rush. Miners voluntarily formed mining 'companies' to regulate operations in a mining camp. These companies in turn negotiated methods for resolving disputes over mining claims, without the involvement of any government.[13] In all these modern examples, legal norms were enacted, complied with, and applied in dispute resolution mechanisms independently of States.

The idea of equating law and State, or of thinking of the law as intrinsically linked with a State, is anchored in nineteenth and twentieth centuries' thinking. But the oft-cited Hobbesian need for a Leviathan is not self-evident. First, it has been disproved in several natural experiments, which Paul Robinson calls 'absent-law' situations.[14] Second, this notion is historically dated, and does not neatly 'fit' in our modern globalized world where, for decades, non-State actors have grown in number and influence, structuring their activities across (and despite) domestic legal systems. François Ost and Michel Van de Kerchove aptly captured this erosion of the pyramidal model of law in the seminal publication *De la pyramide au réseau? Pour une théorie dialectique du droit*. As they explain, private actors today do not necessarily collaborate in the production of norms by the State, but develop, 'at the margins of State law, or even against it, a private, sui generis [form] of regulation'. That form of law-making is non-pyramidal, developing through networks rather than within the strict confines of domestic legal systems.[15] As the authors put it, Kelsen simply could not have written his pure theory of law in the 21st century.[16]

The possibility of Stateless law has been theorized for some time, outside the world of international arbitration. For instance, the a national, yet juridical, nature of

---

10. *See* Benjamin F. Shambaugh, 'Frontier Land Clubs, or Claim Associations', Annual Report of the American Historical Association (1900), cited in Terry Anderson & P.J. Hill, 'American Experiment in Anarcho- Capitalism: The Not So Wild, Wild West', 3(1) Journal of Libertarian Studies (1979), pp. 9-29.
11. *Ibid.*, at 15.
12. *Ibid.*
13. *Ibid.*
14. Paul Robinson, 'Natural Law & Lawlessness: Modern Lessons from Pirates, Lepers, Eskimos, and Survivors', Faculty Scholarship at Penn Law, 389. https://scholarship.law.upenn.edu/faculty_scholarship/389. A relevant example can also be given of a group of adolescents stranded on a Pacific island and rescued over a year later. The succession of events did not resemble the fictional story in *The Lord of the Flies, n'en déplaise à Monsieur Golding. See* Rutger Bregman, 'The Real Lord of the Flies: What Happened when Six Boys Were Shipwrecked for 15 Months' (The Guardian, 9 May 2020) https://www.theguardian.com/books/2020/may/09/the-real-lord-of-the-flies-what- happened-when-six-boys-were-shipwrecked-for-15-months; Peter Gray, 'Lord of the Flies: A Harmful Distortion of Children's Nature', Psychology Today (23 December 2020) https://www.psychologytoday.com/us/blog/freedom-learn/202012/lord-the-flies-harmful-distortion-children-s-nature.
15. François Ost & Michel Van de Kerchove, *De la pyramide au réseau? Pour une théorie dialectique du droit*, Presses de l'Université Saint-Louis, 2010, at 196.
16. *Ibid.*

lex mercatoria has been the subject of much academic analysis since the 1960s.[17] As early as 1964, Professor Goldman found that several international transactions were exclusively regulated by standard terms such as the International Chamber Commerce's INCOTERMS, and that arbitrators liberally relied upon common principles applicable to international commerce to decide disputes.[18] According to Goldman, these norms present all the characteristics of legal rules.[19]

Perhaps the root of the contestation over the possible existence of non-national or non-pyramidal (or heterarchical to use the terms of Teubner) legal systems can be found in the distinction made by Max Weber between the 'legal' and the 'sociological' points of view when one examines the question of what constitutes law.[20]

As Weber found, the 'legal' point of view is concerned with the following question: 'What is intrinsically valid as law? That is to say: What significance or, in other words, what normative meaning ought to be attributed in correct logic to a verbal pattern having the form of a legal proposition.' This approach essentially 'aims at the correct meaning of propositions the content of which constitutes an order supposedly determinative for the conduct of a defined group of persons: in other words, it tries to define the facts to which this order applies and the way in which it bears upon them'.[21] In contrast, the 'sociological' point of view asks: 'What actually happens in a group owing to the probability that persons engaged in social action … subjectively consider certain norms as valid and practically act according to them, in other words, orient their own conduct towards these norms?'[22]

From the sociological point of view, it is obvious, as Weber notes, that several non-national sets of norms constitute legal systems. For example, Weber notes that ecclesiastical law 'is still law even where it comes into conflict with "State" law, as it has happened many times and as it is bound to happen again in the case of the relations between the modern State and certain churches, for instance, the Roman-Catholic'.[23]

It is this socio-legal approach that we apply below, in order to determine why the *sui generis* norms of international arbitration listed above are complied with. Before delving into this analysis, however, a short summary of the major theories of international arbitration is necessary.

---

17. Berthold Goldman, 'Frontières du Droit et Lex Mercatoria', 9 Archives de Philosophie du Droit (1964), 177-192. For a critical view of Professor Goldman's approach, *see* for example Thomas Schultz, 'Some Critical Comments on the Juridicity of Lex Mercatoria', 10 Yearbook of Private International Law (2008), 667-710.
18. Goldman cites, for example, the presumption of a guarantee against monetary depreciation, or the presumption that the signatory of a contract has knowledge of the general terms and conditions to which it refers.
19. Goldman *supra* n. 17, Albeit, for Goldman, these rules taken together might not form a *self-contained* legal system.
20. *See* Max Rheinstein (ed.) (Edward Shils and Max Rbeinstein, trans.), *Max Weber on Law in Economy and Society*, 20th Century Legal Philosophy Series, Vol. VI, Harvard University Press, 1954, reproduced in Max Weber, *Economy and Society: An Outline of Interpretive Sociology* (Guenther Roth & Claus Wittich, eds), University of California Press, 1978, at 311 et seq.
21. *Ibid.*, at 311.
22. *Ibid.*
23. *Ibid.*, at 316.

§2.03 NON-STATAL LEGALITY AND THE AUTONOMOUS THEORY OF ARBITRATION

[A] Overview of the Major Theories of International Arbitration

Academic discussion on the juridical foundations of international arbitration has a long history. At the risk of oversimplification, legal theories of international arbitration can be classified into three major schools, all of which offer diverging characterizations of the relationship between arbitration and national legal systems.[24]

Two traditional schools of thought portray arbitration as a process that takes place within the confines of one or more domestic legal systems. These two schools of thought converge in finding that arbitration acquires its juridical character on account of its recognition as such by one or several national legal systems. These schools have been referred to as the Monolocal and Westphalian schools by Emmanuel Gaillard, and as the territorial and pluralistic schools by Jan Paulsson. For present purposes we refer to these theories collectively as statist theories, because of the weight (excessive, we argue) they attribute to the role of States and their legal systems in the workings of arbitration.

In contrast to the first two schools of thought, a third school regards international arbitration as a transnational legal order.[25] This school considers the arbitral legal order does not owe its existence to any one or several national legal orders.[26] Instead, international arbitration is seen as 'self-regulating'. This is widely referred to as the 'autonomous' theory of arbitration, of which Professor Lew is a proponent.[27]

At a high level, the main distinction between the proponents of the statist and autonomous theories of arbitration is that the former are typically reticent to accept the

24. Jan Paulsson, 'Arbitration in Three Dimensions' 60 International & Comparative Law Quarterly (2011), 291 (classifying these justifications as either 'territorial', 'pluralistic' or 'autonomous'); Emmanuel Gaillard, *Legal Theory of Arbitration*, Martinus Nijhoff, 2010 (classifying these approaches as being either 'monolocal', 'westphalian' and 'transnational'.). Professor Julian Lew, on the other hand classifies legal theories of arbitration as either 'jurisdictional', 'contractual', 'mixed or hybrid' or 'autonomous'. *See* Julian Lew, 'Chapter 20: Achieving the Dream: Autonomous Arbitration?', in Julian D.M. Lew & Loukas A. Mistelis (eds), *Arbitration Insights: Twenty Years of the Annual Lecture of the School of International Arbitration*, Kluwer Law International, 2007, 455-485.
25. *See* Emmanuel Gaillard, *Legal Theory of International Arbitration*, Martinus Nijhoff Publishers, 2010, at para. 43, citing E. Loquin (1986) 'L'application de règles anationales dans l'arbitrage commercial international', ICC Publication No. 440/1 L'apport de la jurisprudence arbitrale, note 95; Daniel Cohen, Arbitrage et société, LGDJ, 1993, at 21, and Thomas Clay, L'arbitre, Dalloz, 2001, at 211-228.
26. This is a particularly gross oversimplification, as we shall see immediately hereafter.
27. *See* Julian Lew, 'Chapter 20: Achieving the Dream: Autonomous Arbitration?', in Julian D.M. Lew & Loukas A. Mistelis (eds), *Arbitration Insights: Twenty Years of the Annual Lecture of the School of International Arbitration*, Kluwer Law International, 2007, 455-485: 'International arbitration exists in a sphere or domain independent of and separate from national laws and jurisdictions (...) [it] coexists with national laws and jurisdictions to the extent only that it is expected, and international law and comity require, that national laws will recognise and support the international arbitration process (...) [it] is today an autonomous, largely self-regulating dispute resolution mechanism.'

idea that 'law' can exist outside of the State. By contrast, the latter readily acknowledge the possibility of Stateless law.[28]

[B] How Does an 'Autonomous' Set of Rules and Practices Become a Legal Order?

Partisans of the autonomous theory do not share the same views regarding the reasons for which the arbitral order can be regarded as autonomous, and the manner in which such an autonomous order is constituted.

On the one hand, Professor Emmanuel Gaillard's preferred representation of an autonomous arbitral order corresponds to what he calls a 'transnational legal order'.[29] This representation 'contemplates the States collectively, not individually',[30] and such a transnational legal order is 'independent of, **but based on**, national legal orders'.[31] Professor Gaillard regards this legal order as 'as emanating from the States, in the same way that, in a positivist conception of international law, the international legal order stems from the will of the States, without this preventing it from having an autonomous existence'.[32]

On the other hand, Professor Jan Paulsson rejects this vision of arbitration, propounded, according to him, primarily by Professor Gaillard and other French scholars.[33] He considers that '[i]nasmuch as they [the aforementioned French scholars] ultimately seek to establish this [autonomous] order by positing its recognition by the very State orders from which they claim autonomy, their idea is circular'.[34] In other words, Professor Gaillard's thesis attaches itself to a 'self-contradictory premise of an "autonomous" order recognized by the very State orders from which is purports to be free'.[35]

Professor Paulsson prefers a vision of arbitration as one of several 'private social systems which secure the enforcement of rights and obligations defined by its

28. At the risk of oversimplifying, 'Statists' also tend to reason in terms that are reminiscent of the positivist theories of the law; whereas 'Autonomists' sound more like legal realists, being more interested in what actually happens in real life rather than what should happen. In particular, the so-called jurisdictional theory of arbitration contends the following: '[T]he state allows within its territory privately administered justice systems (delegated justice or parallel justice) by way of assignment or tolerance. This follows from the legal effect which a state and its legal system attaches to an arbitration agreement and to an arbitration award. Consequently, arbitrators exercise a public function.' *See* 'Chapter 5 Juridical Nature of Arbitration', in Julian D.M. Lew et al., *Comparative International Commercial Arbitration*, Kluwer Law International, 2003, 71-97.
29. Emmanuel Gaillard, 'Three Philosophies of International Arbitration', in Arthur Rowine (ed.), *Contemporary Issues in International Arbitration and Mediation*, Martinus Nijihoff, 2010, 305-310. *See also* Emmanuel Gaillard, *Legal Theory of International Arbitration*, Martinus Nijhoff, 2010.
30. *Ibid.*, at 307.
31. *Ibid.* Emphasis added.
32. Emmanuel Gaillard, *Legal Theory of International Arbitration*, Martinus Nijhoff, 2010.
33. Jan Paulsson, 'Arbitration in Three Dimensions', 60(2) International & Comparative Law Quarterly (2011), 291.
34. *Ibid.*, at 291.
35. *Ibid.*, at 306-307.

constitutive group'.[36] According to him, 'arbitrants would no doubt on occasion be pleased to qualify for assistance from the machinery of the State ... But the point is that this is a vision of arbitration which functions routinely without judicial assistance'.[37]

To demonstrate that social arrangements can create non-national legal orders, Professor Paulsson relies extensively on the work of the Italian jurist Santi Romano. He summarizes Romano's understanding of non-State legal orders in the following terms:

> For Romano, every organized social group is a kind of legal order. It may be superior or inferior to a nation-state, or even parallel: the international community, an institutionalized church, subnational collectivities, professional and trade organizations, associations of myriad types-even families, including criminal 'families'.[38]

The footnote to the above passage is instructive, as it allows us to distinguish between adherence to a norm as a result of mere coercion by private actors and adherence to the same norm as a result of the norm having a legal character:

> There is a vital difference between enforcing a leader's command 'because he wants your coat' and 'because we depend on discipline'. The former is an arbitrary and personal exercise of power; the latter has to do with the group's self-regard as an enduring normative ordering, however primitive (in this case little more than a rule of recognition of authority). Max Weber was saying as much when he distinguished between enforcement of conduct 'because of considerations of expediency or the other material circumstances' and enforcement of 'conformity to a norm as such, i.e. because of its being formally accepted as binding'.[39]

Theoretical representations of arbitration look to States because of the legitimacy or legality that this offers. Looking to States for juridicity is convenient. It validates international arbitration as a legal order. It strengthens arbitral reasoning as objective reasoning. It legitimizes arbitral awards as binding. Detractors of the autonomous theory submit that the validity of the arbitration agreement, the effectiveness of the arbitral procedure, the enforceability of the arbitral award, and the legitimacy of the whole institution all depend to varying degrees on States: on their national laws, their national courts, on their participation in the creation of international law, or even on their 'widely shared moral values'.[40] Even if one concedes that international arbitration has achieved a certain level of autonomy, that autonomy is still conditional on the level of State deference towards international arbitration.

In contrast, the autonomous theory internalizes to some extent the ultimate guidepost within the community instead of externalizing it elsewhere. In other words, the guidepost is the community itself and its shared expertise, values, and predominantly user-driven objectives, which are the driving force behind autonomy. Ultimately, while we do not necessarily need to dismiss Professor Gaillard's view on the

36. *Ibid.*, at 307.
37. *Ibid.*
38. *Ibid.*
39. *Ibid.*, at 307-308 and note 44.
40. Emmanuel Gaillard and John Savage (eds), *Fouchard Gaillard Goldman on International Commercial Arbitration*, Kluwer Law International, 1999, at para. 1525.

juridical foundations of an autonomous arbitral order, we do accept, just as Professor Paulsson, that legal orders can arise from social arrangements 'outside the conventional statist model'.

Indeed, it is only 'outside the conventional statist model' that one can conceive of norms which, while not recognized as having a legal character by any State or agglomeration of States, create perfectly binding obligations (or generally complied with rules) in the context of an international arbitration.

§2.04 WHY ARE THE AUTONOMOUS NORMS OF INTERNATIONAL ARBITRATION OBEYED?

We contend, in conformity with the sociological approach described by Weber, that the autonomous norms of international arbitration can be said to have a juridical character because practitioners and users 'subjectively consider certain norms as valid and practically act according to them, in other words, orient their own conduct towards these norms'.[41]

But how can compliance with these norms be explained? We briefly examine the various explanations provided by other authors (namely, coercion, legitimacy and organizational theory), before adding a small piece to the puzzle in the form of a purely psycho-social explanation.

[A] Social or Psychological Coercion

Max Weber suggests that even within the framework of a sociological approach, the existence of a State-based or non-statal legal order supposes the existence of 'coercive means, whether of a physical or psychological kind'.[42]

In the absence of such a coercive framework, Weber would distinguish between convention, custom and law.

According to Weber, convention shall be said to exist 'wherever a certain conduct is sought to be induced without, however, any coercion, physical or psychological, and, at least under normal circumstances, without any direct reaction other than the expression of approval or disapproval on the part of those persons who constitute the environment of the actor'.[43]

Obligations arising out of mere conventions would not be legal obligations by themselves, but may be transformed into law over time, as evidenced by the following passage:

---

41. Weber, *supra* n. 20, at 311.
42. *Ibid.*, at 317: 'A "legal order" shall rather be said to exist wherever coercive means, of a physical or psychological kind, are available, i.e., wherever they are at the disposal of one or more persons who hold themselves ready to use them for this purpose in the case of certain events; in other words, wherever we find a consociation specifically dedicated to the purpose of "legal coercion."'
43. *Ibid.*, at 319.

> In consequence of the constant recurrence of a certain pattern of conduct, the idea may arise in the minds of the guarantors of a particular norm, that they are confronted no longer with mere custom or convention, but with a legal obligation requiring enforcement. A norm which has attained such practical validity is called customary law. *Eventually, the interests involved may engender a rationally considered desire to secure the convention, or the obligation of customary law, against subversion, and to place it explicitly under the guarantee of an enforcement machinery, i.e., to transform it into enacted law. Particularly in the field of the internal distribution of power among the organs of an institutional order experience reveals a continuous scale of transitions from norms of conduct guaranteed by mere convention to those which are regarded as binding and guaranteed by law.* A striking example is presented by the development of the British 'constitution'.[44]

A significant amount of literature already exists on how 'soft law' is complied with, the examination of which would exceed the scope of this article. It is nonetheless helpful to refer to an oft-cited article on the subject by Alexandre Flükinger.[45] Flükinger points out the role of emotions in ensuring compliance with both hard and soft law. He then proceeds to study the effects of various emotions on obedience,[46] before examining 'manipulation techniques' that make individuals 'choose to act in ways they otherwise would not'.

The role of emotions must not be contrasted with that of reason, but understood as a complementary mechanism in achieving compliance:

> [W]hile it is reasonable to drive on the right side of continental roads, an emotional reading of the issue might focus on the fear of an accident (not to mention a fine). The rational choice theory might lead someone to prefer a solution that involves deliberately breaking the law, if this is less costly in terms of both of money and image, as studies in law and economics have theorized. On the other hand, an emotional reading would show that desire for wealth, greed or fear of impoverishment would weigh more than pride and honour in compliance with law or the embarrassment that guilt stemming from a violation might evoke. The opposition between reason and emotion is in fact used for persuasive purposes in all decision-making processes, whether legal, political, economic or other: an individual who calls another to reason is actually trying to show him that his decision may be based on other emotions that could prevail or that certain emotions can be appeased.[47]

Flückinger explains that in the case of 'soft' law, it is obvious that in the absence of a legal sanction, the '[o]bservance of non-binding rules cannot be explained solely by the rational choice theory ... .'[48] His explanations of the emotions behind the obedience of soft law resemble the coercive means 'of a psychological' nature identified by Weber. Both Weber and Flükinger nonetheless demonstrate that 'soft' law norms can be

44. *Ibid.*, at 323. Emphasis added.
45. Alexandre Flückinger, 'Why Do We Obey Soft Law?', in Stéphane Nahrath and Frédéric Varone eds, Rediscovering Public Law and Public Administration in Comparative Policy Analysis: A Tribute to Peter Knoepfel, Presses polytechniques romandes, 2009, 45-62.
46. *Ibid.* Flükinger surveys the following emotions: obedience of authority, fear, shame, joy, surprise and empathy.
47. *Ibid.*, at 47.
48. *Ibid.*, at 48.

'binding' – not from the point of view of a positivist-normativist scholar, but from the point of view of the addressee of the norm.

In our view, what Weber refers to as 'conventional' norms do not lose their juridical nature merely because of the absence of a coercive apparatus.[49] Nor are the emotional reasons identified by Flükinger the only means of securing compliance with soft norms. Other reasons for the obedience of these norms can be found in the notions of legitimacy and organizational theory, which we examine below.

[B] Legitimacy and Organizational Theory

Legitimacy of the norm. Flükinger also points out that emotional reasons or rational reasons may not suffice by themselves to explain obedience with soft law, and that law is also observed 'when individuals believe in its legitimacy ... by complying spontaneously with it'.[50]

He finds this explanation to be largely based on natural law theory, such that '[m]oral, ethical and justice-related explanations find in this type of work a welcome foundation: I personally don't kill other humans, not because I fear the criminal penalty, but from a personal conviction of the correctness, fairness and legitimacy of that rule'.[51]

Given the nature of the norms in international arbitration that we are attempting to explain, such an explanation is of limited use to us. In effect, while a soft norm perceived to be 'illegitimate' might not be complied with, mere legitimacy, in our view, does not explain the perception why a certain soft norm is perceived to be 'binding'.

For instance, nothing would prevent the adoption of a norm that *does not* require a party to submit translations of documents which are not in the language of the arbitration, or *does not* require a witness to be sequestered before testifying at a hearing. A close look at the rules of procedure of various States reveals significant divergence on these subjects. And yet, we find uniform adherence to these norms in international arbitration.

Arbitration as an epistemic community. Various authors have submitted sociological takes on each commercial and investment arbitration as an 'organizational field'. Organizational fields comprise 'key suppliers, resource and product consumers,

49. Weber himself concedes that 'from the point of view of sociology, the transitions from mere usage to convention and from it to law are fluid' and that: 'Present ethnological literature does not allow us to determine very clearly the point of transition from the stage of mere custom to the, at first vaguely and dimly experienced, "consensual" character of social action, or, in other words, to the conception of the binding nature of certain accustomed modes of conduct. Even less can we trace the changes of the scope of activities with respect to which this transition took place. We shall thus by-pass this problem. *It is entirely a question of terminology and convenience at which point of this continuum one shall assume the existence of the subjective conception of a "legal obligation."*' Emphasis added. *See* Weber, *supra* n. 20, at 320-321.
50. Alexandre Flückinger, 'Why Do We Obey Soft Law?', in Stéphane Nahrath & Frédéric Varone (eds), *Rediscovering Public Law and Public Administration in Comparative Policy Analysis: A Tribute to Peter Knoepfel*, Presses polytechniques romandes, 2009, at 49.
51. *Ibid.*

regulatory agencies and other organizations that produce similar services or products'.[52] These institutions and actors interact regularly giving rise to 'the development of a mutual awareness among participants in a set of organizations that they are involved in a common enterprise'.[53] The existence of an international arbitration field – in the sociological sense – is hardly debatable.[54]

Importantly, this field is driven by its international arbitration community, the features of which may impact its values, beliefs, and objectives. The international arbitration community 'refers to those who make up and surround the institutions that comprise international commercial arbitration'.[55] Traditionally, this community was dominated by senior European academics and retired judges ('grand old men'), arbitration practitioners in large Anglo-American law firms ('arbitration technocrats'), and a select few women who have managed to make a name for themselves in a male-dominated practice ('formidable women').[56] Over time, this community has grown in diversity and number.[57]

Despite its evolution, the community was and remains reputed for being close-knit. The diversification of stakeholders has seemingly not resulted in any lessening of the convergence that has characterized arbitral practice. Alexis Mourre makes an interesting observation:

> [T]he multiplication of potential rule-makers results neither in an inflation of rules nor in divergence as to their content. Rather, there is growing convergence between the rules promulgated by various players, conducive to greater harmonization of arbitral practices that were previously determined to a larger extent by local judicial culture and domestic procedural rules. Where the pyramidal process of lawmaking that characterizes States conduces on the international scene to conflicts of norms because of the persistent differences between national traditions, the production of norms in the context of a horizontal network leads to fewer conflicts of norms and more harmonization.[58]

52. Paul J. DiMaggio & Walter W. Powell, 'The Iron Cage Revisited: Institutional Isomorphism and Collective Rationality in Organizational Fields', 48 American Sociological Review (1983), 147-160, at 148.
53. *Ibid.*, at 148.
54. Emmanuel Gaillard, 'Sociology of International Arbitration', 31 Arbitration International (2015), 1-17, at 1 ('There is no doubt that the international arbitration world possesses all the key features of a "recognized area of institutional life" with a constellation of actors performing various roles and functions such as key suppliers, consumers, regulatory agents, and organizations, all of which share a "common meaning system" and interact more frequently with one another than with other social agents'.).
55. Bryant G. Garth, *Transnational Arbitration Community, in Max Planck Encyclopedia of International Procedural Law*, Oxford University Press, 2015, at para. 1.
56. Yves Dezalay & Bryant Garth, *Dealing in Virtue*, The University of Chicago Press, 1996 (Offering a sociological description of the arbitration community as they saw it back then; highlighting that the community is close-knit and intertwined by key players that know each other; underlining the importance of 'symbolic capital' and reputation in the social hierarchy).
57. Gaillard, *supra* n. 54.
58. Alexis Mourre, 'Arbitral Institutions and Professional Organizations as Lawmakers', in Jean Engelmayer Kalicki & Mohamed Abdel Raouf (eds), *Evolution and Adaptation: The Future of International Arbitration*, ICCA Congress Series, Volume 20, Kluwer Law International, 2019, 86-111, at 94.

At its core, leading members of the community cumulate roles as scholars, practitioners, arbitrators, experts, or members of arbitral institutions and professional bodies. And in those roles, they may come to interact or cooperate with each other regularly in their different capacities. For example, two members of the community can sit on the same arbitration panel in one dispute or be pitted against each other as party counsel in another dispute. They may even engage each other, when one serves as a legal expert on behalf of a party that the other is representing. These same individuals may sit on the 'court' of an arbitral institution or on the board of a professional body. In doing so, they may participate in the drafting and updating of the rules and guidelines that these institutions develop. Or, these individuals may collaborate with each other as co-authors or editors of academic publications.

Putting aside the concerns that these interactions create for arbitral independence in individual cases, the community is increasingly developing a common arbitration-specific legal culture. This legal culture 'knits together' the international arbitration community to a large extent.[59] That is not to say that the community is homogeneous or unified.[60]

Notwithstanding the community's apparent heterogeneity, it seems sensible to describe it as an epistemic community.[61] Epistemic communities are characterized by 'a network of professionals with recognized expertise and competence in a particular domain and an authoritative claim to policy-relevant knowledge within that domain or issue-area'.[62] This network's common values, skills and policy objectives renders it more specific than the organizational field in which the network operates.[63] The international arbitration community – at its core at least – meets this definition. They share common skill, knowledge, and expertise in international arbitration. And they

59. Joshua Karton, 'International Arbitration Culture and Global Governance', in Walter Mattli & Thomas Dietz (eds), *International Arbitration and Global Governance: Contending Theories and Evidence*, 2014, available at http://ssrn.com/abstract=2363751; *see* generally Joshua Karton, *The Culture of International Arbitration and the Evolution of Contract Law*, Oxford University Press, 2013.

60. *Ibid.*, at 19 (Recognizing the commonalities that community members share, but noting that 'arbitrators are too heterogeneous to constitute a unified community, and second, arbitrators' actions are not reflexively conditioned by a common tradition.').

61. Thomas Hale, *Between Interests and Law: The Politics of Transnational Commercial Disputes*, Cambridge University Press, 2015, at 77. Various authors have described the investment treaty arbitration community as epistemic. *See* Jeswald W. Salacuse, *The Law of Investment Treaties*, 3rd ed., Oxford University Press, 2021, at 21-22; Jeswald W. Salacuse, 'The Emerging Global Regime for Investment', 51 Harvard International Law Journal (2010), 427, at 465-466; Moshe Hirsch, 'The Sociology of International Investment Law', in Zachary Douglas, Joost Pauwelyn & Jorge E. Viñuales (eds), *The Foundations of International Investment Law: Bringing Theory into Practice*, Oxford University Press, 2014, 143-168, at 164 onward.

62. Peter M. Haas, 'Introduction: Epistemic Communities and International Policy Coordination', 46(1) International Organization (1992) 1-35, at 2, cited in Paolo Catenaccio, 'Cultural Variation in Arbitration Journals: The *International Court of Arbitration Bulletin* and *Arbitration International* Compared', in Vijay K. Bhatia, Christopher N. Candlin & Maurizio Gotti (eds), Discourse and Practice in International Commercial Arbitration, Ashgate, 2012, at 163-178, at 163.

63. Hale, *supra* n. 61, at 76.

have common values and policy objectives, even if they may disagree on the hierarchy between them.[64]

Isomorphism. Within the context of the organizational theory explained above, the notion of institutional isomorphism, as proposed by Paul DiMaggio and Walter Powell in 1983 merits a closer examination.[65] Their thesis was that 'individual efforts to deal rationally with uncertainty and constraint often lead, in-the aggregate, to homogeneity in structure, culture, and output'.[66]

DiMaggio and Powell identify two forms of isomorphism that are of particular interest to us: mimetic and normative. Mimetic isomorphism results from 'standard responses to uncertainty'. Thus, '[w]hen organizational technologies are poorly understood ..., when goals are ambiguous, or when the environment creates symbolic uncertainty, organizations may model themselves on other organizations'.[67] Meanwhile, normative isomorphism results from professionalization, defined as 'the collective struggle of members of an occupation to define the conditions and methods of their work, to control "the production of producers", and to establish a cognitive base and legitimation for their occupational autonomy'.[68] It is observed that '[p]rofessions are subject to the same coercive and mimetic pressures as are organizations. Moreover, while various kinds of professionals within an organization may differ from one another, they exhibit much similarity to their professional counterparts in other organizations'.[69]

The authors then proceed to describe the various manners in which normative isomorphism is accentuated. Relevant for our purposes is 'the growth and elaboration of professional networks that span organizations and across which new models diffuse rapidly' and the hypothesis that '[t]he greater the extent of professionalization in a field, the greater the amount of institutional isomorphic change.'[70]

Building on these authors' views, Thomas Hale underlines the professionalization of international arbitration and the isomorphism that likely takes place within it.[71] Once a norm is entrenched in an organizational field, the 'field exerts isomorphic pressures on other actors in the field, and in linked fields'.[72] Actors will – as in other institutions – find it more convenient to 'stick' to the institutions' existing focal points,

64. George A. Bermann, 'What Does It Mean to Be 'Pro-arbitration'?', 1 Arbitration International (2018), 1-14 (Expressing twelve non-exhaustive criteria according to which a policy or practice's ability to advance 'international arbitration's purposes' may be assessed; recognizing that these criteria are non-exhaustive, and that there is 'an extremely wide range of ways by which to measure the pro-arbitration character of any given policy or practice'; noting the 'truly remarkable' number and range of situations where international arbitration's goals oppose – or compete against – each other, thereby requiring trade-offs; highlighting that hierarchization of goals is impossible because a consensus over priorities among the values pursued by arbitration is almost certainly beyond reach.').
65. DiMaggio & Powell, *supra* n. 52.
66. *Ibid.*, at 147.
67. *Ibid.*, at 151.
68. *Ibid.*, at 152.
69. *Ibid.*
70. *Ibid.*, at 156.
71. Hale, *supra* n. 61, at 47 et seq.
72. *Ibid.*, at 81.

even if this produces consequences that run contrary to the institutions' interests.[73] This sort of *sticking to the status quo* approach is more convenient than selecting an institutional alternative, changing the institution or creating a new one.[74] The institution's autonomy is preserved as long as it is able to respond to market demands. But, as he also highlights, market demands operate imperfectly. States and users 'defer to legal expertise particularly when they are uncertain about the costs and benefits of institutional alternatives'.[75]

The nature of epistemic communities generally, and the mechanisms of memetic and normative isomorphism in particular, can therefore explain how certain soft norms can become effectively regarded as 'binding' by mere pressures of conformity within the arbitration community.

[C] A Psycho-social Explanation?

After having examined the theories of obedience above, we can now proceed to suggest an additional mechanism, which, in our view, can explain the juridicity of certain norms in international arbitration.

Our hypothesis is the following: the collective belief among a given community in the fact that a rule is legal and binding can suffice to confer a juridical character to that rule, even in the absence of any social or institutional sanction for non-compliance. To put it otherwise, in the field of international arbitration, the community's shared belief that a certain specific procedural conduct 'is the rule' and not a mere 'frequent practice' may be sufficient to confer a juridical character to that rule.

In effect, our argument is that the symbolic register in which we operate conditions our perception of the propositions put to us. This register can condition us to believe (more or less consciously) in the juridicity of certain prescriptions. And in turn explain (if not guarantee) generalized compliance with these prescriptions. In short, a shared belief suffices to establish the juridicity of the said prescriptions for the community that shares this symbolic register.

Looking to the psychological to explain the nature of 'law' is not new. This approach characterized much of the work of the Scandinavian legal realists such as Axel Hägerström and Karl Olivecrona in the early to mid-twentieth century.[76] That approach also bears much resemblance with the concept of 'opinio juris', one of the two constituting elements of custom in public international law (together with State practice). The International Court of Justice defined opinio juris in its 1969 North Sea

73. *Ibid.*, at 86.
74. *Ibid.*
75. *Ibid.*, at 87.
76. T. Spaak, 'Philosophy of Law of Karl Olivecrona', in M. Sellers & S. Kirste (eds), Encyclopedia of the Philosophy of Law and Social Philosophy, Springer, 2017. Robert S. Redmount, 'Psychological Views in Jurisprudential Theories', 107(4) University of Pennsylvania Law Review (1959) 472-513.

Continental Shelf decision as 'a belief that [a] practice is rendered obligatory by the existence of a rule of law requiring it'.[77]

In international law, it is the emergence, on the back of prolonged and consistent State practice, of a collective 'belief', which cements the juridicity of the custom. The mechanism appears similar with norms of the international arbitration order. Prolonged and consistent conduct by arbitration actors lead, over time, to the emergence of an increasingly shared belief that a given practice has become 'the rule'. It is then, we suggest, this belief that leads arbitration actors to comply with the newly crystallized 'rule'.

It would be interesting to conduct empirical research to test our hypothesis, perhaps on lines similar to studies in the field of medicine on the physiological effects of psychological conditions.[78] This, unfortunately, is beyond the scope of this modest contribution.

Interestingly, even among the strongest critics of autonomous or non-statal theories of law, some concede that leaving aside formal considerations as to the nature of what constitutes law, non-statal norms have a practical effect on their addressees. As Thomas Schultz, a critic of the idea of *lex mercatoria* as law, admits:

> [T]he lex mercatoria does not need a deep and detailed theoretical analysis to work, that is to meet the goal of arbitration as defined by Lord Mustill: serve the commercial person. The businessperson, indeed, barely needs the lex mercatoria, and much less any theoretical considerations about it, to go about his or her business.[79]

As we mentioned before, similar observations can be found in Weber's work, when he deals with the notion of conventions and customs. As Weber explains:

> We shall see that the uniformity of mere usages can be of importance ... At any rate, adherence to what has as such become customary is such a strong component of all conduct and, consequently, of all social action, that legal coercion, where it transforms a custom into a legal obligation (by invocation of the 'usual') often adds practically nothing to its effectiveness, and, where it opposes custom, frequently fails in the attempt to influence actual conduct. Convention is equally effective, if not even more. In countless situations the individual depends on his environment for a spontaneous response not guaranteed by any earthly or

77. North Sea Continental Shelf Cases, ICJ Judgment of 20 February 1969, para. 77.
78. For examples of such research in the world of medicine, *see* Roger S. Ulrich, 'View Through a Window May Influence Recovery from Surgery', *Science* 1984 April 27; 224 (4647): 420-421 doi: 10.1126/science.6143402; Arthur Shapiro, *The Powerful Placebo*, The Johns Hopkins University Press, 1997; Bruce E. Wampold, 'The Placebo Is Powerful: Estimating Placebo Effects in Psychotherapy and Medicine from Randomized Clinical Trials', 61(7) Journal of Clinical Psychology (July 2005), 835-854, https://doi.org/10.1002/jclp.20129; Kathy B. Thomas, 'General Practice Consultations: Is There Any Point in Being Positive?', Br Med J (Clin Res Ed) 1987, 294, 1200; Bruce E. Wampold, 'The Placebo Is Powerful: Estimating Placebo Effects in Psychotherapy and Medicine from Randomized Clinical Trials', 61(7) Journal of Clinical Psychology (July 2005), 835-854, https://doi.org/10.1002/jclp.20129. An article by the anthropologist Claude Lévi-Strauss on 'symbolic treatment' in indigenous cultures is equally relevant to our topic: Claude Lévi-Strauss, '*L'efficacité symbolique*', Revue de l'histoire des religions, tome 135, n°1, 1949. pp. 5-27.
79. Schultz, *supra* n. 17, at 709.

> transcendental authority. The existence of a 'convention' may thus be far more determinative of his conduct than the existence of legal enforcement machinery.[80]

One could evidently question if the mere perception by a community of certain norms as binding could confer upon these norms a juridical character. This would be dictated, not in small part, by the legal philosophies that one adheres to.

A purely statist doctrine would inevitably conclude that these norms do not constitute law. Objections may also be raised if one contends that sanctions are a necessary element of a juridical rule. In contrast, a multi-axiomatic approach such as the one adopted by François Ost and Michel Van de Kerchove would find 'a certain relativity of conclusions that no objective criterion could abolish'.[81]

In either case, it would be difficult to deny that we, as practitioners, do perceive several 'soft' norms of international arbitration as binding and that we apply them as such.

§2.05 FINAL REMARKS

In his sociological take on the legal field, Pierre Bourdieu famously remarked that law is the 'quintessential form of legitimized discourse', and that it 'can exercise its specific power only to the extent that the element of arbitrariness at the heart of its functioning (which may vary from case to case) remains unrecognized'.[82] Arguably, the shared practices and beliefs of the international arbitration community have provided an element of predictability as opposed to one of arbitrariness. If these can offer an element of predictability – including where written legal rules do not – then there is a serious case to be made in how we conceive international arbitration's sources of juridicity.

Cliché as it may sound, it is not because we cannot precisely capture something that it does not exist. Astronomers used to focus their attention on ordinary matter – the kind we see – to explain gravitation pull. But they eventually found that there was not enough of that matter to keep stars and galaxies in orbit. From their observations, they inferred the existence of dark matter. By analogy, there are various indicia that express legal rules do not account for all the law that international arbitrators typically follow. If we were to wait for that law to crystallize into writing – let alone writing in prescriptive form enacted by a State – we would fail to appreciate the gravitational pull that the community's own shared practices and beliefs exert.

From the way in which international arbitration rules have come about and evolved, we can already infer that something other than traditional, statist, notions of law must have been at play. It seems natural to assume that the same 'thing' probably still influences how international arbitration practices are taking – and will continue to

80. Weber, *supra* n. 20, at 320.
81. François Ost & Michel Van de Kerchove, *De la pyramide au réseau? Pour une théorie dialectique du droit*, Presses de l'Université Saint-Louis, 2010, at 567. *See also* p. 643 et seq. on the 'gradual and conditional' validity of juridical norms.
82. Richard Terdiman, 'Translator's Introduction to Pierre Bourdieu's The Force of Law: Toward a Sociology of the Juridical Field', 38 The Hastings Law Journal (1987), 805-853, at 844.

take – shape. No one denies that this thing exists. The only point of contention instead seems to be over the willingness to accept the influence that it does and should exert in practice.

CHAPTER 3

The Role of Arbitral Institutions in Driving Change in Arbitral Practice

Paula Hodges KC & Justin D'Agostino MH

§3.01 INTRODUCTION

'Who will direct the future evolution of international arbitration?'; a question asked and answered as part of the Queen Mary University of London (QMUL) arbitration survey in 2018. The answer made very interesting reading, with an overwhelming majority of respondents (80%) expressing the view that arbitral institutions were best placed to make an impact on the future evolution of international arbitration. But why are arbitral institutions so important for the evolution of international arbitration, and what role have they played to date in driving change in arbitral practice?

The arbitration community provides fertile ground for the sharing of ideas. Yet, with no single overarching governing body, there is a risk that innovation is proposed but not necessarily actioned. It is here that arbitral institutions play a unique role. While many of these institutions may be established as not-for-profit entities, they remain businesses, aiming to build their reputation and attract more users to the fold. As a result, each institution has an incentive to develop, change and respond to demand in order to win business. Institutions are also focused on the whole business of arbitration, operating within the community because the management and operation of each institution is intrinsically part of that community. Typically, each institution has a leadership team, a secretariat, a 'court', national advisory committees, and other related groups. Each of these will draw members from across academia, private and in-house practitioners, and other legal professionals. Institutions not only listen to discourse, but can also drive and direct that discourse. They can benefit from the dialogue of their users and members, but also shape how that dialogue is then harnessed and repackaged at conferences, in user groups and through institutional publications. As respected members of the community, leaders of institutions have a platform from which to drive thought leadership and play an integral part in the innovation that takes place across that community. As such, arbitral institutions can consider a range of ideas, adopt the good ones, and filter out the bad ones. They operate as both gatekeepers and drivers of change, acting (in effect) as the moral compass of the international arbitration community.

§3.02 PROCEDURE

This pivotal role is most apparent when we look at the way in which arbitral procedure has developed. There has been significant procedural innovation in arbitration over the last 15 years, particularly in the last decade.

Let us take emergency arbitration as an example. Back in 1990, the International Chamber of Commerce (ICC)introduced its 'Rules for a Pre-Arbitral Referee Procedure'. This was an 'opt in' process, which did not gain popularity with only 14 cases referred in total.[1]

During the 1990s, we saw various other forms of emergency relief emerge in arbitral rules, including The World International Property Organisation (WIPO)and the American Arbitration Association (AAA).[2] The real innovation came only in 2006, however, when the AAA's international division, the International Centre for Dispute Resolution (ICDR), introduced an opt out 'emergency arbitration' process into Article 37 of its rules.[3] The rest, as they say, is history.

In 2010, emergency arbitration was included in the rules of the Arbitration Institute of the Stockholm Chamber of Commerce (SCC)[4] and the Singapore International Arbitration Centre (SIAC).[5] In 2012 the ICC[6] and the Swiss Chambers[7] followed suit, with similar procedures adopted by the Hong Kong International Arbitration Centre (HKIAC)[8] in 2013, the London Court of International Arbitration (LCIA)[9] in 2014 and the China International Economic and Trade Arbitration Commission (CIETAC)[10] in 2015. Emergency arbitration has now become mainstream.

1. Andrea Carlevaris & José Ricardo Feris, *Running the ICC Emergency Arbitrator Rules; The First Ten Cases*, 25(1) ICC Int/l Ct. of Arb Bull, 25, 27 (2014).
2. WIPO considered this during the mid-1990s, but the innovation was not introduced. Dr Francis Gurry, Director, WIPO Arbitration and Mediation Centre, *The need for Speed,* 24 October 1997 at the Biennial IFCAI Conference. https://www.wipo.int/amc/en/events/conferences/1997/october/gurry.html. AAA Commercial Arbitration Rules and Mediation Procedures (1999), Optional Rules for Emergency Measures of Protection.
3. https://www.adr.org/sites/default/files/Summary%20of%20Changes%20for%20the%20International%20Dispute%20Resolution%20Procedures%20May%2001%2C%202006.pdf.
4. SCC Rules 2010 Article 32(4) and Appendix II.
5. SIAC Rules 2010 Schedule 1.
6. ICC Rules 2012, Article 29 and Appendix V.
7. Swiss Rules 2012, Article 43.
8. HKIAC Rules 2013, Article 23.1 and Schedule 4.
9. LCIA Rules 2014, Article 9B.
10. CIETAC Rules 2015 Article 23 and Appendix III.

Emergency arbitration is not alone. Expedited and early determination procedures, together with provisions enabling joinder of additional parties, consolidation of related arbitrations and a single arbitration under multiple contracts, have all become common and popular features of arbitration in that timeframe, as institutions have sought to improve efficiency and cost-effectiveness for parties arbitrating under their rules. Today, these features appear in the rules or guidance of all the leading arbitral institutions.

Each of these innovations had been aired and discussed by the arbitral community over a period of time before they were introduced. Institutions then played a critical role in codifying and legitimising those innovations. As time passes, the institutions continue to play an important role in stress-testing those procedures, as they learn what works, what does not, and how to improve.

Institutions also respond to criticism. Fifteen years ago, it was not unusual to wait for over 18 months for the release of an award by an arbitral tribunal and practitioners found themselves having to defend a forum for dispute resolution which did not always deliver on some of the most frequently vaunted benefits, such as speed and lower costs. Indeed, in the 2006 QMUL Survey, users of arbitration identified cost and delay as significant issues.[11] By 2010, there was a great deal of discussion around the 'long-standing problem of delay in arbitration proceedings', and several other surveys focused on time and delay.[12] Of particular note in the QMUL Survey that year were comments noting that corporate users 'are not happy with the time it takes between the final hearing and the rendering of the award', and suggesting that '... arbitration institutions are best placed to reduce delay'.[13] Another survey stressed that '0% of respondents considered a delay of more than a year to publish an award to be acceptable', and 66% of respondents confirmed that they were dissatisfied with the length of time that they and their clients had to wait for an award in the previous five years.[14]

Institutions took these complaints seriously and responded to the evident dissatisfaction of users. The ICC's 2012 rules introduced an obligation on arbitrators and parties to 'take every effort to conduct the arbitration in an expeditious and cost-effective manner',[15] required arbitrators to convene case management conferences,[16]

11. Queen Mary University of London, International Arbitration, Corporate Attitudes and Practices 2006 at 2.
12. For example, Event 'Delay in Arbitration Proceedings', Maxwell Chambers, Singapore, Wednesday 14 July 2010; Richard Power, *Delay in arbitration; is it really so bad?* Practical Law Construction Blog 28 August 2012, referring to the Berwin Leighton Paisner report 2012, *International Arbitration Research based report on perceived delay in the arbitration process;* Queen Mary University of London 2010 International Arbitration Survey: Choices in International Arbitration. Articles such as Joerg Risse, *Ten Drastic Proposals for Saving Time and Costs in Arbitral Proceedings*, Arbitration International, Vol. 29, Issue 3, pp. 453-466.
13. QMUL 2010 Survey, p. 32.
14. Berwin Leighton Paisner report 2012, International Arbitration Research based report on perceived delay in the arbitration process.
15. ICC Rules 2012, Article 22.1.
16. ICC Rules 2012, Article 24.1.

allowed tribunals to consider whether parties had conducted the arbitration expeditiously when determining costs,[17] and enabled the ICC to consider the timeliness of the award when setting arbitrator fees.[18] The ICC also introduced guidance on case management techniques.[19] We saw similar innovations from other institutions over the coming months and years, with efficiency in time and cost emerging as key priorities for the arbitral community as a whole.

As part of a major update of its Administered Arbitration Rules in 2013, the HKIAC added an emergency arbitration procedure and radically improved provisions for arbitrations involving more than one contract or more than two parties. The 2013 Rules made it easier to join an additional party to an existing arbitration and introduced rules allowing a single arbitration to proceed under multiple contracts. The HKIAC also gained power to consolidate related arbitrations in certain circumstances. At the time, the HKIAC process was arguably the most comprehensive regime available to address the inefficiencies and costs that were inherent in commercial arbitration. Since 2013, other institutions have followed suit. For example, in 2014 the LCIA built on its existing expedited formation procedure by adding several key procedural changes intended to improve the speed and cost-effectiveness of proceedings while also addressing the growing complexity and diversity of disputes.[20] SIAC's 2016 Rules also introduced mechanisms for consolidation and single arbitrations under multiple contracts, together with an 'early determination' procedure for obviously unmeritorious claims.

It is not only the handful of globally recognised institutions that share and innovate in this way. Newer and more regional institutions are taking their lead from the international players in order to bring their rules into line with international arbitration best practice. For example, when the Arbitration Foundation of Southern Africa (AFSA) overhauled its rules in 2021, it appointed a drafting committee of internationally recognised practitioners whose stated aim was to improve efficiency. AFSA's Rules now provide for emergency arbitration, expedited procedures, consolidation, joinder and single arbitrations under multiple contracts.[21] Also, when the South China International Arbitration Center (Hong Kong) (SCIAHK) launched in April 2022 with rules based on the UNCITRAL Rules, it added similar provisions.[22]

Necessity has also been the mother of invention for arbitral institutions during the COVID pandemic. When faced with 'lockdowns', working from home mandates and travel restrictions across the globe, the practice of international dispute resolution initially looked challenging. Arbitral institutions responded in short order, pivoting quickly towards online hearings, electronic correspondence and online case management. As the world has reopened, we have seen those same institutions retaining changes which have had a positive impact on the arbitral procedure for the longer term.

17. ICC Rules 2012, Article 37(5).
18. ICC Rules 2012, Appendix III Article 2(2).
19. ICC Rules 2012, Appendix IV.
20. *See* https://hsfnotes.com/arbitration/2014/07/28/the-new-lcia-rules/ for an explanation of the changes introduced in the 2014 LCIA Rules.
21. https://arbitration.co.za/international-arbitration/international-rules/ (last accessed 26 May 2022).
22. https://www.scia.org.hk/en (last accessed 26 May 2022).

By August 2020, HKIAC had created and launched a dedicated virtual hearing suite, equipped with state-of-the-art audiovisual equipment, and supported by dedicated technology staff as well as members of the institution's secretariat.[23] Similarly, SIAC directed users to Maxwell Chambers' virtual alternative dispute resolution hearing platform, which allows parties to conduct hearings via videoconferencing facilities and grants worldwide access to the arbitration materials on a secure cloud-based platform.[24] Importantly, despite travel restrictions easing, virtual hearings remain popular, as parties recognise the advantages they bring in reducing the cost, time and environmental impact of an arbitration hearing.

Equally interesting are the innovations that emerge gradually and do not cross-pollinate with quite the same speed. In 2014, the LCIA introduced a new annex to its rules about the conduct of party representatives. At the time, the annex was greeted with some scepticism, in a similar vein to the reaction received by the International Bar Association (IBA) Guidelines on Party Representation.[25] Other institutions considered similar provisions: the ICDR Rules 2014 provided at Article 16 that '[t]he conduct of party representatives shall be in accordance with such guidelines as the ICDR may issue on the subject', although no guidelines have yet materialised.[26] However, as more time has passed, it has been fascinating to watch the broader socialisation of the idea that party representatives and the parties who instruct them, can be held responsible for their behaviour procedurally or via cost sanctions. The International Council for Commercial Arbitration (ICCA) Guidelines on Standards of Practice in International Arbitration of 2021 are proof of this evolution, even if the role of the tribunal in sanctioning conduct may remain a subject of debate.[27]

Similarly, the ICC's current practice of requiring extensive disclosures and policing arbitrator conflicts of interest is perhaps ahead of the market, many national laws and the IBA Guidelines.[28] Yet, we question if it will remain ahead of the market for

23. https://www.hkiac.org/news/hkiac-launches-dedicated-virtual-hearing-suite (last accessed 27 May 2022).
24. https://www.maxwellchambers.com/2020/06/24/hybrid-and-virtual-hearings/ (last accessed 27 May 2022).
25. Wilmer Hale Client Alert 1 October 2014, 'These provisions have attracted significant attention, and are arguably one of the most controversial additions to the 2014 Rules' https://www.wilmerhale.com/en/insights/client-alerts/revised-lcia-arbitration-rules; Christina Bustos, *Empty Rhetoric: The Failings of the LCIA's Ethical Rules for Legal Counsel and Alternatives*, 7 Y.B. Arb & Mediation 307 (2015); *See*, for examples, the ASA view on the IBA Guidelines on Party Representation in International Arbitration 2014, expressing 'serious reservations' about the guidelines and stressing 'It is not the role of arbitrators to enforce standards and ethical rules of professional conduct', https://www.swissarbitration.org/wp-content/uploads/2021/05/asa-board-position-on-iba-guidelines-on-party-representation.pdf.
26. https://www.adr.org/sites/default/files/ICDR%20Rules%20English%20Version%20June%202014.pdf (last accessed 26 May 2022).
27. https://cdn.arbitration-icca.org/s3fs-public/document/media_document/ICCA_Guidelines_on_Standards_of_Practice_in_International_Arbitration.pdf (last accessed 26 May 2022). Likewise, the ICC's Note to Parties was updated in 2021 to encourage parties and arbitral tribunals 'to adopt or otherwise be guided' by the IBA Guidelines on Party Representation in International Arbitration (para. 67).
28. The ICC Arbitrator Statement of Acceptance, Availability, Impartiality and Independence requires that 'any doubt must be resolved in favour of disclosure' and that there are 'no facts of circumstances' that could call into question independence. https://iccwbo.org/content/uploads

long. As parties, arbitrators and practitioners become used to applying and complying with the ICC's practice, it may well set the standard for compliance elsewhere. Indeed, the ICC's approach may drive forward rigour in this area, setting the future benchmark for other initiatives such as the work of the International Centre for the Settlement of Investment Disputes (ICSID)/ United Nations Commission on International Trade Law (UNCITRAL) in respect of conflicts of interest.[29]

In a novel departure, SIAC released a cross-institutional consolidation protocol in December 2017, with a view to institutions consolidating arbitrations subject to different arbitral rules.[30] Little has come of it but, never say never; as users become ever more used to the breadth of arbitration clauses and the scope of consolidated proceedings, this sort of innovation may yet find a wider audience. What is clear is that these sorts of innovations, successful or not, derive from arbitrations because innovation wins business and attracts attention. No such drive is present within ad hoc arbitration which rests on legislative reform or the, far less frequent, updates of the UNCITRAL and other ad hoc rules.

§3.03 DIVERSITY

The arbitral community does not lack advocates for change. Initiatives emerge with regularity and in abundance. But without a global governance structure, there is no one body to monitor and oversee the delivery of change, leading to a risk of 'all talk and no action'. Arbitral institutions step into this vacuum, actively demonstrating their commitments to many initiatives and complying with them.

An excellent example of this is the Equal Representation in Arbitration Pledge (the Pledge).[31] A simple and clearly written document, the Pledge requires its signatories to commit to improving the profile and representation of women in arbitration and appointing arbitrators on an equal opportunity basis. The Pledge is something both authors believe in passionately on a personal and professional level.[32] With over 5,000 signatories as at the date of publication, that belief would appear to be shared widely across the community. Certainly, many law firms, including our own, are taking their Pledge commitments very seriously.

Yet while we believe in and support the Pledge, its committees and spokespeople can only cajole and encourage signatories to assess their own compliance and incite the resolve to improve. They cannot punish, shame or blame those who do not comply or are signatories 'in name only', with little intention to change or adapt. It is here that

/sites/3/2016/06/ICC-Arbitrator-Statement-Acceptance-Availability-Impartiality-and-Independence-Arbitration-Rules-ENGLISH.pdf (last accessed 26 May 2022).

29. ICSID and UNCITRAL Working Group III Draft Code of Conduct for Adjudicators in International Investment Disputes. https://icsid.worldbank.org/resources/code-of-conduct (last accessed 26 May 2022).
30. https://siac.org.sg/69-siac-news/551-proposal-on-cross-institution-consolidation-protocol (last accessed 27 May 2022).
31. http://www.arbitrationpledge.com/ (last accessed 26 May 2022).
32. Justin D'Agostino serves as Co-chair of the Pledge Global Steering Committee. Both authors are Pledge signatories, as is Herbert Smith Freehills LLP.

arbitral institutions have truly carried the torch of diversity and shone a light on party and practitioner appointments of female arbitrators.

All the leading international and regional arbitral institutions are signatories[33] and have begun to report on the gender split of the arbitrators appointed to their cases when publishing their yearly statistics.[34] Importantly, we have seen a concerted effort from those institutions to improve the gender balance of institutional appointments, with more positive figures emerging year on year. Indeed, female arbitrators have made up over 40% of all arbitrators selected by the LCIA Court since 2018.[35] This institutional picture stands in sharp contrast to the disappointingly low number of female arbitrators being appointed by parties and their legal advisors.[36] As recognised in the QMUL Arbitration Survey 2021, the institutions play a vital role as independent bodies, able to draw from a wide pool of candidates.[37] They can also entrust cases into the hands of 'first-timers' with appropriate experience as practitioners, while law firms may take the view that they should only recommend candidates whom they have seen in action, first-hand. Again, the LCIA has adopted a proactive approach in appointing first time arbitrators, with 17% of all appointments made by the LCIA in 2021 being arbitrators sitting for the first time.

It may be no coincidence that the overseers of our compliance with the Pledge are overwhelmingly female. Many of the key arbitral institutions, including the LCIA, ICC and HKIAC, currently have female leadership. In a very practical way, this places women at the forefront of the drive to achieve greater gender diversity on tribunals. However, as the institutions execute their diversity policies so effectively, the failings of parties (and perhaps more importantly) their lawyers are being thrown into sharp relief.

Where will the institutions' focus on gender diversity lead? The authors hope that the contrast between the gender split in institutional and party appointments will continue to provoke discussion and prompt action. We hope it is pivotal in making us all look at how we draw up shortlists of candidates and talk about the candidates with our clients.

This extends to action on more than just gender diversity. Arbitral institutions are well-placed to bring their laser focus to bear in addressing regional and ethnic imbalances on tribunals and in the wider arbitration community. We are already seeing

---

33. *See* http://www.arbitrationpledge.com/organisations for the list of signatories (last accessed 27 May 2022).
34. *See*, for example, HKIAC statistics 2021 https://www.hkiac.org/about-us/statistics (last accessed 27 May 2022); LCIA statistics 2021 https://www.lcia.org/media/download.aspx?MediaId=890 (last accessed 27 May 2022).
35. *See* LCIA Casework reports for 2018 (43%), 2019 (48%), 2020 (45%), and 2021 (47%). All available athttps://www.lcia.org/lcia/reports.aspx.
36. *The ICCA Report of the Cross-Institutional Task Force on Gender Diversity in Arbitral Appointments and Proceedings*, The ICCA Reports No. 8, 2020, https://cdn.arbitration-icca.org/s3fs-public/document/media_document/ICCA-Report-8-Gender-Diversity_0.pdf.
37. QMUL International Arbitration Survey 2021, p. 17, 59% of respondents identified 'Appointing authorities and institutions adopting an express policy of suggesting and appointing diverse candidates as arbitrators' as their most chosen option for the most effective initiative to encourage greater diversity in arbitral appointments.

some institutions reporting on the nationality of parties and users, and the region in which the dispute has arisen, seeking to compare that data to the seat, governing law and nationality of the arbitrators.[38] The statistics show a fairly stark picture. The proportion of arbitrators originating from Western Europe and North America is extremely high, and not reflective of the diversity of the users of international arbitration. Here, regional institutions can play a very important part by appointing arbitrators from the relevant region and giving those arbitrators the experience, and exposure, they need to secure appointments from the global institutions and parties too.[39] Arbitral institutions are also able to shine a light on other forms of diversity and inclusion. Efforts made by the ICC to build a LGBTQIA+ network and launch a disability task force should be applauded, supported and replicated.[40]

The global arbitral institutions can also effect change by continuing to lead by example. Just as these institutions have sought to promote female candidates for institutional appointments as sole arbitrators and presiding arbitrators, so too can they promote other forms of diversity. First appointments are often in the gift of the institutions, and they have a significant role to play in trying to ensure that ethnic and regional diversity are a factor in their decision-making. Similarly, they can give a voice to those same candidates as panellists, as authors, as members of institutional bodies and as spokespeople for the institutions. This does not absolve counsel from our own responsibility to commit to change, but it will help to shape a more diverse and vibrant community and provoke behavioural change through observation and experience of a broader pool of arbitrator candidates.

§3.04 TRANSPARENCY

A more controversial role that arbitral institutions have played in driving change in arbitral practice relates to transparency and confidentiality. Transparency has become a key focus for the community in seeking to 'legitimise' the arbitral process. Legitimacy fears have arisen in the context of investment treaty arbitration and the community's response to criticism has been quick and widespread.[41]

---

38. For example, HKIAC statistics 2021 highlight the geographical origin or nationality of the parties, seat, governing law and geographical origins of the arbitrators (divided into institutional and party appointment) https://www.hkiac.org/about-us/statistics (last accessed 27 May 2022); LCIA statistics 2021 includes geographical origin of the parties, the seat and applicable law, arbitrator nationalities and the number of first-time appointees, https://www.lcia.org/media/download.aspx?MediaId = 890 (last accessed 27 May 2022).
39. The ICC 'Hold the Door Open' scheme is an excellent example of how an arbitral institution can train future leaders of international arbitration around the globe, with its pilot programme focused on African practitioners https://iccwbo.org/media-wall/news-speeches/meet-the-2022-icc-hold-the-door-open-scholars/#: ~ :text = The%20ICC%20Hold%20the%20Door,held%20virtually%20or%20in%20person (last accessed 27 May 2022).
40. https://iccwbo.org/media-wall/news-speeches/icc-receives-equal-representation-in-arbitration-pledge-award/ (last accessed 27 May 2022).
41. UNCITRAL Rules on Transparency in Treaty-based Investor-State Arbitration, 2014; United Nations Convention on Transparency in Treaty-based Investor-State Arbitration (New York,

While little criticism has been raised against commercial arbitration in terms of legitimacy, the push for transparency has permeated into the commercial sphere too. Some argue that a lack of openness limits access to new entrant practitioners, keeps arbitration a 'secret science', 'imposes secrecy systematically' and causes a 'serious impediment' to the development of the law.[42] Transparency in some form also appears to be welcomed by end users, with the QMUL Survey 2018 suggesting that 43% of in-house counsel respondents wanted more transparency of information to make an informed choice about arbitrators.[43]

The authors see only benefits in offering transparency around the process of arbitration, particularly around institutional statistics, decision-making and the interpretation and application of rules. This relates to the 'business' of arbitration, and the institutions seeking that business should be offering far greater openness to users across the board.

So how are arbitral institutions driving forward transparency? At present, all the main arbitral institutions publish annual reports providing statistics about their caseloads. As already discussed, typically these include the nationality of parties and arbitrators, the number of cases, the seats of arbitration and the sectors which are most frequent users of the institution. However, there is perhaps less transparency than one might expect in other areas. Some arbitral institutions have been, and continue to be, surprisingly reluctant to share information about their inner workings, their cost-effectiveness, and their efficiency. This is particularly surprising given the move to make arbitrators and parties focus on the efficiency of the process themselves. Arbitral institutions should be publishing information about the time and costs involved for parties using that institution to enable them to make informed choices. Institutions should also publish information about how procedural decision-making is carried out where that rests in the hands of arbitral institutions (for example, statistics about the number of emergency arbitrator appointments and consolidation applications,). This is all information which can, and should, be made available to users.

Some institutions have made progress in this respect. In 2010, the LCIA began to share its arbitrator challenge decisions on an anonymised basis and has done so ever since.[44] The aim of disclosing that data was to share the decision-making process of the institution and how its rules on arbitrator conflicts of interest are applied. This, we

2014) (the 'Mauritius Convention on Transparency'); Working Group III: Investor-State Dispute Settlement Reform https://uncitral.un.org/en/working_groups/3/investor-state, Last accessed 30 April 2021; ICSID Rules.

42. New York City Bar Report on the Publication of International Arbitration Awards and Decisions in February 2014; Philip Wimalasena, *The Publication of Arbitral Awards as a Contribution to Legal Development – A Plea for More Transparency*, ASA Bulletin, Volume 37, Issue 2, pp. 279-288, p. 281; Constantine Partasides and Simon Maynard, *Raising the Curtain on English Arbitration*, Arbitration International, Volume 33, 197, 201-202; The Right Hon. The Lord Thomas of Cwmgiedd, Lord Chief Justice of England and Wales, 'Developing Commercial Law Through the Courts: Rebalancing the Relationship Between the Courts and Arbitration', The Bailii Lecture 2016, 9 March 2016, https://www.judiciary.uk/wp-content/uploads/2016/03/lcj-speech-bailli-lecture-20160309.pdf.
43. QMUL Survey, 2018, The Evolution of Arbitration, p. 21.
44. https://www.lcia.org/challenge-decision-database.aspx.

would argue, is achievable transparency, as it clarifies the approach taken by the institution without disclosing information about the parties' disputes.

In a similar vein, we have the Secretariat's Guide to ICC Arbitration[45] and HKIAC Case Digest,[46] both of which illustrate how the institution applies its rules in practice when making procedural decisions. There are also many and varied guidance notes and practice notes published by arbitral institutions seeking to raise the curtain on how their rules are interpreted and applied. The ICC now publishes case information about the sector, arbitrators and law firms involved in an excellent move designed to increase information available to parties 'without compromising expectations of confidentiality'.[47] Provided the arbitrators have consented to their personal data being shared in this way, users of arbitration are able to identify potential arbitrator candidates whom they might otherwise not know, without any intrusion into the underlying dispute or release of data about the parties.

Where we see less consistent transparency is on time and cost data. A handful of the leading organisations, including the LCIA[48] and HKIAC,[49] publish statistics on the average cost and duration of an arbitration under their rules. The authors encourage more institutions to follow suit, so that parties can assess as accurately as possible the likely investment - in hours as well as dollars - involved in pursuing an arbitration.

However, without exercising care, a quest for institutional transparency could quickly become an unnecessary and unjustified intrusion into a private contractual dispute resolution procedure. We should recognise that confidentiality is consistently cited by users as one of the most valuable features of arbitration. This is not inconsistent with a wish for greater transparency. Parties may indeed want greater institutional, organisational, and procedural transparency. They may want to find out more about other parties' disputes; how they are run and how much they cost. But this does not mean that parties want to share details of their own disputes in public.

Commercial arbitration is, and always has been, a party-led, party-controlled process. Its codification into domestic laws and international treaties has been designed to facilitate and support that. Where an arbitration runs without the need to trouble the courts to supervise its process or enforce its outcome, there can be no justification for requiring the parties to share any aspect of that proceeding publicly unless they choose to do so or are required to do so by law, regardless of whether they use an arbitral institution or agree to ad hoc proceedings. Arbitral institutions must therefore look to deliver what the parties want and need from that party-led process, rather than what the institutions believe that users should want.

Most arbitral institutions are carefully navigating this balance between institutional transparency and party confidentiality. Some institutions, including the LCIA, HKIAC and SIAC, provide expressly for the confidentiality of arbitral proceedings,

45. Secretariat's Guide to ICC Arbitration (ICC, 2012).
46. https://www.hkiac.org/Case-Digest.
47. https://iccwbo.org/dispute-resolution-services/arbitration/icc-arbitral-tribunals/.
48. https://www.lcia.org/LCIA/reports.aspx.
49. https://www.hkiac.org/arbitration/costs-duration#: ~ :text = Under%20the%20Rules%2C%20parties%20have,on%20an%20hourly%20rate%20basis.

leaving it open to parties to 'opt-out' of that provision in the rules when drafting their arbitration clauses, or to waive their rights to confidentiality later by agreeing to share the content of their award.[50] It is perhaps noteworthy just how few parties choose to do so. Others such as the ICC have taken a different approach, seeking to encourage the sharing of awards through 'opt-in' provisions, albeit carefully and thoughtfully executed by the Secretariat in practice.

We may be extremely interested in the allocation of risk and responsibility between private parties or the way in which the law has been applied and interpreted. We may want to find out more about how arbitrators make decisions, both legal and procedural. Indeed, it is very useful to be able to have public access to these awards.[51] However, the system of arbitration has not been established in that way. It is not, despite calls to the contrary, a precedential system,[52] nor one in which the public has any right to access the content of an award.

To this end, we caution against arbitral institutions assuming the role of gatekeeper in terms of confidentiality, in a bid to prioritise the 'common good' over their individual users in what is, at root, a contractual process. Provisions in rules that make confidentiality 'opt-in' rather than 'opt-out' may not override party choice entirely, but they do place the onus on the parties to act to protect that contractual process. We are entirely supportive of parties choosing to allow their awards to be published (usually in redacted form), but they should not be forced to do so, nor should their awards be published by default due to inertia or inaction.

Arbitral institutions wield significant power in their ability to drive change in arbitral practice. But in this area of transparency in particular, institutions must take care that they do not overstep their role or seek to impose views on their end users that those users neither share nor appreciate. Otherwise, there is a risk that we may render the process of arbitration unattractive and undermine one of the very elements that make users turn to it in the first place.

§3.05 CONCLUSION

Arbitral institutions have a unique role within the arbitral community. The leaders of these institutions are respected members of the community, invited to speak and share their personal views at external events. Similarly, the courts, secretariats and advisory bodies of the institutions are drawn from well-known figures across the arbitration spectrum including academia, law firms, counsel and in house practitioners. This cannot fail to lead to a melting pot of innovation through sharing best practice and new ideas freely between those various stakeholders, and then developing and improving them in the process.

50. LCIA Rules 2020, Article 30; HKIAC Rules 2018, Article 45; SIAC Rules 2016, Article 39.
51. For example, through the ICC and Jus Mundi open access database of ICC awards.
52. Alexis Mourre, 'Precedent and Confidentiality in International Commercial Arbitration: The Case for the Publication of Arbitral Awards' in Yas Banifatemi (ed.) *Precedent in International Arbitration*, IAI Series on International Arbitration No 5 (Juris Publishing 2008).

However, arbitral institutions are also businesses. They must win work and adapt to meet user needs. Here, institutions benefit from the unusual legal framework underpinning the word of international arbitration, which enables them to react with speed and introduce change in a way that legislatures typically cannot. This enables arbitral institutions to be gatekeepers of ideas and innovation, where good ideas get adopted and bad ones are left to the pages of journals and conference schedules. In this sense, institutions act as the arbitral community's moral compass, driving forward initiatives, monitoring compliance and preventing complacency.

Without the institutions, arbitration would remain a disjointed, disparate process heavily reliant on the slow-moving wheels of national governments to update national legislation, and the many and varied sets of rules which can be applied to ad hoc proceedings. Instead, arbitration benefits from a consensual approach, honed and finessed by the institutional process, peppered with enough differences to provide choice and inspire change. The authors do not doubt that arbitral institutions will continue to inspire, lead, and drive forward that change into the future.

CHAPTER 4

Reflections on the 25th Anniversary of the Arbitration Act 1996

John Uff CBE KC

This author of this chapter is one of the, now few, surviving members of the original Department of Trade and Industry (DTI) Advisory Committee on Arbitration Law which became known as the DAC. This body was tasked with reviewing and providing advice to the DTI on a range of matters concerning arbitration which were current in the 1990s and which culminated in the successful launch of the Parliamentary Bill which became the Arbitration Act 1996. The process, which occupied some four years, thus ended in a successful outcome. But this was the result not only of hard work and the gathering of expertise but also of a large element of good fortune and good timing as this paper will show.

Most practitioners and certainly their clients will, today, have little notion of how the 1996 Act came into being. Sadly, two of the original chairmen, Lord Mustill and Lord Steyn, are no longer with us but both left a rich legacy of reports as did the third and final chairman, Lord Saville. The final reports on the Bill, commenting on the sections in detail, give the impression that that production of the Bill was simply the result of applying the best available expertise; and the two reports on the working of the Act after 10 and after 20 years in operation have confirmed that there is no strong case for any major change to the substance of the Act. However, the Law Commission has, at the time of writing, embarked on a review of the Act and has put forward proposals for possible amendment of the Act including the introduction of a summary judgement-style procedure, a power to strike out unmeritorious claims, review of the procedure for challenge and appeal of awards and other issues. But it presently seems clear that the basic structure of the Act will remain in its present form and it is fitting, after a quarter-century of use in practice, to recall how, to put it colloquially, the Act came to be as good as it is.

The 1996 Act replaced the Act of 1950 which was itself largely inherited in its form and content from the 1934 Act. Vestiges of both these Acts are still seen in various parts of the British Commonwealth where the local statute law has not yet been updated. One to the features of English Arbitration Law is the provision of various routes by which an award may be challenged, particularly by an appeal on a point of law. In the older statutes this was by way of 'case-stated' which required the arbitrator to express the decision in the form of a question of law to be referred to the court for decision. This reflects the long-standing English tradition of appointing 'trade arbitrators' who were not expected to know the law, in contrast to the Civil Law system in which arbitrators were invariably lawyers thereby avoiding, supposedly, any need to appeal. By the 1970s the use of case stated had become a serious problem for the increasing volume of international cases being heard in London, such that London was being accused (mostly by the French) of no longer being a fit place to conduct international arbitration.

So come 1979, enter the Law Lords who, led by Lord Diplock, promoted and largely drafted the Arbitration Act of that year in which case stated was abolished but replaced by a right of appeal, apparently intended to be available in only the rarest case, save that the Act itself did not make this clear. There were other 'improvements' to the existing legislation but by the mid-1980s it was apparent to both users and practitioners that a new Arbitration Act was needed by the commercial community. But to convert a need into a new statute required a great deal more than good intentions. Something was needed to spur the government into giving priority to Arbitration Law over many other competing good causes. This was a challenge that was taken up by Arthur Marriott, a London solicitor and international arbitration practitioner. He took on the task, with a group of supporting law firms and chambers, to raise funds to instruct a specialist draftsman to produce a model Arbitration Law, which was duly presented to the Department for Trade and Industry (DTI) and publicised throughout the profession.

At the same time as these developments, however, the DTI was also faced by a new issue arising from the UNCITRAL Model Law on commercial arbitration, a draft law which had been issued in 1985 and was by the late 1980s being adopted by many states throughout the world. The new issue for the DTI was whether England and Wales should adopt the model law, a major issue which led to the setting up of the DTI Advisory Committee and the appointment of Lord Mustill to chair the committee. At the same time as considering the model law issue the DAC was, from the outset, very much aware of the views being expressed by many practitioners and focused in the Marriott draft Bill, that the overall need was for a new Arbitration Act. The DAC, however, had first to address the issue of the model law.

The outcome of the model law issue, which was not without controversy, was that Arbitration Law in England and Wales was regarded as so well developed and so well embedded in commercial practices, that the model law should not be adopted but should be taken into account in the drafting of a new Bill. So it was that the DTI then turned to its second task of producing a new updated Arbitration law for England and Wales. But with little support from the government, the DTI insisted on adhering to its traditional practices of producing recommendations in committee, which were then treated as instructions to be turned into draft legislation by the DTI's own parliamentary draftsman and simply presented back to the committee without any direct discussion or debate. The DTI also declined to take any account of the Marriott private draft despite its wide support.

The DAC did succeed in producing a draft Bill which contained much from the 1950 Act including the extensive use of 'implied terms' imported into the arbitration agreement. A full draft of the new Bill was circulated in 1993 and was the subject of a major conference held at Kings College London, jointly organised by the Centre of Construction Law and Dispute Resolution at Kings, and the Centre for Commercial Law Studies, Queen Mary University, London, and effectively organised by the writer and by Prof Julian Lew. The theme taken up by many of the distinguished speakers was whether the commercial community should settle for what was regarded as 'half a loaf'. The overwhelming response of delegates was a resounding NO. The commercial community wanted something better!

At this point external factors began to play a role. The UK Government under John Major lost its parliamentary majority and, although it was to remain in office until 1997, it was clear that no controversial legislation could be put forward. Instead, the government turned to draft legislation which would command general support and, high on the list of potential Bills, was that dealing with Arbitration Law and, incidentally, a Bill on construction contract reform. For the Arbitration Bill the rejection of the 1993 draft was duly noted and steps put in hand to produce a new draft. Two important changes were made at this point: first, Lord Saville was appointed, in 1994, to chair and oversee the work of the DAC; and second, the DTI's parliamentary draftsman was replaced by a new team which had a forward (and European) approach to drafting. The new draftsman was Geoffrey Sellars who was, incidentally, also given the job of drafting the new proposals for construction contracts in what became the Housing Grants, Construction and Regeneration Act, 1996, which explains the appearance of common provisions in the two Acts. Lord Saville also brought into his secretarial team Toby Landau, (QC 2008) who became responsible for much of the research and collating needed to ensure the workability of the new Bill.

The new team was thus able to start afresh with a new draft Bill which bore little or no resemblance to the previous drafts and indeed started with an entirely new (and European) approach of setting out the General Principles on which the new Act was deemed to be founded (section 1). At the outset, therefore, the Act declares that the object of arbitration is *to obtain the fair resolution of disputes by an impartial tribunal without unnecessary delay or expense*; that the parties should be *free to agree how their disputes are resolved* subject to safeguards in the public interest; and that *the court should not intervene except as provided* in the Act, thereby settling many matters which had previously been either controversial or in doubt. For the still controversial issue of appeals, the Bill adopted the now well-embedded procedure of requiring leave, drafting into the Act the basis on which leave should or should not be given. It is of interest that this model has been adopted and adapted in other common law countries where the merits of allowing some form of appeal on a point of law is recognised. Following the general principles, particularly on what is now universally known as 'party autonomy', most of the rules governing the conduct of arbitration are drafted as provisions applying subject to the parties' agreement. Party autonomy also means that parties to an arbitration can, by contractually inserted rules, introduce major changes and enlargements to the powers of the tribunal, subject only to the parties' agreement.

The Arbitration Act 1996, as we now know it, was passed in the dying days of the Major government and came into force on 31 January 1997. Later that year Arthur Marriott's work was recognised by his appointment, along with Lawrence Collins, as the first solicitor QCs. But what of the model law? Lord Steyn in his 1993 Freshfield Lecture referred to the model law as the single most important influence in the shaping of the Bill and that influence remained in the final draft Bill produced under Lord Saville. England had decided against adoption of the model law as such. But one of the members of the DAC, Lord Devaird, a former Scottish judge, was asked after the DAC's activities had been concluded, to chair a Scottish committee to consider whether, by contrast to England and Wales, Scotland should adopt the model law. Unsurprisingly, the Scottish committee decided to take the opposite course to England and Wales, and to adopt the model law for Scotland, the relevant provisions now being found in the Arbitration (Scotland) Act 2010. In the result both the English Act and the Scottish Act have been used as a model for Arbitration Law reform in other common law countries including Australia, New Zealand and Singapore. In most cases the model law has been made available as an option, following the principle of party autonomy.

The DAC, by the time the final drafting process was underway, included two construction practitioners, being the writer and the late John Sims FRICS. They were able, during the debates on the new Act, to put forward proposals to meet the particular problems of potentially long-drawn-out technical disputes which had been largely responsible for the bad press arbitration had generated in previous decades. Among these was a proposal to empower an arbitrator to give a 'provisional' decision, equivalent to an interim order available in the High Court, in a case where liability could be substantially established but where quantum remained seriously in issue. The provision was based on a power formerly included in the ICE Arbitration Procedure 1973, the effect of which remained uncertain. The new provision finally enacted was section 39 of the Act, as follows:

> Power to make provisional awards
> (1) The parties are free to agree that the tribunal shall have power to order on a provisional basis any relief which it would have power to grant in a final award.
> (2) This includes, for instance, making –
> (a) a provisional order for the payment of money or the disposition of property as between the parties, or
> (b) an order to make an interim payment on account of the costs of the arbitration.
> (3) Any such order shall be subject to the tribunal's final adjudication; and the tribunal's final award, on the merits or as to costs, shall take account of any such order.

> (4) Unless the parties agree to confer such power on the tribunal, the tribunal has no such power. This does not affect its powers under section 47 (awards on different issues, &c.).

This provision, whilst requiring the parties' consent, is included in the Construction Industry Model Arbitration Rules (CIMAR), widely adopted throughout the industry including by the JCT (which issues the most widely used domestic standard form contract). The provision has the potential to allow arbitrators to cut through long complex disputes by giving a decision which would reduce the extent and amount of the dispute, allowing the parties to attempt to resolve or further reduce the matters in issue. It was adopted in one reported shipbuilding case where the arbitrators made a provisional award on the quantum of sums payable where liability had been established.[1]

Unfortunately, the potential of section 39 has not been further developed by the United Kingdom construction industry. As already noted, the Housing Grants etc Act was enacted at the same time as the Arbitration Act and brought in an alternative 'short' procedure for construction disputes. This is the statutory right to adjudication, enacted by section 108 of the Housing Grants, Construction and Regeneration Act 1996, which establishes the right to adjudication in respect of any dispute falling within that Act. Adjudication is a dispute resolution process in which the decision is to be given within 28 days (or such extended period as may be agreed) subject to a detailed contractual or regulatory procedure. The process has proved highly popular with contractors and subcontractors seeking to recover disputed payments under construction contracts and has resulted in the great majority of domestic construction disputes being diverted from arbitration to adjudication. However, once the adjudicator has given a decision, he or she is functus, unlike the position of an arbitrator using powers under section 39, who remains seized of the full dispute referred and can give further provisional awards or a final award as the parties may request.

Arbitration remains an alternative procedure for domestic construction disputes and continues to be adopted for larger and more complex disputes. Arbitration is also the forum for a rehearing where the adjudicator's decision is challenged. But for international construction disputes, arbitration remains the overwhelmingly preferred forum, whether the dispute is seated in London or elsewhere. Annual statistics from the International Chamber of Commerce (ICC) and elsewhere regularly confirm London as one of the most favoured venues for multinational arbitrations, where in most cases the Arbitration Act 1996 will apply including the supportive powers of the English courts and, unless contracted out, the procedures for challenge and appeal. The 1996 Act has thus come of age but can look forward to more decades of successful application in the service of both the United Kingdom and the international commercial community.

1. *BMBF (No 12) v. Harland & Wolff* [2001] EWCA Civ 862.

CHAPTER 5
Arbitration in Changing Times

Norah Gallagher

§5.01 INTRODUCTION

I started working with Professor Lew in 2001. The arbitration framework was very different then. The IBA Guidelines on the Taking of Evidence had recently been adopted in 1999 and there was much discussion on how Article 3 might impact document disclosure in international arbitration. It was not clear whether these rules would be overly prescriptive or indeed be used by parties and tribunals at all. In the intervening years these rules - as updated - are widely accepted as the reference point for document disclosure in international arbitration - commercial or investment.

The UNCITRAL Model Law and Arbitration Rules had yet to be updated. The growth in international investment treaty cases was only just beginning with the International Centre for the Settlement of Investment Disputes (ICSID) as an example moving from a handful of cases each year to over 60. In 2001 there were 14 cases filed at ICSID three of which were related to the Argentinean financial crisis. These claims generated much commentary, many arbitration conferences and became central when teaching international investment treaty arbitration at the School of International Arbitration (SIA).[1]

§5.02 THE SIA

The SIA was and remains a very personal project for Professor Lew. Since obtaining his own PhD in Belgium he has been interested in dispute resolution as a discipline distinct from litigation, private international law or commercial law. He has taught at the

1. *See* ICSID concluded cases at: https://icsid.worldbank.org/cases/concluded. Azurix, CMS Continental and Enron were the three Awards issued that year.

Centre for Commercial Law Studies at Queen Mary University[2] since 1982 and specifically arbitration once the SIA was created in 1985. He is particularly proud of having been appointed as Head of the SIA in 1986. Julian could see that there was a growing significance for arbitration as the dispute resolution of choice for international business. It had many positive attributes including its flexibility, potential speed (should Parties so desire) and privacy. I did not use the term 'confidentiality' as Julian would always ask students whether arbitration was in fact confidential. If so, who enforces that confidentiality? Much of course will turn on the relevant applicable law. The SIA stated aim in Julian's owns words was:

> to provide our students with an understanding of the aims, structure and workings of international arbitration as an independent, flexible and appropriate mechanism to determine disputes arising from international transactions of all kinds in an efficient and effective manner.[3]

Central to the ethos of the SIA was Julian's Socratic approach to teaching. He wanted students to be able to think outside the box in a logical way applying the underlying principles. In this way he sought to prepare them for the challenges of working in a dynamic area of international law. His students will recall fondly his question of 'which came first – the chicken or the egg?' This would be the at the start of the academic year when running through what is required from parties to contract out of the national courts – the usual place for disputes to be resolved. Party autonomy in the guise of the arbitration agreement was the central focus. This separable contractual provision was required for the parties to refer future disputes to arbitration – a private dispute resolution mechanism.

Julian has been a consistent proponent of the independent nature of arbitration existing outside the national court system. 'An essential criterion for international arbitration was its non-nationality.'[4] The national courts ought to be supportive of the process but not overly interventionist.[5] In his presentation at the 20th Anniversary of the Annual SIA Freshfields lecture in 2005 Julian expanded on this autonomous theme confirming that the 'ideal and expectation is for international arbitration to be established and conducted according to internationally accepted practices, free from the controls of parochial national laws, and without the interference or review of national courts'.[6] In that lecture he looks at the historical evolution of international arbitration and how the process has changed over time. Ultimately concluding that

2. CCLS was created by Sir Roy Goode in 1980 to bring together commercial law practitioners and academics.
3. Julian Lew, The Development of International Arbitration as a Mechanism For Determining International Business Disputes, Kluwer Blog 6 February 2021. Professor Lew identified three geo political factors that lead to the creation of the SIA in 1985.
4. *Ibid.*
5. *See* for example the recent decision of the High Court decision in *QBE Europe SA/NV v. Generali Espana de Seguros Y Reaseguros* [2022] EWHC 2062 (Comm) where an anti-suit injunction was granted by the court in London in favour of the underlying arbitration clause in the insurance policy.
6. Julian DM Lew QC, 'Achieving the Dream: Autonomous Arbitration' (2006) 22(2) Arbitration International 179.

'international arbitration is today an autonomous largely self-regulating dispute resolution mechanism'.[7]

Julian's extensive experience as counsel and arbitrator in hundreds of commercial and investment[8] cases added much to the students experience at the SIA. He not only taught the legal regime within which arbitration took place he also peppered it with war stories and warnings bringing the subject alive. The aim was to prepare the next generation of dispute resolution lawyers for the challenges they would face. Julian has always been supportive of students and junior lawyers who wanted to work in international dispute resolution. He has also always been progressive in his approach. The first two speakers for the Annual SIA Freshfields lecture were Professor Pierre Lalive and Lady Hazel Fox in 1986 and 1987 respectively. He continues to give guest lectures at the SIA and supervise PhD students. He is firm in the view that the focus should be on the future and teaching the skills the next generation of dispute resolution lawyers will need to succeed in a challenging market. To equip them to address the changes that may arise.

§5.03 THE FUTURE

The type of disputes that will arise in the future is set to change. Much of this is down to the energy transition and actions required of States and corporations to mitigate climate change.[9] It is evident from a review of the climate change litigation database of the range of disputes that can arise.[10] On the commercial side it is expected there may be an increase in claims based on failures to meet Environmental Social & Governance (ESG) targets.[11] The UN Sustainable Development Goals and the UN supported Principles of Responsible Investment have brought these obligations to the fore. It is now an essential part of corporate risk planning. It will potentially increase the number of disputes and may also impact directors duties.

There has also been a significant number of changes in the field of international investment protection in the past twenty years. The number and types of claims being filed under relevant investment treaties whether bilateral (BITs) or multilateral (MITs) like the Energy Charter Treaty (ECT) have changed. In addition, the content of BITs and MITs have also evolved. States have moved away from the short, less prescriptive treaties towards long and very detailed ones. This applies to both procedural and

7. *Ibid.*, p. 203.
8. Concluded investment cases include: *Raymond Charles Eyre and Montrose Developments (Private) Ltd v. Sri Lanka* ICSID Case No. ARB/16/25 *Interocean Oil Development Company and Interocean Oil Exploration Company v. Nigeria* ICSID Case No. ARB/13/20; *Europe Cement Investment and Trade SA v. Turkey* ICSID Case No. ARB(AF)/07/2; and *Parkerings-Compagniet AS v. Lithuania* ICSID Case No. ARB/05/8. Pending investment cases include: *Security Services v. Colombia* (ICSID Case No. ARB/20/7); *ČEZ AS v. Bulgaria* ICSID Case No. ARB/16/24; and *Muhammet Çap & Bankrupt Sehil Inşaat Endustri ve Ticaret Ltd. Sti v. Turkmenistan* ICSID Case No. ARB/12/6.
9. *See* the IEA 'Net Zero by 2050: A Roadmap for the Global Energy Sector' (2021) and the IEA World Energy Outlook 2022 Part B on Road to Net Zero.
10. *See* http://climatecasechart.com/.
11. ESG a much broader concept than corporate social responsibility.

substantive aspects. Transparency being a significant feature as reflected in the newly adopted ICSID Arbitration Rules[12] and the Mauritius Convention 2014.[13]

Recent examples of the more detailed treaties include the Model Dutch BIT which contains references to 'sustainable development' as well as corporate social responsibility. Article 6(6) of the Dutch Model confirms that the parties 'reaffirm their obligations under the multilateral agreements in the field of environmental protection, labour standards and the protection of human rights to which they are party, such as the Paris Agreement, the fundamental ILO Conventions and the Universal Declaration of Human Rights ...'.[14] There is also reference to corporate social responsibility in Article 6 and 7 as well to the UN Guiding Principles on Business and Human Rights and the OECD Guidelines for Multinational Enterprises. The focus of the Dutch Model has changed quite significantly from the earlier versions. These new provisions will have important implications in disputes arising under this new format. This trend is also clear to see for example in the Model BIT of the Southern African Development Community 2012 where there are extensive references to sustainable development throughout the text. It also proposes restrictions on the fair and equitable treatment provision and has a positive assertion of the States right to regulate in a non-discriminatory manner. Other recent examples include the New Zealand UK Free Trade Agreement of February 2022 and the Hungary Oman BIT of February 2022 which also refers to 'sustainable' development. This change in focus of the investment treaties will impact the outcome of any future disputes.

Many of these changes in treaty practice are as a direct result of being involved in an investment claim. It also is influenced by the voluble criticism levelled at the Investor State Dispute Settlement (ISDS) regime more broadly. This has lead for example to the work of the UNCITRAL Working Group III on ISDS Reform since 2017.[15] The remit of this Working Group was on procedural aspects only rather than substantive protections. It is looking at several areas including cost & duration; counterclaims and transparency and the appointment as well as impartiality of arbitrators. Work is ongoing and it remains to be seen how much consensus around the reforms there will be. The Draft Code of Conduct, as an example, was not without controversy among the delegations. As noted by Shane Spelliscy, Chair of the Working Group 'One area where such different views exist is on what has been called "double-" or "multiple" hatting ... Initially, views here were very divergent ... .'[16] This polarisation is also mirrored in the work on the modernisation process of the ECT.

---

12. ICSID Arbitration Rules adopted 1 July 2022.
13. UN Convention on Transparency in Treaty-Based Investor-State Arbitration in force 18 October 2017.
14. Netherlands Model Investment Agreement 22 March 2019 https://investmentpolicy.unctad.org/international-investment-agreements/treaty-files/5832/download.
15. All documents and meetings of Working Group III are available here: https://uncitral.un.org/en/working_groups/3/investor-state.
16. Interview with Shane Spelliscy, Chair of UNCITRAL Working Group III on Investor-State Dispute Settlement Reform, Kluwer Arbitration Blog, 24 August 2022. The current text of the Draft Code of Conduct for Adjudicators in International Investment Disputes is available here: https://uncitral.un.org/sites/uncitral.un.org/files/media-documents/uncitral/en/220825_initial_draft_commentary_to_coc_upload_version.pdf.

§5.04 THE ENERGY CHARTER TREATY

In my view, the ECT is one of the most important multilateral treaties in force. The ECT was negotiated at a significant historical time after the collapse of the Soviet Union entering into force in April 1998. There were no cases decided under the ECT back in 2001. Julian would ask regularly if there was any news as we waited with interest to see how the provisions of this important treaty would be applied. There was no database of details like we have now.[17] I heard in 2001 that there might be a case filed under the ECT and tried to find out more but in vain. It finally emerged that the UK company AES Summit Generation had filed an ICSID claim against Hungary under the ECT.[18] There was much disappointment when this case settled as it would have helped when teaching students about the ECT to have an example of an award applying its terms. We remained in the realm of speculation until the first award under the ECT was rendered several years later in December 2003.

The *Nykomb* award related to a cogeneration plant in Latvia and the tariffs payable. It is worth noting that this was an early example of a State trying to move to cleaner power generation. Latvia as early as the mid-1990s, just after the United National Framework Convention on Climate Change (UNFCCC) 1992 came in to force, took action to attract foreign investment in this area. The award noted that it was undisputed between the parties that in order to 'increase domestic generating capacity and the use of cleaner fuels, the Republic needed to attract private investments in the electricity industry ... .'[19] This would not be possible without attractive tariff payments. This approach is now quite familiar in light of the many arbitrations that arose under the ECT after the global financial crisis relating to feed in tariffs for renewable – predominantly solar – investment. The *Nykomb* Award was short and slim on detailed discussion of the substantive provisions but it provided a frame of reference for students on the application of the ECT. Since then there has been a large increase in the number of claims filed each year under the ECT. Some have become very prominent including the *Yukos* saga and the renewables claims against Spain after its successful campaign to attract foreign investors in the solar sector. This proved problematic after the global financial crisis when the favourable tariffs were withdrawn. There are now 150 cases that appear on the ECT database with the most recent filed in May 2022 relating to legal reforms in the renewable energy sector.[20]

This significant growth in cases under the ECT is likely to continue for the coming years. It has had some impact. Russia terminated its provisional application of the ECT sending a formal notice on 20 August 2009.[21] Then Italy withdrew amidst much speculation for the reasons behind that decision. Italy gave notice of withdrawal on 30

17. https://www.energychartertreaty.org/cases/list-of-cases/.
18. *AES Summit Generation Limited v. Hungary* ICSID Case No. ARB/01/4. The claim was registered on 15 April 2001 but discontinued on 3 January 2002.
19. *Nykomb Synergetics Technology Holding AB v. Latvia* SCC Case No. 118/2001 Award 16 December 2003 p. 11.
20. *Aderlyne Limited v. Romania* ICSID Case No. ARB/22/13.
21. In accordance with ECT Article 45(3)(a) termination of provisional application took place 60 days later. It has been suggested this was as a direct result of the *Yukos* Awards but there were

December 2014 under Article 47 of the ECT which became effective a year later.[22] It noted at the time that it wanted to reduce its expenditure on international organisations although payments due to the ECT Secretariat could not have been considered significant. It may also have been to align itself with the European Union (EU) position that an intra-EU arbitration mechanism was not consistent with EU law (though the EU was involved in the ECT process and signed the treaty). Perhaps the potential claims against Italy relating to the renewable cases may have been another incentive. More recently, the Netherlands, Poland and Spain have commenced the withdrawal process from the ECT. France on 21 October 2022 announced that it would also withdraw from the ECT.[23] It is not clear yet what the implications will be. Under the terms of the treaty the substantive protections continue to apply for a further twenty years to all investments made in France until withdrawal is effective.[24] The inclusion of a 'sunset clause' in an investment treaty is not unusual. Nearly every BIT or MIT will have a period of time within which the provisions will continue to apply ranging from 6 to 15 years.[25] The longer period of time under the ECT reflected the long-term, high risk and large upfront costs of energy investments.

In the recent *Rockhopper* decision, filed in 2017 after Italy had withdrawn from the ECT, the Tribunal found in favour of the investor awarding damages of 190 million Euros plus interest. The dispute arose after a decision of the Italian government in 2015 to ban oil and gas exploration within 12 nautical miles of the coast. This decision was taken due to public opinion and environmental concerns. This award has been criticised at a time when the world is being asked to transition away from fossil fuels towards more sustainable power generation. This is reflected in the review process of the ECT going on over the past five years.

This ongoing modernisation process of the text of the ECT commenced in 2017. This review covers both procedural aspects, for example transparency, third-party funding and security of costs, as well as substantive protections.[26] This is in contrast to the remit of UNCITRAL Working Group III though both processes have evoked very strong views on specific reforms. It is not entirely clear whether agreement will be

---

also some fundamentals difference between the EU and Russia as was evident in the negotiations on the ECT Transit Protocol. *See* https://www.energycharter.org/what-we-do/trade-and-transit/transit-protocol/.

22. In accordance with Article 47(2) if the ECT. *See* generally Anna de Luca, Renewable Energy in the EU, the Energy Charter Treaty, and Italy's Withdrawal Therefrom, (May 2015) 12(3) OGEL/TDM.
23. Toby Fisher, 'France joins rush to exit ECT' GAR 24 October 2022.
24. This aspect of the ECT created a lot of commentary back at the time of adoption in 1994. It was seen as quite an inroad into the States sovereignty. In fact, Contracting States could not withdraw for the first five years, then had to give one year's notice of withdrawal. After which time the protections endured for all investments made up to the point of withdrawal for a further 20 years. Article 47(3) ECT.
25. In the case of the termination of the Czech Republic Ireland BIT 1996 the State Parties agreed that Article 13(3) contained a 10-year sunset clause would no longer apply. The BIT was terminated in 2011.
26. *See* for example suggested policy options for modernisation of the ECT approved by the Conference as well as the Public Communication Explaining the Main Changes Contained in the Agreement in Principle (Ad Hoc Meeting of the Energy Charter Conference, 24 June 2022) at: https://www.energychartertreaty.org/modernisation-of-the-treaty/.

reached on a new ECT text. Article 36 of the ECT requires unanimity of the parties for such a change. There have been some strong diametrically opposing views on the need to modernise the treaty and those who are happy with it as it exists. A final draft text was sent to the parties in August 2022 with a view to its adoption by the Conference on 22 November 2022.

The ECT does have reference to the environment in Article 19 and a Protocol on Energy Efficiency and Related Environmental Aspects signed at the same time as the ECT in 1994. The ECT also refers to the UNFCCC in the Preamble as well as: 'Recognising the increasingly urgent need for measures to protect the environment, including the decommissioning of energy installations and waste disposal, and for internationally-agreed objectives and criteria for these purposes.'[27] A Tribunal can read the provisions of the ECT looking at the object and purpose of its Preamble. This may recalibrate the balance between investors and States in the coming years.

It is clear that many of the disputes in the future will relate to stranded assets both under BITs and the ECT. Climate change and actions required from both governments and corporations will have a fundamental impact.[28] RWE and Uniper have filed claims under the ECT against the Dutch government based on the order to shut coal power plants. This action was taken after the Supreme Court decision in *Urgenda* where the Supreme Court rejected the appeal of the Netherlands, the court confirmed that it needed to reach the 25% reduction in emissions by 2020 compared to the 1990 levels. The Supreme Court stated that: 'This case involves an exceptional situation. After all, there is the threat of dangerous climate change and it is clear that measures are urgently needed ... .'[29] As a direct result the Netherlands announced it would be phasing out all coal power plants by 2030. RWE had built the plant at great cost and at the request of the government who wanted to ensure energy security at the time. The plant was only operational from 2015. It is clear that there will be an intricate balance to be made by the Tribunal[30] on where the financial burden should lie: the tax payer or the corporation. The State undoubtedly has a right to regulate to achieve its climate commitments. Much will depend on any assurances given to the claimants in both cases on the longevity of the projects at the time of construction.

Going forward, it would be hard for an investor in a fossil fuel project not to factor in the risk that they may ultimately be ordered to leave the resources, for example coal or oil, in the ground. An interesting aspect of the proposed modernised ECT text is to allow States to exclude protection for fossil fuel investments. Under this 'flexibility mechanism' 'the EU and the UK have opted to carve-out fossil fuel related investments from investment protection under the ECT, including for existing investments after 10 years from the entry into force of the relevant provisions and for new investments

27. ECT Preamble.
28. Lucy Greenwood, 'The Canary Is Dead: Arbitration and Climate Change' (2021) 38(3) Journal of International Arbitration 310.
29. *Urgenda Foundation v. Netherlands* ECLI:NL:HR:2019:2007 Decision 20 December 2019 para. 8.3.4.
30. Lucy Reed Appointed by the Parties; James H. Boykin – Appointed by the Claimant and Toby Landau – Appointed by the Respondent.

made after 15 August 2023 … .'[31] This will clearly have important implications, if adopted in November 2022, for future disputes. Twenty years on we now have a raft of awards under the ECT with which to teach our students on its remit. Julian has also had to grapple with applying its terms in the complex ICSID Additional Facility case of *Europe Cement Investment & Trade SA v Turkey*.

§5.05 CONCLUSION

Julian has taught generations of young lawyers how to best present their case or 'tell their story' to international tribunals. There has been dramatic changes in the past two decades in the international legal framework – both hard and soft laws – as well as the type of cases that are emerging. The work of the UNCITRAL Working Group III and the modernisation process of the ECT reflect some of these changes and propose ways to improve some of the dispute mechanisms. Climate related disputes will increase. Arbitration may no longer be the preferred dispute resolution in international treaties. Over regulation of the arbitral process may diminish the attributes mostly highly prized by the end users. Julian had a dream almost twenty years ago of autonomous arbitration and it remains to be seen if it will persist. The changes that Julian has seen since the start of his arbitration career have been immense. I am sure he could not have predicted half of them in much the same way that it is hard to imagine today what future changes to international arbitration will occur. What is certain is that Julian's legacy will be lawyers he has taught to be flexible and adapt to the circumstance of each case. I am certain that is exactly what will be needed in the challenging years ahead.

31. Energy Charter Secretariat, Public Communication Explaining the Main Changes Contained in the Agreement in Principle, 24 June 2022.

CHAPTER 6

The Cultural Factor in International Arbitration

Alfonso Gómez-Acebo

International arbitration is a crossroads where multiple cultures meet. Culture can here be defined as the ideas, customs and social behaviour of a particular people or society. A given culture is associated with a certain community, which, in turn, is usually connected to a particular country. In virtually all international arbitrations, parties, arbitrators and counsel of different nationalities are involved.

While this mixture of cultures is enriching, it is also challenging for everyone. Practitioners in international arbitration have a privileged opportunity to become acquainted with and to learn from other cultures. Yet, different cultural approaches also pose risks of disagreement that go far beyond those just stemming from the fact that different people may see things in different ways. Values, customs, tastes, manners...divergences from one country to another can be profound.

The main cultural challenge in international arbitration is to enhance cultural convergence, the process by which cultures change and become closer or more similar to one another through exposure and interaction among them. This convergence is not an end in itself, but a means to enhance the neutrality of arbitration as a cross-border dispute resolution mechanism.

Neutrality is vital for parties from different parts of the world who agree to abandon their national judges and to instead refer their dispute to an arbitral tribunal that will resolve it through a final and binding decision. In every international arbitration, the parties seek to place themselves and their dispute settlement mechanism in a neutral, non-national domain.[1] Ideally, parties resorting to international arbitration, regardless of their country of origin, should be able to feel comfortable with

1. Julian D.M. Lew, *Achieving the Dream: Autonomous Arbitration*, Arbitration International 2006, Vol. 22, No. 2, p. 180.

the process and to genuinely expect that the arbitral tribunal will resolve their dispute fairly. Cultural sensitivity from everyone involved is needed to attain this goal.[2]

Significant progress in ensuring arbitration is conducted according to internationally accepted practices has been achieved throughout history. This progress gained particular momentum in the twentieth century. The Hague Conventions of 1899 and 1907, followed by the Geneva Protocol on Arbitration Clauses of 1923 and the Geneva Convention on the Execution of Foreign Arbitral Awards of 1927, gave great impulse to the international dialogue on arbitration as a valuable means to resolve international disputes. In the first half of the century, there was a boom of initiatives from various organizations such as the International Law Association, the International Chamber of Commerce (ICC), the International Institute for the Unification of Private Law (UNIDROIT) and the United Nations, all with the shared goal of achieving internationally accepted standards.

This progress was not easy to achieve. For example, in 1922, when the ICC presented its first set of arbitration rules, the committee that prepared them, made up of members from seven European countries and the United States, noted the following about the rules: 'They are the result of a great deal of very difficult work, owing to the wide differences regarding commercial arbitration which exist between the various legislations of the countries affiliated to the Chamber. The members of the Committee were obliged to make strenuous efforts in order to conciliate as far as possible the various national points of view.'[3]

A remarkable comparative report on arbitration that René David prepared under the auspices of UNIDROIT in 1932,[4] followed by several proposals from UNIDROIT and others on a uniform law on arbitration during that decade and the ones that followed, sowed the seeds for the UNCITRAL Model Law of 1985, 'a compromise which has stripped out national characteristics and contains provisions acceptable to most systems.'[5] At the onset of the second half of the twentieth century, the New York Convention on the Recognition and Enforcement of Foreign Arbitral Awards, to which 170 states are now party, was born. Between then and the present day, several organizations that have produced soft law in the form of international guidelines, such as the International Bar Association and the Chartered Institute of Arbitrators, have entrusted the task to committees representing diverse legal cultures with the aim of

---

2. Khawar Qureshi, *Cultural Sensitivity and International Arbitration*, International Journal of Arab Arbitration 2009, Vol. 1, No. 2, p. 44: 'parties must (insofar as possible and consistent with fairness/equality of arms) feel that they have been heard and understood in a manner consistent with their cultural context.' In the same vein, Mary Howard, *International Arbitration and Cross-Cultural Issues*, in Stavros Brekoulakis (ed.), *Arbitration: The International Journal of Arbitration, Mediation and Dispute Management*, Kluwer Law International 2020, Vol. 86, No. 3, p. 340, who also stresses the importance of giving proper consideration, not only to legal differences, which are more easily identifiable, but also to social cultural differences, which are less tangible and often invisible (pp. 332 et seq.).
3. Rules of Procedure for Arbitration of the International Chamber of Commerce, 1922, Introduction, p. 15.
4. René David, *Rapport sur l'arbitrage conventionnel en droit privé – Étude de droit comparé*, UNIDROIT, Études III, S.d.N. 1932.
5. Julian D.M. Lew, Loukas A. Mistelis & Stefan M. Kröll, *Comparative International Commercial Arbitration*, Kluwer Law International 2003, Foreword by Julian D.M. Lew.

ensuring that the guidelines gain wide acceptance within the international arbitration community.

Nowadays, it is fair to say that international arbitration has formed and consolidated its own culture as far as important principles of arbitration are concerned. The need for national courts to respect arbitration agreements, the duty of impartiality and independence of arbitrators, equality and due process as the overriding principles in arbitration procedure, the standards applicable to the taking of evidence and the limited grounds on which arbitral awards can be set aside or refused recognition and enforcement, among others, are topics on which views around the world are quite aligned. We have reached some consensus on what the basic arbitration procedures should be, and the development of international arbitration has been responsive to the commercial community's needs.[6] International private justice has become recognized almost universally as legitimate for business disputes.[7]

Over the past few decades, the perception of neutrality in international arbitration appears to be increasing among users from ever more countries. Looking at statistics from the ICC International Court of Arbitration (which, despite having a certain degree of Europe-centric bias for historical reasons, remains the most international arbitral institution if we consider its caseload since it was created in 1923), the number of nationalities represented in arbitrations has increased by 56% over 29 years, from 1992 to 2020. In 1992, there were parties from 93 nationalities; in 2020, this increased to 145 nationalities. The origin of the parties has also evolved. In 1992, 18% were from America, 5.2% from Africa, 11.4% from Asia-Pacific and 64.8% from Europe. In 2020, 26.6% were from America, 6.8% from Africa, 26.1% from Asia-Pacific and 40.4% from Europe.[8] Over the past 20 years, European parties have decreased by more than 24 percentage points; in contrast, the proportion of parties from all other regions has increased: by over 15 percentage points in Asia-Pacific, 8 in America and 1 in Africa.

With respect to arbitrators, the number of nationalities has increased by 77% in nearly three decades, from 52 nationalities in 1992 to 92 nationalities in 2020. Over the years, the geographical origin of arbitrators in ICC cases has also changed. For example, in 1992, 11.3% came from America, 2.9% from Africa, 6.8% from Asia-Pacific and 78.8% from Europe. However, by 2020, 28.8% came from America, 2.3% from Africa, 11.7% from Asia-Pacific and 58.2% from Europe.[9] These figures show that, from 1992 to 2020, the geographical origin of approximately 20% of arbitrators has shifted from Europe to America and Asia-Pacific, while the percentage of arbitrators from Africa has barely changed and remains below 3%.

6. Whitmore Gray, *Is There a Growing International Arbitration Culture?*, in Albert Jan Van den Berg (ed.), *International Dispute Resolution: Towards an International Arbitration Culture*, ICCA Congress Series No. 8, Kluwer Law International 1998, p. 24.
7. Yves Dezalay & Bryant G Garth, *Dealing in Virtue: International Commercial Arbitration and the Construction of a Transnational Legal Order*, University of Chicago Press 1996, p. 33.
8. Figures available in the ICC International Court of Arbitration statistical report for 1992 (Volume 1 of the 2013 ICC International Court of Arbitration Bulletin) and in the ICC International Court of Arbitration statistical report for 2020 (Volume 1 of the 2021 ICC Dispute Resolution Bulletin).
9. *Ibid.*

On certain topics, a process of cultural convergence is currently underway. One example of this is found in the way parties can choose to combine mediation and arbitration in particular cases. Traditionally, practitioners in Europe and America have considered arbitration and mediation as separate processes where mediation always comes first: the failure of mediation opens the door to arbitration. However, more recently, a growing number of American and European members of the international arbitration community have acknowledged the potential value of the Arb-Med-Arb process, which is a different way of combining mediation and arbitration and was initially explored and developed in Asia. Arb-Med-Arb is an arbitration process in which the parties agree to attempt to resolve the dispute through mediation during one or more mediation periods — mediation windows — within the arbitration proceedings. If the mediation is successful, the arbitration comes to an end and the parties may request the arbitrator to record their settlement as a consent award. If the mediation fails, the arbitrator resumes the arbitration proceedings and renders an arbitral award. Although the arbitrator and the mediator are often different persons, nothing prevents the parties from agreeing otherwise.[10] In the future, it may become common to see a growing number of arbitrators explaining, at the first procedural conference and for the parties' consideration, the potential benefits of a mediation window within an arbitration procedure. A mediation window after the parties have exchanged their main submissions may enable them to explore zones of possible agreement based on information about the strengths and weaknesses of their cases that is more complete than the information that was available to them before the arbitration started.

Although progress has been — and continues to be — made towards an international arbitration culture, there is still significant room for improvement. Many questions have not yet received a uniform answer at international level: e.g., the arbitrator's power (or lack thereof) to communicate his or her preliminary views on the case to the parties, the situations where the arbitration agreement can be applied to non-signatories, the recognition and enforcement of arbitral decisions on interim measures in countries other than that of the place of arbitration, how to solve the problems caused by parallel arbitral or judicial proceedings on related matters, what the threshold for evidence required to prove corruption is, what all the acceptable remedies for breach of contract are, the circumstances in which civil liability of arbitrators is justified, the recognition and enforcement of arbitral awards that have been set aside at the seat of the arbitration, the notion of international public policy and how to apply the Shari'a in international arbitration.[11] Further efforts are also needed to address the concern still present in some Latin American, African and Asian countries that arbitration is a system formulated to protect the interests of more developed states.[12]

10. *See, e.g.*, Singapore International Arbitration Centre-Singapore International Mediation Centre (SIAC-SIMC) Arb-Med-Arb Model Clause ('Arb-Med-Arb Clause') and SIAC-SIMC Arb-Med-Arb Protocol; CPR Global Rules for Accelerated Commercial Arbitration (2009), Accelerated Rule 19.
11. With respect to the last topic, *see, e.g.*, Ibrahim Fadlallah, *Arbitration Facing Conflicts of Culture*, Arbitration International 2009, Vol. 25, No. 3, pp. 303-317.
12. Rizwan Hussain, *International Arbitration – Culture and Practices*, Asian International Arbitration Journal 2013, Vol. 9, No. 1, pp. 3 et seq.

It is interesting to note the conflicting positions that state courts from France and the United Kingdom still hold on the issue of the application of the arbitration agreement to non-signatories. In 2010 the Supreme Court of the United Kingdom, in the *Dallah* case, refused recognition of an award rendered in an ICC arbitration in Paris against the Government of Pakistan, as it held that the state was not party to the arbitration agreement under French law. The Supreme Court of the United Kingdom held that the arbitral tribunal had erred by deciding that Pakistan's participation in the underlying transaction made it party to the arbitration agreement.[13] However, months later, the Paris Court of Appeal upheld the award.[14] And a decade later, in the *Kabab–Ji* case, the London Court of Appeal refused enforcement in the United Kingdom of an award rendered in another ICC arbitration in Paris, as it held that English law, and not French law, was applicable to the question of whether the debtor was bound by the arbitration agreement. According to the London Court of Appeal, the parties' choice of English law to govern their contract was also an express choice for it to govern their arbitration agreement, and this choice was not affected by the fact that the contract also stated that the seat of arbitration was Paris.[15] However, the Paris Court of Appeal refused to set aside the award and expressly rejected being bound by the English court's decision.[16]

Another point on which common ground has yet to be reached is the role of party-appointed arbitrators. Today, there is general consensus on the duty of impartiality and independence of all arbitrators, regardless of how they are appointed, and there also seems to be general consensus on the differing roles of arbitrators and mediators. It took centuries to reach international consensus on these two points. However, some members of the international arbitration community nowadays suggest that party-appointed arbitrators have a 'special role' that consists of a certain behaviour that each party-appointed arbitrator may deploy in relation to the appointing party's case. The presumption of such a special role, if this goes beyond mere cultural assistance to avoid misunderstandings when the appointor and the appointee share a common cultural background, brings ambiguity and confusion to the arbitration process. To avoid this confusion and ambiguity, clear international guidelines are needed.[17] Recommendation 73 of the 2019 Code of Best Practices in Arbitration of the Spanish Arbitration Club took an initial step in this direction: 'Arbitrators who are unilaterally nominated by one party do not have the special role or duty of ensuring that their nominating party's case is adequately understood by the other members of the arbitral tribunal, or any other special role or duty with regard to their nominating party's case, except as otherwise agreed by the parties.'

13. *Dallah Real Estate and Tourism Holding Company v. The Ministry of Religious Affairs, Government of Pakistan*, [2010] UKSC 46, 3 November 2010.
14. *Gouvernement du Pakistan, Ministère des Affaires Religieuses v. Société Dallah Real Estate and Tourism Holding Company*, Paris Court of Appeal (1st Ch.), 17 February 2011.
15. *Kabab–Ji v. Kout Food Group*, [2020] EWCA Civ 6, 20 January 2020.
16. *Kabab–Ji v. Kout Food Group*, Paris Court of Appeal (1st Ch.), 23 June 2020.
17. Alfonso Gómez-Acebo, *A Special Role of Party-Appointed Arbitrators?*, in Albert Jan Van den Berg (ed.), *Evolution and Adaptation: The Future of International Arbitration*, ICCA Congress Series No. 20, Kluwer Law International 2020, p. 394.

All legal backgrounds, such as common law, civil law and Islamic law, should have a say in the shaping of international arbitration law, both on procedural and substantive matters. A good way to overcome the legal cultural conflict is an increased interactive approach among the participants in each arbitration.[18] Convergence also results from educational and training activities led by arbitral institutions, universities and arbitral organizations.[19] Attention to different cultural perspectives is particularly important when the differences carry the risk of making some arbitration users feel there is an imbalance or lack of fairness in the arbitration process. Adopting a comparative perspective is essential to tackle the cultural challenges posed by international arbitration.

One other quality is needed to overcome all such challenges, and that quality is one of a rare nature. It is an attitude of respect and curiosity for what is different from us. An unfailing readiness to question one's certitudes, the courage to put one's own convictions to the test when we encounter the thoughts and opinions of others. It is the intuition that, when it comes to certain topics, watertight distinctions between what is right and what is wrong are poor oversimplifications that barely scratch the surface of reality. This intuition is not relativism but quite the opposite: it is a clear vision that what is essential, as Saint-Exupery put it, is invisible to the eye. It is having the intelligence to see that only a careful reflection on the differences in others enables us to understand where we stand today and where we should be going in the future to ensure that no one feels like a foreigner or a stranger. Ortega y Gasset depicted this quality (and its absence) with insight:

> Let our intelligence be hospitable, and let us teach it to rejoice when a foreigner, a stranger, or an idea or emotion we had not counted on, knocks at our door. Operating upon our spirit is a terrible power of inertia, which induces us to be content with the portion of life which habitually is ours. As soon as we become negligent, that stale and sluggish propensity will create in us the firm conviction that there is no reality but the one presently before our eyes. This inclination, above all others, must be mistrusted by whoever aspires to make of himself a delicate instrument of humanity.[20]

I see this rare personal quality in Julian Lew. I saw it the first time I met him twenty years ago, after five minutes of listening to him speak. Thank you, Julian, for your extraordinary contribution to the development of international arbitration. Your immense knowledge and your delicate outlook on humanity are examples to follow.

18. Bernardo M. Cremades, *Overcoming the Clash of Legal Cultures: The Role of Interactive Arbitration*, Arbitration International 1998, Vol. 14, No. 2, p. 160.
19. Bernard Hanotiau, *International Arbitration in a Global Economy: The Challenges of the Future*, Journal of International Arbitration 2011, Vol. 28, No. 2, p. 96.
20. José Ortega y Gasset, *Thoughts on Pío Baroja*, 1916, original in Spanish.

CHAPTER 7

Changing Dynamics of the Hearing Room

John Beechey & Niccolo Landi

§7.01 INTRODUCTION

An appreciation of the professional career of a man whom I have known for over 40 years, variously as an opponent when our then firms were on opposite sides, as a colleague when we were both involved with the International Court of Arbitration of the International Chamber of Commerce (ICC) and served on tribunals together, and as a valued friend of many of those years, gives one pause. Julian honed his skills in what was then regarded as the leading (and, by general consensus, most aggressive) litigation practice in the city: seemingly, no letter was ever knowingly issued with the pleasantries of a prefatory 'Thank you'; Herbert Smith either 'had' one's letter or 'referred' to it. But Julian chose his mentors well, no less than the exceptional lawyer and polymath, Francis Mann, and the formidably able Lawrence Collins, now Baron Collins of Mapesbury PC, KC, FBA. But while that background and his ever present academic 'itch' rather set him apart, what gave rise to an element of common cause between us was an ambition to establish ourselves in the emerging field of international arbitration and, specifically, to venture on to what had long been the Bar's turf by taking on the presentation of cases before international arbitral tribunals where the rules (and conventions) of rights of audience did not apply. The fact that something which has become a matter of routine today should have been regarded as exceptional in the early 1980s is indicative of the extent of the changes in hearing room dynamics in the intervening period.

This article considers how the interactions between tribunals, parties and counsel have evolved and the way in which that evolution has transformed the interactions between these actors in the hearing room.

§7.02 THE CHANGING TRIBUNAL

[A] Role of Arbitrators Through the Years

The first hearing in which I was involved as an advocate was heard by a tribunal presided over by a prominent German academic lawyer, who had a particular view about the way in which a hearing should be run, no matter what agreement the parties might have reached on that score. His colleagues were a distinguished public international jurist and a then serving senior Commonwealth jurisdiction commercial judge. While they might have balked at the idea, they would have been apt for inclusion among the cadre of arbitrators memorably described by Dr Yves Dezalay and Dr Bryant Garth in their celebrated work '*Dealing in Virtue*' as 'grand old men' of arbitration.[1] The members of this pre-eminent and select body were not full-time professional arbitrators. Many of them were serving or retired judges and professors of international renown, who took on arbitral appointments as an adjunct to their principal fields of interest and practice. At that time, the field was dominated by senior, and, without exception, male, European jurists, and academics, steeped in the traditional values of the legal elites of Western Europe[2] and selected for their experience, wisdom, and judgment.[3]

Already by the 1980s, the grand old men's enjoyment of a near monopoly of appointments had been challenged by the appearance on the international scene of a generation of younger arbitrators drawn from diverse backgrounds. Some had gained their experience in practice as counsel at the Iran-US Claims Tribunal, possibly one of the single most significant pools of new talent, or as members of the secretariat of an arbitral institution, who had then entered private practice as counsel. Others had learned 'on the job' as administrative secretaries to tribunals or they had specialised in international disputes resolution within an existing litigation practice, rather than developing a practice solely in litigation work in the domestic courts. Dezalay and Garth defined this younger generation as 'arbitration technocrats'[4] whose professional credibility was dependent upon a perceived technical expertise in arbitration and, crucially, who found fulfilment in full-time careers in arbitration as both counsel and, as they became more senior, increasingly as arbitrators. 'Double-hatting' had yet to become an issue.

The critical difference between this younger generation of arbitrators and their elders was summarised succinctly by Julian's contemporary, Professor Jan Paulsson, himself a prominent member of this emerging group, in his introduction to the very first issue of Arbitration International:

---

1. Yves Dezalay & Bryant G. Garth, *Dealing in Virtue: International Commercial Arbitration and the Construction of a Transnational Legal Order* 10 (Chicago: University of Chicago Press 1996).
2. *Ibid.*, 34.
3. Alan Redfern, *The Changing World of International Arbitration* in *Practising Virtue: Inside International Arbitration* 46, 45-52 (David D. Caron et al. eds, Oxford: Oxford University Press, 2015).
4. Dezalay & Bryant, *supra* n. 1.

> The age of innocence has come to an end ... the subject has inevitably lost some of its charm. Once the delightful discipline of a handful of academic *aficionados* on the fringe of international law, it has become a matter of serious concern for great numbers of professionals determined to master a process, because it is essential to their business. They labor, but not for love.[5]

Although the idea was anathema to the purists, international arbitration was on its way to becoming big business and a significant source of revenue for law firms astute enough to grasp the opportunity presented by the growth of international trade and cross-border investment[6] and the increasing use of arbitration as the preferred mechanism through which cross-border business and investment disputes were resolved. As a result of this proliferation in recourse to arbitration, there was a demand for more arbitration counsel and arbitrators and more than enough work to sustain arbitration teams at leading international law firms globally.[7]

In London, Alan Redfern and the late Martin Hunter might properly lay claim to have broken the mould by demystifying international arbitration with their seminal eponymous text, Redfern and Hunter on International Arbitration, now running to a seventh edition. This important work placed as much emphasis upon the practical issues to be faced by arbitrators and counsel as upon the conceptual and legal framework within which an arbitration was conducted. Martin Hunter (at King's College London and latterly at the Universities of Nottingham, Victoria University in Wellington New Zealand and the KIIT Law School, Bhubaneswar, India among others) and Julian Lew combined practice with academia as international arbitration became a subject for postgraduate study. Julian Lew was instrumental in establishing and leading the School of International Arbitration at Queen Mary University of London since 1985.

The mid-1980s saw the adoption of the United Nations Commission on International Trade Law (UNCITRAL) Model Law on International Commercial Arbitration (the 'Model Law').[8] The Model Law proposed a uniform legal framework for the conduct of arbitrations, which has been adopted (wholesale or in amended form) around the world. The Model Law also contained provisions relating to the composition of arbitral tribunals. It set out, *inter alia*, the mechanisms by which an arbitrator was to be appointed, a procedure for the challenge of an arbitrator, the basis upon which arbitral proceedings were to be conducted and the grounds upon which awards could be recognised or challenged.

5. Jan Paulsson, *Introduction*, 1(1) Arbitration International 2-5 (1985).
6. Esteban Ortiz-Ospina & Diana Beltekian, *Trade and Globalization*, Our World in Data (October 2018), https://ourworldindata.org/trade-and-globalization.
7. Professor Julian Lew DM KC, *The Development of International Arbitration as a Mechanism for Determining International Business Disputes*, Kluwer Arbitration Blog (6 February 2021), http://arbitrationblog.kluwerarbitration.com/2021/02/06/the-development-of-international-arbitration-as-a-mechanism-for-determining-international-business-disputes/ (Julian himself has highlighted the geo-political reasons that led to the arbitration boom in this blog post).
8. UNCITRAL Model Law on International Commercial Arbitration (UN) Document A/40/17, annex I (as adopted by the United Nations Commission on International Trade Law on 21 June 1985). The Model Law was amended in 2006.

The Model Law was a major step towards the harmonisation of the practice and procedure of arbitration, irrespective of the place of arbitration and the nationalities of the parties, their counsel, and the arbitrators themselves. But as is always the case, the benefits of uniformity and predictability are susceptible to a degree of rigidity in their application in practice to the detriment of the flexibility of approach that would have been familiar to a generation of distinguished international arbitrators unencumbered by prescriptive rules and codes of conduct.

Some fifteen years on from Dezalay and Bryant's study, Professor Thomas Schultz and Dr Robert Kovacs published a survey,[9] which postulated the emergence of a third generation of arbitrators, whom they identified as 'dispute managers':

> Probably the most striking attribute revealed in the results is that arbitrators today must possess strong management abilities. It was very important to participants that an arbitrator must be able to manage the proceedings, the deliberations of the arbitral tribunal and the organisation of work within the tribunal. Management abilities were also cited by a number of participants as the single most important attribute to consider when appointing an arbitrator. In the words of one participant, the current generation of arbitrators are 'professional dispute managers.[10]

The development of this skill set, it was suggested, was a response to a fundamentally different approach to disputes resolution on the part of the business community:

> Put bluntly, this evolution is evocative of arbitration as a dispute resolution process of business, by business, for business. Even more brutally summarised, today more than in the past, parties seem to see disputes going to arbitration as just another business problem, to be dealt with – 'managed' – just as another business problem, and neither as a problem of justice for grand old people, nor as a problem of eminent legal intricacy for super-technicians.[11]

[B] The Evolving Procedures

As recourse to institutional and 'ad hoc' arbitration has increased and ever more service providers (arbitral institutions, document management and transcription specialists and, a phenomenon of the COVID pandemic, remote hearing platforms) find themselves competing for business, users of arbitration services and arbitrators alike are faced with a plethora of rules and guidelines on issues such as arbitrator disclosure, the conduct of counsel, conflicts of interest, the taking of evidence and the cost and time-efficient conduct of proceedings.

Hearings of many days', if not weeks', duration (formerly common place in common law jurisdictions at least) have become the exception and hard copy evidence is no longer routinely delivered to a hearing room by the shelf length. But if the duration of hearings has reduced, for all the guidance now available, there is no doubt

9. Thomas Schultz & Robert Kovacs, *The Rise of a Third Generation of Arbitrators? Fifteen Years after Dezaley and Garth*, 28(2) Arbitration International 161-171 (2012).
10. *Ibid.*, 170.
11. *Ibid.*, 162-163.

that the increased formality and sophistication of international arbitration proceedings and the complexity and scale of the disputes being arbitrated has led to an exponential increase in cost, driven in very large part by party-incurred (and party-controllable) costs.

However proactive a tribunal may be in the management of an arbitration, no arbitrator has coercive powers to control the manner in which the parties go about their case presentation. If the stakes are high enough, every last possibly relevant case or commentary will find its way into a soft copy library of authorities of daunting size. Large teams of lawyers will be beavering away 'back of house' to support the lead advocate(s) in their oral presentations and examination of witnesses and to produce written (often repetitive) memorials which seem to expand rather than be distilled down with each successive round. Experts, many of whom have become experienced trial witnesses, will be retained to produce ever more comprehensive reports. It is not uncommon for costs submissions to seek recovery of fees and expenses running into the multi-millions of dollars. Arbitrators can encourage the maintenance of a sense of perspective and, ultimately, they can penalise in costs, but any real exercise of control over the most significant elements of the costs explosion in international arbitration lies in the hands of the parties themselves.

[C] Diverse Tribunals

Not only has the role of the arbitral tribunal changed, but they have become more representative in terms of gender, ethnicity, and geography.

[1] Gender Diversity in Arbitration

Historically, there was no cadre of women arbitrators akin to the 'grand old men'. Looking back, Louise Barrington recalls that she was one of only six women (out of 250 delegates) who attended the ICCA Congress in Bahrain in the late 1980s.[12] In 2003, Focus Europe's first study of arbitrators presiding over significant arbitrations included only two women, Professor Gabrielle Kaufmann-Kohler, and the equally redoubtable Professor Brigitte Stern.[13] About 12 years ago, the percentage of arbitral appointments filled by women was still a mere 7.2%.[14] The table enumerates the percentage of women appointed as arbitrators between 1990 and 2010.[15]

12. Louise Barrington, *Then and Now: A Quarter Century of Women in Arbitration*, (1) NYSBA New York Dispute Resolution Lawyer 16-17, Vol. 5 (2012).
13. *Ibid.*, 16; Michael D. Goldhaber, *Madame La Presidente: A Woman Who Sits as President of a Major Arbitral Tribunal Is a Rare Creature. Why?*, 1(3) Transnational Dispute Management (2004).
14. ICCA, *The Cross-Institutional Task Force on Gender Diversity in Arbitral Appointments and Proceedings: 2022 Update*, The ICCA Reports No. 8 (20 September 2022) (Lucy Greenwood has laboriously collected and compiled historical data regards gender diversity in arbitration, this has been relied upon in the ICCA Report).
15. *Ibid.*, at 27.

Year	*Percentage of Men Appointed as Arbitrators*	*Percentage of Women Appointed as Arbitrators*
1990	99	1.0
1995	98	2.0
1998	98.5	1.5
2006	96.1	3.9
2010	92.8	7.2

When I began my term of office at the ICC in January 2009, the picture had not altered significantly. Women comprised 11% of the membership of the ICC International Court of Arbitration, 5% of the membership of the International Council of Commercial Arbitration (ICCA), 5% of the ICSID Panel of Conciliators and Arbitrators and 4% of those listed in the Guide to the World's Leading Experts in Commercial Arbitration.[16] One of my first acts as President of the ICC Court was to appoint the first four women Vice-Presidents of the ICC Court and thereafter to encourage the appointment by ICC National Committees of more women to serve on the Court.

The promotion of women arbitrators by the institutions, a number of which are now led by women,[17] and by dint of party and co-arbitrator selection, has resulted in a dramatic shift within the past decade.

The 2022 update of the ICCA Cross-Institutional Task Force on Gender Diversity in Arbitral Appointments and Proceedings notes a considerable increase in the proportion of women being appointed as arbitrators between 2015 and 2021.[18]

Institution	*2015*	*2016*	*2017*	*2018*	*2019*	*2020*	*2021*
CAS	3.9%	8.3%	2.1%	4.5%	11.9%	0.0%	[U/R][19]
CEPANI	[U/R]	22.0%	9.1%	24.4%	9.3%	13.6%	35.0%
CRCICA	[U/R]	[U/R]	[U/R]	[U/R]	[U/R]	5.0%	7.3%
DIS	13.4%	12.5%	15.2%	12.4%	17.5%	20.8%	20.2%
HKIAC	9.7%	12.1%	14.4%	12.7%	18.0%	19.9%	16.9%
IAC	[U/R]	[U/R]	[U/R]	[U/R]	[U/R]	55.6%	44.1%
ICAC	[U/R]	[U/R]	41.7%	37.4%	36.5%	42.4%	37.9%
ICC	10.4%	14.8%	16.7%	18.4%	21.1%	23.4%	24.3%
ICDR	17.5%	15.5%	21.8%	22.4%	23.7%	24.7%67	26.2%
ICSID	11.4%	13.2%	19.0%	23.8%	19.3%	22.7%	27.2%

16. Goldhaber, *supra* n. 13.
17. Prominent examples are American Arbitration Association/ICDR (India Johnson), ICC (Claudia Salomon), ICCA (until September 2022 Lucy Reed), ICSID (Meg Kinnear) LCIA (Jacomijn van-Haersolte van Hof and Paula Hodges KC) and SCC (Kristin Campbell-Wilson).
18. The ICCA Reports No. 8, *supra* n. 14, at 25-26.
19. [U/R] indicates no appointments (of men or women) were reported by the relevant institution. Unreported data were not counted in the report when calculating the global average.

Institution	*2015*	*2016*	*2017*	*2018*	*2019*	*2020*	*2021*
LCIA	15.8%	20.6%	23.5%	22.9%	28.6%	32.8%	31.6%
MIAC	[U/R]	[U/R]	[U/R]	[U/R]	[U/R]	0.0%	83.3%
PCA	12.8%	10.5%	15.2%	19.6%	18.5%	7.4%	13.6%
SCC	14.0%	16.4%	18.1%	24.1%	23.0%	31.0%	28.7%
SIAC	[U/R]	12.9%	17.5%	23.1%	22.2%	19.4%	23.2%
Swiss Arb. Centre	18.0%	15.3%	15.8%	31.0%	20.0%	34.6%	[U/R]
VIAC	14.3%	17.1%	16.7%	24.6%	16.4%	31.7%	16.4%
Global Average	12.6%	14.6%	19.7%	20.8%	22.8%	24.8%	26.1%

Although these data are limited to institutions and present an incomplete picture, they are indicative of a trend which reflects the growing prominence of the new generation of women practitioners in international arbitration.

[2] Ethnic and Regional Diversity

Only 38% of those polled in the 2021 International Arbitration Survey undertaken by Queen Mary University of London and White & Case considered that over the past three years, positive progress had been made in terms of geographic diversity. And over the same period, as few as 31% of respondents believed that progress had been made, so far as ethnic diversity was concerned.[20]

The numbers are stark: only 55 of the 298 arbitrators appointed by the LCIA in 2021 were not nationals of North America or Europe.[21] Further, 70.5% of the ICC's appointees in 2020 were from North America and Europe.[22] The most striking example is perhaps that of the Singapore International Arbitration Centre (SIAC). One-third of appointments at the SIAC were made from the Asia-Pacific region,[23] but nonetheless, 183 appointments out of a total of 371 for the year were of arbitrators from Europe and North America. Yet among the principal user communities of SIAC services are India, China, Malaysia, Vietnam, and Indonesia.[24] Singapore's former Attorney General, Mr VK Rajah SC, has pointed out Asian arbitration practitioners were going 'toe to toe' with the world's best. He suggested that it was now up to the institutions, particularly

20. White & Case and Queen Mary University of London, *2021 International Arbitration Survey: Adapting arbitration to a changing world*, 16.
21. LCIA, *Annual Casework Report*, 17-19 (2021) (Count excludes appointments from transcontinental countries).
22. ICC, *ICC Dispute Resolution 2020 Statistics* 14, 4-31 (2021).
23. SIAC, Annual Report, 23 (2021) (116 Singaporean arbitrators were appointed or confirmed by the SIAC in 2021).
24. *Ibid.*, at 18-20.

those, which aspired to be 'international in their outlook and remit', to promote geographical as well as gender diversity in arbitral appointments.[25]

§7.03 THE CHANGING PARTIES

The ICC Dispute Resolution statistics for 2020 record that 2,507 parties were involved in cases filed that year of which 48.8% were from outside Europe and North America.[26] A similar number of parties from outside Europe and North America comprise the LCIA user community.[27] The data from the SIAC offer a very different perspective. In 2021, none of its top 10 foreign users came from Europe and the United States was a distant fourth. India topped the board: 187 Indian parties participated in SIAC arbitrations.[28]

Further, an increasing number of disputes are of high value, indicative of the complexity and/or importance of the claims referred to arbitration. Over the past nine years, the LCIA has seen a rise in disputes of over USD 20 million in value from 11.5% to 25%. Data from the ICC and SIAC show a similar trend.[29] This speaks volumes to the increased value of claims brought before arbitral tribunals around the world.

§7.04 AN INCREASING POOL OF ADVOCATES

It is no longer axiomatic that parties to high value arbitrations will look first to the London Bar or its equivalent in other common law jurisdictions or to recognized practitioners in the leading civil law jurisdictions for their representation before an arbitral tribunal. The fetters of rights of audience imposed by domestic bars have never been applicable in international arbitration proceedings and parties are now more inclined than ever to choose 'horses for courses'. Advocates of the highest calibre will always be in demand, bringing to the arbitration their background of advocacy training and experience gained in practice in their home courts. But a successful advocate in a domestic litigation setting will be astute to recognize that it cannot be assumed that what plays well before a domestic court will chime with a multinational and culturally diverse arbitral tribunal operating under international rules. What will not change is a tribunal's appreciation of well-prepared argument and examination, and its ability to be confident in the integrity of the arguments advanced by counsel for the parties, whether or not ultimately the tribunal accepts them.

While there is no uniform style of arbitration advocacy, there has been a marked transition towards the exchange of rounds of written submissions ahead of the oral hearing, such that oral opening submissions are, more often than not, essentially summary in nature and of limited duration, albeit often supported by a weighty

25. GAR Live Singapore 2022 and *see* Cosmo Sanderson, *Former Singapore AG Calls for More Asian Representation*, GAR (23 August 2022) https://globalarbitrationreview.com/article/former-singapore-ag-calls-more-asian-representation.
26. *ICC 2020 Statistics, supra* n. 22, at 10.
27. LCIA Report, *supra* n. 21, at 18-20.
28. SIAC Report, *supra* n. 23, at 20.
29. *ICC 2020 Statistics, supra* n. 22, at 17, SIAC Report, *supra* n. 23, at 19.

PowerPoint presentation. Likewise, written statements and expert reports are exchanged in advance of the hearing and stand in lieu of traditional direct examination. The reliability of witness evidence prepared with the input of a party's counsel remains controversial. One of the 'fathers' of the New York Convention, Professor Pieter Sanders, opined that:

> Witness Statements may alleviate the hearing but, drawn up with the party or its legal advisors, the witness may be influenced in formulating his or her Statement which has to be signed and affirmed by him or her as being the truth. In my opinion, these Witness Statements, preceding the hearings of the witnesses in person, are not in accordance with the expectations of many parties in an international arbitration.[30]

Proponents of the use of witness statements point to savings of time and costs, because (i) the adverse party is not taken by surprise, (ii) it is in a position to prepare for cross-examination; and (iii) it can focus its examination upon what is said about the real issues in the case.[31] The sceptics remain to be persuaded, but there can be no doubt about the influence of the respected and widely adopted 2010 International Bar Association (IBA) Rules on the Taking of Evidence in International Arbitration (IBA Guidelines), which were updated in 2020.

Written witness testimony and cross-examination based upon such evidence is now so commonplace that the real debate has shifted from the worth of such evidence in itself to the manner in which it is to be collated and prepared. The IBA Guidelines at Article 4(3) state:

> It shall not be improper for a Party, its officers, employees, legal advisors or other representatives to interview its witnesses or potential witnesses and to discuss their prospective testimony with them.

This, in itself, is a significant move away from the situation in many domestic jurisdictions in which counsel were not permitted to play any part in witness training and preparation. The English High Court observed that:

> [T]he principle that a witness's evidence should be his honest and independent recollection, expressed in his own words is at the heart of civil litigation.[32]

Such an approach is foreign to practice in the United States, where lawyers have long been permitted, and arguably are required, to engage in the extensive preparation of witnesses. As one experienced United States practitioner put it:

30. Pieter Sanders, *Quo Vadis Arbitration? Sixty Years of Arbitration Practice* 262 (Massachusetts: Kluwer Law International 1999).
31. Michael Hwang, *Advocacy in International Commercial Arbitration: Singapore* in *The Art of Advocacy in International Arbitration* 413, 422 (Doak Bishop & Edward G. Kehoe eds, Huntington, New York: Juris Publishing 2004).
32. *Ultraframe (UK) Ltd v. Fielding*, [2005] EWHC 1638 (Ch), at para. 25.

> In the world in which I have practiced law the failure of counsel adequately to prepare the witness both for direct and cross-examination would be regarded as a serious dereliction of professional duty.[33]

The lack of uniformity in the approach to witness preparation and the potential for the creation (or at the least, the perception) of an unequal 'playing field' between the parties is a matter to which every tribunal needs to be alive as part of its management of the procedure.

It is, in fact, an element of a much wider problem and that is the management of the tension between the role of the tribunal in seeking to maintain a balance between the parties and that of counsel upon whom it is incumbent to act in the best interests of their client, not least in ensuring that its case is presented to best advantage. As Mr Philippe Pinsolle and the late Professor Emmanuel Gaillard wrote:

> In our view, advocacy encompassed all the aspects of the dispute and all the strategic decisions to be made in the case. Strategy in arbitration is multidimensional. Unlike court proceedings, arbitration leaves open a wide range of possibilities for litigants and it is for their advocate to make the best possible use of these possibilities. The role of the advocate should thus not be limited to delivering the best oral performance, but it should also extend to any important strategic decision to be made.[34]

Happily, overall standards of professionalism remain reassuringly high, but that tension can, on occasion, lead to something akin to a confrontation between counsel and the tribunal. In certain instances, it is a tension deliberately exploited to lay the ground for a challenge, however unjustifiable that might be. Such a situation would have been almost unheard of 20 or 30 years ago, but in the eyes of some parties (and, regrettably, their counsel), arbitrators have come to be regarded simply as another variety of paid service providers, who are owed little professional courtesy or respect. In the more extreme cases, tribunal members might be justified in assuming that they have come to be regarded almost as an adversary by the complainant party.

[A] Challenging Appointments

While the number of challenges to arbitral tribunals seems inexorably to rise, the right to challenge is one of very long standing. As in court, so in arbitration: 'justice must not only be done, but it must also be seen to be done'.[35]

Challenge procedures are available under both institutional rules and national arbitration statutes. While different rules and regulations might set a variety of prescriptive bars, they have essentially the same object, which is to evaluate whether

33. Robert Rifkind, *Practices of the Horseshed* in *Arbitration and Oral Evidence* 55 (Laurent Levy & Johnny Veeder eds, Paris: ICC Institute Dossiers 2004).
34. Emmanuel Gaillard & Philippe Pinsolle, *Advocacy in Practice: The Use of Parallel Proceedings* in *The Art of Advocacy in International Arbitration* 173, 173-191 (Doak Bishop & Edward G. Kehoe eds, New York: Juris Publishing 2004).
35. *R v. Sussex Justices, ex parte McCarthy*, [1924] 1 KB 256, 259.

the circumstances upon which a challenge is based give rise to justifiable doubts as to an arbitrator's independence and impartiality.

There is a concern (for which there is some justification) that the challenge procedure is ripe for abuse. The tactical use of a challenge as a cost-effective means of securing a delay is not infrequent. Challenges may not require extensive work on the part of a complainant, and they are not especially onerous to launch. Absent a very strong risk of a costs sanction, they are not particularly expensive to maintain.[36] If the goal is to stall a proceeding or to draw the opposing party into settlement negotiations, a party may consider that its interests would be best served by challenging an arbitrator even if there is not a strong case to make that challenge, and that any challenge actually made will likely fail.

When the IBA Guidelines on Conflicts of Interest for International Arbitrators (the 'IBA Conflict Guidelines') were introduced in 2004, they provoked some controversy. It was said that they had not only expanded the scope for arbitral disclosure, but also given parties the opportunity to challenge the arbitrators by whom they were made. The late 'Johnny' Veeder QC observed that:

> [The] IBA Conflict Guidelines have provided a well-sprung platform for new tactical challenges to arbitrators, a malign practice that appears to be increasing everywhere. These black arts do not always survive judicial exposure in the English courts; but they can muddy only too easily the 'pristine clear waters of international commercial arbitration'[37]

That is a view shared by Gary Born. In his treatise on international commercial arbitration, he reasons that the IBA Conflict Guidelines have added additional grounds on the basis of which arbitrators may be challenged 'without excluding any existing ground for challenge (and disclosure) under national law or institutional rules'.[38] While Gary Born acknowledges that it may not be possible conclusively to determine that there is a direct causal link between the introduction of the IBA Conflict Guidelines and the increase in the numbers of challenges,[39] he argues that the rise in disclosure

36. Although, in an effort to alleviate concerns that arise from increasing unmeritorious challenges, costs are being imposed on parties for bringing forth such challenges. For instance, in *Fábrica de Vidrios Los Andes, CA and another v. Bolivarian Republic of Venezuela* (ICSID Case No. ARB/12/21) the unchallenged members of the tribunal imposed costs associated with the challenge on the Respondent when dismissing the Respondent's Third Proposal for Disqualification.
37. Grant Hanessian, *BRICs, Not CRIBs: The 'Rebalancing' of International Arbitration* in *Contemporary Issues in International Arbitration and Mediation: The Fordham Papers (2011)* 256 (Arthur W. Rovine ed., Leiden: Martinus Nijhoff Publishers 2012); *see* footnote 42 citing *The English Arbitration Act 1996: Its 10th and Future Birthdays*.
38. Catherine A. Rogers & Idil Tumer, *Arbitrator Challenges: Too Many or Not Enough?* in *Contemporary Issues in International Arbitration and Mediation: The Fordham Papers (2011)* 128-137 (Arthur W. Rovine ed., Leiden: Martinus Nijhoff Publishers 2014); *see* footnotes 2 and 3 citing Gary Born, *International Commercial Arbitration* 1895 (2d ed. Alphen aan den Rijn: Wolters Kluwer 2014).
39. *Ibid.*, *see* footnote 4 citing Gary Born, *International Commercial Arbitration*, 1856-1857 (2d ed. Alphen aan den Rijn: Wolters Kluwer 2014).

requirements and grounds for challenge could lead to an increased number of challenges.[40]

Whether or not that is the case, an examination of recent challenges and the basis on which they were made would suggest that parties have become more aware of, and sensitive to, issues, relationships and even everyday activities of an arbitrator and more prone to analyse them minutely from the perspective of protecting their own interests rather than any altruistic aim to preserve the integrity of the arbitration.

An example was the challenge made in *EURL Tecso v Neoelectra SAS Group*, which arose at the stage of enforcement of the arbitral award. Tecso had petitioned for annulment of the award before the *Cour d'appel de Paris*.[41] It argued that the constitution of the arbitral tribunal was irregular, because two of the three members of the tribunal had failed to make disclosure of their connections with the Respondent. Tecso contended that the non-disclosures created doubts as to the independence and impartiality of the two arbitrators. One such asserted non-disclosure arose out of the fact that one of the co-arbitrators was a 'friend' of Respondent's counsel on the social media networking site Facebook.

In the annulment proceedings before the *Cour d'appel de Paris*, Tecso contended that the non-disclosure by the co-arbitrator of the fact that the Respondent's counsel was a Facebook 'friend', and that the counsel had in the past 'liked' a Paris Bar campaign post shared by the co-arbitrator on Facebook, created reasonable doubts as to the arbitrator's independence and impartiality with respect to the counsel concerned. The *Cour d'appel de Paris* accepted Tecso's arguments in respect of both asserted non-disclosures[42] and set aside the award. The Respondent then appealed this decision to the *Cour de Cassation*. On 10 October 2012, the *Cour de Cassation* reversed the decision. In its judgment, it noted that the *Cour d'appel de Paris* had not explained the reasons for its conclusion that these non-disclosures could create reasonable doubts in the minds of the parties. The *Cour de Cassation* remanded the case to the *Cour d'appel de Lyon*.[43] The *Cour d'appel de Lyon* held that the plea of nullity on the basis of irregularity in the composition of the tribunal was unfounded.[44] The court concluded that neither case of non-disclosure was likely to create a reasonable doubt as to the impartiality or independence of the challenged arbitrators vis-à-vis Tecso In the case of the Facebook 'like', it observed that it had been posted one year after the arbitration. The court held that there was no obligation to disclose these matters in the arbitration.

This case raises a new dimension in the context of which challenges to the appointment of arbitrators are now being made. The conflicting judgments of two different courts of appeal (and the intervention of the apex court) in France demonstrate the issues that can arise when challenges based on such new grounds become the

40. *Ibid.*
41. CA Paris, 11 March 2011, *Société Tecso v. Société Neoelectra Group*, 09/28537 and 09/28540.
42. The other arose out of a failure by one co-arbitrator to disclose historic and ongoing links with the law firm of Respondent's counsel.
43. Cass Civ 1, 10 October 2012, *Société Tecso v. Société Neoelectra Group*, 11-20.299.
44. CA Lyon, 11 March 2014, *Société Tecso v Société Neoelectra Group*, 13/00447. *See* Suar Sanubari, *Arbitrator's Conduct on Social Media*, 8 Journal of International Dispute Settlement 483, 485 (2017).

subject of judicial rulings. The case is also representative of how varied challenges and disclosure obligations have become over time. Some challenges stray beyond the ingenious into the realms of the absurd. A recent case in point was an (unsuccessful) attempt to annul an ICC Award rendered by a tribunal of which a prominent Italian arbitrator and head of an arbitral institution was a member. The complaint was raised that he had failed to disclose that he played in a football match at the margins of the ICCA Congress in Rio de Janeiro some 10 years previously in which a counsel in the arbitration had also participated.[45]

What is absolutely clear is that arbitrators and those aspiring to become arbitrators must give careful consideration to their online presence and their use of social media.

The impact of social media on arbitral appointments was the subject of a recent conference jointly organised by the Madrid International Arbitration Centre, the Chartered Institute of Arbitrators' Young Members Group, Arbitrator Intelligence, AMCHAM Quito and CyberArb.[46] One of the panels at the conference discussed the potential risks faced by arbitrators in handling their online identities. A question put to the panellists was whether social media connections gave rise to conflicts of interest and consequent challenges in light of the IBA Conflict Guidelines. Article 4.3.1 of the Green List states:

> The arbitrator has a relationship with another arbitrator, or with the counsel for one of the parties, through membership in the same professional association, or social or charitable organisation, or through a social media network.

It was the view of one of the panellists that because the reference to social media networks was part of the Green List, there was no requirement for any disclosure of a social media connection and that it was unlikely that a successful challenge could be brought based on such a claim. It was also suggested that no successful challenge had yet been brought on such a basis.

But the discussion then dug deeper into the question of arbitrators' social media identities. The question posed was:

> Whether the different types of reactions available for LinkedIn posts which go beyond a simple 'like' – *i.e.* 'celebrate', 'support', 'insightful', 'curious' and their different interpretation in foreign languages – may reflect different degrees of intensity in the relationship between the involved users.[47]

In the days when Julian Lew and I were first appointed as arbitrators, the notion of any such discussion would have been the stuff of science fiction (and likely dismissed as

45. Cosmo Sanderson, *Copacabana Kickabout Cited in Conflict Challenge*, Global Arbitration Review (22 June 2022) https://globalarbitrationreview.com/article/copacabana-kickabout-cited-in-conflict-challenge.
46. Carolina Mauro & Wendy Gonzales, *Arbitration Tech Toolbox: Arbitrators and Their Online Identities, a Double-Edged Sword?*, Kluwer Arbitration Blog (4 May 2021). http://arbitrationblog.kluwerarbitration.com/2021/05/04/arbitration-tech-toolbox-arbitrators-and-their-online-identities-a-double-edged-sword/.
47. *Ibid.*

the product of a fevered imagination). But such a discussion has now been had. The panellists unanimously agreed upon the general proposition that while arbitration proceedings were pending, arbitrators should avoid interacting through social media with all interested parties in the arbitration. But there was no consensus as to the degree of self-restraint to be observed. The most cautious view in the room was that arbitrators should be proactive in filtering their own contact lists and remove parties' counsel and their law firms from their social media networks. Some may think that excessive, but in the present climate, it might be the most prudent course.

It is not a conclusion to be drawn with any great enthusiasm, but all the indications are that as the stakes get higher, more arbitrators may find themselves subject to challenge on grounds ranging from the respectable and arguable to the downright opportunistic and mischievous, intended to goad an arbitrator into a response which might itself then be used as evidence of antipathy towards the challenging party. It has become, sadly, a fact of professional life. As parties become ever more technologically savvy and familiarity with methods such as data mining in order to vet and challenge future appointees increases, caution is likely to remain the watchword.

§7.05 THE HEARING ROOM

And what of the hearing room itself? It too has undergone a transformation. Purpose built hearing centres are offered in a number of cities. Some have been updated to the point that they offer state of the art facilities to users and are much sought after venues for arbitral hearings.

However, the transformation goes beyond the improvement of infrastructure. The COVID-19 pandemic has perforce caused users to look to remote means of holding hearings. In the course of the pandemic, every party's, counsel's and arbitrator's office or home became part of a hearing room as videoconferencing became the norm.[48] Participants Zoom'ed into hearings at all sorts of hours from any number of time zones and deliberations took place in 'virtual' break-out rooms. The move towards sustainable arbitration was also boosted during the pandemic. Hard copy hearing bundles have largely been foregone in favour of hyperlinked electronic bundles suspended in the Cloud. A new cohort of document management providers now controls the presentation of evidence in soft copy and 'shares' it on screens online. The days of exhibits being printed on large sheets of paper and then being displayed on boards in hearing rooms are long gone.

The adoption of remote hearing has been embraced by users and arbitrators alike. And it works. A recent survey undertaken by the ICC, revealed that by the fourth quarter of 2020, 71 % of ICC users had participated in a remote hearing – almost double

48. On one memorable occasion, a witness appeared for cross-examination from her very well-stocked wine cellar.

the number of users (36%) in the first quarter of 2020.[49] As a result of this move towards remote hearings, several countries and a number of arbitral institutions, have updated their laws and rules to reflect this change. Article 19.2 of the LCIA Arbitration Rules 2020 is a case in point. It provides that:

> the Arbitral Tribunal shall have the fullest authority under the Arbitration Agreement to establish the conduct of a hearing, specifying that as to form, a hearing may take place in person, or virtually by conference call, videoconference or using other communications technology with participants in one or more geographical places (or in a combined form).

Similarly, Article 26(1) of the ICC Arbitration Rules 2021 provides:

> The arbitral tribunal may decide, after consulting the parties, and on the basis of relevant facts and circumstances of the case, that any hearing will be conducted by physical attendance or remotely by videoconference, telephone or other appropriate means of communication.

Guidelines and guidance such as the SCC's COVID-19: Information and Guidance in SCC Arbitrations released on 27 March 2020, the ICC's Guidance Note on Possible Measures Aimed at Mitigating the Effects of the COVID-19 Pandemic dated 9 April 2020 and the HKIAC's Guidelines for Virtual Hearings from 14 May 2020 are among a proliferation of materials published to assist arbitration users.

The Dutch, Hong Kong and Austrian governments have also amended their arbitration legislation to allow for witnesses and experts to be examined without being physically present at a hearing.[50]

These changes have not only impacted the international centres of arbitration, but regional centres, too. The Cairo Regional Centre for International Commercial Arbitration (CRCICA) records that between 1 January and 31 December 2020, a total of 78 hearings took place using its remote hearing protocols. Eleven of those hearings were held entirely via videoconference, 2 hearings were held entirely via teleconference and over 10 hearings were held as 'hybrid' hearings, part in-person and part by remote attendance.[51]

The hearing room was undergoing gradual change, as recourse to electronic document management became more commonplace, but the COVID-19 pandemic has been a catalyst for dramatic change, which is here to stay. The reliability and security of the electronic hearing platforms which have been adopted worldwide have changed the expectations of users, practitioners and arbitrators alike. While it is unlikely that

---

49. Freshfields, *The Future of Remote Hearings in a Post-pandemic World* (2021), https://www.freshfields.com/en-gb/our-thinking/campaigns/international-arbitration-in-2021/the-future-of-remote-hearings-in-a-post-pandemic-world/.
50. *See* Dutch Code of Civil Procedure Book 4 Arbitration of 2015, Article 1072(b) (Netherlands), Austrian Arbitration Act 2013 section 595(2) (Austria), Hong Kong Arbitration Ordinance 2011 Article 20(2) (Hong Kong).
51. Mohamed Hafez, *The Future of Remote Hearings in a Post-pandemic World*, Global Arbitration Review (29 April 2022) https://globalarbitrationreview.com/review/the-middle-eastern-and-african-arbitration-review/2022/article/remote-hearings-and-the-use-of-technology-in-arbitration.

parties, counsel and tribunals will once again embark without a second thought on trips across a continent for a hearing of a day or two's duration or less, there will always be a place for a physical in-person hearing. First, time zones remain the Achilles heel of the lengthy remote hearing to be attended by participants on different continents. Second, and I sense Julian Lew nodding in agreement, there is something about the 'cordite' of the hearing room and the immediacy of the presence in one place of the parties, counsel and the tribunal that no amount of technical wizardry could ever replicate.

§7.06 CONCLUSION

Alan Redfern recently observed that over the past thirty years, the practice of international arbitration had become 'relentlessly professional'.[52] He is, I think, quite right and I am sure that he was not being entirely unreserved in his appreciation of the phenomenon. There has been a tendency to overlook the role of the arbitrator as the professional adjudicator and to focus on the service provider element of the role. It would be no bad thing as we adjust to the 'new normal' in the wake of the pandemic, if attention were to be refocused on the former at the expense of the latter. Otherwise, there is a risk that one will lose sight of professionalism in the race to keep pace with change, whether or not one pauses (or is allowed to pause) to consider whether it would necessarily be for the better or not.

52. *See Practising Virtue*, *supra* n. 3, at 45.

CHAPTER 8

The Concept of Transnational Public Policy in International Commercial Arbitration

*Domenico Di Pietro**

In 1977 a young barrister of the Middle Temple, a research fellow at the City of London Polytechnic, completed his PhD course at the University of Leuven analysing 'The Choice of the Applicable Law in International Commercial Arbitration – a Study in Decided Arbitration Awards.' The Study devoted a sizeable part of its scope to public policy, one of the most significant and perhaps elusive issues in international commercial arbitration. In the preface of his work, he acknowledged the support received from several thought leaders of international arbitration, a status that our young barrister would achieve not so long thereafter.

The brilliant academic, of course, was Prof. Julian Lew. In that PhD thesis it is possible to detect the prodromic traits of a brilliant jurist who, in the following years, would become one of the leading lights of international arbitration. In 1985 Julian Lew created the School of International Arbitration at the Centre for Commercial Law Studies (CCLS), Queen Mary, University of London, together with Sir Roy Goode, another giant of commercial law.

Julian Lew has been an inspiration to the thousands of students, including the author of this inconsequential paper, who have been lucky enough to attend his classes and appreciate his qualities as a human being and, of course, as a jurist.

Public policy has been a constant interest in Julian Lew's academic endeavours. As suggested in one of his publications on the subject, public policy 'reflects the fundamental economic, legal, moral, political, religious and social standards of every State or extra-national community. Naturally public policy differs according to the character and structure of the State or community to which it appertains, and covers those principles and standards which are so sacrosanct as to require their maintenance

* The author is grateful to Jose Angelo (Anjo) David of GST LLP, Washington D.C. for his insightful comments on a draft of this chapter.

at all costs and without exception'.[1] Indeed, public policy is the mirror of our social values at the domestic and international level. It is the ideal line drawn by our sense of morality that we believe should not be crossed if we want to preserve the world of values we elect to live by.

Public policy remains an important subject years after Julian Lew's initial foray into the topic. Indeed, it is likely to become even more relevant in the future because of ever-increasing global interaction and the seemingly faster shift in core policies and values at an international level. As observed by Julian Lew: 'Public policy [...] is often perceived as a national concept; a safety valve concerned with safeguarding the state's most fundamental national interests. However, owing to globalisation, the extensive cultural interactions, and the exposure to other legal systems and practices, the concept of public policy now includes anational dimensions reflecting fundamental principles and interests shared by the international community.'[2]

As suggested by Julian Lew, there is indeed wide consensus on the idea that there exist at least three different levels of public policy in international commercial arbitration, including some form of *a*-national *corpus* of public policy rules operating at a 'transnational' level, even though the actual scope and function of a-national public policy is still open to debate. As observed by Pierre Lalive back in 1986: 'In the whole field, in full expansion, of commercial international arbitration, few subjects are more vague, more difficult to seize and more controversial than that of the existence, contents and function of a public policy which would be "really" or "truly" international, and which it is better, if only for the sake of convenience, to call "transnational."'[3]

As is now well-known, the first two levels of public policy, national and international, are both expression of domestic law. The first level applies necessarily to all purely national legal relationships. Numerous national laws and courts recognize that in the presence of a legal relationship characterized by an international element, such as the nationality of the parties or the international scope of the underlying transaction, only a more limited set of national public policy rules should apply. That more limited set of public policy rules is described as (domestic or national) international public policy. The public policy described as international under domestic law is nothing but a selection of domestic public policy rules that the domestic legal system operating through its legislative or judiciary branches believes should always apply irrespective of the nature of the issue at hand. The two domestic levels of public policy are aimed at protecting the domestic legal system. However, they do so with different

1. Julian Lew, *Applicable Law in International Commercial Arbitration* (Oceana, 1978), p. 532.
2. Julian Lew, *Transnational Public Policy: Its Application and Effect by International Arbitration Tribunals*, IX Conferencia Internacional Hugo Grocio de Arbitraje (Fundación Universitaria San Pablo CEU, 2018), p. 17.
3. Pierre Lalive, *Transnational (or Truly International) Public Policy and International Arbitration*, in P. Sanders (ed.), Comparative Arbitration Practice and Public Policy in Arbitration, ICCA Congress Series, Volume 3 (Kluwer, 1986), 257.

intensity depending on whether the instance under scrutiny is fully domestic or it has an international connotation limiting its impact on the domestic legal system.[4]

The third level of public policy, branded by Pierre Lalive as transnational public policy, is not the direct creation of domestic law, but rather the result of an international *idem sentire*, i.e., a set of shared values that is common to the majority of countries and persons, natural and legal, operating internationally. Those shared values permeate not just the domestic laws of a vast number of jurisdictions but also international instruments, including binding international treaties, aspirational declarations, soft law instruments, and, last but not least, international jurisprudence (including international commercial arbitral awards and the decisions of public international law courts and tribunals).[5]

Transnational public policy is believed to be an even smaller collection of rules compared to (domestic) international public policy because only a limited number of principles and rules demonstrably can be said to have achieved widespread acceptance. By way of example, as suggested by Stavros Brekoulakis, substantive and procedural transnational public policy rules definitively include the prohibition of transactions tainted by bribery and good faith prescriptions qualifying the right to object to the jurisdiction of arbitral tribunals.[6]

A liberal approach to transnational public policy is normally favoured by commentators who have embraced a concept of international arbitration as an autonomous legal order that, as such, should enjoy a degree of autonomy from domestic legal systems.[7] However, it would be wrong to entangle transnational public

4. On the issue of public policy in international arbitration *see ex multis* Linda Silberman & Franco Ferrari, *Getting to the Law Applicable to the Merits in International Arbitration and the Consequences of Getting It Wrong*, in Franco Ferrari and Stefan Kröll (eds) Conflict of Laws in International Arbitration, ((Sellier, 2010), pp. 257-324. Loukas Mistelis, *'Keeping the Unruly Horse in Control' or Public Policy as a Bar to Enforcement of (Foreign) Arbitral Awards*, 2(4) International Law Forum du droit international (2000), pp. 248-253. Bernard Hanotiau & Olivier Caprasse, *Public Policy in International Commercial Arbitration*, in Emmanuel Gaillard & Domenico Di Pietro (eds), Enforcement of Arbitration Agreements and International Arbitral Awards: The New York Convention 1958 in Practice (Cameron May, 2008). Domenico Di Pietro, *Party Autonomy and Public Policy Awards by Consent*, in Franco Ferrari (ed.), Limits to Party Autonomy in International Commercial Arbitration, (Juris, 2016), pp. 383-399.
5. Julian Lew, *Transnational Public Policy: Its Application and Effect by International Arbitration Tribunals*, at p. 64.
6. Stavros Brekoulakis suggests '[...] only a limited number of rules and principles of transnational public policy can be identified in relation to only some aspects of international commercial and trade law, notably, the transnational policy prohibiting contracts of, and arising out of bribery, and the principle of good faith in the form of specific rules to deny spurious objections to the jurisdiction of international tribunals.' Stavros Brekoulakis, *Transnational Public Policy in International Arbitration*, in Thomas Schultz & Federico Ortino (eds), *Oxford Handbook of International Arbitration* (OUP, 2020) p. 149.
7. This issue cannot be meaningfully addressed here. For thorough analysis and discussion *see* Emmanuel Gaillard, *Legal Theory of International Arbitration* (Nijhoff, 2010); Jan Paulsson, *The Idea of Arbitration* (OUP 2013); Julian Lew, *Achieving the Dream: Autonomous Arbitration*, 22(2) Arbitration International (2006), pp. 179-203. Julian Lew seemed to capture that aspiration of autonomy and self-sufficiency when he observed, even though only with respect to the enforcement of arbitration agreements and arbitral awards, that 'the ideal and expectation is for international arbitration to be established and conducted according to internationally accepted

policy in the much broader discussion of a theoretical systemic nature often complicated by personal intellectual beliefs. There is no need to establish the existence of an autonomous arbitral legal order to prove the existence of a self-standing set of rules that the international community recognizes as necessary to protect the legality and fairness of international trade. Indeed, it is no longer possible to deny that a close-knit community of human beings has developed into a pluralist society where rules are created outside the traditional paradigm of State and sovereignty.[8] The two elements genuinely necessary to establish the existence and binding force of a set of rules are positive practice (as in positive conduct) and *opinio juris*, the shared belief that a certain rule is fair and necessary.

Some doubts have been raised about the actual scope or practical application of transnational public policy. The general concern is rooted in the fact that a rarefied concept of transnational public policy can only exist as a legal aspiration, but it cannot be regarded as an operational system of positive norms. Indeed, it has been questioned how transnational public policy, being an even more limited iteration of international public policy adopted at domestic level, could effectively preserve the integrity of international arbitration and international commerce.[9] It has also been observed that, unlike domestic public policy, which is normally enshrined in statutes, transnational public policy relies on norms the identification of which might prove problematic.[10]

---

practices, free from the controls of parochial national laws, and without the interference or review of national courts'. Julian Lew, *Achieving the Dream: Autonomous Arbitration*, at p. 179.

8. As observed by Catherine Kessedjian: 'Whether we like it or not, we are living in a world of legal pluralism. This means that transnational human activities, whether commercial or not, are no longer regulated only by State-made law. We may take a positivist attitude and deny the existence of legal pluralism. However, taking such an attitude will make it very difficult to describe with accuracy the world as it has evolved at least in the past two or three decades.' Catherine Kessedjian, *Transnational Public Policy*, in Albert Jan Van den Berg (ed.), International Arbitration 2006: Back to Basics?, ICCA Congress Series, Volume 13 (Kluwer, 2007) pp. 857-870, at p. 858.
9. As observed by Stavros Brekoulakis '*Ordre public* international is a slender version of international public policy which forms the lowest common denominator of very fundamental state policies. Such a narrow concept of international public policy naturally fails to cover anything more than the very obvious, blatant and really uncommon cases of violation of international law, such as "drug or human organ trafficking", "violation of embargo or boycott laws", "assembling a mercenary army to support an insurrection against a legitimate government", "agreements to transport children intended for slavery of under age labour", "supplying armaments to a terrorist organisation and the supply of illicit drafts", "bribery and corruption of public officials" or "smuggling of goods of individuals into another country". Although public policy was always seen as a dynamic concept, *ordre public* international in effect operates as the counterpart of *jus cogens* in international public law. Therefore, *ordre public* international has a rather static concept that fails to take into account the developments of the evolving civilisation of arbitration, and it hardly corresponds to the increasing complexity and nuances of contemporary transnational commerce.' Stavros Brekoulakis, *Public Policy Rules in English and International Arbitration Law*, 84(3) The International Journal of Arbitration, Mediation and Dispute Management 205-220, at pp. 218-219 (2018).
10. Stavros Brekoulakis explains that 'Public policy at such a high level of general legal norms and abstract principles exists only as a matter of legal aspiration. When transnational arbitration scholars talk about principles of transnational public policy that are broadly shared "among the community of states" they probably mean principles of transnational public policy that ought to be universally shared, according to their own legal and moral considerations.' Stavros Brekoulakis, *ibid.*, at p. 219. *See also* for a complete illustration of the issue, Stavros Brekoulakis,

However, the suggested objective difficulties are not a sufficient argument to disprove the existence and operativity of transnational public policy rules, which are necessary to preserve the integrity of international law and commerce irrespective of the rules of domestic law otherwise applicable. Indeed, those same concerns could be levied with regard to domestic law, yet it cannot reasonably be claimed that domestic law should cease to exist, develop, or operate. The creation of new rules, and particularly the codification of rules expressing fundamental values, has never been easy.

The domains of (national) public policy, including its narrower international declination, and transnational public policy are distinguishable theoretically. However, their respective contents may coincide to a large extent. But this overlap of rules should neither surprise nor detract from the concept of an autonomous transnational public policy. The objectives of domestic (including international) public policy and transnational public policy are clearly distinguishable. It has been correctly observed that the rules of transnational public policy exist to prevent or correct a public policy breach affecting the international community, while domestic public policy rules, irrespective of whether or not they coincide with transnational public policy, are adopted and implemented to preserve the integrity of a domestic legal system.[11]

Having said that, a complete uniformity between domestic and transnational public policy, in addition to being unharmful, is also unlikely. Indeed, transnational public policy rules might also stem from sources other than domestic laws. The most obvious examples of transnational public policy rules that may or may not have an immediate or identical counterpart at domestic level are the collections of principles and rules contained in international treaties, international declarations, international soft law instruments, and international case law. As suggested by Pierre Lalive '[...] there can be no total identity or assimilation between the two kinds of "public policies", inasmuch as the State international public policy inevitably retains a particular or even selfish character, at least in part. Similarly, the fundamental values and interests of a given State can hardly coincide fully with the values and fundamental interests of the international community, just as the national concept of "international public policy" cannot be identified with that of transnational public policy'.[12]

The tripartite representation of public policy is reflected on the endeavours of the International Law Association on the topic of 'Public Policy as a ground for Refusing Recognition and Enforcement of international Arbitral Awards.' The Committee in charge of that effort, chaired by Pierre Mayer and Audley Sheppard, produced an Interim Report that included a clear demarcation of the different levels of public policy.[13] In its Final Report, the Committee agreed upon several Recommendations as

---

Transnational Public Policy in International Arbitration, in Thomas Schultz & Federico Ortino (eds), Oxford Handbook of International Arbitration (2020) OUP pp. 120-149.

11. Martin Hunter and Gui Conde E. Silva, *Transnational Public Policy and Its Application in Investment Arbitrations*, 4 The Journal of World Investment, 367, (2003).
12. Pierre Lalive, *Transnational (or Truly International) Public Policy and International Arbitration* in Pieter Sanders (ed.), Comparative Arbitration Practice and Public Policy in Arbitration, ICCA Congress Series, Volume 3 (Kluwer, 1986), at p. 313.
13. 'International public policy is understood to be narrower than domestic public policy: not every rule of law which belongs to the *ordre public interne* is necessarily part of the *ordre public externe*

to the application of public policy by State courts. The Report confirmed transnational public policy as a set of rules common to many States but substantially independent from national law.[14] Existence and relevance of transnational public policy has been recognized also under the 2016 UNIDROIT Principles. The commentary to Article 1.4, amongst other things, suggests that 'the arbitral tribunal may consider it necessary to apply those overriding mandatory rules that reflect principles widely accepted as fundamental in legal systems throughout the world (so-called transnational public policy or *ordre public* transnational)'.[15] Several leading courts and arbitral tribunals also have recognized both the existence of transnational public policy and the important role played by such principle.[16]

---

or international. [...] The concept of "transnational public policy" or "truly international public policy" is of even more restricted scope, but of universal application - comprising fundamental rules of natural law, principles of universal justice, *jus cogens* in public international law, and the general principles of morality accepted by what are referred to as "civilised nations"', International Law Association - Committee on International Commercial Arbitration Interim Report on Public Policy as a Bar to Enforcement of International Arbitral Awards at pp. 6-7.

14. Recommendation 1(b) 'In these Recommendations, the expression "international public policy" is to be understood in the sense given to it in the field of private international law; namely, that part of the public policy of a State which, if violated, would prevent a party from invoking a foreign law or foreign judgment or foreign award. It is not to be understood, in these Recommendations, as referring to a public policy which is common to many States (which is better referred to as "transnational public policy") or to public policy which is part of public international law. International public policy is generally considered to be narrower in scope than domestic public policy.' Pierre Mayer & Audley Sheppard, *Final ILA Report on Public Policy as a Bar to Enforcement of International Arbitral Awards*, 19(2) Arbitration International, 251 (2003).
15. International Institute for the Unification of Private Law (UNIDROIT), UNIDROIT Principles of International Commercial Contracts 2016 (integral version) commentary to Article 1.4, at p. 13. Available at www.unidroit.org. Article 1.4 states: 'Nothing in these Principles shall restrict the application of mandatory rules, whether of national, international or supranational origin, which are applicable in accordance with the relevant rules of private international law.'
16. In *Niko Resources Ltd. v. Bangladesh*, the Tribunal stated 'It is widely accepted that the prohibition of bribery is of such importance for the international legal order that it forms part of what has been described as international or transnational public policy. [...] Arbitral awards and learned writers have supported this position. The matter was considered in particular detail and with admirable erudition in the World Duty Free case by a distinguished tribunal. This tribunal concluded that "bribery is contrary to the international public policy of most, if not all, States or, to use another formula, to transnational public policy". The tribunal reached this conclusion on the basis of an analysis of a large number of international conventions, the decisions of national and international courts and tribunals, and legal writings. [...] The consequence of this conclusion is that, as a principle of international public policy, the prohibition of bribery overrides the general principle of party autonomy which is widely recognised in international and comparative law. Normally, arbitral tribunals respect and give effect to contracts concluded by the parties which agreed on the arbitration clause from which they derive their powers. However, party autonomy is not without limits. In international transactions the most important of such limits is that of international public policy. A contract in conflict with international public policy cannot be given effect by arbitrators.' Also, the then House of Lords in *Kuwait Airways Corp v. Iraqi Airways Co & Anor* 16 May 2002, UKHL 19 at para. 115: 'This conclusion on English public policy does not reflect an insular approach. Our domestic public policy on the status of Resolution 319 does not stand alone. In recent years, particularly as a result of French scholarship, principles of international public policy (*l'ordre public veritablement international*) have been developed in relation to subjects such as traffic in drugs, traffic in weapons, terrorism, and so forth [...].' *Niko Resources Ltd. v. Bangladesh Petroleum Exploration & Production*

The protection of the international community should not be exclusively delegated to domestic law that may exist at a certain time and the jurisdiction of domestic courts. Indeed, international arbitrators are better placed to recognize the existence of transnational public policy rules and can operate more efficiently, at an early stage, to address any potential public policy issues. Pierre Mayer, seems to agree by suggesting that 'transnational public policy is a necessary device in international arbitration. Since, unlike a court, an international arbitrator is not an organ of a State - even the State where he sits - it is neither easy nor satisfactory for him to rely on the public policy of any given State. He needs to have his own public policy. Evidence of such a consensus will most often result from a scrutiny of the legal systems of the various States, or from the existence of one or more international treaties'.[17]

The identification of transnational public policy rules should not be limited to a comparative law exercise. Transnational public policy is not the exclusive result of certain public policy provisions coincidentally existing at a certain period of time in the majority of domestic systems. The widespread acceptance at domestic level of a certain rule is corroborative of the exercise but not a constitutive element of the principle. The existence of a transnational public policy rule can also be evidenced by looking at international treaties, international declarations, international case law, and international soft law instruments.[18] Indeed, transnational public policy seems particularly well-placed to incorporate new principles and rules taking into account for the fast-developing needs and challenges of the international community.[19] Irrespective of the different form and binding nature of international instruments, the principles adopted therein may form part of transnational public policy.[20] If a State signs a

---

Company Limited and Bangladesh Oil Gas and Mineral Corporation, ICSID Case No. ARB/10/18, Decision on Jurisdiction 19 August 2013, paras 431-434.

17. Pierre Mayer, *Effect of International Public Policy in International Arbitration*, in Julian D. M. Lew and Loukas A. Mistelis (eds), Pervasive Problems in International Arbitration, International Arbitration Law Library Series, Volume 15 (Kluwer, 2006) pp. 61-69.
18. George Bermann, *Mandatory Rules of Law in International Arbitration*, in Franco Ferrari & Stefan Kroll (eds), Conflict of Laws in International Arbitration (Sellier 2011), at p. 336. *See also* Stavros Brekoulakis: '[...] to ascertain policy consensus requires the review of a wide number of international legal documents, including arbitral awards and court decisions, as well as international conventions and legal instruments promulgated by international or intergovernmental organizations'. Stavros Brekoulakis, *Transnational Public Policy in International Arbitration*, in Thomas Schultz & Federico Ortino (eds), Oxford Handbook of International Arbitration (OUP, 2020) pp. 120-149 at p. 147.
19. According to Pierre Lalive: 'Thanks to its evolutive and dynamic character, so often emphasized above, the concept of transnational public policy allows today, and will allow in the future, the incorporation in arbitration of the new needs and ideas of the international community, in particular of the interests of developing States as expressed, for instance, by or implied in the concept of "new international economic order". Also from this point of view, therefore, the concept of transnational public policy appears to be an indispensable and important dynamic factor in the development, through arbitration, of a law of international trade.' Pierre Lalive, *Transnational (or Truly International) Public Policy and International Arbitration*, in Pieter Sanders (ed.), Comparative Arbitration Practice and Public Policy in Arbitration, ICCA Congress Series, Volume 3 (Kluwer, 1986), at 315.
20. Catherine Kessedjian suggests: '[...] we would say that transnational public policy is composed of mandatory norms which may be imposed on actors in the market either because they have been created by those actors themselves or by civil society at large, or because they have been widely accepted by different societies around the world. These norms aim at being universal.

convention but does not actually ratify it, that State is not technically bound by the convention, and the convention does not form part of that domestic legal system. However, that State has contributed to forming consensus around the set of values and principles contained in the convention, which may be used by international arbitrators to identify transnational public policy rules that may be relevant to settle an international commercial dispute. Widely accepted treaties should also apply irrespective of signing and ratification by States the domestic law of which is applied to settle a dispute.[21]

Issues of transnational public policy have arisen and might arise at any stage of the proceedings and in different forms. Arbitral tribunals are sometimes faced with the enforcement of transactions potentially tainted by corruption, or in breach of international conventions for the protection of health[22] or climate change.[23] Arbitrations might also be commenced to manage bogus proceedings part of money laundering schemes.[24] Arbitrators are therefore required to exercise caution, possibly pushing their analysis beyond the seemingly legitimate façade of an arbitration. Similar attention should be paid with respect to procedural issues.[25] An arbitral tribunal might be presented with evidence seemingly or potentially gathered in breach of a transnational public policy principle, such as the so-called exclusionary rule codified under international instruments prohibiting evidence obtained by torture.[26] Where the *lex arbitri* or the law

---

They are the sign of the maturity of the international communities (that of the merchants and that of the civil societies) who know very well that there are limits to their activities.' Catherine Kessedjian, *Transnational Public Policy*, in Albert Jan Van den Berg (ed.), International Arbitration 2006: Back to Basics?, ICCA Congress Series, Volume 13 (Kluwer, 2007) pp. 857-870, at p. 861.

21. According to Pierre Lalive, with respect to transnational public policy resulting from international treaties: 'A distinction should of course be drawn in this context between general principles recognized or implicitly accepted by international treaties in force, on the one hand, and those principles recognized in treaties which are not in force or not yet in force. One should also distinguish, of course, the influence of treaties from that of other instruments of international origin, and among the latter a distinction should be made between the texts adopted by international governmental organizations (such as UN Organizations, the OECD, etc.) and, on the other hand, texts adopted by NGOS like the International Chamber of Commerce.' Pierre Lalive, *Transnational (or Truly International) Public Policy and International Arbitration*, in Pieter Sanders (ed.), Comparative Arbitration Practice and Public Policy in Arbitration, ICCA Congress Series, Volume 3 (1986), at 315, at p. 307.
22. For example, the Basel Convention on the Control of Transboundary Movements of Hazardous Wastes and their Disposal entered into force on 5 May 1992.
23. Take, for example, the Paris Agreement on climate change, adopted in 2015. It covers climate change mitigation, adaptation, and finance. The Agreement was negotiated by 196 parties at the 2015 United Nations Climate Change Conference near Paris, France.
24. Kenneth Beale & Paolo Esposito, *Emergent International Attitudes Towards Bribery, Corruption and Money Laundering*, 75(3) Arbitration: The International Journal of Arbitration, Mediation and Dispute Management, Kluwer Law International, 360-373 (2009).
25. Fernando Mantilla-Serrano indicates that 'A survey of the sources of arbitral procedure shows that a transnational procedural public policy has indeed evolved, and that its baseline is relatively undemanding, comprising the fairness or equality principle that is embodied in the most basic notions of natural justice or due process.' Fernando Mantilla-Serrano *Towards a Transnational Procedural Public Policy*, 20 Arbitration International at p. 336 (2004).
26. Convention against Torture and Other Cruel, Inhuman or Degrading Treatment or Punishment New York, 10 December 1984, https://legal.un.org/avl/ha/catcidtp/catcidtp.html. Article 15 it provides: 'Each State Party shall ensure that any statement which is established to have been

otherwise applicable to the arbitration does not contain an express provision reflecting that principle, the arbitral tribunal would be nonetheless in a position to address the issue by turning to any relevant rule of transnational public policy that the arbitral tribunal would deem applicable.[27]

Arbitrators should ascertain whether the mere application of domestic law may fail to identify an inconsistency with wider and universally recognized public policy principles. According to Georgios Petrochilos, 'The point is not about using international law as a device to alter the bargain of the parties. Rather, it is about the proper function of international law in commercial and economic matters.' The author suggests that there is a body of international economic law codified in four principal sources including: bilateral investment treaties, the UNCITRAL Model Law on International Commercial Arbitration, specialized treaties such on the corruption of State officials or the protection of cultural heritage objects, which may be relevant in disputes settled by arbitration, and resolutions issued by international organizations affecting trade of certain commodities or in specified geographical areas.[28]

As already suggested above, transnational public policy may also play a corrective role. In the presence of an international commercial dispute, arbitral tribunals should indeed consider the overall nature of the underlying transaction, irrespective of the choice of applicable law made by the parties, to verify compliance with transnational public policy.[29] As observed by Julian Lew: 'transnational public policy is directly applicable in international arbitration. Further, it is international arbitral tribunals which determine the content of the transnational public policy and how it applies in the particular case. In looking at transnational public policy in whatever form, arbitral tribunals, while owing their responsibility to the parties, also have the right and perhaps the responsibility to uphold that policy in the international arbitration environment. Whilst there are principles behind this transnational public policy in each case, it is for the arbitrators to decide if and how applicable'.[30] As it has been

made as a result of torture shall not be invoked as evidence in any proceedings, except against a person accused of torture as evidence that the statement was made.'

27. For a thorough analysis of *decisions on public policy see* Monique Sasson, *Public Policy in International Commercial Arbitration*, 39(3) Journal of International Arbitration 411-432 (2022).
28. Georgios Petrochilos, *Three Pillars of International Public Policy*, in Photini Pazartzis, Maria Gavouneli, Anastasios Gourgourinis and Matina Papadaki (eds), Reconceptualising the Rule of Law in Global Governance, Resources, Investment and Trade. (Hart, 2006), pp. 309-318 at p. 312.
29. In ICC Case No. 15300 of 2011, the Tribunal remarked that 'while it is true that the parties subjected their contractual relationship to Swiss law, the matter between Claimants and Respondent is purely international with no specific relation to the Swiss legal order. The place of arbitration is France. Therefore, the yardstick of public policy against which the Parties' relationship must be measured is clearly an international or universal one'. ICC Dispute Resolution Bulletin (Issue 1) (2016), at p. 82.
30. Julian Lew, *Transnational Public Policy: Its Application and Effect by International Arbitration Tribunals* (Fundación Universitaria San Pablo CEU, 2018), at p. 64.

observed, international arbitrators are best placed to apply rules of a transnational nature.[31]

Of course, arbitrators should exercise restraint when identifying and enforcing a rule of transnational public policy. A too liberal approach aimed at creating rules rather than just identifying and enforcing established ones would be problematic.[32]

A balanced approach was adopted by the Tribunal in *WDF v. Kenya* where the underlying transaction was tainted by corruption. The Tribunal noted that arbitral tribunals often base their decisions on universal values including transnational public policy. Because bribery is, *inter alia*, against transnational public policy, the Tribunal concluded that claims based on contract obtained by bribery could not be upheld. However, at the same time, the Tribunal raised a systemic issue by observing that tribunals should be cautious in resorting to transnational public policy, and they should ascertain the actual existence of a given transnational public policy rule through the analysis of international conventions, comparative law, and arbitral awards.[33]

Conclusions

Safeguarding the integrity of the international community through transnational public policy rules may be perceived as an aspiration rather than the exercise of a mandatory task. But transnational public policy, as vague a concept as it may seem, is just another set of mandatory rules that the members of the international community believe are necessary to protect certain fundamental values. The genetics of transnational public policy rules is not so different from the genetics of rules meant to regulate legal relationships at a domestic level. They develop in similar ways but operate in different

31. According to Alexis Mourre 'no judge is better placed than an international arbitrator to void contracts which seriously violate *bonos mores* or international public policy'. Alexis Mourre, *Arbitration and Criminal Law: Reflections on the Duties of the Arbitrator,* 22 Arbitration International 95, 116 (2006).
32. According to Stavros Brekoulakis: 'Appealing as this normative account of transnational public policy may be, it must be resisted, because it dangerously conflates the judicial function and legislative function and substitutes political expediency for legal reasoning. As this chapter suggests transnational public policy is a legal doctrine which includes legal norms, in the form of either legal rules or legal principles. Non-legal standards such as morals and values may underpin some of the rules and principles of transnational public policy, but they are not distinct public policy grounds.' Stavros Brekoulakis, *Transnational Public Policy in International Arbitration,* in Thomas Schultz and & Ortino (eds) Oxford Handbook of International Arbitration (2020) pp. 120-149 at p. 148.
33. 'Arbitral tribunals have more often based their decisions on universal values in using various formulations such as "good morals", "*bonos mores*", "ethics of international trade" or "transnational public policy" But it has been rightly stressed that Tribunals must be very cautious in this respect and must carefully check the objective existence of a particular transnational public policy rule in identifying it through international conventions, comparative law and arbitral awards.' At para. 157: 'In light of domestic laws and international conventions relating to corruption, and in light of the decisions taken in this matter by courts and arbitral tribunals, this Tribunal is convinced that bribery is contrary to the international public policy of most, if not all, States or, to use another formula, to transnational public policy. Thus, claims based on contracts of corruption or on contracts obtained by corruption cannot be upheld by this Arbitral Tribunal.' *World Duty Free Company Limited v. Republic of Kenya,* ICSID Case No. ARB/00/7, Award, 4 October 2006, at para. 141.

though interrelated spheres. The development of such important transnational concepts is in part the result of the endeavours of enlightened jurists. Julian Lew is one of them. And this paper is just a humble attempt to express gratitude to him.

CHAPTER 9

Integrity in International Arbitration and among International Arbitrators

Catherine A. Rogers

In 1985, Julian Lew founded the School of International Arbitration (SIA) at Queen Mary University of London. It was the first ever programme dedicated specifically to the law and practice of international arbitration. Since that time, more than 2,000 students from over 80 countries have graduated from the SIA and innumerable other universities around the world have followed suit by offering programmes and courses on international arbitration.

Because international arbitration is ubiquitous today, it is difficult to imagine how truly innovative Professor Lew's educational initiative was at the time. Back in the 1980s and even up through the 1990s, international arbitration was not considered a distinct field, either of study or research. It existed in this nebulous space between public international law, domestic alternative dispute resolution (ADR), comparative law, and international economic law (in the United States) or private law (in Europe). In 1980, even the vaunted United Nations Convention on the Recognition and Enforcement of Foreign Arbitral Awards (better known as the "New York Convention") had only a relative handful of signatures, with the United States having signed only four years earlier.

Today, an LLM is considered an almost essential credential to become an international arbitration specialist. The degree is a means for young lawyers to study foreign law, to write in English if they are not native speakers, and to move away from home, for many for the first time. The SIA is set in the heart of London, a stone's throw from the Inns of Court. For many of its students, the LLM is also the implied promise of a chance to work in a premier international law firm.[1]

1. Many of these same observations have already been made by Professor Patricia Shaughnessy in her book chapter: *The Proliferation of Specialist LLM Programs—The Challenges They Present, The*

I had the distinct pleasure of teaching in the Queen Mary LLM program for over 10 years. Every year, there was a new assortment of bright, eager young minds. They came to London and to Lincoln's Inns Fields from every corner of the globe. Many of them have since taken their learning from the SIA and gone off to vibrant, interesting careers, again in every corner of the world.

Meanwhile, the SIA has also become a meaningful academic platform for leading arbitration specialists to teach and write. International arbitration is one of the relatively few legal fields in which the leading practitioners are also leading authors and teachers in the field. These multiple, overlapping roles have contributed to the growth and development of international arbitration, which is unlike any other field of legal practice.

In this brief tribute essay, I will trace twin developments in international arbitration over the years: its evolution into a fully mature legal dispute resolution regime and the increasing focus on the professionalism and professional conduct of its participants. These two developments are interrelated, but also—I believe—at least partially attributable to the existence of the School of International Arbitration (SIA) that Professor Lew founded.

§9.01 THE EARLY DAYS OF INTERNATIONAL ARBITRATION

Although the origins of international arbitration date back to antiquity, the origins of modern international arbitration can be traced to the 1920s. During this earlier era, international commercial arbitration was not the mature, intricate mechanism we find today. The foundations for the modern system were, however, being laid. The Geneva Protocol on Arbitration Clauses of 1923 and the Geneva Convention on the Execution of Foreign Arbitral Awards of 1927 were more effective for international arbitration than the League of Nations was for global governance. These Geneva Conventions established the framework for modern international arbitration. Despite their achievements, under the Geneva Protocol and the Geneva Convention, arbitration agreements were still routinely voided and arbitral awards were subject to intense judicial scrutiny, sometimes even rewriting. Only by virtue of domestic courts' respect for principles of international comity were arbitral awards enforced at all.

The early modern era of international arbitration can be marked by the drafting and implementation of the United Nations Convention on the Recognition of Foreign Arbitral Awards, commonly known as the New York Convention, was drafted to resolve the deficiencies of the Geneva Protocol and the Geneva Convention. This major advance for international arbitration was precipitated by members of what Oscar Schachter called the 'Invisible College of International Lawyers'.

Schachter argued that, even though international lawyers were ostensibly performing ordinary legal services on behalf of individual clients, they were effectively engaged in a legislative function, contributing to creation of a global legal order.

Development of Programs, Including Specialized Courses, *in* THE EVOLUTION AND FUTURE OF INTERNATIONAL ARBITRATION (Stavros Brekoulakis et al., eds. 2016).

Although Schachter did not single out the founders of modern international arbitration specifically, he was undoubtedly describing them.

Expectations about what international arbitration could accomplish were much lower than they are today. There were relatively few cases, and their resolution was inherently less predictable in both processes and outcomes. Early international arbitration procedures were primarily compromise-oriented, and characterized by informality and flexibility. Arbitral decisions were revered not so much for their legal accuracy or precision as for their sense of fairness and practical wisdom. Because, as noted, judicial enforcement was questionable, awards were generally only as good as they were likely to be complied with voluntarily.

In keeping with this approach, the arbitrator of yesteryear was often already personally known to the parties or counsel, and typically an expert from the same industry as the parties. He exercised a paternalistic authority and was expected to render a just and equitable result. This objective sometimes meant disregarding the express terms of the contract or the clear provisions of applicable substantive law to achieve unanimity among the arbitrators and satisfy both parties.

The soft-edged standards and procedures suited the international marketplace at the time. In that era, there were relatively few companies, primarily concentrated in specific industries, such as maritime, construction, and engineering, and certain commodities, such as oil, cotton, and steel. Parties that were disputing one day would have to do business with each other another day. The need to continue a business relationship made sharp business tactics and scorched earth litigation strategies counterproductive. International businesses needed to resolve disputes through a kinder, gentler process that would not impair their ability to do business together in the future.

In this earlier era, the small cluster of professionals who acted as arbitrators and counsel generally had shared understandings about what it meant to act honourably and behave ethically. Just like other members of Schachter's Invisible College, they were a self-regulating club of gentlemen (there were virtually no women) who needed no external guidance or regulatory oversight.

§9.02 MODERN INTERNATIONAL ARBITRATION

Contemporary international arbitration practice stands transformed from earlier eras. Arbitration is the unrivalled preference for resolving international commercial disputes. With the success and related growth of international arbitration, several other important trends have transformed its once cosy community.

International arbitration is increasingly and consistently used to resolve many of the world's most high-stakes, high-drama disputes. When the New York Convention was opened for signature in 1958, the vast majority of international arbitrations involved relatively simple private contact disputes. In that era, the non-arbitrability doctrine was alive and well.[24] Under that doctrine, arbitrators were generally precluded from exercising jurisdiction over many categories of claims, including securities fraud, antitrust or competition claims, and claims that implicated issues of corruption.

Arbitrators also frequently lacked the authority to order provisional measures, order consolidation, or issue a host of other procedural measures due to the mistrust in arbitration.

In the last 30 years, the power of international arbitration and international arbitrators have not only expanded in number but dramatically increased in their power and autonomy.

Interim relief provides a useful example. In international arbitration's early days, parties had no real choice but to go to national courts because interim relief granted by arbitrators was generally unenforceable and was not available until potentially months after a dispute arose.[31] Today, by contrast, the UNCITRAL Model law and some other national arbitration laws ensure that national courts are statutorily authorized to support the enforceability of interim relief granted by tribunals or issue their own interim measures in support of arbitration. Meanwhile, the introduction of 'emergency arbitrators' can make such relief available within days.

The reach and potency of arbitral jurisdiction has also expanded in other important ways. Today, numerous doctrines may be invoked to make non-signatories subject to arbitration agreements; arbitrators determine matters of joinder, intervention, consolidation, and participation of amici. Meanwhile, arbitrators in individual cases, both through procedural orders and formal rulings, are increasingly asserting power over the conduct of counsel and the rights and interests of third-party funders.

Finally, crucial issues like bribery and corruption are no longer beyond the jurisdictional reach of international arbitrators. Today, arbitrators seem to have not just a starring role, but a director's seat, in how various international bribery and corruption scandals play out. More than occasionally, international arbitrations involve criminal intrigue promiscuously intertwined with the merits and arbitral proceedings themselves. As a result, arbitrators are with increasing frequency being pressed to engage directly with corollary criminal investigations and proceedings. They are asked to order suspension of criminal prosecutions by State parties, to investigate allegations of criminal misconduct, to take (or decline to take) evidentiary account of them, or to refer potential criminal conduct for police action.

Although taken for granted on a case-by-case basis, the importance of these interactions between international arbitration and criminal matters should not be underestimated. How and how well international arbitration handles allegations of illicit and unlawful conduct is critically important for the future of international arbitration and its perceived legitimacy. This increasingly high stakes, however, has brought new scrutiny from critics of international arbitration.

International arbitration is not the only international institution that has been under siege. From the United Nations to the World Trade Organization (WTO), international institutions are facing challenges in light of what has been called an apparent retrenchment of globalization and concerns about a rise in national economic protectionism. More recently, the economic crisis wrought by COVID-19 has caused a breakdown in supply chains and an increase in contract breaches. That breakdown is predicted to produce a significant spike in commercial disputes.

These potential crises for the rest of the world provide potential for international arbitration to confirm its essential value securing international rule of law for commercial disputes. The key is that as arbitration specialists must, as they tend to the needs of their clients, their organizations, their institutions, and their own professional goals – also look beyond the most immediate, short-term self-interests. We need to train our focus better on how our individual actions affect the system, and hence our own long-term enlightened self-interest.

Over the years, arbitrators, counsel, and arbitral institutions have dedicated time and energy to establish their own legitimacy and that of international arbitration more generally. Part of that work has been investments in educating future generations. In addition, academic institutions like the SIA at Queen Mary have promoted a professional identity for these experts.

Over the years, as international arbitration has expanded, those who pre-cited in the field have themselves developed numerous practices and policies, as well as more formalized soft law instruments, to regulate their own professional conduct to promote and ensure that arbitration works fairly and efficiently. These efforts have been essential to ensure that international arbitration maintains the aura of legitimacy that is a necessary predicate for parties to entrust their more important and high-stakes disputes to the process.

It does not do anyone – not lawyer, not client, not arbitrator, not outside funder, and not institution – any good to have their case become the poster child for some endemic problem or controversy in international arbitration. When one actor in a particular setting does not have the wherewithal to see or act beyond immediate strategic considerations, others should be incentivized by longer-term self-interests to step in.

Thanks to programmes like the SIA and now others around the world, those interested in taking up the mantle of international arbitration have clearer path for their learning and professional development. we have

§9.03 CONCLUSION

International arbitration does not have the majestic buildings, the elaborate protocols, the black robes, or the bailiffs and marshals that national legal systems use to promote a sense of legitimacy and ensure compliance with their decisions. The legitimacy of international arbitration, instead, is predicated in substantial part on the integrity and professional conduct of its founders and its modern adherents.

These individuals also serve as its custodians – the arbitrators, counsel, experts, and administrators of arbitral institutions who manage and decide the disputes. These participants build and sustain the legal frameworks and procedures on which the legitimacy of international arbitration is founded. Foremost among these custodians are the arbitrators, who are endowed with incredible, virtually unreviewable discretion.

International arbitration's elevation from a small practice area to an important field for both formal education and scholarship owes a significant debt to Julian Lew and the SIA.

CHAPTER 10
The International Operation of Civil Legislation in Common Law

Stuart Dutson

Stuart first met and worked with Julian in 1996 when finished his PhD at Cambridge and joined the arbitration and conflict of laws group at Herbert Smith "group 2 litigation". Stuart worked with Julian again at the CCLS QMW before Stuart re-entered private practice. Stuart has appeared before Julian as counsel in numerous arbitrations, from investment treaty arbitrations defending States and representing investors, to commercial arbitrations under the International Chamber of Commerce (ICC), London Court of International Arbitration (LCIA) and China International Economic and Trade Arbitration Commission (CIETAC) rules.

§10.01 INTRODUCTION

Many statues lay down rules of substantive law without any indication of their application in space. For example, Part I of the Consumer Protection Act 1987 (England and Wales) operates where 'any damage ... is caused ... by a defect in a product',[1] and Part VA of the Trade Practices Act 1974 (Commonwealth of Australia) operates 'if a corporation supplies good manufactured by it ... and because of [a defect] an individual suffers injuries'.[2] Generally, these otherwise all pervasive words must be given a limited territorial meaning because the courts presume that parliaments do not intend to legislate for the whole world.

1. Section 2(1).
2. Sections 75AD, 75AE, 75AF, and 75AG.

Three methods have been employed by common law courts and proffered by jurists to reach a decision on a statute's territorial application.[3] They are the presumption against extraterritorial legislation, the purpose of the legislation, and application of the rules of private international law.

§10.02 THE PRESUMPTION AGAINST EXTRATERRITORIAL LEGISLATION

There is a presumption that parliament intends its statutes to operate only on persons and matters within its territory and that its legislation must be construed accordingly.[4]

The presumption can be rebutted where the court can identify a legislative intention that the statute is to have an extraterritorial operation.[5] The legislature's intention must be provided for by express words[6] or it must arise by 'necessary implication' where the policy, object or purpose of the statute so requires.[7]

§10.03 THE PURPOSIVE METHOD 1.0

Courts have attempted to interpret a statute in light of its subject matter, policy or purpose so as to read into it territorial limitations which the legislature would have expressed had it addressed itself to the matter, and to determine whether or not a statute has extraterritorial operation.[8]

Kelly, in his treatise on choice of law and statutes, concluded that it is the statute's purpose which must be pre-eminent, and the purposive method 'indicates that territorially unlimited application will be inappropriate whenever the object of the statute will not thereby be significantly furthered'.[9]

---

3. *See* David St. Ledger Kelly *Localising Rules in the Conflict of Laws* (Adelaide: Woodley Press, 1974), 14-15 and Chapter III generally; C.G.J Morse, 'Product Liability in the Conflict of Laws' (1989) 42 *Current Law Problems* 167, 180-186.
4. *See, e.g., Holmes v. Bangladesh Biman Corporation* [1989] 1 AC 1112, 1126, 1132-1133, 1135-1138, 1145-1148; *Morgan v. White (1912)* 15 CLR 1, 13 *per* Isaacs J; F.A. Mann, 'Statutes And The Conflict Of Laws' (1972-1973) 46 *BYIL* 117, 127ff.
5. *Goliath Portland Cement Co Ltd v. Bengtell* (1994) 33 NSWLR 414, 427-428 *per* Kirby P (Cole A-JA agreeing on this point); *Irish Shipping Ltd v. Commercial Assurance Co plc* [1992] 2 QB 206, 219-221 *per* Staughton LJ.
6. *See Theophile v. Solicitor-General* [1950] AC 186, 195 *per* Lord Porter; cf. *Wilson v. Nattrass* (unreported, Supreme Court of Victoria, Full Court, 16 May 1995) *per* Brooking J at 6.
7. *See Clark v. Oceanic Contractors Inc* [1983] 2 AC 130, 145 *per* Lord Scarman; *Morgan v. White* (1912) 15 CLR 1, 13 *per* Isaacs J.
8. *See, e.g., Kay's Leasing Corporation Pty Ltd v. Fletcher* (1964) 116 CLR 124, 142 *per* Kitto J; *Attorney-General for Alberta v. Huggard Assets Ltd* [1953] AC 420, 441 *per* Lord Asquith of Bishopstone; *Re Greenfield* [1985] 2 NZLR 662, 666; *In re Paramount Airways Ltd* [1993] Ch 223, 235-239 *per* Sir Donald Nicholls V-C (Taylor and Farquharson LJJ agreeing).
9. David St. Ledger Kelly, *Localising Rules in the Conflict of Laws* (Adelaide: Woodley Press, 1974), 85.

It appears that if the court can identify a relevant policy and/or purpose for the statute, then this will be the preferred method.[10]

§10.04 THE POSITIVE METHOD 2.0: MANDATORY LAWS OF THE FORUM

If an enactment is an international mandatory law of the forum then it will be applicable in a case in which a court has jurisdiction over a party notwithstanding that, according to the normal rules of private international law, the law of another jurisdiction should govern the case. An otherwise applicable foreign law will be displaced because its application is contrary to the public policy (order public) of the forum, or, a rule of the forum is regarded as mandatory and it will be applied directly such that no question of referring the matter to foreign law will ever arise.

Mandatory rules of the forum have been described by the Law Commission as 'rules of ... domestic law ... regarded as so important that as a matter of construction or policy they must apply in any action before a court of the forum, even where the issues are in principle governed by a foreign law selected by a choice of law rule'.[11]

In *The Hollandia*[12] the House of Lords considered the provisions of the Hague-Visby Rules as enshrined in the 1968 Brussels Protocol Amending the 1924 Brussels Convention. These international conventions were enacted in England by the Carriage of Goods by Sea Act 1971. At the relevant time the Hague-Visby Rules had not been ratified by the Netherlands. The case concerned whether an English court should stay its own proceedings on the ground that the bill of lading granted exclusive jurisdiction to the Netherlands courts and limited the carrier's liability in a manner that was not in accordance with the rules, but was allowed under Netherlands law. An article of the rules rendered provisions that 'lessened' the liability of a carrier or the ship otherwise than in accordance with the rules, null and void.[13]

In applying the rules in that case and accepting jurisdiction notwithstanding the Dutch arbitration agreement, Lord Diplock[14] stated that international conventions:

> should be given a purposive rather than a narrow literalistic construction, particularly wherever the adoption of a literalistic construction would enable the stated purpose of the international convention, viz., the unification of domestic laws of the contracting states relating to bills of lading, to be evaded by the use of colourable devices that, not being expressly referred to in the Rules, are not specifically prohibited.[15]

10. *Goliath Portland Cement Co Ltd* 428 *per* Kirby P (Cole A-JA agreeing on this point), cf. Acts Interpretation Act 1901 (Commonwealth) section 15AA(1).
11. The Law Commission and the Scottish Law Commission, *Private International Law: Choice of Law in Tort and Delict, Working Paper No 87* (London: HMSO, 1984) para. 4.5.
12. [1983] AC 565.
13. Article III para. 8.
14. Lords Keith of Kinkel, Roskill, Brandon of Oakbrook and Brightman agreeing.
15. At 572-573; cf. *Holmes v. Bangladesh Biman Corporation* [1989] 1 AC 1112.

Accordingly, their Lordships rejected a narrow construction of the relevant article of the rules and refused the stay.

In *The Hollandia*[16] mandatory effect was warranted because the statute aimed to harmonise domestic laws and a number of its provisions evidenced the legislature's intention that this law was not to be evaded. Statutory provisions have also been accorded international mandatory status because to do so upholds the protection that they give to individuals.[17]

§10.05 THE APPLICATION OF THE RULES OF PRIVATE INTERNATIONAL LAW

The courts have applied the rules dealing with choice of law to statutes.[18] According to this method a forum statute is only applicable if the *lex causae*, according to the choice of law rule applicable to that statute, is the lex fori.[19] This was the method preferred by the Australian Law Reform Commission in its 1992 Report on Choice of Law.[20]

In *Wanganui-Rangitikei Electric Power Board v. AMP Society*[21] Dixon J[22] of the High Court of Australia referred to what he described as a 'well settled rule of construction':[23]

> an enactment describing acts, matters or things in general words, so that, if restrained by no consideration lying outside its expressed meaning, its intended application would be universal, is to be read as confined to what, according to the rules of international law administered or recognized in our Courts, it is within the province of our law to affect or control. The rule is one of construction only, and

16. [1983] AC 565.
17. *Kays Leasing v. Fletcher* (1964) 116 CLR 124 esp *per* Kitto J at 143-144, *English v. Donnelly* [1958] SC 494, *Golden Acres Ltd v. Queensland Estates Pty Ltd* [1969] StRQd 378, and *Akai Pty Ltd v. The People's Insurance Co Ltd* (unreported, Court of Appeal Supreme Court of New South Wales; Kirby P, Meagher and Sheller JJA, 28 April 1995) *per* Kirby P (dissenting).
18. *See, e.g., Barcelo v. Electrolytic Zinc Co of Australia Ltd* (1932) 48 CLR 391 *per* Dixon J at 423Fff and cf. Starke J at 410; *Nalpantidis v. Stark (No 2)* (unreported, Full Court Supreme Court of South Australia; 19 March 1996) *per* Doyle CJ (Bollen J agreeing) at 6; *Custodian of Israeli Absentee Property* [1954] 1 WLR 139, 152-132; *Monterosso Shipping Co Ltd v. International Transport Workers Federation* [1982] 3 All ER 841; *Apple Corps Ltd v. Apple Computer Inc* [1992] FSR 431, 469-471; *Arab Bank plc v. Mercantile Holdings Ltd* [1994] 2 WLR 307, 313; *Young v. Industrial Chemicals Co* [1939] 4 DLR 392, 394, 398-399; *Stewart v. Honey* (1972) 2 SASR 585, 592-593 *per* Bray CJ; *Lucas v. Cagnon* (1992) 99 DLR (4th) 125.
19. For example, *Barcelo v. Electrolytic Zinc Co of Australia Ltd* (1932) 48 CLR 391, 428 *per* Dixon J, and *Francis Travel Marketing Pty Limited v. Virgin Atlantic Airways Limited* (1994) ATPR 41-332, 42, 395.
20. Australian Law Reform Commission *Choice of Law, Report No 58* (Canberra: Australian Government Publishing Service, 1992) para. 5.21.
21. (1934) 50 CLR 581, 601.
22. Later Dixon CJ.
23. Burchett J of the Federal Court of Australia described it as 'an entrenched rule of construction': *Re Doyle (dec'd): Ex Parte Brien v. Boyle* (1993) 112 ALR 63, 664, and Scalia J (O'Connor, Kennedy and Thomas JJ agreeing) of the United States Supreme Court in a dissenting judgment in *Hartford Fire Insurance co v. California* (1993) 125 L Ed 2d 612, 653 described it as 'firmly established in [American] jurisprudence'. The Senate Standing Committee on Legal and Constitutional Affairs (1992) described it as the 'Traditional Approach' (at 79).

> it may have little or no place where some other restriction is supplied by context or subject matter. But, in the absence of any countervailing consideration, the principle is, I think, that general words should not be understood as extending to cases which, according to the rules of private international law administered in our Courts, are governed by foreign law.[24]

Dixon J stated that this method allowed a statute to comply with the common law and statutory presumptions against extraterritorial legislation such that the scope of operation of the statute is intra-territorial as opposed to extraterritorial.[25]

The application of this method must be subordinate to the terms of the Act being characterised and the context, subject matter or object of the Act.[26] If, for example, the statute provides that it applies only to acts of a person within the United Kingdom, then it can have no application to acts which take place outside the United Kingdom notwithstanding the determination that the application of the applicable choice of law rule may generate.[27]

This method requires that the relevant statutory provision must itself be characterised as relating to a particular juridical concept or category.[28]

One difficulty in the application of the choice of law rules is that if a statute cannot be characterised according to the traditional categories then the rules cannot be applied to it.[29] It has been suggested that in these cases the statute should be characterised as sui generis and a choice of law rule specifically tailored for the statute would have to be developed by the courts.[30] This specifically tailored rule would reflect the purpose of the statute.

---

24. *Wanganui-Tangitikei Electric Power Board v. AMP Society* (1934) 50 CLR 581, 601 *per* Dixon J; cf. *Kemp v. Piper* [1971] SASR 25, 29 *per* Bray CJ.
25. *Wanganui-Tangitikei Electric Power Board v. AMP Society* 601; and *Barcelo v. Electrolytic Zinc Co. of Australia Ltd* (1932) 48 CLR 391, 424-247 *per* Dixon J; cf. *Young v. Industrial Chemicals Co* [1939] 4 DLR 392; *Wilson v. Nattrass* (unreported, Supreme Court of Victoria, Full Court, 16 May 1995) *per* Ashley J (Hedigan J agreeing) at 19; *Kemp v. Piper* [1971] SASR 25, 29 *per* Bray CJ; Richard Ladbury, Peter Fox and Geoffrey Nettle, 'Forum Statutes and International Financing - A Reply' (1882) 4 *Australian Mining and Petroleum Law Journal* 218, 221; S.D. Robb, 'The Tort Rule of Private International Law - The Chimera Incarnate?' (1977) 8 *Sydney Law Review* 146, 177.
26. *Arab Monetary Fund v. Hashim* (unreported, High Court of Justice Chancery Division, Chadwick J, 29 July 1994, digested at *The Times* 11 October 1994 at 503) 11-14; *Kay's Leasing Corporation Pty Ltd v. Fletcher* (1964) 116 CLR 124, 143 *per* Kitto J; *Wanganui-Tangitikei Electric Power Board v. AMP Society per* Gavan Duffy CJ and Starke J at 595-596 and 597 and Dixon J at 601; *Wilson v. Nattrass per* Brooking J at 6-9 and *per* Hedigan J (Ashley J agreeing) at 8ff; *Molnlycke AB v. Procter & Gamble Ltd* [1992] RPC 21, 28; *Def Lepp Music v. Stuart-Brown* [1986] RPC 274; *Myer Emporium v. Commissioner of Stamp Duties* (1967) 85 WN (pt 2) (NSW) 115 *per* Walsh JA (Jacobs JA agreeing) at 127.
27. *See Hartford Fire Insurance Co v. California* (1993) 125 L Ed 2d 612 (S Ct) *per* Scalia J (O'Connor, Kennedy and Thomas JJ agreeing) in a dissenting judgment at 652, and *Def Lepp Music v. Stuart-Brown* [1986] RPC 274.
28. Cf. Robert J. Sharpe, *Inter provincial Product Liability Litigation* (Toronto: Butterworths, 1982) 80-81; S.M. Waddams, *Products Liability* (Toronto: Carswell, 3rd ed., 1993) 157; Nancy Hennessey, *Choice of Law Rules, Australian Law Reform Commission Discussion Paper No 44* (Sydney: Australian Law Reform Commission, 1990) 37.
29. *See, e.g., Mynott v. Barnard* (1939) 62 CLR 68, 91 *per* Dixon J.
30. *Plozza v. South Australia Insurance Company* [1963] SASR 122, 127-128.

§10.06 THE INTERRELATIONSHIPS OF THE THREE METHODS

In a number of cases the courts have considered more than one of the three methods for determining the spatial application of a forum statute. In *Pugh v. Pugh*[31] the court employed both the purposive and private international law methods.[32] In *Re Perkins, Deceased*[33] McLelland J followed Dixon J's reasoning in *Wanganui-Rangitikei Electronic Power Board v. AMP Society,*[34] in applying the rules of private international law to the statute, and in so doing he refused to apply the presumption to it.[35] He also found that the statute's purpose was not of any assistance. In *Wilson v. Nattrass*[36] three judges determined whether the Transport Accident Act 1986 (Victoria) had extraterritorial operation and what the territorial scope of the Act was, by the application of different methods.[37] Brooking J found in the 'specific provisions of the Act' a specific direction as to the Act's territorial scope which, he stated, ousted the application of the choice of law rule in tort.[38] He also stated that he and Ashley J had reached the same conclusion as to the Act's territorial scope in different ways.[39] Ashley J and Hedigan J relied upon the rules of private international law.

The application of the presumption against extraterritorial legislation merely supplies the court with a positive or negative response to a particularised version of the question 'does this statute apply to the foreign person or matter?' It does not attempt to provide more generalised formulae for the determination of the spatial application of the statute.[40] If the rules of private international law are applied they will generate criteria for the determination of the territorial scope of the statute. If these criteria are satisfied then the statute will be applicable regardless of any considerations of whether or not the statute is operating extraterritorially. Indeed, some judges have stated that the operation generated by the application of the rules of private international law must *ipso facto* be intra-territorial. If the presumption against extraterritorial legislation and the method of applying the rules of private international law to statutes do coexist the only possible operation of the presumption can be in those cases in which a party wishes to have the statute applied in circumstances which go beyond those for which the relevant private international law rule would provide. The extraterritorial operation of a statute (the existence of which is determined by the application of the presumption

31. [1951] P 482.
32. J. Unger, 'Capacity to Marry in the Conflict of Laws' (1952) 15 *MLR* 88, 89.
33. (1958) 58 SR (NSW) 1.
34. (1934) 50 CLR 581, 596-506, 597.
35. At 8.
36. Unreported; Supreme Court of Victoria; Full Court; Ashley, Brooking, and Hedigan JJ 16 May 1995.
37. The trial judge had determined the matter by the application of the presumption against extraterritorial legislation (*Wilson v. Nattrass,* unreported, Supreme Court of Victoria, O'Bryan J 5 May 1994, 3-4), a method which was not so much as referred to on appeal.
38. At 6-9. Brooking J's judgment was criticised in Martin Davies, 'Too Little Imagination or Too Much? Phillips v Eyre Revisited Yet Again' (1995) 3 *Torts Law Journal* 273, 285-286. Davies stated that there appears to be very little indication of section 93's territorial scope in either section 93 itself or the subject matter or purpose of the Act.
39. At 7.
40. Cf. *Mynott v. Barnard* (1939) 62 CLR 67, 76-77 *per* Latham CJ, and Kelly (1974) 79-80.

against extraterritorial legislation) will be, at least, that operation beyond which the relevant rule of private international law will allow a statute to operate.

In a number of decisions dealing with sui generis statutes (such as statutes which regulate conduct rather than create private rights), the courts have utilised the object, purpose, or policy of the statute by way of the presumption against extraterritorial legislation.[41] These cases have often gone beyond merely using the object to rebut the presumption and have supplied positive criteria for a statute's territorial scope. Accordingly, in this way these two methods can be brought to bear on the one statute and this appears to be the predominant approach in cases of sui generis statutory provisions.

Of course the terms of a statute may expressly provide that a statute is to have extraterritorial operation and/or provide the statute's territorial scope. In those cases in which it does not, the three methods discussed above will be relevant. Of them, the purposive method is clearly the dominant method – if the subject matter, object or purpose of the statute requires a particular territorial scope, albeit extraterritorial, then this must be adhered to. Neither the presumption against extraterritorial legislation nor the application of the rules of private international law can modify this result because both methods will be rebutted or ousted by a legislative subject matter, policy, object or purpose that requires a scope that differs from that provided by either of these methods.

A number of jurists have suggested that the solution is the adoption of the purposive method as the sole method to determine the territorial scope of a statute.[42] The courts have yet to develop a systematic approach to these cases and their approach to a given statute cannot be predicted with certainty. In the absence of such an approach, the following may be suggested.

In cases in which the relevant statutory provision is sui generis the purposive method will be the appropriate method (where a relevant purpose can be ascertained). This appears to adequately reflect the general trend away from a purely literal and towards a purposive construction of statutory provisions. However, where the purpose cannot be ascertained, the presumption against extraterritorial legislation may be relied upon.

In cases in which the relevant statutory provision creates a non-sui generis cause of action or private right or affects a pre-existing cause of action or private right, the application of the rules of private international law will be the appropriate method to employ. However, if the subject matter, object or purpose of the statute requires a particular territorial scope, albeit extraterritorial, then the purposive method must be adhered to despite what the rules of private international law would prescribe.

---

41. *In re Paramount Airways Ltd* [1993] Ch 223 *per* Sir Donald Nicholls V-C (Taylor and Farquharson LJJ agreeing) at 232-233 and 235-241; *In re Seagull Co Ltd* [1993] Ch 345 (CA) *per* Peter Gibson J (Lloyd and Hirst LJJ agreeing) at 349 and 353-356; and *Trade Practices Commission v. Australian Meat Holdings Pty Ltd* (1988) 83 ALR 299, 355-356 *per* Wilcox J.
42. Kelly (1974), 6-10, 14-15, 84; cf. Gary Born, 'A Reappraisal of the Extraterritorial Reach of U.S. Law' (1992) 24 *Law & Policy in International Business* 1.

B Applicable Law

CHAPTER 11
Julian Lew and the Applicable Law in International Courts and Tribunals

Hans van Houtte

Ours is a tale of two PhD-theses: some 50 years ago, Julian and I happened to prepare our PhD-thesis at the same time on the same topic in the same town.

Arbitration was quite an exotic topic in the early 1970s. Belgium and the United Kingdom had not yet ratified the New York Convention. Arbitration was at a low ebb in England. The 1950 Arbitration Act made the arbitration process quite cumbersome. The London Court of Arbitration was not as international as it is today: 'International' was only added to its name (LC*I*A) in 1985.

That our theses focused on the applicable law in arbitration, was no coincidence. In those years, not the procedural aspects of arbitration but the law to be applied intrigued arbitration scholars. Arbitrators applying *lex mercatoria* was the big hype.

I do not know how Julian ended up at the Law School of the Catholic University of Louvain, Belgium, which at that time cohabited with its Flemish sister university, where I was lecturer.

We occasionally shared findings. We both spent some weeks at the excellent library of the Hamburg Max Planck Institute, and got in Paris full access to the ICC-vaults where its awards were stocked.

Julian entertained us with the most amusing anecdotes (which I discreetly will keep for myself). He introduced us to the intricacies of Jewish cuisine, and we even compared the notion of heaven in Judaism and Christianity. He was my first (pro bono) 'client' for whom I claimed compensation from a Leuven cleaning shop, which had ruined his silk shirt, bought in Delhi while attending one of the first International Council for Commercial Arbitration (ICCA) conferences.

We defended our theses around the same time and went our own ways. However, our paths crossed from time to time: at Richoux when his office was at New Bond Street while I was teaching in London; at Queen Mary; at his home; at different conferences. Julian was always a pleasure to meet with his wit, anecdotes, and fresh ideas.

In time, Julian contributed to my Festschrift.[1] It is now my turn to do the same for him. In this contribution I will examine how young Julian's PhD-proposals to find the applicable law in international commercial arbitration are relevant for international courts and tribunals as well.

By 'international courts and tribunals' I understand legal fora, which have been created under international law, e.g., by a treaty or other international law instruments, to decide legal disputes. The difference between 'International Courts' and 'International Tribunals': the former have broader jurisdiction and are the judicial branch of a legal system (e.g., the International Court of Justice); the latter handle specific matters (e.g., an arbitral tribunal or a claims tribunal).

Although his focus was on international commercial arbitration, in his thesis Julian touched briefly also on the most prominent international fora for dispute resolution: the International Court of Justice, the Permanent Court of Arbitration and ad hoc (international public law) arbitral tribunals.[2] International Centre for Settlement of Investment Disputes (ICSID) was in its early years and had only four investment contract cases.[3] Since then, ICSID has taken a high flight: at present it has handled over 850 arbitrations, 70% of them investment treaty arbitrations.[4] Moreover, several new international fora have been established in recent times, such as the International Criminal Court, the International Tribunal for the Law of the Sea, the Iran-United States Claims Tribunal, the United Nations Compensation Commission, the Bosnian Real Property Claims Commission, the Eritrea-Ethiopia Claims Commission, etc.[5]

As a general and simple rule, these international courts and tribunals have to apply international law. However, 'international law' is a broad notion which encompasses many fields and sub-systems, going from bilateral agreements to *ius cogens*. Moreover, disputes to be decided under international law, may require some aspects to be solved under national law. Consequently, like international commercial arbitrators, international courts and tribunals must find which rules to apply. This contribution will examine how Julian's suggestions for the international commercial arbitration may also be relevant for international courts and tribunals (hereafter for brevity's sake: 'international fora').

1. J. Lew, *Fusion of Common Law and Civil Law Traditions in International Arbitration*, in P. Wautelet, T. Kruger and G. Coppens (eds), The Practice of Arbitration, Essays in Honour of Hans van Houtte (Hart Publishing, 2012), 1.
2. J. Lew, *Applicable Law in International Commercial Arbitration* (Oceana - Sijthoff, 1978), 608-609.
3. As Julian observed at the time: '[It] was not called upon to flex its muscles ... It is not clear how in practice Article 42 of the Washington Convention will actually be interpreted.' *Ibid.*, para. 301.
4. ICSID Case Load Statistics, 2021-2 - Worldbank.
5. HvH was President or Member of several international tribunals (Commission for Real Property Claims-Bosnia, United Nations Compensation Commission, Claims Resolution Tribunal foir Dormant Accounts, Eritrea-Ethiopia Claims Commission, Iran-US Claims Tribunal, Appeals Committee European Patent Office, investment arbitration tribunals).

   See i.a., the excellent overview of claims compensation commissions: N. Wühler & H. Nierbergall, *Property Restitution and Compensation* (IOM 2008).

After an extensive examination of arbitral practice and scholarship, Julian offered five guidelines to find the applicable law in international commercial arbitration:[6]

(1) The answer to every dispute is to be found *prima facie* in the contract itself.
(2) Whenever some law has to complete or interpret the contract terms and/or to determine the parties' rights and obligations and the parties have identified a law, that law should be applied.
(3) Otherwise, the arbitrators must determine the applicable law themselves.[7] Rather than applying some national legal provision, they should follow some 'non-national' or generally accepted rule.[8]
(4) Whenever arbitrators cannot find an appropriate non-national rule, as an ultimate backstop or guide, they should refer to the conflict rules of the arbitral lex fori.[9]
(5) In all events the rules found with the guidelines mentioned above, do not apply when the result would be in breach of truly international public policy.[10]

To what extent are these guidelines also relevant for international fora to find the applicable law?

§11.01 THE PROVISIONS AGREED BY THE PARTIES THEMSELVES

Julian's first guideline for commercial arbitration is that the provisions of the contract, agreed by the parties, often contain the rules to settle contractual disputes.

Although international fora sometimes must decide whether a party to a contract breached international law, it is rather exceptional that they have to settle contractual disputes as such.

Investment tribunals, however, may directly apply contract provisions, agreed by the parties. This may occur either in investment contract arbitrations (where the terms of the investment contract impose themselves) or in treaty arbitrations (where an umbrella clause may grant the arbitrators jurisdiction to assess the contractual obligations).[11] The Iran-United States Claims Tribunal, which sometimes had to decide contract claims, was explicitly instructed to apply the contract provisions.[12]

Some tribunals, on the other hand, have been specifically created by a treaty provision to review the correct application of this treaty and/or to settle claims under

6. Paragraphs 438-454.
7. Paragraphs 439-442.
8. Paragraph 444.
9. Paragraph 450.
10. Paragraphs 451-455.
11. *See* for the different approaches to an umbrella clause: A. Rigo Sureda, *The Umbrella Clause*, in M. Kinnear et al. (eds), *Building International Investment Law – The First 50 Years of ICSID* (Wolters Kluwer, 2015), pp. 375-388.
12. Claims Settlement Declaration, Articles II and V: 'taking into account contractual provisions', Algiers 19 January 1981.

this treaty. Investment treaties thus provide that arbitrators must assess the State's behaviour against its treaty obligations.[13] Or international organizations have created administrative tribunals in service regulations to settle staff claims for breaches of these service regulations.

Instances, where States or organizations have agreed on a basic set of rules and mandated an international forum to apply these rules, are akin to parties to a contract which request arbitrators to settle disputes arising out of this contract. The forum must apply these rules as its primary law.

§11.02 THE LAW IDENTIFIED TO COMPLETE OR INTERPRET THE PARTIES' PROVISIONS

When the provisions, agreed by the parties, are not sufficient to establish the parties' rights and obligations, the parties may have specified by which other rules, these provisions needed to be completed or interpreted. In such case, the commercial arbitrators, so Julian suggested, should apply these other rules.

Similarly, the international instrument, creating an international forum, sometimes instructs the forum where to look for rules to interpret or complete the parties' provisions. A bilateral investment treaty, for instance, may stipulate that its obligations must be interpreted '*in accordance with the Vienna Convention on the Law of Treaties and other rules and principles of international law, applicable between the Contracting Parties*'.[14]Another example: the Iran-United States Claims Tribunal was instructed '*to take into account ... the relevant usages of the trade, contract provisions and changed circumstances*'.[15]

In all these situations, the forum must follow the given instructions.

§11.03 THE FORUM'S OWN DETERMINATION OF THE APPLICABLE RULES

For Julian, whenever the basic provisions were insufficient to decide the case and the parties did not specify which rules to apply, arbitrators themselves must select the applicable rules.[16] Rather than applying some national law, they should look for 'non-national' or generally accepted rules.

For international fora the situation is somewhat different. In principle, these fora decide claims under international law (unless, as mentioned above, they must decide on a contract or other issue of domestic law).

13. *See e.g.*, the Belgium-Luxemburg Model Investment Treaty, 2018, Article 19.A. 1.
14. *Ibid.*, Article 19, I.
15. Claims Settlement Declaration, 1981, Article V.
16. *Ibid.*, paras 439-442.

However, even in the course of a settlement under international law, some elements may require to be decided under a specific domestic law.[17] For instance, the nationality of the claimant is sometimes crucial: diplomatic protection may only be granted to own nationals; or, only nationals of a party to an investment treaty can instal an investment claim against another Contracting State. Moreover, is the claimant entitled to claim because he/she is the 'spouse' or 'heir' of the initial beneficiary?; or, has the claimant adequate ownership rights over the items which he claims restitution or compensation?

Professor Rigaux, Julian's '*Doctorvater*', labelled these issues '*concepts préjudiciels*', i.e., data, which are relevant for the settlement of the dispute, but which have to be established under their own legal rules.[18]

Some international tribunals avoid '*concepts préjudiciels*'. For instance, the Bosnian Real Property Claims Commission, which had to reinstal entitlement to dwellings after the war ended in 1996, got around deciding who had inherited or otherwise acquired housing by 1996 and merely established ownership as it had been in 1991, i.e., before the war started. It was then for the local courts to sort out what may have happened to ownership in the chaotic wartimes between 1991 and 1996. Administrative Tribunals also may merely follow the instructions of the international organization that a same-sex marriage or registered partnership is not equivalent to a marriage and ignore whether the applicable law considers same-sex marriage or registered partnership equivalent to a marriage, and simply instruct that they are not.[19]

When an international forum has to apply national law, selection of the applicable legal system is often not complicated, and the forum does not elaborate how it arrives at the relevant system. However, matters are not always as simple: what to do when several legal systems grant their nationality to a claimant? What when a company has the nationality of its '*siège social*' as well as of the country of its incorporation? Does the '*lex loci situs*' or the proper law of the contract convey transfer of property when the asset is located in a State where property is transferred by delivery but the sales contract is governed by a legal system where property is transferred as of the conclusion of the contract?

Julian suggested that in such case international commercial arbitrators should construe their own conflict of laws rules because their arbitrations are 'denationalized'. *A fortiori* should international fora, which are governed by international law and operate outside of any national legal system, not borrow conflict rules from a national legal system, but construe their own, a-national rules.

The way was shown by the Permanent Court of International Justice in its decisions on the Payment of Serbian and Brazilian Loans. The question at stake was whether pre-1914 Serbian and Brazilian bonds, issued in France, should be reimbursed

17. *See* D. Arroyo & M. Mbengue, *Public and Private International Law in International Courts and Tribunals: Evidence of an Inescapable Interaction*, 56 Columbia J. Transn'l. Law 597, 804-812 (2018).
18. F. Rigaux & M. Fallon, *Droit international privé*, Vol. I (Larcier, 2004), paras 488-494.
19. ILOAT Judgment No. 2193, Judgment No. 3702; Judgment No. 2643. In other instances, however, they meticulously applied the relevant law: ILOAT Judgments No. 2590; No. 2860 (*see* www.ILO.org > dyn > triblex).

on the basis of the 'French 'paper-franc' or of the 'gold-franc'. Each case turned on the same question: which law applied to the loan contracts and to the currency in which payments were to be made? The court construed its own conflict of law rules, based upon general principles of conflict of laws and concluded that, although the law of the lender State governed the essence of the loan agreement, the currency aspects were governed by French law because French currency was used.[20] For our subject, it is not important that the court was heavily criticized for having settled what was in fact a contractual dispute and not a dispute under international law as Article 38 of its Statute required. More important is that the Permanent Court paved the way for other international fora to construe their own conflict of laws rules.

Many international fora have thus coined their own conflict rules. To cite only one example: The Iran-United States Claims Tribunal was instructed by the Claims Settlement Declaration, Article V, to apply '*such choice of law rules ... as the Tribunal determines to be applicable*'. For a contract, governed by Iranian law, it had to decide whether ownership of machinery, located in the United States, was transferred from the American seller to the Iranian buyer when the sales contract was concluded (as Iranian law provides for) or when the machinery was delivered (when US law would apply). After a comparative analysis of national legislation and jurisprudence and the practice of post-WWI international mixed tribunals, the tribunal opted for the *lex rei situs* so that ownership was transferred at delivery.[21]

§11.04 TOWARDS INTERNATIONAL LAW CONFLICT RULES?

For Julian, whenever the other approaches do not work, as ultimate backstop or guide, commercial arbitrators must refer to the conflict rules of the arbitral lex fori.[22]

However, as the *ARAMCO v. Saudi Arabia* Award already observed in 1958, international law, the lex fori of international courts and tribunals, does not contain conflict rules:

> It is a principle universally admitted in private international law that the law governing relations which were not established between States is to be determined by resorting to the conflict rules of the lex fori. But for an arbitration tribunal which is directly subject to international law ... there is no lex fori to indicate what conflict rules should be used, since general international law does not contain any such rules.[23]

The rules, occasionally construed by international fora, may in the long term constitute a coherent legal system of conflict of laws. However, they probably will remain piecemeal rules of thumb for still a long time.[24]

---

20. Judgments 12 July 1929, Series A, Nos 20 and 21.
21. Partial Award A15 II A of 10 March 2020, paras 142-164.
22. Paragraph 450.
23. *ARAMCO v. Saudi Arabia*, 23 August 1958, 27 Int'l L. Rep. 117 at p. 156.
24. *See* T. Viehweg, *Topik und Jurisprudenz*, 1969.

§11.05 THE SAFEGUARD OF INTERNATIONAL PUBLIC POLICY AND INTERNATIONAL LAW

Finally, for Julian, commercial arbitrators should not apply rules which lead to a decision in breach of truly international public policy.[25]

In international courts and tribunals, not international public policy, but international law safeguards against unacceptable results. For instance, it is international law which serves as touchstone and yardstick to assess whether domestic law is in breach of the State's international law obligations with regard to investment or human rights. In this context, it is not excluded that principles of public policy, universally accepted by the States, may become part of international law and block in this capacity domestic law which goes against international public policy.[26]

§11.06 CONCLUSION

The Julian Lew's methodology for the applicable law in international commercial arbitration fits remarkably for international courts and tribunals as well. Of course, there are differences: conflict rules are not part of international law while they are part of any national law; in international fora, international law takes over the role of public policy in commercial arbitration. However, the priority for the rules the parties conceived or to which they referred, and, when such rules lack, the subsidiary requirement to construe non-national conflict rules, prevails in both international commercial arbitrations and international courts or tribunals.

25. Paragraphs 451-455.
26. Lauterpacht, Separate Opinion, Guardianship of an Infant, Judgment, 1958 CJ Rep. 55, paras 92-94.

CHAPTER 12

Revisting Applicable Law in International Arbitration

Wendy Miles KC

§12.01 INTRODUCTION

International economic law facilitates foreign direct investment by insulating cross-border property rights from state intervention through both public and private international law instruments and mechanisms,[1] including international arbitration. Although the law of nations preserves state sovereignty in respect of the function of law within a state's own territory, structures regulating foreign direct investment may directly or indirectly impede the state's ability to give effect to its own national laws.[2] The potential conflict between domestic laws and international economic law is especially acute in the regulatory and legislative context of reform to achieve climate change mitigation and adaptation commitments.

§12.02 A GLOBAL TRANSITION

Within the United Nations Framework Convention on Climate Change 1992 (UNFCCC), Paris Agreement 2015 established global mitigation and adaptation goals,[3] and

1. AV Dicey et al., *Dicey, Morris and Collins on the Conflict of Laws* (15th edn, Sweet & Maxwell, London 2006) [32-049]-[32-051]. *See also* AFM Maniruzzaman, 'The Pursuit of Stability in International Energy Contracts' (2008) 1(2) Journal of World Energy Law & Business; R Brown, 'Choice of Law Provisions in Concession and Related Contracts' (1975) 39(6) The Modern Law Review 625; Christoph Schreuer et al., *The ICSID Convention: A Commentary* (2nd edn, CUP, Cambridge 2009).
2. A Mills, 'The Private History of International Law', in A Mills (ed.) *The Confluence of Public and Private International Law* (CUP, Cambridge 2010).
3. IPCC, 2018: *Global warming of 1.5°C. An IPCC Special Report on the impacts of global warming of 1.5°C above pre-industrial levels and related global greenhouse gas emission pathways, in the*

a commitment to make 'finance flows consistent with a pathway towards low greenhouse gas emissions and climate-resilient development'.[4] Scientists largely agree that this requires net zero additional greenhouse gas emissions by 2050, with a 45% reduction by 2030,[5] requiring trillions of dollars of investment in systems transition. Investment must focus on energy, infrastructure, transport, industry and land use sectors, including extractive industries. Most finance will be sourced from private sector, likely through foreign direct investment, and public-private partnerships.[6]

States already rely on foreign investment to provide utilities and services for public purpose, as well as to build a foundation for sovereign economic stability, peace and security.[7] At the same time, the key sectors in transition are highly regulated.[8] Transition will involve myriad changes to local operational regulations and legislation and emerging jurisprudence from national courts and administrative bodies.

This rapidly changing host state operating environment creates challenges for private investors. They seek to enhance certainty and mitigate risk, including by insulating investments from state interference by utilising international economic law mechanisms, including international arbitration. The 1958 New York Convention on the Recognition and Enforcement of Foreign Arbitral Awards (the 'NY Convention'), reinforced by the 1985 UNCITRAL Model Law on Commercial Arbitration (the 'UNCITRAL Model Law'), and the 1966 Convention on the Settlement of Investment Disputes between States and Nationals of Other States (the 'ICSID Convention') codify basic principles of procedure in international arbitration, prioritising party autonomy and finality.

Narrow review by enforcing courts protects party autonomy and the right to choose a final and binding outcome through arbitration. Parties elect to arbitrate to avoid undue interference from national courts, including in respect of an error in law.[9] Ultimately, individual outcomes on substance (including application of substantive law) are subsidiary to the systemic outcome of the process. In this regard, the mid-twentieth century American jurist Professor Lon L. Fuller 'rejected a narrowly instrumentalist view that legal processes are to be judged by the quality of their outcomes; the workings of the processes themselves involve important values'.[10] He

---

context of strengthening the global response to the threat of climate change, sustainable development, and efforts to eradicate poverty V Masson-Delmotte et al. (eds).

4. Paris Agreement, Article 2(1)(c). *See* OECD/The World Bank/UN Environment, 'Financing Climate Futures: Rethinking Infrastructure', 2018, 1.
5. IPCC Report 'Summary for Policymakers' 2.
6. *Public-Private Partnerships: Reference Guide Version 2.0 (English).* Washington, D.C.: World Bank Group, http://documents.worldbank.org/curated/en/600511468336720455/Public-private-partnerships-reference-guide-version-2-0; cf.: Christopher Greenwood, 'State Contracts in International Law: The Libyan Oil Arbitrations' (1982) 53(1) British Yearbook of International Law 27-81; and Brown (*supra* n. 1).
7. C Lipson, *Standing Guard: Protecting Foreign Capital in the Nineteenth and Twentieth Centuries*, (University of California Press, Berkeley CA 1985) Chapter 1.
8. *See* https://ppp.worldbank.org/public-private-partnership/sector/energy/laws-regulations.
9. G Born *International Commercial Arbitration* (3rd edn, Kluwer Law International, 2021) §§25.04[F][4][e] and 26.05[c][e].
10. RS Summers, *Lon L Fuller* (Hodder & Stoughton Ltd, 1984) 76, cited by S Toope, 'Arbitrations Involving States and Foreign Private Parties: A Study in Contemporary Legal Process' (DPhil

took the view that 'adjudication should be viewed as a form of social ordering, as a way in which the relations of men to one another are governed and regulated'.[11]

Existing international economic law offers a framework for attracting and mobilising private sector investment into low greenhouse gas emission and climate resilient system infrastructure and transitioning from existing infrastructure. At the same time, state regulatory reform provides the framework for scaling up investment in low greenhouse gas emission and climate resilient systems, and phasing down high greenhouse gas emitting investment activity, within a state's territory. Climate change goals will be achieved only if those two legal frameworks work in harmony, and not in conflict, to meet the Paris Agreement commitments.

§12.03 THE ROLE OF APPLICABLE LAW IN ARBITRATION

The conventional approach of enforcing courts to enforcing arbitral awards pursuant ot the NY Convention may pose a serious threat to a harmonised approach that also achieves the Paris Agreement commitments.

Arbitral procedure is governed by the national law of the parties' selected juridical seat (or place) of arbitration, in accordance with the national arbitration statute. National courts of the seat maintain limited supervisory powers over the arbitration based on the provisions in the UNCITRAL Model Law. If governing law is not expressly stated or otherwise clearly agreed, it is for the tribunal to determine applying conflict of law principles.[12] A tribunal may be required first to determine which conflict of law principles to apply to the question.[13]

According to Dicey, 'the law relating to the conduct of international commercial arbitration, including the conflict of laws issues ..., has been profoundly influenced by international developments',[14] which:[15]

> subjects them to a separate regime, which is partly the product of private regulation, and partly the result of developments in international treaties and national law, which themselves permit a considerable scope for party autonomy in arbitration.

---

thesis, University of Cambridge 1986), 542. Toope argues, at 224, that '*consideration of free choice and the desire to protect reputation do not overcome the fact that for many reasons – often political or economic rather than strictly legal – states sometimes do refuse to comply with arbitral awards ...*', citing to *Libyan American Oil Co v. The Government of the Libyan Arab Republic*, Decision of 12 April 1977, reprinted in (1981) 20 I.L.M.1.

11. L Fuller 'The Forms and Limits of Adjudication' (1978) 92(2) Harvard Law Review 353-409, at 357.
12. The governing law of the underlying contract may differ from the governing law of the separate arbitration agreement.
13. L Silberman & F Ferrari, 'Getting to the Law Applicable to the Merits in International Arbitration and the Consequences of Getting It Wrong', in Stefan Kroll & Franco Ferrari (eds), *Conflict of Laws in Commercial Arbitration* (Seller de Gruere, Munich, 2010); Dicey (*supra* n. 1) [16-002-16-028].
14. Dicey (*supra* n. 1) [16-003].
15. *Ibid.*, [16-006].

The touchstone in arbitration is party autonomy; provided the parties expressly (or sometimes implicitly) agree on an approach, and the tribunal otherwise acts in accordance with due process and within its jurisdiction, the system is somewhat indifferent as to whether or not the tribunal applied the law correctly or even applied the correct law at all.[16] Dicey concludes that modern practice is that subject to the parties' choice of conflict rules, the tribunal '*shall apply the rules which it determines appropriate*',[17] as reflected in most arbitral institution rules and the UNCITRAL Model Law.

[A] Applicable Substantive Law

In *Lesotho Highlands Development Ltd v. Impreligo* SpA,[18] the English House of Lords discussed a tribunal's alleged excess of mandate for non-application of law.[19] It described the Model Law approach as permitting a tribunal to take a 'natural and commercially sensible construction', based on a 'businesslike meaning that will assist the arbitral process'.[20] Although it found no error in law, it went on to reason that section 68(2)(b):

> required the courts below to address the question whether the tribunal *purported to exercise a power which it did not have* or whether it erroneously exercised a power that it did have. If it is merely a case of erroneous exercise of power vesting in the tribunal no excess of power under section 68(2)(b) is involved.

The court considered section 68 to be a 'legislative technique', which UK policymakers had observed 'is really designed as a long stop, only available in extreme cases where the tribunal has gone so wrong in its conduct of the arbitration that justice calls out for it to be corrected'.[21] The court said that 'nowhere in section 68 is there any hint that a failure by the tribunal to arrive at the "correct decision" could afford a ground for challenge under section 68'.[22]

---

16. This is a distinct departure from the Montevideo Convention Article 2, which provided that 'Judges and authorities of the State Parties shall enforce the foreign law in the same way as it would be enforced by the judges of the State whose law is applicable, without prejudice to the parties' being able to plead and prove the existence and content of the foreign law invoked.' Dicey (*supra* n. 1) [16R-001].
17. UNCITRAL Model Law Article 35(1).
18. *Lesotho Highlands Development Authority v. Impreglia SpA* [2006] 1 AC 221.
19. Edward Ti Seng Wei, 'Why Egregious Errors of Law May Yet Justify a Refusal of Enforcement Under the New York Convention' (2009) 12 Singapore Journal of Legal Studies 597-617, at 597, argues that egregious misapplication of the law would amount to failure to apply the law in commercial arbitration and in investor state arbitration, *see also Hussein Nuaman Soufraki v. The United Arab Emirates*, ICSID Case No. ARB/02/7, Ad Hoc Committee decision [86] ('Misinterpretation or misapplication of the proper law may, in particular cases, be so gross or egregious as substantially to amount to failure to apply the proper law').
20. *Lesotho* (*supra* n. 18) [22].
21. *Ibid.*, [27] citing to DAC Report 58 [280].
22. *Lesotho* (*supra* n. 18) [29].

The House of Lords considered that section 68(2)(b) 'assumes that the tribunal acted within its substantive jurisdiction',[23] and is 'aimed at the tribunal exceeding its powers under the arbitration agreement, terms of reference or the 1996 Act',[24] which it describes as meaning that it:

> does not permit a challenge on the ground that the tribunal arrived at a wrong conclusion as a matter of law or fact. It is not apt to cover a mere error of law. This view is reinforced if one takes into account that a mistake in interpreting the contract is the paradigm of a 'question of law' which may in the circumstances specified in section 69 be appealed unless the parties have excluded that right by agreement.

In *B v. A*,[25] the High Court applied *Lesotho* to misapplication of foreign law.[26] It reiterated that 'it would be odd indeed if an error in the application of foreign law could give rise to the possibility of an unconstrained challenge under section 68'.[27] The court described the essence of the applicant's case as an error 'under the relevant Spanish rules of contractual interpretation', which 'cannot possibly be a valid ground of challenge'.[28]

Subsequently, in both *C v. D*[29] and *National Iranian Oil Co v. Crescent Petroleum*,[30] the English court found that non-mandatory provisions in the Arbitration Act (on interest and separability respectively) would apply even if the governing law provided otherwise, unless the parties had expressly opted out of those provisions.[31]

Other national courts take a similar approach. In Singapore, two relatively recent decisions in *Quarella SpA v. Scelta Marble Australia Pty Ltd*[32] and *Quanzhou Sanhong Trading Ltd v. ADM Asia-Pacific Trading Ltd*,[33] considered the issue. The Singapore court found each to be an appeal against the tribunal's choice of governing law. In both cases, the tribunal applied a conflict of laws analyses to reach a decision as to applicable law, and then proceeded to determine the case in accordance with that law. Neither involved a tribunal failing to apply the expressly agreed and undisputed governing law.

Commentary and judgments from other national courts suggest that the situation should be different where the choice is clear or, alternatively, the tribunal failed properly to determine choice of law.[34]

---

23. *Ibid.*, [32].
24. *Ibid.*, [32].
25. [2010] EWHC 1626.
26. *B v. A* [2010] EWHC 1626 [26].
27. *Ibid.*, [27].
28. *Ibid.*, [29].
29. *C v. D* [2008] 1 Lloyd's Rep 239 (CA) [19].
30. *National Iranian Oil Company v. Crescent Petroleum Co Int* [2016] EWHC 510 (Comms).
31. This decision has been subject to some criticism. *See* R Merkin & L Flannery *The Arbitration Act 1996* (Informa Law from Routledge, London 2019) 52.
32. *Quarella SpA v. Scelta Marble Australia Pty Ltd* [2012] SGHC.
33. *Quanzhou Sanhong Trading Co Ltd v. ADM Asia-Pacific Trading Pty Ltd* XLIII YB Comm Arb 549.
34. *See* Kröll (*infra* n. 45) 345; S Jarvin, 'Irregularity in the Composition of the Arbitral Tribunal and the Procedure', in Gaillard, E. and Di Pietro, D. (eds.), Enforcement of Arbitration Agreements and International Arbitral Awards: The New York Convention in Practice, 2008, 730; ICC Case

[B] Applicable Law of the Arbitration Agreement

In the context of the law governing the arbitration agreement, the application of conflict of laws principles was ventilated in the English Supreme Court in *Enka Insaat Ve Sanayi AS v. OOO 'Insurance Company Chubb'*[35] and *Kabab-Ji SAL v. Kout Food Group.*[36] In both cases, the first instance English court conducted a *de novo* review of the tribunal's choice of law and application of law to the validity of the arbitration agreement.[37] As *Kout* involved a foreign award, the Supreme Court noted that its conclusions in *Enka* under Arbitraiton Act section 68 'are not directly applicable' because in *Kout* 'the rules are those in section 103(2)(b) of the 1996 Act, which transposes into English law the text of the [NY] Convention'.[38]

The jurisdiction decisions demonstrate that the English courts are willing and able to conduct *de novo* review of the application of foreign conflict of laws rules and, indeed, the substantive application of foreign law by a tribunal as to jurisdiction.[39] However, jurisdiction is treated as a separate category for review purposes pursuant to the English Arbitration Act 1996 section 67 and the NY Convention Article V(1)(a), and is subject to a different standard of court review.[40]

[C] Mandatory Law

Mandatory rules comprise a particular aspect of applicable law that are treated somewhat more deferentially.[41] Commentators describe these as having 'an exceptional status in each legal system, since they are its backbone'.[42] Parties may not

No. 11264 (2002), in E Gaillard, 'The Role of the Arbitrator in Determining the Applicable Law', *in* L Newman & R Hill (eds), *The Leading Arbitrator's Guide to International Arbitration* (Juris, 2004) 196. Silbermann in Kröll (*supra* n. 13) 120.

35. [2020] UKSC 38.
36. [2021] UKSC 48.
37. This also occurred some years prior in the decisions that culminated in *Dallah Real Estate and Tourism Holdings Co v. Ministry of Religious Affairs of the Government of Pakistan* [2011] 1 AC 763.
38. *Kout* (*infra* n 45). Similar provisions exist in the French Code of Civil Procedure, Article 1502, Austrian ZPO, §-611, German ZPO, §-1059, Swiss Law on Private International Law, Article 190; US Federal Arbitration Act, §§9-11 USC.
39. The English courts are not alone. The US Supreme Court took the same approach in: *BG Group PLC v. Republic of Argentina* 572 U.S. __ (2014). Although the approach is by no means universal: *Four Seasons Hotels & Resorts BV v. Consorcio Barr SA* 613 F Supp 2d 1362, 1369 (Florida court aid: '[a] holding in an arbitration award that is contrary to the substantive law governing the arbitration is not a defense under the Convention, and therefore a district court generally may not review an award on the merits').
40. Dicey (*supra* n. 1) [16-002-16-013].
41. 'ILA Report on Ascertaining the Contents of the Applicable Law in International Commercial Arbitration', Arbitration International (2010) 26(2) 193, at 198, citing only to the ICSID Convention Article 42(2).
42. P Wiliński, *Excess of Powers in International Commercial Arbitration*, Eleven International Publishing (The Hague, 2020), p. 62; P Mayer, *Mandatory Rules of Law in International Arbitration* (1986) 2 Arbitration International 274; A Barraclough & J Waincymer 'Mandatory Rules of Law in International Commercial Arbitration' (2005) 6(2) Melbourne Journal of International Law 205; 'ILA Report' (*supra* n. 41) 23 (Recommendation 13); J Paulson, 'Thinking

contract out of applicable mandatory law.[43] Failure to apply mandatory law should result in a set aside or non-enforcement of an award, if not pursuant to excess of mandate then at least pursuant to public policy.[44] This may appear to be a straightforward proposition, but there are questions as to which mandatory rules apply (i.e., the place of arbitration, governing law of the contract, place of performance or another),[45] the practical challenge of ascertaining the scope, content and effect of mandatory law (including whether or not it is in fact mandatory) and the difficult issue that arises when that mandatory law was never raised in the arbitration or, alternatively, was raised and the tribunal determined in its discretion it was not applicable.

According to George Berman:[46]

> The notion of mandatory rules of law occupies a central place in the world of private international law, chiefly as a limitation on party autonomy. [...] The notion of mandatory rules of law is not, however, without ambiguity; the meaning and effect attributable to them are subject to discussion.

In practice, court decisions suggest that failure to apply mandatory law, alongside public policy, is rarely the basis for a national court to refuse to enforce a foreign judgment or award, or to set aside a domestic award, due to the pro-enforcement deference to tribunal decision-making.[47] This may be contributed to in practice by mandatory rules being treated, as Berman suggests, 'basically as legal data, or facts, for the purpose of applying legal principles drawn from the applicable law, whether the law chosen by the parties or the law that the court otherwise considers applicable'.[48] National courts are even more reluctant to refuse to enforce an award on the basis of error of fact than law.

Simply About Public Policy', in *Liber Amicorum: Mélanges en l'honneur de Serge Lazareff* (L Lévy & Y Derains Pedone, Paris 2011); Luca Radicati di Brozolo 'Mandatory Rules and International Arbitration' (2012) 23(1) ARIA.

43. *See, e.g.*, B Audit, 'How do Mandatory Rules of Law Function in International Civil Litigation', (2007) 18(1) American Review of International Arbitration 37; N Voser, 'Mandatory Rules of Law as a Limitation on the Law Applicable in International Commercial Arbitration', (1996) 7 American Review of International Arbitration.
44. *Desputeaux v. Éditions Chouette (1987) Inc* [2003] 1 SCR 178, 2003 SCC 17 (CanLII), http://canlii.ca/t/ig2jh ('An error in interpreting a mandatory statutory provision would not provide a basis for annulling the award as a violation of public order, unless the outcome of the arbitration was in conflict with the relevant fundamental principles of public order').
45. *National Iranian Oil Company v. Crescent Petroleum Co Int* [2016] EWHC 510 (Comms); G Berman 'Mandatory Rules of Law in International Arbitration', in Kröll (*supra* n. 42) 331-335.
46. Berman (*supra* n. 45) 325.
47. V Pavić, 'Bribery and International Commercial Arbitration (2012) 43 VUWLR 661, at 844 ('Complete deference seems to be an ill-suited protector of public policy principles, and it is understandable why courts and arbitrators attempt to devise a test ("trigger") for further inquiry. It is also notable that the approach of complete deference to the findings of the arbitrators requires parties to furnish fresh, new evidence of illegality. This will be available only in the rarest of circumstances'). *See, e.g.*, *RBRG Trading (UK) v. Sinocore International* [2018] EWCA Civ 838; *PT Asuransi Jasa Indonesia (Persero) v. Dexia Bank* [2006] SGCA 41; *Gutnick v. Indian Farmers Fertiliser Cooperative Ltd* [2016] VSCA; *Hebei Import & Export Corporation v. Polytek Engineering Company Limited*; *A v. R* [2009] 3 HKLRD 389.
48. Berman (*supra* n. 45) 331-335.

Therefore, it is simply not enough to assume that climate change laws will be implemented as a matter of course in international arbitration proceedings, simply because those laws are deemed to be mandatory in the place of performance or registration of a party. With revision only in the rarest of circumstances, even in the case of bribery and corruption,[49] this will not be a reliable foundation upon which to ensure that climate change laws are implemented in relation to investment.

§12.04 CONCLUSION

If one accepts that a dogmatically narrow approach to review for failure to apply the law could inhibit states' ability to meet their Paris Agreement commitments, then it is time to re-evaluate that approach. Such a re-evaluation - or re-imagination - of the 'social order' of international commercial arbitration does not necessarily need to be radical. It may suffice simply to factor the Paris Agreement commitments into each stage of the arbitration and enforcement process in a more careful, deliberate and strategic manner.

After all, the existing approach to enforcement under the NY Convention emerged mid-twentieth century when the global economy was transitioning from a post-colonial past to a modern transnational system of property-based legal protection. A strict uniform pro-enforcement approach by enforcing courts that largely insulates foreign investment from state interference may not account for shifting geopolitical order and global priorities over the intervening 60 years. As a subsequent international instrument has invested individual states with 'bottom up' rights and responsibilities to implement climate change mitigation, adaptation and alignment of finance flows within their territorial borders, an indiscriminate approach to enforcing arbitral awards even where tribunals fail to apply relevant national (and, if relevant, international) climate change laws, may not be the way forward.

49. Pavić (*supra* n. 47).

CHAPTER 13

Reflections on the Law Governing Confidentiality in Arbitration

Lawrence Collins[*]

The purpose of this piece is to make a modest contribution to the debate on the question of what law governs confidentiality[1] in international arbitration. It will be limited to common law jurisdictions. There is no definitive authority on the question, and it has been suggested that there is a binary choice between the law governing the arbitration agreement and the law of the seat of the arbitration.[2] The thesis of this author is that not only is there no binary choice, but also that the solution may depend upon the forum in which the issue arises, and that it will be only very rarely that the issue will need to be addressed directly.

To put the issue in context, it is important to bear in mind that the obligation of confidentiality in international commercial arbitration has many potential sources: an express term (or, less plausibly) an implied term in the commercial agreement, an implied term or (less frequently) an express term in the arbitration agreement, an express provision in the law of the seat of the arbitration (as in those countries, such as Hong Kong and South Africa, which have supplemented the UNCITRAL Model Law to include confidentiality provisions), or an express provision in the institutional rules governing the arbitration (e.g., SIAC, LCIA, Swiss Rules), or a provision in a procedural order made by the tribunal.

* The author is proud to have been a partner and colleague of Julian Lew, and a friend for almost 50 years, and is privileged to contribute to this collection on a topic on which he has long been interested: see his opinion in *Esso Resources Ltd v. Plowman* (1995) 193 C.L.R. 10, published in (1995) 11 Arb. Int. 283.

1. Although the privacy of arbitrations will be touched on, this paper does not directly address the question of what law governs the privacy of arbitral hearings, as distinct from confidentiality in relation to, e.g., documents, pleadings and awards.
2. *See, e.g.* Clifford and Scogings, *Which law determines the confidentiality of commercial arbitration?* (2019) 35 Int Arb 391 (favouring the law of the seat).

A close reading of an article under the title 'Which Law Determines the Confidentiality of Commercial Arbitration?'[3] reveals that it devotes at most about one page to the question (limited to English law) raised by the title. According to the authors: (a) there is no judicial authority on the question whether the issue is determined by the law governing the arbitration agreement or the procedural law of the seat; (b) where the seat or the governing law refers[4] to a jurisdiction which does not recognise confidentiality, parties may wrongly assume that they are not under an obligation of confidentiality; (c) determining confidentiality by the law of the seat would promote greater certainty, because the law of the seat is often clear, whereas the law determining the arbitration agreement is commonly not stipulated and can be unclear; and (d) consequently the law of the seat should be the determining factor. The article does not say what it means by the law of the seat.

Gary Born[5] has a more nuanced treatment. He acknowledges that little attention has been paid to the question of the law governing confidentiality. He discusses the following possible governing laws: first, the law governing the arbitration agreement, which would be consistent with the notion (adopted in England and Singapore) that confidentiality is an implied obligation of the agreement to arbitrate; second, the procedural law of the arbitration, the seat of the arbitration, which would be consistent with the notion that confidentiality obligations derive from the privacy of the hearing and related proceedings; third the law applicable to the underlying contract, particularly where it contains an express confidentiality obligation which could be interpreted to apply to alter or address implied obligations arising from the arbitration agreement.[6] After giving reasons for the argument that the parties' obligations of confidentiality should be governed by the law governing the arbitration agreement (particularly where there is an express obligation of confidentiality), especially because implied obligations of confidentiality are derived from the agreement to arbitrate, he suggests an alternative analysis (which he appears to favour) that would apply both the law governing the arbitration and (if different) the law of the arbitral seat, on the basis that 'implied confidentiality obligations should apply if they exist under the law of either the arbitral seat or the jurisdiction whose law applies to the arbitration agreement'. This appears to suggest a cumulative application of rules of confidentiality, and not a true choice of law. The thesis appears to be a narrow one limited to implied obligations of confidentiality, and that the law or laws most favourable to confidentiality should be applied.

There are several cases in the United States in which the issue of arbitral confidentiality has arisen in a cross-border context, but in none of them was there any serious discussion of what law applied.

In the first case, *United States v. Panhandle Eastern Corp*,[7] by contrast with others mentioned in this piece, the claim to confidentiality had some merit. The action by the

3. *Ibid.*
4. The authors do not explain how this could occur.
5. Born, *International Commercial Arbitration* (3rd ed. 2020), para. 20.08.
6. This is not entirely clear, and what may be meant is that an express confidentiality provision in the underlying contract may be interpreted to apply to arbitral proceedings under the contract.
7. 111 F.R.D. 346 (D.Del. 1988).

US Government was a civil action to protect its security interests as guarantor of ship-financing bonds. Panhandle sought to avoid disclosure of documents generated in an ICC arbitration in Switzerland between the defendant and Sonatrach, the Algerian national oil and gas company. Its argument was that disclosure to third parties of documents related to the Sonatrach Arbitration would severely prejudice its business relationship with both Sonatrach and the Algerian Government. Its motion failed because there was no basis for its contention that the ICC Rules required the documents to be kept confidential. It had relied on the internal rules of the ICC Court of Arbitration which had no application to the parties or the tribunal.[8] The court did not address the question of applicable law, and in particular whether it was treating the application of the ICC Rules as a matter of party choice or as part of the applicable rules in Switzerland as the seat of the arbitration.

Contship Containerlines, Ltd. v. PPG Industries., Inc.[9] was an action in the New York federal court by cargo-owners against charterers and owners for damage to cargo arising out of an explosion and fire on a ship. The cargo-owners sought discovery of documents generated in a London arbitration between the charterers and the owners. The charterers and owners produced the documentary evidence which was submitted in the arbitration (presumably on the basis that they were not confidential) but refused to produce: expert submissions, correspondence with, and briefs and other submissions to the tribunal, and hearing transcripts. The charterers and owners claimed that those materials were protected by the confidentiality which attached to the London arbitration proceedings. The claim to confidentiality was put on the basis that under English law an obligation of confidentiality was implied in law as part of the agreement to arbitrate.[10]

The claim to resist production was rejected on the basis that the charterers and owners had neither cited any contractual provision between them giving rise to an obligation of confidentiality, nor a regulation of any arbitral body as the source of confidentiality. Even assuming that the contention as to the state of English law was correct, it did not preclude the disclosure sought. The court held that the documents were undeniably relevant, since they related to the very incident which was in issue, and their disclosure was necessary for disposing of the matter fairly and inexpensively. The court followed the decision in *Caringal v. Karteria Shipping, Ltd*[11] in which a similar argument had been made, also based on *Hassneh Insurance Co v. Mew.*[12] The court in the *Contship* case purported to apply English law in holding, based on the *Caringal* case, that the court could order disclosure, even though the documents were confidential if (1) the documents were relevant and (2) 'disclosure is necessary for disposing fairly of the cause or matter or for saving costs'.[13] But the quotation was from the then current Rules of the Supreme Court (now the Civil Procedure Rules (CPR))

8. *See* Statute of the International Court of Arbitration, Article 8; and the Internal Rules, Article 1.
9. 2003 WL 1948807 (S.D.N.Y. 2003).
10. Citing *Hassneh Insurance Co v. Mew* [1993] 2 Lloyd's Rep. 243; *Insurance Co v. Lloyd's Syndicate* [1995] 1 Lloyd's Rep. 272.
11. 2001 WL 874705 (E.D.La.2001).
12. *Supra* n. 10.
13. *Ibid.*, at 250.

concerning discovery in general. It is a commonplace that procedure is governed exclusively by the *lex fori*, and the US court overlooked the point that these were English procedural rules which had no application in the United States.

Neither of these cases, therefore, applies defensible choice of law rules on confidentiality. The most which could be said is that each of these tribunals had regard to English law, which was very likely the governing law of the arbitration agreement and certainly the law of the seat of the arbitration. But each of them wrongly applied English procedural discovery rules to determine whether the documents should be disclosed.

On the contrary, because all three of these US cases involved applications for discovery under US rules, they should have applied those rules. The two cases which applied English law misunderstood the English case law. As in English law, confidentiality is not a bar to an order for discovery. In the United States there is a large body of case law and practice surrounding the use of protective orders to prevent the misuse or dissemination of confidential material produced on discovery. By contrast with privilege, confidentiality does not rule out disclosure. But it is a factor to be taken into account when the court considers whether to order disclosure, and on what terms. The latter decisions should have first considered whether the material was confidential under English law (which they did) and then applied US discovery rules (which they did not).

If English law had been properly applied, the US courts would have been referred to the juridical basis of the obligation of confidentiality in arbitration in England. The crucial point is that the law of arbitration in England contains no statutory provision for confidentiality. No recommendation for a provision for confidentiality was made in the February 1996 Departmental Advisory Committee Report on what was then the Arbitration Bill.[14] It follows that, where England is the seat of an arbitration, there is no provision of the law of the seat which deals with the confidentiality of arbitration as such.

There are procedural rules which have some relevance to the privacy and confidentiality of arbitral proceedings, but these, by virtue of their character, will have no impact in foreign proceedings. Thus CPR, rule 39.2 lays down the general rule that court hearings are to be in public, but allows (rule 39,2(3)) the court to sit in private if (inter alia) the hearing involves confidential information and publicity would damage that confidentiality, and that it is necessary to sit in private to secure the proper administration of justice. In *CDE v. NOP*[15] the claimants alleged that the defendants had orchestrated a fraud. An arbitral tribunal had found that companies which had some connection with the defendants had been guilty of fraud, and that the defendants had given false evidence. The claimants sought to amend their pleadings in the fraud action, to rely on the arbitral award. The narrow question was whether under the CPR rule 39.2 the case management hearing should take place in public. There was an express obligation of confidentiality in the LCIA rules applicable to the arbitration. The

14. *See* paras 10-17.
15. [2021] EWCA Civ 1908, [2022] 4 W.L.R. 6.

Court of Appeal held that the fact that the arbitration and/or the award is confidential was sufficient to demonstrate confidentiality. The tension between the principle of open justice and the confidentiality of the award had to be addressed and it had been necessary for the judge to sit in private to secure the proper administration of justice. But by CPR, rule 62.10, in principle 'arbitration claims' (i.e., claims under the Arbitration Acts) are heard in private, other than hearings for determination of a preliminary point of law under the Arbitration Act 1996, or an appeal under the 1996 Act on a question of law arising out of an award. In *Moscow City Council v. Bankers Trust Co*[16] the Court of Appeal said that the courts were acting in the public interest to facilitate the fairness and well-being of a consensual method of dispute resolution, and could take into account the parties' expectations regarding privacy and confidentiality when agreeing to arbitrate.[17]

What the US courts were endeavouring to apply was the main source of confidentiality in English arbitration law, which is the term of confidentiality said to be implied in the arbitration agreement, that the arbitration. *Emmott v. Michael Wilson & Partners Ltd*[18] was one of almost 50 English judicial decisions in a long-running international dispute involving arbitration in London and litigation in many fora (including England, Australia, New Zealand, and the BVI) between former law partners in connection with events which took place in Kazakhstan.[19] Ultimately Mr Emmott succeeded in obtaining a large arbitration award in the London arbitration. In this phase of the litigation, he was seeking the permission of the English court to disclose pleadings in the London arbitration, so that he could show to the courts in New South Wales and the BVI, where allegations of fraud were being made against him, that similar allegations of fraud had been dropped in the London arbitration. The Court of Appeal confirmed that there is a confidentiality term implied into the arbitration agreement ('really a rule of substantive law masquerading as an implied term'[20] or 'in reality a substantive rule of arbitration law reached through the device of an implied term'[21]).

Since the application was made in England, and English law was both the law governing the arbitration agreement and English law was the procedural law of the arbitration, no question of the conflict of laws arose. In particular the court rejected the contention on the part of the Wilson party that Mr Emmott should have applied for the documents by a request under the Evidence (Proceedings in Other Jurisdictions) Act 1975. This contention was rejected because the 1975 Act only applies to requests for

16. [2004] EWCA Civ 314, [2005] Q.B. 207. *See also AZT v. AZV* [2012] SGHC 116.
17. *See also* rule 5.4C on inspection of court records, on which *see Glidepath BV v. Thompson* [2005] EWHC 818, [2005] 2 All ER (Comm.) 833.
18. [2008] EWCA Civ 184, [2008] Bus. L.R. 1361.
19. In *Emmott v. Michael Wilson & Partners Ltd* [2019] EWCA Civ 219, [2019] 4 WLR 53, para. 70, Peter Jackson LJ said: 'This pathological litigation has already consumed far too great a share of the court's resources and if it continues judges will doubtless be astute to allow the parties only an appropriate allotment of court time.'
20. At [84], cited with approval in *Halliburton Co v. Chubb Bermuda Insurance Ltd* [2020] UKSC 48, [2021] A.C. 1083 at [83].
21. At [106].

evidence and there was no case for suggesting that the arbitral material was evidence in that sense.

This chapter is not concerned with the limits of arbitral confidentiality which this author endeavoured to restate in his judgment in the Court of Appeal. For present purposes it is sufficient to mention that Thomas LJ emphasised that in determining whether there has to be disclosure in the litigation it will have regard to the ambit of the obligations of privacy and confidentiality between the parties to the arbitration agreement (whether express or implied), but can compel disclosure not withstanding any such terms. Although the English court would pay high regard to the obligations of privacy and confidentiality of arbitrations when considering whether to order disclosure, the court is ultimately no more bound to give effect to the agreement of the parties than it is to give effect to obligations of privacy and confidentiality which arise by agreement between the party to litigation and a non-party in other contexts. There is a balancing exercise in which the exercise of the court's discretion may ultimately turn on balancing the obligations of privacy and confidentiality between the parties to the arbitration as against the public interest of disclosure of documents in litigation.[22]

But it follows that where a foreign court is considering whether to treat as confidential documents or pleadings or an award generated in an arbitration in England, it should look to whether the arbitration agreement is governed by English law, in which event the expert evidence will reveal that there is an established body of case law on the content and limits of the implied obligation of confidentiality (much influenced by the rules on banking confidentiality).

Where the application in the foreign court is for discovery, the applicable law of the confidentiality obligation is in practice not likely to be of crucial importance, since in applications for disclosure/discovery there will in any event be a balancing exercise, with a strong policy in favour of confidentiality in arbitration.[23] The point can be illustrated by some examples of cases where the confidentiality issue has arisen. None of them has an international element, but they can be used to test the utility of the theories on choice of law.

In *CDE v. NOP*[24] the claimants alleged that the defendants had orchestrated a fraud. An arbitral tribunal had found that companies which had some connection with the defendants had been guilty of fraud, and that the defendants had given false evidence. The claimants sought to amend their pleadings in the fraud action, to rely on the arbitral award. In England the narrow question was whether the application should be held in private or in public. That is purely a question of procedure and could not apply in foreign proceedings. In foreign proceedings the question would be whether the English implied term of confidentiality would preclude reliance on the arbitral award. The answer would almost certainly be in the negative.

So also in *Chartered Institute of Arbitrators v. B*[25] the institute brought disciplinary proceedings against an arbitrator arising out of the circumstances in which he had

22. At [127].
23. At [75]-[77].
24. [2021] EWCA Civ 1908, [2022] 4 W.L.R. 6.
25. [2019] EWHC 460 (Comm), [2020] Bus. L.R. 285.

been removed by the court as arbitrator. The institute applied to the English court (1) to obtain copies of witness statements and exhibits filed in court, the transcript of the arbitral hearing, and correspondence relating to the arbitrator's appointment and skeleton arguments, and (2) for a declaration that, in the disciplinary proceedings, the institute and the arbitrator were entitled to refer to and/or rely on the documents sought, and also on the circumstances of the arbitrator's appointment in other arbitrations concerning the arbitration claimant. It was decided that (1) the institute had a legitimate purpose in seeking most of the documents in order to pursue disciplinary proceedings against the arbitrator, which was also in the public interest; (2) the declaration was granted in relation to those documents, but not in relation to other arbitrations in which the arbitrator had been appointed, since the court had not heard the parties in those arbitrations. If this point had arisen in England in relation to foreign proceedings, but where the arbitrator was a member of the institute and the English court had personal jurisdiction over the arbitrator, and where the institute sought an order against the arbitrator for the documents, then (subject to issues of self-incrimination) English domestic law would determine whether the documents should be produced. Whether they were confidential would depend on a cumulation of the law governing the arbitration agreement and the law of the seat. If they were confidential under either of those systems of law, they would be treated as confidential in England, but their confidential character (if any) would be a factor, but not a decisive one.

So also confidentiality would not be an absolute bar in cases where a prospective claimant sought to sue the defendant for its conduct of an arbitration. In English law it would come within the exception for the protection of the claimant's legitimate interest.[26]

It is apparent that there is very little authority on the question of the applicable law. This author is satisfied that the solution suggested by Clifford and Scogings, that the question should depend solely on the law of the seat of the arbitration, is neither consistent with the very little authority on the point, nor with the needs of the international community. Very few legal systems have express provisions for arbitral confidentiality. In practice the main sources of the obligation of confidentiality are those institutional rules which provide for it (such as LCIA, SIAC and the Swiss Rules) and those systems of law which follow the English model of an implied term in the arbitration agreement. That suggests that the main source of the obligation will be contractual, and that the primary governing law should be the law governing the arbitration agreement (to include the institutional rules chosen or accepted by the parties). That said, if the law governing the arbitration agreement does not expressly or impliedly provide for confidentiality, and the law of the seat does do so (although this

26. *Webb v. Lewis Silkin LLP* [2015] EWHC 687 (Ch). *See also Westwood Shipping Lines Inc, Weyerhaeuser NR Co v. Universal Schiffahrtsgesellschaft MBH* [2012] EWHC 3837 (Comm), [2013] 1 Lloyd's Rep. 670 (claimants allowed to rely on documents deployed in arbitration proceedings for the purposes of an unlawful means conspiracy claim); *Gray Construction Ltd v. Harley Haddow LLP* [2012] CSOH 92, 2012 S.L.T. 1035 (defendant in damages claim for expenses incurred in arbitration entitled to arbitration documents).

is an unlikely event[27]) then the law of the seat should supply the obligation. This author would, therefore, support Gary Born's 'alternative' analysis that if either the law of the seat or the law governing the arbitration agreement imposes implied confidentiality obligations, then those obligations would apply, subject to two reservations in contentious cases. The first is that the analysis should not be limited to implied obligations, but extend also to express obligations. The second is that it is apparent from the cases in England and elsewhere that the issue of whether there is a confidentiality obligation is usually a preliminary or incidental issue to the discretionary of whether the confidentiality should be displaced by the interests of justice. It is striking that in most of the reported cases on confidentiality in arbitration, the party seeking to rely on confidentiality had very little merit, and that justice prevailed.[28]

27. There is room for an argument that if England is the seat, the implied term theory of confidentiality might be applied to an arbitration agreement governed by a foreign law which does not have the theory, on the basis that the reference to the law of the seat is to its internal law, and not its rules of the conflict of laws, with the result that the implied term would be held to apply even to an agreement the governing law of which did not recognise the implied term. But this would be contrary to common sense and the expectations of the parties.
28. *See* for a good example *AAY v. AAZ* [2009] SGHC 12, with a very full discussion of the authorities.

C Evidence and Procedure

CHAPTER 14

Access to U.S. Discovery in International Commercial and Investor-State Arbitration

George A. Bermann

§14.01 INTRODUCTION

A provision of U.S. law—28 U.S.C. section 1782 has for decades enabled litigants in foreign courts and international tribunals to avail themselves of U.S.-style discovery. Litigants and even so-called other interested parties have access to documentary and testimonial evidence even though the parties and dispute have no connection with the U.S. and such discovery is unavailable in the fora where the proceedings are pending. Use of this powerful evidence-gathering tool section 1782 in proceedings before foreign courts and international tribunals has become commonplace.

Among the most controversial issues in the U.S. law of international arbitration in recent years has been whether U.S. courts should make section 1782 discovery available for use in proceedings before international arbitral proceedings conducted abroad. For a long period U.S. courts and commentators have been deeply divided over the matter and awaited impatiently an authoritative ruling from the Supreme Court. That ruling has now come in the form of a pair of cases before the court: *ZF Automotive US, Inc. v. Luxshare, Ltd.*[1] (an international commercial arbitration case) and *AlixPartners, LLP, et al. v. Fund for Protection of Investors' Rights in Foreign States*[2] (an international investor-State case). (For ease, reference below will be made to *ZF Automotive* only, unless *AlixPartners* is specifically implicated.) These rulings have dramatically altered the landscape. As of now, section 1782 discovery is categorically unavailable for use in international commercial arbitral proceedings and, except in extremely rare cases, in international investor-State disputes as well.

1. 596 U.S. ___ 2022, 142 S.Ct. 2078 (June 13, 2022).
2. 596 U.S. ___ 2022, 142 S.Ct. 1204 (June 13, 2022).

§14.02 SECTION 1782

Analysis of the question decided at hand begins, as it should, with the legislative text. The critical statutory language reads as follows:

> The district court of the district in which a person resides or is found may order him to give his testimony or statement or to produce a document or other thing for use in a proceeding in a foreign or international tribunal, including criminal investigations conducted before formal accusation. The order may be made pursuant to a letter rogatory issued, or request made, by a foreign or international tribunal or upon the application of any interested person and may direct that the testimony or statement be given, or the document or other thing be produced, before a person appointed by the court.[3]

The provision goes on to say that in securing the requested information, a district court could follow "the practice and procedure, which may be in whole or part the practice and procedure of the foreign country or the international tribunal." If neither is chosen, the Federal Rules of Civil Procedure are available. The statute further makes it clear that a district court is under no obligation to provide the relief sought. Its decision is discretionary and no indication is given as to how that discretion is to be exercised. Applications for judicial assistance are often made on an *ex parte* basis.

§14.03 PRE-*ZF AUTOMOTIVE*

At the time the *ZF Automotive* decision came down, the U.S. courts of appeal were not of one mind on the applicability of section 1782 to international arbitral tribunals. The Fourth and Sixth Circuits had held that section 1782 could be invoked in aid of arbitrations conducted abroad,[4] while the Second, Fifth and Seventh Circuits had held it could not. The principal arguments of the Fourth and Sixth Circuits were essentially these:

- International arbitral tribunals fall squarely within the plain meaning of the statute.
- Legislative history suggest that Congress intended, through earlier amendments to the statute, to expand the reach of section 1782 beyond formal judicial proceedings.
- There is no suggestion in the statute or legislative history that the adjudicatory body in question must be State-sponsored.
- Section 1782's discretionary character enables district courts to deny the application when granting it would be for any reason inappropriate.

---

3. 28 U.S.C. section 1782.
4. *Servotronics, Inc. v. Boeing Co.*, 954 F. 3d 209 (CA4 2020); Abdul Latif, 939 F. 3d 710, with *National Broadcasting Co. v. Bear Stearns & Co.*, 165 F. 3d 184 (CA2 1999); *Republic of Kazakhstan v. Biedermann Int'l*, 168 F. 3d 880 (CA5 1999); *Servotronics, Inc. v. Rolls-Royce PLC*, 975 F. 3d 689 (CA7 2020).

By contrast, the Second, Fifth and Seventh Circuits thought otherwise, doing so for the following reasons:

- The statutory context implies an exclusion of private arbitration from the definition of "tribunal."
- The term "tribunal," as used in other federal statutes, is limited to government-sponsored body.
- Allowing access to section 1782 by parties to private international arbitration would favor them over parties to domestic arbitration, as limited by the Federal Arbitration Act (FAA).

The international arbitration community in the U.S. was as divided as the federal appellate courts over the matter. This is remarkable because, historically, when other international arbitration issues have come before the Supreme Court, this community has presented a largely united front. The division is all the more remarkable in that both those favouring section 1782's application to private international arbitration and those opposing it maintained that their position was the more "pro-arbitration" one. The former viewed bringing private arbitration into the ambit of section 1782 as arbitration-friendly because it could make much-needed, otherwise unavailable, evidence available to the parties and the tribunal, thus enhancing the record upon which tribunals make their decisions. The latter considered that section 1782's application to private international arbitration was incompatible with the parties' intentions, in having resort to arbitration, to keep judicial intervention in arbitral proceedings to a minimum and enjoy the relative procedural informality with which they are associated. In addition, it would impair the tribunal's control, subject to party agreement otherwise of course, over all procedural aspects of the arbitration.

§14.04 THE *ZR AUTOMOTIVE* RULING

The court in *ZF Automotive* properly focused initially on the term "foreign or international tribunal," beginning with the term "tribunal." The court found the term "tribunal" to be ambiguous in that it could be understood either as including all bodies performing adjudicatory functions or only those that do so under a governmental aegis.[5] However, the court quickly erased the ambiguity by relying on the fact that the term "tribunal" was directly preceded in the text by the term "foreign or international." It thought it more appropriate to analyze the compound formulations "foreign tribunal" and "international tribunal" than the word "tribunal" standing alone.[6]

Turning first to the term "foreign," the court allowed that it too was ambiguous in this context because it could signify, in Justice Barrett's words, either a tribunal that "is" in a foreign State or a tribunal "of" a foreign State.[7] To decide the proper meaning of "foreign" in this context, the court reverted to the term "tribunal," finding that it lent

5. 596 U.S. ___ 2022, No. 21-401, slip op., June 13, 2022, p. 6.
6. *Ibid.*, p. 7.
7. *Ibid.*

the term "foreign" what the court called "potential governmental or sovereign connotations."[8] On that basis, it concluded that the term "foreign tribunal" signifies a tribunal *belonging to* a foreign nation, not one that is simply *located in* a foreign nation. Reinforcing this conclusion was the fact that the statute, as noted, authorizes the person appointed to take evidence to "prescribe the practice and procedure, which may be in whole or part the practice and procedure of the foreign country or the international tribunal." The court thought it "odd" for a privately constituted tribunal to follow the procedures and practices of national courts.[9]

The upshot is that a tribunal cannot qualify under section 1782 unless it exercises governmental authority, which private adjudicatory bodies do not. The court was willing to extend the notion of "governmental" to "intergovernmental" to accommodate adjudicatory bodies established by agreement between or among sovereign States,[10] but to go no further.

The court dealt with the term "international" in a broadly similar way. It too was found ambiguous because it could refer either to bodies on which arbitrators from different jurisdictions sit or to bodies authorized by two or more States to adjudicate disputes.[11] The court rightly rejected the former as making little sense, and so opted for the latter. On that basis, the court arrived at the following definition: a tribunal is "international" when "two or more nations ... have imbued the tribunal with official power to adjudicate disputes."[12] ... . Accordingly, just as a foreign tribunal "is a tribunal imbued with governmental authority by one nation," so too is an international tribunal "imbued with governmental authority by multiple nations."[13]

Turning to legislative history, the court noted that, as originally enacted in 1855, understanding the statute by its terms covered only "courts," but that it was amended in 1964 to introduce the words "or tribunals" alongside "courts."[14] The court held that, while those words expanded section 1782's scope of application, they only did so to bring within the ambit of section 1782 bodies other than courts that, like courts, perform government functions of an adjudicatory character, a category that would include quasi-judicial entities, such as administrative agencies that perform adjudicatory functions. They did not expand section 1782's scope of application to private bodies adjudicating private disputes. Supportive of this conclusion was the fact that the background work leading up to the 1964 amendment was entrusted to a body—the Commission on International Rules of Judicial Procedure—whose charge was to promote cooperation "between the United States and foreign countries." The reference to "foreign countries" confirmed that section 1782 contemplated assistance only to bodies performing governmental functions.[15]

---

8. *Ibid.*
9. *Ibid.*, p. 8.
10. *Ibid.*, p. 9.
11. *Ibid.*, pp. 8-9.
12. *Ibid.*, p. 9.
13. *Ibid.*
14. *Ibid.*, pp. 9-10.
15. *Ibid.*, p. 10.

The court further observed that the animating purpose of section 1782 was international comity, a well-established concept embodying respect for foreign nations and encouragement of reciprocity among nations. Since comity drove the enactment of section 1782 and is owed to foreign States alone, section 1782 could not have contemplated the rendition of judicial assistance to private adjudicatory bodies.[16]

Finally, invoked by the court in support of its position was the view that bringing private adjudicatory bodies within the definition of "tribunal" under section 1782 would "be in significant tension" with the FAA.[17] Under FAA section 7, which governs domestic arbitration, tribunals alone may request judicial assistance from U.S. courts, whereas section 1782 allows litigants and "any interested person" to do so. Further, the Supreme Court had previously held that section 1782 could be invoked in aid not only of proceedings already underway, but also proceedings "within reasonable contemplation."[18] Section 7 does not go that far either. The court saw no justification for according parties to foreign arbitral proceedings such measurably broader access to evidence in the U.S. than is accorded to parties to domestic arbitration.

In sum, the court distinguished sharply between those international arbitral tribunals that qualify under section 1782 and those that do not, making exercise of governmental authority the decisive factor.[19] It then proceeded to examine international commercial arbitration (in the *ZF Automotive* case) and international investor-State arbitration (in the *AlixPartners* case) in that light.

Having posited that exercise of governmental authority was an essential feature of the foreign or international body contemplated by section 1782, the court had little pause in determining that privately constituted international commercial tribunals could not qualify as "tribunals" under the statute. Such tribunals are not formed by the government. Nor do they operate under the aegis of the government, but rather under the aegis of an arbitral institution or on a purely ad hoc basis. The court was unimpressed by the fact that arbitral tribunals are subject to governance by the State in which they are seated or that national courts may be called upon to enforce agreements to arbitrate. That did not suffice to render such tribunals "governmental."

The Supreme Court's 2004 decision in *Intel Corp. v. Advanced Micro Devices, Inc.*[20] did not alter the court's conclusion. That opinion had been widely read to suggest section 1782's applicability to international arbitral tribunals, the court in *Intel* had no occasion in that case to make that determination. What the court did there was allow application of the statute to proceedings before the European Commission Directorate-General for Competition which, while plainly not a court, qualified as an intergovernmental body vested with the required governmental authority.

Thus, application of the principles it had earlier announced was, in the court's view "straightforward,"[21] and the message was clear. International commercial arbitral

16. *Ibid.*
17. *Ibid.*, p. 11.
18. *Intel Corp. v. Advanced Micro Devices, Inc.*, 542 U.S. 241 (2004).
19. 596 U.S. ___ 2022, No. 21-401, slip op., June 13, 2022, p. 11.
20. *Intel Corp. v. Advanced Micro Devices, Inc.*, 542 U.S. 241 (2004).
21. *Ibid.*, p, 12.

tribunals are categorically not "tribunals" within the meaning of section 1782. In the immediate wake (within nine days) of *ZF Automotive*, the Third Circuit, citing *ZF Automotive*, summarily denied a section 1782 application in connection with an international commercial arbitration conducted under the aegis of the German Arbitration Institute.[22]

Attention then turned to the companion *AlixPartners* case which arose, not in connection with an international commercial arbitration as *ZF Automotive* had, but with an international investor-State arbitration. The court allowed that this case was more difficult because the two species of arbitration are distinguishable in ways that favor extending section 1782 to the latter. In investor-State arbitration, unlike commercial arbitration, one of the parties is necessarily a State and the proceeding typically arises under a treaty between States, rather than a private contract.[23] Significantly, while the lower courts had been, as noted, divided over the applicability of section 1782 to international commercial arbitration, they had not been divided over its applicability to international investor-State arbitration; all courts asked to afford access to section 1782 in investor-State cases entertained the request on the merits.

But this ultimately made no difference to the court because the signatory States of the treaty, in this case Lithuania and Russia, had merely consented in their bilateral investment treaty to subject the dispute to arbitration. They had not conferred governmental authority on the tribunal to adjudicate it.[24]

The court further noted that the treaty offered investors four fora in which they could pursue their treaty-based claim against the State: (i) a court of the host State, (ii) the Arbitration Institute of the Stockholm Chamber of Commerce, (iii) the International Court of Arbitration of the International Chamber of Commerce, and (iv) an ad hoc arbitration conducted under the rules of the United Nations Commission on International Trade Law (UNCITRAL).[25] Of these, only the first—a court of the host State—could be said to exercise governmental authority, and the claimant had not chosen that one. Under the other three options, the States have no role in connection with the proceedings. They do not create the tribunal (as they do in State-to-State *arbitration*); the parties do. They operate either under the aegis of an arbitral institution or ad hoc, and in either case independently of the government. Such a body cannot be said to possess governmental authority merely because nations agree in a treaty to submit cases to its jurisdiction.[26] The court cited as additional indicia of a nongovernmental entity both the absence of government funding and the presumption of confidentiality.[27] In sum, this tribunal was simply a product of the States' consent and had not been "clothed" with governmental authority.

While the court ultimately found investor-State tribunals such as the one in *AlixPartners* outside the scope of section 1782, it did not fully close the door to its

22. *See In re Application of EWE Gasspeicher-GmbH*, no. 20-1830, WL 2233915 (3d Cir. June 22, 2022).
23. 596 U.S. ___ 2022, No. 21–401, slip op., June 13, 2022, p. 12.
24. *Ibid.*, p. 13.
25. *Ibid.*
26. *Ibid.*, pp. 13-15.
27. *Ibid.*, p. 14.

application to other international investor-State tribunals, leaving the scope of any opening to another day.[28] But the opinion makes it clear that any such tribunal must have a demonstrable governmental or intergovernmental nature, as understood by the court. There is already speculation that, due to the distinctive multinational character of the International Centre for the Settlement of Investment Disputes (ICSID) stemming from a treaty, the intergovernmental character of its Center for the Settlement of Investment Disputes, and its situation in the World Bank, ICSID tribunals might make the grade. It all depends on whether courts are prepared to view specific international arbitral tribunals as sufficiently imbued with governmental authority to qualify. The court allowed that mixed claims commissions qualified.[29] The court did however provide some guidance by identifying indicia of tribunals that exercise governmental authority, presumably none of which is indispensable: namely that the body at issue preexisted the dispute; that it was created by treaty; that it has in its operations some affiliation with one or more States; that it receives government funding; and that its proceedings and/or awards are public. It is not enough that nations agree in a treaty to submit to arbitration before it. The relevant question is whether the nations intended that the ad hoc panel exercise governmental authority. This tells us that, while *ZF Automotive* drew a bright line with respect to arbitral tribunals hearing international commercial disputes, *AlixPartners* did not quite do so with investor-State tribunals. Fact-specific litigation over whether particular types of investor-State tribunals qualify under section 1782 can be expected in the years ahead, and their resolution will be far from easy.

§14.05 *ZF AUTOMOTIVE*: AN ASSESSMENT

All will agree that the Supreme Court contributed importantly to the international arbitration regime by at last settling a question of enormous practical importance over which both courts and commentators were widely split. The correctness and cogency of the ruling is another matter. While there were more than respectable positions to be taken on both sides of the controversy, and while international arbitration would certainly thrive regardless of the way the court went, its path of reasoning in *ZF Automotive* leaves a great deal to be desired. Each of its arguments suffers under scrutiny.

To begin, the court's treatment of the statutory term "foreign" is quite unconvincing. As will be recalled, the court, finding ambiguity in the term "tribunal," turned to the modifier "foreign," which it similarly found to be ambiguous. To resolve the ambiguity in "foreign," the court reverted to the term to which the term "foreign" was juxtaposed, namely "tribunal." That term, which the court had said at the outset was ambiguous, now evidently has "potential governmental or sovereign connotations" sufficient to require a tribunal, in order to qualify under section 1782, to be one that exercises governmental authority:

28. *Ibid.*, p. 15.
29. *Ibid.*, pp. 15-16.

> The word "foreign" takes on its more governmental meaning when modifying a word with potential governmental or sovereign connotations.[30]

This is a truly remarkable exercise in textual interpretation. Circular is the only way to describe it. To determine the meaning of the ambiguous term "tribunal," the court turns to the adjacent ambiguous term "foreign," whose ambiguity the court then dispels the court by returning to the term "tribunal," where it began and that, despite its ambiguity, now has sufficient "connotations" to require that only tribunals that exercise governmental authority can qualify under section 1782.

The fact is that the term "tribunal" has a plain meaning—an adjudicatory body other than a court—that clearly encompasses arbitral tribunals. "Foreign," too, has a plain meaning, namely "located abroad." It is no wonder that the court went back and forth between "tribunal" and "foreign." It had to do so because in fact neither term was ambiguous. The notion of tribunal is properly understood not by its pedigree but by its function, which is to adjudicate disputes. In point of fact, both the ambiguity of "tribunal" and the ambiguity of "foreign" are entirely of the court's invention, and nothing in either word justifies the court in interposing the otherwise absent term "governmental."

The court does not help itself by enlisting the provision in section 1782 authorizing proceedings under the statute to be conducted pursuant to "the practice and procedure of the foreign country or the international tribunal." Here, the court does nothing more than reiterate its contention that the juxtaposition of the word "foreign" with the word "tribunal" dictates the conclusion that section 1782 contemplates only bodies exercising governmental authority. But making the argument twice makes it no stronger. In any event, section 1782 merely authorizes a U.S. court entertaining an application to follow "the practice and procedure of the foreign country or the international tribunal." It is not required to do so. Also, the practices and procedures that a court is invited under the statute to borrow may be not only those of the "foreign country," but also those of the "international tribunal." Why is an international arbitral tribunal not an "international tribunal" whose practices and procedures a court entertaining a section 1782 may follow? The court has at no point offered any reason why an "international tribunal," within the meaning of section, must necessarily be acting in a governmental capacity.

Worse than the court's disposal of the term "foreign" is its disposal of the term "international." That term too the court finds conveniently ambiguous, resolving the ambiguity by rightly finding one definition of international tribunal—as a tribunal that "ha[s] adjudicators of different nationalities"[31]—to be implausible. The court then offers what it apparently thinks is the only alternative definition, one according to which "[a] tribunal is 'international' when 'two or more nations … have imbued the tribunal with official power to adjudicate disputes.'" But that is hardly the only alternative way of conceiving the term "international." There are numerous others, but the court satisfies itself by positing that a tribunal can be international only if it is

30. 596 U.S. ___ 2022, No. 21-401, slip op., June 13, 2022, p. 7.
31. 596 U.S. ___ 2022, No. 21-401, slip op., June 13, 2022, p. 9.

governmental in its activity. But where exactly is the inevitable link between "international," on the one hand, and "sovereign authority" or "official power," on the other? That link too is pure invention on the court's part.

Plainly, activity need not be either "official" or "governmental" in order to be international. A contract between parties from different States is nothing short of an international contract. A wrongful cross-border act is an international tort. A communication between parties from different countries is an international communication. It is as if the court cannot conceive of anything being international and at the same time private. Perhaps the court believes that all international law is public international law and that there can be no such thing as private international law.

The court's use of language throughout this portion of the opinion in *ZF Automotive* is also telling. The term "foreign" acquires its so-called *more* governmental meaning[32] due to the fact that the term "tribunal" has "*potential* governmental or sovereign *connotations*."[33] We are also told that the term foreign tribunal "*more naturally* refers to a tribunal belonging to a foreign nation than to a tribunal that is simply located in a foreign nation."[34] Finally, for section 1782 to have given a private adjudicatory body the option of following the practices and procedures prescribed by a foreign government would be "*odd*."[35] None of the italicized terms are ones that a court with conviction would use.

The court's use of legislative history is not much better. It maintains that, since the charge of the Commission on International Rules of Judicial Procedure, alluded to above, was to promote international cooperation and render assistance to foreign courts, section 1782 could not possibly contemplate assistance to international arbitral tribunals. Admittedly, facilitating evidence-gathering for use in international arbitral proceedings cannot genuinely be characterized as assisting foreign courts. But we know, based on the 1964 amendment to section 1782, that an entity need not be a court in order for its proceedings to receive aid under the statute; it may also be a quasi-judicial tribunal. In any event, by its very terms, the Commission's charge was not limited to assisting foreign courts; it also included prompting international cooperation. And assisting arbitral tribunals seated overseas *is* clearly a form of international cooperation.

The court acknowledges that the 1964 amendment inserted the general words "or tribunals" after the word "courts." But, as observed earlier, the court never satisfactorily explains why, in this context, a "tribunal" can only be a body that exercises governmental (or intergovernmental) authority, thus excluding international arbitral tribunals from consideration as tribunals within the meaning of section 1782. To reduce the term "tribunal," within the meaning of the amended section 1782, to an official tribunal exercising governmental authority is to assume the very proposition that the court needs to establish.

32. *Ibid.*, p. 7.
33. *Ibid.*
34. *Ibid.*
35. *Ibid.*, p. 8.

The court is doubtless correct that enactment of section 1782 was animated by considerations of comity, in the sense of displaying respect for foreign nations and encouraging reciprocity.[36] But there is no basis, other than some form of intuition or instinct, to assume that comity can only justify international assistance in evidence-gathering assistance when it is given to the courts of foreign States, and cannot justify such assistance when it is given to arbitral tribunals seated in a foreign State.

This proposition assumes that foreign States have no interest in the arbitration activity that takes place in their territory. But that is not the case. States regulate that activity and its courts invalidate local awards that do not meet the State's standards. That international arbitral tribunals do not "belong" to the States in which they sit does not mean that States do not appreciate and benefit from the assistance given by foreign States to locally seated tribunals. If nothing else, States see real economic value and prestige in becoming a known international arbitration center the likes of London, Paris, New York, Geneva or Singapore, and the perceived efficacy of arbitrations conducted on a State's soil contributes to both. The reciprocity dimension of comity is also implicated. A willingness to assist arbitral tribunals seated abroad is no less apt to prompt reciprocity by foreign States than willingness to assist foreign courts.

Ironically, whatever one thinks of the court's ruling, it can be circumvented. A party seeking U.S.-based evidence for use in a foreign or international tribunal need only initiate litigation in any court in the world having personal jurisdiction over the defendant. (Under *Intel*, that litigation need not even be pending but simply contemplated.) It is then indisputably before a "foreign court" and section 1782-eligible. Whatever evidence may be obtained in that fashion may then be put to use in the pending arbitral proceeding.

§14.06 CONCLUSION

The very fact that the federal appellate courts and the international arbitration community were as divided as they were prior to *ZF Automotive* demonstrates that reasonable people can disagree over whether international arbitral tribunals, whether commercial or investor-State, constitute foreign or international tribunals within the meaning of section 1782. Before the Supreme Court ruled in the case, and even after oral argument, it was unclear which way the court would go. But whichever way the court was to go, it owed us a much more logical and cogent set of rationales.

36. 596 U.S. ___ 2022, No. 21-401, slip op., June 13, 2022, p. 10.

CHAPTER 15

The Elusive Standard of Proof in International Commercial Arbitration: The Common Law, Civil Law Divide, Dr Jekyll and Mr Hyde?

Simon Greenberg & Alix de Zitter

§15.01 INTRODUCTION

Black's Law Dictionary, a Common Law reference, defines the 'standard of proof' as "the degree or level of proof demanded in a specific case [...]; a rule about the quality of evidence that a party must bring to prevail"'.[1] Most Civil Law legal dictionaries do not even mention the standard of proof, much less define it, because the concept is virtually unknown to them. In Civil Law systems there is usually no fixed standard of proof for civil claims; the evaluation of proof is rather left to the judge's 'inner conviction', meaning his or her entirely subjective appreciation of the facts.

Where does that leave the standard of proof in the practice of international arbitration? When the standard of proof is the subject of detailed submissions in an arbitration and/or thorough reasoning in an arbitral award, it invariably relates to allegations of illegality - for example fraud, corruption, falsification of documents, etc. In those cases, there is frequently a question as to whether the standard of proof should be 'higher'. But higher *than what*?

Overall, there is confusion surrounding the standard of proof in international arbitration. First, should the concept apply at all, or should we rather embrace the Civil Law notion that the assessment of evidence is incapable of objective definition and is best entrusted to the arbitrator's inner conviction? That liberal approach appears to

1. Bryan Garner, *Black's Law Dictionary* (Thomson Reuters, 11th ed., 2019), p. 1694.

have inspired most arbitral instruments, such as the UNCITRAL Model Law on International Commercial Arbitration ('UNCITRAL Model Law'),[2] the IBA Rules on the Taking of Evidence in International Arbitration ('IBA Evidence Rules'),[3] and many institutional rules.[4] Second, if an ostensibly objective standard of proof is to be applied at all, which one?

There are broadly three approaches in international arbitration. One approach is to characterise the standard of proof as a question of substantive law. If the governing substantive law stipulates a standard of proof for civil claims, the arbitral tribunal applies it. If the governing substantive law contains no applicable standard of proof, such as most Civil Law legal systems, the arbitral tribunal does not apply one and essentially ignores the concept. A second approach is to characterise the question of the standard of proof as procedural and apply the standard of proof, if any, required by the civil and commercial law of the seat of arbitration. A third approach is to characterise the question as procedural but apply *only* the international arbitration law of the seat of arbitration, which will most often be silent or very vague, leaving the question of standard of proof to the arbitral tribunal's discretion.[5] This third approach is accordingly rather circular: its application may lead to one of the other approaches.

For those practitioners who think about the standard of proof at all, which does not appear to be a majority save where there are allegations of illegality, views are strongly divided as between the first and third approaches set out above. Few practitioners would endorse the second given the limited role the general law (as opposed to the international arbitration law) of the seat of arbitration should be permitted to play.

The few scholars who have thoroughly considered this topic express widely divergent opinions.[6] Yet it can be important. International arbitrations usually involve large factual records and frequently require the arbitral tribunal to make findings on

2. UNCITRAL Model Law, Article 19(2), cited *infra* n. 5.
3. IBA Evidence Rules (2020), Article 9(1) ('The Arbitral Tribunal shall determine the admissibility, relevance, materiality and weight of evidence').
4. *See, e.g.*, ICC Arbitration Rules (2021), Article 25(1) (the arbitral tribunal shall 'within as short a time as possible to establish the facts of the case by all appropriate means'); UNCITRAL Arbitration Rules (2021), Article 27(4) (arbitrators have the power to 'determine the admissibility, relevance, materiality and weight of the evidence offered'); LCIA Arbitration Rules (2020), Article 22.1(vi) (the arbitral tribunal may 'decide whether or not to apply any strict rules of evidence (or any other rules) as to the admissibility, relevance or weight of any material tendered by a party on any issue of fact or expert opinion'); HKIAC Administered Arbitration Rules (2018), Article 22.2 ('The arbitral tribunal shall determine the admissibility, relevance, materiality and weight of the evidence, including whether to apply strict rules of evidence'); SIAC Arbitration Rules (2016), Article 19.1 ('The Tribunal shall determine the relevance, materiality and admissibility of all evidence. The Tribunal is not required to apply the rules of evidence of any applicable law in making such determination').
5. *See, e.g.*, UNCITRAL Model Law (1985 with 2006 amendments), which provides simply at Article 19(2), that the 'power conferred upon the arbitral tribunal includes the power to determine the admissibility, relevance, materiality and weight of any evidence'; English Arbitration Act 1996, Chapter 23, section 34(1) ('It shall be for the tribunal to decide all procedural and evidential matters, subject to the right of the parties to agree any matter'). The French Code of Civil Procedure is completely silent on this matter.
6. *See* section §15.02 below.

disputed questions of fact. Those findings of fact are often pivotal in the outcome of cases. It follows that arbitral tribunals should not underestimate the importance of rigorously considering whether there is a standard of proof that they should apply and whether it is met as regards critical, disputed elements of fact. A better understanding of the standard of proof would also assist parties to know whether to make certain factual allegations or, indeed, whether to bring certain claims at all.

The first part of this article analyses the main differences between the standard of proof applied in Common and Civil Law jurisdictions. The second part explores whether there is a default standard of proof in international commercial arbitration and the overall impact of the discretion generally conferred upon arbitrators adjudicating evidentiary issues as to the standard of proof to be applied. Finally, the third part of this article focuses on whether it is proper and desirable for the standard of proof to vary depending on the issue at stake.

§15.02 DIVERGING CIVIL LAW AND COMMON LAW APPROACHES: SAME SAME OR SAME DIFFERENCE?

Many features of international commercial arbitration are a sensible hybrid between various legal traditions. One inherent difficulty in determining the right approach to the standard of proof finds its root in the different approaches of the Common Law and Civil Law traditions.

[A] Common Law: Rigorously Applied, Ostensibly Objective Standards of Proof

The standard of proof is an emblematic element of the law of evidence in Common Law countries. Common Law students study evidence as a specific subject, including the standard of proof, as part of virtually any undergraduate law degree. As a result, the Anglo-Saxon doctrine regularly and extensively deals with this question, whereas it is often ignored by the continental doctrine.[7]

In many Common Law jurisdictions, the default standard of proof for civil cases is the 'balance of probabilities' or 'preponderance of evidence' standard. Under this standard, a tribunal will find a fact to be established if it is more probable than not to have occurred. As explained by Lord Denning in 1947: '[i]f the evidence is such that the tribunal can say 'we think it more probable than not' the burden is discharged, but if the probabilities are equal it is not'.[8] In the words of one of the leading authors on the IBA Evidence Rules, the standard is met if the tribunal 'is convinced by the evidence that the claim is more likely than not true'.[9] The balance of probabilities thus requires

7. Frédérique Ferrand, *Preuve*, Répertoire de Procédure Civile (Dalloz, December 2013), paras 564-565; Olivier Leclerc, Etienne Vergès and Géraldine Vial, *Droit de la preuve* (Presses Universitaires de France, 2015), para. 109.
8. *Miller v. Minister of Pensions* [1947] 2 All ER 372.
9. Nathan D. O'Malley, *Rules of Evidence in International Arbitration: An Annotated Guide* (Informa Law, 2012), p. 208.

a party to present evidence greater in weight than the other party's evidence.[10] It is the quality of the evidence rather than its volume that is being judged.[11]

The balance of probabilities standard is to be clearly distinguished from the higher 'beyond a reasonable doubt' standard applied in criminal cases in Common Law jurisdictions. That is a much higher standard, reflecting important differences between the nature of criminal as compared to civil actions.

In civil actions in certain Common Law jurisdictions, a higher standard of 'clear and convincing evidence' is sometimes applied. US courts have retained this standard of proof in the face of quasi-criminal allegations in civil matters such as fraud, undue influence or gross negligence.[12] It lies between the lower balance of probabilities standard and the higher beyond a reasonable doubt standard. This intermediate standard of proof requires a finding based on evidence so clear that it leaves no substantial doubt. Evidence is 'clear' when it 'is certain, unambiguous, and plain to the understanding', and it is 'convincing' if it is 'reasonable and persuasive enough to cause the trier of fact to believe it'.[13]

[B] Civil Law: What Is a 'Standard of Proof'?

By contrast, most Civil Law jurisdictions apply no standard of proof and the whole concept is unknown. The standard of proof is very rarely, if ever, part of the study of law in a Civil Law jurisdiction. For example, the law of evidence is not taught at all to French law students.

Civil Law systems tend to be silent on the standard of proof or, at best, refer to facts being decided on purely subjective grounds such as the judge's sovereign appreciation or inner conviction. These expressions illustrate the judge's vast discretion as to evidence. It is ultimately the subjective satisfaction of the judge that needs to be met.[14] It follows that in most Civil Law countries the whole notion of standard of proof does not really exist. It is not set forth in statutes or codes and is not taught in law schools. It is only occasionally debated in the jurisprudence or secondary sources.[15] Unlike in Common Law jurisdictions, there is no principle of a quantifiable or identifiable standard of proof. As a result, the term 'standard of proof' has no real

10. Kevin F. O'Malley et al., *3A Federal Jury Practice and Instructions* (Thomson West, 6th ed., 2006), §154:20; *see, e.g.*, *Miller v. Minister of Pensions* [1947] 2 All ER 372.
11. Jennifer M. Smith and Sara Nadeau-Séguin, *The Illusive Standard of Proof in International Commercial Arbitration*, 'Legitimacy: Myths, Realities, Challenges', ICCA Congress Series, Volume 18 (ICCA and Kluwer Law International, 2015), p. 139.
12. *See, e.g.*, *ODECO Oil & Gas Co v. Nunez*, 532 So. 2d 453 (La. App. 1st Cir. 1988), writ denied, 535 So. 2d. 745 (La. 1989); *Lutz v. Orinick*, 184 W.Va. 531, 401 S.E.2d 464 (1990).
13. *See, e.g.*, *Foster v. Alliedsignal*, Inc., 293 F.3d 1187 (10th Cir. 2002).
14. Frédérique Ferrand, *Preuve*, Répertoire de Procédure Civile (Dalloz, December 2013), para. 566.
15. Michele Taruffo, *Rethinking the Standards of Proof*, The American Journal of Comparative Law, Summer, Volume 51, Issue 3 (2003), pp. 664-665.

resonance.[16] Ultimately, the '*intime conviction*' of the judge refers rather to a description of how the judge decides the facts, through a 'deeply personal, secret, subjective and intimate process'.[17]

Under French law, for example, the degree of conviction required of the judge is not subject to any particular rule purporting to require an objective standard of proof. Instead, it is entirely left to the discretion of the judge. Article 1382 of the French Civil Code provides:

> Presumptions not established by statute are left to the discretion of the judge, who shall only admit serious, precise and consistent presumptions, and only in cases where the law admits evidence by all means.[18]

The term 'presumption' in Article 1382 refers to any indicia or facts arising from the documents on the record, also referred to as 'presumptive evidence' or 'man-made presumption'. This indicates that the evidence is left to the judge's free appreciation and judgment (as opposed to legal presumptions under French law, where the judge is bound by the consequence provided for in the law).

Moreover, under French law, there is no formal difference in the standard of proof applicable in civil and criminal matters. For criminal matters, Article 427 of the Code of Criminal Procedure provides:

> Except in cases where the law provides otherwise, offences may be established by any means of proof and the judge shall decide *according to his or her own inner conviction.*[19]

On first reading, it could be understood that the degree of conviction required is more demanding in civil matters than in criminal matters since Article 1353 of the Civil Code refers to 'serious, precise and consistent presumptions' while Article 427 of the Code of Criminal Procedure refers only to 'inner conviction'. However, the adjectives 'serious, precise and consistent' should not be understood literally. As Professor Goubeaux explains:

> The strength of man-made presumptions *depends entirely on the judge's personal conviction*. His *freedom of appreciation* is not even limited by Article [1382] of the Civil Code, which nevertheless states that the judge 'must admit only serious, precise and consistent (presumptions)'. Taken literally, this text would prohibit the judge from being convinced on the basis of a single indicia. But the prevailing opinion in doctrine and case law considers that it is a *simple precautionary advice*

16. Michael J. Bond, *The Standard of Proof in International Commercial Arbitration*, Arbitration: The International Journal of Arbitration, Mediation and Dispute Management, Volume 77, Issue 3 (2011), p. 309.
17. *Ibid.*, p. 313; *see also* Gippini-Fournier, *The Elusive Standard of Proof in EU Competition Cases*, World Competition: Law and Economics Review Volume 33, Issue 2 (2010), p. 6; *Continental Automotive GmbH v. Acushnet Rubber Company*, Final Award in ICC Case No. 17297/JHN/GFG of 12 January 2012, para. 74.
18. Translation from French.
19. Translation from French. Emphasis added.

> *to the judge, who remains entirely free in his assessment and may be satisfied that a single piece of evidence is sufficient if it appears decisive.*[20]

As a result, the reference to 'serious, precise and consistent presumptions' is not a standard of proof. The role of the lower court judge (or arbitrator) is characterised as a mere discussion of fact entrusted to his or her '*appréciation souveraine*'. It follows that, unlike in the Common Law tradition, appellate courts have no power to overturn a judgement because of a wrong application of the standard of proof; an appellate court cannot interfere with a judge's sovereign appreciation of the evidence. The French Court of Cassation has thus ruled that 'appeal judges, who outline a set of presumptions which they list and assess pursuant to their sovereign appreciation powers, are not required to reaffirm the legal requirement of serious, precise and consistent presumptions in their decision'.[21]

It follows that, under French law, the judge or arbitrator is free to decide what weight to give to the evidence, the assessment to be made is purely subjective rather than objective, and this sovereign assessment cannot be changed by higher courts.

There is only one hypothesis in which the French Court of Cassation clearly refers to a standard of proof. That is when European Union law is at issue, essentially in the field of competition law. That is because these rules of European Union law, in some respects inspired by Common Law, expressly require a standard of proof.[22]

To conclude, the Common Law tradition provides a legally fixed standard of proof based on the quality of the evidence and a lower judge's decision can be reviewed by appellate courts. Conversely, a Civil Law judge rules upon disputed facts via his or her inner, personal conviction,[23] in a decision that cannot be overruled by appellate courts on the ground that some legal standard was not met. Commentators thus often refer to the fact that the Common Law standard of proof is objective, at least ostensibly,[24] whereas Civil Law countries emphasise the subjective process of assessing evidence (even if this conviction should not be understood in a purely subjective way as authorising arbitrary decisions).[25]

---

20. Jacques Ghestin, Gilles Goubeaux, *Introduction générale* (LGDJ, 4th ed., 1994), para. 719. Translation from French.
21. Decision of the Court of Cassation, 3rd civil chamber, 18 April 1972, No. 71-10.237. Translation from French.
22. *See, e.g.*, Decision of the Court of Cassation, commercial chamber, 7 October 2014, No. 13-19.476; Decision of the Court of Cassation, commercial chamber, 27 September 2017, No. 15-20.291; Decision of the Court of Cassation, commercial chamber, 18 February 2014, No. 12-27.643; Decision of the Court of Cassation, commercial chamber, 11 June 2013, No. 12-13.961; Decision of the Court of Cassation, commercial chamber, 7 April 2010, No. 09-11.853.
23. Frédérique Ferrand, *Preuve*, Répertoire de Procédure Civile (Dalloz, December 2013), para. 566.
24. Simon Greenberg, *Le standard de la preuve en arbitrage international*, Revue de l'Arbitrage, Comité Français de l'Arbitrage Volume 2020, Issue 1 (2020), p. 114.
25. Frédérique Ferrand, *Preuve*, Répertoire de Procédure Civile (Dalloz, December 2013), para. 566.

[C] Is It Just Optics or Can the Approach to the Standard of Proof Affect Outcomes?

Some commentators argue that the different expressions of the standard of proof between Civil Law and Common Law is nothing more than optics and should make no difference to the resulting decision in practice,[26] assuming the same decision maker. One author even contends that 'there appears to be little practical difference between these standards, as shown by the frequency with which arbitrators from different legal systems concur in the fact finding process'.[27] Considering the paucity of publicly available arbitral awards that analyse the standard of proof in any meaningful way, this conclusion appears to be intuition and not based on empirical evidence.[28]

According to another commentator, one reason why it is unlikely that there is any material practical difference between the applications of the standard of proof in different legal systems is that 'no system allows a party to succeed if their opponent's contentions are preferred'.[29] It is correct that any approach towards the standard of proof ultimately aims at convincing the adjudicator of the 'truth', which involves juggling two or more versions of that truth that are favoured by the litigants.

Under both the Civil and Common Law systems, if one side's evidence is deemed more convincing, the other's position in respect of that evidence will eventually fail. Yet, what is arguably left unanswered is the degree of conviction the adjudicator must reach in order to rule in favour of a claim or defence.[30] Empirical studies conclude that there are considerable differences in criminal conviction rates depending on the applicable standard of proof. For instance, the data of one of these studies showed that the probability of a guilty verdict was almost five times as likely under the preponderance of evidence standard as compared to the beyond a reasonable doubt standard.[31] There is no doubt that the standard of proof applied can affect the final verdict. This parallel is only helpful for comparison purposes as there are of course differences between criminal and civil matters. In a criminal trial, the state's prosecutor is not a party to the proceeding and cannot 'lose' as such. The question is rather whether or not there is sufficient evidence to convict a criminal. Civil cases are very different. The

26. Arthur L. Marriott, *Evidence in International Arbitration*, Arbitration International, Volume 5, Issue 3 (1 September 1989), p. 283; Simon Greenberg, *Le standard de la preuve en arbitrage international*, Revue de l'Arbitrage, Comité Français de l'Arbitrage, Volume 2020, Issue 1 (2020), p. 114.
27. Robert Pietrowski, *Evidence in International Arbitration*, Arbitration International, Volume 22, Issue 3 (2006), p. 379.
28. Michael J. Bond, *The Standard of Proof in International Commercial Arbitration*, Arbitration: The International Journal of Arbitration, Mediation and Dispute Management, Volume 77, Issue 3 (2011), p. 306.
29. Jeffrey Maurice Waincymer, *Procedure and Evidence in International Arbitration* (Kluwer Law International, 2012), p. 767.
30. Jennifer M. Smith and Sara Nadeau-Séguin, *The Illusive Standard of Proof in International Commercial Arbitration*, 'Legitimacy: Myths, Realities, Challenges', ICCA Congress Series, Volume 18 (ICCA and Kluwer Law International, 2015), p. 144.
31. Andreas Glöckner and Christoph Engel, *Can We Trust Intuitive Jurors: Standards of Proof and the Probative Value of Evidence in Coherence-Based Reasoning*, Journal of Empirical Legal Studies, Volume 10, Issue 2 (June 2013), p. 238.

adjudicator must choose between competing positions. On any given claim or issue, one of the litigants will win and another will lose.

§15.03 WHICH STANDARD OF PROOF FOR INTERNATIONAL COMMERCIAL ARBITRATIONS?

Most arbitration rules and arbitration laws do not contain principles governing the standard of proof. William W. Park submits that the silence in arbitration rules is deliberate and unsurprising because leading arbitral institutions seek to avoid taking sides on the delicate division on this issue between the Common Law and Civil Law.[32] Indeed, being seen to favour one legal framework over the other could be harmful to the perception of neutrality of the process and potentially also to the institution.

Whatever the applicable law or governing rules, they usually provide for very broad flexibility on evidentiary matters, subject only to any contrary agreement of the parties. For instance, Article 19(2) of the UNCITRAL Model Law provides that '[t]he power conferred upon the arbitral tribunal includes the power to determine the admissibility, relevance, materiality and weight of any evidence'. Similar language can be found in leading arbitration rules,[33] other national laws[34] and in the IBA Evidence Rules.[35]

This broad evidentiary discretion is said to allow arbitrators to 'tailor the conduct of the proceedings to the specific features of the case without being hindered by any restraint that may stem from traditional local law, including any domestic rule on

32. William W. Park, *The 2002 Freshfields Lecture – Arbitration's Protean Nature: The Value of Rules and the Risks of Discretion,* Arbitration International, Volume 19, Issue 3 (2003), p. 285.
33. UNCITRAL Arbitration Rules (2021), Article 27(4) ('The arbitral tribunal shall determine the admissibility, relevance, materiality and weight of the evidence offered'); ICC Arbitration Rules (2021), Article 25(1) ('The arbitral tribunal shall proceed within as short a time as possible to establish the facts of the case by all appropriate means'); ICDR International Arbitration Rules (2021), Article 22(7) ('The tribunal shall determine the admissibility, relevance, materiality, and weight of the evidence'); HKIAC Administered Arbitration Rules (2018), Article 22.2 ('The arbitral tribunal shall determine the admissibility, relevance, materiality and weight of the evidence, including whether to apply strict rules of evidence'); LCIA Arbitration Rules (2020), Article 22.1(vi) (the Arbitral Tribunal may 'decide whether or not to apply any strict rules of evidence (or any other rules) as to the admissibility, relevance or weight of any material tendered by a party on any issue of fact or expert opinion'); SIAC Arbitration Rules (2016), Article 19.1 ('The Tribunal shall determine the relevance, materiality and admissibility of all evidence. The Tribunal is not required to apply the rules of evidence of any applicable law in making such determination').
34. English Arbitration Act 1996, Chapter 23, section 34(1) ('It shall be for the tribunal to decide all procedural and evidential matters, subject to the right of the parties to agree any matter'); French Civil Code, Article 1382 ('Presumptions not established by statute are left to the discretion of the judge, who shall only admit serious, precise and consistent presumptions, and only in cases where the law admits evidence by all means') (translation from French); Swiss Federal Act on Private International Law, Article 184, para. 1 ('The arbitral tribunal takes the evidence itself') (translation from French).
35. IBA Evidence Rules (2020), Article 9(1) ('The Arbitral Tribunal shall determine the admissibility, relevance, materiality and weight of evidence').

evidence'.[36] Flexibility has indeed long been perceived as a feature and an advantage of international commercial arbitration, as it allows the development of bespoke, case-specific solutions.[37] However, the risk of flexibility concerning an issue as important as the manner in which evidence is assessed is that arbitrators may fail to appreciate the need for rigour in determining whether a particular fact has been sufficiently proven. This broad evidentiary flexibility therefore prompts the question of how it is, or should it be, exercised.

Both in theory and in practice, there are three main approaches: (i) an autonomous standard derived from arbitration practice; (ii) the domestic law of evidence of the applicable substantive law (*lex causae*); or (iii) the domestic law of evidence of the seat of arbitration (*lex arbitri*). The choice between the *lex causae* and the *lex arbitri* is usually described as a question of characterisation (i.e., whether the standard of proof is characterised as a procedural or substantive legal issue).[38]

[A] No Default Standard of Proof in International Commercial Arbitration

The question of whether there is a default standard of proof in international commercial arbitration remains unsettled. Some commentators and tribunals, predominantly from a Common Law tradition, submit that arbitrators usually apply the standard of 'preponderance of evidence' or 'balance of probabilities'.[39] For instance, *Redfern and Hunter on International Arbitration* summarise the issue as follows:

> The degree of proof that must be achieved in practice before an international arbitral tribunal is not capable of precise definition, but *it may be safely assumed that it is close to the 'balance of probabilit*[ies]*' (that is, 'more likely than not')*. This standard is to be distinguished from the concept of 'beyond all reasonable doubt' required, for example, in countries such as the United States and England to prove guilt in a criminal trial before a jury.[40]

---

36. UNCITRAL Model Law (1985 with amendments as adopted in 2006), Explanatory Note, para. 35; *see also* Gary B. Born, *Chapter 15: Procedures in International Arbitration, International Commercial Arbitration* (Kluwer Law International, 3rd ed., 2021), p. 2361.
37. Julian D.M. Lew et al., *Chapter 22 Taking Evidence in International Arbitration, Comparative International Commercial Arbitration* (Kluwer Law International, 2003), p. 558; *see also* Queen Mary University of London, *2018 International Arbitration Survey: The Evolution of International Arbitration*, https://arbitration.qmul.ac.uk/media/arbitration/docs/2018-International-Arbitration-Survey-report.pdf, p. 7.
38. Gary B. Born, *Chapter 15: Procedures in International Arbitration, International Commercial Arbitration* (Kluwer Law International, 3rd ed., 2021), p. 2363.
39. George M. Von Mehren and Claudia Salomon, *Submitting Evidence in an International Arbitration: The Common Lawyer's Guide*, Journal of International Arbitration, Volume 20, Issue 3 (2003), pp. 290-291 ('the degree or level of proof that must be achieved in practice in an international arbitration is not capable of precise definition, but it may be safely assumed that it is close to the balance of probabilities'). *See also* Charles N. Brower, *Evidence Before International Tribunals: The Need for Some Standard Rules*, The International Lawyer, Volume 28, No. 1 (1994), p. 49.
40. Alan Redfern, Martin Hunter, Nigel Blackaby and Constantine Partasides, *Redfern and Hunter on International Arbitration* (Oxford University Press, 6th ed., 2015), p. 378 (emphasis added).

In 2004, the American Law Institute (ALI) and the International Institute for the Unification of Private Law (UNIDROIT) adopted the Principles of Transnational Civil Procedure aimed at setting standards for adjudication of transnational commercial disputes transcending national jurisdictional rules and the divide between Civil and Common Law jurisdictions. The proposed standard of proof under these Principles is that '[f]acts are considered proven when the court is reasonably convinced of their truth'.[41] While this standard seems very close to the Civil Law approach to the standard of proof, somewhat surprisingly, the commentary to this provision states that the standard of 'reasonably convinced' is '*in substance that applied in most legal systems*' and is '*essentially the same*' as the standard of 'preponderance of evidence'.[42]

In practice, arbitral tribunals must necessarily apply a standard of proof of some sort each time they rule on an contested issue of fact. Unfortunately, arbitral awards all too rarely articulate how the arbitral tribunal approached the standard of proof, except sometimes if there have been issues of alleged illegality to consider. The lack of articulation as to what standard of proof is applied makes it difficult, if not impossible, to identify the most common standard of proof. Occasionally, an arbitral award simply dismisses the notion of the standard of proof, although by doing so they are essentially applying the Civil Law approach to the matter.[43] Where an award does express and ally a standard of proof, it is most frequently the 'balance of probabilities' (or equivalent)[44] and this may well simply result from the fact that there is a preponderance of Common Law lawyers among the arbitrators and/or counsel involved.

Applying the 'balance of probabilities' standard may appear logical and indeed evident to a Common Law lawyer, but not to a Civil Law lawyer. Civil Law lawyers may either not understand the concept of an objective standard of proof or, quite possibly,

41. ALI/UNIDROIT Principles of Transnational Civil Procedure (2004), Article 21.2.
42. *Ibid.*, Comment P-21B.
43. *Niko Resources Ltd. v. Bangladesh Petroleum Exploration & Production Company Limited and Bangladesh Oil Gas and Mineral Corporation*, Decision on the Corruption Claim in ICSID Case No. ARB/10/18 of 25 February 2019, paras 805-806 ('In this complex situation of facts and allegations, the Tribunals do not find much assistance in terms such as "preponderance of evidence" and "heightened standard of proof." In the end the question is whether the Tribunals are persuaded that the JVA and GPSA were procured by corruption or not').
44. For ICC cases, *see, e.g.*, *Grupo Unidos por el Canal SA v. Autoridad del Canal de Panama*, ICC Case No. 20910/ASM/JPA (C-20911/ASM, Partial award, 21 September 2020, para. 461 ('in international arbitration, the applicable standard of proof is the "balance of the probabilities" or "more likely than not" standard'); for ad hoc cases, *see, e.g.*, *European Median Ventures S.A. v. The Czech Republic*, Partial award on liability, 8 July 2009 (Lord Mustill, Sir Christopher Greenwood, Dr Julian Lew K.C.), para. 35 ('Whatever standard of proof is required to establish an assertion of contemplated blackmail, *it must at least be for the party who asserts such conduct to show that it is more likely than not to be true.*') (emphasis added). For ICSID cases, *see, e.g.*, *Bernhard von Pezold and others v. Republic of Zimbabwe*, ICSID Case No. ARB/10/15, Award, 28 July 2015, para. 177 ('In general, the standard of proof applied in international arbitration is that a claim must be proven on the "balance of probabilities." There are no special circumstances that would warrant the application of a lower or higher standard of proof in the present case. It is also unclear what standard the Respondent considers should apply, if not the balance of probabilities'); *Tokios Tokelés v. Ukraine*, ICSID Case No. ARB/02/18, Award, 26 July 2007, para. 124; *Marion Unglaube v. Republic of Costa Rica*, ICSID Case No. ARB/08/1, Award, 16 May 2012, para. 34; *Republic of Croatia v. MOL Hungarian Oil and Gas Company Plc*, PCA Case No. 2014-15, Final Award, 23 December 2016, para. 115.

understand it but dismiss it as nonsense. Indeed, applying the 'balance of probabilities' standard theoretically requires an arbitrator to allow a party's claim if the arbitrator is 51% satisfied that the necessary facts are proved, but to deny the claim if the arbitrator is only 50% satisfied. Yet, deciding whether it is 50% or 51% can only be subjective meaning that, in cases where the factual outcome is not obvious, Common Law lawyers are arguably just dressing up their 'inner conviction' with objective terminology.

While it can be reasonably contended that the 'balance of probabilities' standard is widely accepted in international arbitration, asserting that it as a default rule would be an overstatement.[45] Considering the broad discretion granted to arbitrators, and the fact that statistically at least 50%, but probably more, arbitrators hail from non-Common Law traditions, it seems much more likely that the application of the 'balance of probabilities' (or equivalent) standard is only the typical standard where Common Law lawyers are involved or where a Common Law legal system provides the governing law.

[B] The Applicable Law to Determine the Standard of Proof: *Lex Causae* or *Lex Arbitri*?

International arbitrators are expected to apply any applicable laws. Yet there is a lack of consensus in national legal systems as to the proper issue of characterisation of the standard of proof. This is not surprising: as noted above, Civil Law systems generally do not recognise the concept at all and so have not developed characterisation rules in respect of it.

If the standard of proof is considered substantive, it is governed by the *lex causae*, whereas if it is considered procedural, it is governed by the *lex arbitri* or some international arbitral standards.[46]

Some authors generally present the divide between these two approaches as a difference between Common Law and Civil Law countries. It has been suggested that Common Law countries would characterise the standard'of proof as falling within the scope of procedural law, and Civil Law countries as a substantive law issue.[47] This is

45. Pedro Francisco da Silva Almeida, *Burden and Standards of Proof in International Arbitration: Practice and Challenges*, Revista Brasileira de Arbitragem, Kluwer Law International, Volume XVIII, Issue 69 (2021), p. 76.
46. Jennifer M. Smith and Sara Nadeau-Séguin, *The Illusive Standard of Proof in International Commercial Arbitration*, 'Legitimacy: Myths, Realities, Challenges', ICCA Congress Series, Volume 18 (ICCA and Kluwer Law International, 2015), p. 146.
47. Phillip Landolt and Barbara Reeves Neal, 'Chapter 5: Burden and Standard of Proof in Competition Law Matters Arising in International Arbitration', in *EU and US Antitrust Arbitration: A Handbook for Practitioners* (Kluwer Law International, 2011), p. 158; Jeffrey Maurice Waincymer, 'Part II: The Process of an Arbitration, Chapter 10: Approaches to Evidence and Fact Finding', in *Procedure and Evidence in International Arbitration* (Kluwer Law International, 2012), p. 764.

however an inaccurate oversimplification.[48] In the United States, for instance, the standard of proof is categorised as a matter of substantive law, governed by the same law that establishes the claim on the merits.[49] On the other hand, in England, the standard of proof in international arbitration appears to be a matter for the *lex arbiri*.[50]

In Civil Law countries, the issue is rendered more complex by the paucity of codes and case law on the subject. In France, no general statutory provision articulates the civil standard of proof, as both the Civil Code and the Code of Civil Procedure are silent on the subject. The code articles that are arguably relevant to the standard of proof, as set out above, are found in the Civil and Criminal Procedure Codes, suggesting that they are considered to be questions of procedure. Further, in some Civil Law countries, such as Germany and Switzerland, the inner conviction of the judge is explicitly considered a procedural matter,[51] and therefore referred to the *lex arbitri*. One notable exception in the Civil Law world is Quebec, where the rules on the standard of proof can be found in the Civil Code, suggesting that it is a matter of substantive law.[52]

It may appear logical, at least *prima facie*, to characterise the standard of proof in international commercial arbitration as a procedural question for at least two main reasons. *First*, it has been asserted that issues arising from the law of evidence could be considered as procedural in nature.[53] Major arbitration rules and statutes give much discretion to tribunals to determine the admissibility, relevance, materiality and weight of evidence – although not establishing or even suggesting a standard of proof *per se*. Accordingly, some commentators submit that it would follow logically that the standard of proof is also a matter of procedure which must be established, like any other question of procedure, by agreement of the parties or decision of the arbitral

48. Jennifer M. Smith and Sara Nadeau-Séguin, *The Illusive Standard of Proof in International Commercial Arbitration*, 'Legitimacy: Myths, Realities, Challenges', ICCA Congress Series, Volume 18 (ICCA and Kluwer Law International, 2015), p. 146.
49. *See, e.g.*, *Baum v. U.S.*, 541 F.Supp. 1349 (M.D. Pa. 1982) (noting that federal courts look to the substantive state law applicable to the dispute to ascertain standard of proof in a diversity action).
50. *See, e.g.*, *Fiona Trust v. Privalov*, [2010] EWHC 3199 (Comm), para. 138 ('it is a matter for the *lex fori*, in this case English law, to determine how the relevant facts are proved and the standard of proof').
51. *See, e.g.*, German Code of Civil Procedure (Zivilprozessordnung) (2006), section 286(1) ('the court is to decide, at its discretion and conviction, and taking account of the entire content of the hearings and the results obtained by evidence being taken, if any, whether an allegation as to fact is to be deemed true or untrue') (translation from German); Swiss Federal Code of Civil Procedure (2008), Article 157 ('The court forms its opinion based on its free assessment of the evidence taken') (translation from French).
52. Quebec Civil Code (1991), Article 2804. For an analysis *see* Jennifer M. Smith and Sara Nadeau-Séguin, *The Illusive Standard of Proof in International Commercial Arbitration*, 'Legitimacy: Myths, Realities, Challenges', ICCA Congress Series, Volume 18 (ICCA and Kluwer Law International, 2015), p. 146.
53. Francisco Blavi and Gonzalo Vial, *The Burden of Proof in International Commercial Arbitration: Are We Allowed to Adjust the Scales*, Hastings International and Comparative Law Review, Volume 39, Issue 1 (2016), p. 67.

tribunal.[54] *Second*, this approach can be said to respect party autonomy in international commercial arbitration. According to proponents of this approach, the parties' broad powers to determine the applicable arbitral procedure would encompass the standard of proof.[55] As a result, the parties should be free to determine it or modify it in accordance with their broad freedom to determine any procedural issue. But this does not resolve the question of *how* the arbitral tribunal should decide in the absence of agreement.

There are also compelling reasons for characterising the standard of proof as a substantive issue, as explained by proponents of this approach.[56] *First*, a distinction should arguably be made between issues connected to the production of evidence, such as the admissibility, relevance, materiality and weight of evidence, which are procedural in nature, and issues connected to the burden and standard of proof, which are closely tied to the substantive claims and defences. As one commentator noted, the issue of the standard of proof is 'such an important consideration in the decision of the case that it has the quality of substance rather than procedure'.[57]

The burden and sufficiency of evidence will most often be assessed - even if not expressly by reference to a standard of proof - before the commencement of proceedings in order to decide whether a claim or defence should be asserted, its value, and may also be relevant to determine whether an arbitration shall be initiated at all.[58] The evidence will be critical in assessing how easy or difficult it will be for the claimant to win.

Characterising the standard of proof as a question of substance is indirectly supported by the European Union Regulation on the law applicable to contractual obligations (Rome I Regulation). Although not directly applicable to international commercial arbitration, Article 18(1) of the Rome I Regulation provides that '[t]he law governing a contractual obligation under this Regulation shall apply to the extent that, in matters of contractual obligations, it contains rules which raise presumptions of law

54. Florian Haugeneder and Christoph Liebscher, *Chapter V: Investment Arbitration – Corruption and Investment Arbitration: Substantive Standards and Proof*, Austrian Arbitration Yearbook (2009), p. 546.
55. Francisco Blavi and Gonzalo Vial, *The Burden of Proof in International Commercial Arbitration: Are We Allowed to Adjust the Scales*, Hastings International and Comparative Law Review, Volume 39, Issue 1 (2016), p. 53.
56. *Ibid.*, p. 67; Florian Haugeneder and Christoph Liebscher, *Chapter V: Investment Arbitration – Corruption and Investment Arbitration: Substantive Standards and Proof*, Austrian Arbitration Yearbook (2009), p. 545; Abhinav Bhushan, *Standard and Burden of Proof in International Commercial Arbitration: Is There a Bright Line Rule?*, The American Review of International Arbitration, Volume 25 (2014), pp. 607-608.
57. Robert Von Mehren, *Burden of Proof in International Arbitration*, Planning Efficient Arbitration Proceedings: The Law Applicable in International Arbitration, ICCA Congress Series, Volume 7 (Kluwer Law International, 1994), p. 123 at fn. 3 ('The "truth" found in both judicial and arbitral proceedings is relative rather than absolute. It is derived from the evidence presented by the parties and is dependent upon the standard of proof applied to the evidence').
58. Alan Redfern et al., *The Standards and Burden of Proof in International Arbitration*, Arbitration International, Volume 10, Issue 3 (1994), p. 331; Jennifer M. Smith and Sara Nadeau-Séguin, *The Illusive Standard of Proof in International Commercial Arbitration*, 'Legitimacy: Myths, Realities, Challenges', ICCA Congress Series, Volume 18 (ICCA and Kluwer Law International, 2015), p. 149.

or determine the burden of proof'.[59] Since the level of required proof varies greatly between jurisdictions, these differences determine how difficult or easy it is for a party to enforce a claim. This directly affects not only the value of the claim but most importantly impacts the assessment of whether a claim exists at all.[60]

Second, applying the *lex causae* could increase foreseeability for the parties, even prior to the commencement of any proceedings,[61] and may also be deemed the most in line with party autonomy. The parties choose the substantive law governing the dispute, or in the absence of choice, the arbitrator decides on a law, usually selecting the law that has the closest connection to the case. Hence, as Von Mehren explains:

> [i]f the governing law attracts the standard of proof, the factual aspect of the determination of the dispute is most closely assimilated to the legal rules which are being applied. This would seem to harmonize with the presumed intent of the parties in choosing the controlling law, or, if the law is to be selected by the arbitrator, to be consistent with the approach of applying the standard of proof which has the closest connection with the case.[62]

The standard of proof in the substantive law does not only affect the existence of a claim but could potentially even impact the parties' behaviour when performing their contractual obligations. Again, this links it to the substantive law. Conversely, the seat of the arbitration is often chosen for its neutrality, arbitral legal system and/or convenience and may not bear further connection to the underlying dispute.[63] The law of the seat is often associated with issues that are external or ancillary to the substantive claims and defences, i.e., being process issues like how the arbitral procedure should be conducted, annulment proceedings, etc.

Finally, characterising the standard of proof as a substantive law issue may also preserve the finality of the award. Article V(1)(d) of the New York Convention on the Recognition and Enforcement of Foreign Arbitral Awards (New York Convention') recognises as a ground for setting aside that 'the arbitral procedure was not in accordance with the agreement of the parties, or, failing such agreement, was not *in accordance with the law of the country where the arbitration took place*'.[64] Neither Article V(1)(d) nor any other part of Article V of the New York Convention refers to the *lex causae*. It follows that awards should not be subject to attack for error of application of the substantive law. Although some attempts have been made to frame such challenges within broad exceptions, such as public policy, due process or unequal

59. Rome I Regulation (2008), Article 18(1).
60. Alan Redfern et al., *The Standards and Burden of Proof in International Arbitration*, Arbitration International, Volume 10, Issue 3 (1994), p. 331.
61. *Ibid.*, p. 332.
62. Robert Von Mehren, *Burden of Proof in International Arbitration*, Planning Efficient Arbitration Proceedings: The Law Applicable in International Arbitration, ICCA Congress Series, Volume 7 (Kluwer Law International, 1994), p. 125.
63. Julian D.M. Lew et al., 'Chapter 22 Taking Evidence in International Arbitration', in *Comparative International Commercial Arbitration* (Julian Lew KC, Loukas Mistelis & Stefan Kröll eds, Kluwer Law International, 2003), p. 560.
64. New York Convention (1958), Article V(1)(d) (emphasis added).

treatment violations, courts tend to reject them as they imply a review of the merits.[65] If the standard of proof were characterised as procedural, this would arguably mean that an award could be challenged where an arbitrator had failed to apply the standard of proof correctly.

To conclude, although the standard of proof can be seen as either procedural or substantive in nature, there are persuasive reasons to characterise it in international commercial arbitration as substantive, and thus governed by the *lex causae*. If that approach is to be adopted, then this would resolve any doubt as to what standard of proof is applied. The arbitral tribunal would apply the standard of proof required by the governing law; and if the governing law does not contain one (as for most Civil Law jurisdictions) then none is applied, and the arbitral tribunal seeks to apply its evidentiary discretion consistently with that governing law.

§15.04 DIFFERENT STANDARDS OF PROOF FOR CERTAIN KINDS OF ALLEGATIONS, SUCH AS ILLEGALITY

Arbitral tribunals sometimes take into account the substantive nature of the allegations in order to determine the applicable standard of proof, irrespective of the applicable law. A higher standard of proof is sometimes applied to allegations of a particular gravity. For instance, the Court of Arbitration for Sport (CAS) tends to apply the standard of 'comfortable satisfaction' to sporting disputes, in order to take into account the serious impact of doping charges against professional athletes.[66] Conversely, some tribunals apply a lower standard of proof when measuring damages based on equity on the damage finding[67] or for requests of interim measures (e.g., security for costs).[68]

This question is particularly controversial when it comes to proving illegalities such as allegations of fraud or corruption. There are still some arbitrators who consider it proper to apply a higher standard of proof in the face of such allegations even where this is not required by the governing law.

65. Pedro Francisco da Silva Almeida, *Burden and Standards of Proof in International Arbitration: Practice and Challenges*, Revista Brasileira de Arbitragem, Volume XVIII, Issue 69 (2021), p. 69. *See, e.g.*, Swiss Federal Tribunal, First Civil Law Court, 27 March 2014, *X. v. The Football Federation of Ukraine* (FFU), No. 4A_362/2013; Swiss Federal Tribunal, First Civil Law Court, 27 March 2014, *A. v. The Football Federation of Ukraine (FFU)*, No. 4A_448/2013 (rejection of the argument that the misapplication of the standard of proof would amount to a public policy violation).
66. Nathan D. O'Malley, *Rules of Evidence in International Arbitration: An Annotated Guide* (Informa Law, 2012), p. 210; Chris Davis, *The 'Comfortable Satisfaction' Standard of Proof: Applied by the Court of Arbitration for Sport in Drug-related Cases*, University of Notre Dame Australia Law Review, Volume 14, 1-24 (2012), p. 1.
67. Simon Greenberg, *Le standard de la preuve en arbitrage international*, Revue de l'Arbitrage, Comité Français de l'Arbitrage, Volume 2020, Issue 1 (2020), p. 130; George M. Von Mehren and Claudia Salomon, *Submitting Evidence in an International Arbitration: The Common Lawyer's Guide*, Journal of International Arbitration, Volume 20, Issue 3 (2003), p. 291; Andreas Reiner, *Burden and General Standards of Proof*, The Standards and Burden of Proof in International Arbitration, Arbitration International, Volume 10, Issue 3 (1994), p. 336.
68. Nathan D. O'Malley, *Rules of Evidence in International Arbitration: An Annotated Guide* (Informa Law, 2012), p. 211.

In a number of historical cases, arbitrators relied on the heightened standard of proof of 'clear and convincing evidence' or even 'beyond a reasonable doubt', which is generally only used in criminal proceedings.[69] For instance, in the Westinghouse case the tribunal relied on the laws of the United States and the Philippines as governing laws and required 'clear and convincing evidence' of corruption amounting to 'more than a mere preponderance'.[70] Similarly, in the Hilmarton case the tribunal applied Swiss law and requested proof 'beyond doubt' of corruption.[71] While these tribunals applied a higher standard of proof relying on the applicable law, other tribunals have simply asserted that a higher standard of proof applies without engaging in any discussion on the applicable standard of proof pursuant to the governing law. Interestingly, a study conducted by Antonio Crivellaro twenty years ago explained that in fourteen out of twenty-five cases involving allegations of corruption, the tribunal applied a high standard of proof.[72] It is sometimes observed that allegations of serious wrongdoing in international arbitration require more convincing evidence in light of their gravity.[73]

The appropriateness of using such an enhanced standard of proof for allegations of illegality is increasingly challenged both in practice and in doctrine. A higher standard of proof is justified in criminal cases because the trial can result in a criminal punishment for the guilty party. Yet, in international commercial arbitration, tribunals are asked to draw only civil consequences. An arbitral tribunal cannot find a party guilty of a criminal offense or impose upon it a criminal punishment. As a result, the application of a higher standard of proof in international commercial arbitration appears unwarranted.[74]

Many arbitral tribunals proceed on the premise that the 'balance of probabilities' standard of proof applies regardless of the nature of the allegation. Others decide to lower the standard of proof, in the interest of fairness, to take into account the difficulty

---

69. *See, e.g.*, Robert Pietrowski, *Evidence in International Arbitration*, Arbitration International, Volume 22, Issue 3 (2006), pp. 379-380 ('A higher standard of proof may be applied in cases involving particularly sensitive allegations of wrongdoing such as conduct *contra bonos mores*').
70. *Westinghouse Int'l Projects Co., Westinghouse Elec. S.A. and Barns & Roe Enterprises, Inc. v. Nat'l Power Corp. and The Republic of the Philippines*, ICC Case No. 6401, Preliminary Award (19 December 1991), paras 33-35.
71. *Hilmarton Ltd. v. Omnium de Traitment et de Valorisation S.A.*, ICC Case No. 5622, Final Award, 1988, para. 23.
72. Antonio Crivellaro, *Arbitration Case Law on Bribery: Issues of Arbitrability, Contract Validity, Merits and Evidence*, Arbitration: Money Laundering, Corruption and Fraud, Dossier of the ICC Institute of World Business Law (ICC, 2003), pp. 115-117.
73. George M. Von Mehren and Claudia Salomon, *Submitting Evidence in an International Arbitration: The Common Lawyer's Guide*, Journal of International Arbitration, Volume 20, Issue 3 (2003), p. 291 (citing examples).
74. Markus Wirth, *Production of Documents and Fraud in International Arbitration*, Written Evidence and Discovery in International Arbitration: New Issues and Tendencies, Dossiers of the ICC Institute of World Business Law, Volume 6 (2009), pp. 182-183; Emmanuel Gaillard, *La Corruption Saisie par Les Arbitres du Commerce International*, Revue de l'Arbitrage, Comité Français de l'Arbitrage, Volume 2017, Issue 3 (2017), p. 834; Jean-Yves Garaud, *L'Office de l'Arbitre en Arbitrage Commercial: Caractérisation de l'Illicéité et Mise en Oeuvre des Sanctions*, Revue de l'Arbitrage, Comité Français de l'Arbitrage, Volume 2019, Issue 1 (2019), pp. 181-182; Sophie Lemaire, *La preuve de la corruption*, Revue de l'Arbitrage, Comité Français de l'Arbitrage, Volume 2020, Issue 1 (2020), pp. 191-192.

of proving allegations of illegality such as corruption.[75] Indeed, the nature of illegal activities is that parties engaging in them seek to hide their tracks, thus making them harder to prove, especially in civil proceedings where neither parties nor arbitrators possess the powers of criminal investigators. Paradoxically, the difficulty of proving allegations of corruption is also used by those in favour of a heightened standard of proof.[76] There is no logical reason why the difficulty of proving a fact should justify a heightened standard of proof. Finally, some tribunals simply refrain from ruling on this thorny issue and avoid discussing the standard of proof.[77]

There appears to be no justification for an arbitral tribunal to lower or raise the standard of proof in cases involving alleged illegality – or in any other cases – unless this is required by the applicable substantive law.[78] The only exception appears to be where the parties have specifically agreed on a different standard of proof being applied. And if the standard of proof is in essence discretionary, whether by application of the substantive law or not, then in our view there are few, if any, persuasive arguments to change it based on the nature of the allegations. Either a fact is sufficiently proved or it is not.

§15.05 CONCLUSION

Despite being essential to the adjudication of a case, there is little agreement on, or attention given to, the question of the standard of proof in international commercial arbitration. Institutional rules and arbitration laws provide very limited guidance on this issue and rather appear to cloth the arbitral tribunal with discretion. Further, while arbitral tribunals necessarily always apply a standard of proof of some kind, they rarely explain it in their awards.

The varied approaches come at least partly from the differences among different legal traditions. In the Common Law, the issue of the standard of proof is extensively documented with different applicable thresholds depending on the nature of the claim, from 'balance of probabilities' to 'beyond a reasonable doubt'. On the other hand, Civil

75. *See* Michael Hwang and Kevin Lim, *Corruption in Arbitration – Law and Reality*, Asian International Arbitration Journal Kluwer Law International, Volume 8, Issue 1 (2012), p. 30 ('given the difficulty in proving corruption, a criminal standard of proof would be almost impossible to satisfy and plays directly into the hands of unscrupulous parties, who can simply deny wrongdoing and exploit the high threshold of proof to avoid liability').
76. *See, e.g., EDF (Services) Limited v. Republic of Romania*, ICSID Case No. ARB/05/13, Award, 8 October 2009, para. 221 ('In any case, however, corruption must be proven and is notoriously difficult to prove since, typically, there is little or no physical evidence. The seriousness of the accusation of corruption in the present case [...] demands clear and convincing evidence.').
77. *See, e.g., Saipem S.p.A. v. People's Republic of Bangladesh*, ICSID Case No. ARB/05/7, Award, 30 June 2009, paras 114 and 148; *Niko Resources v. Petrobangla and Bapex*, ICSID Case No. ARB/10/18, Decision on the Corruption Claim, 25 February 2019, para. 803; *Ampal-American and others v. Egypt*, ICSID Case No. ARB/12/11, Decision on Jurisdiction, 1 February 2016, paras 305-306; *Flughafen Zürich v. Venezuela*, ICSID Case No. ARB/10/19, Award, 18 November 2014, paras 142-143.
78. Jennifer M. Smith and Sara Nadeau-Séguin, *The Illusive Standard of Proof in International Commercial Arbitration*, 'Legitimacy: Myths, Realities, Challenges', ICCA Congress Series, Volume 18 (ICCA and Kluwer Law International, 2015), p. 150.

Law systems have typically not conceptualised an objective standard of proof and judges decide cases based on their 'inner conviction'. The two systems also appear to diverge on whether the standard of proof is a matter of procedure, governed by the *lex arbitri*, or substance, governed by the *lex causae*. In the interests of predictability and respect for the parties' agreement (at least where they have chosen the substantive law), there are compelling reasons to treat the standard of proof as substantive rather than procedural.

CHAPTER 16

Legal and Litigation Privileges in the 'Redfern Schedule' Phase of Arbitral Proceedings

Monique Sasson

§16.01 INTRODUCTION

Dr Julian Lew's writings and lectures on international arbitration have addressed virtually every important aspect of a vast field that continues to grow. He has had the advantages of experience, energy and a combined career in academia and law practice when he writes and teaches. He was an active participant when the field of international commercial arbitration began to flourish, and – with an unflagging work ethic – he has been able to forecast and report on significant developments. As a successful counsel, arbitrator, scholar and teacher across decades, he has cultivated a perspective that only a handful of practitioners possess.

At the centre of Dr Lew's scholarship and approach to practising international arbitration is his embrace of internationalism or 'autonomous arbitration':[1] i.e., his view that that the conduct of an arbitration should not be tethered to parochial national court procedures and laws. Counsel and arbitrators need to find procedures suitable to a transnational process, in which the parties are not disadvantaged because of any of the participants' home jurisdictions. Throughout his career Dr Lew has focused on what may be termed the 'art' of the international arbitral process, whereby arbitrators – hopefully assisted by counsel – design innovative solutions when facing divergent national procedures and practices.

1. Julian D.M. Lew, 'Achieving the Dream: Autonomous Arbitration', 22 *Arbitration International* 179 (2006).

One key topic on which national procedures diverge is the operation of legal privilege. The intensity of this divergence is perhaps at its highest when the issue is document production. The early years of international commercial arbitration – as manifested by the terms of the earliest iteration, in 1983, of the IBA Rules on the Taking of Evidence in International [Commercial] Arbitration ('IBA Rules')[2] – were not marked by the continual, major disputes over document production that are now a feature of the arbitral process, usually in the form of warring 'Redfern Schedules'.[3] However, by the 1999 iteration of the IBA Rules, there was already a provision, Article 3(7), in which objections to production of documents arguably covered by legal privilege (or 'litigation privilege'[4]) might need to be addressed:

> In exceptional circumstances, if the propriety of an objection can only be determined by review of the document, the Arbitral Tribunal may determine that it should not review the document. In that event, the Arbitral Tribunal may, after consultation with the Parties, appoint an independent and impartial expert, bound to confidentiality, to review any such document and to report on the objection. To the extent that the objection is upheld by the Arbitral Tribunal, the expert shall not disclose to the Arbitral Tribunal and to the other Parties the contents of the document reviewed'.

The 2013 'IBA Guidelines on Party Representation in International Arbitration', Article 15,[5] further notes that counsel should assist its party in taking reasonable steps to produce '*all non-privileged, responsive Documents*' that the party has undertaken or been ordered to produce. The problematic foundational question for counsel, parties, the arbitral tribunal, and the possible independent reviewing expert is what criteria should be applied to determine whether the designation of 'privilege' may be appropriate and thereby protect a document from inclusion in the arbitral case file.

National legal systems and national ethical rules for lawyers may offer varying conceptions of 'privilege', and thus create significant complexity in resolving this foundational question in an international arbitration. One side's understanding that it will enjoy protection from disclosure because of a privilege applied in its home jurisdiction may (and often does) clash with its opponent's view that 'privilege' is improperly being invoked to shield damaging documents from disclosure, thereby preventing the arbitral tribunal from reaching a sound result.

This is precisely the type of complexity that would attract, and has attracted, Dr Lew's attention. He published a well-known article in 2015 on legal privilege and

2. Titled 'The IBA Supplementary Rules Governing the Presentation and Reception of Evidence in International Commercial Arbitration', issued in 1983.
3. Named After Alan Redfern, a 'column' method for organizing document request and objections, often tracked to the requirements of Article 3 (with relevant elements also in Article 9) of the IBA Rules.
4. That is, documents created in anticipation of or in preparation for the conduct of a dispute.
5. 'A Party Representative should advise the Party whom he or she represents to take, and assist such Party in taking, reasonable steps to ensure that: (i) a reasonable search is made for Documents that a Party has undertaken, or been ordered, to produce; and (ii) all non-privileged, responsive Documents are produced'.

document production.[6] He commented that the first task for the tribunal is to verify whether the privilege claim is prima facie justified in the circumstances in which it has been raised, and the next is to reach a determination of the parties' respective rights and obligations in relation to the privilege claim based on the relevant contract terms, the applicable law and the nature and significance of the evidence for which the claim of privilege has been made.

Issues concerning privilege claims are often confronted by arbitral tribunals in a vacuum of predetermined rules, even when the parties may agree on how privilege would otherwise apply under the *lex arbitri* or the substantive law. For example, rules on privilege in many civil law jurisdictions are tied to criminal law proceedings and have little or no applicability in a non-criminal, commercial case in the context of document production (since, for example, document production might not even be part of the civil trial process). Further, it is a commonplace that privilege enjoyed by in-house counsel in common law jurisdictions may not apply to in-house counsel in some civil law jurisdictions. In circumstances where counsel for the parties come from jurisdictions with diverging privilege frameworks, the arbitral tribunal is left with the need and usually the discretion to develop rules that will apply for the resolution of 'privilege disputes' in the Redfern Schedule-document production phase of the arbitration. The risks attending such arbitrator discretion are discussed in Professor William W. Park's 2002 Freshfields Lecture, in which he highlighted the importance of having more precise procedural protocols and the 'discomfort that a litigant may feel when arbitrators make up the rules as they go along, divorced from any precise procedural canons set in advance'.[7]

I propose to broadly follow Dr Lew's 2015 roadmap for reducing the risks of arbitrator discretion on the issue of privilege claims in document production. Dr Lew's roadmap combines academic rigour with practical suggestions arising from international practice, to which he has been a major contributor. This chapter will focus more on the practical aspects of resolving claims of legal privilege. It will propose a definition of privilege, examine the 'rules' on privilege in international arbitration, and consider whether privilege logs and independent reviewing experts are the correct answer to the lack of a uniform discipline on privilege in international arbitration.

§16.02 DEFINITION OF PRIVILEGE

Dr Lew referred to the concept of privilege as encompassing a broad range of private and confidential communications, and he limited his analysis to legal privilege. There is now an abundant literature on privileges in international arbitration,[8] and a useful

6. Julian D.M. Lew, 'Document Production and Legal Privilege in International Commercial Arbitration' in *Practising Virtue: Inside International Arbitration*, David D. Caron et al. (eds), OUP, 2015, pp. 347-356.
7. William W. Park, 'The 2002 Freshfields Lecture – Arbitration's Protean Nature: The Value of Rules and the Risks of Discretion', 19 *Arbitration International* 279 (2003), at p. 286.
8. *See, generally*, Gary Born, *International Commercial Arbitration*, Third Edition, Volume II, International Arbitral Procedures, Kluwer, 2020, pp. 2549-2562; Klaus Peter Berger, 'Chapter 13:

definition is provided by Professor Klaus Peter Berger: privileges are 'legally recognized rights to withhold certain witness or documentary evidence from legal proceedings, including the right to prevent another from disclosing such information'.[9] Four broad types of privileges are often identified: (i) the attorney-client privilege;[10] (ii) the business secrets privilege; (iii) the 'without prejudice' privilege and mediation privilege; and (iv) the government information privilege.[11]

The first category, the attorney-client privilege, is probably the most frequently invoked in international arbitral proceedings. However, the coverage of attorney-client privilege differs substantially in the common law system compared to the civil law system. In the former, the rules protect clients from extensive disclosure, while in civil law countries the rules typically concern the obligation of secrecy imposed on the lawyer, and is applied particularly in the context of criminal sanctions.[12] Thus, common law rules concerning legal privilege are, as a general matter, more extensive and intricate compared to those in civil law jurisdictions.

The four above-identified privilege categories actually find expression in the 2020 IBA Rules on the Taking of Evidence in International Arbitration.[13] Article 9.4 refers to protection of confidentiality of legal advice. The business secrets privilege is addressed in Article 9.2. (e): 'grounds of commercial or technical confidentiality that the Arbitral Tribunal determines to be compelling'. The privilege covering settlement communications, which is regulated under English law and in the United States,[14] is included in Article 9.4. (b): documents, statements and communications '*made in connection with and for the purpose of settlement negotiations*'). Article 9.2(f) concerns the State secrets privilege: 'grounds of special political or institutional sensitivity (including evidence

Evidentiary Privileges' in *Handbook of Evidence in International Commercial Arbitration: Key Concepts and Issues*, Franco Ferrari & Friedrich Jakob Rosenfeld (eds), Kluwer, 2022, pp. 301-320; Klaus Peter Berger, 'Evidentiary Privileges: Best Practice Standards versus/and Arbitral Discretion', 22 *Arbitration International* 501-520 (2006); Guido Santiago Tawil & Ignacio J. Mirorini Lima, 'Chapter 2: Privilege-Related Issues in International Arbitration', in *Written Evidence and Discovery in International Arbitration: New Issues and Tendencies*, Teresa Giovannini & Alexis Mourre (eds), Dossiers of the ICC Institute of World Business Law, Volume 6, Kluwer-ICC, 2009, pp. 29-55; Virginia Hamilton, 'Document Production in ICC Arbitration', 2006 Special Supplement, ICC International Court of Arbitration Bulletin, pp. 63-81; Zara Shafruddin, 'Privilege in International Arbitration' in *40 under 40 International Arbitration*, Carlos Gonzales-Bueno (ed.), Dykinson S.L., 2018, pp. 297-311; Diana Kuitkowski, 'The Law Applicable to Privilege Claims in International Arbitration', 32(1) *Journal of International Arbitration* 65-106 (2015); F.von Schlabrendorff and A. Sheppard, 'Conflict of Legal Privileges in International Arbitration: An Attempt to Find a Holistic Solution', in Aksen, et al., editors, *Liber Amicorum in Honour of Robert Briner* (Paris, 2005).

9. Klaus Peter Berger, 'Chapter 13: Evidentiary Privileges' in *Handbook of Evidence in International Commercial Arbitration: Key Concepts and Issues, supra* n. 8, at pp. 303-304.
10. *Ibid.*, at p. 305: Professor Berger refers to a worldwide survey made in 2014, which indicates that this privilege is known in more than sixty jurisdictions worldwide.
11. *Ibid.*, at pp. 304-310.
12. *Ibid.*, p. 305.
13. The 2020 IBA Rules on the Taking of Evidence in International Arbitration is available online: https://www.ibanet.org/MediaHandler?id=def0807b-9fec-43ef-b624-f2cb2af7cf7b.
14. Klaus Peter Berger, 'Chapter 13: Evidentiary Privileges' in *Handbook of Evidence in International Commercial Arbitration: Key Concepts and Issues, supra* n. 8, p. 308.

that has been classified as secrets by a government or a public international institution) that the Arbitral Tribunal determines to be compelling').

Although there is a broad policy consensus that the protection of privilege serves the public interest in protection of privacy for individuals and security of operations for companies as well as States,[15] there are some systems where legal privilege has little relevance in terms of application. In common law countries, it is linked to disclosure and rules of evidence; the privilege belongs to the client and there is a detailed regimen concerning waivers and inadvertent disclosure. In civil law countries where there is no general obligation to disclose documents in civil litigation, it rests with the lawyers, and it is regulated by professional rules of the Bar.[16] Documents and communications exchanged between lawyers are considered confidential and breach of this confidentiality may lead to a criminal offence. Clients in some civil law systems cannot waive the privilege that their lawyers possess. Further, as Dr Lew reports, the European Court of Justice has limited legal privilege to independent lawyers and law firms and has thus denied legal privilege in communications exchanged internally in a company, even if in-house counsel were part of the exchange and the communications concern pending or potential litigation.[17]

§16.03 RULES ON PRIVILEGE IN INTERNATIONAL ARBITRATION

While, as noted above, the IBA Rules identify and recognize privileges, there is not an accepted, detailed set of rules concerning privileges and their application in international arbitration. There is, at best, general guidance as to the question of application. For example, in the 2020 IBA Rules, several provisions are relevant:

(i) Article 2 provides that the arbitral tribunal 'shall consult' the parties to agree on an '*efficient, economical and fair process of taking of evidence*'; this consultation may include addressing '*the level of confidentiality protection to be afforded to evidence in the arbitration*'.

(ii) Article 3.8 (following on from the original provision in the 1999 IBA Rules) accepts that in '*exceptional circumstances*', if an objection can be determined only by review of the document, the tribunal may decide not to review the document and, having consulted the parties, may appoint an '*independent and impartial*' expert, bound to confidentiality, to review the document and to report on the objection.

(iii) Article 9.2 provides that the arbitral tribunal '*shall*' exclude from evidence or production any document or statement for '*legal impediment or privilege under the legal or ethical rules*' determined by the arbitral tribunal to be applicable.

---

15. Julian D.M. Lew, 'Document Production and Legal Privilege in International Commercial Arbitration', *supra* n. 6, p. 348.
16. *Ibid.*
17. *Ibid.*

(iv) Article 9.4 states that in considering privilege, and if permitted by the '*mandatory legal or ethical rules that are determined to be applicable*', the tribunal may take into account: (a) the need to protect confidentiality of documents/statements created for the purpose of providing or obtaining legal advice; (b) the need to protect the confidentiality of documents /statements rendered in connection with settlement negotiations; (c) the expectation of the parties at the time the legal privilege is said to have arisen; (d) any possible waiver or affirmative use of the document; and (e) the need to maintain fairness and equality between the parties in particular when they are subject to different legal or ethical rules.

The commentary to the IBA Rules[18] ('IBA Commentary') states that the consultations envisioned in Article 2.2 may refer to various techniques in connection with taking of evidence, which include privilege logs to specify the particulars of documents that have been withheld on grounds of privilege and redaction of portions of documents to avoid disclosing protected information.[19] Where a party has raised an objection on grounds of legal privilege, commercial confidentiality or special political or institutional sensitivity, the IBA Commentary indicates that 'it is generally preferable that the arbitral tribunal does not review any such documents itself'. The reasons listed are: (i) if the tribunal upholds the objection, it could not eliminate its knowledge of the document once it had been reviewed; and (ii) there may be confidentiality concerns. The IBA Commentary nonetheless observes that in circumstances where time and cost factors are considered to be compelling, the arbitral tribunal may decide to review the document(s) on which a privilege/confidentiality objection has been lodged.

Although an independent reviewing expert, if engaged, will provide a report on the objection, '*the arbitral tribunal is to make the final ruling as to its validity*'.[20] In this regard, the 2020 IBA Rules Task Force deleted from the previous iteration of the IBA Rules the sentence in Article 6.3. comparing the authority of the expert to request information to the authority of the arbitral tribunal, because it could be misinterpreted to suggest that the tribunal-appointed expert would have the same power as the tribunal to resolve disputes over, for instance, privileged information. Article 6.7 clarifies that the arbitral tribunal will determine the issues in the case.[21]

Many institutional arbitration rules do not mention the issue of privilege, thereby remitting the decision on the issue to the arbitral tribunal's discretion, absent a mandatory provision in the *lex arbitri*. However, there some notable exceptions. One such exception is Article 25 of the International Centre for Dispute Resolution (ICDR) Rules, which is titled 'Privilege', and states as follows:[22]

18. Commentary on the revised text of the 2020 IBA Rules on the Taking of Evidence in International Arbitration is available online: https://www.ibanet.org/MediaHandler?id=4F797338-693E-47C7-A92A-1509790ECC9D.
19. *Ibid.*, at pp. 6 and 12.
20. *Ibid.*, at p. 12.
21. *Ibid.*, at p. 23.
22. 2021 ICDR International Dispute Resolution Procedures Arbitration (Arbitration Rules) available online: https://www.icdr.org/sites/default/files/document_repository/ICDR_Rules_1.pdf?utm

> The arbitral tribunal shall take into account applicable principles of privilege, such as those involving the confidentiality of communications between a lawyer and client. *When the parties, their counsel, or their documents would be subject under applicable law to different rules, the tribunal should, to the extent possible, apply the same rule to all parties, giving preference to the rule that provides the highest level of protection.* [Emphasis added]

Again, in this instance, as seen above with the IBA Rules, there is only a general guideline ('the tribunal should, to the extent possible'). However, there is a clear direction that there should be equal treatment ('apply the same rule to all parties') and, importantly, there is a further clear direction that the tribunal should 'give preference to the rule that provides the highest level of protection' (i.e., supports the broadest applicability of privilege). This is by no means a solution without complications: if, for instance, both parties are subject to civil law system that does not regulate waiver or inadvertent disclosure, what rules would be applicable?

§16.04 SELECTION OF THE RELEVANT APPLICABLE LAW

The selection of the applicable law, referenced in ICDR Article 25, also raises complications for arbitral tribunals. The predicate questions are whether 'privilege' is a matter of substantive or procedural law and whether the tribunal should be considering this question under the substantive law of the contract or the *lex arbitri*. It has been suggested that a comparative analysis of evidentiary privileges leads to the conclusion that these issues are substantive in nature.[23] However, even if privilege were to be assessed in accordance with the applicable substantive law, this may not respect the parties' expectations of the appropriate level of protection, if privilege under the substantive law conflicts with the law of the jurisdiction where the communication between the lawyers and their client occurred.[24]

Dr Lew has suggested that in the absence of a definitive answer as to whether privilege is a substantive or a procedural issue, the arbitral tribunal has many options to work through: it may look to the law of the seat, or the jurisdiction with the strongest interest in the privilege, or the jurisdiction where the communications took place (or where they are being stored), or the jurisdiction where the lawyer in question is a member of the Bar, or the home jurisdiction of the client or international law or general principles of law.[25] Dr Lew emphasized that the *ex post facto* selection of applicable law

_source = icdr-website&utm_medium = rules-page&utm_campaign = rules-intl-update-1mar. *Se e* Klaus Peter Berger, 'Chapter 13: Evidentiary Privileges' in *Handbook of Evidence in International Commercial Arbitration: Key Concepts and Issues, supra* n. 8, at p. 310.

23. KP Berger, 'Chapter 13: Evidentiary Privileges' in *Handbook of Evidence in International Commercial Arbitration: Key Concepts and Issues, supra* n. 8, at p. 310.
24. *Ibid.*
25. Julian D.M. Lew, 'Document Production and Legal Privilege in International Commercial Arbitration', *supra* n. 6, p. 352. *See also* KP Berger, 'Chapter 13: Evidentiary Privileges' in *Handbook of Evidence in International Commercial Arbitration: Key Concepts and Issues, supra* n. 8, p. 312.

may require disclosure of communications that lawyers and parties believed, at the time they were made, would be privileged.[26]

Complications also may remain when the most 'appropriate' applicable law is domestic law in which a document production regime is unknown. In this case, the issue is not a matter of applying the least or most protection; rather, the difficulty is a total lack of rules because the document production procedure is non-existent or is so circumscribed as to make it a useless basis for international arbitral practice. Here, the discretion left to arbitral tribunals is decidedly broad.

§16.05 PRIVILEGE LOGS

Privilege logs, long a feature of, *e.g.*, USA and English national court litigation, have in recent years become more prevalent in arbitral proceedings to enable the tribunal to assess to assess a party's efforts to withhold production of documents, otherwise responsive to a Redfern Schedule request, on the grounds of an asserted privilege claim. The purpose of the log is to describe the nature of the information withheld so that the tribunal may determine (usually upon the challenge of the other side) whether the claim of privilege is valid. Typically, a log contains a brief description of each document for which privilege is claimed, the date the document was created, the individual/party that issued the document and the individual/party that received it, and a brief description of the reason for which the party claims it is privileged.[27]

One drawback of such logs that is particularly pertinent for arbitration is that they are often very time-consuming and expensive to produce. Moreover, many civil law practitioners have limited experience, because the practice of producing such logs does not feature in their national courts. Further, the production of the log does not necessarily enable the arbitral tribunal to make a reasoned decision on whether the assertion of privilege should be upheld; there may still be a need to review the document itself (or documents themselves), which creates the very risk that the log is meant to avoid – i.e., the possibility that the tribunal reviews a document that it eventually rules is privileged, and therefore should not have been seen by the tribunal. As noted below, this is where the role of the independent reviewing expert comes in, though the time and expense of engaging the expert – and the need to ensure that her role does not usurp that of the tribunal – may also entail significant procedural complications.

The parties may take steps at the outset of their arbitration, with the tribunal's guidance, to seek to reach agreement on how issues of privilege can be addressed efficiently and fairly in cases where document production is likely to be both important and contentious and privilege claims will inevitably arise. For example, the parties may agree on dispensing with privilege logs entirely (unlikely) or agree on how such logs

26. Julian D.M. Lew, 'Document Production and Legal Privilege in International Commercial Arbitration', *supra* n. 6, p. 352.
27. Julian D.M. Lew, 'Document Production and Legal Privilege in International Commercial Arbitration', *supra* n. 6, p. 355. *See also* Virginia Hamilton, 'Document Production in ICC Arbitration', *supra*, p. 77.

should be composed. For example, the parties may reach an agreement on identifying categories of documents rather than recording individual document references in the log, and/or the parties (with the tribunal's approval) may agree on how detailed the reasons for the claimed privilege need to be. Reasons accompanied by more details may usefully circumscribe the tribunal's exercise of discretion in reviewing the log and may also lessen the need for an independent reviewing expert.

§16.06 THE INDEPENDENT REVIEWING EXPERT

As discussed above, for some arbitral tribunals, as provided for in the IBA Rules, one solution to avoid the risk of a tribunal reviewing a document that it ultimately determines to be inadmissible on the grounds of privilege – thereby defeating the underlying protection afforded by the privilege – is the appointment of an independent reviewing expert. The expert has the ability to read the documents for which privilege has been asserted – assuming that the log entries do not permit a sound decision on production – and report to the tribunal. As indicated above, this procedural mechanism raises time and costs issues, as well as the potential issue of the expert displacing the tribunal's decision-making authority, thereby creating a potential due process issue. However, in circumstances where the party whose assertion of privilege is challenged and (a) the challenging party contends that the privilege can only be reasonably assessed if the document is read, and (b) the party asserting privilege contends that the tribunal will be irreparably prejudiced against it if the tribunal reads the document, the engagement of an independent reviewing expert may be the prudent and appropriate course, despite the risk of a party later arguing that the independent reviewer has improperly assumed the tribunal's exclusive decision-making authority.

§16.07 CONCLUSION

The assessment of a party's assertion of privilege in the document production phase of an international arbitration has recently become a major feature in many, if not most, complex, high-value proceedings. The complications attending this assessment can be substantial: (i) the applicable privilege rules, taken from national jurisdictions, must be determined, which is often enormously difficult and may raise due process/equal treatment concerns; and (ii) a procedure must be adopted for testing the assertion of privilege pursuant to the applicable rules, which increasingly entails the time and expense of preparation (and tribunal review) of a privilege log. Devising *internationally* accepted practices in relation to these tasks is an intellectually challenging exercise for arbitrators. An approach adopted by a number of tribunals, along the lines of ICDR Article 25, has been to extend one party's set of national privilege rules to the counterparty if the counterparty's national rules would provide lesser protection. But this in itself may provide skewed treatment, based on the counterparty's expectations, rather than equal treatment. Moreover, this approach may have very limited usefulness if both parties hail from a civil law system regime.

Dr Lew's scholarship has emphasized the importance in international arbitral proceedings of the parties placing their 'cards face up' on the table from the outset. The treatment of privilege issue clearly would benefit from such an approach: discussions in the first case management conference about how to select the applicable privilege rules and how the arbitral tribunal should assess an assertion of privilege in the Redfern Schedule phase would enhance the soundness of the process, as well as participants' confidence that they are being treated fairly.

CHAPTER 17

Remote Proceedings and Their Impact on Stakeholders in the Arbitral Process

Claus von Wobeser[*]

§17.01 INTRODUCTION

I am honored and humbled by the opportunity to contribute to this well-deserved book in honor of Professor Lew's extraordinary career and contributions to international arbitration theory and practice. Julian's academic work as Head of Queen Mary University of London's School of International Arbitration has formed hundreds—if not thousands—of successful arbitrators and arbitrations practitioners since its foundation in 1985. Moreover, his extensive scholarly work has shaped several aspects of today's arbitration practice. Moreover, his written work has the virtue of aging well; I confess that, despite being over twenty years old, his paper on Interim and Conservatory Measures in ICC Arbitration[1] continues to be an essential reference for me when dealing with interim relief questions.

Julian's presence in the international arbitration practice spans over four decades, which are also the four decades in which arbitration and legal practice have changed the most in centuries. Perhaps the starkest change in arbitration practice in these four past decades is the one brought about by the COVID-19 pandemic, which forced all the arbitration stakeholders to adapt and completely transform the way we practice international arbitration.

The pandemic brought massive challenges for arbitration practitioners, particularly during the extended lockdowns of 2020 and 2021. However, unlike most national courts and domestic litigation that virtually stopped during those years, the arbitration

* The author thanks Rodrigo Macin for his help in the preparation of this essay.

1. Julian D.M. Lew, *Commentary on Interim and Conservatory Measures in ICC Arbitration Cases* 11(1) ICC Ct Bull. 23 (2000).

practice showed incredible resilience, as most cases continued relatively smoothly. The secret, I believe, was that most arbitration stakeholders embraced remote proceedings quickly and efficiently.

Remote proceedings had been a theoretical possibility since long before the COVID pandemic. The technology upon which remote proceedings rely has been around for several years. However, before the pandemic, arbitration practitioners would seldom be open to considering the advantages of remote proceedings for all stakeholders. In this sense, the migration from in-person to remote proceedings was imposed rather than voluntarily adopted by arbitration stakeholders. Nevertheless, now that arbitration stakeholders have witnessed the undeniable advantages of remote proceedings, it is, in my opinion, improbable that we will go back to the way we practiced before the pandemic. However, it is also unlikely that now that the world has assimilated COVID, arbitration practice will continue to be fully or almost fully remote. I believe that arbitration stakeholders will take the best of both worlds to heal one of arbitration's Achilles heels: cost and time efficiency.

In this sense, this essay briefly dissects remote proceedings before and during the pandemic and where I believe it is heading now as we finally see the light at the end of the tunnel, i.e., hybrid proceedings. Additionally, I try to identify which stakeholders in arbitration win and lose with remote and hybrid proceedings and some potential concerns regarding this type of proceedings.

§17.02 THE PRE-PANDEMIC ERA: FULLY IN-PERSON

Email, FTPs, and video conferencing platforms, the tools that allowed arbitrations to continue even during the worst moments of the pandemic, have been around for many years now. However, arbitration practitioners seldom used them to conduct entirely remote proceedings or hearings. Although parties and tribunals communicated via email, the main filings of the parties were traditionally filed in hard copies and with hundreds—or thousands—supporting exhibits. Similarly, some witnesses or experts occasionally would attend hearings remotely due to exceptional circumstances, such as the impossibility of a certain witness or expert to obtain a visa for the place of the hearing, and in even fewer occasions, the illness or imprisonment of a witness. However, at least in my experience, remote examination of witnesses and experts was never smooth, there were always technical difficulties, and it was generally a disruptive situation for the tribunal and the parties.

Beyond the interaction between parties and tribunals, the preparation of cases was almost always fully in person. Counsel would constantly travel to interview witnesses and meet with experts in different parts of the world, and arbitrators would fly across half the globe to deliberate in physical reunions. During my career as an arbitrator, I have traveled several times to other continents to have one-day deliberations on procedural matters that could undoubtedly have been decided over a phone or video call.

Needless to say, this was not the most time and cost-efficient way of conducting an arbitration, and it certainly was not environmentally friendly. However, it was just the norm, and few stakeholders seriously questioned it.

§17.03 THE PANDEMIC ERA: FULLY REMOTE

The fully in-person arbitral practice completely shut down in early 2020. As borders closed and local governments imposed lockdowns, hearings were postponed and memorial fillings suspended, arbitration virtually halted. Many, including myself,[2] thought that COVID would be an ephemeral disruption and that things would return to "normal" in some weeks. However, as it became evident that COVID would not go away in the foreseeable future, and precisely because of the COVID crisis, the number of disputes grew significantly, arbitration stakeholders were forced to adapt to fully remote practice.

This adapting process was remarkably fast. For instance, the very day the EU closed its borders, the International Chamber of Commerce (ICC) began requiring that all new requests for arbitration and emergency arbitration be filed electronically. Further, as soon as April 9, 2020, the ICC Court had already issued an extensive Guidance Note on Possible Measures Aimed at Mitigating the Effects of the COVID-19 Pandemic, which among other things, included a protocol for virtual hearings and suggested clauses for cyber protocols.

The resilience shown by arbitration stakeholders was remarkable. Within a few weeks, most cases resumed, albeit remotely. The things that we assumed required in-person interaction, such as witness and expert interviews, meetings with clients, or hearings and deliberations, continued remotely seamlessly. Much to my surprise, I found myself and my team working more efficiently. In hindsight, it seems clear that less travel implied that we could work with fewer disruptions.

§17.04 LOOKING FORWARD TO POST-PANDEMIC ARBITRATION: HYBRID PROCEEDINGS

We still cannot talk about a post-pandemic arbitration, as COVID continues to be a real threat to many lives, and everything points to the fact that we will have to continue to live with it. However, thanks to widespread vaccination and social resilience, our lives are starting to look more like they did in 2019. That is not the case for arbitration practice. I believe that arbitration stakeholders were wise enough to take the best of remote working and continue to apply it today that in-person meetings are again a reality. I anticipate this trend will continue, as certain aspects of remote practice have proved to be far more efficient. Most of the work done before the hearing, such as

2. In 2009, Mexico, my home country, saw the outbreak of the swine flu pandemic. Soon after the outbreak, the Mexican government ordered a lockdown, and after a couple of weeks everything was back to normal.

meeting with the client, interviewing witnesses, working with experts, and drafting memorials, can be done more conveniently remotely.

However, I consider that in-person hearings are more convenient, as oral arguments and physical cross-examination of witnesses and experts tend to be, in my opinion, more compelling than those made through video conferences. Additionally, in-person hearings have the benefit of having all the involved stakeholders in the same time zone, which allows for maximizing the hours of the day that can be used for the hearing, which is not possible when the parties and tribunal are in different time zones.

Notwithstanding the above, in every hearing I have participated in since in-person hearings resumed, at least one expert or witness appeared remotely. As I mentioned, this was by no means the reality before the pandemic, when the remote appearance of witnesses or experts was scarce. At least in my experience, not only hybrid proceedings but hybrid hearings are now the norm. Further, I predict that we will continue to rely on remote hearings even when in-person hearings are available to reduce costs. Accordingly, I believe that we will see more and more completely remote proceedings and hearings, especially in smaller cases.

In this sense, I believe that moving forward from the pandemic arbitration stakeholders will build upon the efficacy lessons brought by the multiple lockdowns and will continue to learn how to combine the best aspects of remote and in-person proceedings in the pursuit of one of arbitration's main commonly unfulfilled promises: cost and time efficiency. In sum, as arbitration stakeholders cope with the pandemic and its effects, I believe the new norm for arbitration practice will be hybrid, instead of fully remote or fully in person.

§17.05 THE WINNERS AND THE LOSERS

It is not my aim to identify all the arbitration stakeholders that potentially "win" or "lose" with remote and hybrid proceedings. That would require a lengthy interdisciplinary analysis across multiple jurisdictions. Therefore, I intend to present the primary examples of stakeholders that, in my opinion and based on my experience, will benefit the most from the widespread implementation of remote and hybrid proceedings and those that, in my opinion, would prefer to preserve the fully in-person practice.

[A] The Winners

I am convinced that the two main "winners" when implementing widespread remote and hybrid proceedings are the environment and the parties.

As the environment rapidly and steadily deteriorates, it should be in everyone's interest, including arbitration stakeholders, to do everything in our power to preserve the environment and reduce our carbon footprint. Unfortunately, entirely in-person proceedings are extraordinarily damaging to the environment. Before the pandemic, parties' counsel normally printed thousands or even hundreds of thousands of pages during an ordinary international arbitration. Furthermore, they would often fly many times to the same destination to meet with their client or experts and interview witnesses. All these are things that the lockdowns showed us that can be easily done through zoom meetings.

The parties would also exchange hard copies of their submissions along with hundreds or thousands of exhibits, normally transmitted by air freight, just to end up never being used by the counterparty, as sadly, the common practice in many firms would be for each lawyer to print their own hard copies. Additionally, large teams of lawyers, experts, and witnesses would often travel to other continents to attend evidentiary hearings at a tremendous environmental cost.

The Campaign for Greener Arbitration conducted a study of the environmental impact of a medium-large scale arbitration that considered the impact of printing of submissions, long and short haul flights, train and car journeys, hotel stays, and coffee cups, concluded that just under 20,000 trees are required to offset the carbon footprint of the arbitration studied.[3] Central Park has less than 20,000 trees! I knew that the fully in-person arbitration practice was not good for the environment, but I certainly did not know to what extent.

Thanks to remote and hybrid proceedings, arbitration practitioners can drastically reduce a case's carbon footprint by implementing simple measures such as using only electronic files and submissions and avoiding nonessential travel.

As I mentioned before, I believe that the other big winners when it comes to remote and hybrid proceedings are the parties, specifically, their pockets. Coincidentally, all the things that harm the environment in in-person proceedings, such as printing and flying, are also things that impact the cost of the arbitration and, therefore, the parties' pockets.

Therefore, arbitration stakeholders' actions to reduce arbitration's carbon footprint also have the benefit of making arbitration more cost-efficient, which is in the parties' best interest.

[B] The Losers

Arbitration's original promise to its users was to be a cost and time-efficient means for settling business disputes. However, today's arbitration stakeholders no longer find the main appeal of arbitration in its cost and time efficiency as they have become arbitration's main unfulfilled promise. In my opinion, remote and hybrid proceedings present an unparalleled opportunity to improve time and cost efficiency in arbitration drastically. Therefore, it is hard to speak about "losers."

However, I believe that the biggest losers will be the old-school practitioners that are reluctant or refuse to adapt to the new reality in arbitration practice. Many prominent practitioners of my generation and older have been unable to adapt to the technologies that allow remote and hybrid arbitrations. Some prominent arbitrations continue to require the parties to file hard copies of all submissions and to hold in-person meetings to decide on issues that can easily be settled remotely.

3. A significant impact, Campaign for Greener Arbitration. https://www.greenerarbitrations.com/impact.

Just like in evolution, those who fail to adapt fail to survive, arbitration practitioners unable or unwilling to adapt to the undeniable benefits of remote and hybrid proceedings will no longer be the preferred choice for the stakeholders that have embraced these benefits.

§17.06 AREAS OF POTENTIAL CONCERN

[A] Due Process Concerns

During the initial months of the COVID pandemic, many stakeholders expressed their concerns regarding the ability of remote proceedings to preserve the due process of law, specifically regarding remote hearings. During that period, many parties requested stays in their proceedings, arguing that they were entitled to an in-person hearing as a matter of due process. To settle the question, the International Council for Commercial Arbitration (ICCA) partnered up with Giacomo Rojas Elgueta, James Hoskings, and Yasmine Lahlou to conduct an impressive survey on the right to a physical hearing.[4] The study concluded that no jurisdiction analyzed expressly recognizes a right to a physical hearing. The overwhelming majority do not recognize such a right, only a handful of jurisdictions recognize such right by inference.[5]

Moreover, some of the most salient arbitral institutions, such as the ICC[6] and the London Court of International Arbitration (LCIA)[7] swiftly modified their arbitration rules to expressly recognize or clarify that hearings may be remote.

In view of the above, I believe that it is now settled that remote or hybrid proceedings do not themselves pose any threat to the parties' due process rights.

[B] Cyber Security and Data Protection

An undeniable truth of remote and hybrid proceedings is that they heavily rely on informatics technology. Therefore, all the information of any given proceeding is exposed to cyberattacks that compromise the integrity of the proceeding and the confidentiality of sensitive information.

Cyberattacks in international arbitration are a real threat and have even been raised as grounds to challenge awards.[8] However, I believe that cybersecurity threats are one of the main problems that arbitration stakeholders currently face. It is a problem that would exist regardless of the existence of remote or hybrid proceedings,

---

4. Rojas Elgueta et al., *Does a Right to a Physical Hearing Exist in International Arbitration? General Report* (https://cdn.arbitration-icca.org/s3fs-public/document/media_document/Right-to-a-Physical-Hearing-General-Report.pdf).
5. Rojas Elgueta et al., *Does a Right to a Physical Hearing Exist in International Arbitration? General Report*, p. 39.
6. *See* ICC Rules 2017 and 2021 Article 26.
7. *See* LCIA Rules 2014 and 2020 Article 19.2.
8. Cosmo Sanderson, *ICC Rejects Challenge over Alleged Cyber-Attack*, July 14, 2021, Global Arbitration Review, (https://globalarbitrationreview.com/article/icc-rejects-challenge-over-alleged-cyber-attack).

as all arbitration stakeholders are to various extents dependent on informatic technologies. They all use different protection systems, and their effectiveness may significantly vary from user to user.[9]

This is also a threat that has no clear-cut solution. However, arbitration stakeholders can mitigate risks by implementing uniform security protocols, like the one jointly published in 2020 by the ICCA, the New York City Bar Association (NYC BAR), and the Conflict Prevention & Resolution (CPR).[10]

§17.07 CONCLUSION

The COVID pandemic drastically changed how we practice law and arbitration. The pandemic forced arbitration stakeholders to quickly adapt to a fully remote practice based on technologies that have been available for years. Now that we have embraced the benefits of the remote practice, it would be foolish to go back to the way we practiced arbitration as it is undeniable that some aspects of remote proceedings significantly improve time and cost efficiency.

9. Anca M. Sattler, *Cybersecurity Threats in Arbitration Are Real: Why Take a Risk?,* ADR Institute of Canada, October 2018 (https://adric.ca/cybersecurity-threats-in-arbitration-are-real-why-take-a-risk/).
10. ICCA-NYC BAR-CPR Protocol on Cybersecurity in International Arbitration (2020 Ed.) https://cdn.arbitration-icca.org/s3fs-public/document/media_document/Report-6-icca-nyc_bar-cpr_cybersecurity_protocol_for_international_arbitration.pdf.

CHAPTER 18

Quo Vadis Arbitration Post-COVID?

Neil Kaplan CBE KC & Noam Zamir

§18.01 INTRODUCTION

Julian Lew is a leading figure in the world of arbitration. His work at both Herbert Smith and Queen Mary College (QMC) ensured that he would have a stellar career as an arbitrator. Several generations of students at QMC rightly look on him as a father figure and many current counsel and arbitrators are alumni of QMC. One of the authors of this chapter, Neil Kaplan, has known Julian Lew for over 50 years and has had the great pleasure of sitting with him and sharing panels together. It is thus an honour that we can contribute this short reflection to Julian's Liber Amicorum on the occasion of his 75th birthday. Happy birthday Julian!

The Coronavirus disease 2019 ('COVID-19') has dramatically affected most countries across the globe throughout 2020 and 2021. Millions of lives were lost, borders were closed, and millions of people were under curfew and subject to various quarantine requirements. At times it seemed that the pre-pandemic world would become the world of yesterday.[1] However, as we write this chapter, it appears that most parts of the world have returned to pre-pandemic reality. Borders have now reopened, vaccines have become efficient in preventing serious illness in the majority of cases, international tourism seems to be flourishing again, and masks are no longer mandatory in Europe and the United States.

As we return to some extent to pre-pandemic reality it is time to assess, whether international arbitration should retain anything from the pandemic period.

1. *See* Stefan Zweig, 'The World of Yesterday: Memoirs of a European' (1964) *University of Nebraska Press*.

§18.02 INTERNATIONAL ARBITRATION DURING COVID-19

As one may well expect, one clear ramification of the pandemic on international arbitration was the abundance of academic writing on the impact of international arbitration of COVID-19.[2] Another more practical ramification was the increasing reliance of stakeholders in international arbitration on online technology to conduct proceedings – and in particular, online hearings.

The idea of online arbitration is not new.[3] Various institutions like the World Intellectual Property Organization and the Hong Kong International Arbitration Centre have, years before the pandemic, relied on online services to solve various specific disputes such as domain name disputes where all submissions are done electronically. Even in the context of international arbitration, both commercial and investor-state, various stakeholders such as the United Nations and the International Chamber of Commerce have realized the importance and have since encouraged the use of online arbitration. For example, the General Assembly of the United Nations noted that *online dispute resolution can assist the parties in resolving the dispute in a simple, fast, flexible and secure manner, without the need for physical presence at a meeting or hearing.*[4]

Nevertheless, prior to the pandemic, the use of online technology in international arbitration was somewhat limited. Usually parties uploaded all their submissions onto online platforms. However, it was also customary to produce hard copies of all the submissions. Similarly, while procedural meetings were often held via audio conference calls, these meetings were also held in person. The use of private computers and the Internet in conducting these calls via video was limited.

Importantly, hearings were conducted in person. While it was not uncommon for some witnesses to give evidence by way of videoconferencing if health or distance prevented their attendance, the idea of conducting the whole hearing online was not

2. For example, Maxi Scherer, Niuscha Bassiri and Mohamed S. Abdel Wahab (eds), *International Arbitration and the COVID-19 Revolution* (Wolters Kluwer 2020); Stephan Wilske, 'The Impact of COVID-19 on International Arbitration – Hiccup or Turning Point?' (2020) 13(1) *Contemporary Asia Arbitration Journal* 7; Matt Reynolds, 'Could Zoom Jury Trials Become the Norm During the Coronavirus Pandemic?' (2020) *ABA J* https://www.abajournal.com/web/article/could-zoom-jury-trials-become-a-reality-during-the-pandemic accessed 30 May 2022.
3. While online hearings can mean the determination of cases online without any formal hearing (in this regard, *see* Richard Susskind, *Online Court and the Future of Justice* (Oxford University Press 2019)), in this chapter we refer to online arbitration and hearings to describe the use of online technology to facilitate arbitration proceedings (including hearings) that are managed by real persons – counsel and arbitrators.
4. UNCITRAL, *Technical Notes on Online Dispute Resolution* (United Nations Commission on International Trade Law April 2017), viii-ix https://uncitral.un.org/sites/uncitral.un.org/files/media-documents/uncitral/en/v1700382_english_technical_notes_on_odr.pdf accessed 30 May 2022; *see* the conference in Paris entitled 'Equal Access to Information & Justice: Online Dispute' organized by the International Chamber of Commerce, 'Three Takeaways on How Digital Technologies Are Transforming Arbitration' (2017) https://iccwbo.org/media-wall/news-speeches/three-takeaways-digital-technologies-transforming-arbitration/ accessed 30 May 2022. *See also* Noam Zamir, Online arbitration: the perspective of the arbitrator and the secretary, in Pietro Ortolani, André Janssen, Pieter Wolters (eds), 'International Arbitration and Technology' (Kluwer Law International, 2022).

even contemplated in big international cases. The fascinating fact is that despite the technology being present for years it took a pandemic to introduce it into everyday life.

In 2020, due to the COVID-19 pandemic, borders were closed or subject to quarantine requirements and states imposed various restrictions on public gatherings. This has affected the world of international arbitration in various ways. In this chapter, we wish to address two aspects: the culture of filing legal submissions and the conduct of hearings.

First, due to COVID-19, in more and more cases parties to arbitration did not produce hard copies of their submissions. Frequently, many arbitrators required only hard copies of the main submissions which are often comprised of the parties' pleadings, witness statements, expert reports and the main - but not all - exhibits and legal authorities. The change in the culture of filing legal submissions has various explanations. Many arbitrators and counsel had to work from home. Arbitrators were naturally not thrilled about the idea of having voluminous submissions and hundreds of binders stored in their homes. Moreover, counsel were often not in a position to produce hard copies of the submissions, and disruptions in mail services meant that it was not possible to rely on timely mail services.

The second biggest change in international arbitration during the pandemic related to online hearings. At the start of the pandemic, parties to arbitration often requested postponement of hearings and related procedural meetings. As a result, hearings were deferred to the end of 2021 and into 2022. As it became apparent that the COVID-19 related restrictions were not going to disappear, more and more hearings began to be fully conducted online. These online hearings were conducted when the arbitrators, counsel and witnesses all sat in different locations. This was a major development. In the end, during the pandemic, online hearings became the new norm.

The use of online arbitration has raised various legal issues, such as the circumstances under which a tribunal is permitted to compel parties to arbitration proceedings to participate in online hearings.[5] While it is beyond the scope of this chapter to address these legal issues, we do note that it is now accepted that arbitrators have authority to order online hearings, unless there is a mandatory requirement by national law (whether it is the law of the seat or the national law where the award is likely to be enforced) for a physical hearing, or the parties have expressly agreed that a hearing would only be conducted in person.[6] We also note that it has become common ground that to have one party appearing in person with the other only attending remotely is problematic in terms of due process unless both parties have

5. *See* Maxi Scherer, 'The Legal Framework of Remote Hearings' in Maxi Scherer, Niuscha Bassiri and Mohamed S. Abdel Wahab (eds), *International Arbitration and the COVID-19 Revolution* (Wolters Kluwer 2020) 78.
6. *See* Scherer (*supra* n. 5). The International Council for Commercial Arbitration found that none of the 78 jurisdictions it examined expressly guarantee the right to in-person hearings. *See* the General Report on 'Does a Right to a Physical Hearing Exist in International Arbitration?' https://www.arbitration-icca.org/right-to-a-physical-hearing-international-arbitration. In addition, after examining different jurisdictions, ICCA noted that 'the parties' agreement to hold a physical hearing is not binding on the arbitral tribunal in the Czech Republic. In Brazil, France and Indonesia it is binding, but only when such agreement was made prior to the constitution of the tribunal'. *See* 'Right to a Physical Hearing Project: The Release of 22 New Reports Reveals

agreed to it. The common view was that disputes must be resolved even during the pandemic.[7] Indeed, courts all over the world, including the US Supreme Court and UK Supreme Court, conducted online hearings in 2020 and 2021.[8] In order to avoid a potential conflict regarding the authority of the arbitrators to order online hearings it is now a standard practice for many arbitrators to include a clause in the first procedural order that provides that the tribunal has authority to conduct an online arbitration in cases of pandemics.[9]

With the ease of COVID-19 related restrictions in most parts of the world, it seems that the world is returning to what it used to be before COVID-19. This positive development raises the question of the way in which we should move forward in the way we conduct international arbitration.

§18.03 WHAT HAVE WE LEARNED FROM COVID-19?

In the post-pandemic world, we believe that the culture of producing hard copies of all submissions should remain in the past. In practice, arbitrators and opposing counsel might look at all the exhibits only once and therefore there is no reason to print all of them. Similarly, many of the legal authorities might not be crucial to the cases and there is a chance that arbitrators and opposing counsel are already familiar with the key legal authorities. While we understand that some stakeholders, whether arbitrators or counsel, require hard copies of the submissions to prepare for a case, we believe that production of these hard copies can be limited to the main pleadings, witness statements, experts reports and key exhibits. This approach is better for the environment and should also reduce some of the costs of arbitration.[10]

Interesting Trends and Significant Convergences', 8 February 2021. https://www.arbitration-icca.org/right-physical-hearing-project-release-22-new-reports-reveals-interesting-trends-and-significant.

7. *See* Toby Landau QC expressing the view that the 'world of justice cannot stop'. *See* Toby Landau QC, 'An Inside Guide to International Practice' (Oxford University, 19 May 2020) https://www.youtube.com/watch?v=u4fdYro32oc accessed 30 May 2022.
8. *See, e.g.*, Supreme Court of the United States, press release of 30 May 2022 https://www.supremecourt.gov/publicinfo/press/pressreleases/pr_04-13-20 accessed 30 May 2022.
9. For example, Linklaters model law: 'In the event of a declared public health emergency by either the World Health Organisation (the "WHO") or a national Government, as a consequence of which it is inadvisable or prohibited for the parties and/or their legal representatives to travel to, or attend any hearing ordered by the tribunal, the following shall apply: i. any such hearing shall be held via video or telephone conference upon the order of the tribunal; ii. The parties agree that no objection shall be taken to the decision, order or award of the tribunal following any such hearing on the basis that the hearing was held by video or telephone conference; and iii. In exceptional circumstances only the tribunal shall have the discretion to order that a hearing shall be held in person, but only after full and thorough consideration of the prevailing guidance of the WHO and any relevant travel or social distancing restrictions or guidelines affecting the parties and/or their legal representatives and the implementation of appropriate mitigation.' *See* Linklaters, 'Drafting for Virtual Hearings in Arbitration: Helping to Keep Matters Moving in Light of COVID-19' (*Linklaters online publication*, 16 April 2020) https://www.linklaters.com/en/insights/blogs/arbitrationlinks/2020/april/drafting-for-virtual-hearings accessed 30 May 2022.
10. On the notion of costs in arbitration, *see* Noam Zamir, 'The Issue of Costs: How Much Does ISDS Cost and Who Bears the Cost?' in J Chaisse, L Choukroune & S Jusoh (eds), *Handbook of International Investment Law and Policy* (Springer 2020); Neil Kaplan, 'Decision on Costs – A

The more difficult question is online hearings. In terms of costs, online hearings are obviously less expensive as parties need not pay for travel expenses and hearing facilities. Moreover, based on our experience online hearings work well in many respects. The management of most hearings has been smooth. There is some value in the ability to focus on the facial expressions of the witnesses, experts and counsel through a camera. In some ways, online hearings were also easier for arbitrators and counsel as they did not require long commutes. Therefore, less time was wasted on travelling and jet lag, which is something that stakeholders in international arbitration know all too well.

However, online hearings are far from a perfect experience. The move to online hearings was a result of necessity as the alternative of not conducting hearings was not possible. As the alternative of in-person hearing is now available, it is time to assess whether we should stick to online hearings in light of its advantages and disadvantages.

There are obviously various problems with online hearings. First, as the hearing participants are often based in different time zones, it can be challenging to find appropriate hearing hours. Some of the solutions adopted during the pandemic were far from ideal. One solution was to sit shorter hours, which was often hard to implement due to conflicting schedules of busy counsel and arbitrators. Another solution was to sit long hours, even through the night. While it is impossible to gauge the exact effect that this solution had on cases, the truth is that one cannot expect arbitrators or counsel to be focused in the middle of the night.

Another problem with online hearings is the phenomenon of 'Zoom fatigue'.[11] When sitting in front of the screen, people tend to have shorter attention spans and can be more easily distracted. Again, while it is possible to overcome the problem of Zoom fatigue by sitting shorter hours and having longer breaks, this solution is not always possible due to scheduling conflicts. While some scholars suggest the idea that at least some parts of the hearings might be conducted 'asynchronously',[12] we do not believe that this solution is adequate as it deprives the ability of counsel to interrupt, raise objections and for the tribunal to ask questions.

Putting the above problems aside as they can be solved, the main problem with online arbitration is connected to the precise point that it is online. One well understands that counsel prefer cross-examining in front of a live audience. They like to see the effect of their questions on the audience in the room which includes their

---

Mind Field for Arbitrators and Uncertainty for Participants' (Harbour Lecture, 19 October 2016) https://static1.squarespace.com/static/5fc4c63ed27ff856c265d945/t/5fd03811c0a29916a5643830/1607481362682/Decision+on+Costs+-+A+Mind+field+for+Arbitrators+and+Uncertainty+for+Participants.pdf accessed 30 May 2022.

11. *See* Liz Fosslien & Mollie West Duffy, 'How to Combat Zoom Fatigue' (2020) *Harvard Business Review* https://hbr.org/2020/04/how-to-combat-zoom-fatigue (accessed 30 May 2022). *See also* Manyu Jiang, 'The Reason Zoom Calls Drain Your Energy' (2020) *BBC Worklife* https://www.bbc.com/worklife/article/20200421-why-zoom-video-chats-are-so-exhausting accessed 30 May 2022.
12. Maxi Scherer, 'Asynchronous Hearings: The Next New Normal?' (2020) *Kluwer Arbitration Blog* http://arbitrationblog.kluwerarbitration.com/2020/09/09/asynchronous-hearings-the-next-new-normal/ accessed 30 May 2022.

adversaries and their witnesses. From the arbitrator's point of view, the main importance of in-person hearings is the interaction between arbitrators and the process of deliberation in person. This importance cannot be overstated. That in-person interaction enables the arbitrators to discuss the case from different angles. Often, dinners are the moments where some of the diverging opinions between the arbitrators are settled or narrowed. No amount of virtual breakout rooms can substitute for sitting around a dinner table having a good discussion about the merits of a particular argument. Furthermore, by traveling to hearings, the arbitrators also disconnect themselves from other matters and become fully engaged with the case. When working from home, it is evidently much harder to disconnect from other matters. In addition, in-person hearings provide a better chance for new arbitrators to bond and foster professional links with leading arbitrators. In that sense, online hearings are detrimental to the new generation of arbitrators because they cannot properly bond with other arbitrators. The social contact should never be underestimated and that is why some tribunals are insisting on sitting together even if the parties wish to attend virtually.

Therefore, we consider that online hearings should not substitute in-person hearings *in toto*, despite the fact that the latter are more expensive and are less environmentally friendly.[13] Nevertheless, in light of the clear cost-savings effect, time-saving effect and environmental reasons, there are many instances when online hearings would be preferable. These instances must be decided in consultation with the participants in the arbitration proceedings. However, as a benchmark, we believe that small-sum disputes and cases involving simple matters of legal interpretation that do not require the cross-examination of many witnesses are the typical cases that might be conducted online. Even in big and complex cases, while the main hearings should be conducted in person, it is evident that the days of long flights for short procedural meetings should end. While having these meetings in person has some value as it often breaks the ice between the parties and might even facilitate settlement discussions, in most cases, there is no justification to pay for the all tribunal members and counsel to fly to a specific location simply to discuss issues such as the timetable of the proceedings and procedural orders.

To conclude, COVID-19 might be remembered, among other things, as a health crisis that at least had a positive impact on arbitration as it pushed forward the use of online technology to conduct arbitration proceedings. However, while we hope that the world of international arbitration will continue to rely on online technology as described above, we do believe that in-person hearings should remain the default position in most international cases, especially in more complex disputes or high-profile cases. Our conclusion is in line with the saying that every cloud has a silver lining.

13. *See* GAR, 'Towards Greener Arbitrations: Carbon Footprint and Costs of In-Person and Virtual Hearings Compared' (12 April 2022) (concluding that virtual hearings are significantly less carbon-intensive and cheaper for arbitration parties than in person hearings).

CHAPTER 19

Interim Measures: The Critical Impact They May Have on International Arbitration

Isabelle Michou

I am one of the lucky ones who worked with Professor Lew when he was still at Herbert Smith Freehills. I witnessed first-hand the creation of one of the first dedicated international arbitration practices in a large law firm and the amazing ability he had to jungle with multiple roles: head of a successful arbitration practice, counsel, arbitrator, academic and founder of the School of International Arbitration of Queen Mary University of London. He was a great mentor for the younger associates and one of the first to welcome non-English lawyers in the firm's London office believing they could bring cross-border skills that are essential to a real international arbitration practice.

In furtherance of the tradition to mix practice and academic, this chapter is excerpted from the inaugural lecture that I gave at the Geneva Master of International Dispute Settlement (MIDS) in September 2022.

The recent events in Ukraine have brought into focus the potential power of interim measures in international disputes. Ukraine requested, and obtained in March 2022, an order for provisional measures from the International Court of Justice under the 1948 Convention on the Prevention and Punishment of the Crime of Genocide.[1] After the ICJ expressed regret that the Russian Federation did not appear at the hearing, it indicated provisional measures, including by thirteen votes to two, that Russia shall immediately suspend its military operations, and by unanimous vote, that both parties shall refrain from any action which might aggravate or extend the dispute or make it more difficult to resolve.[2] This has not stopped Russia, but the decision has been commented widely. Several states have since then intervened in the proceedings. The European Commission has issued a joint statement emphasizing that the ICJ's order 'is

1. *Allegations of genocide under the Convention on the prevention and punishment of the crime of genocide (Ukraine v. Russian Federation)*, Order, 16 March 2022.
2. *Ibid.*, para. 86.

legally binding' and any failure to comply with it constitutes a further 'breach' of international law.[3]

Nowadays, requests for interim measures have become a matter of course in most international proceedings, before international courts or arbitral tribunals, in disputes between states, between a foreign investor and a state, or in pure commercial disputes between private parties.

Focusing on international arbitration, a review of the decisions rendered by the International Centre for Settlement of Investment Disputes (ICSID) arbitral tribunals on interim measures shows that from 2006, the number of decisions has reached an average of 10 decisions a year, with some exceptions.[4]

The purpose of this chapter is to draw attention to the critical impact that interim measures may have on international arbitration proceedings. They have become a powerful procedural tool in modern resolution of international disputes. Their practical importance is obvious. They provide interim protection of the parties' rights during the potentially considerable length of the proceedings, and may even be decisive of the outcome of a case. As equally important, they can serve as guardian of the parties' behaviour throughout the proceedings and as such, are an essential part of the integrity of the process.

Many national laws and all major arbitration rules now confirm that international tribunals have a broad power to grant interim relief. This is not to say that the rules are exactly the same or that all tribunals have found the same answers as to how to exercise that power. The exercise of that power requires a delicate assessment: the denial of the interim remedy may prejudice the claimant, but its grant may prejudice the respondent.

A review of the practice of international arbitral tribunals shows that there are broadly two different approaches, which in turn depend, at least in part, on the rules applicable.

If the rules only make a general reference to the broad power to grant interim measures without any guidance (such as Article 28 of the International Chamber of Commerce (ICC) Arbitration Rules[5]), some tribunals have considered that they can simply exercise their power and grant the measures that they consider as appropriate without applying any particular standards. The rationale underlying this approach is that granting interim relief is purely a matter of discretion in light of the specific circumstances. In exercising their discretion, tribunals will however – at a minimum – assess the respective impact on each party if the measure is granted or if it is not granted. The decision will be one that appears to carry the lower risk of injustice.

3. Joint statement on supporting Ukraine in its proceeding at the International Court of Justice, European Commission, 13 July 2022.
4. Data collected from https://icsid.worldbank.org/cases/content/tables-of-decisions/provisional-measures.
5. Article 28 of the ICC Arbitration Rules states that: 'the arbitral tribunal may, at the request of a party, order any interim or conservatory measure it deems appropriate'.

By contrast, if the arbitration rules set out specific conditions for the grant of interim measures (such as Article 26 the UNCITRAL Arbitration Rules[6]), tribunals will need to apply them. However, even there, there is a large degree of discretion. This second approach will often consist in, first, assessing if the conditions are satisfied, second, if they are, assessing if there are grounds for the tribunal to exercise its discretion to order such measures, and third, if so, what measures should be ordered.

There are two key moments when a party can obtain interim relief:[7] prior to the constitution of an arbitral tribunal, or once a tribunal has been constituted. First, subject to some preliminary requirements that must be satisfied, a party may obtain interim relief that cannot await the constitution of the arbitral tribunal through emergency arbitration. That party can apply to the arbitral institution for it to appoint an emergency arbitrator on an interim basis, who will hold the fort until the main tribunal is fully constituted and can take over. This is only available under some institutional arbitration rules such as the ICC, Stockholm Chamber of Commerce (SCC) or London Court of International Arbitration (LCIA) Rules for instance, but it is not available under the ICSID Rules or the UNCITRAL Rules. The second moment is throughout the proceedings once an arbitral tribunal is fully constituted.

There is a range of objectives that the requests for interim relief may be pursuing, and correspondingly there is a large diversity of interim measures that can be granted. As a preliminary point, it is important to bear in mind that, in deciding a request for interim measures, each arbitral tribunal is solely concerned about the integrity of its own proceeding. The tribunal is not a global policeman. It is not a permanent court with general or inherent jurisdiction such as the ICJ. As a result, the objectives pursued in international arbitration are less far-reaching that the ones of the ICJ. In its recent order against Russia, the Court noted that it was mindful of 'its own responsibilities in the maintenance of international peace and security as well as in the peaceful settlement of disputes ...'. This is indeed the prime objective of international law, as enshrined in the United Nations Charter, of which the International Court is a principal organ. The International Court regularly emphasizes the 'duty' of the parties not to exacerbate the dispute. This was already described by the Court's predecessor in 1939 as a universal principle.[8]

By contrast, in international arbitration, there are two broad objectives that interim measures can pursue: first, measures designed to protect the integrity of the process itself and/or the procedural rights of a party, and second, measures designed to protect the substantive rights of a party.

---

6. Article 26 of the UNCITRAL Arbitration Rules states that: 'The arbitral tribunal may, at the request of a party, grant interim measures [...] the arbitral tribunal orders a party, for example and without limitation, to: (a) Maintain or restore the status quo pending determination of the dispute; (b) Take action that would prevent, or refrain from taking action that is likely to cause, (i) current or imminent harm or (ii) prejudice to the arbitral process itself; (c) Provide a means of preserving assets out of which a subsequent award may be satisfied; or (d) Preserve evidence that may be relevant and material to the resolution of the dispute.'
7. I will not address interim measures granted by national courts.
8. *Electricity Company of Sofia and Bulgaria* case in 1939

Starting with the first ones. Arbitral tribunals should not – and do not – hesitate to use their interim measures power in cases where they are confronted with situations where, if the measures are not granted, would otherwise frustrate a party's right to due process or the integrity of the proceedings. Typically, these include orders for the preservation of evidence, orders forbidding public statements in breach of any confidentiality obligations or otherwise likely to aggravate the parties' dispute, injunctions restraining a party from pursuing litigation elsewhere in violation of the arbitration agreement, and so on. However, as mentioned, the interim protection in international arbitration will be strictly limited to the specific proceedings and to the parties' procedural rights that are before the arbitral tribunal. In the *Plama Consortium Ltd v. Republic of Bulgaria* case,[9] the tribunal made it clear that the procedural rights that may be protected, including the general right to the preservation of the *status quo* and non-aggravation of the dispute, must relate to the requesting party's ability to have its claims in the arbitration fairly considered and decided by the arbitral tribunal. To illustrate the point, in a case *DP World v. The Republic of Djibouti*, a LCIA tribunal ordered that the state 'shall not take any steps that cause, or result in, any interference with [the claimant's] lawfully instituted and authorised legal claims against the Republic in these arbitration proceedings'.[10] But the tribunal made it clear that the interim measure was designed to protect the rights in issue, and not any other rights that may have been asserted in other parallel proceedings.

In *Quiborax v. Bolivia*,[11] the tribunal ordered the state to suspend the local criminal proceedings, even though criminal matters are generally within the exclusive scope of state sovereignty. The tribunal decided in this way because the factual accusation in the criminal proceedings was precisely that the claimants had allegedly forged documents to establish their shareholding to gain access to ICSID arbitration.[12] The status as shareholders was one of the components of the alleged crimes prosecuted. This was precisely what the tribunal had to protect in the arbitration: the ability of the claimants as investors to pursue their claims before the ICSID tribunal.

By contrast, in *ABCI v. Tunisia*,[13] the ICSID tribunal refused to order the state to suspend the ongoing criminal proceedings because it was not established by the claimant that these proceedings had a direct impact on the claimant's substantive or procedural rights in issue in the arbitration.

I would include in this category orders for security for costs because they are designed to protect the financial procedural position of a party, often the respondent,

9. *Plama Consortium Limited v. Republic of Bulgaria*, ICSID Case No. ARB/03/24, Order, 6 September 2005, para. 40: 'The rights to be preserved must relate to the requesting party's ability to have its claims and requests for relief in the arbitration fairly considered and decided by the arbitral tribunal.'.
10. *Doraleh Container Terminal SA and DP World Djibouti FZCO v The Republic of Djibouti*, LCIA Arbitration No: 183886, unpublished.
11. *Quiborax S.A., Non-Metallic Minerals S.A. & Allan Fosk Kaplún v. Plurinational State of Bolivia*, ICSID Case No. ARB/06/2, Decision on provisional measures, 26 February 2010.
12. *Ibid.*, para. 164.
13. *ABCI Investments Limited v. Republic of Tunisia*, ICSID Case No. ARB/04/12, unpublished.

in case the claimant is unsuccessful. The security serves to guarantee that the respondent will be reimbursed of its legal costs incurred to defend itself.

The other broad objective seeks to preserve or restore the *status quo*, or otherwise clarify the parties' substantive rights that are the subject of the merits of their claims. Typically, these include orders to refrain from disposing of the object of the dispute, orders requiring a contractor to continue construction works, orders requiring specific performance of a contract, order prohibiting a party from calling upon a bank guarantee, orders requiring a board meeting to take place, or suspending the effect of a board resolution, orders providing access to company records or to a site, orders appointing a neutral manager for some or all of the company's activities, orders maintaining a contract in place regardless of the purported termination notice given by the other party, and so on.

To illustrate this second objective, in seven parallel emergency arbitrations that I recently handled under two sets of rules (one SCC and six ICC), we were able to obtain interim relief of specific performance. The dispute arose out of seven contracts with seven counterparties all belonging to the same group. On the same day, they terminated the seven contracts and took aggressive actions overnight against our client. The seven emergency arbitrators agreed with us and granted the relief requested including ordering the respondents 'to immediately revert to the *status quo ante*', i.e.,. to reinstate our client in the position it was before the contracts were terminated. This is a good example of the benefits of using emergency arbitration to protect a party's substantive rights in the face of sudden and aggressive action. Not only was it a powerful tool but it also ended the dispute before the main arbitrations even took off. The parties eventually settled their dispute on very favourable terms for our client.

This leads me to my first preliminary conclusions. Whatever the applicable rules, international tribunals exercise their broad discretion in granting (or not) interim measures in a rather consistent way (with some exceptions), in light of the specific circumstances of each case. The regime of interim measures is autonomous in the sense that tribunals exercise their broad power separately from any examination of the merits of the claims. Also, the applicable law on the merits of the claims, whether national law or international law, is irrelevant when examining a request for interim measures. Another important rationale for the grant of interim measures is to combat bad conduct of the parties and protect the integrity of the process. There is often an element of good faith, whatever the purpose pursued by the interim measure.

Now turning to the question of compliance and enforceability of the decisions on interim measures. It is now widely accepted that decisions on interim measures are binding on the parties, but that was not always the case. Just to give a little bit of history. The binding nature of interim decisions was debated in the early days of ICSID arbitration because of the use of 'recommend' in Article 47 of the Convention, which meant, for a prevailing view, that the decisions were likely not legally binding. Only a minority view considered that they were binding because the parties were under an implied obligation to do nothing to frustrate their agreement to arbitrate. The binding nature of these decisions was first clearly recognized in 1999, in the case *Maffezini v.*

Spain.[14] The tribunal noted that its power to recommend interim measures was 'no less binding than that of a final award' and the word 'recommend' was 'deemed to be of equivalent value to the word "order"'.[15] Three years later, in 2001, the tribunal in *Pey Casado v. Chile* said the same thing.[16] Note the timing: 1999-2001. Shortly after, in 2006, the decisions on interim measures started to increase before ICSID tribunals. But the recognition of the binding nature of these decisions has not prevented states to refuse to comply with the decisions.

The binding nature is in fact just the starting point. To have a real impact, interim measures decisions need to be complied with by the party to whom the decision is directed, and if not, they need to be enforced if possible. But arbitral tribunals have no coercive power. We all know that an arbitral tribunal cannot send a bailiff to compel compliance with its order of interim measures. Enforcement can only be done through national courts.

That said, parties and tribunals are not short of procedural tools to ensure compliance. A party can request 'super' interim relief. This measure may be quite effective when it is granted, but it is valid only for a very limited duration, i.e., pending the outcome on the request for interim measures itself. Indeed this 'super' interim relief is likely to be complied with voluntarily by the parties because at that point, the parties have not yet set out their positions in full on the request for interim measures and may still be hoping to receive a ruling in their favour. In a way, this relief is self-efficient. There are several examples in international arbitration where this 'super' interim relief was granted by tribunals. Just to cite one: in *Igor Boyko v. Ukraine*,[17] a UNCITRAL tribunal granted the emergency relief on the ground of 'immediate danger to [the claimant's] life and safety'.[18] The tribunal noted that its power to do so was part of its broader power to grant interim measures. The measure was said to be akin to 'a form of temporary restraining measure'.[19] The respondent state was ordered to 'forthwith' refrain from taking any measures that could endanger the claimant's life and integrity pending the determination of the interim measures request. In most cases, this 'super' interim relief is granted in cases where there is compelling evidence of 'imminent injury' to the claimant.[20] By contrast, the 'super' interim relief will not be granted in cases where there is only a concern expressed by the claimant to have 'a dispassionate and serene climate' pending the examination on the request for interim measures.[21]

14. *Emilio Agustín Maffezini v. Kingdom of Spain*, ICSID Case No. ARB/97/7.
15. *Ibid.*, Procedural Order No. 2, 28 October 1999, para. 9: 'Consequently, for the purposes of this Procedural Order, the Court considers that the word "recommend" has the same value as the word "dictate [...] The Tribunal's authority to decide on the adoption of interim measures is no less binding than that of a final arbitral award."' (Translation from the original in Spanish).
16. *Víctor Pey Casado and President Allende Foundation v. Republic of Chile*, ICSID Case No. ARB/98/2, Decision on provisional measures, 25 September 2001, para. 21.
17. *Igor Boyko v. Ukraine*, PCA Case No. 2017-23, Procedural Order No. 3, 3 December 2017.
18. *Ibid.*, para. 1.
19. *Ibid.*, para. 2.3.
20. *See Igor Boyko v. Ukraine*, PCA Case No. 2017-23, Procedural Order No. 3, 3 December 2017; *Mohammed Munshi v Mongolia*, SCC Award on Emergency Measures, 5 February 2018.
21. *Mr Ayoub-Farid Michel And Mr Fadi Michel Saab (Lebanon) v. the Republic of Cyprus*, ICC Case, Procedural Order No. 1, 20 February 2015, unpublished.

A party may also seek ex parte relief. While I found this somehow foreign to the consensual nature of arbitration, it is yet contemplated in the revised UNCITRAL Model Law on commercial arbitration since 2006. Article 17B allows a party to obtain a 'preliminary order ex parte', i.e., without notice to the other party, if the tribunal considers that prior disclosure of the request for the interim measure, to the party against whom it is directed, would risk frustrating the purpose of the measure. Only 17 jurisdictions have to date adopted that particular provision including Australia, New Zealand, Hong Kong, Costa Rica.[22] Swiss law, while not an UNCITRAL-based jurisdiction, appears to recognize the power of an arbitral tribunal to issue ex parte orders.[23] The Swiss Arbitration Rules also have a provision to that effect, but allow for ex parte orders only in 'exceptional circumstances'.[24]

Other tools exist that may prompt a recalcitrant party to comply voluntarily with a decision on interim measures. For example, repeated orders by the same tribunal with some 'escalation' involving the use of increasingly mandatory language by the tribunal. This worked in *Abengoa v. Mexico*.[25] The tribunal first issued a recommendation asking the respondent state to 'take the necessary measures to restore [claimant]'s right of access to the Plant'.[26] The respondent did not comply, and, two days later, the arbitral tribunal sent a message to the parties requesting their cooperation.[27] Two weeks later, the respondent had still not complied. Claimants requested and obtained that the tribunal issued another decision ordering Mexico the same interim measures but this time using stronger language asking the respondent that it 'shall immediately take the necessary measures to reinstate SDS's right of access to the Plant'.[28] A few weeks later the respondent complied with the order.[29]

The tribunal can also find that there is a clear violation by the non-compliant party and order sanctions. This was requested, for instance, by the claimant in the *Tokios Tokėlės* case, but refused by the tribunal, because it considered that the state respondent was not in breach of its previous order. The tribunal took a restrictive definition of 'proceedings' that the state had been ordered to suspend and considered

22. Ajar Rab, *Interim Measures in International Commercial Arbitration: A Comparative Review of the Indian Experience*, 2022, pp. 449-464.
23. Georg von Segesser and Christopher Boog, 'Chapter 6: Interim Measures', in Elliott Geisinger and Nathalie Voser (eds), International Arbitration in Switzerland: A Handbook for Practitioners (Second Edition), pp. 116-118: 'Under Swiss law, it is well established that an arbitral tribunal has the power to issue interim measures on an ex parte basis.'
24. Article 29(3) of the Swiss Arbitration Rules of the Swiss Arbitration Association: 'In exceptional circumstances, the arbitral tribunal may rule on a request for interim measures by way of a preliminary order before the request has 21 been communicated to any other party, provided that such communication is made at the latest together with the preliminary order and that the other parties are immediately granted an opportunity to be heard.'
25. *Abengoa, S.A. y COFIDES, S.A. v. United Mexican States*, ICSID Case No. ARB(AF)/09/2, Final award, 18 April 2013.
26. *Ibid.*, para. 60. (Translation from the original in Spanish).
27. *Ibid.*, para. 64. (Translation from the original in Spanish).
28. *Ibid.*, para. 71. (Translation from the original in Spanish).
29. *Ibid.*, para. 75. (Translation from the original in Spanish).

that a tax investigation launched against the claimant was outside the scope of the previous order.[30]

Tribunals can, arguably, order penalties in case of non-compliance. This was requested in an ICSID case *Hydro v. Albania*[31] but was refused by the tribunal. However, interestingly the tribunal did not say it did not have the power to do so. Simply, it considered that it was not warranted in this case because it '[was] not persuaded that the conduct of the Respondent was such as to involve a contravention of the recommendation'.[32] The tribunal also noted that 'even if it had [ie. it had been persuaded], [...] monetary compensation awarded in the Final Award [would] adequately compensate the Claimants for their loss, whatever that may be'.[33] It can be argued that, in appropriate circumstances, a tribunal has the power to order a penalty, for instance a daily penalty for each day of non-compliance. This is in fact not entirely foreign to some arbitration national laws. Take for instance, French arbitration law. Article 1468 of the French Code of Civil Procedure provides that an arbitral tribunal may order any provisional measure that it deems appropriate, set conditions for such measure including if necessary, attach penalties to its order. More generally, a tribunal could monitor the situation and asks the party who has to comply with the order to inform the tribunal about progress. This is what the International Court of Justice is seeking to do. An Article 11 was added in December 2020 to the Court's Internal Judicial Practice in order to 'enhance compliance by the parties of the Court's orders on provisional measures'.[34] An ad hoc committee of three judges can assist the Court in monitoring the implementation of the provisional measures that the Court indicates. However, what we see in practice is that arbitral tribunals simply invite the requesting party to apply again for interim measures if compliance has not taken place within the specified time limit.

In case of persistent non-compliance in international arbitration, a party who has obtained interim relief is often left with no other choice but to apply to the competent national courts to seek to enforce the interim decision if that is available. The question of enforcement of interim measures is still, however, debated. Enforcement of interim measure decisions will depend on the nature of the decisions, the nature of the measures and the jurisdiction where enforcement is requested.

The decisions may take the form of a procedural order, an award or an emergency decision. The ICSID tribunal in *Hydro* clearly refused to render a partial award on the basis that a decision for interim relief can be revoked, modified or terminated at any time.[35] But more generally, intermediary decisions in the ICSID system are not in the

30. *Tokios Tokelés v. Ukraine*, ICSID Case No. ARB/02/18, Procedural Order No. 3, 18 January 2005, para. 16.
31. *Hydro Srl, Francesco Becchetti and others c. Albanie*, ICSID Case No. ARB/15/28.
32. *Hydro Srl, Francesco Becchetti and others c. Albanie*, Claimants' request for a partial award and respondent's application for revocation or modification of the order on provisional measures, 1 September 2016, para. 4.30.
33. *Ibid.*
34. https://www.icj-cij.org/en/other-texts/resolution-concerning-judicial-practice.
35. *Hydro Srl, Francesco Becchetti and others c. Albanie*, Claimants' request for a partial award and respondent's application for revocation or modification of the order on provisional measures, 1

form of an award; they are binding but are not *res judicata* until they have been incorporated into the final award.

In non-ICSID arbitration, some arbitration rules such as the SCC or UNCITRAL Arbitration Rules provide that interim measures' decisions may take the form of an order or an award. If the decision is an award, enforcement will be easier but even there, this is not guaranteed. There has long been a debate, not least because of the interim nature of the decision and whether it could be considered as an award enforceable under the New York Convention. There were some attempts in the past to tackle this issue but in vain. In 1998, at the 40th anniversary of the New York Convention, several speakers called for the need to strengthen the enforceability of interim measures. In particular, the late Johnny Veeder noted that an arbitral interim measure 'could be at least as [important as], if not more important than, an arbitral award' because, without such measures, 'it is sometimes possible for a recalcitrant party to thwart the arbitration procedure – completely and finally'.[36]

The first real attempt by the arbitration community to address the issue was in 2006 when the UNCITRAL Working Group revised the Model Law on International Commercial Arbitration. They added an Article 17H and 17I that established an explicit right and mechanism to enforce arbitral interim measures in the national courts of any relevant jurisdiction. However, only a few jurisdictions have adopted an arbitration legislation based on all or part of the Model Law.[37] In all the other jurisdictions, which have not adopted the 2006 Model Law, it is necessary to examine each national arbitration legislation, on a case-by-case basis. That said, a few courts have shown to be receptive to enforcing arbitral interim measures, even in the absence of an express statutory provision to that effect. In the US, for instance, some courts have enforced arbitral interim measures on the basis that they finally dispose of a particular request in relation to the dispute.[38] The same in Singapore.[39]

Enforcement of an emergency decision raises specific questions. In practice, parties tend to comply voluntarily with emergency arbitrators' decisions to avoid appearing uncooperative or non-compliant to the subsequent main arbitral tribunal

September 2016, para. 4.29, cited in Philippe Pinsolle, *'L'impact décisif des mesures provisoires (et sa justification théorique)'*, Revue de l'Arbitrage 2022

36. V.V. Veeder, 'Provisional and Conservatory Measures in Enforcing Arbitration Awards Under the New York Convention: Experience and Prospects' 21, UN Publication Sales No. E.99.V.2 (1999), also cited in 'Enforcement of Interim Measure', GAR, 8 June 2021, J. Castello and R. Chahine.
37. https://uncitral.un.org/en/texts/arbitration/modellaw/commercial_arbitration/status.
38. *See, e.g.*, Y Lahlou, A Poplinger and G Walters, 'Other Issues in Enforcement Proceedings', in Frischknecht et al. (eds), Enforcement of Foreign Arbitral Awards and Judgments in New York, 235, 245 to 249 (2018); *ibid.*, at 247: 'preliminary awards that require parties to take certain provisional actions during the pendency of the arbitration, such as providing pre-hearing security on the potential award, paying the advance on costs, or making a preliminary payment, have been found to satisfy the requirement for a "specific act" and enforced as "final" in New York' (footnotes omitted); *see also* the case of *Polydef kis Corp v. Transcontinental Fertiliser Co*, 1996 WL 683629 (ED Pa.), cited in 'Enforcement of Interim Measure', GAR, 8 June 2021, J. Castello and R. Chahine.
39. *PT Perusahaan Gas Negara (Persero TBK) v. CRW Joint Operation* [2015] SGCA 30, cited in 'Enforcement of Interim Measure', GAR, 8 June 2021, J. Castello and R. Chahine.

that will ultimately decide the merits of the dispute. The ICC Arbitration Rules, for instance, specifically give the arbitral tribunal the authority to decide on 'any claims arising out of or in connection with the compliance or non-compliance with the order' of the emergency arbitrator.[40] However, when a party refuses to comply with an emergency arbitrator's order, recourse to local state courts appears necessary. If the emergency decision is in the form of an award - and this is possible under the SCC Rules - the enforcement will be facilitated. But again, enforcement will depend on where enforcement is requested. In 2016, in an investor-state case, the Supreme Court of Ukraine was willing to consider enforcement of the interim relief decision granted by the emergency arbitrator under the SCC Arbitration Rules.[41] A handful of countries have addressed the uncertainties surrounding the enforceability of the emergency arbitrator's decisions by amending their arbitration law. For example, Singapore amended its Arbitration Act in 2012 providing that an emergency arbitrator constitutes an arbitral tribunal and that the decision rendered, whether an 'order' or an 'award', shall be enforceable.[42] The same in Hong Kong and New Zealand.[43] The UK Law Commission is working on a reform of its Arbitration Act to the same effect at the time of writing this chapter.[44]

This leads me to my second conclusion. Parties may find some incentive in complying voluntarily with interim decisions to avoid appearing uncooperative or non-compliant to the tribunal that will ultimately decide the merits of the dispute. But when they do not comply, enforcement of interim decisions still raises today challenges.

Even if an interim measures decision is not complied with or is not enforced, it can still have a critical impact on the proceedings.

It has been reported by the ICC Task Force on Emergency Arbitration that an order by the emergency arbitrator not to call a performance bond - that was not complied with by the respondent - was nevertheless relied upon as a fact to get a court order to stop the payment. In this case, as I understand it, the first ranking bank paid the respondent. The party who had obtained the emergency relief then applied to the national court of the counter-guarantor bank. Although the order of the emergency arbitrator was not binding on the court, the court took it into account - and enjoined the counter-guarantor bank from paying.[45]

The ultimate sanction of non-compliance of interim measures' decisions is the power of the arbitral tribunal to render the final award.

Tribunals may draw adverse inferences in their decisions on the merits. This is a recurrent theme in the area of preservation of documents. In *Gerald International*

40. Article 29(4) of the ICC Arbitration Rules.
41. *JKX Oil & Gas plc, Poltava Gas B.V. and Poltava Petroleum JV v. Ukraine,* Decision of the Supreme Court of Ukraine, 24 February 2016.
42. https://hsfnotes.com/arbitration/2012/04/27/amendments-to-singapores-arbitration-laws/.
43. Section 22 B (1) of the Arbitration Ordinance of Hong Kong; Article 2 of the New Zealand Arbitration Act states that arbitral tribunal includes 'any emergency arbitrator appointed'
44. The Law Commission, Review of the Arbitration Act, Summary of Consultation Paper, 7.97.
45. ICC Commission Report on Emergency Arbitrator proceedings, p. 34, para. 207.

Limited v. Sierra Leone,[46] documents were seized by the respondent state and the claimant had been unsuccessful in its request for restitution of the documents. The tribunal however ruled that: 'In case the seized documents were no longer available in the course of these ICSID proceedings, the Tribunal would be entitled to eventually draw adverse inference.'[47]

Another, more frequent, way to sanction non-compliance is by a decision on costs. The new ICSID Arbitration Rule 52(1) now says it explicitly. In allocating the costs of the proceeding between the parties, the tribunal shall consider the conduct of the parties during the proceeding which includes 'the extent to which they complied with the orders and decisions of the Tribunal'.[48]

Interim measures may also have a decisive impact on the outcome of the claims even if not complied with, as I mentioned earlier with the seven emergency arbitrations.

However, these ultimate sanctions have some limits. What is the point in waiting for the final award if the party's ability to pursue the arbitration, or its ability to present its case, has been hindered by the conduct of the other party? This can rarely be compensated with monetary relief in the final award.

But there is also a political impact that may be critical - even in case of non-compliance. This is true especially in the context of disputes involving states.

Lord Collins noted in his Course at The Hague in 1992, commenting about the International Court's practice, that: 'A Claimant, well knowing that the order may be ineffective, nevertheless desires a judicial forum for its grievances, and a political forum in which to complain of the Respondent's disregard of the Court's judgment.'[49]

As mentioned at the outset of this chapter, when the ICJ ordered Russia to suspend its military operations in Ukraine, there was an incredible response and support from the international community, governments and institutions to coordinate sanctions and export controls levied, adding to Russia's increasing isolation on the international scene. Several states have intervened in the proceedings before the International Court in support of Ukraine. The European Commission has issued a joint statement to remind that non-compliance constitutes a further breach of international law.

The need for more transparency in investor-state arbitration also responds to the same need to make public the state respondent's claimed failures.

All of these confirm the critical effectiveness - albeit indirect - of interim measures.

To conclude, interim measures form an autonomous, international and rather consistent regime that has been shaped over the years. Their practical importance is obvious. They provide interim protection of the parties' rights (whether procedural or

46. *Gerald International Limited v. Sierra Leone*, ICSID Case No. ARB/19/31, Procedural Order No. 2, 28 July 2020.
47. *Ibid.*, para. 215.
48. Article 52(1) of the 2022 ICSID Arbitration Rules.
49. L. Collins, *Provisional and Protective Measures in International Litigation* (Volume 234), Collected Courses of the Hague Academy of International Law, 1992, pp 219-220.

substantive) during the proceedings, and may sometimes be decisive of the outcome of a case. They also protect the integrity of the process itself. As such they can play a critical role in modern resolution of international disputes - by making the process more efficient, fair and peaceful. However, parties should be well advised to articulate their requests properly and only where circumstances justify it. Arbitral tribunals have no tolerance for fanciful requests. They also, generally, make careful decisions with the use of their powers in order to ensure that they retain the confidence of both parties.

As enforcement still raises some challenges today, this should be tackled by the arbitration community to increase even more the effectiveness of interim measures. Tribunals do not like to see that their decisions are deprived of effects. Looking at the outcome on the ICSID decisions that have been made public, about 35% of the requests have been accepted in full or in part by ICSID tribunals.[50] One can wonder if that percentage would not increase if tribunals knew that enforcement of their decisions was better guaranteed in case of non-compliance.

50. Data collected from https://icsid.worldbank.org/cases/content/tables-of-decisions/provisional-measures.

CHAPTER 20

Forced Joinder: Arbitration Without Privity or Consent in Disguise?

Maxi Scherer & Ole Jensen

§20.01 INTRODUCTION

Some 20 years ago, Professor Julian Lew, together with his colleagues Loukas Mistelis and Stefan Kröll, published a treatise on *Comparative International Commercial Arbitration*.[1] It has since become one of the main reference works for international arbitration law, cited widely across court decisions, arbitral awards and scholarship.[2] It has also remained remarkably accurate. Through a combination of succinctness and foresight the book presents solutions to pervasive issues that still hold true today – despite entering its third decade.

The authors' treatment of joinder in international arbitration is a case in point. As a fundamental difference to litigation – where state courts possess the sovereign power to coerce third parties into joining ongoing proceedings – arbitration's nature as a consent-based dispute resolution mechanism makes tools like joinder and intervention

1. Julian Lew, Loukas Mistelis & Stefan Kröll, *Comparative International Commercial Arbitration* (Kluwer 2003).
2. *See, e.g.*, *PT First Media TBK v. Astro Nusantara International BV* [2013] SGCA 57, para. 177 (Singapore Court of Appeal); *Dallah Real Estate and Tourism Holding Company v. The Ministry of Religious Affairs, Government of Pakistan* [2010] UKSC 46, 3 November 2010, paras 108, 117 (U.K. Supreme Court); *Enka Insaat Ve Sanayi AS v. Insurance Company Chubb and Chubb European Group SE* [2020] UKSC 38, 9 October 2020, para. 130; Partial Award of 15 January 2007 in *Sonera Holding B.V. v. Çukurova Holding A.S.*, ICC Case No. 13856/AVH/EC/GZ, para. 188; Partial Award on Jurisdiction of 6 December 2004 in *UEG Araucária Ltda. v. Companhia Paranaense de Energia (COPEL)*, ICC Case No. 12656/KGA, para. 80; Final Award of 12 November 2010 in *Frontier Petroleum Services Ltd. v. The Czech Republic*, PCA Case No. 2008-09, paras 486, 528; Nigel Blackaby & Constantine Partasides, *Redfern and Hunter on International Arbitration*, paras 3.12, 3.34, 9.44, *passim* (Oxford University Press 2015); Gary Born, *International Commercial Arbitration*, pp. 551, 641, 707, *passim* (3rd ed. Kluwer 2021).

less accessible. As Lew, Mistelis and Kröll aptly put it, '[t]he problem ... is that due to the consensual nature of arbitration in general an agreement to arbitrate between all parties is required'.[3] Given that in a dispute there is typically at least one party who considers it more beneficial for a joinder not to occur, the authors shift perspective to the pre-dispute stage. According to them, the necessary consent 'may be given at an earlier stage ..., for example by agreeing to arbitration under one of the few arbitration rules which allow for joinder or the intervention of third parties'.[4]

Back in 2003 there were indeed only few arbitration rules that provided for the joinder of third parties.[5] In the following twenty years, this landscape has changed. Many of the leading arbitral institutions have realized that their users consider the 'lack of power in relation to third parties' one of the 'worst features' of arbitration.[6] To improve this perceived shortcoming and make arbitration more appealing to companies involved in large multi-party projects, virtually all arbitral institutions have introduced rules addressing joinder.[7]

Most of them, however, stop short of addressing the most delicate issue. They only provide for joinder where all parties are subject to the same arbitration agreement or agree on a joinder post-hoc, once the dispute has arisen.[8] The obvious downside of this approach is that '[t]here will usually be at least one party who sees advantages in separate proceedings' and will thus object to a joinder.[9] What is needed, then, is a mechanism by which a third party can be joined without the need for a post-hoc agreement of all disputing parties.

This is where rules like the 2020 LCIA Rules (and equally their 1998 and 2014 iterations), the 2021 Swiss Rules and the 2021 Vienna Rules come in. The 2020 LCIA Rules only require the consent of one of the disputants and the third party, and thus allow for joinder despite the objection of one of the parties.[10] The Swiss and Vienna Rules are worded even more broadly, essentially providing the tribunal with full

3. Julian Lew, Loukas Mistelis & Stefan Kröll, *Comparative International Commercial Arbitration*, para. 16-37 (Kluwer 2003).
4. Julian Lew, Loukas Mistelis & Stefan Kröll, *Comparative International Commercial Arbitration*, para. 16-42 (Kluwer 2003).
5. As discussed below, the 1998 LCIA Rules were an exception.
6. Queen Mary University & White & Case, *2018 International Arbitration Survey: The Evolution of International Arbitration*, p. 8 (2018). *See also* ICC, *Final Report on Multi-Party Arbitrations*, 6(1) ICC Ct. Bull., section 5 (1995); Nathalie Voser & Anke Meier, *Joinder of Parties or Need to (Sometimes) Be Inefficient*, in Christian Klausegger et al. (eds), *Austrian Yearbook on International Arbitration Volume 2008*, p. 115 (Manz 2008).
7. *See, e.g.*, 2018 HKIAC Rules, Article 27; 2021 ICC Rules, Article 7; 2021 ICDR Rules; 2016 SIAC Rules, Rule 7; 2021 AFSA Rules, Article 29; 2018 DIS Rules, Article 19; 2015 NAI Rules, Article 37; 2017 SCC Rules, Article 13.
8. 2018 HKIAC Rules, Article 27.1; 2016 SIAC Rules, Rule 7.1; 2017 SCC Rules, Article 13(5); 2021 AFSA Rules, Article 29(1)(a) and Article 29(1)(b).
9. Julian Lew, Loukas Mistelis & Stefan Kröll, *Comparative International Commercial Arbitration*, para. 16-38 (Kluwer 2003).
10. 2020 LCIA Rules, Article 22.1(x) ('The Arbitral Tribunal shall have the power ... to allow one or more third persons to be joined in the arbitration as a party provided any such third person and the applicant party have consented expressly to such joinder in writing').

discretion whether to order joinder without any express requirement of consent.[11] As joinder under these provisions can result in a tri- or multipartite arbitration to which one more of the parties object, this mechanism has been dubbed 'forced joinder'.[12]

At first blush, the notion of forcing parties to arbitrate with others with whom there is no pre-existing arbitration agreement in place 'appears to be in conflict with [a] basic principle of arbitration'.[13] Typically, the parties' consent is required not only with respect to whether but also with whom they wish to arbitrate.[14] A forced joinder could then be perceived as an attack on the 'citadel of privity', as Professor Jan Paulsson seminally put it in addressing investor-state arbitration.[15] Similarly, some commentators depict the device of forced joinder as 'a departure from the principle of party autonomy'.[16]

And yet forced joinder has existed under the LCIA Rules at least since 1998 and is now also available under other arbitration rules. According to Lew, Mistelis and Kröll, there is no issue because all disputants have given their advance consent to forced joinder by agreeing to arbitrate under the LCIA (or parallel) rules.[17] As a consequence of this agreement, 'none of the parties can object when a third party wants to join with the consent of another party'.[18]

---

11. 2021 Swiss Rules, Article 6(3) ('After the constitution of the arbitral tribunal, any crossclaim, request for joinder or request for intervention shall be decided by the arbitral tribunal, after consulting with all parties, taking into account all relevant circumstances.'); 2021 Vienna Rules, Article 14.1 ('The joinder of a third party in an arbitration, as well as the manner of such joinder, shall be decided by the arbitral tribunal upon the request of a party or a third party after hearing all parties and the third party to be joined as well as after considering all relevant circumstances.').
12. Gary Born, *International Arbitration: Law and Practice* 275 (3rd ed. Kluwer 2021). *See also PT First Media TBK v. Astro Nusantara International BV* [2013] SGCA 57, para. 176 (Singapore Court of Appeal) (citing Gary Born, *International Arbitration: Law and Practice* 228-229 (Kluwer 2012)). In this sense, the term 'forced joinder' neither applies to cases in which the third party is a party to the underlying arbitration agreement nor to cases in which the third party objects to being joined.
13. Julian Lew, Loukas Mistelis & Stefan Kröll, *Comparative International Commercial Arbitration*, para. 16-40 (Kluwer 2003).
14. *See also* Peter Ashford, *The Power to Join Parties or Consolidate Separate Arbitrations in International Arbitration*, 87 Int'l J. Arb. Med. & Disp. Mgmt 381, 383 (2021) ('In [concluding an arbitration agreement], parties agree to arbitrate with certain other parties (their contractual counterpart) according to specified procedures. They do not typically merely agree to arbitrate with anybody, in any set of proceedings.'); Manuel Gómez Carrión, *Joinder of Third Parties: New Institutional Developments*, 31 Arb. Int'l. 479, 481 (2015).
15. Jan Paulsson, *Arbitration Without Privity*, 10(2) ICSID Review 232, 255 (1995).
16. *See* Gordon Smith, *Comparative Analysis of Joinder and Consolidation Provisions under Leading Arbitral Rules*, 35(2) J. Intl. Arb. 173, 181 (2018). *See also* Bernard Hanotiau, *Complex Arbitrations: Multi-party, Multi-contract, Multi-issue – A Comparative Study* 330 (2nd ed. Kluwer 2020) ('Arbitral tribunals are likely to be reluctant to join a third party if there is no arbitration agreement binding that third party with the parties to the arbitration or if not all parties involved agree to the joinder.'); Alexis Mourre, *L'Intervention des Tiers à l'Arbitrage*, IV(16) Rev. Bras. Arb. 76, 90 (2007) ('The condition of agreement by all parties … disappears here, leaving only that of the consent of the third party') (authors' translation); Moritz Keller & Paul Hauser, *Balancing Procedural Flexibility with the Parties' Right to Equal Treatment under the 2021 ICC Joinder Rules*, SchiedsVZ 68, 71 (2022).
17. Julian Lew, Loukas Mistelis & Stefan Kröll, *Comparative International Commercial Arbitration*, para. 16-44 (Kluwer 2003).
18. *Ibid.*, para. 16-42.

The purpose of the present contribution is to revisit and test this hypothesis. Is the mere agreement to arbitrate under rules that do not require all parties' consent a sufficient basis for a tribunal to force a joinder? Or are we then faced with an unprincipled arbitration without privity?

§20.02 CONSENT IN DISGUISE: DE-CONSTRUCTING THE DOGMATIC FOUNDATION OF FORCED JOINDER

The question whether provisions such as those contained in the 2020 LCIA Rules and 2021 Swiss Rules sufficiently encapsulate parties' advance consent to a forced joinder has engaged courts and commentators. Perhaps the most famous instance is the Singapore Court of Appeal's 2013 decision in *PT First Media TBK v. Astro Nusantara International BV*.[19] In the underlying arbitration, an arbitral tribunal constituted under the 2007 SIAC Rules had ordered a forced joinder based on Article 24(b) of the 2007 SIAC Rules. According to this provision 'the Tribunal shall have the power to ... allow other parties to be joined in the arbitration with their express consent'.[20] The tribunal reasoned that this broadly worded provision allowed it to order the joinder of a third party against the objection of one of the disputing parties.[21]

The Singapore Court of Appeal disagreed. It emphasized the importance of consent, stating that '[t]he terms of any arbitration reference must ultimately lie within the limits described by the arbitration agreement'.[22] However, '[i]f there is consent given in any form, either under the arbitration agreement or through subscription to a set of institutional rules which ***unambiguously*** permits forced joinders, that would suffice to negative any subsequent allegation that there was no agreement to arbitrate with the joined party'.[23] The court thus established the standard that the applicable arbitration rules must 'unambiguously' provide for forced joinder. Without saying so expressly, the underlying reasoning appears to have been that if arbitration rules are indeed clear in providing for forced joinder, parties choosing these rules must be presumed to have accepted in advance that they might be forced to ultimately arbitrate with third parties.

This would appear to apply to the LCIA Rules. Since their 1998 version, they have only required the consent of the 'third person and the applicant party'.[24] Notably, the Singapore Court of Appeal also confirmed the unambiguous availability of forced

19. *PT First Media TBK v. Astro Nusantara International BV* [2013] SGCA 57 (Singapore Court of Appeal).
20. 2007 SIAC Rules, Article 24(b) (emphasis added). *See also PT First Media TBK v. Astro Nusantara International BV* [2013] SGCA 57, para. 180 (Singapore Court of Appeal).
21. *PT First Media TBK v. Astro Nusantara International BV* [2013] SGCA 57, para. 178 (Singapore Court of Appeal).
22. *PT First Media TBK v. Astro Nusantara International BV* [2013] SGCA 57, para. 181 (Singapore Court of Appeal).
23. *Ibid.*, para. 177 (Singapore Court of Appeal) (emphasis added).
24. 1998 LCIA Rules, Article 22.1(h). *See also PT First Media TBK v. Astro Nusantara International BV* [2013] SGCA 57, para. 180 (Singapore Court of Appeal); Maxi Scherer, Lisa Richman & Rémy Gerbay, *Arbitrating under the 2020 LCIA Rules: A User's Guide* 311 (Kluwer 2021); Gary Born, *International Commercial Arbitration* 2801 (3rd ed. Kluwer 2021).

joinder under the more broadly worded Swiss Rules. At the time, the Swiss Rules provided that 'where a party to pending arbitral proceedings under these Rules requests that one or more third persons participate in the arbitration, the arbitral tribunal shall decide on such request, after consulting with all of the parties, including the person or persons to be joined, taking into account all relevant circumstances'.[25] The court contrasted this provision with Article 24(b) of the 2007 SIAC Rules which refers to the tribunal's power 'to ... allow other ***parties*** to be joined'.[26] From this reference to 'parties' the court deduced that the joining party needed to be a party to the underlying arbitration agreement.[27] It held that 'the overarching imperative of clarity in setting out standard rules, and the internal logic of the consensual basis of an agreement to arbitrate all militate against the Tribunal's [order of a forced joinder]'.[28]

Conversely, 'a differentiating term like "third person", as with the ... Swiss Rules, would have been a straightforward solution' to 'unambiguously' provide for forced joinder.[29] At least implicitly, the Singapore Court of Appeal thus confirmed that parties consent to a forced joinder if they choose to arbitrate under the 2012 Swiss Rules.[30] Notably, the 2021 Swiss Rules now also refer to the joinder of an 'additional party' rather than a 'third person'.[31] Based on the logic of the *PT First Media* court, this reference to a 'party' would mean that forced joinder has ceased to exist under the revised Swiss Rules. It is doubtful whether this was really the intention behind the 2021 Swiss Rules.[32]

Although establishing the criterion of 'unambiguity', and confirming at least implicitly that the LCIA and Swiss Rules meet this threshold, the Singapore Court of Appeal was hesitant to fully embrace the concept of pre-existing consent to forced joinder. It criticized the wording of Article 24(b) as 'com[ing] precariously close to creating on the part of the existing parties to an agreement to arbitrate under the 2007 SIAC Rules, a unilateral offer to arbitrate with an indeterminate class of potential

25. 2012 Swiss Rules, Article 4(2).
26. 2007 SIAC Rules, Article 24(b) (emphasis added). *See also PT First Media TBK v. Astro Nusantara International BV* [2013] SGCA 57, para. 180 (Singapore Court of Appeal).
27. *PT First Media TBK v. Astro Nusantara International BV* [2013] SGCA 57, paras 180-187 (Singapore Court of Appeal).
28. *PT First Media TBK v. Astro Nusantara International BV* [2013] SGCA 57, para. 215 (Singapore Court of Appeal). Thus, the Court only allowed partial enforcement of the award and denied the enforcement with respect to the additional parties (para. 247).
29. *Ibid.*, paras 180 and 187 (Singapore Court of Appeal).
30. *But see PT First Media TBK v. Astro Nusantara International BV* [2013] SGCA 57, para. 176 ('[The LCIA and Swiss] rules are not before us and we therefore shall not express any views on them.') (Singapore Court of Appeal).
31. 2021 Swiss Rules, Article 6(1) ('[A] party asserting a claim against an additional party (joinder) ... shall do so by submitting a notice of claim.') and Article 6(3) ('[A]ny ... request for joinder ... shall be decided by the arbitral tribunal, after consulting with all parties, taking into account all relevant circumstances').
32. *See, e.g.*, Daniel Girsberger and Nathalie Voser, *International Arbitration: Comparative and Swiss Perspectives*, at paras 582-583 (4th ed. Schulthess 2021) (who do not address the change in wording but nevertheless opine that (even under the old Swiss Rules) 'Art. 4(2) of the 2012 Swiss Rules (Art. 6(3) and (4) as revised in 2021) cannot be a substitute for the consent of the parties').

disputants'.[33] This was problematic as, in the court's view, '[a] tribunal cannot extend its jurisdiction to disputes over which it has no jurisdiction by simply purporting to rely on Article 24'.[34] As the court considered such pre-existing jurisdiction necessary, it considered Article 24(1)(b) merely 'as a procedural power, rather than a means for a tribunal to extend its jurisdiction.'[35] The court therefore concluded that:

> [w]e do not think that any set of arbitration rules, unless explicitly stated otherwise (and even then, we would reserve our views), could provide for such unlimited jurisdiction. ... In our judgment, the general position must be that the arbitration agreement sets the parameters of the tribunal's jurisdiction. This follows from the premise that arbitration references spring from the continuous agreement to arbitrate future disputes.[36]

Thus, while initially endorsing the solution provided in the LCIA and Swiss Rules, the Singapore Court of Appeal ultimately considerably caveated its 'unambiguity' criterion. It appears to have perceived the question primarily as one of the tribunal's power under a given set of arbitration rules. It did not consider it likely that the parties' choice of such rules indicates their willingness to arbitrate with 'an indeterminate class of potential disputants'. Ultimately, the court appears to have made a distinction between forced joinder provided for in an arbitration agreement (or unambiguously in arbitration rules) and an agreement on forced joinder that was formed later (which it appears to have had more difficulty to accept).

This is an unprincipled approach to the issue. The core question should not be by which means the parties agree on the participation of a non-party to the arbitration agreement but whether they do so at all. Accordingly, the *PT First Media* decision has been criticized for its hesitancy:

> Where institutional rules (or an arbitration agreement) expressly permit a non-party to the arbitration agreement to be joined into an arbitration, regardless of the consent of the existing parties to the arbitration agreement, there should be no questions as to validity.[37]

Indeed, there is an oft-cited dogmatic explanation of how the (post-hoc) arbitration agreement between the disputing and the joining parties is formed. A party's choice to

33. *PT First Media TBK v. Astro Nusantara International BV* [2013] SGCA 57, para. 179 (Singapore Court of Appeal).
34. *Ibid.*, para. 181.
35. *Ibid.*
36. *Ibid.*
37. Gary Born, *International Commercial Arbitration* 2805 (3rd ed. Kluwer 2021). *See also* Peter Ashford, *The Power to Join Parties or Consolidate Separate Arbitrations in International Arbitration*, 87 Int'l J. Arb. Med. & Disp. Mgmt 381, 403 (2021) ('[C]onsent to joinder is usually manifested by the incorporation of institutional rules that provide for joinder or consolidation'); Gordon Smith, *Comparative Analysis of Joinder and Consolidation Provisions under Leading Arbitral Rules*, 35 J. Int'l Arb. 173, 176 (2018) ('Parties, by agreeing to institutional arbitral rules in their arbitration agreement, are taken to have impliedly consented to the joinder and consolidation provisions contained in the rules, together with the consequences arising from their operation'); Julian Lew, Loukas Mistelis & Stefan Kröll, *Comparative International Commercial Arbitration*, para. 16-44 (Kluwer 2003) ('[T]he second party to the arbitration agreement does not have to expressly consent to the joinder. It has done so by agreeing to the LCIA Rules').

arbitrate under the rules of an arbitral institutions that foresee the possibility of joining initially unidentified third parties is understood as that party's standing offer to join such a third party once arbitration proceedings have commenced (*offerta ad incertas personas*). The third party accepts this offer when it asks to be included in the ongoing proceedings (intervention) or consents to being added (joinder). Thus, a tri- or multipartite agreement between the original disputants and the joining party is formed which provides for the tribunal's jurisdiction over all parties - or so the argument goes.[38]

§20.03 ARBITRATION WITHOUT PRIVITY? QUESTIONING THE TRUE EXISTENCE OF A STANDING OFFER FOR THIRD PARTIES TO JOIN

Although the construct of a new multilateral arbitration agreement is perpetuated in legal commentary, there is good reason to revisit its reliability. Indeed, there are at least four plausible arguments why the standing offer to join unidentified third parties is a pure fiction and may have to be rejected.

First, the assumption of a standing offer is divorced from what most commercial parties can be reasonably presumed to understand and expect when agreeing to any set of arbitration rules. As noted above, a standing offer is readily assumed under the LCIA Rules which stipulate on their face that only the consent of the applicant and third party is required.[39] But already under the Swiss and Vienna Rules consent is one step removed. These rules are much less express with respect to the availability of forced joinder as they simply do not exclude it.[40] Even a close review of the language of those rules does not reveal that their choice entails the extension of an offer to add third parties.

Realistically, it is thus unlikely that all parties to arbitration agreements designating the LCIA, Swiss or Vienna Rules will be aware of their standing offer to join third

38. *See* Gary Born, *International Commercial Arbitration* 2805 (3rd ed. Kluwer 2021); Maxi Scherer, Lisa Richman & Rémy Gerbay, *Arbitrating under the 2020 LCIA Rules: A User's Guide*, 311-312 (Kluwer 2021); Dongdoo Choi, *Joinder in International Commercial Arbitration*, 35(1) Arb. Intl. 29, 44-45 (2019); Manuel Gómez Carrión, *Joinder of Third Parties: New Institutional Developments*, 31(3) Arb. Intl. 479, 487 (2015); Shai Wade et al., *A Commentary on the LCIA Arbitration Rules 2014*, para. 22-027 (Sweet & Maxwell 2015); Peter Turner and Reza Mohtashami, *A Guide to the LCIA Arbitration Rules*, para. 6.49 (OUP 2009). *See also CJD v. CJE* [2021] SGHC 61, para. 45 (Singapore High Ct.).
39. *See above*, at §20.2.
40. *See* 2021 Swiss Rules, Article 6(3) ('After the constitution of the arbitral tribunal, any crossclaim, request for joinder or request for intervention shall be decided by the arbitral tribunal, after consulting with all parties, taking into account all relevant circumstances.'); 2021 Vienna Rules, Article 14(1) ('The joinder of a third party in an arbitration, as well as the manner of such joinder, shall be decided by the arbitral tribunal upon the request of a party or a third party after hearing all parties and the third party to be joined as well as after considering all relevant circumstances.'). *See also* Stavros Brekoulakis, *Third Parties in International Commercial Arbitration*, paras 1.11, 3.95 (OUP 2010); Cristian Conejero Roos, *Multi-Party Arbitration and Rule-Making: Same Issues, Contrasting Approaches*, in Albert Jan van den Berg (ed.), *50 Years of the New York Convention* 411, 423 (Kluwer 2009).

parties to an arbitration they might become involved in. It is considerably more likely that those parties have chosen a reputable institution to conduct their arbitration without going over its rules with a fine-tooth comb, assessing for each provision what the potential consequences of their choice may be. It is also likely that those same parties expect to arbitrate with the party with whom they concluded their arbitration agreement – not with unidentified third parties which might later wish to take part in proceedings.

The surprise parties might feel when suddenly a third party is added to 'their' arbitration becomes even more pronounced in the case of forced intervention. Some commentators understand Article 4(2) of the 2012 and 2004 Swiss Rules to allow the intervention of a third party against all disputing parties' objection.[41] Again, this is explained by those parties' advance consent or standing offer for any third party to intervene in their arbitration, which the third party accepts with its request to be joined.[42] Most if not all parties would be surprised, however, that by the mere wish of a third party, which is not privy to the underlying arbitration agreement, that third party can join and arbitrate with parties even if they unanimously object. This shows that there is a measure of artificiality in feigning a standing offer by the choice of institutional rules with broad language.

Second, one might also consider the situation where arbitration rules are changed after the original arbitration agreement is concluded to introduce an unambiguous

---

41. Richard Bamforth & Katerina Maidment, *'All Join In' or Not? How Well Does International Arbitration Cater for Disputes Involving Multiple Parties or Related Claims?*, ASA Bulletin 3, 12 (2009); Filip de Ly, *Third Party Participation*, in Markus Wirth (ed.), *Best Practices in International Arbitration*, ASA Special Series No. 26, 57, 69 (2006); Philippe Gilliéron & Luc Pittet, *Article 4*, in Tobias Zuberbühler, Christoph Müller & Philipp Habegger (eds), *Swiss Rules of International Arbitration* 36, 41 (1st ed. Juris 2005). *See also* Dorothee Schramm, *Commentary on the Swiss Rules: Article 4*, in Manuel Arroyo (ed.), *Arbitration in Switzerland: The Practitioner's Guide* 483, 494 (2nd ed. Kluwer 2018); Philippe Bärtsch & Angelina M. Petti, *Article 4*, Tobias Zuberbühler, Christoph Müller & Philipp Habegger (eds), *Swiss Rules of International Arbitration* 53, 63 (2nd ed. Juris 2013); Nathalie Voser, *Multi-Party Disputes and Joinder of Third Parties*, in Albert Jan van den Berg (ed.), *50 Years of the New York Convention* 343, 395-96 (Kluwer 2009).
42. Filip de Ly, *Third Party Participation*, in Markus Wirth (ed.), *Best Practices in International Arbitration*, ASA Special Series No. 26, 57, 69 (2006) ('I interpret Article 4 Swiss Rules as an anticipatory consent of the parties to authorize the arbitral tribunal to order joinder or intervention and as an irrevocable offer to the third party to arbitrate with it if joinder or intervention is ordered.'); Richard Bamforth & Katerina Maidment, *'All join in' or Not? How Well Does International Arbitration Cater for Disputes Involving Multiple Parties or Related Claims?*, ASA Bulletin 3, 12 (2009); Philippe Gilliéron & Luc Pittet, *Article 4*, Tobias Zuberbühler, Christoph Müller & Philipp Habegger (eds), *Swiss Rules of International Arbitration* 36, 41 (1st ed. 2005). *But see* Daniel Girsberger and Nathalie Voser, *International Arbitration: Comparative and Swiss Perspectives*, at para. 583 (4th ed. 2021) ('This provision does not refer to consent at all .... Given the consensual nature of arbitration, it is argued that Art. 4(2) of the 2012 Swiss Rules (Art. 6(3) and (4) as revised in 2021) cannot be a substitute for the consent of the parties.'); Paolo Patocchi, *National Report for Switzerland (2018 through 2022)*, in Lise Bosman (ed.), *ICCA International Handbook on Commercial Arbitration* 1, 29-30 (2022) ('Art. 4(2) of the Swiss Rules does not state that consent is not required under the Swiss Rules with regard to intervention and joinder. The general principle of the parties' consent which governs (international) arbitration in Switzerland therefore also applies to arbitration under the auspices of the Swiss Rules. The departure from such a general and fundamental principle would have required express language').

provision on forced joinder. Typically, there is no question that the parties' agreement to arbitrate under a certain set of arbitration rules refers to the iteration of those rules in force at the time of commencement of the arbitration.[43] But what does this mean for the standing offer to join third parties supposedly made when submitting to those arbitration rules? Are parties presumed to make a standing offer to unidentified third parties at the moment the new arbitration rules enter into force – even if that is years after they concluded their arbitration agreement and they are unaware of the rule change? Feigning such an offer is a conceptual stretch – and potentially far removed from the parties' expectations when agreeing to arbitrate under the respective rules.

Third, it is curious that the alleged standing offer is supposedly irrevocable. Most proponents of a forced joinder argue that by choosing relevant arbitration rules parties extend a standing offer which they later cannot revoke.[44] That too requires closer scrutiny. There is no question that parties cannot unilaterally denounce an arbitration agreement. It is a contract which must be honoured. But a unilateral standing offer is a different creature. Under more than a few contract laws, standing offers to an uncertain group of recipients can be revoked before accepted.[45] This means that a party agreeing to arbitrate under the LCIA Rules would have to be able to revoke its offer to join an unidentified group of third parties until such time as a third party accepts the standing offer (by consenting to be joined). But if that is true, the instrument of forced joinder would lose most of its teeth: once a dispute involving a potential third party arises a party fearing that the other party might attempt to join that third party could simply revoke its standing offer.

Fourth, all rules providing for forced joinder ultimately subject this joinder to the tribunal's discretion.[46] Thus, even where the presumed standing offer is accepted by a third party, the tribunal might still exercise its discretion to not allow the third party to participate. If, however, the standing offer and its acceptance create a binding arbitration agreement (in the form of a submission agreement) it would appear difficult

43. 2021 ICC Rules, Article 6(1); 2020 LCIA Rules, Preamble; 2021 Swiss Rules, Article 1(2); 2021 Vienna Rules, Article 1(2); Simon Greenberg & Flavia Mange, *Institutional and Ad Hoc Perspectives on the Temporal Conflict of Arbitral Rules*, 27 J. Int'l Arb. 199, 200 (2010). *See also China Agribusiness Development Corp. v. Balli Trading*, [1998] 2 Lloyds Rep. 76, para. 733 ('if an arbitration agreement requires an arbitration to be held according to the rules of a particular institution, that agreement prima facie refers to the rules current at the time when the arbitration is begun').
44. *See, e.g.*, Filip de Ly, *Third Party Participation*, in Markus Wirth (ed.), *Best Practices in International Arbitration*, ASA Special Series No. 26, 57, 69 (2006) ('I interpret Article 4 Swiss Rules as an ... irrevocable offer ... If the arbitrating parties have consented in advance to arbitrate with third parties, that party may request to intervene in the proceedings and the arbitrating parties cannot object'); Maxi Scherer, Lisa Richman & Rémy Gerbay, *Arbitrating under the 2020 LCIA Rules: A User's Guide* 312 (2021) ('[a] subsequent unilateral objection to the joinder by the other party is without effect to the original agreement to arbitrate under the LCIA Rules and the standing offer to join non-parties contained therein'); Gary Born, *International Commercial Arbitration*, 2805 (3rd ed. Kluwer 2021).
45. *See, e.g.*, Hugh Beale (ed.), *Chitty on Contracts*, Vol. I, paras 2-094 and 2-097 (33rd ed. Sweet & Maxwell 2018); UPICC, Article 2.1.4(1); CISG, Article 16(1); Italian Civil Code, Article 1328.
46. 2020 LCIA Rules, Article 22.1(x); 2021 Swiss Rules, Article 6(3); 2021 Vienna Rules, Article 14(1).

for a tribunal to decline jurisdiction. Thus, once again, the assumption of a newly created arbitration agreement by way of a standing offer reaches its conceptual limits.

§20.04 UNDERSTANDING FORCED JOINDER AS PART OF THE PARTIES' FUNDAMENTAL INTEREST IN EFFICIENT PROCEEDINGS

Yet, none of these four counterarguments withstands closer scrutiny. Any concern about artificiality can be alleviated when considering the parties' fundamental interest in effective and innovative dispute resolution; and all supposed conceptual issues can be resolved satisfactorily.

First, there will indeed be more than a few commercial parties who are unaware that their choice of a particular set of arbitration rules entails the extension of a standing offer for third parties to join their proceedings. Yet, the same can be said of other aspects of the chosen arbitration rules. Few parties choosing the LCIA Rules will be acutely aware that the tribunal has the power to abridge time limits on which the parties have agreed,[47] and to dismiss a claim on the merits by means of a mere 'early determination'.[48] But parties need not be aware of these features of arbitration rules for their choice to be effective. In reality, their choice of arbitration rules is much more global. It is guided by their trust that the respective institution has promulgated rules that provide for balanced and efficient proceedings. The decisive point in time is thus not the moment when a third party wishes to join ongoing proceedings but rather when parties conclude their arbitration agreement. At that time, it is unclear who will benefit from which aspect of the chosen rules. It is only clear that both parties agree that those rules provide an objective, efficient and comprehensive means of dispute resolution.

Indeed, empirical evidence demonstrates that parties are particularly interested in arbitration rules that provide for the tribunal's 'power in relation to third parties'.[49] Thus, parties' fundamental trust in arbitral institutions ensuring efficient dispute resolution entails that they consent to mechanisms that objectively enhance efficiency but subjectively may not be in their interest once a specific dispute has erupted. Although the standing offer to join third parties may come in disguise, it does not disadvantage any party when viewed from the pre-dispute perspective. Accordingly, an agreement on joinder through the acceptance of a standing offer is no less effective than a post-hoc agreement.

Second, similar considerations apply to the agreement to be bound by the latest iteration of arbitration rules. This agreement, too, is geared towards achieving maximum efficiency by benefitting from the latest innovations in institutional arbitration.

---

47. 2020 LCIA Rules, Article 22.1(ii); Klaus Peter Berger & Ole Jensen, *Due Process Paranoia and the Procedural Judgment Rule: A Safe Harbour for Procedural Management Decisions by International Arbitrators*, 32 Arb. Int'l 415, 432 (2016).
48. 2020 LCIA Rules, Article 22.1(viii).
49. Queen Mary University & White & Case, *2018 International Arbitration Survey: The Evolution of International Arbitration*, p. 8 (2018). *See also* ICC, *Final Report on Multi-Party Arbitrations*, 6(1) ICC Ct. Bull., section 5 (1995); Nathalie Voser & Anke Meier, *Joinder of Parties or Need to (Sometimes) Be Inefficient*, in Christian Klausegger, et al. (eds), *Austrian Yearbook on International Arbitration Volume 2008*, p. 115 (Manz 2008).

The institution acts as the parties' agent in devising procedures that lead them to an efficient resolution of their dispute. There is no conceptual reason why this agency relationship could not entail the issuance of a standing offer for third parties to be joined – even if that offer remains implied in the updated arbitration rules. There is thus no insurmountable conceptual hurdle with respect to the issuance of the standing offer to join a third party.

Third, there is also no dogmatic issue with assuming that the standing offer is irrevocable. Indeed, given that provisions on forced joinder are only effective if the offer is binding, it is clear to all parties that irrevocability is intended. An irrevocable standing offer to arbitrate is also not uncommon. It is the very basis of investor-State arbitration. With its request for arbitration, the investor accepts the State's *offerta ad incertas personas*, thus 'create[ing] privity at the time of initiating arbitration'.[50] If the State could revoke its consent to arbitrate by simply making a corresponding declaration, the entire purpose of the investment treaty would be frustrated (and so too its termination and sunset provisions). Accordingly, it is beyond doubt that State parties to investment treaties understand their respective offer to arbitrate with investors of the other State(s) as irrevocable (unless specifically provided otherwise). There is no reason why the same should not apply with respect to the standing offer for the joinder of third parties contained in some commercial arbitration rules.[51]

Fourth, the fact that the tribunal retains discretion once a joinder agreement has been formed is not incompatible with the agreement. To the contrary, this discretion is a crucial safeguard in the absence of which parties might not be provide their advance-consent in the first place. Properly construed, the standing offer must not be understood as a binding offer to arbitrate with any third party that comes along and accepts the offer. Instead, the offer is to endow a future tribunal with the discretion to decide whether, in the circumstances of the particular case, a forced joinder is appropriate. Thus, if the offer is accepted, the decisive factor for ordering forced joinder will always remain the circumstances of the particular case.[52] This ensures that no party will be forced to arbitrate with a third party in circumstances where this would be truly inequitable or entirely unexpected.[53] The arbitral tribunal thus remains the

50. Jan Paulsson, *Arbitration Without Privity*, 10(2) ICSID Review 232, 247 (1995).

51. *See also* Gary Born, *International Commercial Arbitration*, 2805 (3rd ed. Kluwer 2021) ('A 'standing offer' to arbitrate disputes with non-parties should be no less valid in the case of commercial arbitrations than investment arbitrations, where such provisions are standard; the fact that consent to arbitration takes a different form from most agreements to arbitrate is no basis for denying recognition to the resulting arbitration agreement. Indeed, failure to do so would violate Article II of the New York Convention and parallel provisions of many national laws.').

52. *See also* Philippe Gilliéron & Luc Pittet, *Article 4*, in Tobias Zuberbühler, Christoph Müller & Philipp Habegger (eds), *Swiss Rules of International Arbitration* 36, 41 (1st ed. Juris 2005) ('This of course does not mean that any third party wishing to intervene in pending arbitration proceedings under the Swiss Rules shall *eo ipso* become a party. ... It remains at the discretion of the arbitral tribunal to allow the intervention').

53. *See* Maxi Scherer, Lisa Richman & Rémy Gerbay, *Arbitrating under the 2020 LCIA Rules: A User's Guide* 313 (Kluwer 2021) ('Aspects Tribunals will consider when weighing whether to order joinder ...: the efficiencies that can be gained by joining the third party and the potential to prevent parallel proceedings with potentially incompatible results. At the same time, Tribunals

ultimate gatekeeper to ensure a just and reasonable decisions on forced joinder. In practice, this has kept the number of actual forced joinders comparable low.[54]

§20.05 CONCLUSION

In conclusion, while seemingly a 'delicate mechanism',[55] the conceptual foundation of forced joinder remains strong. Although disguised, the parties' consent to arbitration is contained in their agreement to submit their disputes to an arbitral institution that ensures efficient dispute resolution by providing for the possibility of forced joinder. In principle, this means that even where a provision on forced joinder is introduced only subsequently, parties would be bound by it. Nevertheless, the arbitral tribunal remains the ultimate guardian of ensuring fair proceedings. By exercising discretion, the tribunal can ensure that forced joinder is not ordered in circumstances where this would be plainly against the parties' legitimate expectations and inequitable in the circumstances. The essence of the solution provided by Professor Lew thus holds true today as it did then: '[T]he second party … does not have to expressly consent to the joinder. It has done so by agreeing to the … Rules'.[56]

should take into account any prejudice the joinder would cause to the other disputing party/parties. Other circumstances to consider include: (i) the proximity of the claim(s) pending before the original parties and the claim(s) to be brought against the third party; (ii) the law applicable to the substance of the dispute(s) and (iii) the stage of the proceedings').

54. Bernard Hanotiau, *Complex Arbitrations: Multi-party, Multi-contract, Multi-issue – A Comparative Study* 330 (2nd ed. Kluwer 2020) ('It seems that only one [LCIA] case has been reported in which the third party was joined in spite of the objection of an original party.'); Nadia Darwazeh & Pierre Johnson, *The More the Merrier or How Different Arbitral Institutions Tackle Multiparty and Multi-contract Disputes*, in Dirk De Meulemeester, Maxime Berlingin, et al. (eds), *Liber Amicorum CEPANI (1969-2019): 50 Years of Solutions* 87, 90 (Kluwer 2019).
55. *See* Jan Paulsson, *Arbitration Without Privity*, 10(2) ICSID Review 232, 257 (1995) ('Arbitration without privity is a delicate mechanism.').
56. Julian Lew, Loukas Mistelis & Stefan Kröll, *Comparative International Commercial Arbitration*, para. 16-44 (Kluwer 2003).

CHAPTER 21

Summary Dismissal: Useful but Risky

*Pierre Tercier**

In arbitration due process and efficiency are often in tension. Throughout his career, Julian Lew QC has demonstrated how to find the right balance between the two. Below is a short essay in acknowledgment and celebration of his incomparable skills as a practitioner and as an academic.

§21.01 INTRODUCTION

Summary dismissals have been the subject of some recent developments in the field of international arbitration. In particular: on 1 July 2022, the amended Regulations and Rules of the International Centre for Settlement of Investment Disputes (ICSID Rules) came into effect; these rules were the first to expressly provide for summary dismissal in 2006 and the new version provides more detail on the scope of the power. The English Arbitration Act 1996 (EAA 1996) is currently the subject of consideration by the Law Commission. In its recent consultation paper, the Commission proposed to explicitly provide for the power of summary dismissal in the EEA 1996.[1] The UNCITRAL Working Group III charged with investigating the areas for reform of the investor-state dispute settlement system has also been considering possible reforms of the 'means to address frivolous claims'. The academic interest in the issue also remains vivid.

This short essay contributes to the debate by making a case for cautious exercise of the now widely accepted power of the tribunal to summarily dismiss claims.

* I would like to thank my associate, Ms Victoria Barausova, for her very efficient and valuable assistance in the preparation of this contribution.

1. Law Commission, Review of the Arbitration Act 1996: A Consultation Paper, September 2022, available at https://s3-eu-west-2.amazonaws.com/lawcom-prod-storage-11jsxou24uy7q/uploads/2022/09/Arbitration-Consultation-Paper.pdf, date of last access 13 February 2023.

§21.02 DEFINITION AND ORIGINS OF SUMMARY DISMISSAL POWERS

Summary dismissal is disposition of a claim, a counterclaim or a defence without full evidentiary hearing, often very early in the proceedings. The concept is widely used in civil litigation before national courts in common law jurisdictions; it is aimed at saving taxpayers' money in circumstances where the use of full procedure 'would be disproportionate to what it could achieve'.[2] For instance, an English court may strike out a statement of case if it appears that it discloses no reasonable grounds for bringing or defending the claim.[3] It can also enter a summary judgment where the claimant has no real prospect of success and there is no other reason why the matter should be disposed of at trial.[4] In applications to strike out, the court only looks at the statement of the case, while in case of summary judgment applications, the court also looks at the evidence submitted and can draw inferences from it.[5]

Given the often-expressed dissatisfaction of arbitration users with the speed of proceedings and efficiency,[6] it is hardly surprising that arbitration practitioners turned to summary procedures before national courts for inspiration.

It should be noted that, even before the power to summarily dismiss claims was embraced, some institutional rules already provided for an initial screening by the institution. For instance, under the ICC Rules, the initial screening is carried out by the Secretary General who may refer the matter to the Court in certain circumstances.[7] The Court then determines whether prima facie there is a valid arbitration agreement.[8] Similarly, the ICSID Convention gives the Secretary General a power to refuse registration of a request for arbitration if he or she finds that the dispute is manifestly outside the jurisdiction of the Centre.[9]

§21.03 STATE OF THE LAW AND ACADEMIC DEBATE

Originally, the power to summarily dismiss claims was not found in any institutional rules. The academic debate naturally focused on whether this was part of the tribunal's inherent powers. Arguments were made in favour of recognising it as such in order to enhance efficiency of arbitration.[10] The main concern was whether summary dismissal

2. Adrian Zuckermann, *Zuckermann on Civil Procedure: Principles of Practice* § 9.53 (4th ed. Sweet & Maxwell 2021).
3. CPR 3.4(2)(a).
4. CPR 24.2(a).
5. Adrian Zuckermann, *Zuckermann on Civil Procedure: Principles of Practice* § 9.83 (4th ed. Sweet & Maxwell 2021).
6. Queen Mary University of London and White & Case LLP, *2018 International Arbitration Survey: The Evolution of International Arbitration* 8.
7. Article 6(3) ICC Rules 2021.
8. *Ibid.*
9. Article 36(3) ICSID Convention.
10. Kenneth Beale and Gary Born, *Party Autonomy and Default Rules: Reframing the Debate Over Summary Disposition in International Arbitration*, 21 ICC International Court of Arbitration Bulletin 19, 23 (2010); Adam Raviv, *No More Excuses: Toward a Workable System of Dispositive Motions in International Arbitration*, 28 Arbitration International 487 (2012).

would be in line with the due process principle and the right to be heard. Failure to observe those rights might lead to annulment and refusal of enforcement of the resulting decision (e.g., Article V(1)(b) and V(1)(d) of the New York Convention (NYC), Article 52(1)(d) of the ICSID Convention, and analogous provisions of national arbitration legislation). Commentators argued that the right to be heard and the right to fair trial do not require 'giving a plaintiff or defendant an exhaustive opportunity to advance hopeless claims or defences',[11] nor do they mean that 'in each and every case an oral hearing must take place'.[12]

Over time, the arguments of the proponents of summary dismissal became widely accepted. As mentioned, in 2006, the ICSID pioneered the inclusion of an express power to summarily dismiss frivolous claims into its institutional rules.[13] Some years later other institutions followed suit.[14] While the International Chamber of Commerce Arbitration Rules 2021 (ICC Rules 2021) do not contain an express power of the tribunal to summarily dismiss claims early in the proceedings, the Note to the Parties and Arbitral Tribunals on the Conduct of the Arbitration mentions that such power is encompassed in the broad case management powers under Article 22.[15] These developments have caused the academic debate to shift towards the question of *whether and how* such powers should be exercised.

The data on the application of the mentioned provisions suggests that the tribunals have been exercising the power with extreme caution. According to the ICSID's most recent data, as of 11 March 2021, 40 requests under Rule 41(5) have been filed in the 754 arbitration and post-award remedy proceedings registered during the same period; out of 40 cases, the objection was upheld in full in 7 cases and in part in 4 cases.[16] Singapore International Arbitration Centre (SIAC) received 10 applications for early dismissal in 2021, out of which only 3 have been allowed to proceed.[17] Two applications were submitted to Hong Kong International Arbitration Centre (HKIAC) arbitral tribunals in 2021, none of which have been granted.[18] The London Court of International Arbitration (LCIA) stands out with 7 out of 15 applications for early determination granted in 2021.

11. Constantine Partasides and Ben Prewett, *Rediscovering the Lost Promise of International Arbitration*, in *Expedited Procedures in International Arbitration, Dossiers of the ICC Institute of World Business Law, Volume 16* 110, 121 (Laurent Lévy and Michael Polkinghorne eds, Kluwer Law International, ICC 2017).
12. Albert Jan van den Berg, *The New York Arbitration Convention of 1958* 306 (Kluwer Law International 1981); James P. Duffy, *Dispositive Motions and the Summary Disposition of Claims in International Arbitration*, in *International Arbitration in the United States* 275, 297 (Laurence Shore and Tai-Heng Cheng eds, Kluwer Law International 2017); Adam Raviv, *No More Excuses: Toward a Workable System of Dispositive Motions in International Arbitration*, 28 Arbitration International 487, 501-505 (2012); Ryan and Dharmananda, *Summary Disposal in Arbitration: Still Fair or Agreed to Be Fair*, 35 Journal of International Arbitration 31 (2018).
13. Rule 41(5) ICSID Rules 2006; revised and elaborated in Rule 41 ICSID Rules 2022.
14. Article 29 SIAC Rules 2016; Article 39 SCC Rules 2023; Article 43 HKIAC Rules 2019; Rule 22.1(viii) LCIA Rules 2020.
15. ICC, *Note to Parties and Arbitral Tribunals on the Conduct of the Arbitration* §§ 109–114 (2021).
16. ICSID, *In Focus: Objections that a Claim Manifestly Lacks Legal Merit (ICSID Convention Arbitration Rule 41(5)* (2021).
17. SIAC, *Annual Report 2021*, 26.
18. HKIAC, *2021 Statistics* (2021) https://www.hkiac.org/about-us/statistics.

This essay argues that the tribunals are right to approach such applications with a degree of caution.

§21.04 RES JUDICATA EFFECT AND LIMITED REVIEW OF SUMMARY DISMISSAL DECISIONS

If an application for a summary dismissal is made, the tribunal can reach one of the following decisions: (i) to uphold the application and to dismiss the claim or (ii) to dismiss the objection and continue with the proceedings. The former decision has some characteristic features that are relevant for the present discussion:

- First, summary dismissal can be made *in respect of all aspects*, jurisdictional issues, as well as the merits. Most rules state so expressly.[19] As for the ICC Rules, it is mentioned in the Note.[20]
- Second, such summary dismissal *has res judicata effect*. This doctrine is concerned with the policy of preventing retrial of determined matters. Its precise requirements vary from one jurisdiction to another. In broad terms, it provides that an earlier and final adjudication by a court or tribunal is conclusive in later proceedings that involve the same parties, claims and relief.[21] Recognising res judicata effect of a decision to summarily dismiss a claim means that the claimant cannot re-litigate the matter before a different court or tribunal.

  It is undisputed that, in national court proceedings, a summary judgment dismissing a claim has res judicata effect and is considered to be a final judgment for all purposes.[22] However, the issue has not been widely discussed in arbitration commentary. Some institutional rules contain express provisions on the matter. Rule 41(6) of the ICSID Rules 2006 and Rule 41(3) of the ICSID Rules 2022 provide that a decision dismissing claims for lack of legal merit is made in the form of an award and this has also been recognised by arbitral tribunals deciding the matter.[23] Other institutional rules provide that the

19. For example, Rule 41 ICSID Rules 2022 (this is a development from the previous version of the ICSID Rules that did not expressly state whether the provision applied to jurisdictional issues); Rule 22.1(viii) LCIA Rules 2020; Article 43.1 HKIAC Rules 2018; Article 39(2) SCC Rules 2023; Article 29.1 SIAC Rules 2016.
20. ICC, *Note to Parties and Arbitral Tribunals on the Conduct of the Arbitration* § 110 (2021).
21. Jeffrey Maurice Waincymer, *Procedure and Evidence in International Arbitration* 687 (Kluwer Law International 2012).
22. Adrian Zuckermann, *Zuckermann on Civil Procedure: Principles of Practice* § 9.78 (4th ed. Sweet & Maxwell 2021). The same is true for the US: *see* Kenneth Beale & Gary Born, *Party Autonomy and Default Rules: Reframing the Debate over Summary Disposition in International Arbitration*, 21 ICC International Court of Arbitration Bulletin 19, 24 (2010).
23. *Trans-Global Petroleum, Inc. v. Hashemite Kingdom of Jordan*, ICSID Case No. ARB/07/25, Decision on the Respondent's Objection Pursuant to Rule 41(5) of the ICSID Arbitration Rules, 2 February 2009, para. 92.

tribunal renders 'an order or award', without further elaboration.[24] It is submitted that tribunals' decisions summarily dismissing claims must indeed have res judicata effect because they constitute final adjudication of a matter. Ultimately, the tribunal dismisses a claim, just as it would in an award concluding full proceedings with an oral hearing. The only difference is that in cases of summary dismissal it does so upon a more limited examination of the evidence.

- Third, a decision summarily dismissing claims *can only be reviewed on limited grounds*. In view of the limited nature of judicial cognition that underpins summary determinations, it is important to consider the guarantees that are put in place to ensure correctness of such decisions.

Summary judgments rendered by the courts in England and Wales are susceptible to appeal. Such appeal 'will be concerned with the correctness of the summary judgment decision on the basis of the materials available to the court below'.[25] The appellate court is entitled to consider and draw inferences from all the material that was before the first instance court that entered a summary judgment.[26]

By contrast, in international arbitration, a resulting decision can only be reviewed on very limited grounds contained in national legislation for domestic awards and the NYC for foreign awards.

With respect to the merits, there is no de novo review, with some very limited exceptions. One such exception is section 69 of the EAA 1996 that allows a party to appeal to the court on a question of law. However, the parties may exclude the possibility of the appeal by their agreement.[27] Even if they do not exclude the appeal, it can only be brought where all the parties agree or there is a leave of the court that can only be given in limited circumstances.[28] Another exception is public policy ground for review that is available under national law and Article V(2)(b) of the NYC. The review on this ground, although may pertain to the merits, is very limited and is concerned merely with the outcome of the proceedings and not with the correctness of the tribunal's findings. The ICSID Convention creates a special legal regime where awards can only be annulled on the limited grounds listed in Article 52(1) which do not concern the merits of the decision, but only the process through which it was reached.[29]

24. Rule 22.1 LCIA Rules 2020; Article 43.6 HKIAC Rules 2018; Article 39(6) SCC Rules 2023; Article 29.4 SIAC Rules 2016; ICC, *Note to Parties and Arbitral Tribunals on the Conduct of the Arbitration* § 113 (2021).
25. Adrian Zuckermann, *Zuckermann on Civil Procedure: Principles of Practice* § 9.78 (4th ed. Sweet & Maxwell 2021).
26. *McFaddens v. Guru Paran Chanrdasekaran* [2007] EWCA Civ 220.
27. Section 69(1) English Arbitration Act 1996 ('*Unless otherwise agreed by the parties*').
28. Section 69(2) English Arbitration Act 1996.
29. *A Commentary on the Convention on the Settlement of Investment Disputes Between States and Nationals of Other States* 901 (Schreuer, Malintoppi, Reinisch & Sinclair eds, CUP 2010).

With regards to jurisdictional objections, the courts usually carry out de novo review in annulment setting. This is the case under the UNCITRAL Model Law,[30] French law,[31] English law[32] and German law.[33] Under Swiss law, judicial reconsideration is limited to the findings of law, but not the findings of fact.[34] In recognition and enforcement setting, the courts also independently examine jurisdictional objections on a de novo basis when they fall within one of the grounds under Article V of the NYC.[35] Similarly, under the ICSID Convention, annulment committees investigate jurisdictional objections under Article 52(1)(b) independently, but do not 'rectify incorrect decisions' or 'annul unjust awards'.[36]

To conclude, decisions summarily dismissing a claim in international arbitration (i) may pertain to jurisdiction or the merits, (ii) have res judicata effect, (iii) are susceptible to independent review on jurisdictional objections but (iv) almost no review on the merits.

§21.05 IMPACT ON CORRECTNESS

In international arbitration, the principle of finality and efficiency is often in tension with the principle of correctness. The importance of accuracy and truth-seeking has been highlighted by William W. Park in the following passage:

> Although justice delayed can mean justice denied, a sense that truth matters remains vital to a perception that justice is being done. ... Although good case management values speed and economy, it does so with respect for the parties' interest in correct decisions. The parties have no less interest in correct decisions than in efficient proceedings. ... In the long run, little satisfaction will come from awards that are quick and cheap at the price of being systematically wrong.[37]

Finality and efficiency often take precedence over correctness.[38] This is acceptable in cases where the tribunal enjoys full judicial cognition in the original proceedings. However, when its judicial cognition is limited, as in summary dismissal proceedings, the balance inevitably shifts. This is the reason why limited review is acceptable for awards resulting from a full review of the evidence and full proceedings, but becomes an issue in summary proceedings. This problem arises mainly in respect of dismissals for reasons pertaining to the merits.

---

30. Gary Born, *International Commercial Arbitration* 1198 (3rd ed. Kluwer Law International 2021). Although in fact sometimes courts demonstrate a degree of deference to the tribunal's findings, especially findings of fact resulting from careful and extensive fact-finding exercise.
31. *Ibid.*, 1206.
32. *Ibid.*, 1308.
33. *Ibid.*, 1216. But under German law only in relation to positive findings of jurisdiction.
34. *Ibid.*, 1213.
35. *Ibid.*, 3728, 3797.
36. *Ibid.*, 906.
37. William W. Park, *Arbitrators and Accuracy*, 26 Arbitration International 25 (2010).
38. *A Commentary on the Convention on the Settlement of Investment Disputes Between States and Nationals of Other States* 903 (Schreuer, Malintoppi, Reinisch & Sinclair eds, CUP 2010).

As mentioned above, annulment courts, courts at the seat of enforcement and ad hoc committees under the ICSID Convention consider jurisdictional objections de novo; this ensures that there is an additional layer of review of their correctness. Further, in some (but not all) cases where the claim is summarily dismissed for lack of jurisdiction, even if the reviewing court or ad hoc committee agrees with the tribunal's findings, the claimant may still have recourse to alternative fora of dispute resolution, such as national courts.

By contrast, when a claim is summarily dismissed on the merits, there is no review of the decision that would provide an additional safeguard for correctness which may be put at risk by the limited nature of judicial cognition. Further, following summary dismissal on the merits, the claimant cannot pursue its claims before a different forum because of the decision's res judicata effect. In such situation, the claimant may be left with an incorrect decision that cannot be reviewed, on the matters that cannot be reopened in a new forum. Hence, in cases of summary dismissals on the merits, the risk of incorrect decisions is particularly acute. This demands greater caution from the tribunals when exercising the power.

This is not to say that summary dismissal on the merits should never be possible. It is an invaluable tool for ensuring that the parties' expectations of cost- and time-efficiency of the proceedings are met. Where, accepting the facts alleged by the claimant as true, it is obvious, clear and uncontroversial that there is no case on the merits and the legal issue is well-settled, the tribunal should use the power.

In investment arbitration, many legal issues remain unsettled, at least when it comes to the detail. First, disputes are often decided under an investment treaty whose provisions may be rather vague, thus leaving it to the tribunals to develop the detail of the law. Second, in investment treaty arbitration, disputes often arise under different treaty texts which makes legal findings of earlier tribunals less transposable. Finally, there is no doctrine of precedent in investment arbitration, in contrast with national courts in common law jurisdictions. The absence of the doctrine of precedent means that there may be conflicting authorities on a given legal issue. This makes it harder to determine whether the law is settled and what it is. These factors mean that the instances where the claimant cannot point to an 'arguable case'[39] would be rare because the law is inherently less settled.

The cautious approach to summary dismissal on the merits advocated here does not need to considerably undermine efficiency of arbitration proceedings. There is a wealth of other mechanisms that tribunals and parties may resort to for achieving this aim.[40]

39. *Lotus Holding Anonim Şirketi v. Turkmenistan*, ICSID Case No. ARB/17/30, Award, 6 April 2020, para. 158.
40. *See, e.g.*, Yas Banifatemi, *Expedited Proceedings in International Arbitration*, in *Expedited Procedures in International Arbitration* 9, 15-16 (Laurent Lévy and Michael Polkinghorne eds, ICC 2017).

§21.06 JURISPRUDENCE ON SUMMARY DISMISSAL

Consideration of arbitral jurisprudence reveals that arbitrators have been awake to the foregoing considerations. The concern about the lack of appeal or de novo review has been featured in the tribunal's reasoning on the threshold for summary dismissal in the past:

- The tribunal in ICC Case No. 11413 recognized this fact as a 'serious concern [that] makes its position fundamentally different from that of a [national] court'.[41] This has led the tribunal to set a high threshold for the exercise of the power: 'a motion to dismiss ... should not be granted unless the arbitrators are confident that it is crystal clear that the claim may have no legal basis'.[42]
- In *Elsamex v. Honduras*, the ad hoc committee was invited to dismiss the application for annulment on the basis of ICSID Rule 41(5). The committee observed that the detrimental effect on the claimant in cases of summary dismissal is greater in annulment proceedings because there is no further recourse against the decision.[43] In view of the committee, this warranted a higher standard when determining an application under ICSID Rule 41(5) in annulment proceedings.[44] Similar observations were made by the annulment committees in *Venoklim v. Venezuela*[45]and *Dominion Minerals Corp. v. Panama*.[46]
- In *Trans-Global Petroleum v. Jordan*, the tribunal compared the ICSID Secretariat's screening powers under Article 36 of the ICSID Convention and the power of summary dismissal under Rule 41(5) which 'may produce an ICSID award finally disposing of the claimant's claims, with all its attendant legal effects under the ICSID Convention, the New York Arbitration Convention and national legislation'.[47] This, in the tribunal's view, warranted the application of the power only to 'clear and obvious' cases.

Even though the tribunals did not distinguish between the different grounds on which a claim can be dismissed and how the level of review varied across those different grounds, they did identify the limited review as a factor warranting a higher threshold for summary dismissal.

---

41. First Interim Award in ICC Case No. 11413, published in *Decisions on ICC Arbitration procedure: A Selection of Procedural Orders issued by Arbitral Tribunals acting under the ICC Rules of Arbitration (2003-2004)*, ICC ICArb. Bull., 2010 Special Supplement 41 (ICC 2011).
42. *Ibid.*
43. *Elsamex, S.A. v. Republic of Honduras*, ICSID Case No. ARB/09/4, Decision on Preliminary Objections, 7 January 2014, paras 124-125.
44. *Ibid.*
45. *Venoklim Holding B.V. v. Bolivarian Republic of Venezuela*, ICSID Case No. ARB/12/22, Decision on the Respondent's Preliminary Objection under ICSID Arbitration Rule 41(5), 8 March 2016, paras 75-82.
46. *Dominion Minerals Corp. v. Republic of Panama*, ICSID Case No. ARB/16/13, Decision on the Respondent's Applications for the Stay of Enforcement of the Award and under Arbitration Rule 41(5), 21 July 2022, paras 157-158.
47. *Trans-Global Petroleum, Inc. v. Hashemite Kingdom of Jordan*, ICSID Case No. ARB/07/25, Decision on the Respondent's Objection Pursuant to Rule 41(5) of the ICSID Arbitration Rules, 2 February 2009, para. 92.

§21.07 CONCLUSION

The express confirmation of the power to summarily dismiss claims has been a long-awaited and welcome development in international arbitration. Despite this fact, tribunals have exercised the power with a considerable degree of caution. The power is undoubtedly valuable for ensuring efficiency and its employment is particularly welcome when a party is using arbitration as a tool for abuse. Nevertheless, the tribunals' cautious approach must be approved, especially when the application pertains to the merits. The limited judicial cognition underpinning such decisions, the absence of review and res judicata effect create a greater risk for correctness.

D Jurisdiction and Substantive Issues

CHAPTER 22

Pathological and Hybrid Arbitration Clauses*

Bernard Hanotiau

I had the pleasure to become acquainted with Julian Lew as early as in 1971 when he was preparing his thesis on the law applicable to the arbitration agreement under the supervision of Professor François Rigaux while I was myself assistant of the same professor at the Center for International Law of Louvain University in Belgium. Our careers have developed in parallel and over the years we have had many opportunities to meet in conferences and seminars, to collaborate in academic projects and to sit together in a number of arbitrations. It is therefore with great pleasure that I dedicate these few lines to Professor Lew, one of the most prominent specialists of international arbitration.

Normally, the wording of an arbitration clause should not hinder the setting in motion of arbitration proceedings. But this is not always the case. This article will deal with two types of problematic clauses: pathological arbitration clauses and hybrid arbitration clauses.

§22.01 PATHOLOGICAL ARBITRATION CLAUSES[1]

What is a pathological arbitration clause? It is a clause whose defective drafting complicates, disrupts, delays or sometimes makes impossible the setting in motion of the arbitral proceedings. A defect in an arbitration clause does not necessarily negate the agreement thereby constituted. It depends on the nature or the substance of the

* Amended version of a presentation made at the ICC Arbitration Conference held in Paris on 28 March 2022.

1. The term was used for the first time by Frederic Eisemann in 'La Clause d'Arbitrage Pathologique' in Essais d'arbitrage commercial à la mémoire d'Eugenio Minoli (Turin), Unione Tipografico-editrice Torinese, 1974.

defect, or whether the defect can be cured. In practice – as will be seen below – state courts, institutions and imaginative arbitrators will be able to make pathological clauses work, in the greatest majority of cases.

There are different types of defective clauses:

- in some cases, what is in question is the intention of the parties to refer to arbitration;
- in other cases, it is not clear which institution the parties had in mind to resolve their disputes through arbitration;
- in still other cases, it is not clear what disputes can be submitted to arbitration.

[A] In the First Type of Pathological Arbitration Clauses, the Issue Is: What Is It the Real Intent of the Parties to Refer Their Disputes to Arbitration?

This is for example the case where the contract provides that all the disputes will be submitted to arbitration and a subsequent paragraph of the contract provides that only the courts of a particular city have jurisdiction to hear the disputes between the parties. What needs to be done in such a case is to determine whether the two provisions are compatible, whether the parties did not provide for court jurisdiction for certain procedures which would fall outside the scope of the arbitration clause. When the two provisions do not appear to be compatible, the usual approach of many arbitrators and courts is to give priority to the arbitration clause from the moment the parties have expressed their intention to go to arbitration.

[B] In the Second Type of Pathological Clauses, the Issue Is: What Institution Did the Parties Have in Mind?

This is one of the most common types of pathological arbitration clauses. The parties refer for example to:

- the 'official Chamber of Commerce in Paris'; or
- the 'Arbitration Court at the Swiss Chamber for Foreign Trade in Geneva'; or
- the 'International Trade Arbitration Organisation in Zurich'; or
- the 'Amsterdam Court of Arbitration'; or
- the 'International Chamber of Commerce of Geneva'; or
- 'arbitration in Paris in conformity with the rules and procedures of the Commercial Court'; or
- 'the parties will endeavour to resolve their disputes through Swiss arbitration'.

The pathology of these clauses is not difficult to solve since they show clearly that the parties intended to submit their disputes to arbitration. This is why courts and tribunals are reluctant to consider these clauses void for uncertainty. In general, the reference to a particular city will allow the courts to identify the chosen institution: the

International Chamber of Commerce (ICC) in Paris, the Swiss Arbitration Centre in Geneva or in Zurich, the Netherlands Arbitrage Institute in Amsterdam.

[C] In the Third Type of Pathological Clauses, There Is Uncertainty as to the Claims That Can Be Submitted to Arbitration

One category of such clauses are clauses which provide for the submission of certain claims to expertise and others to arbitration without great precision as to the division between both. The author of this article was confronted to this scenario in a Eurotunnel arbitration. The arbitral tribunal had in the first place to determine whether the claims in dispute were to be submitted to experts or were within the jurisdiction of the arbitral tribunal.

Another frequent situation in this third category concerns groups of contracts. For example, the parties enter into a framework agreement which envisages the conclusion of subsequent implementation agreements. The framework agreement provides that all the claims under the agreement and the implementation agreements will be submitted to arbitration. But it subsequently appears that one ancillary agreement provides for a different type of arbitration, that another one provides for jurisdiction of the courts of a particular city and a third one for jurisdiction of still other courts. When the parties start an arbitration to settle the disputes arising under the various contracts, the arbitral tribunal is confronted to the question whether it has jurisdiction over all of them or only part of them.

But there are also situations where determining which claims fall within the jurisdiction of the arbitral tribunal appears impossible and the arbitration clause will be declared inoperable and therefore invalid. This was the case of the arbitral clause in Lovelock v. Exportles[2] which provided that the parties would submit '*any dispute and/or claim to arbitration in England*' and '*any other disputes to arbitration to the USSR Chamber of Commerce Foreign Trade Association Commission in Moscow*'. Lord Denning found that the two references were impossible to reconcile. It was not possible to determine which dispute came within which part of the arbitration clause.

[D] Conclusion

It may be concluded from the above that drafters should to the extent possible adopt the arbitration clause proposed by the relevant institution. If the clause which is included in the agreement is pathological, the approach of institutions and arbitral tribunals is to try in general by all means to solve the pathology of the clause in a positive manner; in other words, to try to make it work. As the Singapore Court of Appeals has recently decided:

> [w]here the parties have evinced a clear intention to settle any dispute by arbitration, the court should give effect to such intention, even if certain aspects of

2. [1968] 1 Lloyd's Rep. 163.

> the agreement may be ambiguous, inconsistent, incomplete or lacking uncertain particulars ... so long as the arbitration can be carried out without prejudice to the rights of either party and so long as giving effect to such intention does not result in an arbitration that is not within the contemplation of either party.[3]

§22.02 HYBRID ARBITRATION CLAUSES

[A] The Various Types of Hybrid Arbitration Clauses

The second type of problematic arbitration clauses are hybrid arbitration clauses.

Hybrid arbitration clauses can come in a variety of forms. One example is the mutual or unilateral option clause when one or both parties have the right to choose between arbitration and litigation, so that they can select the most appropriate forum after the dispute has arisen. It seems that unilateral option clauses are popular with the banking and finance sector, particularly in the context of loan agreements. However, these clauses raise the fundamental issue of their validity in many jurisdictions.[4]

The two other categories of hybrid arbitration clauses are those which provide for arbitration administered by one arbitral institution but conducted under the arbitration rules of another arbitral institution and *ad hoc* arbitration clauses providing for arbitration under the rules of an arbitral institution.

The author of this article was confronted to this last category of clauses in two disputes involving North Atlantic Treaty Organization (NATO). The arbitration clauses that NATO included in their contracts thirty years ago provided for *ad hoc* arbitration but under the rules of the ICC. The first task of the tribunal was then to determine, with the agreement of the parties, which provisions of the ICC Rules were applicable because some of these provisions cannot apply to an *ad hoc* arbitration, like for example the scrutiny process. In both cases, the proceedings worked well and the awards were not challenged.

The most problematic hybrid arbitration clauses are those which provide for arbitration administered by one institution under the rules of another institution. Five examples of such clauses are available on line and in each case, their application has raised a multiplicity of problems. Two of these cases took place in Singapore: *Insigma Technology Co. Ltd. v. Alstom Technology Ltd.*[5] and *HKL Group Co. Ltd. v. RIZQ International Holdings Pte Ltd.*[6]

---

3. *Insigma Technology CO Ltd. v. Alstom Technology Ltd.*, [2009] SGCA 23, at paragraph 31.
4. *See, e.g.*, the decisions of the French Supreme Court in *X v. Banque Privée Edmond de Rothschild Europe*, 26 September 2012, Cass. Civ. (1ère) No. 11-26.022 and in *ICH v. Crédit Suisse*, 25 March 2015, Cass. Civ. (1ère) No. 13-27.264, commented by Maxi Scherer, The French Rothschild Case: A Threat for Unilateral Dispute Resolution Clauses, Kluwer Arbitration Blog, 18 July 2013 and by Victoria Clark and Jonathan Cowe, Beware the Hybrid Arbitration Clause in Thomson Reuters Practical Law Arbitration Blog, 28 January 2022.
5. Cited *supra* n. 3.
6. [2013] SGHCR 5. The two cases are commented by Jae Hee SUB, Interpretation of Pathological Clauses: A Cautionary Tale, Thomson Reuters Practical law Arbitration Blog, 31 January 2019.

[B] *Insigma Technology Co. Ltd. v. Alstom Technology Ltd*

In *Insigma*, the arbitration clause provided that:

> Any and all such disputes shall be finally resolved by arbitration before the Singapore International Arbitration Centre in accordance with the Rules of Arbitration of the International Chamber of Commerce then in effect and the proceedings shall take place in Singapore and the official language shall be English ... .

When Alstom initially commenced an ICC arbitration, Insigma objected, arguing that Singapore International Arbitration Centre (SIAC) could administer the arbitration under the ICC Rules. Alstom enquired with SIAC whether they would in fact administer such arbitration. Having received a positive answer, Altsom withdrew the ICC arbitration with Insigma's consent and started arbitration at SIAC which agreed to apply the ICC rules. And so did the three members tribunal put in place by SIAC.

The arbitral tribunal noted that the arbitration agreement was not contrary to the law as the rules of an arbitral institution can be legally divorced from the administration of an arbitration by that institution.[7] It also noted that the arbitration agreement was not inoperable as SIAC was capable of administering the arbitration in accordance with the arbitration agreement, performing mutatis mutandis the functions assigned by the ICC Rules to the ICC and that it would not make any difference to the outcome.

The award was challenged by Insigma. It argued in particular that tribunal had rewritten the arbitration agreement, that an arbitration without the involvement of the ICC Secretariat and the ICC Court would not bear the 'ICC's hallmark of quality' which was what Insigma had bargained for.

The appeal was however dismissed by both the High Court and the Singapore Court of Appeal. The Court of Appeal set out a number of general principles to be applied in such cases including the following:

- first, it stated that when the parties have evinced a clear intention to settle any dispute by arbitration, the court should give effect to that clear intention even if certain aspects of the agreement are ambiguous, inconsistent or incomplete;
- second, where a clause can be interpreted in two different ways, the interpretation enabling the clause to be effective should be adopted in preference to that which prevents the clause from being effective;
- third, as far as possible, a commercially logical and sensible construction is to be preferred over another that is commercially illogical;
- fourth, there was no reason why a clause providing for the rules of one arbitral institution to be applied by a similar institution should be too uncertain to be given effect to;
- five, a defect in an arbitration clause does not necessarily render it unworkable, since it may often be cured by the assistance of state courts, arbitral institutions and arbitrators and in this case the clause was rendered workable

7. Citing *Bovis Lend Lease Pte. v. Jay-Tech Marine &Projects Pte Ltd.* [2005] SGHC 91 at 104.

by SIAC agreeing to administer the arbitration in accordance with the ICC Rules;
- and finally, the court of appeal found that there were no policy considerations that would bar SIAC from agreeing to administer an arbitration under the ICC Rules.

[C] *HKL Group v. RIZQ International Holdings*

In the other Singapore case, *HKL Group v. RIZQ International Holdings*, the arbitration clause was hybrid and pathological. It provided that:

> Any dispute shall be settled by amicable negotiation between [the] two Parties. In case both Parties fail to reach [an] amicable agreement, all dispute (sic) out of in connection with the contract shall be settled by the Arbitration Committee at Singapore under the Rules of the International Chamber of Commerce [the ICC Rules] of which awards shall be final and binding [on] both Parties ... .

A dispute arose and an action was started before the Courts of Singapore by HKL. Rizq applied for the court proceedings to be stayed in favour of arbitration. The High Court noted that in general, '*an incorrect reference to the arbitral institution has not prevented the courts from referring the matter to arbitration*'. It then found that the arbitration clause was operable for various reasons:

(1) first, it clearly demonstrated the intention of the parties to resolve disputes by arbitration;
(2) it required the mandatory consequence of a matter being referred to arbitration if a dispute arose;
(3) it provided for the place of arbitration (Singapore); and
(4) it provided that the arbitration was governed by a particular set of rules, the ICC Rules.[8]

The High Court further found that although the arbitration clause was uncertain in relation to the arbitral institution, it was open to the parties to approach any arbitral institution in Singapore to administer the arbitration while applying the ICC Rules. The court therefore stayed the proceedings and imposed the condition that parties obtain the agreement of SIAC or any other arbitration institution in Singapore to conduct a hybrid arbitration applying the ICC Rules, with liberty to apply to the court should they fail to secure such agreement.[9] The court further stated that its decision did not impede the parties from resolving the matter in a more practical manner by agreeing to submit the dispute to another form of arbitration, for instance a straightforward SIAC

8. At §27.
9. At §37.

arbitration, '*in order to avoid the procedural gymnastics of having the SIAC conduct a hybrid arbitration by applying the ICC Rules*'.[10]

[D] The 21 August 2018 Decision of the Austrian Supreme Court

The Austrian Supreme Court was also seized of the issue of validity of an award rendered under a hybrid arbitration clause[11] which provided as follows:

> Every dispute arising out of or connection with this contract that cannot be solved amicably within 60 days shall be decided by an arbitral tribunal in accordance with the arbitration rules of the International Chamber of Commerce that were in force when this contract was signed. The tribunal shall consist of three arbitrators appointed according to these Rules. The arbitral award shall be final and binding to the parties. The arbitral proceeding, including oral hearings and the issuance of the award shall take place at the Vienna International Court of Arbitration in Vienna, Austria.

In that case, the arbitral tribunal had been constituted and the proceedings had been conducted under the ICC Rules. The oral hearing was held at the offices of the presiding arbitrator in Vienna. An action to set aside the award was initiated by the claimant who argued that the agreement had called for arbitration under the Vienna International Arbitration Centre (VIAC) Rules. The action to set aside was dismissed in a decision of 21 August 2018.

The court found that the parties had agreed that an arbitral tribunal would decide the dispute; that the tribunal would consist of three arbitrators and be constituted in accordance with the ICC Rules; and that the proceedings would take place at the VIAC. The court further found that these provisions were not contradictory: it was possible for an arbitral tribunal to be constituted according to the ICC Rules and to conduct the proceedings at VIAC. The court also noted that the clause contained no clear designation of VIAC as the arbitral institution but rather merely provided that proceedings would take place there. It conceded that it was unclear whether the agreement required that the proceedings (and not only the constitution of the tribunal) were to be made under the ICC Rules or the VIAC Rules. But, said the court, such a decision must be made by an arbitral tribunal which must in any case be constituted under the ICC Rules. The Supreme Court also held that even if the arbitration clause had called for conducting the proceedings under the VIAC Rules, the failure to do so would still not reach the level of procedural public policy.

[E] The 23 January 2015 Decision of the Svea Court of Appeal

The next case is a decision of 23 January 2015 of the Svea Court of Appeal in Sweden.[12] The agreement provided as follows as regards arbitration:

10. At §38.
11. 3 Ob 127/20b. The case is commented by Nikolaus Pitkowitz, *Supreme Court evaluates hybrid arbitration agreement*, International Law Office, 18 July 2019.
12. Case n° T2454-14.

Arbitration rules: International Chamber of Commerce (ICC, Paris).

Court of arbitration: Chamber of Commerce and Industry, Stockholm, Sweden.

Number of arbitrators: three (3).

Language of arbitration: English, official and Russian, unofficial translation.

Place of arbitration: Stockholm, Sweden.

An arbitration took place. It was administered by the Stockholm Chamber of Commerce and the arbitration tribunal applied the ICC Rules. An action to set aside the award was filed by the losing party. The Svea Court of Appeal rejected the request. It held that the approach to interpreting a pathological or hybrid clause was as follows:

> If an arbitration agreement in some respect provides a self-contradicting or otherwise ambiguous procedure, which is not practicably doable, the general principle is that the agreement should, to the extent possible, be interpreted in line with the parties' basic intentions with the arbitration agreement, i.e., that disputes between the parties should be settled by arbitration. This could entail that the court will disregard a contradicting provision, if it is clear that the remainder of the arbitration otherwise represents the parties' actual intentions. In some particular instances, the natural order could, however, be to disregard the arbitration agreement in its entirety.

Upon a review of the facts, the court held that the arbitration clause had to be interpreted as follows:

> The arbitration between the parties must be understood so that the main purpose was that possible disputes between the parties would be resolved by arbitration and that the purpose was that the arbitration should take place in Stockholm before the SCC.

The Court further held that: '[i]t is undisputed that the SCC agreed to and also did administer the arbitration', that the arbitration clause was enforceable and was not invalid. In these circumstances, the arbitral tribunal could not 'be deemed to have disregarded a joint instruction from the parties by adapting ICC's rules of arbitration to the organisation of the SCC'.

One judge dissented and concurred. He considered that in principle the arbitration agreement was invalid. The Rules of the ICC – which by way of an incorporation have been agreed between the parties – provide that it is that institution that shall take measures, assess and decide on various issues. Thus, the wording of the rules makes it impossible that another institution could apply them; only the ICC can do what is provided by the ICC Rules. The judge however noted that it was of determining importance that the parties had agreed on an application of the ICC Rules by another institution. Therefore, if the other institution does as well as possible, the result is that the parties have achieved what they had agreed upon. Then, it ought not to be possible to complain that various measures, assessments and decisions by the administering arbitration institution might not have been exactly as they would have been if they had been applied by the ICC.

[F] *Flashbird v. Compagnie de Sécurité Privée et Industrielle SARL*

The last hybrid arbitration clause which recently generated judicial proceedings was the clause *Flashbird Ltd. v. Compagnie de Sécurité Privée et Industrielle SARL* (CSPI), which was finally decided by the Privy Council on 13 December 2021.[13]

In that case, the arbitration clause provided as follows:

> 14. The law applicable and the settlement of disputes.
>
> Mauritius has a permanent Court of arbitration at the Chamber of commerce and industry.
>
> All disputes arising out of this Contract or in connection with it, such as with regard to additional clauses, shall be finally determined according to the Arbitration Rules of the International Chamber of Commerce by one or more arbitrators appointed in accordance with those Rules.
>
> The applicable law shall be Malagasy law.
>
> The arbitration shall be held at Port Louis, Mauritius.

Flashbird filed a request for arbitration with the Secretariat of the Arbitration and Mediation Centre (MARC) of the Mauritius Chamber of Commerce and Industry. The institution appointed a sole arbitrator to decide the dispute. CSPI objected and applied to the Permanent Court of Arbitration at The Hague for the appointment of three arbitrators. The application was rejected. The arbitration proceeded. CSPI defaulted. The arbitrators issued a final award in favour of Flashbird. CSPI applied to the Supreme Court of Mauritius to set aside the award arguing that the procedure had not been in accordance with the agreement of the parties, that the constitution of the tribunal should have been in accordance with the Rules of the ICC rather than the Rules of MARC.

The parties agreed that paragraph 2 of the arbitration clause referred to the ICC Arbitration Rules and that this created a contradiction between the chosen arbitration institution, MARC, and the chosen arbitration rules, the ICC Rules. Moreover, although the MARC Rules provide that by nominating MARC as the institution, the parties are bound by the MARC Rules,[14] the ICC Rules provide that the ICC Court is the only organisation authorised to administer arbitration under the ICC Rules.[15] CSPI submitted that MARC was to administer the arbitration but should do so in accordance with the ICC Rules. The arbitrator resolved the contradiction by holding that paragraph 1, the choice of the institution, should prevail over paragraph 2 and that the reference to 'international' in paragraph 2 was an error and should properly be interpreted as being a reference to the Mauritius Chamber of Commerce and to MARC. In his view, the choice of the seat of arbitration at Port Louis, Mauritius, reinforced the connection to an arbitration centre physically located in Mauritius.

The Supreme Court held that it was not demonstrated that the constitution of the tribunal would not have been any different under the ICC Rules. Three arbitrators

13. [2021] UKPC 32.
14. Article 1.2.
15. *Ibid.*

would also have been appointed by the ICC. The Privy Council agreed with the Supreme Court. It further noted that there had not been any demonstration that 'substantial prejudice' had been suffered as a result of the arbitration procedure not being in accordance with the agreement of the parties.

§22.03 CONCLUSION

As already noted above, subsequently to the Insigma award issued in Singapore, the ICC has amended its arbitration rules. They now provide that the ICC Court is the only body authorised to administer arbitrations under the ICC Rules and is exclusively responsible for the scrutiny and approval of awards rendered in accordance with the rules.[16] On the other hand, one may have some doubts concerning the effectiveness in all cases of Rule 1.1 of the SIAC Rules which provide that 'whether the parties have agreed to refer their disputes to SIAC for arbitration or to arbitration in accordance with SIAC Rules, the parties shall be deemed to have agreed that the arbitration shall be conducted pursuant to and administered by SIAC in accordance with the SIAC Rules'. If the parties have clearly mentioned in their arbitration clause that any dispute will be decided in accordance with SIAC Rules but will be administered by another institution, their intention to have the dispute administered by that other institution should prevail, at least if that other institution accepts to administer the case under different rules.

In any case, the above demonstrates the problems that can arise from hybrid clauses. They generate jurisdictional disputes and procedural uncertainty, particularly where an arbitral institution is requested to act with an unfamiliar procedural framework and to apply different institutional rules. These issues are definitely significant. They compromise the efficiency of the arbitration process and open up the possibility of challenges to an arbitration award with significant cost consequences for the parties, not to mention the deference that each institution should have vis-à-vis other arbitral institutions. Such clauses should therefore be definitely avoided.

16. Article 1(2) of the 2017 and 2021 Arbitration Rules.

CHAPTER 23

Application of Investment Treaties in the Pre-investment Stage

Matthew Weiniger KC[*]

The first contemporaneously published investment treaty award is *AAPL v. Sri Lanka*, dated 27 June 1990.[1] In the following few years further awards trickled into the public domain without receiving much attention. The current intense focus on bilateral investment treaties (BITs) was not yet underway. I started working for Julian in 1995 and I recall a day shortly afterwards when he summonsed me into his office. An eccentric and irritable client, whom he knew personally and did not like, had sought his advice on a matter relating to arbitration. Although I was junior, my time was more expendable than the established associates, and he asked me to go to the client and see what the issue was.

Upon my arrival, the client directed someone to show me into a windowless room. I was given a two-page memo of supposed facts, some documents and a copy of an instrument, the likes of which I had never seen before, being a BIT between the United Kingdom and a third country. The client ordered me to knock on the door of his office in one hour to let him know whether he would have a claim in arbitration under the treaty.

All I had to go on were a few contemporaneous documents and the treaty itself. I could do little more than read the treaty and guess the answer. With some trepidation I told the client that as he had merely been negotiating a state contract but had not actually signed it, I doubted he would have a claim. I was shown the exit.

In those days, and probably now also, Julian was an extremely busy man, so I am not sure whether I actually had an opportunity to fill him in on the advice I gave that

* I would like to thank Maria Bisila Torao Garcia for her help with this chapter.

1. *Asian Agricultural Products Ltd. v. Republic of Sri Lanka*, ICSID Case No. ARB/87/3, Final Award, 27 June 1990, https://www.italaw.com/cases/96 (accessed 21 July 2022).

afternoon. So, I am taking the opportunity in this article to set out some thoughts about the coverage of pre-investment expenditure under BITs.

A useful precedent for my advice arrived some years later in the form of *Mihaly v. Sri Lanka,*[2] an award published in 2002. Here the claimants brought an International Centre for Settlement of Investment Disputes (ICSID) case under the provisions of the United States-Sri Lanka BIT over the building and operation of a power plant. The case involved compensation for expenditures incurred by the claimant after a formal bidding process and an exclusive right to enter a letter of intent establishing targets to obtain final approval.[3] After the claimant had incurred substantial pre-contractual development expenditures the government refused to sign the agreement. The tribunal dismissed the claim concluding that such expenditures did not qualify as an investment based on the case's particular facts and the document exchanged between the parties.[4] However, in a concurring opinion, arbitrator David Suratgar averred that the ICSID Convention should be available for investors who 'embark on expensive exercises'.[5]

A further award arrived in similar terms in 2003, *Nagel v. Czech Republic.*[6] In May 1993, Mr Nagel, a British national, concluded a Cooperation Agreement with Millicom International Cellular and Sprava Radiokomunikaci Praha (**Sra**), a state entity, for the purchase and operation of a mobile phone licence. This Cooperation Agreement would enable the claimant to obtain rights for a new Global Systems Mobile (GSM) system in the Czech Republic. Despite the existence of the Cooperation Agreement and the fact that Nagel obtained reassurances from senior government officials, months after the agreement was concluded, the government resolved to issue licences to two different companies (Sra's successor and an American investor). Consequently, the anticipated licence never materialised.[7]

As a result of the government actions, Nagel initiated arbitration under the Czech Republic-United Kingdom BIT, claiming that taking his exclusive right to acquire the licence under the agreement was discriminatory. Additionally, Nagel alleged breaches of the treaty's Fair and Equitable Treatment (FET) standard and expropriation.[8] However, the tribunal found that Nagel's rights under the Cooperation Agreement did not constitute an investment protected under the treaty because Nagel failed to prove he had made an investment within the scope of the treaty.[9] When examining the

2. *Mihaly International Corporation v. Democratic Socialist Republic of Sri Lanka,* ICSID Case No. ARB/00/2, Award, 15 May 2002), https://www.italaw.com/cases/702 (accessed 21 July 2022).
3. *Ibid.*, paras 36-48.
4. *Ibid.*, paras 60-62.
5. *Mihaly v. Sri Lanka,* Individual Concurring Opinion by Mr. David Suratgar, 7 March 2002, para. 10, https://www.italaw.com/sites/default/files/case-documents/ita0533.pdf (accessed 21 July 2022).
6. *William Nagel v. The Czech Republic,* SCC Case No. 049/2002, Final Award, 9 September 2003, https://www.italaw.com/cases/728 (accessed 21 July 2022).
7. *Ibid.*, paras 53-59.
8. *See* Czech Republic-United Kingdom BIT (1990), Articles 2(2), 2(3), 3(1), 3(2) and 5(1), https://www.italaw.com/sites/default/files/laws/italaw6082.pdf (accessed 21 July 2022).
9. *Nagel, supra* n. 6, paras 335-336. *See also* Article 1 (a) of the Czech Republic-United Kingdom BIT, which provides 'the term investment means every kind of asset belonging to an investor of one Contracting Party in the territory of the other Contracting Party under the law in force of the latter Contracting Party'.

definition of investment under the treaty, the tribunal indicated that the relevant treaty language specified Czech law should determine and define the term 'investment' for the purpose of treaty protection. The Cooperation Agreement did not qualify under that definition because the agreement itself was preparatory and its financial value speculative.[10]

§23.01 STANDARD APPROACH TO PRE-INVESTMENT PROTECTION: FROM *MIHALY* TO PRESENT

Following *Mihaly* and *Nagel*, there have been a number of treaty cases where claimants have sought to invoke pre-investment protection.

In *Zhinvali v. Georgia*,[11] a case involving the rehabilitation of a Georgian waterpower plant, exclusive rights were granted to enter a concession agreement. After executing a memorandum of understanding with a state-owned company, which held the lease for the operation of the plan, a draft contract circulated. However, a concession agreement was never signed.[12] The claimant, a company incorporated in Ireland, contended having an investment under Georgian domestic law[13] because the Georgian Civil Code recognised protection of preliminary agreements in the pre-investment phase.[14] The investor also contended having contributed to the project by sharing intellectual property rights as well as incurring development costs.[15]

The tribunal did not side with the claimant and explained that the pre-investment costs could not qualify as an investment under Georgian law because the state never assumed such obligation. When analysing the scope of investment protection, the tribunal, referencing *Mihaly v. Sir Lanka*, concluded that based on the evidence presented, the government never consented to undertake state responsibility for development costs.[16]

Similarly, in *Generation Ukraine v. Ukraine*,[17] a US company brought a claim under the Ukraine-United States BIT before ICSID over the development of an office building project in central Kyiv. Generation Ukraine was involved in this project through a company vehicle (Heneratsiya Ltd) in which it had a majority shareholding interest.[18] Heneratsiya Ltd had faced issues while investing in the building project, which never came to fruition. The claimant argued that as a result of the government's

10. *Ibid.*, paras 181-185; 328-329.
11. *Zhinvali Development Ltd v. Republic of Georgia*, ICSID Case No. ARB/00/1, Final Award, 24 January 2003, https://www.italaw.com/cases/3273 (accessed 21 July 2022).
12. *Ibid.*, para. 116.
13. Law No. 473 of 1996 On Promotion and Guarantees of Investment Activity [Georgia], 12 November 1996, https://www.italaw.com/sites/default/files/laws/italaw6309.pdf (accessed 21 July 2022); *See also* the Georgia Civil Code, 26 July 1997, matsne.gov.ge (accessed 21 July 2022).
14. *Zhinvali*, *supra* n. 11, para. 197.
15. *Ibid.*, paras 183, 194-196.
16. *Ibid.*, paras 415-416.
17. *Generation Ukraine, Inc. v. Ukraine*, ICSID Case No. ARB/00/9, Award, 16 September 2003, https://www.italaw.com/cases/482 (accessed 21 July 2021).
18. *Ibid.*, paras 1.1-1.3.

misconduct the project never materialised, which amounted to an unlawful denial of property rights.[19]

While the tribunal held that under the BIT, the claimant's shareholding constituted an investment, it dismissed all claims. It reasoned that the fact that the government officials made it difficult for the claimant to implement its investment through the company vehicle did not entitle the investor to claim pre-investment protection. In particular, the treaty itself did not provide such protection, and Generation Ukraine's ownership in the company vehicle was not affected by the alleged misconduct of the government or state organs.[20] The tribunal further clarified that a protocol of intentions could not qualify as an investment as it was not a binding contract under Ukrainian domestic law.[21]

In another ICSID award, *F-W Oil Interest v. Trinidad & Tobago*,[22] the claimant, a Delaware incorporated company, won a public tender bidding process to negotiate an oil exploitation contract. At the time of negotiations, the claimant was under the belief that it would be granted a licence or proprietary interests. However, while the bidding process was running, the state companies that owned the licences decided that the successful bidder would only operate as a service contractor.[23] As a result, F-W Oil sought assurances that it would be paid and compensated for the work carried out in the event an agreement was not concluded. Soon after, the majority state company suddenly withdrew from the negotiations and, consequently, F-W Oil filed for arbitration, arguing that it was entitled to compensation because its contractual rights were frustrated. The tribunal reasoned that the question as to whether an investment exists or not should be approached in the context of the 'intention animating the BIT',[24] which means in light of the object and purpose of the treaty and its terms. In that vein, the tribunal determined that, realistically, there cannot be an investment without the existence of entitlement or legal rights. Further, a key aspect highlighted by the tribunal was the fact that it was clear that the parties did not intend to be bound before the execution of a formal contract.[25]

§23.02 SWIMMING AGAINST THE TIDE: *BOSCA* AND *NORDZUCKER*

While the predominant line of authority is clear, the jurisprudence does not all point in one direction. There are a limited number of cases where investors have persuaded tribunals to accept jurisdiction over investments that never came to fruition.

19. *Ibid.*, para. 5.1.
20. *Ibid.*, paras 8.4-8.7, '[a]fter analysing how the claimant's investment had materialised, the tribunal noted that Generation Ukraine had acquired its investment through a number of transactions that could not give raise to a dispute within the meaning of Article VI(1)(a) or (b) of the BIT'.
21. *Ibid.*, para. 6.14 (a)-(i).
22. *F-W Oil interest Inc v. Republic of Trinidad & Tobago*, ICSID Case No. ARB/01/14, Award, 3 March 2006, https://www.italaw.com/cases/469 (accessed 21 July 2022).
23. *Ibid.*, paras 1-9, 'changed the basis of the proposed transaction … the successful bidder would no longer be granted a licence or other proprietary interest … but would instead operate as a "Service Contractor", remunerated by a rate per barrel of oil produced'.
24. *Ibid.*, para. 124.
25. *Ibid.*, paras 162-166.

Bosca v. Lithuania[26] was an UNCITRAL arbitration where the investor succeeded in showing a treaty breach. The claim arose from Lithuania's handling of a tender awarded to the claimant over four state-owned beverage makers after the claimant was declared the winning bidder. Despite the novelty of the finding that pre-investment expenditures were protected, the case can be analysed along conventional grounds. The BIT in question included a protocol specifically treating '*associated activities*' as investments.[27] The claimant had already made substantial investments in Lithuania prior to the tender and the tribunal concluded that the claimant's tender expenditures could be considered associated activities and thus be entitled to protection in accordance with the terms of the BIT.[28]

A more unusual claimant-friendly award is *Nordzucker v. Poland*.[29] This award was rendered in 2008 but was only published in 2013 on the IAReporter website.[30] This may be a reason for its novel approach receiving less exposure than it would otherwise be due. Here the claimant sought to recover pre-investment expenditure after being designated the winning bidder in a privatisation process to purchase two state-owned sugar plants where the state, after initiating a privatisation procedure, ultimately did not sell.[31] Nordzucker filed for arbitration and argued that it had an investment within the meaning of the BIT. Poland contended, relying on *Mihaly*, that pre-investments were not protected under the treaty.[32] After examining the wording of the BIT, the tribunal concluded it covered investments '*in the making*'.[33] Its conclusion was based upon a close reading of the BIT and its use of the word 'investment'. Article 2(1) of the BIT limited its protections to '*investments that have been admitted in accordance with the respective law of one Contracting Party*'. While this would limit the BIT's protections to concluded investments, the article went on to say, '*Each Contracting Party shall in any case accord investments fair and equitable treatment*'.[34] The tribunal relied upon the phrase '*in any case*' to say that the FET standard covers more than merely concluded investments.[35] This conclusion is questionable from a policy standpoint as the FET standard is a wider treatment standard than the lesser standard, which is strictly limited to 'proper' investments. However, as a literal reading of the treaty text, the tribunal's conclusion cannot be faulted.

26. *Luigiterzo Bosca v. Lithuania*, UNCITRAL, Award, 17 May 2013, https://www.italaw.com/cases/2076 (accessed 21 July 2022).
27. *Ibid.*, para. 104; *see also* the Protocol to the Italy-Lithuania BIT (1994), p. 8.
28. *Ibid.*, para. 264.
29. *Nordzucker v. Poland*, UNCITRAL, Partial Award on Jurisdiction, 10 December 2008, https://www.italaw.com/cases/750 (accessed 21 July 2022).
30. Filip Balcerzak & Luke Eric Peterson, *Germany-Poland BIT award in Norzucker case adopts novel approach to claims centered on events that occurred before arbitral consent was given* (10 December 2013), https://www.iareporter.com/articles/ (accessed 21 July 2022).
31. *Nordzucker, supra* n. 29, paras 36-51.
32. *Ibid.*, para. 137.
33. *Ibid.*, para. 211.
34. *See* Germany-Poland BIT (1993), Article 2(1), https://www.italaw.com/sites/default/files/laws/italaw6127.pdf (accessed 21 July 2022).
35. *Ibid.*, paras 182-185, 'the Tribunal is inclined to accept that the "fair and equitable treatment" is applicable to both admitted investments and to the promotion and admission of investments'.

§23.03 WHEN CAN AN INVESTOR INVOKE PRE-INVESTMENT PROTECTIONS?

I am pleased, in retrospect, that my guess that day in the 1990s turned out to be correct. Tribunals have repeatedly highlighted that investments typically consist of several cumulative interrelated economic activities that should be considered conjunctively.[36] Nevertheless, foreign direct investment processes for the purpose of treaty protection are usually divided into the establishment stage (pre-investment phase) and the investment phase. The vast majority of BITs cover only the post-establishment stage.[37]

This makes sense from a legal point of view as investment treaties by their very nature are supposed to protect investments. The legal status of an investor's property rights is usually assessed by reference to the domestic law of the host state. If that law would not recognise the rights as amounting to a concluded investment (for example, because a contract had yet to come into force) then it is reasonable to conclude that such non-rights do not constitute an investment. However, this conclusion can lead to gaps in property protection under investment treaties. An investor can expend a great deal of money at the pre-investment stage, either in participating in a tender process or on reliance of a future contract. Such pre-investment expenditures can themselves be subject to unfair administrative actions, in the same way as concluded investments. Nevertheless, absent specific treaty wording they do not amount to covered investments.

36. *Fedax N.V. v. Venezuela*, Decision on Jurisdiction, 11 July 1997, paras 25-26; *Ceskoslovenska Obchodni Banka, A.S. v. The Slovak Republic*, Decision on Jurisdiction, 24 May 1999, para. 72, 'the Tribunal agrees with the interpretation adopted in the *Fedax* case. An investment is frequently a rather complex operation, composed of various interrelated transactions'; *ATA Industrial and Trading Company v. The Hashemite Kingdom of Jordan*, Final award, 18 May 2010, para. 96, 'an investment is ... correctly conceived of as a bundle of rights'; *Electrable S.A. v. Hungary*, Decision on Jurisdiction, 30 November 2012, paras 5.44-5.45; *Magyar Farming Company Ltd v. Hungary*, Final Award, 13 October 2019, paras 274-275; *Inmaris Perestroika Sailing Maritime Services GmbH and Others v. Ukraine*, Decision on Jurisdiction, 8 March 2010, paras 92-94.
37. UNCTAD, *World Investment Report* (2015), p. 110; Borzu Sabahi et al., *Investor-State Arbitration* (2nd ed., Oxford University Press 2019), pp. 47-74, 'Despite some significant variations, modern BITs are broadly similar in their provisions ... The majority of BITs follow the OECD model, which only protects investment [once their made]'.

CHAPTER 24

Loss of Chance Damages

Audley Sheppard KC[*]

§24.01 *ENPH V. NIGERIA*

In the case of *Enron Nigeria Power Holding Ltd (ENPH) v. Lagos State Government & ors,*[1] ENPH, which was part of the US Enron Corporation, entered into a Power Purchase Agreement (PPA) whereby it was to, *inter alia*, design, construct, finance, own and operate an onshore 538 MW natural gas fired power plant to be located in Lagos, Nigeria (and a gas pipeline). The Purchaser was the Lagos State Government. The National Electric Power Authority of Nigeria (NEPA) was also a party to the PPA, as was the Federal Republic of Nigeria (FRN) as Guarantor. The PPA was governed by Nigerian law.

The PPA was signed on 6 December 1999. Just nine days later, the NEPA gave notice to ENPH that implementation of the PPA had been stayed until further notice. Four weeks later, on 13 January 2000, the President of Nigeria sent a letter to the Governor of Lagos State informing him that the Attorney-General of the FRN had advised that the PPA was to be considered inoperative. ENPH sought to persuade the Nigerian government to reverse its decision. In September 2000, AES Corporation, another US power company, was granted an option by ENPH to acquire its interests in

* This contribution to the *Liber Amicorum* for Julian considers the application of the 'loss of chance' / 'loss of opportunity' doctrine in determining damages, including in investor-state dispute settlement (ISDS).

1. *Enron Nigeria Power Holding Ltd v. (1) Lagos State Government, (2) Power Holding Company of Nigeria, (3) Federal Republic of Nigeria*, ICC Case No. 14417. The tribunal comprised Julian Lew (UK) (P), Robert H Smit (USA) and Ms Tinuade Oyekunle (Nigeria) (the Lew tribunal).

the onshore project, valued at USD 34 million, but conditional upon certain amendments to the PPA being agreed by the Nigerian authorities (AES Option).[2] No agreement was reached with the FRN. At the end of 2001, Enron Corporation filed for US Chapter 11 bankruptcy protection. Some years later, ENPH (which had been sold and taken out of the bankruptcy proceedings) commenced ICC arbitration seeking substantial damages for wrongful termination.[3] A tribunal chaired by Professor Julian Lew was constituted.

In a partial final award on liability,[4] the tribunal found against the NEPA (by then Power Holding Company of Nigeria plc – PHCN[5]) and the FRN.[6] In a further partial final award on remedies,[7] the tribunal determined that ENPH was entitled to be put in the position it would have been in had the contract been performed after taking into account the contingencies that would have reduced ENPH's expectation of net profits. In this respect, the tribunal stated that ENPH would 'have to prove, on the balance of probabilities, the actual losses it has suffered taking into account its abilities, capabilities and those of third parties to perform their obligations' and that the tribunal would 'reduce the level of lost profits projected to reflect the level of likelihood that the outcome would have in fact produced'. It added that, in the alternative, ENPH could seek reliance damages.

In the third stage of the arbitration, ENPH sought damages on several bases: (i) lost profits that it would reasonably have been expected to make as at the date of the breach, which it quantified on a Discounted Cash Flow (DCF) basis at USD 475 million (expectation damages); (ii) alternatively, damages quantified on the basis of a loss of a chance to make profits; (iii) alternatively, damages quantified according to the amount the respondents would hypothetically have been willing to pay to be released from their obligations under the PPA (i.e., *Wrotham Park* damages[8]); and (iv) alternatively, the costs and expenses in fact incurred (reliance damages).

In its final award,[9] the tribunal first considered the claim for expectation damages, which were based on 1999 pre-contractual financial projections, as updated in 2011. The tribunal accepted that had the project gone ahead as originally intended it would have been profitable. However, it did not go ahead and the Enron group had done very little to progress the project at the time of termination. The tribunal considered that the project would have faced many hurdles and developments which would have tested the income and cost projections. These included the designing of the power plant, obtaining designation of the route of the gas pipeline and the necessary

2. AES acquired Phases I and III of the PPA for the supply of small power plants on offshore barges. The AES Option was for Phase II, being the onshore power plant. References hereinafter to the PPA are to Phase II only.
3. The author was counsel to the Claimant, assisted by Professor Edwin Peel of Oxford University.
4. Partial Final Award on Liability, dated 9 December 2008.
5. The successor in title to the NEPA.
6. The claims against Lagos State were dismissed.
7. Partial Final Award on Remedies, dated 28 February 2011.
8. *See infra* n. 11.
9. Final Award, dated 19 November 2012, available at: https://jusmundi.com/en/document/decision/en-enron-nigeria-power-holding-enph-v-federal-republic-of-nigeria-final-award-monday-19th-november-2012#decision_5262.

permissions, the hazards of building both the pipeline and the power plant, obtaining the equity and debt finance for the project, appointing a contractor capable of undertaking the project on time and on budget, ensuring a guaranteed supply of gas, and general political uncertainties in Nigeria. Moreover, the assumptions concerning Enron Corporation as an experienced contractor and operator changed; initially when it changed its policy and sought to sell its assets, and then when it went into bankruptcy. The tribunal concluded that ENPH's projections were not the most appropriate and reliable basis for determining the quantum of damages, because there were too many uncertainties as to the amount of realistic profits which would have been earned. Even applying discounts for the various contingencies, as suggested by ENPH in its alternative request, would not have given any realistic calculation of a fair and realistic loss. However, the PPA was a valuable and profitable asset for a company that had the ability, capacity and interest to perform it.

The tribunal then turned to consider 'loss of chance' and noted that the parties agreed that the tribunal could determine the damages to be recovered by the claimant on that latter basis. The tribunal stated that 'loss of chance' is the alternative to the calculation of actual loss, or expected lost profits, which cannot be satisfactorily proved. It said that the test here is to determine the loss of opportunity to make a profit due to the wrongdoer's breaches. The tribunal noted that two principal issues must be identified: first, what was the loss suffered by the innocent person, or the value of that loss; and second, what are the chances that - but for the other party's breaches - the benefit or gain would have been received.

The tribunal considered the AES Option to be the most stable figure from which to calculate the lost chance (i.e., the 'base loss'). The option price of USD 34 million was a cap to be negotiated downwards depending on the terms of the new PPA. There were at least four discounting factors: (i) would a final agreement have been reached by AES and the respondents; (ii) would AES in fact have exercised the option; (iii) would AES have been able to raise the necessary finance and otherwise been able to perform the new PPA; and (iv) would ENPH have been able to obtain a parent company guarantee as required under the original PPA. After considering each of these, the tribunal concluded that there was a one-third (33%) chance that the contingencies would have been met and the project assigned to AES. Accordingly, the tribunal fixed damages at USD 11.22 million (plus interest).[10]

The tribunal therefore neither needed to consider the *Wrotham Park* doctrine (i.e., 'negotiating damages')[11] nor reliance damages. It did note, however, which is of

10. The tribunal's analysis and award of damages can be contrasted with that in *Process and Industrial Developments Ltd v. The Ministry of Petroleum Resources of the Federal Republic of Nigeria*, Final Award, dated 31 January 2017 (Lord Hoffmann (P), A Evans and B Ojo dissenting). The claimant had not acquired the site nor built the NGL plant, but was awarded USD 6.597 billion (plus interest), without any discounting.
11. The award of damages for breach of contract on the basis of a hypothetical negotiation between a willing buyer (the contract-breaker) and a willing seller (the party claiming damages) in which the subject matter of the negotiation is the release of the relevant contractual obligation and in relation to which both parties are assumed to act reasonably; *see e.g.*, *Wrotham Park Estate Co v. Parkside Home Ltd* [1974] 1 WLR 798; *Pell Frischmann Engineering Ltd v. Bow Valley Iran Ltd*

interest, that given the *de minimis* amount of ENPH's actual expenses (USD 213,555), an award of approximately that amount would unfairly let off the respondents from the consequences of the unlawful repudiation of the PPA.

§24.02 ENGLISH LAW

The parties and the Lew tribunal looked to English law principles, because the English common law applies in Nigeria, subject to contrary intention.[12]

'Loss of chance'[13] arises both in claims of breach of contract[14] and tort,[15] and – if applicable – will inform the award of damages.[16]

Professor Peel, in *Treitel – The Law of Contract*, notes that it has been said that there are two different types of 'loss of chance' claim.[17] In the first type, the very thing which the claimant has lost is a 'chance', or an opportunity, to obtain something else, such as taking part in a beauty contest or a tender. A claimant must prove that the loss of opportunity was due to the defendant on the balance of probabilities. It is then a question of quantifying such loss and that may be done on a percentage basis.

Chaplin v. Hicks (1911)[18] is generally regarded as having introduced the 'loss of chance' doctrine into the law of England. Mr Hicks offered to engage 12 actresses to be chosen by a process which reduced the 6,000 applicants down to 300, and those down to 50 finalists, who would then be interviewed. Ms Chaplin succeeded in becoming one of the 50 finalists but, in breach of contract, she was not given adequate notice of the interviews and the 12 winners were chosen in her absence. A jury awarded her GBP 100, the equivalent of over GBP 800 today,[19] being between 13% and 22% of the financial benefit of winning the contest.[20] The Court of Appeal upheld the award. Vaughan Williams LJ stated: '... the presence of all the contingencies upon which the gaming of the prize might depend makes the calculation not only difficult but incapable of being carried out with certainty or precision', but wished to 'deny with emphasis that, because precision cannot be arrived at, the jury has no function in the assessment of damages'. In this case, Ms Chaplin was deprived of the opportunity, which was

---

[2009] UKPC 45; *Morris-Garner v. One Step (Support) Ltd* [2018] UKSC 20 (which preferred the term 'negotiating damages'); and *Treitel*, *infra* note 14, paras 20-014-20-021.

12. By section 32 of the Interpretation Act, Cap 123, LFN (2004), the common law of England, the doctrines of equity, together with the statutes of general application that were in force on 1 January 1900, will be in force in Nigeria.
13. Variously 'loss of chance' as referred to in *Treitel* or 'loss of a chance' as referred to in *Clerk & Lindsell* and *McGregor*.
14. Edwin Peel, *Treitel – The Law of Contract* (15th edn, 2020, Sweet & Maxwell) ('*Treitel*'), para. 20-063.
15. Michael Jones (gen. ed.), *Clerk & Lindsell on Torts* (23rd edn, 2020, Sweet & Maxwell), paras 2-76-2-99.
16. James Edelman, *McGregor on Damages* (21st edn, 2021, Sweet & Maxwell) ('*McGregor*'), paras 10-041-10-110.
17. *See Treitel*, *supra* n. 14, para. 20-063.
18. [1911] 2 KB 786 (CA).
19. *See McGregor*, *supra* n. 16, para. 10-041.
20. The winners were awarded contracts which paid out between GBP 450 and GBP 700 over three years (*see Treitel*, para. 20-063, footnote 384).

caused by Mr Hicks on the balance of probabilities, and that was compensable in damages.[21] A more recent (and prosaic) example is *Mallino v. Essex Demolition Contractors* (2022)[22] where the claimant was deprived of the right to be included in the re-tendering of certain construction works.

The second type of claim is not so much that the claimant has lost a valuable right, but rather the opportunity of gaining a benefit which depends on a third party, whose conduct is a critical link in the chain of causation, acting in a particular way, An example is a solicitor's negligence preventing the claimant negotiating capped liability protection, which would have been dependent upon the contractual counterparty agreeing to those terms, as in *Allied Maples* (1995).[23] A percentage assessment is applied to the chance of that eventuality occurring (and not-occurring).

In both types of claim, the claimant must prove as a matter of causation that it had a real or substantial chance as opposed to a speculative one. If it succeeds in doing so, the evaluation of the chance is part of the assessment of the quantum of damages, the range lying somewhere between something that just qualifies as real or substantial on the one hand and near certainty on the other hand.[24]

However, Justice James Edelman, in *McGregor on Damages*, states that loss of a chance appearing in the process of quantification does not fall within the 'loss of a chance' doctrine proper.[25] He opines that there are three stages of enquiry: first, it must be ascertained whether loss of a chance is recognized as a head of damage or loss in itself; second, it must be shown on the balance of probabilities that the claimant has lost the particular chance; and third, the lost chance must be quantified and the quantification is expressed in percentages and proportions.

Where a claim is assessed on a 'loss of chance' basis, this will benefit the claimant in those cases where the chance is assessed as real or substantial, but less than 50%, as he/she will still recover the proportion of chance proved. It will benefit the defendant where the chance exceeds 50%, since the claimant cannot in such a case claim that he/she has proved his/her loss on the balance of probabilities and therefore recover in full.

Given that the determination of loss of future profits is always uncertain and depends on how third parties might act (such as customers, commodity markets,

21. It has been said that *Chaplin v. Hicks* opened a legal Pandora's box: *McGregor, supra* n. 16, para. 10-042, footnote 165, per Lord Neuberger; and that 'authorities which in modern times have cascaded over the law reports': *McGregor*, para. 10-043. However, these are largely in the fields of personal injury and professional malpractice.
22. *Mallino Development Ltd v. Essex Demolition Contractors Ltd* [2022] EWHC 1418 (TCC). The judge determined that the value of the benefit had the claimant won the tender to be GBP 321,000 and assessed the chance at 66% and so awarded damages of GBP 212,000.
23. *Allied Maples Group Ltd v. Simmons & Simmons (a firm)* [1995] EWCA Civ 17. *See* more recently, e.g., *Perry v. Raleys Solicitors* [2019] UKSC 5.
24. For a recent decision reviewing the jurisprudence, *see Bugsby Property LLC v. LGIM Commercial Lending Ltd & anor* [2022] EWHC 2001 (Comm), per Knowles J. The defendant breached a contractual obligation of exclusivity, which allowed another party to bid for and acquire a development. The judge assessed the chance of the claimant being the successful bidder as a near certainty (90%) if it could raise the finance (40%) = 36% of lost profits.
25. *See McGregor, supra* n. 16, para. 10-048; *see also Treitel, supra* n. 14, para. 20-064.

government authorities and the economy generally), why are not all such determinations assessed on the basis of 'loss of chance'? The answer is that it is a matter of judicial policy. Professor Peel observes:[26]

> 'To some extent, all claims for damages for breach of contract depend on the contingency of what would or might have happened if there had been no breach, but it is only in the two types of case referred to above that a 'loss of chance' approach is taken. For example, they can be distinguished from a case where what is claimed is the loss of the opportunity to trade generally and the claimant seeks recovery of the profits he would have made. The claimant will need to prove on the balance of probability that he would have traded profitably and, if he does so, the court will seek to 'quantify the loss'. At this stage, an element of 'chance' may still be in play, as in the example of a restaurant which is prevented from trading, where the extent of the loss depends on the actions of multiple third parties in the form of potential customers. Nevertheless, in such a case the court simply does its best to assess the loss and since that will have involved an assessment of all the chances involved in trading, even if not in such terms, it is not appropriate to further discount the figure which is reached by the court.'

The restaurant example is taken from *Vasiliou v. Hajigeorgio*u (2010).[27] In that case, the claimant sued for lost profits while his restaurant was closed due to the defendant. The first instance judge received expert evidence on the number of covers at the restaurant, the number of cover turns per week, and the average cover price. The defendant sought to have the outcome discounted to reflect Mr Vasiliou's alleged (in)competence as a restaurateur and the chance that the restaurant would fail. The Court of Appeal held that no discounting was appropriate (unlike in a 'loss of chance' case such as *Allied Maples*). It endorsed[28] the approach that the claimant has first to establish an actionable head of loss. Once the claimant has established, on a balance of probability, that – but for the breach – it would have traded profitably, the next task is to quantify the loss. Where that involves a hypothetical exercise, the court does not apply the same balance of probability approach as it would to the proof of past facts. Rather, it estimates the loss by making the best attempt it can to evaluate the chances, great or small (unless those chances amount to no more than remote speculation), taking all significant factors into account, and reaching an amount equating to lost profits of the restaurant. (This is akin to the 'income approach' used in ISDS cases, discussed below.)

As a final observation on English law, it might be said that application of a percentage discount in 'loss of chance' cases is arbitrary.[29] Certainly, any determination has to be reasoned. But in the arbitration context, the court has allowed a degree

26. *See Treitel, supra* n. 14, para. 20-063.
27. *Vasiliou v. Hajigeorgiou* [2010] EWCA Civ 1475.
28. At [25], quoting Toulson LJ, in *Parabola Investments Ltd v. Browallia Cal Ltd & ors* [2010] EWCA Civ 486, at [23].
29. The courts have recognized that the assessment of damages cannot always be particularly scientific and may involve 'the exercise of a sound imagination and the practice of the broad axe', *see Morris-Garner, supra* n. 11, at [37] per Lord Reed.

of flexibility. In *Pakistan v. Broadsheet*,[30] Broadsheet had been retained to recover monies from the family of former President Nawaz Sharif. The contract had been terminated and Broadsheet brought a claim for loss of the chance to be paid a commission in relation to recoveries and was awarded USD 21.6 million. Pakistan complained that the tribunal had failed to give reasons as to how any 'loss of chance' discount had been applied. Moulder J concluded that the failure to give adequate reasons cannot amount to a serious irregularity under section 68(2)(c) or (h) of the Arbitration Act 1996.

§24.03 UNIDROIT PRINCIPLES

'Loss of a chance' is recognized in other legal systems, such as in French law,[31] but less so in German law,[32] and also in soft law codifications such as the UNIDROIT Principles of International Commercial Contracts 1994, 2004, 2010 & 2016.[33] Article 7.4.3 (*Certainty of harm*) provides:[34]

> '(1) Compensation is due only for harm, including future harm, that is established with a reasonable degree of certainty.

30. *The Islamic Republic of Pakistan & The National Accountability Bureau v. Broadsheet LLC* [2019] EWHC 1832 (Comm). Partial Final Award (Quantum), dated 17 December 2018 (A Evans). Contrast a decision of the Singapore Court of Appeal that a tribunal's flexible approach to proof of damages resulted in an arbitrary decision that could not have been anticipated by the parties: CEF & anor v CEH [2022] SGCA 54.
31. '*Le principle de la perte de chance*' is the present and certain disappearance of a favourable eventuality ('*la disparition actuelle et certaine d'une éventualité favorable*') (*see* Cass. 1re civ., 21 November 2006, n° 05-15.674). Examples of recoverable loss of a chance include a claim where a racehorse which cannot take part in a race because it arrived late due to the carrier's fault or loss of chance of winning a trial due to the lawyer's fault. *See e.g.*, A Bénabent, *Droit des obligations*, July 2021, Lextenso, para. 672, and P Stoffel-Munck, P Malaurie & L Aynès, *Droit des obligations*, September 2022, Lextenso, para. 607.
32. German law generally does not recognize the 'loss of chance/opportunity' ('*Verlust von Gewinnchancen*') as compensable damage because 'chances'/'opportunities' are not sufficiently concrete/material asset positions ('*keine hinreichend verselbständigte Vermögenspositionen*'). *See e.g.*, Grüneberg/Grüneberg, *Bürgerliches Gesetzbuch*, 2022, Vorb v. § 249, para. 53; and BeckOGK/Brand, *Bürgerliches Gesetzbuch*, § 252, paras 78-82. Also *see*: (1) BGH, NJW 1983, 442: A judgment by the German Federal Court of Justice which dismissed damage claims by an architect who had been wrongfully excluded from an architectural competition for a project; and (2) OLG Düsseldorf, VersR 1987, 691: A judgment by the Higher Regional Court Düsseldorf which dismissed a claim for damages based on the assertion that a race horse would have had 'chances of winning' in various races had it not been disqualified because the responsible veterinarian had injected it with a banned doping substance. There are, however, exceptions, e.g.: (a) Procurement law: section 180 of the Act against Restraints of Competition provides for a damages' claim where – by wrongful exclusion from the procurement process – the applicant loses the chance for of award of the contract; and (b) General Act on Equal Treatment: section 15 provides for damages claim in cases where an applicant has been rejected in violation of the prohibition of discrimination.
33. *See*https://www.unidroit.org/english/principles/contracts/principles2016/principles2016-e.pdf, p. 274.
34. *See* Stefan Vogenauer (gen. ed.), *Commentary on the UNIDROIT Principles of International Commercial Contracts* (2nd edn, 2015, OUP), pp. 988-992 (this part written by Ewan McKendrick, Oxford University).

> Compensation may be due for the loss of a chance in proportion to the probability of its occurrence.
> Where the amount of damages cannot be established with a sufficient degree of certainty, the assessment is at the discretion of the court.'

The example given in the Official Comment in each of the editions of the UNIDROIT Principles to illustrate Article 7.4.3 is of a contract under which an express delivery company agrees to deliver a tender for the construction of an airport, but in breach of contract it delivers the tender after the expiry of the closing date for submission. In such a case, the amount of compensation depends upon the degree of probability of the tender being accepted, such that the tribunal will have to compare it with the tenders that were submitted on time. The compensation payable is a proportion of the profit which the aggrieved party might have made.[35]

§24.04 INTERNATIONAL LAW

Based on the statements of principle made in the *Factory at Chorzów* case,[36] the United Nations International Law Commission's (ILC) draft Articles on Responsibility for Internationally Wrongful Acts (2001)[37] at Article 36 (*Compensation*) state that (1) 'The State responsible for an internationally wrongful act is under an obligation to compensate for the damage caused thereby, insofar as such damage is not made good by restitution' and (2) 'The compensation shall cover any financially assessable damage including loss of profits insofar as it is established.'

International law has taken a conservative approach to any harm or damages that were uncertain, also as articulated in *Chorzów*.[38] As explained in the ILC's Commentary on Article 36(2):[39] '... lost profits have not been as commonly awarded in practice as compensation for accrued losses. Tribunals have been reluctant to provide compensation for claims with inherently speculative elements. When compared with tangible assets, profits (and intangible assets which are income-based) are relatively vulnerable to commercial, political and other risks, and increasingly so the further into the future projections are made. In cases where lost future profits have been awarded, it has been where an anticipated income stream has attained sufficient attributes to be considered a legally protected interest of sufficient certainty to be compensable ...'.

However, where there had been a taking by the State, international law has come to accept the market value approach for determining lost profits of a going concern,

35. *See* https://www.unidroit.org/wp-content/uploads/2021/06/Unidroit-Principles-1994-English-i.pdf, at p. 199; and 2016 edition, *supra* n. 33, p. 275. Cf. *Mallino*, *supra* n. 22.
36. *Case Concerning the Factory at Chorzów* (*Germany v. Poland*) (Jurisdiction) 1927 PCIJ Rep Series A No 9, at p. 21; and (Merits) 1928 PCIJ Rep Series A No 17, at pp 47-48 and 51.
37. International Law Commission, *Draft Articles on Responsibility of States for Internationally Wrongful Acts*, with commentaries (ILC Commentary), adopted 2001, available at https://legal.un.org/ilc/texts/instruments/english/draft_articles/9_6_2001.pdf.
38. (Merits), *supra* n. 36, at p. 57, where the Court would not condone: 'possible but contingent and indeterminate damage, which, in accordance with the jurisprudence of arbitral tribunals, cannot be taken into account'.
39. James Crawford, *The International Law Commission's Articles on State Responsibility* (2002, CUP), at para. 27, p. 228.

especially in *fora* such as the Iran-United States Claims Tribunal,[40] and especially by ISDS tribunals[41] (with 'market value' expressly referred to in the expropriation clause of many investment treaties).[42] The fair market value is the price that a willing buyer would pay to a willing seller in circumstances in which each had good information, each desired to maximize its financial gain, and neither was under duress or threat. This 'income approach' typically relies on a DCF methodology to establish a present market value. Future uncertainly and risk should influence the income line and the discount rate (applying the capital asset pricing model) so as to lower the net present value.[43] The CAPM includes a *beta* factor for systemic risk, and can also include an adjustment for country specific risk and/or company specific risk (a so-called *alpha* factor). The market value approach for a going concern is endorsed in the World Bank's Guidelines on the Treatment of Foreign Investment (1992).[44] However, where the enterprise demonstrates a lack of profitability, the Guidelines propose that compensation be based on the liquidation value.[45]

As we see below, while one distinguished tribunal held that 'loss of chance' did not form part of international law (*Chevron v. Ecuador*), another eminent tribunal the same year was willing to assess damages based on the lost opportunity to make a profit (*Gemplus v. Mexico*). Nevertheless, the application of 'loss of chance' is rare.

§24.05 *SAPPHIRE, SOABI* AND *SPP*

The application of 'loss of chance' in international investment cases is often traced back to *Sapphire v. NIOC* and *SPP v. Egypt* (with *SOABI v. Senegal* sometimes mentioned).

In *Sapphire v. NIOC* (1963),[46] NIOC terminated Sapphire's oil concession contract after it had done some work but before prospecting had begun. The claimant sought

40. See e.g., *Starrett Housing Corp v. The Islamic Republic of Iran*, 16 Iran-US CTR 112, Final Award No. 314-24-1, 14 August 1987, para. 274.
41. *See e.g.*, Sergey Ripinsky and Kevin Williams, *Damages in International Investment Law* (2008, BIICL); Irmgard Marboe, *Calculation of Compensation and Damages in International Investment Law* (2nd edn, 2017, OUP); Campbell McLachlan, Laurence Shore & Matthew Weiniger, *International Investment Arbitration: Substantive Principles*, ch. 9 (2nd edn, 2017, OUP); Borzu Sabah, Noah Rubins & Don Wallace Jr, *Investor-State Arbitration*, ch. XXI (2nd edn, 2019, OUP); John Trenor (ed.), *The Guide to Damages in International Arbitration* (4th edn, 2020, Law Business Research); August Reinisch and Christoph Schreuer, *International Protection of Investments: The Substantive Standards*, ch. 1.D-E (2020, CUP).
42. *Cf.* the weight to be given to wording in an investment treaty such as 'just' or 'appropriate' compensation, *see* Separate Opinion on the Issues at the Quantum Phase of *CME v. Czech Republic*, by I Brownlie.
43. *See e.g.*, Marboe *supra* n. 41, paras 4.89-4.132, and as an example of its application *Watkins Holding Sàrl 7 ors v. Kingdom of Spain*, ICSID Case No. ARB/15/44, Award, dated 22 January 2020 (C Abraham (P), M Pryles and H Fabri dissenting), paras 694-744.
44. World Bank Group, *Guidelines on the Treatment of Foreign Direct Investment*, para. IV.5, available at: https://documents1.worldbank.org/curated/en/955221468766167766/pdf/multi-page.pdf.
45. *Ibid.*, para. IV.6(ii).
46. *Sapphire International Petroleum Ltd v. National Iranian Oil Company, ad hoc* tribunal, 35 ILR 136 (1963), Award, dated 15 March 1963 (P Calvin), pp 187-189.

lost profits (of USD 5 million). The Swiss sole arbitrator referred to French law, to *Chaplin v. Hicks* and to US law. He held that there are two steps in dealing with a claim for loss of profits. The first step is to determine whether compensation for the loss of opportunity is recognized in law. If the principle is recognized, then the determination of the amount of compensation is a question of fact to be determined by the arbitrator. He noted that while no one can confirm that the operation would have been profitable, it was nevertheless clear that the claimant had an opportunity to discover oil, which both parties regarded as favourable, and that this opportunity had value. He referred to the risk inherent in the operation in a desolate area, and unfavourable climate, with potential trouble such as wars, disturbances, economic crises or slumps in prices, which could affect the operation over 25 years. He concluded that in his judgment it was reasonable and equitable[47] to fix the amount of compensation for loss of profits at USD 2 million.

In *SOABI v. Senegal* (1988),[48] a contract to construct social housing was cancelled before any sales were made. The claimant sought lost profits of CFA Francs 3.4 billion, which the tribunal reduced to 1.4 billion, but even then thought the possibility of profits was sufficiently uncertain and awarded only 150 million (plus its wasted investment costs).

In the well-known case of *SPP v. Egypt* (1992),[49] a project to build a hotel and sell off parcels of land was terminated. The claimant[50] claimed net lost profits of USD 80 million. The tribunal decided that the DCF methodology was not appropriate because the project was in its infancy with an insufficient history on which to base projected revenues into the future. Only 6% of the lots had been sold. Quoting *Chorzów* and *Amoco* (1987),[51] the tribunal held that speculative or uncertain damages cannot be awarded; however, it was incontestable on the evidential record that the claimants' investment had a value that exceeded their out-of-pocket expenses, and awarded USD 3.1 million.

§24.06 ISDS

With the increase in ISDS claims, so have claims for loss of profits, allegedly caused by expropriation or sometimes breach of the Fair and Equitable Treatment (FET)

47. Although the sole arbitrator had decided that the governing substantive law was 'the principles of law generally recognised by civilized nations', he stated that it is the arbitrator's task to decide damages *ex aequo et bono*, by considering all the circumstances. He may have simply meant that determining damages, especially for loss of chance, requires judicial discretion.
48. *Société Ouest Africaine des Bétons Industriels v. Senegal*, ICSID Case No. ARB/82/1, Award, dated 25 February 1988 (A Broches (P), J Schultz and K Mbaye dissenting).
49. *Southern Pacific Properties (Middle East) Ltd v. Arab Republic of Egypt*, ICSID Case No. ARB/84/3, Award, dated 20 May 1992 (E Jiménez de Aréchaga (P), R Pietrowski and M El Mahdi dissenting), paras 185-189.
50. The claimant was owned by Peter Munk, who 20 years later, represented by the author, appointed Julian Lew as arbitrator in a shareholder dispute.
51. *Amoco International Finance Corp v. Government of the Islamic Republic of Iran, National Iranian Oil Co, National Petroleum Co and Kharg*, IUSCT Case No. 56, Partial Award, dated 14 July 1987, para. 238 ('One of the best settled rules of the law on international responsibility of States is that no reparation for speculative or uncertain damages can be awarded. This holds true for the existence of the damage and to its effect as well.').

standard. Application of 'loss of chance' has increased, but remains uncommon.[52] As described earlier, 'loss of chance' can be applied to loss of an opportunity and separately to the assessment of damages, including where the claimant has yet to establish a profitable business, but there may be overlap between the two. I have sought to characterise the cases in to these two types rather than take them in chronological order, but I start with an unusual example of denial of justice which dismissed the 'loss of chance' doctrine as a general principle of international law.

[A] Denial of Justice

In *Chevron v. Ecuador* (2010),[53] the tribunal held that there had been a denial of justice due to the undue delay in progressing the claimants' claims in the Ecuadorian courts. The claimants requested an award of damages equivalent to that sought before the courts, relying on *Chorzów* and the ILC Articles. The respondent argued that damages should be assessed on the basis of 'loss of chance', referring to the UNIDROIT Principles, and discounted to 14% of the claims. The tribunal stated that its task was to evaluate the merits of the underlying cases and decide them as it believed an honest, independent and impartial Ecuadorian court should have done. It rejected the State's 'loss of chance' argument and stated: 'Finally, the "loss of chance" principle does not have wide acceptance across legal systems such that it can be considered a "general principle of law recognized by civilized nations." At most it can be said that the "loss of chance" principle is applied in exceptional situations where there exists a "harm whose existence cannot be disputed but which it is difficult to quantify," as noted in the commentary to the UNIDROIT Principles cited by the Respondent. In this case, the Tribunal finds no exceptional difficulties in coming to a conclusion as to what should have occurred but for the breach of the bilateral investment treaty (BIT) and what damages result therefrom. The Tribunal therefore declines to apply the "loss of chance" principle.' It awarded USD 354 million (plus interest).

[B] Pre-contractual Treaty Breach

The following cases are examples of the State breaching the applicable treaty before a binding contract has been entered into and where 'loss of chance' has been argued. Generally, no damages are awarded, because, for example, the claimant cannot establish that it has a qualifying investment (such as in a unsuccessful tender)[54] or damages are limited to wasted expenses.

52. The cases summarized below do not purport to be all the cases that address 'loss of chance'. The awards in this contribution can be found on the italaw.com and/or jusmundi.com websites.
53. *Chevron Corp & Texaco Petroleum Co v. Republic of Ecuador*, PCA Case No. 34877, UNCITRAL, Partial Award on the Merits, dated 30 March 2010 (K-H Bockstiegel (P), C Brower and A van den Berg), para. 382.
54. *See e.g.*, *Nagel v. Czech Republic*, SCC, Award, dated 9 September 2003 (H Danelius (P), M Hunter and H Kronke); and *F-W Oil Interests Inc v. Republic of Trinidad and Tobago*, ICSID Case No. ARB/01/14, Award, dated 3 March 2006 (F Nariman (P), F Berman and Lord Mustill).

In *Lemire v. Ukraine II* (2011),[55] the claimant applied for multiple radio licenses. The tribunal found that he had been discriminated against in the award of licenses, in breach of FET. The claimant sought damages based on 'loss of chance', which the tribunal rejected, but did award him lost profits. It asked: is the damage a loss of chance? And answered: the tribunal's certainty that the claimant has indeed suffered a loss has another important implication, it excludes the possibility that Mr Lemire's injury be classified as a simple loss of a chance. The investor's loss does not consist in being deprived of some chance to win additional frequencies; what has been proven is that Ukraine's wrongful acts have resulted, through a foreseeable and proximate chain of events, in the damage suffered by the investor. Once causation has been established, and it has been proven that the *in bonis* party has indeed suffered a loss, less certainty is required in proof of the actual amount of damages; for this latter determination the claimant only needs to provide a basis upon which the tribunal can, with reasonable confidence, estimate the extent of the loss. (This articulation is echoed in many subsequent decisions and is also similar to the English position.)

Consistent with the orthodox approach of awarding little or no damages, in *Bosca v. Lithuania* (2013),[56] the claimant was the successful bidder for a wine producer as part of a privatization process, but after negotiating the share purchase agreement (SPA), its tender was cancelled. The tribunal held that the claimant was entitled to compensation for the lost opportunity resulting from failure of the State Property Fund to respect the legal rules which governed the negotiations of the SPA with the winning bidder who had legitimate expectations that the negotiations would be carried out in accordance with the law and that the SPA could be successfully concluded. However, the claimant, in pre-contractual negotiations, is only entitled to recover direct damages (monies paid to the respondent in the privatization process and costs incurred in this case). It held that lost profits based on the assumption of an agreed SPA were much too remote and speculative.

[C] Early End of an Existing Contract

The next set of cases are examples of breach of treaty by the State after the investor has entered into binding contractual arrangements. Here, the issues more relate to causation and assessment of damages in circumstances where there is an insufficient record of profitability. Generally, tribunals have been reluctant to award lost profits for a beginning industry and underperformed work. Space does not permit a full review of the authorities.[57] The following are examples of where loss of opportunity has been considered.

55. *Joseph Charles Lemire v. Ukraine II*, ICSID Case No. ARB (AF)/06/18, Award, dated 28 March 2011 (J Fernández-Armesto (P), J Paulsson and J Voss dissenting), paras 250-252.
56. *Luigiterzo Bosca v. Republic of Lithuania*, PCA Case No. 211-04, UNCITRAL, Award, dated 17 May 2013 (M Lalonde (P), D Price and B Stern), paras 297-303.
57. *See e.g.*, *Autopista Concesionada de Venezuela CA v. Bolivarian Republic of Venezuela*, ICSID Case No. ARB/00/5, Award, dated 23 September 2003 (G Kaufmann-Kohler (P), K-H Bockstiegel and B Cremades); and *PSEG Global Inc, North American Coal Corp, and Konya Ilgin Elektrik*

In *Gemplus v. Mexico* (2010),[58] the claimants were members of a consortium that won a concession to operate a national vehicle registry. The project ran into difficulties. The operating terms were amended, but eventually the Mexican government revoked the concession. The claimants sought MXN 501 million lost profits. The tribunal held that there had been an expropriation, but rejected the DCF approach for determining damages. It referred to *Chorzów*, the ILC Articles and Commentary, *Sapphire* and *SPP*, the UNIDROIT Principles, *Chaplin v. Hicks,* and the BIT which prescribed compensation to be the market value. The tribunal concluded that although the project never achieved the level of profitability contemplated in the Concessionaire's Business Plan, it still retained a reasonable opportunity to make significant future profits until the respondent's unlawful conduct and that 'opportunity, however small, has a monetary value' for the purpose of Article 36 of the ILC Articles and the BIT. The tribunal was unwilling to apply percentages. Nevertheless, it held that business people would be capable of agreeing a price for the shares. The tribunal determined 'in the exercise of its arbitral discretion' the price that would have been agreed by these hypothetical willing buyer and willing seller was the sum of MXN 130 million.[59]

In *Flemingo v. Poland* (2016),[60] the claimant was the operator of duty-free stores in Warsaw airport. The airport operator terminated the lease two years before it was due to expire. The claimant sought lost profits for that period and for a further period on the 75% probability that the lease would be renewed. Future lost profits were denied. The tribunal noted that 'loss of chance' requires, in a 'but for' scenario, a causal link between the non-breach and the probability that a future event would have occurred if no breach had been committed. The tribunal failed to see the causal link between the termination of the lease agreements on 16 February 2012 - with compensation - and the granting of completely new lease agreements, nearly three years later, also observing the poor relationship between the claimant and the operator.

In *Kontinental Conseil v. Gabon* (2016),[61] the tribunal rejected the claimant's claim based on a loss of opportunity to perform other projects, finding that the investor had failed to prove that it had sufficient capacity and opportunities.

In *Gavazzi v. Romania* (2017),[62] the tribunal held, by majority, that the respondent had breached FET and expropriated the claimant's steelmaking concern. Although the factory had not started operating, the tribunal held that it would be wrong as a matter of principle to limit the claimants' compensation to the return of its capital invested (with interest). Applying loss of opportunity, the tribunal turned to the 'only

Üretim ve Ticaret Limited Sirketi v. Republic of Turkey, ICSID Case No. ARB/02/5, Award, dated 4 June 2004 (F Orrego Vicuña (P), Y Fortier and G Kaufmann-Kohler), paras 310-313.

58. Two conjoined arbitrations: *Gemplus SA, SLP SA and Gemplus Industrial SA de CV v. The United Mexican States, & Talsud SA v. The United Mexican States* ICSID Case No. ARB (AF)/04/03, Award, dated 16 June 2010 (V Veeder (P), Y Fortier and E Magallón Gómez).
59. Which then equated to USD 14.3 million.
60. *Flemingo DutyFree Shop Private Ltd v. Republic of Poland,* UNCITAL, Award, dated 12 August 2016 (H van Houtte (P), W Kühn and J Townsend), paras 921-931.
61. *Kontinental Conseil v. Gabonese Republic,* PCA Case No. 2015-25, Award, dated 23 December 2016 (P Mayer (P), N Ziade and M Audit).
62. *Marco Gavazzi and Stefano Gavazzi v. Romania,* ICSID Case No. ARB/12/25, Award, dated 18 April 2017 (*H van Houtte (P), v. Veeder and M Rubino-Sammartano* dissenting).

solid data available': the amounts invested by the claimants and sought to estimate the probable future return on such investment. The tribunal, by majority, quantified the claimants' loss of opportunity at 50% of the amount of their investment.

[D] Extractive Industries

The extractive industries usually have a period of exploration, followed by exploitation, with possible license extensions, such that there may be uncertainly whether the project will proceed to the next stage, and be profitable. Most breaches occur after there is some contractual arrangement in place. However, unlike many general businesses which depend upon customers liking and buying a product, and are valued on a multiple of free cash flow or EBITDA,[63] companies in the extractive industries can point to the likely existence of the relevant metal, mineral or hydrocarbon, and are valued on the basis of their reserves. The uncertainties relate to the quantity of reserves and the cost of extraction and the selling price. However, in practice, reserves and costs can be assessed with some accuracy[64] and there will often be assignments or farm-ins at substantial value once the reserves have been de-risked, both before and after production starts.

I summarize first those cases where the uncertainty is whether a *new contractual arrangement* (in the form of an extension) will be agreed.

In *Stati v. Khazakhstan* (2013),[65] the claimant had restarted disused oil fields and to build an LNG plant. The claimants sought, among other claims, loss of profits based on an extension of one of its contracts. The tribunal rejected the claim and, after referring to Professor Crawford's ILC commentary said: 'To meet this standard, an investor must show that their project either has a track record of profitability rooted in a perennial history of operations, or has binding contractual revenue obligations in place that establish the expectation of profit at a certain level over a given number of years. This is true even for projects in early stages.' The claimants had not proven that they could have declared a commercial discovery, which would have given them exclusive oil and gas rights, within the extended period. The tribunal award out of pocket expenses of USD 31 million.

In *Burlington v. Ecuador* (2017),[66] the claimant contended that it was deprived of the right to negotiate an extension to its oil field concession of Block 7 and claimed USD 376 million for eight years of lost production. The tribunal recognized loss of

63. Earnings before interest, taxes, depreciation and amortization.
64. 'Proven' reserves are those with a 90-percent or above likelihood of commercial extraction. 'Probable' reserves are those with the likelihood of recovery is over 50% but under 90%. 'Possible' reserves have odds of commercial extraction under 50%, but higher than 10%.
65. *Antolie Stati, Gabriel Stati, Ascom Group SA and Terra Raf Trans Trading Ltd v. Republic of Kazakhstan*, SCC Case No. 116/2010, Award, dated 19 December 2013 (D Haigh (P), S Lebedev and K-H Böckstiegel), paras 1684-1692. The claimant was awarded substantial damages in respect of other oil fields and the LNG plant.
66. *Burlington Resources Inc v. Republic of Ecuador*, ICSID Case No. ARB/08/5. Decision on Reconsideration and Award, dated 7 February 2017 (G Kaufmann-Kohler (P), S Drymer and B Stern), paras 269-283.

opportunity as a head of claim but did not award any damages, noting that that even if the conditions to extension had been satisfied, it was still a decision for the State to make, and the claimants themselves did not expect production to continue.

In the related case of *Perenco v. Ecuador* (2019),[67] the tribunal applied 'loss of chance' to value the lost opportunity to obtain and benefit from a contract extension. The decision in *Gemplus* (above) was distinguished, on the grounds that Block 7 was a proven field with valuable oil reserves, even if there would be a changed contractual model if Perenco wanted to stay, and there was considerable evidence that the State would have preferred Perenco to have stayed (the problem being with Burlington). It concluded that the parties more likely than not would have arrived at a solution whereby Perenco would be operating Block 7 albeit under a different contractual regime. Perenco claimed USD 626 million. The tribunal stated that because it was a loss of opportunity to have the contract extended rather than the loss of a fully crystallized legal right to an extension of a contract, such value must necessarily be significantly lower than the amount claimed by Perenco. The tribunal awarded USD 25 million for loss of opportunity in respect of Block 7. It concluded that: 'It cannot but note that the equities tend strongly in favour of the granting of this relief. This however is not a decision *ex aequo et bono*. It is one grounded in law.' It also awarded Perenco over USD 400 million for damages to the existing concession caused by other breaches.

However, the award of USD 25 million was successfully annulled (2021).[68] The State contended that the proper method for calculating the value of a lost opportunity consists of determining the value of the loss or benefit and multiplying it by the probability of such loss or benefit.[69] The State argued, first, that the tribunal's decision constituted a manifest excess of power, because the tribunal simply came up with a value, exceeding mere discretion. The Annulment Committee rejected this, stating that nowhere in the applicable law is there a mathematical formula to quantify loss of opportunity and it is not for *ad hoc* committees to question the methodology used by tribunals to reach their conclusion on damages or to impose a certain method for calculation of the damages. Second, the State argued that Perenco had not quantified its loss of opportunity nor estimated its probability, and the tribunal had failed to apply the applicable evidentiary standard in that Ecuador never had an opportunity to debate either issue and the tribunal had violated the right to be heard. That too was dismissed. The Committee held that the tribunal is not under an obligation to discuss with the parties every step of its decision-making process and can make its own assessment of the evidence and arguments, so long as its decision remains within the legal and factual framework of the debate in the arbitration. Third, the State argued that the tribunal did not provide a single line of reasoning as to its calculation of the hypothetical loss or benefit and the probability of such loss or benefit occurring. The Committee held that

67. *Perenco Ecuador Ltd v. Republic of Ecuador*, ICSID Case No. ARB/08/6, Award, dated 27 September 2019 (P Tomka (P), N Kaplan and C Thomas), paras 312-326.
68. Decision on Annulment, dated 28 May 2021 (E Zuleta (P), R Knieper and M Pinto), paras 429-326.
69. Perenco countered that had the tribunal complied with this mathematical formula approach, it should have granted damages that were at least 51% of USD 626 million = USD 319 million.

that the tribunal indeed reached a decision that did not follow from its prior analysis and therefore failed to state reasons for its conclusion on loss of opportunity. It concluded that, rather than explaining whether it disregarded the degree of probability as a tool and the reasons therefore, or what, in the tribunal's view, an equitable, reasonable and balanced outcome is, or what could have been the impact of the degree of discretion that Ecuador had to extend the contract in dispute or, generally, refer to a conclusion from the premises contained earlier in the award, the tribunal simply 'acknowledged' that it had discretion and decided to award 'a nominal value.' No explanation whatsoever was given as to what is the concept of a nominal value or the reason to award a nominal value as opposed to any other value.[70]

In *Infinito Gold v. Costa Rica* (2021),[71] the tribunal held that there had been no breach of the treaty, but even if there had been, the claimant's harm would essentially consist of the loss of an opportunity or chance to apply for an exploitation concession. Yet, the claimant had not put forward a quantification for such a loss of opportunity, nor had it provided the tribunal with any elements to calculate it. If one adds the inherent uncertainty and the regulatory risk involved in any application process, the monetary consequences of this 'loss of chance' appeared too speculative to give rise to an award of damages.

There is another set of cases where the breach has caused the early *end of existing contractual arrangements*.

Sapphire (1963), referred to above, is an example of a project expropriated at an early stage, after a concession had been issued but before prospecting had begun. The sole arbitrator pointed to the very favourable reserves, but also the risks to the project, and awarded an equitable amount.

In *RSM v. Central African Republic* (2011),[72] the claimant had its four-year exploration contract ended on grounds of *force majeure* and claimed specific performance, alternatively damages. The tribunal held that loss of a chance can be compensated in principle, but it must be attributable to acts of the respondent, whereas in the present case a loss of a chance resulting from the negligence of the claimant cannot be the basis for awarding damages.

In *Khan Resources v. Mongolia* (2015),[73] the claimant had carried out a drilling programme and conducted a feasibility study before its licenses were invalidated. The tribunal rejected a DCF valuation. It pointed to uncertainties, which included: (i) how the project would have been financed; (ii) whether a strategic partner would have been

70. Given the objective of a loss of chance analysis, this conclusion strikes this author as somewhat harsh. The award of USD 25 million recognized the breach by the State, but balanced that against the uncertainties of what might happen in the future. Paradoxically, the award of 'loss of chance' damages might have survived if the tribunal had applied a formula and awarded USD 319 million (*see supra* n. 69). Instead, it awarded 3.8%, and that aspect of the award was annulled.

71. *Infinito Gold Ltd v. Republic of Costa Rica*, ICSID Case No. ARB/14/5, Award, dated 3 June 2021 (G Kaufmann-Kohler (P), B Hanotiau and B Stern), para. 585.

72. *RSM Production Corp v. Central African Republic*, ICSID Case No. ARB 07/2, Award, dated 11 July 2011 (A Kettani (P), P Merle and B Stern), para. 42.

73. *Khan Resources Inc, Khan Resources BV and CAUC Holding Company v. The Government of Mongolia and MonAtom LLC*, UNCITRAL, Award on the Merits, dated 2 March 2015 (D Williams (P), B Hanotiau and Y Fortier), paras 390-421.

brought in or whether the claimant would have been able to bring the project into production by itself; (iii) whether the claimant would have taken the project to production or sold it; (iv) when and how certain additional property would have been merged into the joint venture; and (v) the signing of various agreement such as an investment agreement and a new joint venture agreement 'to finalise the commercial terms' of the project. The tribunal considered that the true value of Khan's investment was better reflected by the offers made for the mine or for Khan Canada's shares in and around the relevant period than by the more traditional methodologies advanced by the claimants. (This was similar to the AES Option in *ENPH*, but the *Khan* tribunal did not apply any discount to the offers as they were less conditional.)

In *Caratube v. Kazakhstan* (2017),[74] the tribunal held that the claimants had not convincingly established that Caratube ever was a going concern with a proven record of profitability, after five years, and had not sufficiently established that Caratube would have become a going concern but for the termination of the relevant contract. It observed that some international tribunals have awarded damages for lost opportunity, but 'such practice is not widely accepted'. The tribunal did not deem it appropriate to speculate and choose a figure 'likely to reflect [the Tribunal's] views of an equitable and reasonable outcome'.

In contrast, in *Tethyan v. Pakistan* (2019),[75] the mine was not in production when the concession was terminated. The tribunal stated that the first key question is whether, based on the evidence before it, the tribunal is convinced that in the absence of respondent's breaches, the project would have become operational and would also have become profitable. The second key question is whether the tribunal is convinced that it can, with reasonable confidence, determine the amount of these profits based on the inputs provided by the parties' experts for this calculation. If it is not convinced by the inputs provided by the parties' experts, it may conclude that it cannot apply the DCF method or it may conclude that certain deductions have to be made to account for additional risks or uncertainties faced by the project. The tribunal concluded that the DCF approach was appropriate, subject to certain adjustments to the inputs. It resulted in an award of USD 4.087 billion (plus interest).

Finally, while the determination of loss and damages by a tribunal is a matter of 'informed estimation, taking into account the evidence before it' with a margin of appreciation accorded to arbitrators, *Perenco* shows that a degree of reasoning is required when it comes to awarding damages on the basis of 'loss of chance'.[76]

74. *Caratube International Oil Company LLP& Devincci Salah Hourani v. Republic of Kazakhstan*, ICSID Case No. ARB/13/13, Award, dated 27 September 2017 (L Lévy (P), L Aynès and J Salès), paras 1142-1161.

75. *Tethyan Copper Company Pty Ltd v. Islamic Republic of Pakistan*, ICSID Case No. ARB/12/1, Award, dated 12 July 2019 (K Sachs (P), S Alexandrov and Lord Hoffmann), paras 271-307.

76. *Cf. Duke Energy International Peru Investments No. 1 Ltd v. Republic of Peru*, ICSID Case No. ARB/03/28, Decision of the Ad Hoc Committee, dated 1 March 2011 (C McLachlan (P), D Hascher and P Tomka), paras 252-258.

[E] UNCITRAL Working Group Reforms

There is disquiet amongst States at the quantum of some awards. This is being discussed at UNCITAL Working Group III.[77] It has been proposed, for example, that more often adjustments should be made to DCF calculations to account for investor culpability.[78] It is suggested by this author that wider application of 'loss of chance', or discounting for risk, should be considered as part of that review, to greater reflect the uncertainties in predicting lost profits.

§24.07 CONCLUSION

The phrase 'loss of chance' is one that is used in different ways. It can be used to describe the nature of the loss suffered (also 'lost opportunity') and a head of loss. It can be used to describe a doctrine primarily directed to issues of causation. It can also be used in the evaluation of factors which go only to the quantification of economic loss.

Assessing a lost opportunity to earn profits and determining what might happen in the future is inherently uncertain and speculative and nearly always depends on the actions of third parties. As has been said: 'It is difficult to make predictions, particularly about the future.'[79]

This brief review shows that although there may be some movement away from the proposition that 'loss of chance' is not a recognized doctrine in international law, nevertheless ISDS tribunals rarely award damages on the basis of 'loss of chance'. The few notable examples in the last decade include *Gemplus* and *Perenco*. It appears that as a matter of policy, it has very limited application.

Another relevant policy is that a party in breach should not get off lightly. The tribunal chaired by Julian Lew in *ENPH* considered these two policies, and applying the 'loss of chance' doctrine, balanced the uncertainties that existed so that compensation was not speculative with not allowing the respondent to avoid paying some damages resulting from its breach, and reached a pragmatic and just result.[80] That approach is commended to other tribunals.

---

77. *See e.g.*, Report of Working Group III (Investor-State Settlement Reform) on the work of its forty-third session (Vienna, 5-16 September 2022), available at https://documents-dds-ny.un.org/doc/UNDOC/LTD/221/034/0E/PDF/2210340E.pdf?OpenElement.
78. Damages were reduced by 25% to reflect the claimants' contribution to the prejudice they suffered, due to their tax misconduct, in the exercise of the tribunal's 'wide discretion', in *Yukos Universal Ltd v. Russian Federation*, PCA Case No. AA 227, UNCITRAL, Final Award, dated 18 July 2014 (Y Fortier (P), C Poncet and S Schwebel), paras. 1633-1637 and 1827.
79. Variously a Danish proverb and also attributed to, *inter alia*, Niels Bohr, Mark Twain, Sam Goldwyn and Yogi Berra.
80. Rabbi Lord Jonathan Sacks, 'A Sage Is Greater Than a Prophet', available at: https://www.yeshiva.co/midrash/45206 (last accessed20 February 2023).

E Arbitrators

CHAPTER 25

An Arbitrator's Guide to Hearing Preparation: Consolidating Conventional Wisdom and Innovation

Nayla Comair-Obeid

§25.01 INTRODUCTION

The term 'conventional wisdom' results from the association of the words 'convention' and 'wisdom', and refers to a '*generally accepted theory or belief*'. While certain wisdoms can be unconventional, and conventions are far from always being wise, the consolidated term, i.e., '*conventional wisdom*', refers to those principles which are both conventional and wise. In other words, they ally the rooting power of traditions with the insight that comes with wisdom.

John Kenneth Galbraith has defined 'conventional wisdom' in the following way:

> What is conventional wisdom? It will be convenient to have a name for the ideas which are esteemed at any time for their acceptability, and it should be a term that emphasizes this predictability. I shall refer to these ideas henceforth as the conventional wisdom.

Three elements in this definition deserve particular attention. Conventional wisdom refers to ideas which are '*esteemed for their acceptability*', i.e., are generally recognized as sound and as a vehicle of wisdom. The second element of this definition has a time component: a conventional wisdom is not one which is temporarily in vogue but rather one that has endured the test of time. Finally, because the principles which can be categorized as 'conventional wisdom' are generally accepted and have crossed the times, they are a source of reliability and predictability.

As to 'innovation', arbitration has, as a method of dispute resolution, been regularly associated with the notion of 'innovation'. As put by Professor Loukas Mistelis, '[a]*ny form of stimulated change can be considered an "innovation"*.' And arbitration is a form of 'stimulated change' in and of itself, being conceived, and operating ever since, as an alternative to the traditionally predominant court litigation procedure. Yet, rising concerns over the past decades have underscored the need for enhanced efficiency, with the perceived effectiveness of past practices being questioned and new developments being regularly tested against the procedural reality of international arbitration.

Questioning the content of conventional wisdom and identifying the principles which constitute it requires going back to the foundations of international arbitration, which is of particular relevance at a moment when the role of arbitrators and counsel in the field is being criticized. Among the criticisms that international arbitration faces are the increased time and costs of its proceedings and the quality of arbitrators' decisions.[1] In such context, conventional wisdom bears an element of acceptability, and as such, if properly observed, should have an ability to inspire trust, and strengthen the system around which it revolves so that it can meet the ever changing needs and requirements of the end users.

However, does the fact that the principles identified as conventional wisdom are *recognized as 'wise'* means that they represent the *'right'* principles to apply in any circumstances? This is probably not the case, mainly for two reasons:

(1) the way arbitrators work has evolved over the years. This is not only due to technological innovations, but it is also a result of an increased arbitration caseload. Wisdom, therefore, requires a constant adaptation of arbitral procedures to the changing environment in which arbitrators operate.
(2) the specificities of each case do sometimes require deviating from usual practice.

Against this background, this paper attempts to analyse the role of conventional wisdom and innovation in the promotion of efficient arbitration proceedings. In doing so, the paper identifies certain principles and/or ideas which are generally accepted and ensure the good functioning of the arbitration process on the part of arbitral tribunals and counsel (section §25.02). Next, the paper explores some innovative techniques in international arbitration, focusing on the way they can contribute to consolidating conventional wisdom and improving the practice of international arbitration (section §25.03). Finally, it questions the element of acceptability and predictability included in John Kenneth Galbraith's definition by analysing how conventional wisdom is influenced by perceptions (section §25.04).

1. *See, e.g.*, William W. Park, 'Arbitration and Fine Dining: Two Faces of Efficiency', in P. Shaughnessy & S. Tung eds, *The Powers and Duties of an Arbitrator: Liber Amicorum Pierre A. Karrer* (Kluwer 2017) at p. 251; Steven Seidenberg, 'International Arbitration Loses Its Grip' 96 American Bar Association Journal (2010) at p. 50; Peter Yuen and John Choong, 'Is Arbitration Value for Money? Assessing Some Common Complaints about the Costs of International Arbitration' 3 Asian Dispute Review (2008) at pp. 90-95; Leon E. Trakman and Hugh Montgomery, 'The "Judicialization" of International Commercial Arbitration: Pitfall or Virtue?' 30 Leiden Journal of International Law (2017) at p. 405; Jennifer Kirby, 'Efficiency in International Arbitration: Whose Duty Is It?' 32(6) Journal of International Arbitration (2015) at pp. 689-696.

§25.02 'CONVENTIONAL WISDOM' AS SEEN IN PRACTICE

There are a number of principles in international arbitration that are generally recognized as best practices and have been constantly applied in international arbitral proceedings as such. The below is not intended to be an exhaustive list of such principles but rather a description of some accepted wisdoms in international arbitration regularly followed and/or proposed to be followed by counsel and arbitral tribunals, respectively.

[A] Best Practices to Be Followed by Counsel

The increasing use of international arbitration as a means of resolving disputes has led to the creation of an enhanced role for lawyers who are expected to not only assist their client in resolving their dispute, but also master the factual background, applicable law, and arbitration procedure, and be in a position to identify and engage any and all appropriate legal and technical experts, and factual witnesses. The increased responsibilities attributed to arbitration lawyers have triggered the development of a series of best practices that act as 'conventional wisdom': to achieve the best results for their clients, lawyers should adopt the 'conventional wisdom' that has been established through field experience and covers the whole arbitral process from the pre-arbitral stages to the final evidentiary hearing.

[1] Case Strategy and Preparation

One of the first tasks that an arbitration lawyer should perform is a case assessment, i.e., determining whether initiating arbitration proceedings against an opposing party is beneficial from a legal, as well as financial, perspective. Therefore, before advocating, either orally or in writing, counsel should think thoroughly about their case, and assess its strengths and weaknesses, including any issues of jurisdiction and enforcement that may arise. Advocacy – let alone effective advocacy – relies heavily on the contemplation of a properly formulated case strategy that enables counsel to create a road map for the legal team to follow throughout the proceedings. A meticulous case strategy allows counsel to properly assess the factual and legal issues involved in the case, prepare the factual matrices and legal principles to be followed in the submissions, select the most appropriate arbitral tribunal, as well as factual and expert witness, prepare written and oral submissions, review the case materials and determine which exhibits are to be used.

One of the most important – and at the same time, difficult – tasks that counsel is engaged with is, *first*, to understand the factual theory of the case, and develop the legal arguments that will be made in its support; and *second*, to anticipate the factual and legal theories that will be likely used by the opponent. In doing so, counsel must have an excellent understanding of the underlying structure of the parties' relationship. Moreover, case strategy should be easily and readily adaptable to the parties' current relationship. Counsel should remain mindful of whether the parties are still doing business together, or whether the dispute has escalated to such an extent that possible hostile legal steps are to be taken into consideration.

The legal team should start preparing the case strategy as early as possible, i.e., immediately after learning the main facts of the case, seeing the key documents, and conducting a first assessment of the factual and legal bases. This pre-arbitral case assessment will ensure that the case is worthwhile, in terms of both time and costs for the client.

[2] Choosing the Arbitral Tribunal

In a comment published in the *GAR Guide to Advocacy*, Kaj Hobér said:[2]

> Never forget who the decision maker is. In most arbitrations the tribunal is composed of three qualified and experienced lawyers (i.e., colleagues). Your job as counsel is to convince them, not the client, the opposing party or its counsel or anyone else, but the arbitrators. Everything that you do as counsel must be geared towards this goal.

Counsel should carefully choose which arbitrator(s) to appoint. Deciding which individual will be the ultimate decision-maker of all points of fact and law has several implications on the case itself. Counsel should aim to appoint an '*impartial, fair and patient lawyer*' who is competent and suitable to settle the dispute in question in terms of legal and technical expertise, as well as experience. In this regard, counsel should perform a requisite background check to understand the proposed candidate's legal, technical, and cultural background and verify that the identified individual does have any special technical expertise sought for the purposes of arbitrating the case in question, is able to comprehend the underlying commercial and legal issues, and is experienced and credible enough.

At the stage of the constitution of the arbitral tribunal, appointing a three-member tribunal, whenever the economics of a case can bear it, has also been described as conventional wisdom.[3] Having three arbitrators potentially improves the quality of the arbitral process and the resulting award, since having three arbitrators to decide a case allows for *true deliberation—the sharing of ideas, perspectives reasoning and drafting*[4] and a more thorough consideration of the issues from different points of view.[5] Moreover, appointing three arbitrators essentially means that the parties maintain and exercise their right to nominate a co-arbitrator. This generally increases party autonomy, as well as confidence in the arbitral process, since the parties *believe that there*

2. The GAR Guide to Advocacy – Fifth Edition, p. 15.
3. Jennifer Kirby, 'With Arbitrators, Less Can Be More: Why the Conventional Wisdom on the Benefits of Having Three Arbitrators May Be Overrated' 26(3) Journal of International Arbitration (2009) p. 337, at p. 338.
4. Stephen Jagusch, 'Starting out as an Arbitrator: How to Get Appointments and What to Do When you Receive Them' 71 Arbitration (2005) p. 329, at p. 335.
5. Julian D.M. Lew, Loukas A. Mistelis & Stefan M. Kroll, *Comparative International Commercial Arbitration* (Kluwer Law International 2003) at pp. 227-228; Jan Paulsson, 'Ethics, Elitism, Eligibility' 14 Journal of International Arbitration (1997) at p. 13; Wendy Miles, 'Practical Issues for Appointment of Arbitrators' 20 International Arbitration (2003) p. 219 at p. 226.

is at least one member of the arbitral tribunal who will listen attentively and sympathetically to its case, understand its position, and ensure that the party gets a fair hearing and that its views are considered during the deliberations.[6] When arbitrators have the same ethical and professional values, as well as good knowledge of the applicable law, and/or an open and flexible approach to the application of a foreign law, three-member tribunals' deliberations are proven to be very fruitful, particularly in complex procedures where the complementary approaches of three well-versed individuals is indispensable to the decision-making process.

However, criticism of three-arbitrator tribunals has been developed, underlining the potential risks for excesses coming principally from party-appointed arbitrators, including, *inter alia*, co-arbitrators having ex parte communication with 'their' party; resigning at a time designed to disrupt the proceedings; making themselves unavailable for deliberations; encouraging the filing of challenges; secretly feeding information about deliberations to 'their' party; failing to deal with an award that needs only their signature before it can be notified to the parties; secretly sending 'their' party the draft of a forthcoming award; taking months to draft a dissenting opinion and/or filing a dissenting opinion that is designated to undermine the enforceability of the award, etc.[7]

Irrespective of whether the arbitral tribunal consists of one, three, or more arbitrators, counsel should be in a position to anticipate how it will likely approach the procedural and substantive elements of the arbitration, and be prepared to assist the tribunal throughout the arbitral process. This exercise requires an excellent knowledge and understanding of the arbitrators' background given that '*different cultural backgrounds and distinct methodologies may affect the outcome*',[8] be it procedural or substantive.

[3] Factual and Expert Witnesses

Factual Witnesses: the selection of factual witnesses is of the utmost importance for the outcome of the case, as it heavily affects the tribunal's evaluation and consideration of the facts of the dispute. The first step that counsel should take is deciding whether factual witnesses are actually needed; such decision should be made as early as possible in the arbitration. When a documentary case is strong, and there is a clear and effective legal basis for the claims advanced in the procedure, counsel can opt in for a documents-only arbitration. On the contrary, when documents are not helpful in

6. *See* Jennifer Kirby, *supra* n. 3, at p. 342. In a Survey conducted by Queen Mary University London in 2012 on 'Current and Preferred Practices in the Arbitral Process', a significant majority of interviewees further state that they prefer selection of the two co-arbitrators in a three-member tribunal by each party unilaterally, for the following reasons: (i) it gives the parties control over the constitution of the tribunal and inspires confidence in the arbitral process, which consequently raises the legitimacy of the final award; (ii) parties are better placed to know what skills and knowledge are required for resolving the dispute; and (iii) many interviewees expressed some distrust in arbitral institutions selecting arbitrators.
7. Jennifer Kirby, *supra* n. 3, at p. 344.
8. The GAR Guide to Advocacy – Fifth Edition, p. 4.

proving their party's case, counsel are advised to use factual witnesses in order to fill in any factual gaps that may exist in the documentary narrative.

The selection of the most appropriate factual witnesses is an exercise that should factor in all relevant elements and circumstances, including the proposed witness's familiarity with the facts of the case, as well as their ability to narrate the events simply and remain calm when testifying before the tribunal. When preparing for the hearing, counsel should help the witness go through the evidence and narrate the events, confirming that the witness' story makes the requisite correlation between the facts of the case and the legal arguments that counsel is advancing.

Counsel should always prepare their witnesses for giving testimony before the arbitral tribunal. Notwithstanding the veracity that a witness statement may have, the supplementation of written statements with a short and concise direct questioning will allow the witness to present themselves, get acquainted with the hearing process, and also address some of the key points of their testimony.

As far as cross-examination of factual witnesses is concerned, it should primarily focus on the main points in dispute between the parties, without addressing every single element of the case. While there is no right and wrong way of conducting an effective cross-examination, counsel should contemplate in advance and prepare their cross-examination taking account of the particularities of the witness and/or their testimony. Counsel should generally be short and concise, avoid asking overcomplicated, hypothetical and/or legal questions, avoid explanation and/or repetition, and focus on the factual evidence that are within the personal knowledge of the witness. Counsel had always better stop cross-examining a hostile witness when the witness' answers to the questions raised start improving.

Expert Witnesses: equally important with the selection of factual witness is the selection of expert witnesses. Identifying the right expert witness can win a case as '*the version of expert evidence that is accepted by the tribunal* [does] *have a critical effect on the decision in the case*'.[9] Experts must act independently and provide their honest professional opinion. Counsel should choose their preferred candidate wisely considering factors that range from experience to willingness to personally engage with the mandate to locality.

When assigning certain legal and/or technical issues to experts, counsel should make sure that they maintain control over the case. Counsel should confirm that expert witnesses address all issues brought before them for their expert opinion, offer a roadmap that simplifies the tribunal's decision-making, and do not take a position that proves too difficult to properly defend. Counsel's and expert witnesses' credibility should be maintained to the highest standards throughout the proceedings. The ultimate aim is to persuade the tribunal to accept the expert's analysis, and this can only be done when the expert not only is, but also appears to be, independent and impartial.

The cross-examination of expert witnesses is a very delicate exercise. Counsel should be well advised and assisted by their own expert witness in preparing their

9. *Ibid.*, p. 18.

cross-examination, focus on points which are rebuttable and can undermine the expert's credibility, and ask as few questions as possible. Apart from the technical parts of the expert evidence, counsel should focus on the opposing expert's independence and experience, trying to demonstrate that they lack independence and impartiality, as well as the '*requisite qualifications and experience to express an authoritative and reliable opinion on the subject matter*'.[10]

To the extent possible, both factual and expert witnesses should testify in the language of the arbitration. Yet, if they are not comfortable testifying in a language that is not their mother tongue, counsel should consider whether the preferred option from a strategic viewpoint is to have the witness testifying in their native language with systematic translation following or to employ a translator that will assist the witness who is testifying in the language of the arbitration only when needed.

[4] Oral Submissions

The golden rule of oral advocacy is no other than: '*Less is more*'. When orally presenting their arguments before the tribunal, counsel should be clear, fair, and reasonable, taking account of, and paying deference to, both the favorable and the unfavorable facts of the case. In structuring and presenting their submission(s), counsel should always take a step back and consider what is the ultimate goal: to make the tribunal understand and accept their case, while also rejecting the case of their counter-party. Therefore, structure and presentation should make the submission clear, interesting, and easy to follow, so that the tribunal accepts the narrative that is presented by counsel.

Simplification is also of the essence. As international arbitration disputes are generally complex, counsel's goal should be the simplification of the intricate points of the dispute, thus assisting the tribunal in following the case and rendering an informed decision. In this regard, a chronological presentation of the facts is always helpful, while non-important and/or irrelevant information should not be included in the submission. Counsel should refer to key facts and documents in a manner that supports their narrative. This does not mean that they should hide or intentionally fail to address difficult issues. Quite on the contrary, the experienced counsel is expected to address difficult issues upfront; this attitude is very much appreciated by the tribunal, which will gain more confidence in counsel and remain focused on the case, without unnecessary distractions intervening.

Precision is also key. The tribunal should be able to understand the fundamentals of counsel's case theory before diving into the details of the case. Additionally, the use of a visual presentation including tables, schedules, chronologies and diagrams may well support the written and oral submissions as it can enhance the tribunal's understanding of the factual background.

10. *Ibid.*, p. 115.

[B] Best Practices to Be Followed by the Arbitral Tribunal

[1] Conventional Wisdom at the Preliminary Stages of the Arbitral Proceedings

The experiences encountered in the course of international arbitration proceedings highlight the fact that the initial stages of the arbitral proceedings are essential for the conduct of the rest of the proceedings, as they constitute the key moment to set the tone for the arbitration and to build the basis for an efficient arbitral process.

As no arbitration is self-effectuating, the arbitral tribunal should be very proactive. The procedural planning of an arbitration requires that the arbitral tribunal identify and ascertain as quickly as possible in the arbitration the source of the dispute, the pertinent factual and legal issues, as well as the manner in which the parties contemplate the arbitral proceedings and timetable.[11] The tribunal is generally expected to identify all procedural issues that will likely arise during the course of the arbitration, and guide the arbitral process in a way that will enable each party to engage in the proceedings and present its case.

In this regard, the ICC Rules refer to a number of specific 'Case Management Techniques' which arbitral tribunals are encouraged to consider in conjunction with the 'Case Management Conference' or 'Preliminary Meeting'. The Preliminary Meeting (or, preliminary hearing) allows for a dialogue between the arbitrator(s), and both counsel for the claimant(s) and the respondent(s). The purpose of the Preliminary Meeting is to enable the tribunal to identify the main issues in dispute, and develop a procedural calendar. The tribunal should consider preparing an agenda with the items it wishes to be addressed at the Preliminary Meeting between the tribunal and the parties. The presence of the parties themselves at this stage is highly recommended, since it represents the best occasion for the arbitrator(s) to explain to them how the arbitration proceedings work, particularly when they are unfamiliar with such proceedings. Further, the Preliminary Meeting allows the arbitrator(s) to ensure that the parties are aware of other mechanisms available for the resolution of their dispute, and is the best occasion to encourage settlement.

[2] Conventional Wisdom in the Conduct of the Arbitration

As put forward by Gary Born, some of the most important characteristics of the arbitral procedure are procedural fairness, efficiency, expertise and tailoring procedures to specific disputes and parties.[12] With international arbitration disputes involving parties coming from different jurisdictions, one of the fundamental objectives of international arbitration is that disputes will not be resolved in accordance with the procedures of any of the parties' home jurisdictions, but rather in accordance with a neutral,

11. Gary B. Born, 'Chapter 15: Procedures in International Arbitration' in *International Commercial Arbitration* 2nd edn (Kluwer Law International 2014).
12. Gary Born, *supra* n. 11, p. 2120.

tailor-made, procedure in the course of which both parties should be treated fairly and equally. Arbitral proceedings should also be as efficient and as expeditious as possible, with most arbitral institutions imposing extendable time limits for the rendering of the arbitral award.

In order to achieve this twofold mission, arbitrators should approach their duties fairly, making sure that each party has the opportunity to duly present its case, and that any determinations made are objective, based solely on the facts of the case and the arguments presented by the parties. Moreover, arbitral tribunals should prepare in the background while the case between the parties is advancing towards the final evidentiary hearing. The best way to do so is through the preparation of preparatory memorials and/or working documents by one or more arbitrators for internal circulation among themselves. Such preparatory memorials and/or working documents are intended to cover the main aspects of the dispute between the parties, and form the structural and substantive basis for the drafting of the final award. They should make reference to, and analyse, *inter alia,* the identity and characteristics of the parties involved, the main provisions of the contract under which the dispute arises, including the arbitration clause, as well as the particularities of the dispute, including the parties' legal submissions, and relief sought.

Structure-wise, a working document can take the form of a word.doc table where two separate columns are dedicated for the respective arguments advanced by the claimant(s) and the respondent(s):

	Case No. YYYYY
CLAIMANT	*RESPONDENT*
[INSERT ISSUE 1]	
[INSERT SUB-ISSUE A]	
[Claimant's argumentation, with references to submission, exhibits, witness statements and expert reports (if any)]	[Respondent's argumentation, with references to submission, exhibits, witness statements and expert reports (if any)]
[INSERT SUB-ISSUE B]	
[Claimant's argumentation, with references to submission, exhibits, witness statements and expert reports (if any)]	[Respondent's argumentation, with references to submission, exhibits, witness statements and expert reports (if any)]
[INSERT SUB-ISSUE C]	
[Claimant's argumentation, with references to submission, exhibits, witness statements and expert reports (if any)]	[Respondent's argumentation, with references to submission, exhibits, witness statements and expert reports (if any)]

	Case No. YYYYY
CLAIMANT	*RESPONDENT*
[INSERT ISSUE 2]	
[Claimant's argumentation, with references to submission, exhibits, witness statements and expert reports (if any)]	[Respondent's argumentation, with references to submission, exhibits, witness statements and expert reports (if any)]
[INSERT ISSUE 3]	
[Claimant's argumentation, with references to submission, exhibits, witness statements and expert reports (if any)]	[Respondent's argumentation, with references to submission, exhibits, witness statements and expert reports (if any)]

The arbitral tribunal should pay particular attention to the contractual provisions that come into play when deciding the issues in dispute. Preparing a table that directly refers to the most important provisions of the contract applicable between the parties in dispute presents a highly effective way of doing so, as it grants the tribunal direct access and easy reference to provisions that could otherwise be 'hidden' within lengthy contractual arrangements.

Key Contractual Provisions

Type	*Clause Number*	*Content*
Definition	X1	'FINAL ACCEPTANCE CERTIFICATE' or 'FAC' shall mean the certificate issued by [xx] as per Article [xx]
Definition	X2	'TAKING OVER CERTIFICATE' shall mean the certificate issued by the [xx] as per Article [xx]
Claimant's Obligation	X3	The [xx] undertakes to [xx]
Respondent's Obligation	X4	The [xx] undertakes to [xx]
Effective Date of Contract	X5	The CONTRACT shall come into effect on the date of signature of both the parties on the contract (Effective Date) and shall remain valid until the completion of the obligations of the parties under the CONTRACT.
Respondent's Obligation	X6	PAYMENT TERMS and BANK GUARANTEES: he total CONTRACT price for FOREIGN and INDIAN SUPPLY as per Article [xx] shall be paid by [xx] to [xx] in the following manner: [xx]

Type	*Clause Number*	*Content*
Liquidated Damages	12.1	In the event of [xx]'s failure to complete the final acceptance within [xx] months from the effective date of CONTRACT, [xx] may, at their discretion withhold any payment until the completion of the CONTRACT.

The arbitrators should also start reviewing the factual exhibits, witness statements, and expert reports, if any, produced by the parties as early as possible. The witness statements will help them to clearly comprehend the factual background of the dispute, while the expert reports will assist them in making an informed decision in technical matters. The main exhibits should also be tabularized with appropriate reference being made to the exhibit number, its description, as well as its contents:

Exhibit Number	*Description*	*Summary*
C-X1	Contract [XX] dated [XX] between [XX] and [XX]	[Add brief description; recite where necessary]
C-X2	Letter by [XX] to [XX] dated [XX]	[Add brief description; recite where necessary]
C-X3	Letter by [XX] to [XX] dated [XX]	[Add brief description; recite where necessary]
C-X4	Letter by [XX] to [XX] dated [XX]	[Add brief description; recite where necessary]
C-X5	MOM dated [XX]	[Add brief description; recite where necessary]
C-X6	Tender [XX] by [XX] dated [XX]	[Add brief description; recite where necessary]

§25.03 CONSOLIDATING CONVENTIONAL WISDOM AND INNOVATION

The use of technologically innovative tools in international arbitration represents yet another way to improve the arbitral process and ensure respect for both the parties' intentions and conventional wisdom. Arbitral proceedings should be quick, efficient and predictable to ensure access to justice. This is also essential to make sure that they maintain the advantages attributed to alternative means of dispute resolution over national court proceedings which often suffer the consequences of an overloaded schedule.[13] The development of innovative tools is even more necessary in an

13. *See, e.g.* Frank Sander's 1976 speech at the Pound Conference on 'The Causes of Popular Dissatisfaction with the Administration of Justice', widely seen within the legal academy as the birth of the Alternative Dispute Resolution (ADR) movement in the United States and then worldwide. During this speech, Franck Sander explained that ADR should help avoid case overload in courts, which slows down the judicial process.

ever-evolving society with an increasing need for speed and swift resolution of disputes.

Once a swift and cost-efficient method of resolving international disputes, international arbitration is now often stalled by long and costly procedures.[14] Yet, long and costly procedures can definitely be avoided if the proceedings are effectively organized and managed. A number of ideas have been developed over the time to improve the efficiency of the arbitral process. The '2015 International Arbitration Survey: Improvements and Innovations in International Arbitration' conducted the School of International Arbitration of the Queen Mary University of London, in partnership with White & Case LLP,[15] the procedural innovation perceived as most effective at controlling time and cost in international arbitration is the requirement for tribunals to commit to a schedule for deliberations and delivery of final awards.[16] Such internal commitment of the arbitral tribunal is essential and can be achieved only if the proceedings are efficiently organized, an efficiency which can be maximized when arbitrators are fully knowledgeable in the details of the case when they attend the evidentiary hearing.

Against this background, the below are examples of procedural innovations which can improve both time and cost-efficiency of the arbitral process.

[A] Remote Hearings

Technology and innovation have played a key role in enhancing the efficiency of international arbitration as a result of, and during, the COVID-19 pandemic. In order to limit the various geographic restrictions prescribed by COVID-19-related measures, the arbitration community implemented and willingly employed a series of innovative tools that kept arbitration alive and made it even more accessible despite COVID-19 restrictions.

One of such innovative tools was the conduct of fully remote virtual hearings, whereby the participation of all actors involved, i.e., the arbitral tribunal, party representatives, factual and expert witnesses, as well as counsel, is achieved through the use of video and audio technology. Now, what had initially started as a temporary alternative to traditional physical hearings, where all participants were physically present in a single room, has been established into the primary means of conducting procedural and evidentiary hearings in international arbitrations. Witnesses, both factual and expert, now regularly undergo direct and cross-examination remotely via appropriate means of virtual communication. As a result of this turn towards technologically backed means of communication, a multitude of remote hearing platforms has emerged over the past few years providing various availabilities that are merely dependent on the participants' Internet connection and bandwidth.

14. *See supra* n. 1.
15. Queen Mary University London Survey, 'Improvements and Innovations in International Arbitration' (2015).
16. *Ibid.*, at p. 24.

Going forward, the end users of international arbitration are seen as preferring 'a "mix of in-person and virtual" formats for almost all types of interactions, including meetings and conferences [with] [w]holly virtual formats [being] narrowly preferred for procedural hearings [...].'[17]

Bearing this innovation in mind, counsel should be mindful of the downfalls that are associated with remote hearings, the most important of which is the participants' – including the tribunal's – limited attention span. Holding an arbitral hearing remotely essentially means that counsel advocating in favour of their client will appear as small squares in a virtual screen that features not only the main speaker but also many other individuals attending the hearing. As the hearing progresses, and depending on the overall duration of the hearing in days, as well as in hours per day, counsel should focus on getting the tribunal's full attention. This goal will be achieved through various techniques including, *inter alia*, having the camera focusing on the speaker and making eye contact with the tribunal, to the extent possible; verifying that the speaker is audible and is articulating their speech in a clear and concise manner; being brief while keeping in mind so-called *zoom fatigue*; having full control of the technical equipment.

[B] Electronic Document Management Systems

The case file, including documents obtained through document production and disclosure, are rendered redundant if the relevant material cannot be adequately presented to the tribunal. In cases involving large amounts of documents, the parties' counsel carries out thorough document reviews to eventually agree on what documents should be included in 'common bundles'. Making the appropriate decisions as far as the content, organization, pagination, and production of bundles are concerned makes the function of the tribunal and the conduct of the arbitration in general much more effective.

Against this background, the increased tendency towards the use of technology in conducting virtual hearings, compounded by the participants' willingness to '*adopt paperless practices*',[18] has further enhanced the development of appropriate software and techniques that provide efficient electronic case and document management solutions. Such case management systems permit the collection, storage and retrieval of all documents relating to a case through a single platform. Parties can file and store their submissions and accompanying exhibits on platforms as such, without being required to send their full submission via email and/or regular mail. The case bundle is compiled in one place, set in chronological order, and easily accessible. Moreover, artificial intelligence can enhance the operation of such software and platforms by programming them to 'recognise references to exhibits within a submission and, as a

17. 2021 International Arbitration Survey: Adapting Arbitration to a Changing World, School of International Arbitration of the Queen Mary University of London, in partnership with White & Case LLP, p. 3, available at: https://arbitration.qmul.ac.uk/media/arbitration/docs/LON03200 37-QMUL-International-Arbitration-Survey-2021_19_WEB.pdf.
18. *Ibid.*

result, automatically offer a hyperlink to allow easier access to the referenced exhibit'.[19]

This new feature eliminates size restrictions, does not require huge amounts of paper waste, and avoids the risk of accidentally excluding one or more recipients from the correspondence. Moreover, the complete case record is immediately accessible, with users having merely to employ an electronic device and the Internet. Arbitrators are also assisted in following the development of the parties' arguments, and reviewing the case file.

[C] Online Dispute Resolution

Recourse to Online Dispute Resolution (ODR) through diverse online platforms can be key to saving time and costs, particularly in situations where the parties are not situated in the same countries, and where the amount and nature of the dispute allow for such procedure.[20]

By way of example, the European Commission has sponsored an innovative online platform for ODR, 'The ODR Platform', that can be used for any contractual dispute arising from online purchases of goods or services where the trader and consumer are both based in the European Union or Norway, Iceland, and Liechtenstein. The platform is designed as a mechanism that is aimed to provide the speed and high quality required by the current world business sector.[21]

The WIPO Arbitration and Mediation Center is also developing an online, Internet-based system for administering disputes. Digital communication tools will allow the parties to file requests by completing electronic forms and to submit documents and exchange correspondence online through secure channels. The parties, the neutrals and the Centre will thus communicate electronically (in addition to using any available audio and video facilities), reducing the need for other potentially time-consuming and expensive means of communication and in-person meetings and hearings.[22]

[D] Other Innovative Tools

Three qualitative analytical models have been identified by Iain Sheridan as models that may contribute to the processes and outcomes in international arbitration, namely

19. Sven Lange and Irina Samodelkina, 'Digital Case Management in International Arbitration', Kluwer Arbitration Blog, 13 August 2019, available at: http://arbitrationblog.kluwerarbitration.com/2019/08/13/digital-case-management-in-international-arbitration/.
20. Julio Cesar Betancourt & Elina Zlatanska, 'Online Dispute Resolution (ODR): What Is It and Is It the Way Forward?' 79(3) International Journal of Arbitration, Mediation and Dispute Management (2013). *See also* Derrick Yeoh, 'Is Online Dispute Resolution the Future of Alternative Dispute Resolution?', Kluwer Arbitration Blog (29 March 2018).
21. *See* the website of the European Commission, 'Online Dispute Resolution', at https://ec.europa.eu/consumers/odr/main/?event=main.trader.register last accessed on 22 May 2018.
22. WIPO Arbitration and Mediation Center, at http://www.wipo.int/amc/en/ last accessed on 22 May 2018.

mind map diagrams, simplified evidence charts, and cause and effect diagrams.[23] These are only examples of innovative software, among a myriad of tools which are being developed and used to simplify and organize complex factual matrices and ideas.

Mind Map Diagrams: mind map diagrams summarize a case in a non-linear way, replicating how the human brain often analyses knowledge and problems. The essential elements of any mind map are (1) a main topic represented with a central image; (2) important themes radiating from the central image as branches; (3) branches comprised of a key image or key word printed on an associated line to form a connected nodal structure; and (4) the incorporation of colour to clarify or emphasize connections.[24] This tool allows for complex, voluminous facts to be summarized with links to other types of documents, such as party requests and responses, as well as expert spreadsheets.[25]

Simplified Evidence Charts: can set out with succinct clarity either side's arguments alongside supporting evidence and accepted generalizations.[26] Well-drafted simplified evidence charts help counsel in preparing for, and delivering, their oral arguments. They also assist arbitrators' decision-making. This technique further allows to put forward the main argument with the evidence and generalizations that support it.

Fishbone Diagrams: or cause and effect diagrams can help in brainstorming, as well as in the identification of possible causes of a problem, and in sorting ideas into useful categories. They constitute a visual way to look at cause and effect, and as such can help clarify causation matters in the most sophisticated cases.[27]

§25.04 CONVENTIONAL WISDOM AND PERCEPTIONS

Although the principles which constitute conventional wisdom aspire to a certain universality and are theoretically '*esteemed at any time for their acceptability*', the practice of international arbitration shows that, although there might be general consensus as to the formulation of certain principles, the perception of the way such principles should apply is likely to be influenced by the background of the party representatives or arbitrators involved in a specific arbitration.

[A] Perceptions Influenced by the Legal Background

The legal tradition of an arbitrator or counsel often does influence the perception of the best ways to conduct arbitral proceedings and to apply the substantive law. As Pierre

23. Iain Sheridan, 'Qualitative Analytical Models for Arbitration' 33(2) Journal of International Arbitration (2016) pp. 171-184.
24. Page Vitulli & Rebecca M. Giles, 'Mind Mapping: Making Connections with Images and Colors' 6(2) Delta State University Journal (2016).
25. Iain Sheridan, 'Dispute Resolution: Three Tools to Improve International Arbitration' IFLR1000 (12 October 2015).
26. *Ibid.*
27. *Ibid.*

Tercier explained in a lecture at the American University Washington College of Law, justice is not dispensed in the same way everywhere around the globe, meaning that the preferred way of applying the law in one legal system can be inconceivable in another legal system. This implies that arbitrators, facing the inherently diverse backgrounds of parties and of their representatives in international arbitration, should be ready to understand and apply rules with which they are not necessarily familiar. It also implies that counsel should be ready to adapt to a different way of approaching the legal proceedings from the other party's side.[28]

By way of example, while applying the principle of equality of arms is a conventional wisdom recognized in both civil and common law legal traditions, the application of this principle by counsel in document production differs significantly between both traditions. The common law adversarial approach requires the disclosure of both supportive and adverse documents to a disputing party's case and ensures that 'cards face up on the table' to secure equality of arms.[29] By contrast, in the civil law inquisitorial approach, document production is initiated by the disputing party and is limited to the discharge of each party's burden of proof. Therefore, each party has to make out its own case in reliance on the evidence in its own possession, and document requests are only admissible in the most exceptional circumstances.[30]

[B] Perceptions Influenced by the Cultural Background or the Personal and Specific Industry Experience

At the 2002 ICCA Congress, Shari Diamond, Professor of Law, whose research and interests include the psychology of the decision-making process, described three main psychological influences on an arbitrator's decision-making:

> [D]ecision-makers are influenced by their cultural backgrounds, their prior experiences and their personal associations in formulating their understanding of and judging the behaviour they must consider in reaching their decisions.[31]

While the legal tradition is essential in an arbitrator or lawyer's perception of fairness, due to a developed habit to apply rules in a certain way, the cultural or professional background of arbitrators can also influence the decision-making process and their perception of the best application of conventional wisdoms, e.g., their perception of a fair procedure.

---

28. 'Washington DC: Tercier on Harmonisation', Global Arbitration Review (11 December 2015) available at https://globalarbitrationreview.com/article/1035003/washington-dc-tercier-on-harmonisation.
29. Gordon Blanke, 'Document Production in International Arbitration: From Civil and Common Law Dichotomy to Operational Synergies' 83(4) Arbitration (2017) p. 423 at p. 424.
30. *Ibid.*
31. Shari Diamond, 'Psychological Aspects of Dispute Resolution: Issue for International Arbitration' in *International Commercial Arbitration: Important Contemporary Questions*, ICCA Congress Series no. 11, London 2002 (2003).

Justice Holmes explained how the legal culture in which an arbitrator is schooled can have a significant impact not only on the procedures the arbitrator adopts but also on how they interpret the legal principles applicable:

> The life of the law has not been logic: it has been experience. The felt necessities of the time, the prevalent moral and political theories, intuitions of public policy, avowed or unconscious, even the prejudices which judges share with their fellow-men, have had a good deal more to do than the syllogism in determining the rules by which men should be governed.[32]

A number of studies have been conducted on the influence of arbitrators' industry backgrounds on arbitration outcomes, including with a focus on the securities industry,[33] or the construction industry,[34] some of them concluding that a specific industry experience indeed has an impact on the decisions arbitrators take.[35]

In light of the foregoing, ideas have been developed on how to minimize the impact of cultural differences or of personal experience, in order to ensure a more harmonized approach to the application of conventional wisdom. As explained by Edna Sussman:

> While Arbitrators are often selected because of their backgrounds and experience, arbitrators should take care to assess the case that is actually presented before them, and to consciously endeavor to overcome any affinity they might have for any of the parties as a result of their background. Counsel should take care in the selection of arbitrators to appoint arbitrators accustomed to assessing witness from different cultural backgrounds and who have a reputation for independence and impartiality in their decision-making.[36]

A number of suggestions have been formulated to improve arbitral procedures and to ensure the best application of, and respect for, the principle of due process. Having a thorough review of the evidentiary record and a strong focus on the factual evidence submitted by both parties, for instance, can help to avoid being influenced by internal bias.[37]

---

32. Oliver Wendell Holmes Jr, *The Common Law* (Dover Publishing 1991).
33. Stephen J. Choi, Jill E. Fisch & A.C. Pritchard, 'The Influence of Arbitrator Background and Representation on Arbitration Outcomes', Penn Law: Legal Scholarship Repository (2014).
34. George Ossman III, Mehmet Emre Bayraktar & Qingbin CU, 'Consistency and Reliability of Construction Arbitration Decisions: Empirical Study' 26(2) Journal of Management in Engineering (2010).
35. *See* Stephen J. Choi, Jill E. Fisch & A.C. Pritchard, *supra* n. 21; *see also* Edna Sussman, 'Chapter 3: Biases and heuristics in Arbitrator Decision-Making: Reflections on How to Counteract or Play to The' in Tony Cole ed., *The Roles of Psychology in International Arbitration*, (Kluwer Law International 2017) p. 40 at pp. 45-74.
36. Edna Sussman, *supra* n. 20, at p. 65.
37. Edna Sussman advances that reviewing the evidentiary record before preparing the award, and reviewing evidence in favour of what has preliminarily been assessed to be the losing side can be a remedy to the expression of bias. *Ibid.*, at pp. 67-68.

§25.05 CONCLUSION

Looking to the future of international arbitration and thinking of how to build better arbitration proceedings brings the consolidation of conventional wisdom and innovation at the forefront of preparation and organization of arbitral proceedings.

Essential in many different professions, the concept of 'wisdom' has been extensively analysed by Greek philosophers in the fifth century BCE (Before Common Era) and is central in the five virtues described as follows by Aristotle in 'The Nicomachean Ethics':

(1) Science (*episteme*) allows to draw conclusions in a logical, demonstrable fashion, from given facts and principles.
(2) Intelligence (*nous*) is the intuition of self-evident truths and can be referred to as 'common sense'.
(3) Theoretical wisdom (*sophia*) is a combination of science and intelligence.
(4) Prudence or practical wisdom (*phronesis*) involves not only the ability to decide how to achieve a certain end, but also the ability to reflect upon and determine good ends.
(5) Art (*technē*) is the ability to use one's skills to produce and create.[38]

As practitioners of international arbitration, and particularly as arbitrators, it is useful to keep in mind the five virtues described by Aristotle more than two millennia ago. Arbitrators indeed have to approach the decision-making process in a scientific fashion, while using common sense, wisdom, prudence, and a sense of creation to reach just and fair solutions. According to Aristotle, we learn moral virtue primarily through habit and practice rather than through reasoning or instruction. It is up to us, as members of the arbitration community, to uphold these essential virtues by practising them as habits, if we wish to ensure the perennity of international arbitration in the years to come.

38. Aristotle, *Nicomachean Ethics*, Book VI.

CHAPTER 26

Transparency and Stakeholders' Role in the Selection of the Arbitral Tribunal

Ali Yeşilırmak

§26.01 INTRODUCTION

International arbitration has been ever evolving since the introduction of modernized arbitration rules in the last century.[1] The evolution is very much related to the satisfaction of users and other stakeholders of arbitration. One of the evolving areas is transparency. The issue of transparency mainly derived from investment arbitration[2] for the protection of public interests, but has been adopted to cover wider interests, needs and dynamics in international commercial arbitration.

Transparency touches upon many aspects of international commercial arbitration; selection/appointment of arbitrators, the arbitration process, orders and awards etc. Perhaps one of the most important of all is the selection/appointment of arbitrators. This is because 'arbitration is only as good as its arbitrators.'[3] The selection/appointment of arbitrators generally has a direct effect on the quality of arbitration. The users of arbitration desires to have predictable and just decision-making. Thus, transparency is directly related to independence and impartiality of arbitrators, due process and accountability.

1. On the evolution of arbitration, *see, e.g.*, Gary B. Born, *International Commercial Arbitration* 7 etc. (3rd ed. Kluwer 2021); Ali Yeşilırmak, *Provisional Measures in International Commercial Arbitration* 19 etc. (Kluwer 2005).
2. *See, e.g.*, Judith Gill, *Chapter 11: Transparency: Is It Really Needed and to What Extent?* in *Players Interaction in International Arbitration* 106 etc. (Bernard Honatiou & Alexis Mourre eds Dossiers of the ICC Institute of World Business Law, vol. 9, 2012).
3. *See, e.g.*, Lord Hacking, *Arbitration is Only as Good as Its Arbitrators* in *Liber Amicorum Eric Bergsten – International Arbitration and International Commercial Law: Synergy, Convergence and Evolution* 223 etc. (Stefan Kröll, Loukas A. Mistelis, Perales Viscasillas Maria del Pilar & Vikki M. Rogers eds Kluwer Law International 2011).

Many steps have been taken for greater transparency over the last decade or so, mainly because of the above reasons. Competitive pressures among the arbitral institutions should be added to those reasons.[4]

This note reviews and analyses the following stakeholders' role in respect of transparency in the selection/appointment of arbitrators in international commercial arbitration:[5] (a) the International Bar Association and its soft law on conflicts of Interest, (b) role of arbitration institutions,[6] and (c) private initiatives.

§26.02 IBA GUIDELINES ON CONFLICTS OF INTEREST

One aspect of transparency is the disclosure of any circumstance that may give rise to independence and impartiality of arbitrators. IBA Guidelines on Conflicts of Interest in International Arbitration[7] (IBA Guidelines) deals with conflicts of interest in international arbitration. General Standard 3 of the IBA Guidelines sets out a general disclosure requirement for disclosure by arbitrators:

> (a) If facts or circumstances exist that may, in the eyes of the parties, give rise to doubts as to the arbitrator's impartiality or independence, the arbitrator shall disclose such facts or circumstances to the parties, the arbitration institution or other appointing authority (if any, and if so required by the applicable institutional rules) and the co-arbitrators, if any, prior to accepting his or her appointment 7 or, if thereafter, as soon as he or she learns of them.

This general disclosure standard articulated by non-exhaustive examples of specific situations as set out in the Application List of the IBA Guidelines. There are essentially three lists: Red List, Orange List, and Yellow List. The disclosure is required for situations set out in the Red List. The arbitrator applies the General Standards to decide on a case-by-case basis, whether disclosure should be made for the situations set out in the Orange List. There is no requirement of disclosure for the situations set out in the Yellow List. Some examples of situations from the (Red and Orange) Application List are:

- if the arbitrator is a party to the dispute or representing such party;
- if arbitrator is managing or controlling the party;
- if arbitrator has financial or personal interest in the dispute;

4. Catherine A. Rogers, *Chapter II: The Arbitrator and the Arbitration Procedure, Transparency in Arbitrator Selection* in *Austrian Yearbook on International Arbitration* 75 (Christian Klausegger, Peter Klein, Florian Kremslehner, Alexander Petsche, Nicholas Pitkowitz, Jenny Power, Irene Welser & Gerold Zeiler eds Manz'sche Verlags- und Universitätsbuchhandlung 2016).
5. Transparency in investment arbitration will not be dealt with.
6. This chapter will mainly focus on the approach on disclosure of arbitrators of the most preferred arbitration institutions: the International Chamber of Commerce (ICC), Swiss Arbitration Center (SAC), Hong Kong International Arbitration Centre (HKIAC), London Court of International Arbitration (LCIA), and the Chinese International Economic and Trade Arbitration Center (CIETAC). The list is acquired from the survey of Queen Mary University. *See* 2021 International Arbitration Survey: Adapting Arbitration to a Changing World, https://arbitration.qmul.ac.uk/research/2021-international-arbitration-survey/.
7. Adopted 2004 and revised in 2016.

- if the arbitrator regularly advises to the party or its affiliates;
- if arbitrator has given legal advice/opinion or prior involvement in the case;
- if the arbitrator has a relationship with the parties or counsel;
- if the arbitrator or her law firm has, within past three years, served as counsel for one of the parties or its affiliate;
- if one of the parties, its affiliate or any of the law firm involved has appointed an arbitrator on two or more occasions by within last three years;
- if the arbitrator or her law firm represents, not concerning the current dispute, a party or its affiliate on a regular basis;
- if the arbitrator was affiliated with another arbitrator or any of the counsel in the arbitration;
- if the arbitrator's law firm is currently acting adversely to one of the parties or its affiliate;
- if the arbitrator has publicly advocated a position regarding the case; and
- if the arbitrator holds a position with the appointing authority concerning the dispute.

The IBA Guidelines are of soft law in nature or 'non-binding set of principles'.[8] Despite this fact, the Guidelines are often used and widely accepted in international commercial arbitrations.[9] The Guidelines set the general standard for arbitrator conflicts of interest in international arbitration and will undoubtedly be consulted with by arbitrating parties, arbitrators, arbitration institutions and national courts.

§26.03 INSTITUTIONAL RESPONSES FOR FOSTERING TRANSPARENCY IN ARBITRATOR APPOINTMENT/SELECTION PROCESS

A number of arbitration institutions has taken various steps for fostering transparency.

8. Nigel Blackaby et al., *Redfern and Hunter on International Arbitration* 258 (6th ed. Kluwer Law International; Oxford University Press 2015).
9. Report on the Perception of the IBA Arbitration Soft Law Products, para. 101. In the ICC experience, IBA Guidelines reportedly used 60% of the cases analysed by the ICC Court of International Arbitration. *See also* Simon Greenberg & José R. Ferris, *References to the IBA Guidelines on Conflict of Interest in International Commercial Arbitration when Deciding on Arbitrator Independence in ICC Cases*, 20(2) ICC Court of Arb. Bull. 33 (2009); Andrea Carlevaris & Rocio Dign, *Arbitrator Challenges under the ICC Rules and Practice,* 23(1) ICC Disp. Res. Bull. (2016); Álvaro López de Argumedo Piñeiro, *Interaction Between the IBA Guidelines on Conflict of Interest of Arbitrators and the ICC Arbitration Rules*, 143(44) Spain Arb. Rev.: Revista del Club Español del Arbitraje (2022). For practice regarding the IBA Guidelines under other arbitration institutions, *see* Geoff Nicholas & Constantine Partasides, *LCIA Court Decisions on Challenges of Arbitrators: A Proposal to Publish*, 23 Arb. Int. 1, 3 (2014). For national court decisions referring to the IBA Guidelines *see, e.g.*, Diana Akikol, *Chapter 8: The View from the Swiss Courts on Conflict of Interest, Disclosure, Objection, and Challenges* in *Clear Path or Jungle in Commercial Arbitrators' Conflict of Interest?* 55, 68-70 (Felix Dasser ed. Kluwer Law International 2021); Paula Hodges, *Chapter 10: The View from the English Courts on Conflict of Interest: Halliburton and Beyond* in Dasser, *ibid.*, 91 etc.; Laurence Shore & Federico Alberto Cabona, *The View from U.S. Courts on Conflicts of Interest* in Dasser, *ibid.*, 115 etc. The IBA Guidelines referred to in several free trade agreements and even implicitly referred in Indian national law in 2015. *See* Felix Dasser, *Chapter 7: The View from the State Courts on Conflicts of Interest: Introduction* in *ibid.*, 47, 52.

[A] Submission of Statement of Acceptance, Availability, Impartiality and Independence

The submission of the Statement of Acceptance, Availability, Impartiality and Independence (ICC Statement) has long been the part of the ICC arbitration practice and aimed at enforcing the rules that ICC arbitrators have a duty, at all times, to act in an impartial and independent manner (Articles 11 and 22(4) of the ICC Rules of Arbitration). There are a similar disclosure requirements under the other institutional arbitration rules.[10]

The ICC Court of Arbitration adopted a reform in respect of disclosure requirements under the ICC Statement in 2016. As to what has to be disclosed, there is a general rule and a number of circumstances exemplified in the Note to Parties and Arbitral Tribunals on the Conduct of the Arbitration under the ICC Rules of Arbitration ('ICC Note').

As a general rule in the ICC arbitration,[11] any circumstance that might be of such a nature as to call into question the arbitrator's independence in the eyes of any of the parties or give rise to reasonable doubts as to the arbitrator's impartiality must be disclosed. In making disclosure, the arbitrator should consider the following list of circumstances:[12]

- the arbitrator[13] or her law firm represents or advises, or has represented or advised, a party to the dispute or its affiliates;
- the arbitrator or her law firm acts or has acted against the party or its affiliate;
- the arbitrator or her law firm has a business relationship with the party or its affiliate, or a personal interest of any nature in the outcome of the dispute;
- the arbitrator or her law firm acts or has acted on behalf of the party or its affiliate as director, board member, officer, or otherwise;
- the arbitrator or her law firm is or has been involved in the dispute, or has expressed a view on the dispute in a manner that might affect her impartiality;
- the arbitrator has a professional or close personal relationship with counsel to one of the parties or the counsel's law firm;
- the arbitrator acts or has acted as arbitrator in a case involving the party or its affiliates;
- the arbitrator acts or has acted as arbitrator in a related case; and
- the arbitrator has in the past been appointed as arbitrator by the party or its affiliate, or by counsel to the party or the counsel's law firm.

10. *See* Article 12 of SAC Arbitration Rules; Article 11(4-5) of HKIAC Arbitration Rules; Article 5(4) of LCIA Arbitration Rules and Guidance Note paras 6-14; and Article 31 of CIETAC Arbitration Rules.
11. ICC Rules of Arbitration, Article 11(1).
12. ICC Note, para. 27.
13. For ICC list of circumstances, the reference to arbitrator also cover prospective arbitrator.

The above list contains similarities with and mainly derived from the list of situations set out in the IBA Guideline's Application List. The ICC's standard norms intend to supplement the latter.[14]

The ICC's list of circumstances for disclosure is of hard law in nature; that is to say contractually binding upon the arbitrator.[15] The ICC's standard norms for disclosure is wider as compared the IBA Guidelines.[16] In all circumstances set out in the ICC's list, disclosure from the arbitrator is expected.[17] Thus, the ICC's standards seem to foster further transparency. It is highly likely that other arbitration institutions will follow the ICC approach of having separate and wider standard norms (as compared to the IBA Guidelines) for disclosure of arbitrators.

[B] Availability of Arbitrators

One of the reasons for delay in arbitration proceedings is the overload of arbitrators.[18] Thus, the parties have a legitimate interest in being informed as to how busy the arbitrators are. The ICC, like other most preferred arbitration institutions, expects the prospective arbitrators to disclose relevant information regarding their availability. The prospective arbitrator should, in the ICC Statement, declare the number of arbitrations they are involved, their role[19] in such arbitrations and other commitments and their availability over the next 24 months.[20] If there is an objection of the lack of availability, the ICC may refuse to confirm the appointment.

The declaration on the availability of arbitrators generally demonstrates that the arbitrator has capacity and could spend appropriate time for the case at hand. Such a declaration, thus, in the view of the author, serves the satisfaction of the users' expectation to have a final award in a relatively short period of time. To this end, the author is of the view that other arbitration institutions could consider seeking similar information on the availability from prospective arbitrators.

[C] Sharing Information Regarding Arbitral Tribunals, Industry Sector and Law Firms Involved

In the past, arbitration institutions had shared no or little information about the arbitrators with public at large. The lack of information, in some cases, caused

14. It is rightly argued that the IBA Guidelines can work on a complimentary manner with ICC disclosure norms. Piñeiro, *supra* n. 9, 157.
15. Felix Dasser, *Soft Law in International Commercial Arbitration – A Critical Approach* in *Austrian Arbitration Yearbook on International Arbitration* 112 (Christian Klausegger, Peter Klein, Florian Kremslehner, Alexander Petsche, Nicholas Pitkowitz, Jenny Power, Irene Welser & Gerold Zeiler eds Manz'sche Verlags- und Universitätsbuchhandlung 2016); Piñeiro, *supra* n. 9, 144.
16. Piñeiro, *supra* n. 9, 148.
17. ICC Note, paras 20-21.
18. *See, e.g.*, Blackaby et al., *supra* n. 8, 249.
19. Whether they are acting as the president, sole arbitrator, co-arbitrator, counsel to a party, or funder.
20. ICC Note, para. 33.

criticisms towards arbitration as an institution.[21] In order to avoid those criticisms, certain actions were taken in institutional arbitration.[22] For instance, the ICC started to publish, on its website, the names of arbitrators (after the terms of reference was transmitted or approved by the ICC Court), their nationality, their role with the tribunal, their appointment method, whether the arbitration was pending or closed, industry sectors involved, law firms representing the parties, and the names of the administrative secretaries.[23] The author welcomes the ICC's approach in respect of sharing the above information and urges other arbitration institutions to follow the ICC's example.

[D] Sharing Information Regarding Challenges of Arbitrators

Arbitration institutions generally did not share with the parties the reasons for decisions made in respect of challenges against arbitrators. This approach has recently been changed by many institutions.[24] The leading institution for the reform on sharing reasons is the LCIA.[25] The LCIA not only shares the reasons for challenge with the parties to arbitration but also publishes, on its website, abstracts from the decisions on challenge.[26]

The ICC shares, upon request of a party, the reason for a decision on the challenge for an arbitrator (under Article 14 of the ICC Arbitration Rules).[27] Under exceptional circumstances, the ICC Court may decide not to communicate the reasons without the need of any request from a party.[28] A request could be made prior to the decision on a challenge by the ICC Court.[29]

The approach of both the LCIA and ICC are welcomed. The ICC has a rather cautious approach on sharing information concerning the reasons for challenges of arbitrators. It only shares the information, upon request with the parties with a

21. For those criticisms *see*, José R. Ferris, *New Policies and Practices at the ICC: Towards Greater Efficiency and Transparency in International Arbitration*, ICC Dis. Res. Bull. 13 etc. no. 2 (2016). The ICC Note refers to them as inaccurate or ill-informed criticisms. ICC Note, para. 50.
22. ICC Note, para. 50.
23. *Ibid.*, paras 51-53.
24. For recent initiatives by arbitration institutions, *see, e.g.*, Andrea Carlevaris, *Chapter II: The Arbitrator and the Arbitration Procedure, The Rise of Transparency in Arbitral Institutions' Decision-Makings* in *Austrian Yearbook on International Arbitration* 157, 159-162 (Christian Klausegger, Peter Klein, Florian Kremslehner, Alexander Petsche, Nicholas Pitkowitz, Jenny Power, Irene Welser & Gerold Zeiler eds Manz'sche Verlags- und Universitätsbuchhandlung 2021). Swiss Court of International Arbitration has started providing reasons on arbitrator challenge decisions, *see* Gabrielle Nater-Bass, *Chapter 6: SCAI's Approach to Conflicts of Interest* in Dasser *supra* n. 9, 35, 50.
25. *See, e.g.*, Peter Turner & Reza Mohtashami, *A Guide to the LCIA Arbitration Rules* 79 (Oxford University Press 2009); Thomas Walsh & Ruth Teitelbaum, *The LCIA Decisions on Challenges: An Introduction*, 27(3) Arb. Int. 283 etc. (2011).
26. *See* https://www.lcia.org/challenge-decision-database.aspx.
27. ICC Note, para. 46.
28. *Ibid.*, para. 47.
29. *Ibid.*, para. 49.

caveat.[30] Ultimately, the approach of the LCIA for providing reasons to the parties and disseminating to public at large seems to be followed, in the author's view, by other arbitration institutions.[31] This is due mainly to the fact that, the LCIA's approach (a) assists the parties in better understand of the decision on challenge, (b) promotes predictability through uniform interpretation of standards, and (c) potentially protects arbitral awards from challenges.[32]

[E] Feeding Back to Arbitrators

The 2018 International Arbitration Survey[33] demonstrates that most of the users of arbitration services (mostly lawyers and in house counsels) wish to give feedback to the arbitrators. More than half of the arbitrators participated to the 2018 Survey desires to receive feedback from the parties.

The main benefits of having feedbacks in arbitration have many folds:[34]

- promoting confidence in arbitration;
- assisting arbitration institutions for their future appointments; and
- assisting in improvement of arbitrators' skills.

Some arbitration institutions, like the ICC and the HKIAC, receive feedback from the users (the parties and/or counsels) at the end of an arbitration.[35] The feedback is generally requested after the award is transmitted to the parties. For covering the whole service, it is logical to have feedback after the award is delivered. In such cases, in order to have a better understanding, particular attention should be given to whose (winning or losing party) feedback is being handled.

The feedback given provides, despite a number of impediments,[36] invaluable information about the quality of arbitration and arbitrators.[37] The feedback received is

30. The ICC Court keeps the power, in exceptional circumstances, not to share the reasons for the challenge.
31. Indeed, Born suggests that arbitration institutions must publish arbitrator challenge decisions. *See* Gary Born, *Institutions need to publish Arbitrator Challenge Decisions* (10 May 2010) http://arbitrationblog.kluwerarbitration.com/2010/05/10/institutions-need-to-publish-arbitrator-challenge-decisions/.
32. Carlevaris, *supra* n. 24, 168-171.
33. 2018 International Arbitration Survey: The Evolution of International Arbitration, https://arbitration.qmul.ac.uk/research/2018/.
34. *See* Paula Hodges, *Feeding Back to Arbitrators?*, (13 December 2018), http://arbitrationblog.practicallaw.com/feeding-back-to-arbitrators/.
35. *See* https://www.hkiac.org/news/rate-your-experience-hkiac-launches-arbitration-evaluation-system.
36. The feedback questions for the feedbacks are generally aimed at improvement of the arbitration practice of the institution but not particularly focused on analysing the quality of the arbitrators. Furthermore, not all parties respond to the surveys. *See* Rogers, *supra* n. 4, 79. Furthermore, the losing party may have emotional responses to the feedback questions. In addition, parties may fail to fill up the questionnaire for various reasons. *Ibid.*
37. There is always a risk that the losing party may exaggerate its negative comments on the arbitrators.

currently for internal use of the institution. However, it is the author's view that the transparency and confidence in arbitration could be better fostered if such feedbacks are

- designed to assess the quality of arbitrators and arbitration;
- transmitted to the arbitrators themselves; and
- with the advanced approval of the arbitrators, to third parties for considering arbitrator selection.

§26.04 PRIVATE INITIATIVES ON SELECTION OF ARBITRATORS

The 2018 International Arbitration Survey provides that 70% of the respondents have access to enough information to make an informed selection of arbitrators. Users generally rely on, according to the Survey, word of mouth from internal colleagues and publicly available information. There seems to be a room for improvement for selection of arbitrators. In order to satisfy the need and foster further transparency at the arbitration selection stage, a number of private initiatives emerged. These initiatives mainly are:[38]

- Arbitrator Intelligence (AI)[39]
- Dispute Resolution Data[40]
- Global Arbitration Review Arbitrator Research Tool.

The above tools essentially gather, by using artificial intelligence, publicly available information about the arbitrators and awards. They vary in gathering and putting forward the data gathered and surf through it. AI seems to go a step further to collect information on arbitrators through feedback questionnaires.

All private initiatives are welcomed. As publicly available information becomes more readily available and feedback questionnaires are responded by more participants, the initiatives will provide more accurate information for arbitrator selection. The author believes that the usage of private initiatives will steadily increase.

§26.05 CONCLUSION

Arbitrator disclosure is immensely important for the satisfaction of the users' desires and holding the integrity of arbitration as institution. To this end, the IBA Guidelines set the standard for arbitrator disclosure. The Guidelines are widely accepted and used

38. Daniel Schimmel et al., *Transparency in Arbitration*, Resource ID: W-013-1478 (Thomson Reuters 2018).
39. Initially launched by Queen Mary University and The Pennsylvania State University. *See* Catherine A. Rogers, *The International Arbitration Information Project: From Ideation to Operation* (10 December 2012) http://arbitrationblog.kluwerarbitration.com/2012/12/10/the-international-arbitrator-information-project-from-an-ideation-to-operation/.
40. *See* https://www.disputeresolutiondata.com/about_drd.

by arbitrating parties, arbitrators, arbitration institutions and national courts. Various arbitration institutions has taken steps, within past decade, to further foster disclosure concerning arbitrator selection/appointment:

- A statement of impartiality and independence is a tool that should be used for ensuring wide disclosure. The ICC's standard for disclosure foster wider transparency. Similar standard is expected to be followed by other arbitration institutions.
- The transparency on the availability of arbitrators is useful for satisfaction of users' needs and thus is expected to be used in the near future by major arbitration institutions.
- Sharing information regarding arbitral tribunals, industry sector, law firms involved will assist avoiding or minimizing criticisms towards arbitration. One would expect this trend to be followed by other arbitration institutions.
- Sharing reasons concerning arbitrator challenges with parties will in the near future have a great acceptance among arbitration institutions. However, disseminating such reasons to public at large may have creeping acceptance.
- Feedbacks are used by some arbitration institutions. Sharing feedbacks with arbitration institutions and arbitrators will in principle foster quality in arbitration.

Although, empirical studies demonstrate that word of mouth from internal colleagues and publicly available information is generally used for the selection of arbitrators, there is room for private initiatives that would objectively assist parties in selection of arbitrators. To this end, private initiatives on selection of arbitrators will be used more often in the near future.

CHAPTER 27

Arbitrator Disclosure: Objective Observer or in "the Eyes of the Parties"

Patricia Shaughnessy

§27.01 INTRODUCTION AND BACKGROUND

Ensuring the impartiality and independence of arbitrators is fundamental to safeguarding due-process, fostering user-trust, and protecting the integrity and finality of arbitration. The arbitrator's obligation to disclose facts and circumstances that may relate to their impartiality and independence provides the parties and an administering arbitral institution with needed information when appointing or considering challenges to an arbitrator. Despite guidance through national arbitration legislation, arbitral rules, guidelines, court decisions, and practice, arbitrator disclosure continues to generate robust discussion and arguably leads to more frequent challenges to arbitrators, many of which appear unjustified and statistically, most are rejected. The case-specific and fact-based nature of assessing potential circumstances that might raise concerns of impartiality and independence, makes disclosure difficult for arbitrators to navigate. Abstract regulation offers limited guidance and even categories and examples of potential situations often need to be refined to the actual circumstances. The increasing sources of guidance seek to assist arbitrators in making disclosures. However, various rules and guides may overlap, may apply differing approaches, and may need to be adapted to the relevant national law. This can add to ambiguity in assessing disclosure for arbitrators, parties, arbitral institutions, and courts.

One ambiguous area is the relevant standard for determining disclosures that should be made. It is generally accepted that the standard for disclosure is broader and creates a lower threshold than the standard for a successful challenge. However, there exists a lack of consensus on the standard for disclosure. Many consider that a subjective standard should be applied to disclosure and an objective standard should be applied to challenges, given that disclosure should be broader to enable parties to fully assess potential conflicts that could lead to bringing a challenge and to enhance confidence in the arbitrators, while the objective standard applies to the objective determination of a challenge. Some approaches apply a subjective disclosure standard which adopts the perspective of "in the eyes of the parties," while others apply an objective standard adopting the perspective of "the reasonably informed observer" (or some variation of this).

Arbitrators equipped with extensive experience—particularly those with the range and depth of experience which Professor Julian Lew possesses—can navigate disclosure with acquired wisdom. Less experienced arbitrators may find disclosure obligations fraught with uncertainty and face the "disclosure dilemma" of over or under-disclosure and its consequences. Some may legitimately fear that making a disclosure of a minor matter may prevent the arbitrator appointment. Even experienced arbitrators may underestimate disclosure obligations, the adequacy of which may be viewed differently by a party, an arbitral institution, or a court. Most regulations and guidelines provide that any doubt should be resolved in favor of disclosure thus encouraging broad disclosure.

The competing interests in respecting party selection of arbitrators, ensuring efficiency and finality, and preventing strategic deployment of challenges causing obstruction and delay, as well as protecting confidentiality concerns of arbitrators, make arbitrator disclosure an area difficult to navigate. Even the consequence of inadequate disclosure remains uncertain, although it is generally considered an aggravating factor rather than an independent ground for challenge. In serious cases, failure to disclose can lead to loss in reputation, an annulled or unenforceable award, and even liability claims against the arbitrator.

This essay focuses on the objective and subjective standards for arbitrator disclosure and considers an arbitral institution perspective. Arbitrator disclosure obligations seek to ensure that arbitrators provide essential information to allow the parties to make informed decisions on whether to accept or challenge an arbitrator for lack of impartiality or independence. However, an arbitral institution also has an interest in ensuring the integrity of the arbitration, the enforceability of an arbitral award, and the reputation of the institution. Arbitral institutions are key stakeholders, regulators, decision-makers, and custodians of arbitrator disclosure.

This essay first addresses the regulatory framework for disclosure, before reflecting on the application of disclosure assessment standards. At the time of authoring this essay, International Centre for Settlement of Investment Disputes (ICSID) and the United Nation Commission on International Trade Law (UNCITRAL) Working Group III are actively developing and debating the "Code of Conduct for Adjudicators"; recent case law, such as Haliburton v. Chubb,[1] continues to generate discussions; and the Law Commission has just released Consultation Paper 257 reviewing the 1996 Arbitration Act, including considering potential revisions to introduce express duties of independence and disclosure on arbitrators, which currently do not exist in the Act.[2] The

1. Halliburton Co v. Chubb Bermuda Insurance Ltd [2020] UKSC 48, [2021].
2. Law Commission, Consultation Paper 257, pp. 19-27, available at: Law Commission Documents Template (last accessed September 27, 2022). The Commission has provisionally proposed:

Commission provisionally proposes to introduce a general duty of disclosure but not an independence requirement, allowing for arbitral practice to evolve and "for arbitral rules to offer further particulars of how the general duty applies in the specific factual context of their own area of activity."[3]

These and other developments underscore the ongoing and dynamic evolution of arbitrator disclosure, as well as the important regulatory role of institutions and organizations. This short essay does not analyse these and other developments, as they deserve considerably more discussion than can be addressed here.

§27.02 THE REGULATORY FRAMEWORK

The regulatory framework relating to arbitrator disclosure seeks to protect the rights of the parties and the legitimacy of arbitration. Parties have a legitimate interest in arbitrator disclosure in order to exercise their right to bring a challenge. The aim and nature of disclosure has a party-focus. Arbitrators need to ensure that they have provided all needed information to allow parties to make an early assessment thereby preventing later doubts regarding their independence and impartiality and concerns stemming from an arbitrator failing to fully disclose matters that the parties later discover. The obligation for disclosure continues throughout the arbitration. Arbitral institutions also have an interest in ensuring adequate disclosure as a failure to disclose may cast a shadow of distrust in the arbitrator and the arbitral process, endangering the integrity of the arbitration and even jeopardizing the finality of the award.

The UNCITRAL Model Law on International Commercial Arbitration ("the Model Law") provides a widely accepted standard for arbitrator disclosure. Article 12(1) provides:

> (1) When a person is approached in connection with his possible appointment as an arbitrator, he *shall disclose any circumstances likely to give rise to justifiable doubts as to his impartiality or independence*. An arbitrator, from the time of his appointment and throughout the arbitral proceedings, shall without delay disclose any such circumstances to the parties unless they have already been informed of them by him. (Emphasis added).

This disclosure obligation is significantly wider than the grounds for successfully challenging an arbitrator under the Model Law, Article 12(2), which provides: "[a]n arbitrator may be challenged *only if circumstances exist that give rise to justifiable doubts as to his impartiality or independence*" (Emphasis added). The distinction between "circumstances likely to give rise" and "only if circumstances exist" intentionally provides for a substantially different degree of probability and burden of proof. For a successful challenge, the circumstances which create justifiable doubts must be found to actually exist. The UNCITRAL Rules of Arbitration follow this approach.[4]

"codifying the common law, which requires an arbitrator to disclose circumstances which might reasonably give rise to justifiable doubts as to their impartiality." *Ibid.*, at §3.3, p. 19.

3. *Ibid.*, at para. 3.47, p. 26.
4. Articles 11 and 12(1), UNCITRAL Arbitration Rules (with Article 1, para. 4, as adopted in 2013 and Article 1, para. 5, as adopted in 2021).

The Model Law approach requiring arbitrator disclosure of "circumstances likely to give rise to justifiable doubts" has gained acceptance in many arbitral rules and national legislation. It is commonly considered to provide an objective standard of justifiable doubts from the perspective of an informed reasonable observer. Similarly, the higher threshold for a challenge to succeed relies upon an objective standard from the perspective of an informed reasonable observer. While non-Model Law jurisdictions may use differently formulated provisions and text, the approach to challenge relies on an objective standard to assess the alleged impartiality and independence. The objective approach invites an assessment from the perspective of a detached but reasonable observer rather than from the arbitrator or the parties' perspective.

Arbitral institution rules usually regulate arbitrator disclosure and challenges, frequently containing provisions similar to the UNCITRAL approach, thus employing an objective standard. However, some rules, notably the ICC Rules, contain a disclosure obligation linked to the "eyes of the parties." This introduces a subjective standard of disclosure. Article 11(2) of the ICC Rules (2021) provides:

> Before appointment or confirmation, a prospective arbitrator shall sign a statement of acceptance, availability, impartiality and independence. The prospective arbitrator *shall disclose in writing to the Secretariat any facts or circumstances which might be of such a nature as to call into question the arbitrator's independence in the eyes of the parties*, as well as any circumstances that could give rise to reasonable doubts as to the arbitrator's impartiality. The Secretariat shall provide such information to the parties in writing and fix a time limit for any comments from them. (Emphasis added).

Interestingly, the rule requires both a subjective and objective standard, with the subjective standard linked to the arbitrator's independence and the objective standard linked to the arbitrator's impartiality. The 1998 ICC Rules referred only to "independence" of arbitrators. Article 7(1) ICC Rules (1998) provided: "Every arbitrator must be and remain independent of the parties involved in the arbitration." Article 7(2) ICC Rules (1998) required an arbitrator to submit a statement of independence and "disclose in writing ... any facts or circumstances which might be of such a nature as to call into question the arbitrator's independence in the eyes of the parties."

The 2012 edition of the ICC Rules introduced "impartiality" and linked it to the "circumstances that could give rise to reasonable doubts as to the arbitrator's impartiality."[5] The Secretariat's Guide to ICC Arbitration (2012) noted that the new Article 11 reflected the ICC Court's existing practice of considering challenges based on a lack of impartiality. It also noted the new provision may affect the scope of disclosure obligation.[6]

---

5. This short essay does analyse the discussion on the differences of independence and impartiality.
6. Jason Fry, Simon Greenberg, Francesca Mazza, *Secretariat's Guide to ICC Arbitration*, sections 3.371-3.375 (July 2012, available on ICC Digital Library). The court has always considered challenges based on a lack of impartiality and independence alike, although a challenge based purely on alleged impartiality is more difficult to demonstrate and therefore less likely to succeed. The inclusion of impartiality in the rules is not expected to affect the standard applied by the court in determining objections or challenges to arbitrators. However, the express reference to impartiality in Articles 11(2) and 11(3) may affect the scope of disclosure obligations.

In 2004, the International Bar Association (IBA) introduced the IBA Guidelines to Conflicts of Interest in International Arbitration (IBA Guidelines), which were updated in 2014. The approach of the guidelines was inspired by and adapted to the ICC Rules approach with a subjective standard, but excluded the "green list" category from disclosure.[7] General Standard 3(a) of the 2004 version of the IBA Guidelines provided:

> *If facts or circumstances exist that may, in the eyes of the parties, give rise to doubts as to the arbitrator's impartiality or independence, the arbitrator shall disclose such facts or circumstances* to the parties, the arbitration institution or other appointing authority (if any, and if so required by the applicable institutional rules) and to the co-arbitrators, if any, prior to accepting his or her appointment or, if thereafter, as soon as he or she learns about them. (Emphasis added).

The original IBA Guidelines (2004) Explanation to General Standard 3 comments that this provision introduces a subjective standard. This contrasts with General Standard 2, (applying to conflicts of interest precluding an arbitrator from serving), which adopted an objective standard derived from Article 12 of the Model Law and employing the perspective of a "reasonable third person's point of view having knowledge of the relevant facts." The "eyes of the parties" subjective standard for disclosure requires the arbitrator to consider all known circumstances, "including to the extent known the culture and the customs of the country of which the parties are domiciled or nationals."[8] Any disclosure made pursuant to the subjective standard is not an indication of a lack of impartiality or independence. If the arbitrator considers the disclosed information indicates such a concern, the arbitrator should not accept the nomination/appointment. The disclosure serves to allow the parties to "explore the situation further" if they so wish.[9] Any challenge to the arbitrator should be subject to the higher threshold of the stricter objective test.[10]

The 2014 IBA Guidelines have essentially followed this approach, retaining the language of the 2004 Guidelines for arbitrator disclosure (General Standard 3(a)). Arbitrator disclosures are subject to a subjective test, while challenges to arbitrators are subject to an objective test.

Notably, both the 2004 and 2014 IBA Guidelines not only introduced a subjective test to apply to disclosure, but also made other significant changes to the approach of Article 12 of the Model Law. The Model Law refers to disclosure of "any circumstances *likely to give rise to justifiable doubts* … ." The IBA Guidelines require disclosure "*If facts or circumstances exist that may, in the eyes of the parties, give rise to doubts* … ." There is a significant difference between "circumstances likely to give rise" and those which "may … give rise," the latter providing a lower threshold for requiring disclosure.[11] The IBA Guidelines refer to "doubts," while the Model Law refers to

7. IBA Guidelines, (2004), Explanation to General Standard 3(a).
8. *Ibid.* The 2014 Explanation to General Standard 3(a) does not refer to the parties. culture and customs.
9. *Ibid.*, at 3(b).
10. *Ibid.*
11. *See* Gary B. Born, *International Commercial Arbitration*, Chapter 12, §12.05, (G) 5(b) (ii), updated in the Kluwer Arbitration database in September 2022.

"justifiable doubts." These textual differences combined with the "in the eyes of the parties" subjective standard substantially broadens the disclosure obligation.[12] This approach and the subjective standard to arbitrator disclosure has been criticized as arguably encouraging more frequent and unnecessary challenges to arbitrators.[13]

The IBA Guidelines have broadly impacted arbitrator disclosure obligations and practice throughout the arbitration community, affecting parties, arbitrators, arbitral institutions, and courts across the globe. The IBA Arbitration Committee and its Arbitration Guidelines and Rules Subcommittee is currently surveying the arbitration community for input on the guidelines. A 2016 survey of IBA arbitration-related instruments recommended updating the guidelines every 10 years. This may provide an opportunity to review and if justified, retool the standards for arbitrator disclosure.

§27.03 APPLYING THE SUBJECT STANDARD OF "IN THE EYES OF THE PARTIES"

Applying a subjective standard that takes into account the "eyes of the parties" may be a fiction.[14] In most cases it will be impossible for an arbitrator to actually ascertain the parties' subjective doubts that may be triggered by various facts and circumstances in a particular case. First, it is rare that the parties would have a common perspective. One or more of the parties may find the circumstances create doubts of the impartiality and independence of an arbitrator, while another may not. The arbitrator would have to consider whether one or more of the parties may find the facts and circumstances could give rise to subjective doubts. Thus, the level of disclosure would be set by the most sensitive potential "doubter" based on the arbitrator's assumptions.

As the arbitrator cannot look into the parties' minds, the arbitrator would have to consider the concerns of reasonable parties in the circumstances of the dispute to be arbitrated. The arbitrator necessarily brings her judgment to determining what facts and circumstances might be relevant to these parties in this dispute in assessing their confidence in the arbitrator's independence and impartiality. The consideration of the parties' unique characteristics—including backgrounds, experience, cultural and customs of the parties' nationality and domicile—may be more of guessing endeavour and an invitation to make assumptions about the parties at a very early stage. The parties' state of mind can only be determined from an "outsiders" assessment of observable or expressed indicators, which typically is limited at the outset of a case.

In most commercial arbitrations, the parties are entities not individuals. It would be difficult for an arbitrator to apply a purely subjective standard to an entity, which may include individuals with many different backgrounds and characteristics. The parties may also represent different sectors which have different perspectives. For example, In the context of the Halliburton v. Chubb case, some organizations making

12. *Ibid.*
13. *Ibid.*, at §12.05, (G) 5 C (i).
14. Catherine A. Rogers, *Ethics in International Arbitration*, fn. 126 (and related text), p. 242 (Oxford University Press 2014), referring the "eyes of the Parties" as a "modified objective standard."

amicus curiae submissions to the court, explained the perspectives of parties in their specialized sectors regarding arbitrator multiple appointments.[15]

In determining the disclosures, the arbitrator will need to consider what might reasonably be relevant to the parties in the context of the known or alleged circumstances in the dispute. The arbitrator cannot ascertain the subjective perspective of each party and instead must consider the circumstances of the dispute when conducting reasonably diligent enquiries and checks based on the parties, related entitles, and relevant aspects of the dispute, such as known experts and material witnesses. Arguably, parties should provide the prospective arbitrator and the arbitral institution with relevant known information to assist in identifying related entities and persons that should be checked for potential conflicts. The extent of arbitrators' duty to investigate potential circumstances that would trigger disclosure, as well as the corresponding "duty of curiosity" of the parties is beyond this essay.

There is a risk that a purely subjective standard involving a party-specific approach, could lead to over or under-disclosure. Potential arbitrators need to ensure the confidentiality of other arbitration assignments and other professional work, as well as purely private matters. Over-disclosure can lead to triggering more challenges, some of which may be more strategic than justified. Reports from arbitral institutions demonstrate that most challenges are not accepted. Challenges impose costs, delays, and effort of the parties, arbitrators, and arbitral institutions.

The IBA Guidelines subjective standard can be difficult for arbitrators to apply in practice and can lead to arbitrators in fact applying an objective test.[16] The draft Code of Conduct provision on disclosure, Article 10, has generated debates over whether disclosure should be based on an objective standard of "any circumstances likely to give rise to justifiable doubts" or to include the subjective standard of "in the eyes of the parties."[17] In commenting on the draft Code of Conduct provision on Disclosure (Version Two), Professor Lew (together with Professors Brekoulakis and Mistelis), noted the variation of terminology and the risk of confusion leading to disputes regarding disclosure:

> Two observations only: first, the test for disclosure under Article 10(1) requires clarification as it confusingly provides for cumulative formulations of bias, namely "doubts" as to the Adjudicators' "independence or impartiality," "bias," "conflict

15. Halliburton Co v. Chubb Bermuda Insurance Ltd [2020] UKSC 48, [2021], para. 128, p. 34. The court noted that GAFTA (Grain and Feed Trade Association) and LMAA (*London Maritime Arbitrators Association)* explained in their submissions that multiple appointments are common in their fields of operation. *Ibid.*, at paras. 43 and 44. The court also noted that: "There is also evidence from ARIAS (UK) of such practice in reinsurance arbitrations." *Ibid.*, at para. 43.
16. As was noted by the Swiss Arbitration Association, Comments to the Draft Code of Conduct, Version Three, at p. 17 (November 23, 2021), available at: https://icsid.worldbank.org/sites/default/files/documents/Code_of_Conduct_V3_Comments_by_Article.pdf (last accessed September 27, 2022).
17. *Ibid.*, at pp. 18-19, Bernard Hanotiau, commented that the word "reasonable" has disappeared and that the test only refers to the eyes of the disputing parties. You have therefore to speculate what might be the subjective thinking of somebody that you do not know and who might not share the same common sense than yourself on grounds of personality or culture. The absence of reference to reasonableness is shocking.

> of interest," "impropriety" or "appearance of bias." It is unclear whether the different formulations of bias intend to introduce different tests for disclosure or what exactly is the difference in the scope of their application. It is apprehended that they will give rise to confusion and satellite disputes over which circumstances warrant disclosure.[18]

Anecdotally, some arbitrators overly rely on the IBA categories of situations rather than carefully consider the General Standards when determining any disclosures. The IBA Application Lists are intended to be a non-exhaustive list of situations to provide guidance. At a recent conference panel addressing disclosure, an experienced arbitrator reported that if a potential disclosure falls into the IBA Guidelines orange list and it was within the three-year period, he would disclose, but if it were even one-day past the three-year period, he would not disclose. The three-year period is not a firm limit, and each situation should be assessed according to the specific circumstances. For example, if the relationship between the potential arbitrator and a counsel for the party ended five years ago but had been a very close working relationship for many years, it should be disclosed. It might not lead to a successful challenge, but the parties should be made aware of it by the arbitrator at the outset, rather than perhaps discovering it later during the arbitration. The lack of disclosure may cast a shadow of distrust and undermine the confidence in the arbitrator. The subjective disclosure test contained in the IBA Guidelines General Standards invites the arbitrator to focus on the parties' perspective rather than blindly consulting the Application Lists.

The subjective standard can be justified as the aim is to direct the arbitrator to consider disclosure from the parties' interests in disclosure. This could allow the arbitrator to determine disclosure from the perspective of reasonable parties in the circumstances of the actual case. The arbitrator should consider the purpose of disclosure, which is to facilitate the legitimate interests of the parties to be fully informed of all relevant facts and circumstances to assess the arbitrator's independence and impartiality. The arbitrator should have a "party-perspective" in carrying out the needed "checks" and enquiries for determining disclosures. The party-centric focus encourages arbitrators to avoid viewing disclosure as "what do I need to disclose" as a reasonable objective arbitrator, (which most people tend to equate with themselves as being inherently reasonable and objective), and instead considering "what might these parties want to know to assess my impartiality and independence to serve as their arbitrator in this arbitration."

The approach of the IBA Guidelines and many arbitration rules and guides have purposely widened the scope of disclosure obligations. And most rules and guides provide, when in doubt, the arbitrator should make the disclosure. It is preferable to provide the parties and an arbitral institution with relevant disclosures at the start of an arbitration or as soon as a disclosure matter becomes known, in order that the parties and the institution can react in a timely fashion and limit time, costs and efforts from potential challenges. Disclosure can allow parties or an arbitral institution to request further details to better understand the situation and perhaps avoid an unnecessary

18. *Ibid.*, at 119.

challenge. Disclosure increases transparency which encourages user trust in the arbitration process and confidence in the arbitrators.

It is also in the interest of an arbitrator to have any issues relating to potential conflicts addressed at an early stage and to avoid failing to disclose matters that should have been disclosed. Most legal provisions, rules, and guides provide that the failure to disclose will not in itself lead to a successful challenge but may be considered in assessing the grounds for challenge.

Arbitral institutions have a unique and impactful role as policymakers and regulators of arbitration generally and particularly in arbitrator disclosure.[19] In order to provide more guidance to arbitrators and parties, many arbitral institutions have supplemented their rules relating to disclosures with guides or notes to assist in navigating disclosure."[20]

Arbitral institutions are called upon to determine if an arbitrator failed to adequately and timely make needed disclosure when this is a ground(s) for a challenge. An arbitral institution will apply its own rules and guidelines and typically considers its practice in earlier challenges with similar issues. When an arbitral institution assesses the adequacy and timeliness of an arbitrator's disclosure, it views the matter through the lens of its rules, practice, interests, perspectives, and experience. The IBA Guidelines may be considered but for most institutions, it is not the determinative basis for assessing a challenge, but a source that may be considered. Many arbitrators rely upon the IBA Guidelines in making disclosures, parties consider and often refer to them when bringing and defending challenges, and some courts have referred to them in cases. Reference to the IBA Guidelines may lead to the subjective standard through the "eyes of the parties" and the low threshold for disclosure created by the text "may give rise ... to doubts." But it may also lead to over-reliance on the application lists in a mechanical fashion.

Arbitral institutions are developing and influencing arbitrator disclosure through their rules, guidelines, policies, and practice. Recently many institutions have been providing parties, upon granted requests, with brief summarized reasoned decisions on challenges, which often include assessments of the adequacy of disclosures. Some institutions have been publishing anonymized summaries of challenges to better inform its users and the general public of its practice. Greater transparency regarding disclosures is welcome, as is greater guidance to arbitrators and parties which will contribute to shared expectations.

---

19. *Ibid.*, at pp. 241-243.
20. *See e.g.*, section III A, paras. 22-36, pp. 5-8, ICC Notes to Parties and Arbitral Tribunals on the Conduct of Arbitration (2021), available at: https://iccwbo.org/content/uploads/sites/3/2020/12/icc-note-to-parties-and-arbitral-tribunals-on-the-conduct-of-arbitration-english-2021.pdf (last accessed June 27, 2022). For a review of guides and practice, *See* UNCITRAL WG III—Background Information on a Code of Conduct Annex: Codes of Conduct & Ethics (Updated July 2019), part I and part II, available at: https://uncitral.un.org/sites/uncitral.un.org/files/media-documents/uncitral/en/icsid_code_of_codes_and_ethics_part_1.pdf and (last accessed September 27, 2022).

§27.04 CONCLUSION

Arbitration is a service that invites and relies upon users' trust in its integrity and ability to deliver on its promise of efficient, fair, effective, and final dispute resolution. Its success depends upon protecting its appeal to its users through ensuring the independence and impartiality of the arbitrators who have wide discretion in managing and adjudicating the case. Arbitrator disclosure serves the parties' interest in having relevant information to determine whether to accept the arbitrator, to request further information, or challenge the arbitrator. Disclosure and challenges both protect the rights of parties and the integrity of the arbitration, although there are different standards for determining the adequacy of disclosure and the outcome of a challenge.

Disclosure obligations are broader and should have a party-centric focus to fulfil the aim of the disclosure, which is to provide relevant information to the parties in the particular dispute. The subjective standard of assessing disclosure "through the eyes of the parties" should not entail the arbitrator seeking to read the minds of each party to a dispute and tailoring the disclosure accordingly. The "eyes of the parties" standard should be interpreted and applied to require arbitrators to have the parties, in the circumstances of the specific dispute, at the forefront of their disclosure. The disclosure obligation is not abstract or based upon what the arbitrator considers relevant. It should be focused on what these parties may need to assess this arbitrator's independence and impartiality in this dispute.

The approach of the ICC Rules in providing for both the "eyes of the parties" for independence and the objective standard of "reasonable doubts as to the arbitrator's impartiality" may usefully combine the two tests, leading to a hybrid approach which is both party-centric and objective. But it may also introduce some confusion for arbitrators. Any confusion in what should be disclosed should be resolved—as provided for in the International Chamber of Commerce (ICC) approach—with disclosing when in doubt. This can be challenging in some situations with the need to protect confidential and private information. The distinction between independence and impartiality may justify differing approaches to disclosure, but this is a topic worthy of a separate essay.

In a highly regarded article, Professor Lew posed the question of whether we are achieving the dream of autonomous arbitration.[21] At the beginning of the article he asked this question: "Why has arbitration survived the test of time?" And answered it: "Simply because it has served the users well."[22] Arbitrator disclosure must serve the users well and this should be the focus of disclosure to ensure user trust and the overall integrity of arbitration.

Arbitration will neither achieve the dream of autonomy, nor fulfil its promise to its users, if it does not serve its users well.

---

21. Julian D.M. Lew, *Chapter 20: Achieving the Dream: Autonomous Arbitration?*, in Loukas A. Mistelis and Julian D. M. Lew (eds.), *Arbitration Insights: Twenty Years of the Annual Lecture of the School of International Arbitration*, International Arbitration Law Library, Volume 16, p. 455 (Kluwer Law International 2007).
22. *Ibid.*, at p. 456.

CHAPTER 28

Welcome to the Future: The AI Arbitrator – An Unwelcomed Reality or Science Fiction?

Mohamed S. Abdel Wahab

§28.01 INTRODUCTION

Artificial Intelligence (AI) is a transformative technology that is reshaping almost every aspect of our lives and is drastically changing the world around us. International Arbitration (IA) is no exception. Technological developments, digitization and AI are already playing a major role in redefining, reconfiguring and revolutionizing IA, and we are already witnessing new tools and practices that aim to increase the efficiency and quality of the arbitration process.

This dominance of AI in all sectors was accentuated since 2020 when the world was put off balance by the COVID-19 pandemic. As such, the global market of AI witnessed a rise of 150% in 2020 compared to 2019.[1]

Against the uncertainties brought about by the COVID-19 pandemic, dispute resolution professionals and IA managed to quickly adapt and to find tools and develop approaches to minimize delay and disruption to ongoing proceedings. With the introduction of restrictions, lockdowns and other challenging measures, IA practitioners had to resort to remote working and virtual meetings and hearings, and this involved investing more into many new technologies.

As the market for remote hearings and technology-integrated services grew larger and larger, demand for more sophisticated technological applications increased, and technology-based services gained more traction, especially in relation to (i) case management and remote hearing platforms (e.g., Opus2, Lloyd Michaux, Epiq, etc.),

1. *Artificial Intelligence (AI) Market Size 2022-2029*, Fortune Business Insights, https://www.fortunebusinessinsights.com/industry-reports/artificial-intelligence-market-100114.

(ii) case analytics, expedited data review and analyses (e.g., Luminance), (iii) and possible use of AI in relation to decision-making function (e.g., Lex Machina).

Over the years, and specifically in relation to the dispute resolution field, practitioners tend to think of technology as a simple support tool; a medium of communication or a tool for limited support functions, but not transformative in any way. However, with countries like *Australia* and *South Africa* recognizing that 'an inventor can be non-human',[2] and with the proliferation of online dispute resolution (ODR) technologies, one cannot underestimate the power of technology and its transformative role, which is impacting IA and the way IA proceedings are being prosecuted. In fact, the idea of an AI-arbitrator is not an impossible frontier to conquer.

Evolving, adapting and adjusting to changes are essential for the continuity of life on earth, and law is no different. It evolves, adapts and responds to social, economic, cultural, environmental and technological changes. It is in this respect that one needs to examine the manifestations of Life 3.0 as coined by Max Tegmark in his published work '*Life 3.0:Being Human in the Age of Artificial Intelligence*', which addresses the technological age of humans.[3] The central question in this analysis is whether and to what extent AI would assist or replace human factor in IA (i.e., the arbitrators).

At the outset, it should be noted that Life 3.0 relates to artificial general intelligence (AGI) which is a recurrent theme in science fiction. AGI relates to agents or tools understanding and learning any intellectual task that a human being can undertake.[4] This is a technology that has not yet been achieved.[5] Artificial specific intelligence (ASI) is the only type of AI realized to date which is able to achieve specific tasks, and operate strictly within the specific scope of the scenarios for which it is programmed.[6] It is thus ASI that is the subject of this article.

In an era of 'system reconfiguration' with the transformative role of technology, one must tackle this issue with an open mind that is freed from the shackles of restrain mandated by traditional perceptions of how arbitral proceedings are conducted and how the arbitral process is managed.

In the specific realm of IA, one needs to consider the following questions, which are further addressed below:

- What is the current state of technology with respect to AI?
- Would AI, with its current state, replace a human arbitrator and manage a fair and legitimate arbitration process?
- What are the existing limitations of an AI-arbitrator?
- What are the legal implications of an AI-arbitrator?

2. Deeth Williams Wall, *In a Historic Move, South Africa and Australia Recognize that Artificial Intelligence Can Be Recognized as an Inventor* (4 August 2021), https://www.dww.com/articles/a-historic-move-south-africa-and-australia-recognize-artificial-intelligence-can-be.
3. Max Tegmark, *Life 3.0:Being Human in the Age of Artificial Intelligence* (Alfred A. Knopf, 2017).
4. Henry Shevlin, Karina Vold, Mattew Crosby & Marta Halina, *The Limits of Machine Intelligence*, EMBO Reports (2019).
5. *Ibid.*
6. Nicolas Miailhe & Cyrus Hodes, *The Third Age of Artificial Intelligence*, Field Actions Science Reports (2017).

§28.02 THE CURRENT STATE OF TECHNOLOGY AND AI

With the booming of 'Big Data', the exponential growth and development of AI applications in almost every sector, and the contended promise of elimination of human biases (including subconscious biases) from the decision-making process by the proponents of AI,[7] the IA community is exploring how new technologies, applications and tools can be beneficial in increasing efficiency, reducing time and costs, and boosting the quality of the decision-making process.

As Scherer put it '*AI-savvy lawyers are said to be as rare as vegan butchers*'.[8] However, it should be noted that a deep technical understanding of AI, specifically, machine learning's (ML) fundamental techniques and components, is quintessential to undertake an informed assessment of the potential role of technology and its technical implications when integrated in IA and specifically arbitral decision-making.

[A] AI and ML Demystified

'AI' is a term coined by John McCarthy in 1956, on the occasion of the Dartmouth conference (where AI got its name and mission).[9] It was defined as *making a machine behave in ways that would be called intelligent if a human were so behaving.*[10] Similar definitions also exist with the human intelligence put as a benchmark when defining AI. That said, AI is often defined as a set of scientific theories and techniques or '*machines that mimic human cognitive functions*'.[11]

AI is an umbrella term that is constantly evolving with the development of new systems, applications and techniques. Today, in the age of 'Big Data', the term 'AI' is often used interchangeably with the term ML. As often noted by AI specialists '*if it's written in Python, we call it "machine learning". If it's written in PowerPoint, we call it "AI"*'.[12]

ML as a term, was coined by Arthur Samuel in 1959 as an AI subfield where programs learn from experience and improve their performance overtime. That said, AI can be defined as a set of techniques that can automatically find patterns (or correlations) in data and use such patterns to make predictions or for decision-making purposes.[13] ML necessitates a goal defined by the programmer and a collection of data

7. Solon Barocas, Solon & Andrew D. Selbst, *Big Data's Disparate Impact*, 104 California Law Review (2016) 271.
8. Maxi Scherer, *Artificial Intelligence and Legal Decision-Making: The Wide Open? Study on the Example of International Arbitration*, Journal of International Arbitration 36, no 5 (2019) 542.
9. Blagoj Delipetrev, Chrisa Tsinaraki & Uroš Kostić, *Historical Evolution of Artificial Intelligence: Analysis of the Three Main Paradigm Shifts in AI*, Publications Office of the European Union (2020) 8.
10. Maxi Scherer, *Artificial Intelligence and Legal Decision-Making: The Wide Open? Study on the Example of International Arbitration*, Journal of International Arbitration 36, no 5 (2019) 542.
11. Blagoj Delipetrev, Chrisa Tsinaraki & Uroš Kostić, *Historical Evolution of Artificial Intelligence: Analysis of the Three Main Paradigm Shifts in AI*, Publications Office of the European (2020) 5.
12. Rob Thomas, *The AI Ladder: Demystifying AI Challenges*, O'Reilly Media (2019) 2.
13. David Lehr & Paul Ohm, *Playing with the Data: What Legal Scholars Should Learn about Machine Learning*, 51 U.C. Davis Law Review (2017) 671 ('[M]achine learning refers to an automated

to learn from. Contrary to rule-based programs, in relation to which a programmer hand-code the algorithms into the machine (generally in the form of 'if-then' instructions), in ML, the machine learns the algorithms necessary to achieve the prescribed goal.

The emergence of Big Data allowed a diversion in the AI research from the rule-based programs, known to be insufficient to handle complex and dynamic realities, to ML relying on hidden patterns from observed data. This is referred to as 'data mining'. In that sense, ML may identify patterns and connections that remain unknown to the programmer.[14]

ML has two main categories, these are: (i) supervised learning (SL); and (ii) unsupervised learning (UL).

SL is defined by the use of labelled data, where SL algorithms *map input to output values based on labelled examples of input-output pairs*.[15] In other words, the programmer provides the algorithm with labelled data that is tagged with the correct desired result. The algorithm infers associations from the input to the output of the training data. After that the trained model is put to test on a new dataset to assess its effectiveness at predicting the outcome by applying such pattern to unlabelled data.[16]

UL does not require labelled data. UL algorithm finds unknown patterns in unlabelled datasets. The goal is to identify the data structure, for example, by grouping similar items to form 'clusters'. In this model, the algorithm is provided with dataset without a specific desired outcome. As such, the algorithm finds patterns on its own.

The choice of the specific ML technique depends on several factors, such as, data size, quality and diversity and the answer the programmer wants to derive from that data. For the purpose of this paper, which focuses on the potential AI has to replace human arbitrators, if at all possible, the focus will be on SL as it is the technique usually used to make predictions.[17]

[B] The Different Stages of ML

In this section, the main stages of ML will be briefly explored as an indispensable step to identifying areas of concerns when applying ML methods in the domain of

---

process of discovering correlations (sometimes alternatively referred to as relationships or patterns) between variables in a dataset, often to make predictions or estimates of some outcome.') Also *see* Gizem Halis Kasap, *Can Artificial Intelligence ('AI') Replace Human Arbitrators?: Technological Concerns and Legal Implications*, Journal of Dispute Resolution Vol. No. 2, 2021 212 ('*Machine learning refers to a science of automatic pattern recognition between variables in a dataset, often in order to predict or estimate some result*').

14. Gizem Halis Kasap, *Can Artificial Intelligence ('AI') Replace Human Arbitrators?: Technological Concerns and Legal Implications*, Journal of Dispute Resolution Vol. No. 2, 2021 212.
15. Blagoj Delipetrev, Chrisa Tsinaraki & Uroš Kostić, *Historical Evolution of Artificial Intelligence: Analysis of the Three Main Paradigm Shifts in AI*, Publications Office of the European Union (2020) 6.
16. Gizem Halis Kasap, *Can Artificial Intelligence ('AI') Replace Human Arbitrators?: Technological Concerns and Legal Implications*, Journal of Dispute Resolution (2021) 214, 215.
17. *Ibid.*, 220.

decision-making in IA. While ML is not linear,[18] it can be broken down into six steps that are covered below.

The first step in ML is *defining the problem or the outcome variable* (i.e., defining what the algorithm should predict). In SL, the algorithm is provided with labelled outcome variable,[19] which is the value to be predicted based on input data. As such, in SL, '*defining the problem means defining the outcome variable*'.[20] In this step, the decision-maker first translates an abstract goal into a predictive goal. For instance, for the development of autonomous vehicles, one abstract goal may be minimizing human casualties. In that sense, the programmer would need to create an algorithm that recognizes objects in the vehicle's surroundings (predictive goal). Thereafter, the decision-maker must second translate such predictive goal into a specified outcome variable.[21]

The second step in ML is *data collection*, which is the most time-consuming step, especially that it is well-known in ML processes that an algorithm is only as good as the data. This step is of major importance as it has many crucial consequences.[22] ML models are data-hungry, '*the larger the sample data, the more accurate the model's predictive value*'.[23] The quality of the data collection depends heavily on many factors such as volume, validity, velocity, and veracity.[24]

The third step in ML is the *preparation of the data*. This includes data cleaning and data partitioning. Data cleaning relates to dealing with missing or inaccurate values by deleting, imputing and/or correcting them. These are judgments that an analyst has to make with no mathematical guidance.[25] Data partitioning is the splitting of the collected data into training and test data. Assigning a bigger volume of test dataset would ensure a well-trained algorithm in the real world. Afterall, the ultimate goal of an analyst is to create an algorithm that will make accurate predictions in the real world, and the accuracy of the algorithm is directly linked to the higher volume of dataset. Data partitioning depends on many considerations that require a judgement call by the analyst,[26] which is another form of human intervention in the ML process.

The fourth and fifth steps are the *choice of an algorithm model (or multiple models)* that is suited for the objective and *the training of the model*. This means passing the data to the model to find patterns, and with training, the algorithm does get more accurate at predicting the outcome.

18. David Lehr & Paul Ohm, *Playing with the Data: What Legal Scholars Should Learn about Machine Learning*, 51 U.C. Davis Law Review (2017) 655.
19. *Ibid.*, 673. An outcome variable may be a classification in binary classification (true/false or yes/no) or multi-layered classification. It may also be a regression algorithm used to predict continuous values (numeric value) such as price, salary.
20. *Ibid.*, 673.
21. *Ibid.*, 674.
22. *Ibid.*, 677.
23. Maxi Scherer, *Artificial Intelligence and Legal Decision-Making: The Wide Open? Study on the Example of International Arbitration*, Journal of International Arbitration 36, no 5 (2019) 554.
24. *Ibid.*
25. David Lehr & Paul Ohm, *Playing with the Data: What Legal Scholars Should Learn about Machine Learning*, 51 U.C. Davis Law Review (2017) 682.
26. *Ibid.*, 687.

The sixth step is the *evaluation* of the algorithm model on the test dataset and *deployment of the model* to make predictions in the real world.

These are the material ML steps that are necessary to reach an ultimate goal of predicting outcomes or making decisions. However, the issue remains whether technological limitations exist with respect to AI generally and AI in the context of IA specifically.

§28.03 TECHNOLOGICAL LIMITATIONS OF AI IN THE CONTEXT OF IA

The previous section served as a primer on AI and ML. Learning and understanding the different stages of ML allows us to pinpoint the limitations of such technology with respect to decision-making in the context of IA.

[A] Limitations Related to the Programmer

One may think that the concept of an AI-arbitrator and the automation of the decision-making process would prevent the human biases and would provide 'objective' results free from the constraints and the alleged vices of human intervention. However, as explained above, during the different stages of SL,[27] the analyst is faced with a significant number of subjective judgements that he/she needs to make. In other words, a multi-layered human intervention occurs by programmers, which affects the ML model and algorithms, resulting in a process that is not free from human biases and intervention.

At the outset, translating a predictive goal (*e.g., predicting an individual's potential to commit violent acts in an AI that should help in reducing inmate altercation in a prison*[28]) into a specified outcome variable is not necessarily objective as many possibilities arise.[29] As such, the accuracy of AI prediction will depend on certain choices made by the programmer during the stages of ML. For example, during the preparation of data, the choices made by the programmer during data cleaning and data partitioning are subjective judgements with no strict mathematical guidance for making the relevant choices, and analysts will have to bring the subject matter knowledge to bear.[30] Similarly, an analyst makes judgement calls with respect to the choice of a model and the training of the model which will affect the algorithm's direction and accuracy.

This highlights the role of the human factor in developing and maintaining AI algorithms and ML models that are not devoid from human intervention and the alleged biases that proponents of AI seek to avoid by advocating for an AI-arbitrator in IA.

27. *Supra* §28.02[B].
28. David Lehr & Paul Ohm, *Playing with the Data: What Legal Scholars Should Learn about Machine Learning*, 51 U.C. Davis Law Review (2017) 674.
29. *Ibid.*, 674.
30. *Ibid.*, 682.

[B] Limitations Related to the Training Data

As already explained, an algorithm is as good as its data. Accordingly, good data is at the core of any AI algorithm. The quality of the algorithm is directly correlated to the quality of the dataset.[31] In this sense, an AI-arbitrator would need enough historical data (arbitral awards, opinions and decisions) to formulate a general rule or predict an outcome on a certain matter.[32] Accordingly, the volume, variety, accuracy and veracity of the data are of great importance in the context of ML processes.

In this context, the *volume* of relevant data is not of trivial importance. ML, which is based on probabilistic inferences, necessitates a large sample of data for more accurate predictions. The *status quo* of the IA field suggests that a large sampling of data is problematic, since access to data is still relatively limited, with privacy and confidentiality militating against the publication of a significant percentage of awards and decisions, especially in commercial arbitration proceedings.[33]

Nevertheless, with the rise of transparency and award publication initiatives in IA, arbitral awards are gradually becoming available in the public domain, but the volume, hitherto, remains insufficient to guarantee accurate predictions or decision-making processes in the context of ML. It is thus questionable that AI would produce reliable results on matters in relation to which only a scarce number of decisions are available.[34]

Even if a sufficient volume of data is being made available, another issue arises in relation to the *variety* of the collected data. In IA, given the complexity of certain disputes and the involvement of parties from different jurisdictions, with different applicable laws, and complex factual contexts, another issue may arise in relation to the non-repetitiveness and novelty of the issues in question. The more novel and different the issues being considered are, the less reliable and accurate an AI model is.[35] The increase in the diversity of disputes would '*correspondingly decrease the number of available observations on the dataset for each type of dispute*',[36] and this will lower the accuracy of the algorithm.

Moreover, the *accuracy* and *veracity* of the data are of radical importance.[37] Undoubtedly, the idea of the use of AI-arbitrator to eliminate human bias (*which can*

31. Paul Bennett Marrow, Mansi Karol & Steven Kuyan, *Artificial Intelligence and Arbitration: The Computer as an Arbitrator – Are We There Yet?*, 35 American Arbitration Association, Dispute Resolution Journal (2020) 49.
32. Gizem Halis Kasap, *Can Artificial Intelligence ('AI') Replace Human Arbitrators?: Technological Concerns and Legal Implications*, Journal of Dispute Resolution (2021) 222.
33. *Ibid.*
34. *Ibid.*, 222, 223.
35. Maxi Scherer, *Artificial Intelligence and Legal Decision-Making: The Wide Open? Study on the Example of International Arbitration*, Journal of International Arbitration (2019) 556.
36. Gizem Halis Kasap, *Can Artificial Intelligence ('AI') Replace Human Arbitrators?: Technological Concerns and Legal Implications*, Journal of Dispute Resolution (2021) 223.
37. Maxi Scherer, *Artificial Intelligence and Legal Decision-Making: The Wide Open? Study on the Example of International Arbitration*, Journal of International Arbitration (2019), 557.

either be conscious or subconscious with external and irrelevant factors[38]) sounds interesting, but it has already been seen that ML predictions do include biases and judgement calls by the programmer in more concerning aspects.

First, if the training data is biased (*a certain group is over or underrepresented*) and is not accurately representative of the real world, the results would reflect the same inaccuracies and any conclusion drawn from such data would be distorted.

Second, if the training data is tainted or 'infected' with hidden conscious or subconscious human biases, the AI-arbitrator would detect such biases and hold it as true for its results.[39] This was the case of Amazon's algorithm aiming at automating the employment of top talent. When put in application, the algorithm's results showed that it is not gender neutral and that it discriminates against woman. The algorithm disfavoured resumes that included the word 'woman'.[40] This algorithm detected a hidden pattern of male domination in the technology industry and predicted discriminating results based on such domination.

If one is to consider an example from the IA world, then assume that the investment arbitration awards used as data are unduly favourable to either the investor or the State, an AI-arbitrator would find such bias and automatically generate decisions that are favourable to that side.[41]Even when programmers edit the algorithm to neutralize some biases, this in itself is a level of human intervention that subjectively aims to eliminate other subjective biases, and, in any event, there is no guarantee that the algorithm would not predict other discriminatory factors. The dark history of humanity which is tainted with discrimination, racism, and other forms of biases is embedded in the data and this will infect the ML algorithm that used such data to detect patterns to get a prediction. In that sense, biases may well become '*algorithmized*' and automated. Additionally, since such bias is unintended and results from the allocation of hidden biases in data (*and not a result of the conscious bias of the programmer*), it can even be hard to detect its source, explain it and root it out in full.[42]

[C] Limitations Related to AI as a 'Black Box'

The issue of the opacity of the AI algorithms is central to AI discussions in different fields. AI operates in a 'black box', which makes it hard to understand and trust the result. The inability to explain results obtained by an AI algorithm is even more

38. *Ibid.*, 558. Scherer gives the example of the decision being affected by the judge's food break. In this study, the probability of issuing a favourable decision is much higher after the judge's food break.
39. Gizem Halis Kasap, *Can Artificial Intelligence ('AI') Replace Human Arbitrators?: Technological Concerns and Legal Implications*, Journal of Dispute Resolution (2021) 225.
40. Jeffrey Dastin, *Amazon Scraps Secret AI Recruiting Tool That Showed Bias Against Woman*, Reuters (2018), https://www.reuters.com/article/us-amazon-com-jobs-automation-insight-idUSKCN1MK08G.
41. Gizem Halis Kasap, *Can Artificial Intelligence ('AI') Replace Human Arbitrators?: Technological Concerns and Legal Implications*, Journal of Dispute Resolution (2021) 226.
42. Solon Barocas, Solon & Andrew D. Selbst, *Big Data's Disparate Impact*, 104 California Law Review (2016) 671, 674.

troubling in the IA context where a causal link between an input and output is required.[43]

One of the fundamental features of legal decision-making is the reasoning of the decision. A human arbitrator must provide a well-reasoned decision for the parties unless the parties have agreed otherwise. A well-reasoned award is quintessential for the losing party, in order to understand the basis of such decision either to accept it or to find, in such an explanation, a ground for challenging that award, if the applicable legal system so permits. Another important aspect of a reasoned decision is that it guarantees that parties' legal and factual evidence were heard and taken into consideration by the decision-maker and that it followed the applicable legal rules in issuing such a decision. This gives the process legitimacy and induces trust and confidence in same.

With the development of Explainable Artificial Intelligence (XAI) models, AI researchers promise more transparent models.[44] However, AI-arbitrators built on black-boxed models would still be opaque. In addition, and more importantly, an AI-arbitrator decision would be based on probabilistic inferences, as such, explaining such mathematical or statistical decision (identifying what features were taken into consideration for instance) would not result in a well-reasoned decision in the context of IA as we know it. A probabilistic explanation would not satisfy the users of the system who need a causal explanation.[45]

[D] Limitations Inherent to the Basis upon Which AI Makes Decisions

Crucial questions arise in relation to whether 'AI can replace human arbitrators?', these are: what is the nature of an AI-arbitrator's decision? Does an AI-arbitrator follow the means used by a human arbitrator for the decision-making?

ML analyses past data to develop rules that can offer general outcomes to novel scenarios.[46] An AI-arbitrator will use statistics and probabilities as the 'normative framework' for decision-making which is problematic. Justice is not simply a function of mathematical calculations of probabilities based on past considerations or data; it involves an intellectual exercise with several other considerations that go beyond simple mathematical calculations. An AI-arbitrator cannot produce a new kind of outcome, it simply '*mimic[s] existing thought patterns or combine them to produce what*

43. Gizem Halis Kasap, *Can Artificial Intelligence ('AI') Replace Human Arbitrators?: Technological Concerns and Legal Implications*, Journal of Dispute Resolution (2021) 229.
44. Maxi Scherer, *Artificial Intelligence and Legal Decision-Making: The Wide Open? Study on the Example of International Arbitration*, Journal of International Arbitration (2019) 563. ('the model selects alternative samples with different features, compares the different outcomes under each and is therefore able to identify how and why they differ').
45. *Ibid.*, 564. Taking the example of Scherer where a student gets 50/100 in an exam and the explanation of this grade is that the majority of the class received the same score. This is merely a probabilistic explanation that does not clarify why this particular student got this grade.
46. Harry Surden, *Machine Learning and Law*, 89 Washing Law Review (2014) 105.

appears to be a novel outcome. This [...] will be only a mathematically different version of an already existing pattern',[47] but not a novel approach or outcome altogether.

In this regard, an AI-arbitrator would not be able to reflect on a novel matter or circumstance and produce a decision that would tackle any novelty in light of the legal rule. This would lead to a stagnant rule of law that is purely pattern-based, but not intellectually innovative. For instance, an AI-arbitrator would not be able to create new doctrines or principles, like the arbitral tribunal did in 1982 in *Dow Chemical* where it established the 'group of companies doctrine', irrespective of whether this was good or bad. AI cannot step '*outside the box when exigencies and the demands of international commerce require this*'[48]. An AI-Arbitrator's decisions would undoubtedly be conservative and might not be adapted to policy changes over time. As mentioned earlier, it predicts and develop outcomes in light of past decisions and existing datasets.

Even in the context of investment arbitration where access data and decisions may well be much easier, with more awards being published, an AI-arbitrator could be problematic. For example, if a State has been found in violation of investors' protected rights under a specific investment treaty several times, how would that affect the ML model? Will it mean that the algorithm will find a pattern that leads to an automatic or a default finding of violation of such rights in future claims?[49] This shift in the basis of an arbitral award issued by an AI-arbitrator and a human arbitrator was described by Scherer as a '*paradigm-shift in legal decision making*' from deductive reasoning and logic to probabilistic inference.[50]

All the above limitations are not intended to favour a tech-sceptic approach, but rather aims at understanding and shedding light on the current limitations of AI generally, and in the context of IA more specifically, so that we can appreciate whether and to what extent AI is best-suited for IA.

§28.04 LEGAL IMPLICATIONS RELATED TO THE USE OF AI-ARBITRATOR

After unveiling some of the technical limitations relating to replacing a human arbitrator with an AI-arbitrator, it is necessary to shed some light on few legal implications.

The first issue that comes to mind when discussing the topic of replacing human arbitrators by AI-arbitrators is the enforceability of an AI-arbitrator's award.

In this context, the New York Convention (NYC) which is the benchmark instrument in setting the standards of enforceability of arbitral awards, does not, in anyway, specify that an arbitrator should be a human being, though it is arguable that it was in no one's contemplation that an award could be rendered by any species other

47. Gizem Halis Kasap, *Can Artificial Intelligence ('AI') Replace Human Arbitrators?: Technological Concerns and Legal Implications*, Journal of Dispute Resolution (2021) 250.
48. *Ibid.*
49. Maxi Scherer, *Artificial Intelligence and Legal Decision-Making: The Wide Open? Study on the Example of International Arbitration*, Journal of International Arbitration (2019) 572.
50. *Ibid.*

than humans. However, if a literalist approach to reading and construing the provisions of the NYC is adopted, it can be argued that an award rendered by an AI-arbitrator would still fall within the scope of the NYC. However, would an AI award that is based on probabilistic algorithms meet the requirements of the NYC? That is a tough question, since awards under the NYC were never intended or expected to be premised on ML predictions and algorithms that analysed data that may be insufficient, incomplete, unvaried and/or not accurate. And, if the matter extends to improperly or inadequately reasoned AI awards, then this may lead to challenges to the award and its enforcement.

On a different note, some domestic arbitration laws do not currently permit awards to be rendered by an AI-arbitrator, as they either refer to human arbitrators,[51] or require a standard that only applies to humans.[52] However, as previously said, the rule of law is in a constant state of flux and states may eventually decide to adopt a more neutral language that does not expressly refer to humans as arbitrators, if technology evolves to a level where AI-arbitrators become a reality.

In addition to the issue of enforcement, other legal questions arise, including: (a) the liability of AI-arbitrators and their legal capacity; (b) whether and to what extent due process will have a role to play, if any; (c) whether and to what extent AI-arbitrators can be challenged and/or removed; and (d) how AI-arbitrators can assess the credibility of witness evidence during hearings, etc. All these and more are legal issues that the IA community will need to consider and examine if an AI-arbitrator becomes a reality rather than a fiction.

§28.05 CONCLUDING REMARKS

The IA community is still wrestling with the integration of technology in IA proceedings, and the idea of an autonomous AI-arbitrator replacing human arbitrators is of no appeal to many, though tech-optimists think differently. It is this debate that has prompted the author to consider this article to unveil the particularities, intricacies of ML processes and the associated algorithms that are advocated as having a potential to make and take decisions in IA proceedings.

That said, this article tackled certain important and relevant aspects of AI and ML to examine whether the current state of technology can make the AI-arbitrator a reality, or this is simply science fiction.

In light of the foregoing, the replacement of human arbitrators by AI-arbitrators undoubtedly involves several limitations, complications and implications. It has been seen that even with AI applications for IA, the human factor is not fully neutralized and programmers intervene to make certain judgement calls that may well affect that

51. French Code of Civil Procedures, Article 1450: 'only a natural person having full capacity to exercise his or her rights may act as an arbitrator'.
52. Egyptian Arbitration Law No. 27 of 1994, Article 16(1): 'the arbitrator cannot be a minor, under guardianship, have been deprived of his civil rights by reason of a judgement against him for a felony or misdemeanour contrary to honesty or due to a declaration of his bankruptcy; unless he has been restored to his status'.

trajectory a certain algorithm takes, which in turn influences the outcome and the decision-making process.

Moreover, users of the IA system have not yet pledged their trust and confidence in AI applications and the AI-arbitrator, especially in light of the uncertainties that taint almost every step of developing the algorithm to applying same to arbitration claims.

With the *status quo* of technology and its ASI level, it is clearly foreseeable that a fully functional, trusted and reliable AI-arbitrator can substitute the human arbitrator in the next few years. The ability of an AI-arbitrator to render accurate and well-reasoned awards on existing or novel matters on which datasets are either not available or simply insufficient is dubious, and certainly more transparency in relation to AI applications and algorithm developments is necessary. AI-arbitrators built on black-boxed and not XAI models remain controversial. However, just like George Orwell's predictions from 1984 coming to life, including facial recognition, auto-transcription and music made by AI, an AGI-arbitrator, with an ability to exhibit cognitive functions and to make decisions may become a reality in future. After all, we are just focused on the AI-arbitrator, but if that fiction turns into a reality the whole process may well become automated with a full house of AI-counsel, AI-experts and perhaps even AI-witnesses.

Finally, while the AI and IA communities tend to focus on AI as a threat to human intelligence, it may also be worth exploring the possible infusion of AI and human intelligence, where humans may be subject to implants that heighten senses and cognitive functions in a manner similar to cyborgs in science fiction. Only the future will tell what technology and AI hold for the human race, and whether humans will remain the dominant species on Earth or they will surrender this dominance to other artificial life forms under the confused pretext that this would be the next phase of evolution. Be that as it may, one hopes that when humanity charters its next path to progressive development, it is able to observe the clear dividing lines between '*evolution*' and '*extinction*', and is able to channel the use of the right technology for all good reasons.

CHAPTER 29

Quasi-contractual or Quasi-judicial Nature of Arbitration: Balancing the Powers of the Arbitral Tribunal with the Contractual Rights Between the Parties and the Arbitrators

Silja Schaffstein

§29.01 INTRODUCTION: THE LEGAL NATURE OF ARBITRATION AND THE SOURCES OF THE ARBITRAL TRIBUNAL'S POWERS

The title of this contribution raises the preliminary question of the definition and legal nature of arbitration. Rightly, as one may argue that the definition of arbitration and of its legal nature holds the key to determining the scope of an arbitral tribunal's powers,[1] including in the context of the tribunal's relations with the parties.

There is no generally accepted definition of arbitration. At the same time, there also do not appear to be any fundamental divergences between the various definitions given in legal scholarship and, in particular, there does not appear to be any definition, which is peculiar to any given country.[2] For the purposes of this contribution, arbitration is defined as a contractual method of dispute resolution exercised by private individuals, who have been chosen by the parties and vested with the power to

1. In this sense, *see* Julian D.M. Lew, *Applicable Law in International Commercial Arbitration* (Oceana Publications, Inc. 1978), para. 63, p. 51.
2. Jean-François Poudret & Sébastien Besson, *Comparative Law of International Arbitration* (Sweet & Maxwell Ltd, 2nd ed. 2007), paras 1-2. *See also* Gary B. Born, *International Commercial Arbitration* (Wolters Kluwer, 3d ed. 2021), Ch. 2, §2.02[C][1].

adjudicate the dispute in place of state courts by rendering a decision having effects analogous to those of a court judgment.[3]

A detailed discussion of the doctrinal debate of the legal nature of arbitration is outside the scope of the present contribution. Suffice it to say here that it is generally accepted that arbitration has both a contractual and a judicial component.[4]

As a contractual method of dispute resolution, the parties' arbitration agreement is the 'pillar of the arbitration'[5] such that there can be no arbitration without an arbitration agreement.[6] Moreover, it is widely considered that the parties confer certain powers to the arbitrator and, once they have done so, a contract is formed between the arbitrator and the parties. The arbitrator accepts to perform his or her mandate in conformity with such contract and with the conferred powers.[7]

Arbitration also has a judicial component. Like a judge, the arbitrator is empowered to adjudicate the dispute between the parties by a decision having res judicata effect, even though he or she acts in a private capacity, was chosen by the parties, and has only a temporary mandate.[8] The arbitrator's adjudicative function, namely his or her power to decide the parties' dispute with judgment-like effect, rests on national law (unless one adheres to the theory of 'delocalized arbitration', which views international arbitration as rooted in an autonomous, transnational arbitral legal order rather than national law).[9]

It follows from the quasi-judicial or adjudicative nature of arbitration that the arbitrator cannot be considered as a mere 'service provider' to the parties. As expressed by Gary Born, '[a]rbitrators do not merely provide the parties with a service, but also serve a public, adjudicatory function, possessing binding adjudicatory powers and immunities from suit and liability, that cannot be equated with the provision of service in a commercial relationship'.[10] This means that the arbitrators are not in a position of '*soumission absolue*'[11] with respect to the parties' will. Rather, their adjudicative function entails a certain independence from the parties, including certain powers and, in some circumstances, obligations to refuse to obey their instructions.[12]

3. Poudret & Besson, *supra* n. 2, para. 3. *See also* Gabrielle Kaufmann-Kohler & Antonio Rigozzi, *International Arbitration: Law and Practice in Switzerland* (Oxford University Press 2015), para. 1.16.
4. *See, e.g.*, Kaufmann-Kohler & Rigozzi, *supra* n. 3, paras 1.17-1.18; Pierre Mayer, *The Arbitrator's Initiative: Its Foundation and Its Limits*, ASA Special Series No. 45, p. 2.
5. Luca G. Radicati di Brozolo, *Applying the Rules Governing the Merits in International Commercial Arbitration: What Role for Inherent Powers?*, in Franco Ferrari & Friedrich Rosenfeld (eds), Inherent Powers of Arbitrators Ch. 10 (JurisNet, LLC 2019), p. 275.
6. Kaufmann-Kohler & Rigozzi, *supra* n. 3, para. 1.17.
7. Mayer, *The Arbitrator's Initiative*, *supra* n. 4, p. 7. *See also* Born, *supra* n. 2, pp. 2116-2118.
8. Silja Schaffstein, *The Doctrine of Res Judicata Before International Commercial Arbitral Tribunals* (Oxford University Press 2016), para. 5.43, with references. *See also* Born, *supra* n. 7, pp. 313-317.
9. Kaufmann-Kohler & Rigozzi, *supra* n. 3, para. 1.18. *See also* Radicati di Brozolo, *supra* n. 0, pp. 275-276, 284.
10. Born, *supra* n. 7, p. 2121. *See also* Sylvain Bollée, *Les pouvoirs inhérents des arbitres internationaux*, 418 Recueil des Cours de l'Académie de Droit international 9 (2021), paras 29-31.
11. Bollée, *supra* n. 10, paras 26-31 and paras 125-133.
12. Born, *supra* n. 7, p. 2121; Bollée, *supra* n. 10, para. 126.

In a contribution dedicated to Julian Lew, the discussion of the definition and legal nature of arbitration naturally cannot be limited to a reference to the 'quasi-contractual' and 'quasi-judicial' nature of arbitration, but must include a reference to Julian's 'dream' of autonomous arbitration.[13]

Today the autonomy of arbitration is widely recognized. But *'l'autonomie est affaire de degrés'*.[14] Different national laws recognize this autonomy to a greater or lesser extent. Racine has described the autonomy of arbitration as *'notion expansioniste'*[15] given that it has steadily increased over the past decades.[16] The 1958 New York Convention was 'the beginning of internationalism in arbitration',[17] recognizing that arbitration agreements, proceedings, and awards would have their origin and seek to be effective in different jurisdictions.[18] As a result, the New York Convention also reduced the role of the arbitral seat.[19] According to Emmanuel Gaillard, the Convention broke with the traditional representation of arbitration as equivalent to domestic litigation, drawing its legitimacy solely from the legal order of the arbitral seat.[20]

Against the changing attitude towards arbitration following the adoption of the New York Convention, today's national laws increasingly recognize the autonomy of arbitration at all stages of the arbitration, namely the arbitration agreement, the arbitration procedure, and the award.[21] In the words of Julian Lew, '[t]here are tentacles that descend from the domain of international arbitration to the national legal arena' and '[t]hese tentacles require the recognition and enforcement of the agreement to arbitrate, that the award be recognised and enforced, and that the arbitration process itself be given the effective support it may require'.[22]

The 'dream' of autonomous arbitration is not inconsistent with arbitration being both quasi-contractual and quasi-judicial and with the arbitrator's adjudicative function resting on national law. As just seen, modern national laws are increasingly 'arbitration-friendly' and broadly recognize the autonomy of arbitration. They contain only few rules of mandatory law or public policy, which restrict autonomy and impose obligations and which cannot be altered by the contract between the parties and the arbitrators.[23]

---

13. *See* Julian D.M. Lew, *Achieving the Dream: Autonomous Arbitration?, in* Julian D.M. Lew and Loukas Mistelis (eds), Arbitration Insights: Twenty Years of the Annual Lecture of the School of International Arbiration Ch. 20 (Kluwer Law International 2007), pp. 455-485.
14. Jean-Baptiste Racine, *Réflexions sur l'autonomie de l'arbitrage commercial international*, Revue de l'arbitrage, No. 2 (2005), p. 308.
15. *Ibid.*, p. 305.
16. *See* Lew, *Achieving the Dream, supra* n. 13, paras 20-37; Schaffstein, *The Doctrine of Res Judicata, supra* n. 8, paras 5.53 et seq., with references.
17. Lew, *Achieving the Dream, supra* n. 13, paras 20-43.
18. *Ibid.*
19. Emmanuel Gaillard, *Aspects philosophiques du droit de l'arbitrage international*, 329 Recueil des Cours de l'Académie de Droit international 49 (2007), pp. 86 et seq.
20. *Ibid.*, p. 87.
21. Racine, *supra* n. 14, pp. 311 et seq. *See also* Schaffstein, *The Doctrine of Res Judicata, supra* n. 8, paras 5.56 et seq., with references.
22. Lew, *Achieving the Dream, supra* n. 13, paras 20-100.
23. Born, *supra* n. 7, p. 2117; Kaufmann-Kohler & Rigozzi, *supra* n. 3, para. 2.14.

It follows from the foregoing that the parties are largely free to agree on the rules and principles governing the arbitration and to confer powers to the arbitrators on the basis of which the latter accept to perform their adjudicative function. However, they can do so only to the extent permitted by the law. In the same vein, while the primary source of the arbitrators' powers lies in the parties' will, they must exercise the powers conferred to them as permitted by the law.[24]

Having thus delineated the roles of the parties' will and of national law - respectively the roles of the powers conferred to the arbitral tribunal by the parties, by their adjudicative function, and by national law - the next question is whether and how the tribunal's adjudicative function may affect the contractual rights between the parties and the arbitrators. In other words, the question is whether there are instances where the tribunal's adjudicative function calls for a 'balancing' between the arbitrators' quasi-judicial powers and the contractual rights between the parties and the arbitrators.

The answer to this question will vary on a case-by-case basis, depending not only on the law and rules governing the arbitration, but also on the cultural and legal background of arbitrators. In practice, the arbitrators' exercise of their powers may reflect the powers of the courts of the country in which they are used to working.[25]

In line with this author's legal background, the present contribution will address the question of the balancing of the quasi-judicial and the quasi-contractual nature of arbitration from a Swiss law perspective, namely by discussing a number of specific examples that arbitration practitioners may encounter at different stages of an international arbitration with a seat in Switzerland. This contribution will examine these examples in the context of the arbitral tribunal's powers to rule on its jurisdiction (II.); to apply the law (or rules of law) governing the merits (III.); and to act as settlement facilitators (IV.).

§29.02 THE ARBITRAL TRIBUNAL'S POWER TO RULE ON ITS JURISDICTION

As one of the few mandatory provisions in Chapter 12 of the Swiss Private International Law Act (PILA) - which governs international arbitrations with a seat in Switzerland[26] - Article 186(1) PILA stipulates that '[t]he arbitral tribunal shall decide on its own jurisdiction'. This will usually raise the question of whether there is a valid arbitration agreement covering the parties and the dispute before the tribunal.

Under the case law of the Swiss Supreme Court, if the validity of the arbitration agreement is assessed under Swiss law pursuant to Article 178(2) PILA, the determination of the parties' intent to submit their dispute to arbitration is governed by the general Swiss law principles of contract interpretation. This means that the arbitral tribunal must first attempt to determine the parties' 'real common intent' through a

24. Radicati di Brozolo, *supra*. n. 5, pp. 275-276.
25. Mayer, *The Arbitrator's Initiative*, *supra* n. 4, p. 4; Bollée, *supra* n. 10, paras 134-135.
26. Another mandatory rule is that the choice of a Swiss arbitral seat will trigger the application of Swiss arbitration law (*see* Article 176(1) PILA).

'subjective' interpretation of the arbitration agreement based on evidence. The subjective interpretation is a question of fact.[27]

If the arbitral tribunal concludes that no 'real common intent' can be established, it must then determine the parties' presumed intent to arbitrate in application of an 'objective' interpretation of the arbitration agreement. This means that the tribunal must examine, based on the principle of good faith, how one party's declarations of intent could and should reasonably have been understood by the other. In doing so, the tribunal will consider the text of the agreement and the context in which the parties expressed their intent, namely the circumstances at the time of making the agreement, to the exclusion of subsequent conduct. The objective interpretation is a question of law.[28]

How does the tribunal's power to determine the parties' intent to arbitrate through Swiss law principles of contract interpretation affect the contractual rights between the parties and the arbitrators?

The issue lies in the fact that the tribunal's finding that the parties had a real common intent to arbitrate is a finding of fact. Specifically, under the Swiss Supreme Court's case law, in annulment proceedings against an award on jurisdiction based on Article 190(2)(b) PILA, the Supreme Court can only review the arbitrators' determination on the parties' presumed intent, i.e., a question of law. As a rule, the Court cannot review the arbitrators' finding of fact about the parties' real common intent to arbitrate.[29] This means that if the arbitrators have accepted, respectively declined their jurisdiction based on a subjective interpretation of the arbitration agreement, this would effectively exclude the annulment ground in Article 190(2)(b) PILA.[30]

A number of Swiss commentators have criticized the Supreme Court's case law.[31] They submit that it is incompatible with Swiss law, given that it allows arbitral tribunals with a seat in Switzerland to 'make a final and unreviewable determination' of their jurisdiction. Arbitral tribunals thus have 'absolute competence-competence', without any authorization from the parties, simply by deciding their jurisdiction based on a subjective interpretation of the arbitration agreement.[32] However, Article 190(2)(b) PILA grants the parties the right to challenge the award on jurisdiction 'where the arbitral tribunal wrongly accepted or declined jurisdiction', without providing any further limitations or exceptions to this right.[33] Moreover, so the argument

27. *See*, e.g., ATF 142 III 239, para. 5.2.1.
28. *Ibid.*
29. *See*, e.g., ATF 142 III 239, para. 5.2.2. *See* also Bernhard Berger & Franz Kellerhals, *International and Domestic Arbitration in Switzerland* (Stämpfli Publishers Ltd., 4th ed. 2021), paras 1723-1725; Mladen Stojiljković, *Arbitral Jurisdiction and Court Review: Three Swiss Federal Supreme Court Decisions to Reconsider*, 34 ASA Bulletin 4/2016, p. 899; Kaufmann-Kohler & Rigozzi, *supra* n. 3, para. 8.154.
30. Berger & Kellerhals, *supra* n. 29, para. 1725a.
31. *See, e.g.*, Stojiljković, *supra* n. 29, pp. 897-902; Philippe Hovaguimian, *Non-reviewable Facts in Swiss Annulment Proceedings: Undermining the Safeguards of Art. 190 PILA*, 36 ASA Bulletin 1/2018, pp. 89-108; Berger & Kellerhals, *supra* n. 29, para. 1725a.
32. Stojiljković, *supra* n. 29, p. 899. *See also* Hovaguimian, *supra* n. 0, pp. 100-102; Berger & Kellerhals, *supra* n. 29, para. 1725a.
33. Berger & Kellerhals, *supra* n. 29, para. 1725a. *See also* Stojiljković, *supra* n. 29, pp. 901-902.

continues, while Article 192 PILA allows non-Swiss parties to waive their right to challenge arbitral awards, they can only do so by means of an express agreement that meets the form requirements applicable to arbitration agreements (Article 178(1) PILA – 'evidenced by text'). The waiver cannot result solely from the arbitrators' finding that the parties had a 'real common intent' to arbitrate.[34]

Is the Swiss Supreme Court's case law in line with the arbitral tribunal's adjudicative function and its mandatory power pursuant to Article 186(1) PILA to rule on its own jurisdiction? Is it compatible with the contractual rights between the parties and the arbitrators and the legal framework governing this relationship? Should the Court reconsider its position so to better balance the quasi-contractual and quasi-judicial components of arbitration? While the Supreme Court continues to follow its current position,[35] it appears to somewhat balance its approach by carefully considering the requirements for a valid arbitration agreement, even where the arbitral tribunal has ruled on its jurisdiction based on a subjective interpretation of the agreement.[36]

§29.03 THE ARBITRAL TRIBUNAL'S POWER TO APPLY THE LAW OR RULES OF LAW GOVERNING THE MERITS OF THE DISPUTE

Arbitral tribunals with a seat in Switzerland must perform their adjudicative function by resolving the parties' dispute in application of the rules of law chosen by the parties or, in the absence thereof, according to the rules of law with which the case has the closest connection, unless the parties have authorized them to decide *ex aequo et bono* (Article 187 PILA). Thus, in the words of Sylvain Bollée, '[l]*'arbitre est, fondamentalement, un organe d'application du droit*'.[37]

Since its landmark *Westland Helicopters* decision in 1994,[38] the Swiss Supreme Court has repeatedly held that the maxim *iura novit curia* applies in arbitrations with a seat in Switzerland.[39] This means that arbitrators have the power (and the duty) to apply the applicable law on their own motion;[40] the parties do not have to prove the law.

This being so, a failure by the arbitrators to comply with this duty does not entail any particular sanction. In particular, an incorrect application of the law is not, as such, a ground for challenge under Article 190(2) PILA. Moreover, under the Swiss Supreme

34. Stojiljković, *supra* n. 29, p. 900.
35. *See, e.g.*, Swiss Supreme Court decision 4A_460/2021 of 3 January 2022, para. 3.1.1.
36. *See* Berger & Kellerhals, *supra* n. 29, footnote 95, with reference to case law. According to these authors, 'the case law of the Swiss Federal Supreme Court appears to show that the Court is aware of the problem', namely by making 'extensive considerations as to whether the arbitration clause in question had satisfied the requirements of an arbitration agreement', in a situation where the sole arbitrator had admitted his jurisdiction under Swiss law based on a subjective interpretation of the arbitration agreement. *See also* Swiss Supreme Court decision 4A_460/2021 of 3 January 2022.
37. Bollée, *supra* n. 10, para. 29.
38. ATF 120 II 172, para. 3a.
39. *See, e.g.*, ATF 130 III 35; Swiss Supreme Court decision 4A_214/2013 of 5 August 2013; Swiss Supreme Court decision 4A_56/2017 of 11 January 2018.
40. Berger & Kellerhals, *supra* n. 29, para. 1433.

Court's case law,[41] a breach of *iura novit curia* does not amount to a violation of public policy within the meaning of Article 190(2)(e) PILA; like a Swiss court (under Article 16 PILA), an arbitral tribunal may request the parties to establish the content of the applicable law.[42]

Conversely, an arbitral award rendered in application of the *iura novit curia* maxim is not *ultra petita* within the meaning of Article 190(2)(c) PILA if it is based on a legal ground that was not raised by the parties during the proceedings. Similarly, the arbitrators do not violate the parties' right to be heard within the meaning of Article 190(2)(d) PILA, even though they have not consulted the parties on the legal grounds underlying the award.[43] An exception applies, however, as the arbitral tribunal would violate the parties' right to be heard if it grounds its decision on a legal theory that was not raised or debated in the proceedings and the relevance of which the parties could not have reasonably foreseen.[44]

Subject to this exception, arbitrators sitting in Switzerland are largely free to determine the method of establishing the content of the applicable law.[45] Whether and to what extent they will exercise this power may depend on their cultural and legal background, their knowledge of and access to the applicable law, their own conception of their duties and responsibilities, and on the parties' expectations.[46]

Can the parties balance the arbitrators' adjudicative power to apply the law on their own motion, for instance if the parties are from a legal background that regards foreign law as a fact, to be proven by the parties?

Under Swiss law, the answer would be 'yes': the parties can in principle agree to limit or even exclude the arbitrators' power to ascertain and apply the law ex officio and confine their mandate to legal arguments advanced by the parties.[47] They can also agree on the application of transnational rules, such as the 2008 Recommendations of the International Law Association (ILA) on Ascertaining the Contents of the Applicable Law in International Commercial Arbitration,[48] or the transnational rules proposed by Prof. Gabrielle Kaufmann-Kohler.[49] Both recommend a balanced approach between a strict application of *iura novit curia* and a 'law is fact' approach: while the parties are

41. Swiss Supreme Court decision 4P.242/2004 of 27 April 2005, para. 7.3.
42. Silja Schaffstein, *Switzerland, Supreme Court Confirms 'Iura Novit Arbiter'*, ICC Dispute Resolution Bulletin 3/2018, p. 30, with references. *See also* Gabrielle Kaufmann-Kohler, *The Governing Law: Fact or Law? – A Transnational Rule on Establishing Its Contents*, reproduced in Kaufmann-Kohler & Rigozzi, *supra* n. 3, pp. 377-381, at p. 380.
43. Kaufmann-Kohler, *The Governing Law*, *supra* n. 2, p. 379.
44. Schaffstein, *Supreme Court Confirms 'Iura Novit Arbiter'*, *supra* n. 42, p. 30. *See also* Kaufmann-Kohler, *The Governing Law*, *supra* n. 43, p. 379; Berger & Kellerhals, *supra* n. 29, para. 1435.
45. Kaufmann-Kohler, *The Governing Law*, *supra* n. 43, p. 380.
46. *See* Pierre Mayer, *Reflections on the International Arbitrator's Duty to Apply the Law*, in Julian D.M. Lew & Loukas Mistelis (eds), Arbitration Insights: Twenty Years of the Annual Lecture of the School of International Arbitration Ch. 15 (Kluwer Law International 2007), paras 15-34-15-39; Berger & Kellerhals, *supra* n. 29, para. 1436.
47. Schaffstein, *Supreme Court Confirms 'Iura Novit Arbiter'*, *supra* n. 44, p. 30, with references; Berger & Kellerhals, *supra* n. 29, para. 1437.
48. ILA, *Report and Recommendations on Ascertaining the Contents of the Applicable Law in International Commercial Arbitration*, 26 Arbitration International 191 (2010), pp. 201-205.
49. *See* Kaufmann-Kohler, *The Governing Law*, *supra* n. 43, p. 381.

primarily tasked with establishing the contents of the applicable law, the arbitral tribunal can conduct its own research, giving the parties an opportunity to comment thereon.[50]

§29.04 THE ARBITRAL TRIBUNAL'S POWER TO ACT AS SETTLEMENT FACILITATOR

Chapter 12 of the PILA (and Part 3 of the Swiss Code of Civil Procedure which governs domestic arbitrations with a seat in Switzerland) is silent on the arbitral tribunal's power to act as settlement facilitator, i.e., on the admissibility and extend to which arbitrators may actively assist the parties in bringing about a settlement of their dispute. However, arbitrators from a Swiss legal background may consider it part of their adjudicative power to do so, especially in domestic arbitrations.[51] The degree of such involvement may vary, ranging from arbitrators simply encouraging the parties to enter into settlement discussions to expressing a preliminary non-binding opinion on certain issues or on the outcome of the dispute as a whole. At the request of the parties, the arbitrators may even contribute to the content and wording of the settlement.[52]

Arbitrators (and parties) from other cultures and legal backgrounds may consider such settlement efforts incompatible with the arbitrator's adjudicative powers as they risk threatening the parties' due process rights and the arbitrator's impartiality, especially if the settlement fails. In particular, the arbitrator may receive sensitive information during *ex parte* communications with one of the parties that is not part of the arbitration record.[53]

This being so, there appears to be a growing trend among institutional arbitration rules and professional guidelines in favour of allowing the arbitrators' assistance in bringing about a settlement, namely in view of increasing the efficiency of the dispute resolution process.[54] For instance, Article 4(d) of the IBA Guidelines on Conflicts of Interest in International Arbitration provides that '[a]n arbitrator may assist the parties in reaching a settlement of the dispute, through conciliation, mediation or otherwise, at any stage of the proceedings'. Similarly, Appendix IV of the 2021 ICC Arbitration Rules list 'Settlement of Disputes' among several 'examples of case management techniques that can be used by the arbitral tribunal and the parties for controlling time and cost'.

50. Schaffstein, *Supreme Court Confirms 'Iura Novit Arbiter'*, *supra* n. 44, p. 30.
51. Gabrielle Kaufmann-Kohler, *When Arbitrators Facilitate Settlement: Towards a Transnational Standard*, 25 Arbitration International 187 (2009), pp. 190 and 195-196; Kaufmann-Kohler & Rigozzi, *supra* n. 3, para. 1.28; Bernd Ehle, *The Arbitrator as Settlement Facilitator*, in Walking a Thin Line – What an Arbitrator Can Do, Must Do or Must Not Do, Recent Developments and Trends, Colloquium CEPANI 40, 29 September 2010, pp. 80-83; Berger & Kellerhals, *supra* n. 29, para. 171.
52. Berger & Kellerhals, *supra* n. 29, para. 171.
53. Kaufmann-Kohler, *When Arbitrators Facilitate Settlement*, *supra* n. 51, pp. 190-193; Ehle, *supra*. n. 1, pp. 83-85; Christopher Harris, *Arbitrators and Settlement – A Common Law Perspective*, ASA Special Series No. 45, pp. 92-96.
54. *See* Berger & Kellerhals, *supra* n. 29, para. 172; Paolo Marzolini, *The Arbitrator as a Dispute Manager – The Exercise of the Arbitrator's Powers to Act as Settlement Facilitator*, ASA Special Series No. 45, pp. 99-119.

However, there is a need to balance the (controversial) powers of the tribunal with the contractual rights between the parties and the arbitrators, as well as the advantage of efficiency with the disadvantage of threats to the parties' due process rights and to the arbitrators' impartiality.

To achieve such balance, institutional arbitration rules and guidelines impose several limitations on the arbitrators' intervention as settlement facilitator.[55] In particular, they frequently confine the arbitrator's powers to those conferred by the parties. By way of example, under Appendix IV, letter (h)(ii) of the 2021 ICC Arbitration Rules, '*where agreed between the parties and the arbitral tribunal*, the arbitral tribunal may take steps to facilitate settlement of the dispute, provided that every effort is made to ensure that any subsequent award is enforceable at law'.

Similarly, Article 19.5 of the 2021 Swiss Rules provides that, '[w]*ith the agreement of each of the parties*, the arbitral tribunal may take steps to facilitate the settlement of the dispute before it'. To preserve the tribunal's adjudicative function, this provision further specifies that '[a]ny such agreement by a party shall constitute a waiver of its right to challenge an arbitrator's impartiality based on the arbitrator's participation and knowledge acquired in taking the agreed steps'.

Article 4(d) of the IBA Guidelines contains a similar rule but goes one step further in safeguarding arbitration's quasi-judicial or adjudicative nature. Indeed, Article 4(d) specifies that '[i]f the assistance by the arbitrator does not lead to the final settlement of the case, the parties remain bound by their waiver'. It then adds that, notwithstanding the parties' waiver of their right to challenge an arbitrator's impartiality, 'the arbitrator shall resign if, as a consequence of his or her involvement in the settlement process, the arbitrator develops doubts as to his or her ability to remain impartial or independent in the future course of the arbitration'.

Finally, to avoid the risk of perceived bias and preserve the parties' due process rights, it would appear advisable in principle for arbitrators to refrain from the particularly controversial practice of conducting separate discussions with one of the parties in the absence of the other(s).[56]

§29.05 CONCLUSION

The specific content and contours of the arbitral tribunal's powers and of the relationship between arbitrators and parties will vary from case to case. They will depend on the law and rules governing this relationship and the arbitration, on the cultural and legal background of the parties and the arbitrators, and on individual expectations and conceptions about the scope of the arbitrators' powers and the manner in which such powers should be exercised.

As a result, the need to balance the arbitrators' judicial powers with the contractual relationship between arbitrators and parties will also vary from case to

55. *See also* the 'fundamental rules' identified by Gabrielle Kaufmann-Kohler in Kaufmann-Kohler, *When Arbitrators Facilitate Settlement*, *supra* n. 51, pp. 204-205; Kaufmann-Kohler & Rigozzi, *supra* n. 3, para. 1.28; Berger & Kellerhals, *supra* n. 29, para. 172.
56. *Ibid. See also* Harris, *supra* n. 53, p. 93.

case. As this contribution has shown, the specific legal framework governing international arbitrations with a seat in Switzerland will give rise to particular instances that may call for a certain 'balancing' of judicial powers and contractual rights and obligations. The situation will be different in arbitrations with a seat in another jurisdiction, involving parties and arbitrators from other backgrounds.

Having said this, this contribution has also shown that the act of balancing oftentimes can be performed through transnational rules and the harmonization of international arbitration law. It thus appears appropriate to conclude this contribution with the contention that a balancing of the quasi-judicial and quasi-contractual nature of arbitration may be attained by 'achieving the dream' of autonomous arbitration.

CHAPTER 30

The Concept and Scope of the Arbitrator's Autonomy

Emilia Onyema

§30.01 INTRODUCTION

In this chapter, I shall examine the question of the existence of the concept of arbitrator autonomy, its scope, and relevance in international arbitration. Julian Lew in his 1978 book on *Applicable Law in International Commercial Arbitration*, promotes party autonomy and agrees with its definition as a doctrine that frees the parties to select the law that governs their relations, which, 'is thus accompanied by an initial removal of the responsibility from the judge or arbitrator to the parties'.[1] This description of party autonomy remains true with arbitration laws and rules granting parties greater voice in their arbitration. This chapter argues that there is increasingly a shift from party autonomy to arbitrator autonomy, with the tribunal empowered to determine more procedural issues where the parties have not made any decisions or choices. The idea of the autonomy of the arbitrator arises from the question of who the master of the arbitral process is: the parties or the arbitrator? In this chapter, arbitrator also includes the arbitral tribunal. In the context of this topic, I like the definition of 'autonomy' provided by the Collins Dictionary as, 'the ability to make your own decisions about what to do, rather than being influenced by someone else or told what to do'.[2] This definition ably captures the question of the role of the arbitrator in the international arbitration process and the arbitrator's control over the arbitral process.

This chapter will revisit the concept of autonomy in arbitration linked back as Julian Lew postulates to the autonomous nature of international arbitration (2). A brief

1. Julian D.M. Lew, *Applicable Law in International Commercial Arbitration: a Study in Commercial Arbitration Awards* (Oceana Publications) 1978, para. 87 (references excluded).
2. Collins Dictionary online: https://www.collinsdictionary.com/dictionary/english/autonomy (accessed 15 August 2022).

discussion of the purpose autonomy will follow (3) before the discussion of the shift to arbitrator autonomy and its scope (4); followed by a conclusion (5).

§30.02 THE CONCEPT OF AUTONOMY AND INTERNATIONAL ARBITRATION

Arbitration is widely recognised as an efficient dispute resolution mechanism adopted primarily for the resolution of commercial disputes (whether cross border or domestic). As a dispute resolution mechanism applied by trading organizations, individuals, and firms, it was reputed for being fast in comparison to litigation before national courts.[3] This description may now be contested as some courts have tried to note that their processes can be equally fast. One interesting example can be found in the decision of the Supreme Court of the United Kingdom in the much discussed *Enka v. Chubb* where Lord Hamblen notes:

> It is a striking feature of the English proceedings that the trial, the appeal to the Court of Appeal and the appeal to the Supreme Court have all been heard in just over seven months. This is a vivid demonstration of the speed with which the English courts can act when the urgency of a matter requires it.[4]

It remains correct to assert that most arbitration references take a shorter time to get to a final award than a final decision in litigation from most first instance courts. This is certainly the case in most jurisdictions. It has been noted that in some developing jurisdictions, litigants may wait up to ten or more years to get a first instance judgement.[5] Some arbitration institutions also set out the average time within which final awards should be published by tribunals under their rules.[6]

In his 2005 Freshfields/School of International Arbitration 20th annual lecture titled, *Achieving the Dream: Autonomous Arbitration,*[7] Julian Lew argued that international arbitration occupies an autonomous legal regime the effect of which is to:

> remove the process from the control of national law and courts. The arbitration exists in a different domain, a non-national or international sphere.[8]

It is in the spirit of this autonomy of international arbitration that this chapter argues for the autonomy of the arbitrator vis-a-vis the parties and their autonomy, concluding that

3. *See* for example an account of commercial arbitration in the European Middle Ages in Gary Born, *International Commercial Arbitration*, Volume I (Kluwer Law International 2009) pp. 27-32.
4. *Enka Insaat Ve Sanayi AS v. OOO Insurance Company Chubb* [2020] UKSC 38 at para. 24. We are also aware that some cases at the same time had been pending before the English courts for much longer periods. *See* for example, National Statistics for the Civil Justice Statistics Quarterly: January to March 2022, at: https://www.gov.uk/government/statistics/civil-justice-statistics-quarterly-january-to-march-2022/civil-justice-statistics-quarterly-january-to-march-2022 (accessed 15 August 2022).
5. Examples of such jurisdictions include India and Nigeria.
6. *See* for example, Article 31 of the ICC Arbitration Rules, 2021.
7. Julian Lew, 'Achieving the Dream: Autonomous Arbitration', *Arbitration International*, Vol. 22, No. 2 (2006), 179 (hereafter 'Achieving the Dream').
8. *Ibid.*, at p. 195.

the arbitrator's autonomy overrides that of the parties during the arbitration proceedings. It is however, important to note the cautionary view of the authors of *Redfern and Hunter on International Arbitration* that:

> Such emphasis of the 'autonomy of the parties' might suggest that partis and arbitrators inhabit a private universe of their own. But this Is not so. In reality, the practice of resolving disputes by the essentially private process of international arbitration works effectively only because it is supported by a complex public system of national laws and international treaties.[9]

§30.03 THE PURPOSE OF AUTONOMY IN ARBITRATION

The issue of autonomy leads back to efficiency in arbitration. Arbitration practitioners easily recount delay tactics adopted by a party (usually, not themselves) in an arbitration they were involved. We herald 'party autonomy' as the essence of arbitration: it is the decision of the parties, we hear. This chapter critically examines this view in the context of arbitral practice to understand if this is the full story.

Party autonomy is a phrase that is almost synonymous with arbitration and by its use we basically mean that the law that governs the arbitration agreement grants the disputing parties' powers to determine how they wish to operationalise their arbitration. Examples of these are where most national laws allow the parties to choose the place/seat, language, arbitrator appointment procedure, arbitrator challenge procedure, applicable substantive laws or rules, etc, of the arbitration.[10] These provisions are usually couched in permissive language and act as default rules to apply where the parties do not exercise the power to make those decisions.[11] The parties therefore, as masters of their dispute, are provided with the tools to effect the execution of their arbitration agreement.

It is also this 'autonomy' of the parties that is said to be one of the major attractions of arbitration as a dispute resolution mechanism to commercial parties. The Queen Mary/PWC 2006 survey found that of the top reasons why parties choose international arbitration, flexibility of the procedure and the ability of the parties to select the arbitrators were ranked very highly.[12]

The scope and contours of the autonomy of the parties is also accepted by commentators as being limited by mandatory provisions of the applicable law (which may be the law of the seat of arbitration as the law with the closest connection to the

9. Nigel Blackaby & Constantine Partasides QC with Alan Redfern and Martin Hunter, *Redfern and Hunter on International Arbitration* (6th ed., OUP, 2015) at para. 1.08 (hereafter, *Redfern and Hunter*).
10. *See* for example Articles 10, 19, 20 and 28 of the UNCITRAL Model Law on International Commercial Arbitration, (2006 version) with text available at: https://uncitral.un.org/sites/uncitral.un.org/files/media-documents/uncitral/en/19-09955_e_ebook.pdf (accessed 15 August 2022).
11. This is usually by the use of the word, 'may' instead of 'shall' or 'will'.
12. Queen Mary/PriceWaterHouseCoopers, *International Arbitration: Corporate attitudes and Practices*, (2006) at p. 6 and available at: https://arbitration.qmul.ac.uk/media/arbitration/docs/IAstudy_2006.pdf (accessed 15 August 2022).

arbitration or the law of the place of enforcement) and the public policy of the relevant place which may be the seat of arbitration or the place of enforcement as well. It is correct that some commentators refer to international public policy[13] (and reference the New York Convention,[14] though, the New York Convention does not mention international public policy), and some national laws also refer to international public policy in the context of cross border disputes.[15]

There is no such clarity or even agreement among commentators on the existence and scope of the arbitrator's autonomy. What is however agreed, is that the main obligation of the arbitrator is to resolve the dispute submitted to it by the parties. Lew, Mistelis and Kroll note that this obligation, 'includes in particular a duty to conduct the arbitration in such a way that it leads to a valid award not open to challenge'.[16] This comment aptly captures the relevance of this discussion on the arbitrator's autonomy.

The individual with the primary burden to resolve the dispute between the parties is the arbitrator (not the parties). It is argued that to enable the arbitrator to discharge this fundamental and primary obligation, they require a degree of autonomy that will allow them to (using the definition of Collins dictionary), make their, 'own decisions about what to do, rather than being influenced by someone else or told what to do'. In this case, the arbitrator should not be influenced or told what to do by the disputing parties or arbitral institution. The arbitrator should be solely guided by its obligations under the relevant arbitration agreement, arbitration rules and arbitration law.

As it refers to party autonomy, there is, therefore, no serious contentions on its existence and scope in arbitration, especially as these powers of the parties are regulated under national arbitration laws and arbitration rules. Can we also reach the same conclusion as it relates to the autonomy of the arbitrator?

§30.04 ARBITRATOR AUTONOMY

How then can we describe the 'arbitrator autonomy'? simply put, this refers to the authority or power of the arbitrator to exercise control over the arbitral proceedings. As it stands, the tension is in determining who determines procedural issues in arbitration: the parties or the arbitrator or even the arbitral institution?

The arbitrator becomes involved in arbitration from the moment they accept their appointment (or the full panel is constituted) until their final award is published, or if

13. *See* for example Julian Lew, 'Achieving the Dream', *supra* n. 7, at p. 201.
14. Convention for the Recognition and Enforcement of Foreign Arbitral Awards, New York, 1958. *See* for example, Article V(2)(b) of the New York Convention.
15. For example, Article 1520(5) Arbitration Law of France, 2011 (French Code of Civil Procedure, Decree No. 2011-48); and Article 26 OHADA Uniform Arbitration Act 2017.
16. Julian D.M. Lew, Loukas A. Mistelis & Stefan M. Kroll, *Comparative International Commercial Arbitration* (Kluwer Law International, 2003), at p. 279 (para. 12-12). *See also Redfern and Hunter*, *supra* n. 9 at paras 1.80-1.86.

relevant, any corrections to the final award is completed.[17] These are the periods the mandate of the arbitrator commences and terminates.

From the various arbitration rules, the power to make default decisions rests with the arbitrator from the moment the arbitrator enters into the arbitral proceedings.[18] Examples from the UNCITRAL Arbitration Rules include the general provision under Article 17 which provides:

> Subject to these Rules, the arbitral tribunal may conduct the arbitration in such manner as it considers appropriate, provided that the parties are treated with equality and that at an appropriate stage of the proceedings each party is given a reasonable opportunity of presenting its case. The arbitral tribunal, in exercising its discretion, shall conduct the proceedings so as to avoid unnecessary delay and expense and to provide a fair and efficient process for resolving the parties' dispute[19]

This provision of the UNCITRAL Rules expressly empowers the arbitrator as stated above. However, Article 22.2 of the ICC Rules (2021) limits this power of the arbitrator by reference to the parties. The ICC Rules provide:

> In order to ensure effective case management, *after consulting the parties*, the arbitral tribunal shall adopt such procedural measures as it considers appropriate, *provided that they are not contrary to any agreement of the parties* ... [Emphasis added].

The ICC Rules expressly limit the powers of the arbitrator to the views, comments, or agreement of the parties.

Is there any major difference in these two formulations? In this author's view, there are fundamental differences. Under the UNCITRAL regime, the arbitrator can be described as the master of their procedure. It is for the arbitrator to run or conduct the arbitration as they see fit with the only caveat being to ensure the equality of treatment of the parties, avoiding unnecessary delay and expense and ensuring the efficiency of the proceedings. It is arguable that though in practice, the arbitrator may seek the views of the parties in making procedural decisions, they do not necessarily have to do so, as long as they can justify that their procedural decisions meet the criteria set out under Article 17.1 of the UNCITRAL Rules. However, the situation under the ICC Rules differs. The ICC Rules expressly require the arbitrator to consider the views of the parties and not to make procedural decisions before consulting the parties; and the

17. For example, General Principle I of the IBA Guidelines on Conflicts of Interest in International Arbitration (2014) sets out this time period as, 'Every arbitrator shall be impartial and independent of the parties at the time of accepting an appointment to serve and shall remain so until the final award has been rendered or the proceedings have otherwise finally terminated.' The IBA Guidelines are available at: https://www.ibanet.org/MediaHandler?id=e2fe5e72-eb14-4bba-b10d-d33dafee8918 (accessed 15 August 2022).
18. I have not used the word commencement since arbitration commences at different times under different legal regimes. For example, under the ICC Rules (Article 4(2)) arbitration commences when the request for arbitration is received; while under Article 3(2) of the UNCITRAL Arbitration Rules (2010) arbitration commences when the notice of arbitration is received by the respondent.
19. There are different formulations of this provision in different rules of arbitration.

procedural measures the arbitrator adopts cannot be contrary to the agreement of the parties. Thus, under the ICC Arbitration regime, the arbitrator must take notice and consider the views of the parties in its procedural measures.

Under the English Arbitration Act 1996 (EAA), similar provisions ensure the autonomy of the arbitrator over the arbitral proceedings. Section 33 of the EAA sets out the general duty of the arbitrator as a mandatory provision to:

> (1) (a) act fairly and impartially as between the parties giving each party a reasonable opportunity of putting his case and dealing with that of his opponent, and
>
> (b) adopt procedures suitable to the circumstances of the particular case, avoiding unnecessary delay or expense, so as to provide a fair means for the resolution of the matters failing to be determined.
>
> (2) The tribunal shall comply with that general duty in conducting the arbitral proceedings, in its decisions on matters of procedure and evidence and in the exercise of all powers conferred on it.

Section 33 of the EAA does not condition or subject the exercise of the powers conferred on the tribunal to the, 'view, comments or agreement' of the parties (as in the ICC Rules). The recent decision of the English commercial court in *Union of India v. Reliance Industries Limited and another*, evidences this power of the arbitrator over the proceedings by preventing abuse of the arbitral process through the exercise of its procedural powers.[20]

Having noted these two different regimes: the ad hoc regime of greater arbitrator autonomy and the ICC regime of more or less, greater party autonomy over the procedural phase of the arbitration, the question that arises is which regime better serves the arbitration process. In this author's view and from their practice, the better view is the autonomy of the arbitrator over the arbitral process subject only to due process and efficiency requirements.

Will such a regime negatively impact on party autonomy? It does not appear so since the two regimes: arbitrator autonomy and party autonomy are not contradictory or in opposition but directed in achieving efficiency and due process in the arbitral process. However, it is argued that each 'autonomy' has a separate sphere of influence and period. Party autonomy should and does operate from the period the underlying transaction is completed (leading to the conclusion of an arbitration agreement), commencing the arbitration in accordance with the arbitration agreement,[21] until the arbitrator accepts appointment. Upon the constitution of the arbitral tribunal, it is argued that the arbitrator should take control or charge over the arbitral proceedings without their powers being subjected to the vagaries of the parties. This will greatly enhance the actualisation of the efficiency requirement of the various arbitration laws and rules and reduce the ability of the parties (or one of them) to delay and frustrate the progression of the arbitral proceedings, and of course, abuse of the process.

20. *Union of India v. Reliance Industries Limited and another* [2022] EWHC 1407 (Comm).
21. Which includes exercising all rights to defend and uphold the arbitration agreement.

This discussion raises the question whether the arbitrator or the parties are the masters of the dispute. It is suggested that the phrase 'master of the dispute' may need further clarification to reflect the arguments in this chapter. It is obvious that the parties are the masters of their dispute but the discussion argues that the arbitrator is the master of the arbitral proceedings from the moment the tribunal is constituted.

§30.05 CONCLUSION

This chapter has argued briefly that the arbitrator should be the master of the arbitral proceeding from the moment they enter into the arbitration until their mandate ends. This view ensures that the arbitrators have full authority and power to run the arbitration in an efficient, and time and cost-effective manner. Does this view deprive the parties of control over their dispute? The short answer is, No, it does not and it should not. The parties retain control over their *dispute* while the arbitrator retains control over the *arbitral proceeding* upon accepting appointment, at which moment the parties cede their powers or authority to the arbitrator to enable the arbitrator to perform the terms of their arbitration agreement, which is to determine their dispute in accordance with the terms of the arbitration agreement, relevant arbitration rules and laws.

CHAPTER 31

Self-Created Reasons to Challenge an Arbitrator: Recipe for Success or Disaster?

Stephan Wilske

Is it right for you to attack me, in contempt for what you yourself have made, thus abetting the schemes of the wicked? (Job 10:3, NJB)

§31.01 INTRODUCTION

A pivotal figure of international arbitration, who is to be honoured by this *liber amicorum* Prof. Dr D.M. Julian Lew QC, has set standards in international arbitration in many ways, including through his pioneering work on the perspective of comparative international arbitration.[1] He has also shown a vivid interest in the role of international arbitrators, being not only service providers, but guardians of higher values. This is perhaps best expressed in Julian Lew's 1978 doctoral thesis, where, influenced by Goldman, he writes:

> [A]rbitrators ... have a special responsibility to international commerce. They are the guardians of the international commercial order: they must protect the rights of participants in international trade; give effect to the parties' respective obligations under the contract; imply the presence of commercial bona fides in every transaction; respect the customs followed in international trade practice and the rules developed in relevant international treaties; uphold the commonly accepted views of the international commercial community and the policies expressed and adopted by appropriate international organisations; and enforce the fundamental moral and ethical values, which underlie every level of commercial activity.[2]

1. *See* Julian D. M. Lew, Loukas A Mistelis & Stefan M Kröll (eds), *Comparative International Commercial Arbitration*, 2003.
2. Julian D. M. Lew, *Applicable Law in International Commercial Arbitration: A Study in Commercial Arbitration Awards*, 1978, 540 (footnotes omitted). For a discussion of the role of arbitrators,

As Julian is perfectly aware, also from his work as series editor of the *International Arbitration Law Library*, there are not only good guys in international arbitration, but also arbitration guerrillas who want to delay or derail arbitrations and make life hard for the guardians of international public policy.[3] Certainly, no one is better equipped than the honouree to deal with the question raised in this contribution whether self-created reasons to challenge an arbitrator are a recipe for success or disaster.

§31.02 THE PROVOKED ARBITRATOR

There was once an arbitrator: a sound and honest man who feared God and shunned evil and was as impartial and independent as could be.[4] And then, he was confronted with arbitration guerrilla tactics because one party was not interested in a resolution of the dispute at all, or, at least not by impartial, independent and law-abiding arbitrators. The risk was simply too high that any decision, or, at least a decision in conformity with the law, would go against this party. And because of the disruption or suspension of the arbitration, challenging an arbitrator was discovered to be an excellent weapon for use by parties who wish to sabotage the arbitration.[5] Indeed, there is large consensus that doubts with respect to the bias of an arbitrator must be justifiable on some objective basis.[6] And obviously, if an arbitrator is mad at a party representative - for whatever reason - it is fair enough to review whether this gives rise to doubts as to this arbitrator's independence or impartiality.

[A] Ordeal on Patience and Self-Control in Times of Guerrilla Tactics

Arbitration guerrillas normally commence by insults of the targeted arbitrator(s) or threats, thereby hoping to either infuriate them to a degree that it is easy to accuse them of bias, cause them to resign or intimidate them in order to avoid any adverse decision.

This is not uncommon in criminal proceedings with a political background. In Germany, one needs only think of the '*Stammheim Trial*' (May 1975 - April 1977) in Stuttgart against the leaders of the Red Army Faction (RAF), when Andreas Baader and

see Stephan Wilske & Martin Raible, *The Arbitrator as Guardian of International Public Policy? Should Arbitrators Go Beyond Solving Legal Issues?*, in: Catherine A. Rogers & Roger P. Alford (eds), *The Future of Investment Arbitration*, 2009, 249-272 and Stephan Wilske & Laura Bräuninger, *Arbitrators*, in: Stefan Kröll, Andrea Bjorklund & Franco Ferrari (eds) *Cambridge Compendium of International Commercial and Investment Arbitration*, Vol. 1, 330-362 (forthcoming in 2023).

3. *See* Vol. 28 of the series *International Arbitration Law Library:* Günther J. Horvath & Stephan Wilske (eds), *Guerrilla Tactics in International Arbitration*, 2013.
4. Cf. Job 1:1, NJB.
5. Karel Daele, *Challenge and Disqualification of Arbitrators in International Arbitration*, 2012, 103, para. 2-094. *See also* Gary B. Born, *International Commercial Arbitration*, 3rd edition, 2021, Vol. II, 2034 ('Nonetheless, it is also clear that parties not infrequently abuse the challenge process – both for purposes of delay and, more perniciously, as a so-called "guerilla tactic", for purposes of attempted harassment and intimidation of an arbitrator.')
6. Sam Luttrell, *Bias Challenges in International Commercial Arbitration: The Need for a 'Real Danger' Test*, 2009, 14-15 and Karel Daele, *Challenge and Disqualification of Arbitrators in International Arbitration*, 2012, 25.

Gudrun Ensslin called the presiding judge a '*fascist asshole*' and an '*old pig*', respectively, which was enough at the time to get them excluded from the trial, but not to have the presiding judge disqualified for bias.[7]

One may wonder about the kind of allegations which could be brought forward against arbitrators in order to seek their removal.

In Fall 2021, the Republic of the Congo filed a criminal complaint with the France's Public Prosecutor alleging that a billion-Euro ICC award against the state was obtained through corruption on the part of leading French arbitrator Yves Derains.[8] To no one's surprise, Yves Derains dismissed the allegations as '*pure inventions*' and denied them vehemently.[9] The Republic of the Congo alleged that Yves Derains received gifts including Rolex watches and negotiated a percentage of any recovery from the award.[10] Needless to say that such allegations can be extremely damaging to the reputation of an arbitrator – even though the allegations against Yves Derains lack any plausibility.

Are there any allegations which could be worse? Financing of terrorism? Blasphemy? Child trafficking or pederasty? This author does not want to inspire the fantasy of arbitration guerrillas. However, it is obvious that as we know from Robert A. Zimmerman (aka Bob Dylan), '*the times they are a-changin*'. Filing charges against arbitrators is not unusual anymore, threatening them with malpractice actions should they dare to decide in favour of an opponent is nothing particular and even commencing civil lawsuits for damages while the arbitral proceedings are still ongoing is not unheard of anymore.[11]

[B] The 'Tensions Are Harmful' Test

Charles Brower recommended that '... [an arbitrator] should by all means respond to the challenge .... If, however, the response becomes an attack on the challenging party, the arbitrator faces the risk of creating new grounds to sustain the disqualification request'.[12] And he is correct.

In two connected *ad hoc* arbitrations seated in Milan, brought by an Italian broker against the NASDAQ-listed insurer AmTrust Financial Services and its European

7. *See* Michael Sontheimer, *Stammheim-Urteile: Beispiellose Blamage für den Rechtsstaat* (Stammheim Verdicts: An Unprecedented Disgrace for the Rule of Law), Spiegel Online, 28 April 2007. It was not until the 85th attempt that the challenge was successful, after it emerged that the presiding judge of the Stuttgart trial court had sent case documents to the judge at the Federal Court of Justice who would have been the one to rule on the case, if an appeal on points of law had been made (Sontheimer, *ibid.*).
8. Jack Ballantyne, *Congo Accuses Derains of Corruption*, GAR news, 11 October 2021.
9. *Ibid.*
10. *Ibid.*
11. OLG Frankfurt am Main, Order of 26 June 2008, Docket no. 26 SchH 2/08 (Chairperson of Frankfurt-based DIS arbitration was sued in the US for damages because of alleged breach of confidentiality whereby it was obvious that the costs of legal representation in the US would exceed the arbitrator fees).
12. *See* Charles N. Brower, Sarah Melikian & Michael P. Daly, *Tall and Small Tales of a Challenged Arbitrator*, in: Chiara Giorgetti ed., *Challenges and Recusals of Judges and Arbitrators in International Courts and Tribunals*, 2015, 320, 336.

subsidiary, the respondents challenged the chairperson of the arbitral tribunal on grounds of corruption. The President of the Court of Milan, competent to decide the challenge, upheld AmTrust's application, not on the merits of the corruption allegations, but on the basis of a '*serious divergence of opinions*' between the respondents and the arbitrator after the challenge, such that it was no longer possible to guarantee the absolute independence and impartiality of the arbitrator.[13]

In an LCIA case, the claimant based its challenge, *inter alia*, on the fact that the challenged arbitrator was the President of a local arbitral institution and that there were alleged shortcomings in the fairness of this arbitral institution which the claimant described as 'not famous for being always protective and fair to the justified interest for foreign companies'.[14] The challenged arbitrator took note of the language used by the claimant and was snapping back by using, in particular, the expression '*fictitious, false and malevolent*' in his characterization of the claimant's characterization of 'his' arbitral institution.[15]

The LCIA Division consisting of Prof. William W. Park, Dr Éva Horváth and Jean-Claude Najar took into consideration the language used by the arbitrator and upheld the challenge with the following reasoning:

> Though neither accepting that the grounds originally adduced by the Claimant for the removal of the arbitrator, nor in any way calling into question his reputation or qualifications, the Division considered that the self-evident tension and ill-feeling that had arisen as a result of the challenge had created circumstances that may, of themselves, give rise to justifiable doubts as to the arbitrator's impartiality in this particular case.[16]

Obviously, these two decisions follow a rather rigid approach pursuant to which tensions between a party representative and an arbitrator give rise to justifiable doubts as to this arbitrator's impartiality or independence no matter whether the tensions were knowingly caused by such party or not.

[C] The Balancing Approach Considering Cause and Effect

It is hard to accept that an arbitration guerrilla may derail an arbitration simply by creating tensions between such party and the arbitrator. For such a situation, this author suggests an approach that takes into consideration whether the challenging party purposefully provoked tensions with the arbitrator.

In a case decided by Duisburg Regional Court, an application for disqualification of the arbitrator Dr X on grounds of bias was granted because there were considerable

13. Cecilia Carrara & Lukas Florian Innerebner, *Recusal of arbitrator cannot be appealed* (Italian Court of Cassation, Decision No. 20615/2017), 20 September 2017, PLC Arbitration monthly (The Italian Court of Cassation held that an order for the recusal of an arbitrator cannot be appealed.).
14. *See* Challenge Digests, LCIA Reference No. 1303, Decision Rendered 22 November 2001, Arbitration International Vol. 27 (2011), 342, 344.
15. *See ibid.*
16. *See ibid.*

personal tensions between him and Dr U, counsel for the applicant. Dr U and Dr X had represented opposing sides as counsel in a different case, and Dr X (the subsequent arbitrator) had made the following contentions in a written submission in that case:

- that Dr U was only seeking his own advantage in a more than questionable manner;
- that Dr U thought that everyone - except himself - was a halfwit;
- that, for his own advantage, Dr U was evidently even prepared to go as far as to commit character assassination; and
- that legal opinions held by Dr U were largely erroneous and unclouded by knowledge of the law.

The Duisburg Regional Court ruled that the attacks were of such a personal and hurtful nature that it was hardly likely that it would be possible to resolve the tensions any time soon and that to have such a strained relationship between counsel for one of the parties and an arbitrator was unreasonable for the party concerned. As there could also be no question of the applicant or her counsel having provoked the tensions with the aim of getting the arbitrator Dr X disqualified, the challenge was justified, it held.

Based on this decision, irreconcilable personal tensions between a counsel and an arbitrator constitute grounds for a challenge unless the tensions were provoked with the aim of disqualifying the arbitrator. This implies that a challenge might have been dismissed if the personal irreparable tensions would have been provoked by the challenging party. This, of course, triggers the question: is it acceptable to compromise on a cornerstone of international arbitration, namely the impartiality and independence of arbitrators?

In the ICSID case *Hrvatska v. Slovenia*, the arbitral tribunal argued: 'Even fundamental principles must, however, give way to overriding exceptions. In this case, the overriding principle is that of the immutability of properly constituted tribunals … .'[17] Indeed, the principal role of every legal system should be to protect its integrity by not allowing an actor to benefit from abusive or unlawful action.[18]

This approach should be favoured. It is certainly in line with criminal courts' approach all over this globe because the idea that an accused could easily avoid a verdict by simply insulting the judge(s) cannot be justified.[19]

What should be decisive in accepting the perception of the tainted impartiality and independence of an arbitrator?

17. *Hrvatska Elektroprivreda v. Slovenia*, ICSID Case No. ARB/05/24, Tribunal's Ruling regarding the participation of David Mildon QC in further stages of the proceedings (6 May 2008), para. 25.
18. *See* Bin Cheng's seminal book on *General Principles of Law as Applied by International Courts and Tribunals* (1953) and more recently, Charles T. Kotuby Jr. & Luke A. Sobota, *General Principles of Law and International Due Process*, 2017 on the general prohibition on the abuse of rights with numerous references, 108-103.
19. *See, e.g.*, German Constitutional Court (Bundesverfassungsgericht, BVerfG), 2nd Senate, 2nd Chamber, Decision of 24 April 1996, Docket No. 2 BvR 1639/94 (arguing that criminal charges of a party against the judge would regularly not justify doubts as to the impartiality and independence of the judge because otherwise the challenging party would have full discretion to elude any judge. This reasoning is admittedly result-oriented and dogmatically not very strong. Accordingly, the court conceded that the particulars of each case are decisive).

If an arbitrator loses control of his or her temper, by making inappropriate remarks or taking other action that might display enmity.[20] This should disqualify the arbitrator whether the arbitrator was provoked or not.

However, if an arbitrator needs to defend his or her reputation by, necessarily taking an opposite position to accusations, that should not harm the arbitrator's position. The same applies to a public announcement with respect to the arbitrator's position vis-à-vis unjustified accusations or similar action – at least as long as the language is calm and composed, referring to facts and follows the advice of the wife of the 44th US President: '*When they go low, we go high.*'[21]

Needless to say that our honouree Julian Lew is one of those arbitrators who would not display any irritation but rather continue even under fire with a 'stiff upper lip' in true British fashion.

§31.03 CONCLUSION AND OUTLOOK

Self-created reasons to challenge an arbitrator should not be a recipe for success. That would be disastrous because it would incentivize guerrilla tactics against arbitrators in order to derail or, at least, to intimidate arbitrators. To the contrary: following the wisdom of the *Glimmer Twins* it seems more obvious that '*someone will have to pay the price*'[22] for provocations. This should not be the arbitrator – unless the arbitrator falls into the trap of the provocation. Rather, it is the agitator who should face the consequences, i.e., having wasted time and money for the unsuccessful challenge and now facing – for the further course of the proceedings – the risk of cost consequences[23] and arbitrator(s) who know by then what they have to expect from such party. That would not necessarily lead to a disaster but, possibly, to a situation where a party might want to consider a replacement of its counsel who played along with such dirty tactics. For counsel this would be the right time to consult our honouree or 'his institution' the *School of International Arbitration* at Queen Mary University of London, a school he helped to create in 1985, and go for some extra classes in legal ethics.[24]

20. *See* standard 3.3.7 (orange list) of the *IBA Guidelines on Conflicts of Interest in International Arbitration* (2014): '*Enmity exists between an arbitrator and counsel appearing in the arbitration*'.
21. First Lady Michelle Obama first uttered this now-famous catchphrase at the 2016 Democratic National Convention in Philadelphia on 25 July 2016, https://www.cnbc.com/2020/02/12/michelle-obama-on- famous-catchphrase-when-they-go-low-we-go-high.html.
22. The quote is taken from '*The Last Time*', The Rolling Stones' first original song released on 26 February 1965 in the UK. Luckily, this song was not performed during the Rolling Stones' 2022 '*SIXTY Tour*'. Thus, there is still hope to see them again on stage.
23. *See* Gary B. Born, *International Commercial Arbitration*, 3rd edition, 2021, Vol. II, p. 2035 ('In cases involving abusive or repeat challenges of this character, sanctions against the challenging party are appropriate remedies.').
24. Book of Sirach 51:23, NJB: 'Draw near to me, you who are uneducated, and lodge in the house of instruction.'

F The Seat

CHAPTER 32

Are Arbitral Seats Striking the Right Balance Between Arbitrator Autonomy and Court Supervision?

*Jacomijn J. van Haersolte-van Hof**

The relationship between arbitrator autonomy and court supervision, or in other words the relationship between arbitrators and the courts, is a broad topic which raises essential questions of legitimacy. This relationship is not without tension. While on the one hand, the whole point of arbitration is not to be in court,[1] with courts in many jurisdictions upholding parties' right to arbitrate and in some jurisdictions even adopting 'pro-arbitration' policies,[2] the fundamental right to access the courts[3] implies that the ultimate arbiters of jurisdiction are the national courts.

The courts thus play a crucial role at different stages of the arbitration, potentially at the outset of an arbitration where questions of jurisdiction, including the validity of an arbitration agreement, may arise and also at the end of an arbitration, whether in

* The author thanks Eleanor Scogings for her invaluable help in preparing this contribution.

1. J. Lew, *Applicable Law in International Commercial Arbitration*, Oceana/Sijthoff 1978 ('Lew, Applicable Law'), p. 82 ('By submitting to arbitration, the parties remove their contractual disputes from the jurisdiction of any one country.')
2. *See, e.g.*, the United States' Federal Arbitration Act 1925 which stipulates the fundamental principle that arbitration agreements must be considered valid, irrevocable and enforceable (except on legal or equitable grounds for the revocation of the contract): Section 2: 'A written provision in any maritime transaction or a contract evidencing a transaction involving commerce to settle by arbitration a controversy thereafter arising out of such contract or transaction, or the refusal to perform the whole or any part thereof, or an agreement in writing to submit to arbitration an existing controversy arising out of such a contract, transaction, or refusal, shall be valid, irrevocable, and enforceable, save upon such grounds as exist at law or in equity for the revocation of any contract.'
3. *See, e.g.*, Article 6(1) of the European Convention on Human Rights (signed 4 November 1950) which guarantees 'a fair and public hearing within a reasonable time by an independent and impartial tribunal established by law.'

annulment, enforcement or potentially revocation proceedings. In addition, in particular in *ad hoc* arbitration, the supporting role of the courts is an important safeguard for arbitration to function effectively, including by providing a default mechanism for the appointment of arbitrators.

The precise scope and impact of the supervisory role of the courts depends on the applicability and interpretation of treaties, national law, institutional rules and relevant provisions of the arbitration agreement. It is obvious that a modest contribution to a *liber amicorum* cannot do justice to this panoply of rules and regulations and range of modalities. The focus of this contribution will therefore be on arbitrator autonomy and court supervision in the context of recent cases concerning the review by courts of tribunals' jurisdictional decisions.

Specifically, it will address the concept of de novo review which, for the purpose of this contribution, entails a court reviewing the question of jurisdiction anew, rather than merely reviewing the decision of the tribunal on jurisdiction as such. Or, in other words, the court will review jurisdiction from scratch, rather than through the prism of the arbitral decision.

The question, however, is how to define 'from scratch'? Does it mean that the court will consider new arguments and new evidence, thus allowing a party to change and improve on its initial case? Is there a difference in approach with respect to positive and negative decisions on jurisdiction? How does this concept interact with procedural limitations in national law such as the obligation to raise certain arguments and defences at the earliest opportunity? In other words, how do courts balance the right to a court review on jurisdiction with due process considerations? Are these thrown overboard, or do they limit the scope of subsequent review?

The observations in this contribution are intentionally presented with a bird's eye view. Precisely because the scope and modalities of review are so dependent on the specific legal matrix of each case, it is difficult to perform an 'apples and apples' comparison. In addition, as I will address in my concluding remarks, the variety and disparity of court decisions is compounded by the increasing importance of national law, not merely arbitration law, but the rules and practice of civil procedure.

Then again, there are enough cases from a wide range of jurisdictions addressing similar concepts and scenarios to make a high-level review worthwhile. One of the key benefits of court decisions as a source of research material is that there is plenty of material available. As Julian stated in his foreword to his PhD thesis, 'the most glaring problem' when he embarked on his study of the law applicable in international arbitration was the non-availability of primary source material, i.e., awards.[4] One of the reasons his study was so valuable was because he reviewed a large number of unpublished awards, containing a wealth of information. The topic of publication of awards is not uncontroversial and it remains to be seen how representative any selection of arbitral awards is. While there is generally greater access to court decisions, it remains difficult, at least partly due to the multitude of different languages

4. Lew, Applicable Law, p. ix.

involved, to ensure that any selection of court decisions is genuinely representative and that decisions are properly analysed.[5]

The recent spate of set-aside decisions, frequently involving investment arbitration disputes, has yielded a wealth of insight in the challenging question of the boundary between arbitrator autonomy, and the rights and obligations of arbitrators to determine jurisdiction, and the rights and obligations of the courts to review such arbitral decisions.

In discussing some of these cases, one needs to be conscious of the specificities of each case and in particular the basis for review. For example, the standards imposed by section 67 of the English Arbitration Act 1996 (EAA),[6] Article 1065 Dutch Code of Civil procedure[7] and Article 34 of the UNCITRAL Model Law 1985 (as amended) (UML)[8] insofar as they relate to the jurisdictional view are far from identical. These standards are not set in stone and are subject to development and discussion. For instance, the Law Commission of England & Wales is currently undertaking a review of the EAA and will consider, as part of the potential areas of review, the court's powers exercisable in support of arbitration proceedings and the procedure for challenging a jurisdiction award.

Nevertheless, while there are differences in the bases for review, the scepticism expressed until some years ago is no longer mainstream. Moreover, what this contribution seeks to do is to distil the essence of the level of review by the courts, and to try

5. The challenges interpreting decisions correctly is illustrated by some of the decisions to be reviewed hereafter in this contribution. For example, the Dutch decision, to be discussed, is difficult to understand without a reasonable grounding not only in Dutch law of civil procedure, but also a decent grasp of the intricacies of the rules and limitations applicable to appeal and appeal in cassation procedures.
6. Section 67 EAA provides: '(1) A party to arbitral proceedings may (upon notice to the other parties and to the tribunal) apply to the court—(a) challenging any award of the arbitral tribunal as to its substantive jurisdiction; or (b) for an order declaring an award made by the tribunal on the merits to be of no effect, in whole or in part, because the tribunal did not have substantive jurisdiction.'
7. Article 1065 Dutch Code of Civil Procedure provides: '1. A reversal of the award can take place only on one or more of the following grounds: (a) absence of a valid arbitration agreement; (b) the arbitral tribunal was constituted in violation of the rules applicable thereto; (c) the arbitral tribunal has not complied with its mandate; (d) the award is not signed or does not contain reasons in accordance with the provisions of Article 1057; (e) the award, or the manner in which it was made, violates public policy or good morals.'
8. Article 34 UML provides: '(2) An arbitral award may be set aside by the court specified in article 6 only if: (a) the party making the application furnishes proof that: (i) a party to the arbitration agreement referred to in article 7 was under some incapacity; or the said agreement is not valid under the law to which the parties have subjected it or, failing any indication thereon, under the law of this State; or (ii) the party making the application was not given proper notice of the appointment of an arbitrator or of the arbitral proceedings or was otherwise unable to present his case; or (iii) the award deals with a dispute not contemplated by or not falling within the terms of the submission to arbitration, or contains decisions on matters beyond the scope of the submission to arbitration, provided that, if the decisions on matters submitted to arbitration can be separated from those not so submitted, only that part of the award which contains decisions on matters not submitted to arbitration may be set aside; or (iv) the composition of the arbitral tribunal or the arbitral procedure was not in accordance with the agreement of the parties, unless such agreement was in conflict with a provision of this Law from which the parties cannot derogate, or, failing such agreement, was not in accordance with this Law; or (b) the court finds that: (i) the subject-matter of the dispute is not capable of settlement by arbitration under the law of this State; or (ii) the award is in conflict with the public policy of this State.'

to further a discussion as to what the appropriate level of review is or should be. As this overview will show, there is tension between the notion of a full review (which is necessary to do justice to the fundamental nature of the courts' supervisory powers, and at the same time the recognition that the decision of arbitrators and the arbitral procedure cannot or should not be without consequences) and the notion that where a party has waived or relinquished a procedural right,[9] set-aside proceedings should not be providing the parties with a second bite of the cherry. In other words, due process dictates that there comes a point when enough is enough.

In addition, while terminology is sometimes consistent but has a different connotation, there are also examples of terminology suggesting differences that are in fact not there. What I will seek to distinguish in this limited overview of some recent cases is to what extent review is undertaken through the prism of the arbitral decision, or from scratch.

I will start this *tour d'horizon* in my native country, the Netherlands. On 5 November 2021 the Dutch Supreme Court issued a long-awaited decision in *The Russian Federation v. Yukos Universal Limited (and others)*, ('*Yukos*').[10]

After the bankruptcy of Yukos Oil Company, its shareholders initiated arbitration proceedings against the Russian Federation pursuant to Article 26 of the Energy Charter Treaty (ECT), alleging that the Russian Federation had expropriated their investments in Yukos and had failed to protect those investments. An UNCITRAL Tribunal seated in The Hague issued three awards in favour of the shareholders awarding more than USD 50 billion. The Russian Federation commenced set-aside proceedings, *inter alia*, on the basis that the Tribunal lacked jurisdiction.

The District Court set aside the awards in 2016 on the ground that there was no binding arbitration agreement. The court considered, *inter alia*, that the Russian Federation had not ratified the ECT and that Article 45 of the ECT, which provides that a State that has signed the ECT will provisionally apply the Treaty, could not be invoked as a basis for jurisdiction in light of the so-called limitation clause stipulating that provisional application only applies 'to the extent that such provisional application is not inconsistent with its constitution, laws or regulations'.

The Court of Appeal came to a different conclusion and considered among other things that the shareholders were entitled in the set-aside proceedings, and for the first

9. For instance, section 67(1) EAA provides that '... [a] party may lose the right to object (see section 73) and the right to apply is subject to the restrictions in section 70(2) and (3)'. Among other things, section 73 provides that if a party takes part in the arbitration without making any objection that the tribunal lacks jurisdiction, that party '... may not raise that objection later, before the tribunal or the court, unless [that party] shows that, at the time [it] took part or continued to take part in the proceedings, [it] did not know and could not with reasonable diligence have discovered the grounds for the objection'. Similarly, section 70(2) and (3) set out supplementary provisions that apply to applications challenging the tribunal's award on jurisdiction. Article 4 UML similarly deals with waivers of the right to object. This contribution seeks to further the discussion regarding the interplay between such provisions and the concept of de novo review.

10. *The Russian Federation v. Veteran Petroleum Limited, Yukos Universal Limited and Hulley Enterprises Limited*, Supreme Court of the Netherlands, 20/01595, ECLI:NL:HR:2021:1879, 5 November 2021, https://uitspraken.rechtspraak.nl/inziendocument?id=ECLI:NL:HR:2021:1879 (English translation provided by the court).

time on appeal, to invoke an interpretation of the limitation clause not previously invoked in the arbitration proceedings.

The Supreme Court stressed that while a tribunal is entitled to evaluate jurisdiction, that evaluation is not final. The final word rests with the courts and such review 'should be made without restraint' that is typically applicable in set-aside proceedings '... and is not limited to the question of whether the arbitrators assumed jurisdiction on the correct grounds'.[11] Moreover, while it is unclear whether the Supreme Court's level of review would have been different had the tribunal declined jurisdiction, the Supreme Court made clear that:

> The public interest in effective arbitration implies that the court should not annul the arbitral decision on the sole ground that the arbitral tribunal gave incorrect reasons for its decision that it had jurisdiction to hear the dispute. Therefore, the court is free to decide, on grounds other than those relied on by the arbitral tribunal, that it rightly considered itself competent to take cognisance of the dispute. After all, a different view would mean that a court that finds that the grounds relied on by the arbitral tribunal were insufficient to establish its jurisdiction, but notes that the arbitral tribunal did have jurisdiction on other grounds, would nevertheless have to annul the arbitral award. The consequence of this would be that, even though there is a valid arbitration agreement, the dispute would have to be decided by the ordinary court, unless the parties agree otherwise (former art. 1067 CCP). This would not be consistent with the parties' clear intention to submit their dispute to arbitration rather than to the court system.[12]

Consequently, the Supreme Court considered in considerable detail the scope and meaning of the limitation clause, by reference to the relevant provisions of Vienna Convention on the Law of Treaties and various principles of public international law. It also considered at length whether the requirements of Article 1 ECT had been met and whether the shareholders qualified as 'investors' having made 'investments' pursuant to this provision.

Three issues are worth noting at this stage. First, because of the limitations of cassation proceedings before the Supreme Court, pursuant to which one cannot complain in cassation about the incorrect application of foreign law, the Supreme Court held that it could not revisit the considerations of the Court of Appeal insofar as that court had determined that according to Russian law (which was relevant pursuant to Article 45 ECT) this type of claim is arbitrable.[13]

In addition, the Supreme Court rejected Russia's request to seek a preliminary ruling from the Court of Justice of the European Union (CJEU) on the basis that the Court of Appeal's interpretation of the ECT was inconsistent with the interpretation of Commission, the Council and European Union (EU) Member States, and thus not '*acte claire*' or '*acte éclairé*',[14] requiring the Supreme Court to seek a preliminary ruling.

11. Yukos, para. 5.2.7.
12. *Ibid.*, para. 5.2.7.
13. *Ibid.*, para. 5.2.17.
14. *Acte claire* is a doctrine that permits national courts of last instance to refrain from requesting a preliminary ruling under Article 267(3) Treaty on the Functioning of the European Union (TFEU) from the CJEU when the point of EU law at issue is indubitably obvious.

While beyond the scope of this contribution, the Supreme Court's ambivalent way in which it addressed the potential applicability of EU law by positing that given the difference of opinion the matter was not '*acte claire*', is striking. Despite not considering the point obvious, the Supreme Court refrained from seeking a preliminary ruling holding that the complaints against the Court of Appeal's judgement failed on other grounds.[15]

The reference to this nuanced doctrine is notable because it presupposes that there is a matter of EU law at stake, and as the Advocate General to the Supreme Court had carefully analysed, this was far from clear in the present case. What is even more notable for present purposes, however, is that this aspect of the decision and the reference to the complex doctrine of EU law and its incorporation in the system of civil procedure adds another layer of complication, compounded by the very technical aspects of appeal and appeal in cassation.

Third, the Yukos decision is noteworthy because it did not only involve an application to set aside the original awards, but in appeal in the annulment proceedings, the Russian Federation also argued that the arbitral awards were contrary to public policy due to fraud committed by the shareholders in the arbitration, consisting of submitting false statements and withholding documents, and failing to produce documents in the arbitration. Dutch arbitration law contains a specific remedy, revocation, for situations in which an award has been procured by means of fraud or withholding documents fraudulently. While not strictly speaking part of the section of the decision in which the jurisdictional arguments were considered, the Supreme Court's considerations as to the scope of the right to invoke revocation (which is generally a separate procedure, with different time limits and under the then applicable arbitration law a remedy to be submitted to a different, higher, court) are nevertheless of interest for the discussion of the scope of review proceedings as the wording is broad and the considerations likely applicable more generally.

The Supreme Court noted that the grounds for annulment must be included in the initial summons and that:

> former art. 1064 (5) CCP does not in itself preclude further elaboration, on appeal, of grounds put forward in the initial summons, and if necessary correction of an omission, in response to a defence raised in the further course of the proceedings, or as a result of the decision of the court of first instance. However, the possibility to elaborate, on appeal, on grounds already submitted in the summons, or to make new factual submissions, is not unlimited. This possibility is limited inter alia by the ordinary rules applicable to appeal proceedings, such as art. 130 CCP. In addition, this possibility is limited by specific provisions that prescribe when a certain ground for annulment must be invoked for the first time, on penalty of forfeiting the right to rely on it later. If such a provision is at issue, the court will have to assess in each individual case whether a new factual or legal submission introduced in the course of the annulment proceedings would conflict with the purport of such a provision, partly in view of the requirements of due process.[16]

15. Yukos, para. 5.2.10.
16. *Ibid.*, para. 5.1.14.

Moreover, the Supreme Court's decision in Yukos is interesting for a number of reasons but perhaps most relevant for the purposes of this contribution is the extent to which the Supreme Court did consider issues of jurisdiction afresh, allowing new jurisdictional arguments to be raised and justifying this on policy grounds including the desire to consider favourably a putative agreement to arbitrate.

The next step in this tour around the world is Canada, where another Yukos decision, this one involving a tribunal seated in Toronto, Ontario, also considering an ECT claim, has led to a number of interesting decisions.[17] As with the Dutch Yukos decisions, the various court instances (including different judges dealing with the matter at different points in time) came to different conclusions.

The Russian Federation brought an application under Article 16(3) UML to set aside an interim award on the ground that it had not consented to arbitrate. In its 2018 first decision in this case, the Ontario Superior Court of Justice (Commercial List) held that in reviewing the matter, it was not confined to the record adduced before the Tribunal.[18] The court considered that its role was not to undertake a mere review of the tribunal's decision, and consequently permitted Russia to file new evidence.

In its 2019 decision, however, the Ontario Superior Court of Justice came to a different conclusion in its review of the preliminary jurisdiction decision and considered that this review was not the same as a hearing de novo.[19] Consequently, it considered that allowing new evidence would undermine the principle of competence-competence.[20]

This decision was overruled by the Ontario Divisional Court of the Ontario Superior Court of Justice, which considered that Article 16(3) UML requires the court to 'decide the matter' and not just to 'review' the tribunal's decision.[21] Moreover, the court held that:

17. *The Russian Federation v. Luxtona Limited*, 2021 ONSC 4604, 30 June 2021 ('*Luxtona*').
18. Decision of the Ontario Superior Court of Justice, 2018 ONSC 2419, 13 April 2018.
19. Endorsement of the Ontario Superior Court of Justice, 2019 ONSC 7558, 20 December 2019. Penny J issued judgement having been assigned the case from Dunphy J (who had heard the initial motion to strike out evidence in 2018 ONSC 2419) due to a change in judicial assignments. [8].
20. 'The Court of Appeal also very clearly described what the court is doing on a jurisdictional challenge under the Model Law as a "review." On a true jurisdictional challenge, it is a review on correctness, without any deference, in which the court must come to its own conclusion on whether the tribunal had jurisdiction, but a "review" nevertheless. This is a profoundly different approach from that propounded by the cases from the London Commercial Court, which generally describe the court's role on a challenge under s. 67 of the UK Arbitration Act as a trial *de novo*.' [58] and 'If parties can adduce fresh evidence at will, both parties to the jurisdictional challenge will have an incentive, knowing what the tribunal's decision now is, to file new evidence providing further support for their position and why the tribunal was right or wrong in its determination. This, it seems to me, will result in such evidence being routinely filed and the court routinely conducting a trial de novo on jurisdiction. This will have the further result that the record put before the court will routinely be materially different than that put before the tribunal. The tribunal, in that scenario, will not have, as Article 16(1) requires, the ability to "rule on its own jurisdiction including any objections with respect to the existence or validity of the arbitral agreement" [my emphasis].' [61].
21. *Luxtona*, 2021 ONSC 4604, 30 June 2021.

> the parties are not restricted to the record they placed before the tribunal on the jurisdictional issue. I so conclude because of the language of the *Model Law* and the consensus in the international jurisprudence on this point. Ontario administrative law favours a deferential review of arbitral decisions, but this approach is not invariable, and the Supreme Court of Canada has been clear that the presumptive deferential review can be displaced when the legislature shows a contrary intention by the words chosen to describe the court's role. Further, it is desirable that there be a measure of consistency in the approach taken to these issues across jurisdictions, and this goal is reflected in language in the ICAA adopted by the legislature to implement the *Model Law*. The international consensus on this issue strongly supports the conclusion that the application below is a hearing de novo and not a review of the tribunal's decision. Therefore, for the reasons that follow, I conclude that the application judge erred on this point and that the parties are entitled to adduce evidence on the application as of right. [10]

The court relied on, and quoted, the English Supreme Court in *Dallah v. Pakistan* [2010] UKSC 46[22] that the court's role was '"to reassess the issue [*of jurisdiction*] itself" and not "to review the tribunal's decision'. [30]

The English approach was confirmed in *GPF GP S.A.R.L v. Republic of Poland* [2018] EWHC 409 (*GPF*), which involved a London seated Swedish Chamber of Commerce arbitration brought on the basis of the Bilateral Investment Treaty (BIT) between Poland and Belgium and Luxembourg. The investors applied to set aside the Tribunal's award on jurisdiction under section 67 EAA, arguing that the Tribunal erred in finding that it did not have jurisdiction over all its claims. The High Court set aside parts of the award considering that it was entitled to a full review of jurisdiction. The court noted:

> In such circumstances it is for the Court under section 67 to consider whether jurisdiction does or does not exist, unfettered by the reasoning of the arbitrators or indeed the precise manner in which arguments were advanced before the arbitrators. Ultimately jurisdiction either is, or is not, conferred on the true construction of the arbitration agreement, and that ought not to be fettered by how arguments were advanced below, subject always to the discretion of the court as to the admission of evidence before it ... [70]
>
> An issue has arisen between the parties as to the nature of a section 67 hearing, and what arguments may be advanced, and evidence adduced, by the applicant on such a hearing which I address at Section F below. Suffice it to say at this point that I am satisfied that it is well established that the hearing is in the nature of a rehearing, and to the extent that Griffin advances any particular arguments not argued before the Tribunal, or adduces any new evidence, I am satisfied that Griffin may do so, and to the extent that permission is required to do so, I am

22. 'In my view the text of the Model Law, adopted in Ontario law, prescribes a de novo hearing in a court application "to decide the matter" of the tribunal's jurisdiction. Mexico v. Cargill does not say otherwise. Dallah is strong authority to the contrary, and although the Court of Appeal decision in Mexico v. Cargill does not rule on this point, it does generally approve the reasoning in Dallah. The strong international consensus on this point favours the Dallah approach, and the Model Law itself encourages "uniformity" on such points. The onus is on the challenging party to set aside a tribunal's preliminary ruling on jurisdiction. But because the court is hearing the jurisdictional issue de novo, the parties are entitled as of right to adduce evidence, including expert evidence, relevant to the jurisdictional issue.' [38]

> satisfied that this is an appropriate case for permission to be granted, the Respondent not having adduced any evidence of prejudice in dealing with the same, and indeed having itself addressed such matters at length in its submissions and evidence. [7]

Consequently, the court confirmed that it would undertake a full rehearing, including potentially a review of new arguments and evidence albeit that it stressed that producing evidence would be subject to the generally applicable rules of civil procedure and to the extent required, subject to permission.[23]

Similarly in Singapore a decision in a Singapore seated BIT dispute was initially treated differently in the lower court, but ultimately led to an outcome similar to the English decisions. In *Sanum Investments Ltd v. The Government of the Lao People's Republic* [2016] SGCA 57 ('*Sanum*'), a jurisdictional objection that the BIT should not apply to Macau and the claim in question thus did not fall within the remit of the arbitration clause, was expanded in the context of court review, with Lao trying to adduce two diplomatic letters which had not been before the Tribunal.

The High Court, while emphasising that a party should not have full unconditional power to adduce fresh evidence at will, admitted the new evidence applying

23. *The* court stated: 'the fact that a section 67 application is a re-hearing does not mean that the court cannot control the evidence adduced on a section 67 application – it clearly can ...' [71]. Further, the High Court in its recent judgement in *Gold Pool JV Limited v. The Republic of Kazakhstan* [2021] EWHC 3422 applied the conclusions in GPF, noting: 'The nature of a s.67 claim, and the approach to be adopted by the court, requires no substantial elaboration on this occasion. *It involves and requires a rehearing* de novo *by the court in which the arbitrators' conclusions have no legal or evidential weight. I agree with the explanation of the position in* GPF GP Sàrl v Republic of Poland *[2018] EWHC 409 (Comm), per Bryan J at [64] to [70].* It has been said that nonetheless the arbitrators' conclusions and reasons may be of interest rather more often than it has been explained why that might be so. For example, in *Dallah Real Estate v. Pakistan* [2010] UKSC 46 at [160], Lord Saville (no less) said that "The findings of fact made by the arbitrators and their view of the law can in no sense bind the court, though of course the court may find it useful to see how the arbitrators dealt with the question" without explaining why a court might find it useful to look at conclusions that have neither legal nor evidential weight before it.' [7] and at [8-9]: 'In *Republic of Korea v. Dayyani et al,* [2019] EWHC 3580 (Comm) at [26], Butcher J said that "A challenge under section 67 proceeds by way of a de novo rehearing of the jurisdiction issue(s). The award of the arbitrators has no automatic legal or evidential weight. Nevertheless, and given that the arbitral tribunal has considered the same issues, the court will examine the award with care and interest. If and to the extent the reasoning is persuasive, then there is no reason why the court should not be persuaded by it." *That idea needs to be applied with a degree of caution however as the court's task is to decide the case as presented to it by a party on the rehearing, as Bryan J explained in* GPF v. Poland *at [70].* It should generally be for the parties to decide for themselves to what extent they each may wish to adopt any reasoning of the arbitrators as an argument of their own in court. *In short, a s.67 claim does not operate by way of a review of the arbitrators' decision.* In the present case, in fact the arbitrators formulated the applicable legal rule accurately in the award and both parties accept as much. The arbitrators stated the rule in these terms: "... States may agree to continue a pre-existing treaty relationship following the emergence of one of them as a new State and such agreement may be either explicit or tacit and may lack the ordinary formalities associated with the conclusion of a new treaty. ... whether this represents the formation of a new legal agreement between the States concerned, or constitutes an agreement confirming succession to an earlier agreement represent[s] fine shades of nuance, but in either view the existence of an agreement is paramount."' (emphasis added)

standards previously developed in relation to the submission of evidence in court proceedings and overturned the award on jurisdiction.

The Court of Appeal confirmed that the court was entitled to conduct a de novo review of the Tribunal's decision and upheld the High Court's decision, rejecting the view that the court should apply a restrained approach by according deference to the Tribunal's findings. Nevertheless, the Court of Appeal, citing a different court case, warned that this 'does not mean that all that transpired before the Tribunal should be disregarded, necessitating a full re-hearing of all the evidence ... it simply means that the court is at liberty to consider the material before it, unfettered by any principle limiting its fact-finding abilities'. [43]

Consequently, while the court endorsed the concept of de novo review and reversed the decision by the Tribunal on the basis of evidence, it somehow distinguished this from a full rehearing.

Finally, the perspective from Switzerland. In *Recofi SA v. Vietnam* 4A_616/2015[24] ('*Recofi*'), the Swiss courts reviewed a Geneva seated UNCITRAL award in a BIT case in which the Tribunal declined jurisdiction on the basis that the underlying sales contracts did not constitute an investment.

The Federal Tribunal emphasised that while it would review the Tribunal's jurisdictional decision, it would not do so on its own motion but rather on the basis of the arguments made by the appellant:

> The Federal Tribunal reviews the findings of facts only within prescribed limits, even when it examines an argument based on the lack of jurisdiction of the arbitral tribunal .... The Court must make its decision on the basis of the facts found in the award under appeal (see Art. 105(1) LTF), it may not rectify or supplement ex officio the factual findings of the arbitrators, even if the facts were established in a blatantly inaccurate manner or in violation of the law (see Art. 77(2) LTF, ruling out the applicability of Art. 105(2) LTF). However, there is the possibility that may review the factual findings on which the award under appeal is based if one of the grievances mentioned in Art. 190(2) PILA is raised against such factual findings or if some new facts or evidence are exceptionally taken into account in the framework of the civil law appeal procedure (Judgment 4A_342/20158 of April 26, 2016, at 3). [3.1.2]

Consequently, while the ability to review new facts or evidence is not entirely excluded, the court's emphasis is on the exceptional nature of such review. However, this does not necessitate a starkly different approach as there has also been some suggestion by the Federal Tribunal in a separate case that it will freely examine questions which determine the jurisdiction, or lack of jurisdiction of the tribunal.[25]

Here ends our whirlwind tour of the world. At a superficial level, this range of cases from a variety of jurisdictions, shows a general consensus that courts will not limit themselves to reviewing jurisdictional decisions through the prism of the arbitral award and effectively adopt de novo review as the standard. Beyond this general

24. *Recofi S.A. v. Vietnam,* Federal Supreme Court of Switzerland, 20 September 2016, 4A_616/2015.
25. *See, e.g., Clorox Spain S.L. v. Bolivarian Republic of Venezuela,* Decision of the Swiss Federal Tribunal, 25 March 2020, 4A_306/2019, [3.4.1].

observation, however, the most striking feature of these cases is that the implementation of review is far from straightforward, and very much dictated by rules and doctrine of domestic civil procedure. It is also striking that a number of cases show significant variety of perspective at the different levels of courts involved in particular case, suggesting that the matter is not as clear-cut as this whirlwind tour suggests.

In some cases, such as the Dutch Yukos decision, policy considerations play a role, in particular the desire to consider favourably a putative agreement to arbitrate. Other decisions, however, while endorsing the concept of de novo review (such as the Singaporean decision) may or may not necessarily conduct the same depth of review or conduct such review in the same way.

Moreover, a feature of all the decisions is the sometimes cryptic or offhand reference to systemic limitations that may serve to mitigate the supposedly full review. These limitations require not only an understanding of arbitration law, but much more so an understanding of the rules of evidence and civil procedure applicable in the courts hearing the request for annulment proceedings. For example, while the English GPF decision confirms the right to submit arguments, the right to submit new evidence is generally subject to permission and the discretion of the court. The Swiss Recofi decision refers to the requirement to show exceptional circumstances and refers to the framework of the civil law appeal procedure, while the Dutch Yukos case reads like a manual of cassation procedure, including a treatise on the nature of foreign law being neither fact nor law.

This leads us back to Julian Lew, who started his arbitration career with a magnificent treatise on the applicable law in international commercial arbitration. In his doctoral thesis, Julian addressed the practice of arbitrators and parties in determining the applicable law. This research was conducted on the basis of awards, not merely court decisions. In his thesis, he explores and advocates party autonomy in arbitration.

The overview of court decisions in this contribution demonstrates that arbitrator autonomy is not unlimited, at least not in the sense that arbitrators are allowed to be the final arbiter of their jurisdiction. Equally, however, the extent of court review of the jurisdiction of the tribunal is not without limit either but rather is carefully balanced with due process considerations. I suggest that in principle, this is entirely understandable and in fact desirable. Arbitrators are no Baron Münchhausen, who was able to pull himself - and his horse - out of a swamp by his own hair and equally, court proceedings should not always provide parties with a second bite at the cherry.

More problematic is that perhaps inevitably, while there is a general consensus regarding de novo review (at least superficially), the application of such concept is not uniform and leads to divergence across, and within jurisdictions, thereby exemplifying the need to consult national law. Nonetheless, we should take to heart the considerations of the Ontario Divisional Court of the Ontario Superior Court of Justice in Luxtona, which referred to the Model Law's encouragement of uniformity.

CHAPTER 33

The Legal Fiction of the Seat of the International Arbitration

Eduardo Silva Romero

Professor Julian Lew. Professor Julian Lew has animated many colloquia within the framework of the alliance between Queen Mary University and the ICC Institute of World Business Law. Those colloquia have focused on many topics, including basic concepts of international arbitration, such as the curious 'legal fiction' of the 'seat of the arbitration'.

The 'juridical' seat of the English Arbitration Act. Section 3 of the English Arbitration Act, for example, expressly recognizes that the seat of the arbitration at the international level is a legal fiction:

> The seat of the arbitration. In this Part 'the seat of the arbitration' means the juridical seat of the arbitration designated – (a) by the parties to the arbitration agreement, or (b) by any arbitral or other institution or person vested by the parties with powers in that regard, or (c) by the arbitral tribunal if so authorised by the parties, or determined, in the absence of any such designation, having regard to the parties' agreement and all the relevant circumstances.

The word 'juridical' in the text above makes indeed clear that the seat of the arbitration refers to a 'legal link' between the specific international arbitration and the law of a State, and not to any geographical location; in this sense, the word 'seat' in 'seat of the arbitration' is, at best, a metaphor. This conclusion is corroborated by the universally adopted provisions in arbitration laws and rules pursuant to which (i) the tribunal may deliberate at any location it deems convenient, and (ii) hearings may be held at a place different from and more convenient than the seat of the arbitration.

The legal effects of the juridical seat. It is today common ground that the legal effects of the juridical link between a specific arbitration and the law of a State are, in the end, the following two: first, the seat of the arbitration determines the law on international arbitration, including its mandatory provisions, such as the due process of law, applicable to the specific international arbitration; and, second, the court of law competent to decide upon any setting aside action against the arbitral award is the competent court of law of the seat of the arbitration. It is therefore clear that the legal effects arising out of the seat of the arbitration do not have a direct link with a geographical location but, rather, with a legal system.

Several questions. The propositions above prompt several questions: how should we understand the notion of legal fiction in the circumstances? Is the legal fiction of the seat of the arbitration necessary in the language of international arbitration? Has the legal fiction of the seat of the arbitration been abused? What does the fact that the language of international arbitration contains several legal fictions tell us about international arbitration and, perhaps more generally, about the law? We shall address these questions in turn.

Confusion surrounding the notion of legal fiction. First, we must address the very notion of legal fiction, which, as we will see, has its weaknesses. This notion is defined in multiple ways.[1] It tends to be confused with the notions of legal presumption, legal metaphor, or even analogy.[2] We believe this confusion to be a result of the fact that the origin and functions of legal fictions are poorly understood, as they are rarely analysed, and, even then, often only fleetingly.[3] It is true that, from the perspective of a predominant pragmatism, the study of legal fictions would doubtless be dismissed as a mere pastime without much practical relevance. *Yet, the fact that they exist in the legal language shows us something fundamental about the nature of law.*

Definition of legal fiction. Although there are numerous definitions of legal fiction, especially in the English language literature on jurisprudence,[4] we must logically adopt one of them. For present purposes, therefore, legal fiction will be understood as 'an assumption that something is true even if it may be untrue, made especially in judicial [legal] reasoning to alter how a legal rule operates'.[5] Save for a few minor differences, this definition matches that proposed by Henri Duméril in the nineteenth century. According to Duméril, 'in relation to law, fiction is understood broadly as the supposition, contrary to reality, of a fact or an attribute with the intention of producing certain legal effects'.[6] These definitions explain two corollaries which are essential to understanding the legal fiction both as a concept and as a technique.

As if. (i) First of all, legal fictions assume that a thing is real or an idea true even if they are not. Several legal theorists thus argue that legal fictions operate 'as if' they

1. Cf., for instance, M. Del Mar and W. Twining, eds, *Legal Fictions in Theory and Practice*, Springer, 2015.
2. Cf., for instance, A.-J. Arnaud, ed., *Dictionnaire encyclopédique de théorie et de sociologie du droit*, LGDJ, 1993, second edition, pp. 259-261; Cf. also Ch. Perelman and P. Foriers, eds, *Les présomptions et les fictions en droit*, Bruylant, 1974.
3. Cf., for instance, Ch. Perelman and P. Foriers, *supra* n. 2; A.-B. Caire, ed., *Les fictions en droit – Les artifices du droit : les fictions*, LGDJ, 2015; M. Del Mar and W. Twining, *supra* n. 1; and F.-X. Roux-Demare and M.-Ch. Dizès, eds, *Les fictions du droit*, Institut Universitaire de Varenne, 2018.
4. Cf., for instance, M. Del Mar et W. Twining, *supra* n. 1.
5. B.A. Garner, ed., *Black's Law Dictionary*, West Group, 1999, 7th edition, p. 904.
6. H. Duméril, *Les Fictions juridiques*, extract from Revue générale du droit, Hachette Livre BnF, 1882, p. 5.

were real or true.[7] In other words, the expression 'as if' clearly reveals the nature of legal fictions: they pretend to be something that, in truth and in reality, they are not.

The legal fiction of the autonomy of the arbitration agreement. This first corollary of the definition of legal fiction can be illustrated by an initial example taken from the language of arbitration law. It is the rule referred to as the autonomy or separability of the arbitration agreement.[8] Legal practice, on the one hand, shows that arbitration agreements, especially when in the form of an arbitration clause concluded before a dispute arises, are negotiated and accepted at the same time as the other clauses in what is often referred to as the main contract. As the parties sign only once, the reality thus indicates that the contract forms a single unit. The language of arbitration law, on the other hand, states that 'the arbitration agreement is independent of the contract to which it relates. It is not affected by the latter's unenforceability'.[9] In other words, the language of arbitration law treats the arbitration agreement 'as if' it were independent of the main contract.

The legal fiction of the seat of the arbitration. The seat of the arbitration, in turn, plays out as if the specific international arbitration were located in a specific geographical location. The word seat inevitably links the specific international arbitration with a space. Its ultimate aim, however, is to create a juridical link between a specific international arbitration and a State's legal system.

The function of legal fictions. (ii) The insertion of legal fictions in legal language is never done on a whim. There is always an underlying purpose, be it the interpretation of an existing rule of law or the creation of a new rule of law.

Legal fiction as a tool for interpreting an existing rule of law. In the words of the definition adopted above, the function of legal fiction is 'to alter how a legal rule operates'.[10] The function of a legal fiction could therefore be to interpret a rule of law by broadening its scope, for example. The praetorian law of Ancient Rome contained many legal fictions of this kind.[11] In English law, a very telling example is found in the case *Mostyn v. Fabrigas*:

> Fabrigas, a resident of the Mediterranean island of Minorca then occupied and controlled by England, was imprisoned by Mostyn, at the time the governor of the island. Because no suit could be brought against Mostyn in Minorca without the approval of the governor, and because the governor was the defendant in the very lawsuit Fabrigas wished to pursue, Fabrigas sued instead in the Court of Common Pleas in London for trespass and false imprisonment, and proceeded to win a jury verdict of 3 000 £. On appeal, Mostyn claimed, correctly, that the trial court had been granted jurisdiction only in cases brought by residents of London, but Lord Mansfield, recognizing that denying jurisdiction here would leave someone who was plainly wronged without a legal remedy, concluded that Minorca was part of

7. Cf., for instance, H. Kelsen, *On the Theory of Juridic Fictions. With Special Consideration on Vaihinger's Philosophy of the As-If*, in: M. Del Mar and W. Twining, eds, *supra* n. 1, pp. 3 et seq.
8. We will use in this text the expression 'autonomy of the arbitration agreement'.
9. Article 1447 of the French Code of Civil Procedure.
10. Cf. *supra*, para. 5.
11. Cf., for instance, H. Duméril, *supra* n. 6, p. 5: '*[...] Quiconque a étudié, fût-ce d'une manière superficielle, la législation romaine, connaît le rôle considérable qu'y ont joué les fictions, surtout pendant la période du système formulaire [...]*'.

> London for purposes of this action. That conclusion was plainly false and equally plainly produced a just result, and thus Mostyn v. Fabrigas represents the paradigmatic example of using a fiction to achieve what might in earlier days have been done through the vehicle of equity.[12]

The appeal court's holding that, for the purposes of the action brought in this case, Minorca was part of London is noteworthy enough, but even more so is the use of legal fictions to avoid a denial of justice.

Interpretative legal fictions in investment arbitration. We believe that the greatest number of legal fictions in the language of arbitration law that interpret an existing legal rule are to be found in investment arbitration. Excellent examples are the legal fictions characterizing the notion of investment as provided in bilateral treaties on the promotion and protection of investments; the treatment of companies bearing the nationality of the State where the investment takes place 'as if' they were foreign companies; and the distinction drawn between contract claims and treaty claims. From there, it is but a short step to concluding that the surprising abundance of legal fictions in the language of investment arbitration is at the heart of the crisis that this system of dispute resolution is undergoing.

Legal fiction as a tool for creating new rules of law. The legal fictions on which international commercial arbitration, on the other hand, is based are those that have as a corollary the creation of new legal rules. This is well illustrated by the French legal fiction of the arbitral legal order and the corollary principle of the validity of the arbitration agreement. The rule of the autonomy of the arbitration agreement is also helpful in clarifying the function of this category of legal fictions. In the latter case, the legal fiction serves as a means of empowering the arbitral tribunal to determine any dispute over the existence, validity or scope of the so-called main contract.

The seat of the arbitration, an unnecessary legal fiction. *Second*, it appears that the legal fiction of the seat of the arbitration is, in the end, not necessary. The use of the word seat in that expression is misleading. It would, as a consequence, be clearer to refer to the link between any specific international arbitration and a State's legal system.

The French 'arbitral legal order'. The notion of the seat of the arbitration is even less necessary within French international arbitration law, which is based on the theory of the 'arbitral legal order'. This foundational theory is complex in the sense that it is based on many premises and may have several corollaries.

The implicit premises of the arbitral legal order. The three premises of the theory of the arbitral legal order are these:

(1) there would exist a society of international merchants which, to lend credence to its existence, some authors call the '*societas mercatorum*', where its members trade and conduct business; it is interesting to note that some

12. F. Schauer, *Legal Fictions Revisited*, in: M. Del Mar and W. Twining, eds, *supra* n. 1, p. 122.

investment arbitral decisions and awards refer to the existence of a 'community of investors and States hosting investments',[13] which is not without resemblance to the idea of the *societas mercatorum*;

(2) it is then added that '*ubi societas, ibi ius*' (any society must have its law) and that the law applicable in the *societas mercatorum* is the '*lex mercatoria*'; and

(3) all societies must have a 'natural judge'; the natural judges of the *societas mercatorum* being international arbitrators.

The premises of the arbitral legal order are legal fictions. These very attractive premises (especially those formulated in Latin) are legal fictions (if not 'legal myths'):

- International merchants are not organized in a society (neither are host States or investors for that matter); in other words, the notion of the arbitral legal order operates *as if* international merchants interacted in a society - the *societas mercatorum* is a legal fiction;
- The *lex mercatoria* is, in turn, an invention of some clever professors that has not been universally recognized as a legal order; as a consequence, this premise operates *as if* (a) there were a *societas mercatorum*, and (b) such a society had a legal order, that is, the *lex mercatoria*[14] - the *lex mercatoria* is yet another legal fiction; and
- It is also fictional to hold that international arbitrators are the natural judges of the *societas mercatorum*. In fact, international arbitration does not apply automatically to disputes arising out of international commerce and investment; rather, the participants in international commerce and investment have by law or treaty a choice - when drafting the dispute resolution clause of an international contract or choosing to rely on a bilateral investment treaty - of the dispute resolution forum before which they want to submit potential disputes. Conversely, State judges are natural judges because their jurisdiction applies automatically, that is, by operation of the law, to disputes arising within the territory of their State. As a result, the idea that international arbitrators are somewhere (*societas mercatorum*) natural judges is at best used as a metaphor in the circumstances (*as if*).

13. Cf., for instance, *Burlington Resources Inc. v. Republic of* Ecuador, ICSID Case No. ARB/08/5, Decision on Liability, 14 December 2012, para. 187 ('As stated in the Decision on Jurisdiction, the Tribunal considers that it is not bound by previous decisions. Nevertheless, the majority considers that it must pay due regard to earlier decisions of international courts and tribunals. It believes that, subject to compelling contrary grounds, it has a duty to adopt solutions established in a series of consistent cases. It further believes that, subject to the specifics of a given treaty and of the circumstances of the actual case, it has a duty to seek to contribute to the harmonious development of investment law, and thereby to meet the legitimate expectations of the community of States and investors towards the certainty of the rule of law. Arbitrator Stern does not analyze the arbitrator's role in the same manner, as she considers it her duty to decide each case on its own merits, independently of any apparent jurisprudential trend').

14. Cf., for instance, B. Goldman, 'Frontières du droit et "lex mercatoria"', in: *Archives de Philosophie du Droit, Le droit subjectif en question*, Paris: Sirey, 1964, pp. 177 et seq.

The arbitral legal order, again. These three legal fictions form in any event the basis for the existence of an arbitral legal order. To summarize this idea, one can argue that not only would the *societas mercatorum* have its own material or substantive law, the *lex mercatoria*, but it would also have its natural judges, the international arbitrators, who in turn would be supported by their own legal order, independent of any national legal order, which would be the so-called (international) arbitral legal order. In this sense, the validity (legal force) of international arbitration would come from the arbitral legal order, and it would not be necessary to reflect in terms of the seat of the arbitration to link any specific international arbitration to a State's (national) legal order. The most famous French decision on the notion of arbitral legal order is perhaps the *Putrabali* Decision. In that decision, the French *Cour de Cassation* held that: '[...] *la sentence internationale, qui n'est rattachée à aucun ordre juridique étatique, est une décision de justice internationale* [...]'.[15] Even if this holding does not refer explicitly to the arbitral legal order, its characterization of an international award as a 'decision of international justice' unequivocally implies it.

The abuse of the notion of seat of the international arbitration. Third, the notion of seat of the arbitration has particularly been abused in those cases in which one of the parties argues that, because the seat of the arbitration has been fixed in a given State, the hearings shall be held in such State.

A false argument. The proposition according to which there would be a 'presumption' that hearings should be held at the seat of the arbitration has even often been advanced. Such a position, however, runs against the very nature of the seat of the arbitration as a legal fiction, that is, as a juridical link between a specific international arbitration and a State's legal system. In short, such an argument contradicts the purpose of the seat of the arbitration as a legal fiction. The purpose of the seat of the arbitration is not to fix the place of hearings in a particular city. Its aim is, rather, to define the legal system from which international arbitration derives its legitimacy, that is to say the law providing for its binding nature.

A clear corroboration. It is because of the clear fictitious nature of the seat of the arbitration that arbitration legislations and rules all provide for (i) arbitral tribunals to be allowed to deliberate at any location, and (ii) arbitral tribunals and parties to hold hearings at any convenient place.

A conclusion. Lastly, we cannot but notice that the language of international arbitration is full of surprises. There is a trend in that language to rely on legal fictions in the same way we may rely on shortcuts to arrive faster to a destination. Such a technique, however, may lead to misunderstandings if those who play the arbitration language-game forget what the purpose of the specific legal fiction, such as the one of the seat of the arbitration, really is. Why does the legal mind resort so often to legal fictions? We might try various responses. Suffice it to say, to close, that, in the end, the use of expressions such as the seat of the arbitration shows us the true (and mysterious) nature of the law.

---

15. Civ. 1ere, 29 June 2007, *Sté PT Putrabali Adyamula c/ Sté Rena Holding*, in: I. Fadlallah and D. Hascher, *supra*, p. 325.

G Third Party Funders

CHAPTER 34
The Dynamic Role of Third-Party Funders in International Arbitration

Crina Baltag

In *Greenland Minerals v. Greenland and Denmark,*[1] an arbitration arising out of an exploration licence for a rare earths project in southern Greenland, claimant announced on 5 July 2022 that a funding agreement has been entered into with Woolridge Investment LLC, a wholly owned subsidiary of Burford Capital, to fully fund the arbitration against Greenland and Denmark. As stated in Greenland Minerals' announcement, the funding arrangement 'enables the Company to preserve its cash reserves as it seeks other investments in the technology metals sector'.[2]

Third-party funding (TPF) has become a common feature of international arbitration, being secured not only by impecunious parties, but also, as Greenland Minerals' announcement indicates, by fully solvent companies, in order to preserve their financial resources and to ensure that their investment plans continue to be implemented during the arbitration proceedings. Furthermore, TPF is usually on a non-recourse basis, which offers superior advantage compared to any other form of loan. As to the arbitration proceedings, it is now undisputed that the funded party should disclose the TPF to the opposing party and to the arbitral tribunal, as soon as possible.[3] In addition to disclosure, the requests for security for costs in arbitrations involving third-party funders have increased in commercial and investment arbitrations in the past years.[4] These developments have triggered appropriate responses: first, most of the arbitration rules, including the 2022 ICSID Arbitration Rules, now

1. *Greenland Minerals v. Greenland and Denmark,* UNCITRAL (contract based), Request for Arbitration of 22 March 2012.
2. Greenland Minerals LTD, *Company Announcement of 5 July 2022,* https://wcsecure.weblink.com.au/clients/ggg/v2/headline.aspx?headlineid=61098424 (last visited, 23 July 2022).
3. *See* more recently, the 2022 ICSID Arbitration Rules, entered into force on 1 July 2022, Rule 12.
4. *See* ICSID, *Proposals for Amendment of the ICSID Rules – Working Paper #1,* 3 August 2018, paras 265-266.

include specific provisions on disclosure of TPF and on security for costs;[5] and, second, some of the risks raised by the presence of third-party funders in arbitrations are now addressed by new financial and insurance products, such as the after-event-insurance (ATE) for adverse costs, and which are usually included in the TPF.

Nonetheless, TPF is still a territory to be explored.[6] Three main issues are now emerging and still to be properly addressed by arbitral tribunals and courts: (1) TPF and the legal standing of the funder in international arbitration; (2) TPF and the recovery of the funding costs in the arbitration proceedings; and (3) the increasing arbitration and litigation proceedings arising out of TPF agreements. These three issues reflect the dynamic role of third-party funders in international arbitration and mainly arise out of the fact that TPF is a relatively new concept in international arbitration. These concerns are also generated by and reflected in the difficulty to agree on a generally accepted definition of TPF. For example, Article 8.1 of CETA, defines TPF as 'any funding', 'either through a donation or grant, or in return for remuneration dependent on the outcome of the dispute', 'provided by a natural or legal person who is not a disputing party', thus reflecting both 'for-profit' and 'not-for-profit' funding,[7] while Singapore Civil Law (Amendment) Bill No. 38 of 2016 includes in the meaning of TPF only the 'for-profit' funding.[8]

§34.01 THIRD PARTY FUNDERS AND THE REAL PARTY IN THE ARBITRATION PROCEEDINGS

One of the emerging issues concerning TPF is the status of the funder in the arbitration proceedings. Given the financial interest of the third-party funder in the arbitration, as

---

5. 2022 ICSID Arbitration Rules, Rule 53.
6. Some of the concerns with TPF include the lack of national regulations on two important aspects: (i) the regulation of TPF as an industry, and (ii) the regulation of the relationship between TPF and litigation/arbitration (except for few jurisdictions, such as Hong Kong, regulations introduced in 2019, and Singapore, in 2017). Indeed, when it comes to arbitration rules – 2022 ICSID Arbitration Rules being one recent example – and treaties – for example, 8.26 of the EU-Canada Comprehensive Economic and Trade Agreement (CETA) – TPF is regulated in its main aspects, which mainly concern issues pertaining to conflicts and disclosure. For a detailed commentary of Article 8.26 of CETA, *see* Crina Baltag, *Article 8.26 Third Party Funding*, in Marc Bungenberg and August Reinisch (eds), *CETA Investment Law: Article-by-Article Commentary* (Bloomsbury Publishing, 2022), pp. 576-591.
7. Article 8.1 of CETA:

> Third party funding means any funding provided by a natural or legal person who is not a disputing party but who enters into an agreement with a disputing party in order to finance part or all of the cost of the proceedings either through a donation or grant, or in return for remuneration dependent on the outcome of the dispute.

8. Singapore Civil Law (Amendment) Bill No. 38/2016, Article 5B(10):

> 'ThirdParty Funder' means a person who carries on the business of funding all or part of the costs of dispute resolution proceedings to which the person is not a party;
>
> 'thirdparty funding contract' means a contract or agreement by a party or potential party to dispute resolution proceedings with a ThirdParty Funder for the funding of all or part of the costs of the proceedings in return for a share or other interest in the proceeds or potential proceeds of the proceedings to which the party or potential party may become entitled.

well as the involvement in the conduct of the proceedings – by approving the strategy of the arbitration, the submissions of the funded party in the arbitration etc. – it is claimed that funders are the 'real parties' in the arbitration. This allegation is also fuelled by the fact that TPF agreements are rarely disclosed in the arbitration proceedings, thus not allowing the tribunal and the opposing party to have a full understanding of the relationship between the funder and the funded party. Until now, no arbitral tribunal has accepted the plea that funders are the 'real parties' in the arbitration. Furthermore, scholarship is in agreement that '[a]lthough the funder clearly has an economic interest in the outcome of the dispute, it is not a party to the proceedings'.[9]

In *Teinver v. Argentina*,[10] the respondent State submitted that the third-party funder of the claimants, Burford Capital, was 'the real party interested in this arbitration', as it would be the one benefiting in the case of an award against Argentina.[11] Furthermore, as explained by the respondent, if the funder is the real party in this arbitration, it 'does not meet the basic jurisdictional requirements under the ICSID Convention': it is neither an investor in Argentina, nor is it a company organized in Spain that could invoke the treaty relied upon by the claimants.[12] In sum, as advanced by the respondent, allowing the third-party funder to proceed with this arbitration would 'bypass the limits of Argentina's and Spain's consent to arbitral jurisdiction'.[13] The claimants rebutted these allegations by explaining that the third-party funder is not a party to the arbitration, and that the claimants did not sell or transfer the claim to Burford.[14] The claimants further pointed out that there is a general acceptance by arbitral tribunals, as also pointed out by the respondent, that TPF is not illegitimate, unlawful or inappropriate.[15] The arbitral tribunal took a cautious approach to the issue and relied on the fact that the legal standing must be determined at the date of the filing of the request for arbitration.[16] As the funding agreement with Burford was dated post the filing, the tribunal explained, the respondent's objection must be rejected.[17]

More recently, in *Sehil v. Turkmenistan*,[18] the arbitral tribunal chaired by Professor Julian Lew rejected the respondent's submission that the real party in the

9. Omar Puertas Álvarez et al., *Two's a Crowd, Three's a Party: The Coming of Age of Third-Party Funding in International Arbitration*, 2021 Spain Arbitration Review | Revista del Club Español del Arbitraje 40, 25-41, p. 27. *See also*, John Beechey, *The Pandora's Box of Third-Party Funding: Some Practical Suggestions for Arbitrators in Light of Recent Developments*, in Jean Engelmayer Kalicki and Mohamed Abdel Raouf (eds), *Evolution and Adaptation: The Future of International Arbitration*, ICCA Congress Series, Volume 20 (Kluwer Law International; 2019), 558-586, p. 578.
10. *Teinver S.A., Transportes de Cercanías S.A. and Autobuses Urbanos del Sur S.A. v. The Argentine Republic*, ICSID Case No. ARB/09/1, Decision on Jurisdiction of 21 December 2012.
11. *Teinver v. Argentina*, Decision on Jurisdiction, para. 245.
12. *Ibid.*, para. 246.
13. *Ibid.*
14. *Teinver v. Argentina*, Decision on Jurisdiction, para. 254.
15. *Ibid.*
16. *Ibid.*, para. 256.
17. *Ibid.*, para. 259.
18. *Muhammet Çap & Sehil Insaat Endustri ve Ticaret Ltd. Sti. v. Turkmenistan*, ICSID Case No. ARB/12/6, Award of 4 May 2021.

arbitration is the claimants' third-party funder, La Française.[19] The respondent submitted to the tribunal that there was an assignment of rights by the claimants by virtue of the existence of the TPF, which deprives the tribunal of its jurisdiction.[20] The respondent also explained that on several occasions during the course of the arbitration it sought information from the claimants concerning the existence and name of the third-party funder and to receive a copy of the funding agreement, in order to determine whether the claimants remained the owners of the claims.[21] The claimants refused to provide a copy of the funding agreement, which, as the respondent submitted, has prompted the tribunal to order the claimants to provide the funding agreement in the context of the respondent's request for security for costs.[22] The claimants declined to provide the funding agreement on the basis that it is 'a privileged document that contains not only confidential information, notably regarding the percentages of the success fee to be paid to the fund, and indirect assessment of the case, but also affects elements of claimant's legal strategy regarding the proceeding, in particular in the event of settlement negotiations'.[23] However, the claimants provided an affidavit from La Française detailing the provisions of the Funding Agreement 'directly relevant to the terms and conditions of (i) the costs borne by La Française and (ii) the circumstances under which the Fund can withdraw from the funding arrangement'.[24] In a second affidavit from La Française, it was stated that the funding agreement 'does not provide for any direct, indirect or de facto assignment of the claim, nor does it create joint ownership of the claim, or any part of the claim by the Fund and Claimants, nor a common legal interest in the claim, or any part of the claim between the Fund and Claimants'.[25] In dismissing the respondent's claim that the real party in the arbitration is the third-party funder, the tribunal held that the respondent has presented no evidence to show or even suggest that the claimants are no longer the proper owners of the claims and that they have been replaced by the third-party funder.[26]

§34.02 TPF COSTS AND ARBITRATION

The presence of TPF in arbitration proceedings has also triggered a new development in the way tribunals approach the costs of arbitration. It is presented that arbitral tribunals are ready to accept the recovery of the costs with TPF, given the permissive language of the arbitration laws and rules, as well as the discretion of the tribunals.[27]

19. *Sehil v. Turkmenistan*, Award, para. 692.
20. *Ibid.*, para. 683.
21. *Ibid.*, para. 685.
22. *Ibid.*, para. 686.
23. *Ibid.*
24. *Ibid.*, para. 687.
25. *Ibid.*, para. 689.
26. *Ibid.*, para. 691.
27. It appears to be undisputed that the parties, even funded, may recover the costs of the arbitration, not including the costs of the funding. For example, the Stockholm District Court in *Ascom Group S. A. et al. v. The Republic of Kazakhstan*, Case No. T 10498-17, Final Decision of

At the post-award stage, courts have been confronted with the challenge of arbitral tribunals' decisions awarding the costs with TPF. English courts, have recently accepted that the costs with TPF are recoverable in the arbitration proceedings.[28]

In *Essar v. Norscot,*[29] the English High Court held that the sole arbitrator in the underlying ICC International Court of Arbitration - ICC arbitration has proceeded correctly in retaining that under the English Arbitration Act 1996 and the ICC Arbitration Rules, the reference to 'legal or other costs of the parties' is meant to include 'other costs which relate to the arbitration proceedings'.[30] As such, the court explained that 'where a party to an arbitration is funding it by obtaining specific litigation funding which is now available in a variety of forms, so as to enable him to specifically enforce his legal rights, it is very hard to see how that is excluded for all purposes from the expression "other costs"'.[31] Furthermore, the Court rejected claimant's contention that the expression 'other costs' must be construed to mean that these are costs analogous to legal costs, explaining that '[t]here are legal costs of the arbitration and there are other costs of the arbitration'.[32] As such, in the court's opinion, '[t]he real limiting factor ... is the functional one. Do the costs relate to the arbitration and are they for the purposes of it?'[33] The court also gave weight to the ICC Commission Report of 2015 on *Decisions on Costs in International Arbitration,*[34] indicating that the observations made in the report are 'highly pertinent here'.[35] Among these observations, the report explains that '[u]sually, the third-party funder will require payment of an uplift or success fee. ... As a tribunal only needs to satisfy itself that a cost was incurred specifically to pursue the arbitration, has been paid or is payable, and was reasonable, it is feasible that in certain circumstances the cost of

24 January 2018 held that the fact that a party has obtained funding for the arbitration, does not mean that the party has not incurred costs in the arbitration. *See also, Ioannis Kardassopoulos v. Georgia*, ICSID Case No. ARB/05/18, and *Ron Fuchs v. Georgia*, ICSID Case No. ARB/07/15, Award(s) (3 March 2010), para. 686, *RSM Production Corporation v. Saint Lucia*, ICSID Case No. ARB/12/10, Order of the Committee Discontinuing the Proceeding and Decision on Costs (28 April 2011), paras 68, *ATA Construction, Industrial and Trading Company v. The Hashemite Kingdom of Jordan*, ICSID Case No. ARB/08/2, Order Taking Note of The Discontinuance of the Proceeding (11 July 2011), para. 34 etc.

28. For a discussion on whether a similar conclusion would be reached under the US Federal Arbitration Act, *see* John Fellas, *Third-Party Funding: The Award of Costs and Security for Costs*, in Sherlin Tung, Fabricio Fortese and Crina Baltag (eds), *Finances in International Arbitration: Liber Amicorum Patricia Shaughnessy* (2019), 107 (110 ff.).
29. *Essar Oilfields Services Ltd v. Norscot Rig Management Pvt Ltd* [2016] EWHC 2361 (Comm) (15 September 2016).
30. *Essar v. Norscot*, para. 54. In deciding on the recovery of the costs with TPF, the sole arbitrator also took into consideration the conduct of Essar in triggering the funding of Norscot: 'Norscot had no alternative, but was forced to enter into the litigation funding to the full cost of 300 per cent of the sum advanced by the funder or 35 per cent of the sum recovered, whichever was the higher' (*Essar v. Norscot*, paras 21-27).
31. *Ibid.*, para. 54.
32. *Ibid.*, para. 58.
33. *Ibid.*
34. Published in the ICC Dispute Resolution Bulletin 2015, issue 2. The Task Force behind the Report was co-chaired by Professor Julian Lew, Bernard Hanotiau, Wendy Miles, and Philippe Cavalieros.
35. *Essar v. Norscot*, para. 67.

capital, e.g. bank borrowing specifically for the costs of the arbitration or loss of use of the funds, may be recoverable'.[36]

In a subsequent case, *TFM v. KCS*,[37] the claimant brought a challenge under section 68 of the English Arbitration Act 1996 to an ICC arbitral award by which Tenke Fungurume Mining SA - TFM, among others, was ordered to pay KCS more than USD 1 million in costs relating to the litigation funding agreement.[38] The arbitral tribunal, relying on *Essar v. Norscot*, held that as a matter of English law and under the ICC Arbitration Rules, parties can recover the costs with TPF as 'other costs',[39] and, as such, it only needs to determine whether such costs are 'reasonable'.[40] Although the circumstances of *TFM v. KCS* were slightly different than in *Essar v.* Norscot, in particular because the funding of KCS was obtained from a related company, the English High Court found no reason to depart from the findings in *Essar v. Norscot*.[41]

§34.03 NEW TYPES OF CLAIMS RELATED TO TPF AGREEMENTS

Reflecting the evolution of TPF, the latest developments also show a surge in the disputes arising out of funding agreements.

For example, in *Trinh Vinh Binh v. King and Spalding LLP et al.*,[42] the US District Court for the Southern District of Texas decided that, pursuant to the funding agreement, an arbitral tribunal should decide the dispute between an investor and his former counsel concerning the distribution of funds paid by Vietnam to Trinh Vinh Binh and Binh Chau, pursuant to the arbitral award of 10 April 2019.[43] In 2021, Mr Trinh Vinh Binh commenced court proceedings against King & Spalding before the Texas courts, for legal malpractice. Mr Binh argued that King & Spalding, his counsel in the underlying arbitration, had colluded with the third-party funder, Burford Capital, to obtain overpayment for their services.[44]

In another case, the third-party funder, Buttonwood Legal Capital, has filed suit against Mr Mohamed Abdel Raouf Bahgat before UK courts for the share of the

36. *Ibid.*, para. 66 and ICC Report, para. 92.
37. *Tenke Fungurume Mining SA v. Katanga Contracting Services SAS* [2021] EWHC 3301 (Comm) (7 December 2021).
38. *TFM v. KCS*, paras 1 and 31.
39. *Ibid.*, para 75.
40. *Ibid.*, para. 74.
41. *Ibid.*, para. 94.
42. *Trinh Vinh Binh v. King and Spalding LLP et al.*, US District Court for the Southern District of Texas, Case No. 4:21-CV-02234, Order of 10 January 2022. *See also*, Lisa Bohmer, *US court grants King & Spalding's motion to compel arbitration of dispute over distribution of funds from treaty award against Vietnam*, IAReporter, 12 January 2022.
43. *Trinh Vinh Binh and Binh Chau JSC v. Viet Nam (II)*, PCA Case No. 2015-23, Award of 10 April 2019.
44. *Trinh Vinh Binh v. King & Spalding, Reginald R. Smith and Craig S. Miles*, US District Court of Harris County, Texas, Case No. 2021-35240, Plaintiff's Original Petition of 6 November 2021. *See also*, Lisa Bohmer, *After Vietnam pays hefty UNCITRAL BIT award, investor-claimant files suit against his lawyers accusing them of collusion with third-party funder to take greater share of winnings*, IAReporter, 15 June 2021.

proceeds from the award owed under the funding agreement.[45] In the underlying arbitration, Mr Bahgat was awarded over USD 43.77 million and compound interest to it,[46] which was later partially recovered by way of a post-award settlement with Egypt.[47]

The past years have seen a meteoric evolution of the TPF industry in international arbitration. Equally rapid was the reaction of the arbitration institutions in adapting their rules to reflect the dynamic role of third-party funders. TPF will continue to grow and refine its products in order to satisfy not only the funded parties, but also the rules prescribed by national legislations and arbitration rules. Some issues will require closer consideration in the imminent future, reflecting the position of TPF in international arbitration: (1) the status of the third-party funder in the arbitration proceedings: should limitations be enforced on the involvement of the funder in the arbitration? Should the party disclose the funding agreement so that any doubt as to any assignment of claims to the funder be eliminated?; (2) the recovery of the cost with TPF: should the losing party pay for the costs of funding? If so, would this be the general rule, or only the exception when the impecuniosity of the funded party is caused by the losing party?; and (3) implications of new claims arising out of TPF agreements: are these set to cast doubt on the funding arrangement? Or are these simply contractual disputes in the normal course of the funding process? On this note, Professor Julian Lew's contribution to the topic of TPF and to most of the issues addressed here is essential in advancing the proper solutions to the concerns raised. In particular, the tribunal in *Sehil v. Turkmenistan*, chaired by Professor Julian Lew, was the first investment arbitration tribunal to order the disclosure of a funding agreement.[48]

45. *See Buttonwood Legal Capital Limited v. Mr Mohamed Abdel Raouf Bahgat*, High Court of England and Wales, Particulars of Claim of 11 May 2022. *See also*, Damien Charlotin, *Third-party funder turns to UK courts, seeking payment of proceeds from treaty award against Egypt*, IAReporter, 20 May 2022.
46. *Mohamed Abdel Raouf Bahgat v. Egypt*, PCA Case No. 2012-07, Final Award of 23 December 2019.
47. *Buttonwood Legal Capital Limited v. Mr Mohamed Abdel Raouf Bahgat*, Particulars of Claim, para. 40. The case is particularly interesting as it presents an example of co-funding, Vannin Capital, a third-party funder acquired in 2021 by Fortress Investment Group LLC, being brought to the case at a later stage.
48. *Sehil v. Turkmenistan*, Procedural Order No. 3 of 12 June 2015, para. 13. *See also*, Luke Eric Peterson, *In an apparent first, ICSID tribunal orders claimants to disclose any third-party litigation funders backing their arbitration*, IA Reporter, 16 June 2015.

CHAPTER 35

Third-Party Funding in Investment Arbitration: To Be or Not to Be?

Alice Fremuth-Wolf

I owe my whole career in arbitration to Professor Julian Lew who inspired and challenged me as an LLM student 25 years ago when I had the honour and privilege to sit in his class on arbitration at the School of International Arbitration of Queen Mary University of London which he had founded in 1985. He sparked a fire in me for arbitration back then that is still burning today. His approach was to pose questions, challenge our answers and teach us to be critical, innovative and think outside the box. This was definitely a completely different teaching style that I was used to, especially the fact that there was never the one 'right' answer he was looking for but rather training our ability to think. I am forever thankful that our paths have crossed and I would hereby like to express my sincerest appreciation and congratulations for his birthday.

The topic I have chosen combines my previous career as Secretary General of the Vienna International Arbitral Centre and my current practice as Litigation Funder and pays tribute to Professor Lew's brilliance as arbitrator in commercial and investment arbitration cases.

In the following, I will briefly discuss the provisions on Third-Party Funding (TPF) in the Investment Arbitration Rules of the Vienna International Arbitral Centre (VIAC) and the new ICSID Arbitration Rules and thereafter reflect on the current draft provisions on TPF prepared by the UNCITRAL Secretariat for Working Group III on the Reform of Investor State Arbitration.

§35.01 THE VIAC INVESTMENT ARBITRATION AND MEDIATIONS RULES 2021

One year ago, on 1 July 2021, VIAC's Investment Arbitration Rules 2021 ('Vienna Investment Rules') entered into force. The stand-alone set of arbitral rules are specifically tailored to the resolution of investment disputes involving sovereign parties (States, political subdivisions, State agencies, State-owned enterprises, and international organizations). However, there are no objective requirements as to the nature of the dispute or restrictions as to the parties. The parties are free to qualify a dispute as an investment dispute that they wish to settle under the Vienna Investment Rules. Consent to arbitrate may be expressed in any type of instrument, including a contract, treaty, statute, or other instrument, and may be accepted by the other party by any means, including by simply commencing arbitration under the Vienna Investment Rules.[1]

§35.02 ARTICLE 6 PARAGRAPH 1.11 AND ARTICLE 13A VIAC INVESTMENT RULES ON TPF

TPF is meanwhile an accepted element in commercial arbitration where the main focus of attention is the prevention of conflicts of interest on the part of arbitrators. But also investment arbitration proceedings have seen a steady increase in TPF which is not met with unconditional applause, especially by States. While the issue of impartiality and independence of the decision makers is certainly an issue here as well, the discussion around TPF in investment arbitration has reached another dimension, putting into questions its legitimacy as a whole. As the ICCA Queen Mary Task Force Report on TPF[2] has so aptly formulated:

> In investment arbitration, third-party funding has drawn particular attention, which often extends beyond the existing legal frameworks and decisions in individual cases. Because investment arbitration involves states, it necessarily implicates a range of policy issues more deeply, more regularly, and (in some cases) differently than private commercial disputes. Investment arbitration is, and is expected to be, more transparent than international commercial arbitration and factors that affect the incentives, viability, and scope of investment claims are subject to more intensive scrutiny and to more rigorous assessments of related policy issues.

The VIAC Investment Rules tried to take these concerns into account by providing a balanced solution. Article 6 paragraph 1.11. defines TPF as:

> any agreement entered into with a natural or legal person who is not a party to the proceedings or a party representative (Article 13), to fund or provide any other material support to a party, directly or indirectly financing part or all of the costs of the proceedings either through a donation or a grant, or in exchange for remuneration or reimbursement that is wholly or partially dependent upon the outcome of the proceedings.

1. The most important features have been summarized here: VIAC Rules Revision 2021 Part II: The New VIAC Rules of Investment Arbitration and Mediation - Kluwer Arbitration Blog.
2. ICCA Reports 4_TPF_FINAL for print_26 March_amended 29 March (arbitration-icca.org) at p. 199.

This definition is sufficiently broad to cover any material support *that is dependent on the outcome of the proceedings*, including portfolio funding, non-profit funding as well as after-the-event (ATE) insurance to the extent that premiums are payable only in the event of an award in favour of the insured.

Before-the-event (BTE) insurance, by contrast, is payable before a dispute arises and independent of the outcome of any future arbitration, and thus not covered by this definition. For the same reason, commercial loans are not covered. Funding received from a party's counsel, such as contingency fee arrangements, are likewise not covered since a disclosure of such funding is not necessary to guard against conflicts of interest.

Based on this definition, Article 13a paragraphs 1 and 2 impose an obligation on each party to disclose the existence of any TPF and the identity of the third-party funder in its statement of claim and answer to the statement of claim, respectively. This disclosure requirement continues throughout the arbitration. The purpose of this disclosure obligation is to enable arbitrators to flag any potential conflicts of interest from the outset.

Article 13a contains an additional paragraph 3 (not reflected in VIAC's arbitration rules for commercial disputes) which expressly authorizes the tribunal, *if it deems it necessary*, to order disclosure of (i) 'specific details of the TPF arrangement', and/or (ii) 'the third-party funder's interest in the outcome of the proceedings', and/or (iii) whether the funder 'has committed to undertake adverse costs liability'.

Especially the extension of the disclosure obligation to the litigation funding agreement itself has been heavily criticized[3] for fear of potential disclosure of commercially sensitive information about the funded party and the funder that is not relevant to the dispute. This is a valid concern.

The tribunal's discretionary power under the VIAC Investment Rules to order disclosure is for this reason limited to *specific details* of the funding arrangement. This is not a *carte blanche* for tribunals to order disclosure of the full text of the TPF arrangement. A necessity for the disclosure of certain details (i.e., coverage of adverse costs) might arise for instance, when the tribunal has to decide an application for security for costs or to allocate the costs of the arbitration.[4] The mere existence of a TPF arrangement does, however, *not per* se justify an order for security for costs or the allocation of all costs to a funded party.[5]

§35.03 NEW ICSID AMENDMENTS ON TPF IN RULE 14 AND RULE 53

The amendments to the new ICSID Arbitration Rules have entered into force on 1 July 2022. They also include regulations on TPF, namely in Rule 14 and Rule 53:

Under Rule 14 (1):

3. Can Third-Party Funding Find the Right Place in Investment Arbitration Rules? - Kluwer Arbitration Blog.
4. Cf. *Brekoulakis/Kröll/Riegler* in VIAC Handbook (2019) Excursus to Article 33 mns 66 et seqq.
5. Cf. *Brekoulakis/Kröll/Riegler* in VIAC Handbook (2019) Excursus to Article 33 mns 67 et seqq. and mns 83 et seqq.

> (a) party shall file a written notice disclosing the name and address of any non-party from which the party, directly or indirectly, has received funds for the pursuit or defense of the proceeding through a donation or grant, or in return for remuneration dependent on the outcome of the proceeding ('third-party funding'). If the non-party providing funding is a juridical person, the notice shall include the names of the persons and entities that own and control that juridical person.

The reason for the extension of disclosure to the names of the persons and entities that own and control a funder in paragraph 1 is that several ICSID Member States had expressed concerns that third-party funders were hiding their identities behind complex corporate structures, making it difficult to identify potential conflicts of interest for arbitrators.

In addition, under Rule 14(4) '(t)he Tribunal may order disclosure of further information regarding the funding agreement and the non-party providing funding pursuant to Rule 36(3)'. International Centre for Settlement of Investment Disputes (ICSID) tribunals have the (general) authority under Rule 36(3) to order the disclosure of documents if it is 'relevant in the circumstances'. This might be seen as an open door for tribunals to request details of the funding agreement or the funder's history of cases against the same States. For this reason, the same caveats and considerations should be applied as discussed above for Art 13 a paragraph 3 VIAC Investment Rules.

ICSID has included a detailed rule allowing a tribunal to order any party asserting a claim or counterclaim to provide security for costs. In contrast to the VIAC Investment Rules, Rule 53(4) explicitly mentions the existence of TPF as one of the criterions that should be considered by the tribunal in its assessment. Parties and funders should be prepared and consider arranging for the coverage of adverse costs as part of their funding agreement (by way of an ATE insurance) in order to avoid a security for cost order.

§35.04 UNCITRAL WORKING GROUP III: PROPOSALS FOR REGULATING TPF IN ISDS – THE BEGINNING OR THE END?

What will be the impact of these recent amendments on the ongoing discussion on the reform of Investor-State Dispute Settlement (ISDS) by the UNCITRAL Working Group III where TPF is among the topics currently being considered? In particular, during the deliberations concerns were identified related to the impact of TPF on arbitral proceedings as such and on the ISDS system as a whole.

In May 2021, the UNCITRAL Secretariat has published an initial draft provisions on the regulation of TPF in ISDS, presenting three potential alternatives to regulate TPF in ISDS[6].

6. This Draft has meanwhile been revised in the Report of Working Group III on the work of its forty-third session, Vienna, 5–16 September 2022; to be accessed here: https://documents-dds-ny.un.org/doc/UNDOC/GEN/222/285/3E/PDF/2222853E.pdf?OpenElement.

(1) Total prohibition:

TPF is entirely prohibited in ISDS taking into account the main concern of States that TPF aggravates the structural imbalance in ISDS by increasing the number of ISDS cases and frivolous claims as well as the amount of damages claimed.

(2) Restriction: TPF is permitted but certain types are restricted, differentiating between:

(i) the 'access to justice' model under which TPF is permitted if the funding is necessary for the claimant to bring its claim, particularly when the claimants are micro, small, and medium-sized enterprises;
(ii) the 'sustainable development' model: a claimant is allowed to obtain TPF if its investment meets pre-defined sustainable development requirements of the respondent State; and
(iii) the 'restriction list' model: TPF is generally allowed except for certain prohibited specific types of TPF, such as speculative funding, funding where the amount of the expected return is excessive, or where the funder has already provided funding for several claims against the same respondent State concerning the same measure.

The legal consequences of a party entering into or being provided with TPF that is not permitted would differ depending on the regulation model. For example, the claim may be inadmissible, or the tribunal might lack jurisdiction to consider the case.

(3) No action except for Disclosure:

Following wording for a very broad disclosure obligation was proposed:

(1) The funded party shall disclose to the tribunal and the other disputing parties the following information:
  (a) the name and address of the third-party funder;
  (b) the name and address of the beneficial owner of the third-party funder and any natural or legal person with decision-making authority for or on behalf of the third-party funder; and
  (c) the funding agreement or the terms thereof.
(2) In addition to those set forth in paragraph 1, the tribunal may require the funded party to disclose the following information:
  (a) whether the third-party funder agreed to cover the costs of an adverse cost award;
  (b) the expected return amount of the third-party funder;
  (c) any rights of the third-party funder to control or influence the management of the claim, the proceedings and to terminate the funding arrangement;
  (d) number of cases that the third-party funder has provided funding for claims against the respondent State;

(e) any agreement between the third-party funder and the legal counsel or firm representing the funded party; and
(f) any other information deemed necessary by the tribunal.

Since disclosure might be a prerequisite for obtaining clearance from the tribunal of TPF under the restriction model, this provision has far-reaching consequences.

(4) Comments and concerns

Especially the broad disclosure requirement in the draft proposal is to be seen with a particular concern. A funding agreement is always tailor-made to the specific financial needs of the funded party, containing commercially sensitive information that is very relevant for the funding but not to the dispute. A funding agreement contains not only the pricing model but may reveal the strategy as well as the funder's view of the specific dispute, including tactical assessments such as anticipated costs, procedural milestones, and the envisaged duration of the proceedings. If such information comes into the hands of the tribunal or the counterparty, this may endanger the fairness of the process as a whole.

Many comments have been submitted to this draft[7] among others by International Legal Finance Association (ILFA), the International Legal Finance Association which was founded in September 2020. In its statement ILFA tried to counter the three main arguments raised against TPF in ISDS in general which are alleged increases in (i) the number of frivolous claims; (ii) the number of investor-State arbitration cases, and (iii) the number of cases in which respondent States have been unable to recover their costs. ILFA's counterarguments can be briefly summarized as follows:

Ad i) Increase of frivolous claims through unlimited availability of TPF

Third-party funders do have a very strict due diligence process before agreeing to fund a case and take on only claims with a very high probability of success due to the non-recourse nature of TPF, i.e., in case of loss the funded party does not have to reimburse the funder. Any other approach would not make economic sense. This in itself counters the proposition that non-meritorious claims would increasingly be funded as funders would simply lose all their investment. Quite to the contrary: due to the extensive case assessment on the merits, quantum and procedure performed by funders, TPF can actually lead to more meritorious claims with a more streamlined process and strategy.

Ad ii) Increase of number of investor-State arbitration cases and inflated claims

It is questionable whether the mere increase in cases could be taken as an argument against TPF in investment arbitration. If those cases were based on good-faith assertion of treaty rights, and if they resulted in decisions in favour of investors, the increased numbers of cases should not be a concern – as this is exactly the purpose of investment

7. https://uncitral.un.org/sites/uncitral.un.org/files/media-documents/uncitral/en/compilation_of_comments_tpf_1.pdf.

protection under the respective treaties. Also, the proposition that funded claims are artificially inflated can be countered easily. Third-party funders always perform a commercial 'reality check' on the claim involving experts in financial matters and thus help claimants to have a more realistic view on the value of their claim. So in fact, TPF may help to decrease amounts in dispute.

Ad iii) Increase of number of cases in which respondent States have been unable to recover their costs

There seems to be a common understanding by now that the mere fact of TPF is in and of itself no reason for granting security for costs by tribunals. So, additional factors have to be shown in order to determine that in case of loss, the costs of the opposing party will be not recoverable. An even greater concern of States seems to be that in case of loss, claimants will fail to pay a cost award or simply be unable to do so. The latter is a reasonable concern and needs to be tackled. But it can be done via the existing mechanism of security for costs. In fact, if a funder is involved the chances are much higher that adverse cost awards are being complied with as the adverse cost risk is part of the budget or covered by an ATE-insurance.

§35.05 OUTLOOK: TPF IN ISDS – STATES HAVE TO EMBRACE IT!

I fear that a new 'enemy' has been identified in the form of TPF, which serves to further challenge the current ISDS system as 'unfair' to States. This is a very critical moment in the discussion and should not be brushed away lightly.

If either the Prohibition Model or the Restriction Model or even (only) the Broad Disclosure Model were adopted by the UNCITRAL Working Group III, this would be the end of TPF in ISDS. Whether this would really be in the best interest of the ISDS system as a whole is more than questionable. Surely, it would not be in the interest of investors whose access to justice might be severely hampered. But it would also not be in the interest of States as it cuts them off from funding possibilities as well. States might want (or need) funding in order to afford a good defence and to hedge their risk. The market for defence funding is just developing and a prohibition or restriction could nip it in the bud. Instead, States should start to embrace TPF and develop tailor-made solutions with funders along the lines of, 'If you can't fight them, join them.'

Julian Lew has always been a visionary with a dream of autonomous arbitration free from State-control. He has framed his vision – what else – as a question:[8]

> Do you dream? When do you dream? What do you dream about? Do you dream about international arbitration? Is there a dream for international arbitration? Is the concept of delocalised arbitration, or arbitration not controlled by national law, a dream or a nightmare?

8. Julian DM Lew, 'Achieving the Dream: Autonomous Arbitration', (2006) 22(2) Arbitration International pp. 179-203.

With this in mind, I dream of an ISDS system in which TPF is an accepted financing tool available to all stakeholders, allowing for the settlement of disputes between States and investors on an equal footing, without the need for prohibitions or strict limitations.

PART II Julian Lew's Achievements and Legacy

CHAPTER 36

Prof Dr Julian Lew QC: The Dream Realised

Ariella Lew & Lauren Levin

It is a rare opportunity and honour for us to be able to participate in this special publication and acknowledge our father's contribution to his field of practice.

Having sat in on a few of Dad's lectures in various cities across the globe, we have become accustomed to his trademark use of Socratic questioning. This is a method he also employs when teaching us or discussing our goals. Yet even we were not expecting his maverick opening question to the audience when he set out his vision for autonomous arbitration at the Freshfields lecture in 2005: 'DO YOU dream? When do you dream? What do you dream about? Do you dream about international arbitration?'

In the many scholarly articles and discussions in the field following this, some have questioned the virtue of invoking dreams when discussing shaping legal realities. Does utopian rhetoric have a place in the legal world?

Arguably referencing dreams is more for the realm of philosophy than law. The trouble is that often we get caught between the dreamer and the pragmatist. The pragmatist functions within the imperfections of their reality, but is confined by their limitations. The dreamer will fantasise of paradise, but it remains severed from reality. Our grandfather, a clergyman, lauded Joseph in the Bible as the ideal 'practical dreamer'. His tragic beginnings of being sold into slavery by his brothers, belittled by them as being a mere 'dreamer', developed into a golden age where economic, political, and national survival were credited to his 'dreams'. He did not just dream; he advocated and served for their implementation.

'A practical dreamer' in many ways encompasses who Dad is and what he has worked towards for so many years within the legal profession. As a much younger man, he found his calling within the field of international arbitration and saw the potential for a new area of legal practice to emerge. He worked within international firms as a solicitor and later as a QC to allow, arbitration to not only be a small part of a litigation practice but rather to be accepted as a mainstream area of the law. Ultimately, a dream in isolation remains a fantasy until someone embodies it and gives it reality. Dad became one of these critical voices and helped to ensure that international arbitration was not just an idea but something that is an evolving reality.

Growing up, we witnessed first-hand his unwavering dedication to his field, his colleagues, his clients, his students and to anyone who sought out his counsel. It allowed us to truly learn by example what it means to be immersed in a career that you love and to make personal sacrifices to honour the commitments you have made to those who rely on you.

In addition to his work in the profession itself, our father is a gifted teacher. Not only did he pursue academia to develop the area of law that he was so passionate about, but he mentored young lawyers and empowered his students at the university to ensure that his dream would live on far beyond his retirement.

Dad has been our greatest teacher. He has shown us that when you are in sight of a dream, coupled with focus and dedication, the sky is the limit. No goal is insignificant and by pushing one's self and having ambition, no obstacle is too great. We have watched and heard stories of how he has privately used his expertise to advise people within our own community to navigate complex issues without ever saying that he was involved or expecting honour or credit for it. The knowledge that he has, he shares with those who may benefit from it and he is well respected within our community as an expert on legal matters.

One may assume that Dad's work life and home life are entirely separate entities. In many ways they are. Yet upon reflection, it is clear to us that the professor who taught so many, the partner you looked up to, the arbitrator who ruled on your case, the author whose book you have on your shelf and the dad who raised us are really no different. At the heart of all his personal and professional dealings, seems to be the biblical injunction of 'justice, justice, you shall pursue'. Similarly, the dedication he shows to his work is the dedication he shows to our family. His generosity of time for colleagues and students is palpable in the special relationships he has with his children and each of his grandchildren.

Dad is a traditionalist, and we were brought up with a keen sense of responsibility to the past and reverence for tradition. At the same time, he is a non-conformist, challenging us to be creative, find out-of-the box solutions, and disregard any glass ceilings. This duality is present in his academic writings as well. His references to a possible rudimentary autonomous arbitration system in the Middle Ages are reflective and historical. Do they jive with his vision for the future which is still very much a 'dream'? To us it seems consistent with our upbringing. If you know where you came from, it will propel you forward to where you need to go. The past shapes the present, and we, standing in the present, must dare to shape the future.

Tremendous thanks from all our family to Professor Stavros Brekoulakis, Professor Romesh Weeramantry and Lilit Nagapetyan. Dad has not only treasured your relationship as students as colleagues, but also in time as teachers and friends.

It is our fervent hope that many other fields of the corporate world, both within the legal world and beyond, will be impacted by practical dreamers.

CHAPTER 37

The Centre for Commercial Law Studies and the School of International Commercial Arbitration: The Story of an Adventure

Roy Goode KC

It is both a pleasure and a privilege to be invited to contribute to a *Liber Amico rum* for our dear friend and colleague Professor Julian Lew. Ably supported by his wife Margot, Julian has had a much varied life. Called to the Bar in 1970 he practised there for some 11 years before moving to become a partner of the leading City law firm Herbert Smith. It was while there as a practicing solicitor that he took silk, for which few solicitors were then considered eligible, returning to the Bar in 2005. A leading figure in international commercial arbitration he is also the author of many outstanding publications in the field of international commercial arbitration. One of his early works was *The Applicable Law in International Commercial Arbitration*, a major but previously rather neglected branch of the subject which Julian made peculiarly his own. There followed a steady stream of scholarly publications informed by his deep knowledge of arbitration practice. But what is arbitration? In his *Devil's Dictionary* Ambrose Bierce gave us his own distinctive definition:

> A patent medicine for allaying international heat, designed to supersede the old-school treatment of blood-letting. It makes the unsuccessful party to the dispute hate two or more nations instead of one—to the unspeakable advantage of peace.

Julian's warm and genial character, which has enchanted his friends and colleagues over the years, will have made him an admirable peacemaker and certainly one who is in huge demand as an international arbitrator, holding appointments under the rules of all the major arbitral institutions. And he has been a pivotal figure in the creation and development of the School of International Commercial Arbitration, to which this modest piece is devoted. Long may we continue to enjoy his talents, his leadership and his camaraderie.

§37.01 THE CENTRE FOR COMMERCIAL LAW STUDIES

In the late 1970s, when I was Dean of the Faculty of Law at Queen Mary College, University of London, a random thought floated into my mind. When this happens, it usually floats out again pretty quickly and is lost to posterity, but this time it stuck. Here we were in London, one of the world's leading financial and commercial centers, yet there was no institution in the country—or, indeed, anywhere in the world so far as I knew—devoted to the academic study of commercial law. Surely there was a role for the Centre, and why not at Queen Mary (London), an intellectually lively place with a strong Law Faculty within which the Centre could be established and for which it should be possible to raise substantial funds. My colleagues thought that from being mildly eccentric I had now gone completely mad! 1979, the year in which the idea crystallized, was the time when the economy was widely considered to be a time of the most severe recession since World War II. "Not a hope in hell of raising money at this particular time.! 'Yes', I replied, 'but if by some means we *are* able do it now we shall be well placed to expand when the economy improves'."

Thus began the great adventure. We had no money, no building, no courses and, indeed, no academic posts apart from my own Chair and the Herschel Smith Chair of Intellectual Property Law. This had already established through the generosity of Dr Herschel Smith, via the good offices of the Chartered Institute of Patent Agents, which wanted to celebrate its centenary, and we brought it within the Centre. I had never formed a Centre before. How to begin? My answer: with decent notepaper! The college notepaper was, to say the least, pedestrian, so I spent £200 which we did not have getting a modern design for Centre notepaper. This produced astonishing results. For example, I received a telephone call from the British Council saying they would be interested in funding scholarships for our postgraduate courses. The problem was that at that time we had no students, no courses and no accommodation apart from my own office—but we did have notepaper! However, fortune favours the brave. I wrote to the then Lord Chancellor, Lord Hailsham, inviting him to open the Centre, which he graciously agreed to do. Belatedly I asked myself: what exactly is he going to open? Then a brainwave. I asked the college's maintenance department, which was next door to the Law Faculty building, to put up a sign, "Centre for Commercial Law Studies" (CCLS) below "Faculty of Laws," and bingo, we had a building! So it all started as a massive confidence trick! Still, formally opening the Centre on June 20, 1980 the Lord Chancellor did us proud. In the ensuing five years the Centre built up an enviable program of activities and a strong publication record. It was therefore particularly rewarding when in 1986 in the first research assessment exercise the young CCLS was placed in the top category alongside Oxford, Cambridge and five others a mere six years after it had come into being.

§37.02 THE ORIGINS OF THE SCHOOL OF INTERNATIONAL ARBITRATION

I now come to the kernel of this short contribution to the Liber Amico rum for our distinguished honor and, Julian Lew. The School of International Arbitration had a long gestation period. My very first Director's Report in October 1981 records that through the good offices of Lord Justice Kerr, then Chairman of the Centre's management committee, the new Dean, Professor Graham Zoellick, and I became engaged in preliminary discussions with senior members of some of the leading arbitration bodies with a view to establishing a School of International Arbitration, which at that time had no counterpart in the world. But how to get this off to the ground? I hit on the idea of an international arbitration conference with papers by the world's leading arbitrators and I consulted the estimable Bertie Vigrass, the then Director of the Chartered Institute of Arbitrators. "Roy," he said, "this will cost you a bomb! Top arbitrators will expect a substantial fee, the cost of air travel in the most comfortable class and Accommodation in a five-star hotel." "Bertie," I replied, "I am not paying a fee, air fares or the cost of hotel accommodation, but as they will be giving papers I will graciously waive the registration fee!" "You'll never get away with it." "We'll see." I then wrote to Pieter Sanders, doyen of the arbitration world, Pierre Lalive, Berthold Goldman, and Robert Coulson, inviting them to speak but saying they would have to cover their own expenses (none of them needed help on that!). They were all captured by the idea and generously agreed. I then wrote to some 26 other leading arbitrators around the world asking them to present papers and adding, as an afterthought, that "by the way, Sanders, LA live, Goldman and Coulson have agreed to speak," after which there was no way the other invitees wanted to be left behind! So we launched the School at a three-day conference on March 25-27, 1985 attended, astonishingly, by some 300 participants and it was a brilliant success. All the papers were later reproduced in a book *Contemporary Problems in International Arbitration* skillfully edited and with an introduction by Julian Lew, whose support from the very outset was crucial and who became the first Head of the new School, a post which, amazingly, he continues to hold 37 years later, a tribute to his unswerving dedication and leadership.

In my own short paper I set out my vision for the school. First, it was not to promote any national arbitration system but was to be international in character and comparative in method, its purpose being to inculcate, through its teaching and research activities, a greater knowledge and understanding of the arbitration processes and principles and rules of law in the world's major legal systems. The emphasis on the international and comparative focus of the new School, echoed by the Master of the Rolls Sir John Donaldson in his opening address at the conference, struck a chord with our overseas experts. Second, while the academic could not hope to match the day-to-day expertise of the practitioner the academic's role was to lay out the subject of arbitration in a structured fashion, by surveying current practice, by identifying problems and suggesting solutions and by disseminating knowledge through teaching, research and writings. Underpinning the academic's work in the field of arbitration was a focus on underlying principles of contract and tort law, conflict of laws and public international law.

At the conference dinner in Middle Temple Hall on March 26, 1985 where the principal guest was Lord Roskill, a Lord of Appeal, Pieter Sanders gave a memorable speech, reproduced in the book:

> I am most honoured speak on this happy occasion, and a happy occasion it is, the birth of new institute, the School of International Arbitration. This conference has been very promising. Many fairy godmothers well known in the field of international arbitration stood at the cradle of the School. You have heard them speak these past few days. There was no wicked fairy amongst them. On the contrary, they all wholeheartedly welcomed the newborn and contributed to her their gifts of arbitration wisdom ...
>
> Queen Mary College has been very courageous in starting this new venture. It is an academic approach, but an approach very closely connected with the realities of the international business world... I am sure that I speak in the name of all of you, in wishing the School good luck and great success in the fascinating task it has undertaken.

In his own paper Pierre Lalive, who was later to give the first public arbitration lecture at the School, also emphasized the importance of the comparative approach and the need to have at least one counsel sufficiently trained in foreign law or having a comparative outlook.

I recall arranging a panel session in which the speakers were to speak for no more than 10 minutes each to allow plenty of time for discussion. For this I needed a strong chairman and chose Pierre LA live, who I knew would keep speakers to time. One of these was the beguiling French law professor, Berthold Goldman, a great exponent of the *lex Mercatorian*. He began with characteristic charm:

> Here in London I think I will not speak about the *lex mercatorian*!

Through a heroic effort he maintained this approach for a full two minutes and then went on to speak of nothing else. When I was accompanying him a taxi back to his hotel he remarked:

> You know, Roy, for a Frenchman your 10-minute rule was exceedingly difficult—but it came off!

Aided by an International Advisory Panel the new School went from strength to strength under the leadership of Julian, by now a Professor of International Arbitration Law at Queen Mary, and successive directors, of whom the current post-holder is Professor Stavros Brekoulakis in London, ably assisted by Professor Maxi Scherer, who is herself a professor in international commercial arbitration and runs the Centre's LLM programme in Paris. The school has become a jewel of the CCLS and one of Europe's leading research centrer in the field of international dispute resolution. It offers a wide range of teaching and research programmed in London and Paris and has developed an extensive network of associations around the world. What started as an acorn has become a giant oak—and still growing!

CHAPTER 38

The Multi-faceted Legacy of Julian Lew: The Prism of Immunity in International Arbitration

Susan Franck[*]

Professor Julian D.M. Lew is responsible for the creation, evolution, and longevity of the professional and scholarly life of an entire generation of new international arbitration specialists. In large part, Julian's influence derives from his unique capacity to model critical thinking, to exercise independent judgment, and to demonstrate the vitality (and possibility) of how arbitration scholars must engage in *praxis* to support the positive evolution of international dispute settlement. Somehow, he manages to do so with a smile on his face and hope for the future.

Julian's wit and wisdom has created a multifaceted legacy that offers a treasure trove for the future of arbitration. For my own part, I can say without hesitation that Julian influenced my life in multiple ways. This contribution offers one insight into the myriad of ways in which Julian has made fundamental contributions to the world of international arbitration—whether as a teacher, a scholar, an intellectual inspiration, a mentor, or a colleague. It does through by exploring an area in which Julian both piqued my curiosity and supported my professional evolution. Namely, it discusses how he motivated me to explore the embedded complexities of the immunity and liability of international arbitrators; and this, in turn, taught me to engage in exacting comparative law analyses of arbitration doctrine, conflict of laws, and policy considerations to develop my scholarly voice. Julian's intellectual generosity and personal decency are gifts from which I (and many others) have benefitted; and I, for one, am blessed to know Julian and have benefitted from his tutelage.

* The author is grateful for the aid of her research assistants, Vicky Cheng and Abby Raines.

Julian Lew as Teacher

As a young law student in the United States, I became intrigued by international arbitration and how different forms of dispute settlement, applying different substantive laws and using different cultural perspectives on adjudication, can peacefully resolve transnational disputes.[1] When considering whether to apply a U.S.-U.K. Fulbright Grant, I was regularly told: if I was truly serious about the subject, the obvious choice was to study with was Julian Lew at Queen Mary in London.[2] This advice was spot on,[3] and Professor Lew became a fundamental exemplar that I have used (and continue to use) when assessing academic and professional excellence.

Despite working as an arbitrator and head of Herbert's Smith international arbitration practice, Julian always made time to teach his students and engage in a thoughtful dialogue, sometimes talking about fundamental cases (or his practical experiences) and sometimes in collaboration with John Adams, while they exchanged spicy repartee designed to solidify long-term memory. His late-night commute to the Mile End campus[4] to teach for three hours straight (often longer) told us all we needed to know about his commitment to and love of international arbitration. Even now, that year is memorable, with several fellow students practicing and writing about international arbitration today.

Beyond his commitment to international arbitration, Julian's teaching style and pedagogy was transformative. He explored the material in a novel way, made strategic assignments designed to make us active participants in our own education and evolution, and engaged in self-deprecating humor while demanding excellence. His style offered me a new template for how to teach others and how to become responsible for my own educational advancement.

While studying international arbitration without the aid of a formal textbook (just a ringed binder containing the substantive legal provisions), students were required to self-direct class preparation by identifying and analyzing materials that we theorized might be covered in discussions of the week's topic. I spent hours in the library thumbing through hard copies of journals like *Arbitration International* and the *Journal of International Arbitration* and books like Pieter Sanders' *Handbook of*

1. Susan Franck, *Transforming into an International Lawyer*, ILSA Q., December 2006, at 23, available at https://digitalcommons.wcl.american.edu/cgi/viewcontent.cgi?article=2599&context=facsch_lawrev (last accessed June 14, 2022).
2. The grant process for securing a Fulbright grant from the U.S.-U.K. Fulbright Commission is particularly rigorous, involving extra interviews by the home commission. Although one mentor told me to apply to the Netherlands Fulbright program as it was less competitive, given others' advice and the value of Dr. Lew's program, for me, I knew it was either "London or bust."
3. After doing background research on Julian Lew and the School of International Arbitration in the University of Minnesota Law Library, I discovered a copy of his book *Contemporary Problems in International Arbitration* from 1987, which had an awful cover page when originally published by the Centre for Commercial Law Studies (CCLS) at Queen Mary College. The volume was full of scholarship addressing fundamental topics like jurisdiction, applicable law, procedural matters, and enforcement. *Contemporary Problems in International Arbitration* (Julian D.M. Lew ed., 1986).
4. In those days, the international arbitration class was taught in Mile End, which had become somewhat infamous when Pulp's 1996 song, *Mile End*, appeared in the movie *Trainspotting*.

International Commercial Arbitration. Even if I did not always focus on the most relevant material, I always learned something critical and useful.

Perhaps more importantly, Julian's approach to teaching international arbitration was, at its core, deeply comparative. This meant, before class, it was best to understand how different countries (and different arbitral institutions) addressed the core concepts underpinning the topic of the week. Julian's innovative teaching style, which sometimes felt like the plan of an evil genius, meant that we were prepared to explore three types of questions. First, where was there consistency across the arbitration doctrine and a general approach? Second, what was the scope of variation around the concept and unique innovations in specific countries (and the inherent trade-offs in those choices)? Third, what were the policy underpinnings of an area and the strategic (or inadvertent) decisions to avoid addressing a perennial issue in international arbitration? Our conversations about the week's topic usually occurred with reference to a salient personal example or with dry humor to make the point stick.

Julian Lew as Scholar

As a scholar, Julian has been prolific, contributing to fundamental debates about international arbitration in a myriad of different ways on a variety of topics.[5] One area in which Julian has been a thought leader involves the liability and immunity of international arbitrators. He authored the leading book on the topic, the *Immunity of Arbitrators*,[6] which remains fundamental reading for anyone exploring arbitrators' liability and immunity by providing an intellectual baseline.[7]

The liability and immunity of international arbitrators also happens to be an area where the three elements of Julian's pedagogical approach, described previously, bore unique fruit in the scholarly domain. Specifically, to understand the intricacies surrounding the liability of international arbitrators, it is necessary to appreciate: (1) the silos of convergence (i.e., some jurisdictions permit broad immunity), (2) the core pattens of divergence (i.e., some jurisdictions strip arbitrators of fees and/or otherwise impose broad liability), and (3) tactical silence where—despite the importance of the underlying issues—in the past, strategic decisions were made to avoid the topic rather than wrestle with challenging doctrinal and policy issues.[8]

5. *See, e.g.*, Julian D.M. Lew, Loukas A. Mistelis & Stefan M. Kröll *Comparative International Commercial Arbitration* (2003); Loukas A. Mistelis & Julian D.M. Lew, *Pervasive problems in international arbitration* (2006); *see also supra* n. 3 and accompanying text (noting the influence of Lew's other scholarship).
6. *The Immunity of Arbitrators* (Julian D.M. Lew ed., 1990).
7. *See* Loretta Malintoppi, *Don't Shoot the Sheriff: The Threat of Legal Claims Against Arbitrators and Arbitral Institutions*, 37 Arbitration International 487, 488 (2021); Sarah Schaeffer, *Approaches to Arbitrators' Liability: Immunity or Liability*, 2 Stockholm Arbitration Year Book 249 (2020).
8. This contrasts, however, with modern reality. Rather than avoiding issues of arbitrators' duties, integrity, and conduct, there have been several iterations of the IBA Rules on Conflicts of Interests of International Arbitrators. *See, e.g.*, James Crawford, *The Ideal Arbitrator: Does One Size Fit All?*, 32 American University International Law Review 1003, 1007-1012, 1119 (2017); *see also* Perry S. Bechky, *Investor-State Arbitrators' Duties to Non-parties*, 31 Duke Journal of Comparative & International Law 221, 231, 256 (2021); Caline Mouawad, *Arbitration in A Changing World*, 32 American Review of International Arbitration 1, 13 n. 39 (2021). More recently, there has been a major push in connection with UNCITRAL reform to provide a draft code of conduct for

I owe Julian a debt of gratitude for our conversations on the topic, as they inspired my first article on international arbitration.[9] During my LLM course work, we had a chance to receive preliminary feedback on our knowledge on the acquisition of the course content and were offered a slate of optional essay questions to assess our understanding of course materials. The "small" question (or what appeared to be small) that I selected involved the liability of international arbitrators. Yet, once I started researching and writing, I was hooked. Each question I answered piqued my curiosity and only led me to ask more fascinating questions. Meanwhile, Julian (and John Adams) were patient with and supportive of my enthusiasm on the topic, suggesting other materials to explore. I still recall when it was strongly suggested that I explore the 1989 legislative history of the United Nations Commission on Trade and Investment Law's (UNCITRAL) Model Law on International Commercial Arbitration.[10] When digging into the primary materials, I discovered textual evidence that the UNCITRAL drafters, rather than dealing with challenging issues head on, made a strategic choice to remain silent and fail to expressly identify a salient issue or provide potential alternatives.[11] As Gerold Herrmann (former Director of the UNCITRAL Secretariat) later explained in a public forum, the hope had been to "let sleeping dogs lie,"[12] rather than highlighting the fact that arbitrators who breached their duties (or

international arbitrators. *See, e.g.*, UNCITRAL Secretariat, Possible reform of investor-State dispute settlement (ISDS) Draft Code of Conduct, A/CN.9/WG.III/WP. 209 (September 15, 2022), https://daccess-ods.un.org/tmp/1319963.03796768.html (last accessed June 17, 2022).

9. *See* Susan Franck, *The Liability of International Arbitrators: A Comparative Analysis and Proposal for Qualified Immunity*, 20 New York Law School of Journal of International & Comparative Law 1, 3-15 (2000). That article is regularly cited in scholarship exploring the applicable law to arbitrator immunity and liability; and according to SSRN, this article has been downloaded well over 1,800 times. The article It also formed the core of some of the most recent scholarship on arbitrator liability and immunity. *See* Schaeffer, *supra* n. 7, at §§ 14.01, 14.02, 14.05 (providing the most recent comparative discussion of arbitrator immunity and liability and citing to the article); *see also* Bechky, *supra* n. 8, 227-229 (discussing the article); Peter B. Rutledge, *Toward a Contractual Approach for Arbitral Immunity*, 39 Georgia Law Review 151, 184-85 (2004) (same); Emmanuela Truli, *Liability v. Quasi-Judicial Immunity of the Arbitrator: The Case Against Absolute Arbitral Immunity*, 17 American Review of International Arbitration 383, 395-398 (2006) (same); V.V. Veeder, *Arbitrators and Arbitral Institutions: Legal Risks for Product Liability?*, 5 American University Business Law Review 335, 340-341 (2016) (same). From a practical perspective, multiple lawyers have used the article to motivate recalcitrant arbitrators to finalize their written awards.

10. United Nations Commission on Trade and Investment Law (UNCITRAL), Model Law on International Commercial Arbitration, U.N. Document A/40/17, annex I (1985), https://uncitral.un.org/sites/uncitral.un.org/files/media-documents/uncitral/en/06-54671_ebook.pdf (last accessed June 18, 2022) (hereinafter '1985 Model Law').

11. Howard M. Holzman & Joseph E. Neuhaus, *A Guide to the UNCITRAL Model Law on International Commercial Arbitration: Legislative History and Commentary* (1989); *see also* UNCITRAL, First Secretariat Note, A/CN.9/207, para. 70, https://digitallibrary.un.org/record/22459/files/A_CN.9_207-EN.pdf (last accessed June 18, 2022) (providing additional legislative history about the desire to avoid addressing the immunity or liability of arbitrators and stating "In view of the fact that the liability problem is not widely regulated and remains highly controversial, it may seem doubtful whether the model law could provide a satisfactory solution"); Franck, *supra* n. 9, at 2, 33-34 (noting and providing references to the legislative history of the Model Law's decision to avoid immunity issues).

12. *See* Veeder, *supra* n. 9, at 347 (noting the lack of information on liability and immunity in the 1985 Model Law and stating 'This omission was addressed by UNCITRAL's former Secretary,

otherwise neglected their mandate) were theoretically subject to liability for their professional activities.

Julian Lew as Intellectual Inspiration

Julian's passion for rigorous comparative analysis also inspired my conversations with colleagues outside of class. I recall with fondness one spirited debate about the legal basis for arbitrator liability, which occurred at the Institute for Advanced Legal Studies in Russell Square with my friend, Ali Yeşilırmak, who is now a professor of international arbitration in Turkey. We vigorously debated whether tort or contract law made arbitrators legally responsible for their professional conduct during the arbitration.

As a common law lawyer, I argued that the substantive law must derive from tort law, as misconduct would involve the breach of a professional duty that caused harm and damages to a party. In other words, I assumed the core question was whether liability derived from a tort involving professional malpractice, which made the next question whether the defense of immunity was available. By contrast, Ali was trained in civil law and had different expectations about the genesis of an arbitrator's legal duties. He argued that tort law could not provide a basis for liability; rather, the matter must be governed by contract law, as, depending upon which part of the preexisting civil code applied, the code automatically created both duties and liability for professionals (like arbitrators) who exceeded or abandoned their mandate.[13] Eventually, I realized that we were both arguing for the same thing—namely, that there was some legal basis to regulate the behavior of international arbitrators. We only diverged as to the applicable *source* of that legal obligation. Without the lateral thinking Julian's classroom promoted, the breakthrough would not have occurred.

Perhaps more importantly, that transformative conversation taught me the importance of humility, the value of asking questions to test personal assumptions, and essential value of intercultural competency in international dispute resolution. When and where I can, I try to pass Julian's insights on to my own students, whether it involves reminding them that the concept of "consideration" is an anathema to civil law lawyers, professional duties need not derive from case law (but may come from civil or statutory codes), and different jurisdictions may have different interpretive assumptions. Put another way, understanding that different legal cultures approach similar legal problems with different sets of expectations, legal rules, norms, and applicable analytical frameworks has been fundamental to my professional development.

Gerold Herrmann, in his 1998 Freshfields Lecture. There, he explained that, at UNCITRAL, the national delegations abstained from touching the issue of arbitral immunity, preferring "to let sleeping dogs lie" for the Model Law. The trouble with sleeping dogs is that they eventually wake up. Soon, as a tactical measure, arbitrators were threatened personally with challenges and claims against them. Accordingly, twenty-five years after the Model Law, UNCITRAL reconsidered arbitral immunity when drafting its new UNCITRAL Arbitration Rules 2010.') (footnotes omitted).

13. *See generally* Lew, *supra* n. 6; *see also* Schaeffer, *supra* n. 7, at §§ 14.02, 14.05; *see also* Franck, *supra* n. 9, at 3-15 (discussing potential contract and tort-based approaches for identifying duties and potential liability of international arbitrators).

Julian Lew as Mentor and Colleague

Julian's influence has, however, extended well beyond the classroom. He has been an inspiration to me (and many other contemporaries) in a variety of unique and very special ways. He has been generous with his time and counsel.

Whenever I had professional questions, as I was exploring how I wanted my life to evolve—whether as a practitioner in the United States or England or as a junior scholar seeking to make the transition into the legal academy—Julian always had a kind word, some thoughtful observations to keep me grounded, and the kindness to provide these over a delightful lunch. He was also fond of reminding me about his own experience as a young researcher, cheekily trying to obtain documentation on international arbitration to be used for future intellectual study. When I considered shifting my research trajectory as a young scholar to focus more on empirical analysis of legal phenomena, I was reminded of Julian and the bravery and thoughtfulness he displayed. His conduct and professional dignity was something that I wished to emulate.

Ultimately, the wisdom and kindness that I gained from Julian across a variety of moments in my life is something that I treasure and wish to replicate for future generations.[14] I can only hope that my own legacy will mirror the many kindnesses, thoughtful questions, hard steers, and deep integrity that Julian has consistently demonstrated throughout the years. He is a man for all times. It is therefore with great pleasure that I make this contribution in Julian's honor.

14. When I served as Chair of the Institute for Transnational Arbitration's Academic Council, I wanted to ensure Julian's life story was properly memorialized. Working with colleagues at Queen Mary, including Stavros Brekoulakis, Loukas Mistelis, and Audley Sheppard, we organized a program memorializing the lifetime and career of Julian in July 2019. Although others did much of the work for that event, working with Julian in that context was a delightful experience. The event can be viewed at *Preserving Perspectives: International Arbitrators in Their Own Words*, https://vimeopro.com/user34174610/ita-oral-history-interviews/video/367748394 (last accessed June 24, 2022).

CHAPTER 39

Teaching Lew's Dream: Musings on Teaching Transnational (Autonomous) Arbitration

Loukas Mistelis

§39.01 INTRODUCTORY REMARKS: JULIAN LEW AND AUTONOMOUS ARBITRATION

I first met Julian Lew in February 1999 a couple of months after I joined QMUL as a young lecturer. He invited me to his law firm office to meet and explore how I would fit in with the School of International Arbitration. He was generous with his time, friendly and inquisitive and at the end of the meeting I landed a PhD thesis by one of our students who had to resubmit a revised draft following his viva. I suspect this was the indication that we could work together ... We have worked together ever since: we taught together for well over 20 years as well as co-supervised research students and also co-wrote a treatise[1], as well as co-edited other publications[2] and co-organised numerous events.

From the very beginning it was clear that as much as Julian was (and continues to be) a successful practitioner and talented academic writer,[3] his real passion is teaching. Against this background it is felicitous that Julian is a truly charismatic lecturer and an engaging communicator.

1. Julian Lew, Loukas Mistelis & Stefan Kröll, *Comparative International Commercial Arbitration* (Kluwer Law International, 2003).
2. Loukas Mistelis & Julian Lew (eds), *Pervasive Problems in International Arbitration* (Kluwer Law International, 2006); Julian Lew & Loukas Mistelis (eds), *Arbitration Insights – Twenty Years of the Annual Lecture of the School of International Arbitration* (Kluwer Law International, 2007).
3. The seminal work is Julian Lew, *Applicable Law in International Commercial Arbitration: A Study in Commercial Arbitration Awards* (Oceana, 1978).

Given Julian's background in private international and comparative law he always approached international commercial arbitration as a comparative and international law subject. He also espoused the view that due to party autonomy very little in arbitration is set in stone. On this basis there are two extracts from our treatise which reflect this standpoint (not to call it ideology).

The first is that first para of the book:

> International arbitration is essentially a private, comparative and international mechanism. No two arbitrations are the same. There are few absolutes. There are no fixed rules or procedures. Any factual variation will invariably result in a significant change in the context and structure of the arbitration. The matrix which affects every arbitration varies depending upon the arbitration agreement, the procedure agreed by the parties, the nationality of the parties, the make-up of the tribunal, the applicable arbitration rules, the substantive applicable law or rules, the subject-matter of the dispute, the mandatory law of the place of arbitration and the permissive law where everything else is silent.
>
> All of these factors are directly controlled by party autonomy.[4]

Students over the years would recall how Julian always answers questions with questions: if there are only few absolutes then there is not always one possible (correct) answer. An inquisitive and curious mind and a comparative law sensibility are essential assets for international arbitration lawyers. And Julian has espoused these values and made every effort to inspire generations of students to embrace such values by developing their knowledge and skills.

The second extract comes from the first para of the treatise, our working definition of arbitration:

> International arbitration is a specially established mechanism for the final and binding determination of disputes, concerning a contractual or other relationship with an international element, by independent arbitrators, in accordance with procedures, structures and substantive legal or non-legal standards chosen directly or indirectly by the parties.[5]

It is understandable that some may debate whether this is a definition or not; it certainly is a delimitation of arbitration and does contain all essential features of arbitration. The two extracts do not explicitly refer to arbitration being an autonomous legal order (a concept which Julian Lew fully supports[6]).

The concept of international arbitration as an autonomous legal order is not novel. It denotes that arbitration is emancipated from the law of its (legal) seat,[7] and

4. Lew, Mistelis & Kröll, *supra* n. 1, at p. v.
5. *Ibid.*, at para. 1-1, p. 1.
6. Julian Lew, 'Achieving the Dream: Autonomous Arbitration' (2014) 22 *Arbitration International*, pp. 179-204.
7. This version of autonomy is also referred to as 'delocalisation'. *See also* Jan Paulsson, 'Delocalisation of International Commercial Arbitration: When and Why It Matters' (1983) 32 *International and Comparative Law Quarterly*, p. 53; Pierre Mayer, 'The Trend Towards Delocalisation in the Last 100 Years', in M. Hunter, A. Marriott & V.V. Veeder (eds), *Internationalisation of*

that local national courts and local national law exercise no control[8] over the arbitral process. It is a very attractive proposition as arbitration is typically based on party autonomy and the express or implied will of parties to refer their existing or future disputes to arbitration. At the same time the parties express their will to have their disputes resolved outside the jurisdiction of national courts and opt for arbitration, the most prominent form of private justice.[9] The outcome of the arbitration, the arbitral award is easily enforceable on the basis on the 1958 New York Convention on the Recognition of Foreign Arbitral Awards.[10] The limited and scarce existing evidence suggests that only around 10% of international arbitration cases would have some interaction with local courts,[11] either because of a challenge of arbitrators, challenge of award or requests made to local courts to provide their support in their taking of evidence or to enforce an interim order made by a tribunal.[12] It has even been suggested[13] that any challenge of the award at the seat of arbitration is meaningless since awards may still be enforced;[14] ultimately what matters is enforcement for which

International Arbitration (Oxford University Press 1995), p. 37; and Loukas Mistelis, 'Delocalization and its Relevance in Post-Award Review', in Frédéric Bachand and Fabien Gelinas (eds), *25 Years of the UNCITRAL Model Law* (Juris, 2013), pp. 165-179.

8. This version of autonomy is also referred to as 'denationalisation'. *See also* Klaus Lionnet, 'Should the procedural Law Applicable to International Arbitration Be Denationalised or Unified? The Answer of the UNCITRAL Model Law' (1995) 8(3) *Journal of International Arbitration* p. 1.
9. Stephen J. Ware, 'Private Ordering and Commercial Arbitration: Lasting Lessons from Mentschikoff' (2019) *Journal of Dispute Resolution*, p. 1, at 3. The importance of arbitration as the primary private dispute resolution of commercial disputes is evidenced by a series of surveys ever since 2006. *See* http://www.arbitration.qmul.ac.uk/research/ [last visited on 10 June 2021]; and also Loukas Mistelis, 'International Arbitration: Corporate Attitudes and Practices' (2004) 15 *American Review of International Arbitration*, pp. 525-593.
10. Convention on the Recognition and Enforcement of Foreign Arbitral Awards, adopted on 10 June 1958, and entered into force on 7 June 1959 ('New York Convention'). *See generally* Marike Paulsson, *The 1958 New York Convention in Action* (Kluwer Law International, 2016); Albert Jan van den Berg, *The New York Convention of 1958, Towards a Uniform Judicial Interpretation* (Kluwer Law International, 1981).
11. QMUL, *International Arbitration: Corporate Attitudes and Practises 2008*, p. 10, available at http://www.arbitration.qmul.ac.uk/media/arbitration/docs/IAstudy_2008.pdf [last visited on 10 June 2021].
12. Lew, Mistelis & Kröll, *supra* n. 1, paras 15-1-15-57.
13. On this point, *see* Loukas Mistelis, 'Setting Aside of Arbitral Awards and Forum Shopping in International Arbitration: Delocalization, Party Autonomy and National Courts in Post-Award Review', in Franco Ferrari (ed.), *Forum Shopping in the International Commercial Arbitration Context* (European Law Publishers, 2013), pp. 277-295.
14. Cases on point are, for example, Cour de cassation, 9 October 1984, 'Pabalk Ticaret Limited Sirketi v. Norsolor SA', 112 *Journal du droit international* 679 (1985), with comment by P. Kahn, 681 *Revue de l'Arbitrage* 432 (1985), with note by B. Goldman, 24 *International Legal Materials* 360 (1985), with note E. Gaillard, XI *Yearbook Commercial Arbitration* 484 (1986); Cour de cassation, 23 March 1994, Hilmarton Ltd v. Omnium de traitement et de valorisation - OTV, *Revue de l'Arbitrage* 327 (1994), XX *Yearbook Commercial Arbitration* 663 (1995); Cour d'appel de Paris, 14 January 1997, 'The Arab Republic of Egypt v. Chromalloy Aeroservices Inc', *Revue de l'Arbitrage* 395 (1997), 12(4) *Mealey's International Arbitration* Report B-1 (1997), XXII *Yearbook Commercial Arbitration* 691 (1997); Direction Generale de l' Aviation Civile de l'Emirat de Dubai v. Internationale Bechtel, Paris Court of Appeal, 29 September 2005. Similar cases also exist in few other jurisdictions, such as The Netherlands and the United States (e.g., Chromalloy Aeroservices Inc. v. The Arab Republic of Egypt, 939 F. Supp 907 (D. D. C. 1996).

we have a unified legal regime[15] and the enforcement of foreign awards most often occurs outside the courts of the seat of arbitration.

The autonomous nature of the arbitral legal order is not only attractive to arbitrators who are arguably given wide discretion in designing the proceedings but is also espoused by sociologists,[16] legal scholars who focus on international business transactions (droit des affaires internationales), transnational law and/or law merchant (*lex mercatoria*)[17] or arbitration theorists[18] who some[19] have labelled as 'dreamers'.

Of course the concept of autonomous legal order may require a more precise definition and in some cases we may only see some semi-autonomy rather than full autonomy. It has been suggested by this author that in terms of procedure and in respect of the so-called internal *lex arbitri*; the autonomy of tribunal in making decisions in matters of procedure also ensures a substantial partial autonomy of the arbitral process itself while the interaction of the arbitration with national courts is a matter of external lex arbitri and this is only used (in fact, activated) in very limited circumstances.[20]

While the concept of autonomous arbitration is attractive it has received less support in recent years as most modern arbitration laws, in particular, those based on the UNCITRAL Model Law on International Commercial Arbitration, rely heavily on territoriality and the seat of arbitration. While, of course, the seat was meant to be a connecting factor for the application of the arbitration law in question, territoriality has gained acceptance to the detriment of autonomy. The widely perceived wisdom is that arbitration is regulated by the law of the seat.[21] However, the concept of transnational arbitration, especially if seen as Philip Jessup[22] describes transnationality seems to be unaffected. Jessup describes as transnational law, the concept aimed:

15. Mistelis, *supra* n. 13, and Emmanuel Gaillard, 'Enforcement of Awards Set Aside in the Country of Origin: The French Experience', in Albert Jan van den Berg (ed.), *Improving the Efficiency of Arbitration Agreements and Awards: 40 Years of Application of the New York Convention*, ICCA Congress Series No. 9 (Kluwer Law International 1999), 505.
16. *See generally* the seminal study by Yves Dezalay & Bryant Garth, *International Commercial Arbitration and the Construction of a Transnational Legal Order* (University of Chicago Press, 1996).
17. *See* for example, Chia-Jui Cheng (ed.), *Clive M. Schmitthoff's Select Essays on International Trade Law* (Nijhoff, 1988); Clive Schmitthoff, 'Finality of Arbitral Awards and Judicial Review', in Julian Lew (ed.), *Contemporary Problems in International Arbitration* (Queen Mary and Westfield College / Martinus Nijhoff 1987), 230-240; Berthold Goldman, 'The Applicable Law: General Principles of Law - The Lex Mercatoria', in Julian Lew (ed.), *Contemporary Problems in International Arbitration* (Queen Mary and Westfield College / Martinus Nijhoff 1987), p. 113.
18. Gaillard, *supra* n. 17; Julian Lew, 'Achieving the Dream: Autonomous Arbitration' (2014) 22 *Arbitration International*, pp. 179-204.
19. Ralf Michaels, 'Dreaming Law Without a State: Scholarship on Autonomous International Arbitration as Utopian Literature' (2013) 1(1) *London Review of International Law*, pp. 35-62.
20. Loukas Mistelis, 'Reality Test: Current State of Affairs in Theory and Practice Relating to "Lex Arbitri"' (2006) 17(2) *The American Review of International Arbitration*, pp. 156-180.
21. *See*, critically, Mistelis, *supra* n. 7 and Mistelis, *ibid*.
22. Philip Jessup, *Transnational Law* (Yale University Press, 1956).

> to include all law which regulates actions or events that transcend national frontiers. Both public and private international law are included, as are other rules which do not wholly fit into such standard categories.[23]

It is undisputed that arbitration law has all features of transnational law, some of which do not fit in standard categories: national laws,[24] international law,[25] soft law, codified or uncodified.[26] In that sense arbitration law is truly transnational law.

§39.02 TEACHING OF TRANSNATIONAL (AUTONOMOUS) ARBITRATION

How would then one design and deliver an international arbitration course which supports the autonomy of transnational standpoint while at the same time provides all knowledge and skills needed by those students who would practise in more traditional jurisdictions? In other words, is it possible to teach arbitration in a non-ideological fashion?

Generally, arbitration is not typically taught at undergraduate level, and if it is, it would be a small part of broader classes focusing on either civil procedure or international business law. The former would inevitably address regulation of arbitration and its interaction with national courts while the former would focus on party autonomy and agreements parties make to have their disputes resolved by arbitration. Either way arbitration would be one or two lecturers, often lectures that the students would consider of great interest.

The situation is different when it comes to postgraduate courses. It would be fair to state that until Queen Mary University of London (QMUL) offered year-long arbitration modules (starting in 1983) arbitration was not typically taught. QMUL eventually offered a highly specialised curriculum which has evolved and expanded over the years, in particular, in the last twenty years. It has now developed into an LLM in Comparative and International Dispute Resolution.[27]

For the delivery of a transnational arbitration curriculum two elements are equally critical: *content* and *methodology*. In terms of *content* and in line with Jessup's vision, a transnational arbitration curriculum comprises comparative and international dimensions. Hence, one will have to study not only key domestic legal systems (and certainly all systems which are considered should be given equal treatment) but also focus on international treaties and international instruments (primarily soft law). It is

23. *Ibid.*, at 2.
24. For example, English Arbitration Act, US Federal Arbitration Act, Swiss Private International Law Act.
25. For example, 1958 New York Convention on the Recognition and Enforcement of Foreign Arbitral Awards.
26. For example, Arbitration Rules, such as those issued by ICC, LCIA, UNCITRAL as well as as instruments promulgated under the auspices of International Bar Association (IBA) Rules on Taking of Evidence, or Guidelines on Conflict of Interests, the Chartered Institute of Arbitrators, ICCA and others.
27. *See* https://www.qmul.ac.uk/postgraduate/taught/coursefinder/courses/comparative-and-international-dispute-resolution-llm/.

inevitable that some legal systems will received a higher degree of attention, simply because they are most often used and hence a great deal of data and resources are available. Such legal systems are also used by the major arbitral seats[28] and include:

- London – English Arbitration Act 1996
- Paris – French Code of Civil Procedure 2011
- Switzerland – Swiss Private International Law Act
- Singapore, Hong Kong, Vienna – UNCITRAL Model Law 1985/2005
- US – Federal Arbitration Act 1925.

Other legal systems will also have to be considered depending on the composition of the student body and recent developments. Hence it always makes good sense to look at Brazilian and Chinese laws as well as Sweden and some emerging seats in Africa, Asia and Latin America. The method of teaching comparative law is by having some generic factual scenarios (often inspired by real cases) and explore how these would be dealt by different national laws. In some instances the differences are substantial, in other cases less so.

In terms of international treaties and international instruments a curriculum at the very least would cover the New Yok Convention and a selection of leading arbitration rules, both institutional (International Chamber of Commerce (ICC), London Court of International Arbitration (LCIA), American Arbitration Association International Center for Dispute Resolution (AAA-ICDR), Hong Kong International Arbitration Centre (HKIAC), Singapore International Arbitration Centre (SIAC), Stockholm Chamber of Commerce (SCC), Swiss Arbitration Centre and others) and ad hoc (mainly UNCITRAL Rules) as well as soft law instruments addressing emerging standardisation of procedure[29] or code of conducts and ethics.[30] It would also be useful to look at procedural tools which reflect 'usages' or practices.[31]

Last, not least, there is now a substantial (and ever expanding) body of published case law as well as extracts (and even full text) of arbitral awards[32] in international commercial arbitration.[33] Such publications not only provide guidance (and is referred to by disputing parties in their submission) but also popularise a practice of law where very little was published until the early 1980s.

28. *See* Loukas Mistelis, 'Arbitral Seat: Important Features and the Role of Law' (2012) 23 *American Review of International Arbitration*, pp. 407-416; Loukas Mistelis, 'Arbitral Seats – Choices and Competition', in Stefan Kröll, Loukas Mistelis, Pilar Perales Viscasillas & Vikki Rogers (eds), *International Arbitration and International Commercial Law: Synergy, Convergence and Evolution* (Kluwer 2011), pp. 363-379. *See also* the various QMUL empirical surveys exploring popular arbiral seats: https://arbitration.qmul.ac.uk/media/arbitration/docs/2010_InternationalArbitrationSurveyReport.pdf and https://arbitration.qmul.ac.uk/media/arbitration/docs/LON0320037-QMUL-International-Arbitration-Survey-2021_19_WEB.pdf.
29. Mainly, IBA Rules on Taking of Evidence, and Prague Rules.
30. For example, IBA Guidelines on Conflicts of Interest, IBA Guidelines on Party Representation.
31. For example, Redfern schedule on document production.
32. Major databases such as www.kluwerarbitration.com, and www.jumundi.com and regular publications such as the ICCA Yearnook of Commercial Arbitration and the Institute of Transnational Arbitration (ITA) Report regularly publish arbitral case law, i.e., arbitral awards and national court.
33. There is, by contast, a high degree of transparency in investment arbitration. *See, e.g.*, www.italaw.com.

In terms of *methodology* the challenge is even greater: while it is important to explain the practice of a rather highly specialised area of law it is also crucial to cover theoretical aspects. Indeed, the concept of autonomy and transnationality are primarily theoretical but also have significant practical consequences. Understanding the practical connotations would inform the choice of arbitration rules and choice of arbitral seat (as well as the selection of counsel and arbitrators).

Hence, in addition to teaching the theory/ies of arbitration one has to teach private international law (how applicable law is determined), sources of law and their interpretation, and contract and treaty interpretation too. In this respect the interaction of hard and soft law and the interaction of mandatory law and permissive law is critical as is the understanding of hierarchy of sources.

It also goes without saying that arbitration is best delivered through classes which are structured as seminars or interactive lectures with substantial class participation and input (and a not a French style *conference*). Students take from classes as much preparation as they are putting in themselves.

A significant aspect of teaching methodology of transnational arbitration is the so-called experimental learning. In arbitration there is a significant number of moot courts[34] and several focus on commercial arbitration. This is undisputedly a very insightful way of acquiring skills and a some level of knowledge about transnational arbitration, assuming, of course, one agrees that there are different ways to moot effectively and not one-size-fits all. In other words transnational arbitration is inclusive and accommodates well cultural differences. Hence, in the teaching through moots it is essential to appreciate that different tribunals have different expectation and stylistic and cultural inflexibility may be detrimental to one's case. For example, cross-examination is approached differently in different cultures and therefore it is critical to 'understand' your tribunal. Such learning experiences, via moot or other experiential learning exercises are very useful indeed.

In terms of pedagogy, mooting has its challenges: it is suitable for smaller groups of students and it is very intense in terms of resources. It is, however, more impactful than any traditional lecture.

International commercial arbitration, i.e., arbitration of business disputes with cross-border or international elements, is transnational by nature and hence it has to be studied and experienced as the international subject it is. Comparative approach is not only useful, it is in fact essential. Challenging perceptions and taking nothing for granted is the bread-and-butter of global arbitration lawyers.

Julian Lew has set the foundation of this approach some 40 years ago and it must be rewarding and encouraging to see that nowadays there are dozens or arbitration programmes (most of which developed in the last 15 years) in universities all over the world. One can only hope that all these programmes are transnational by design and in terms of delivery and culture as was envisaged by the pioneer of international arbitration Julian Lew, was and is.

34. Mainly, in English, the Vis International Arbitration Moot and Cross-Examination Moot.

CHAPTER 40
Julian Lew as Mentor

Caroline Croft & Simona Valkova

Caroline Croft

It has been an honour to have been invited by the editors of this Liber Amicorum to reflect on Julian's influence and impact as a mentor. The exercise has been a wonderful opportunity to reflect on common experiences of working with Julian, and on his approach to work and life.

Young professionals today are often searching for mentors to guide them, motivate them and model themselves on. Mentors come in many forms, some overt and formally sought, and some arising simply through their presence in your life. My experience with Julian has had a subtle but profound effect on my approach to arbitration.

First, Julian has a truly international outlook. He launched the School of International Arbitration some 37 years ago which continues to go from strength to strength. Its intakes year after year include some of the best international talent. Julian's vision for the school was to create a forum which would encourage understanding, tolerance and respect for different viewpoints, cultures and systems. Julian's approach could be seen as somewhat militant. He was then (and still is) rejecting the universality of national approaches and recognized arbitration's unique ability to adapt to the mixing of views and cultures. In times of growing concerns over the judicialization or nationalization of arbitration or return to bigotry, it is helpful to reflect on those core values.

Second, Julian belongs to a class of arbitrators that approaches arbitration as a way to smooth out and resolve commercial differences. Julian embodies the values of collegiality, class and respect for the views of others. These values, applied to practice, have enabled him to understand that a good arbitrator is one who is able to provide different inputs depending on the situation – whether that be a facilitator for communication between the parties or an advisor and guide in the taking of hard decisions. Above all the arbitrator must be flexible.

Third, Julian encourages critical thinking in those around him. Thoughtful and reflective, Julian's scholarly work offers some deceivingly simple yet powerful thoughts. His maxim is to make sure you are able to convey your message in a way that is understood to others. Quality is important. Julian would be the first to admit that he is not a 'fuzzy' mentor who is there to make you feel good about yourself, but rather someone who demands high standards from himself and those around him, which forces us to perform beyond what we might think possible.

The common thread to these three reflections will be no surprise to those who know him; Julian likes to challenge and be challenged. Thirty-seven years ago he noticed that arbitration was not a subject taught at university, so Julian challenged the *status quo* in launching the School of International Arbitration. The way he teaches and practises international law is that of a truly comparative lawyer. What is accepted as true is one jurisdiction may be rejected by others. Julian applies this outlook in his work as an arbitrator and shows respect for the parties' multiplicity of views and backgrounds. He understood that the crux of an international outlook, whether in arbitration or otherwise, requires one to challenge the universality of one's own experiences. I have seen him encourage the rise of others, providing opportunities and advice to those attempting to follow in his footsteps. His legacy is one of teaching subsequent generations not just the legal principles of arbitration, but its underlying philosophy, giving them a touchstone for when they encounter a novel or difficult situation.

Simona Valkova

A King's Counsel, an arbitrator, and a professor of international arbitration. Just a few of the many hats that Julian wears daily, and for which he is internationally known. Yet, another hat that fits just as perfectly is that of a mentor.

I had the honour and pleasure of working with Julian for over three years, a period during which, he invested his time and energy in my personal and professional development, as he had done with many before me. Julian consistently showed me what a good lawyer and an arbitrator is and taught me how to think critically and always strive for perfection. His ability to approach issues from different perspectives, his capacity to keep an open mind despite the challenges he faces and his focus on the big picture are skills that I aspire to develop and deploy throughout my career. Julian's experience, scholarly writings and career are testament to the fact that in a world where disputes cross borders, and legal and cultural differences are most expressed, arbitration is the ideal forum of dispute resolution.

Julian is also a true visionary. He has the ability and intelligence to look into the future and the courage and determination to act, leading to a great success in the process. But more importantly, he has the generosity and kindness to then use this success for the benefit of others. Since launching the School of International Arbitration in 1985, Julian has been investing in the intellectual and professional development of numerous generations to come, be it as their LLM or PhD supervisor, their professor of international arbitration, or by simply offering them his invaluable mentorship.

Julian's passion for international arbitration and its development throughout the years is inspirational. He always had 'a dream' of achieving an 'autonomous international arbitration' – one which coexists with the different national laws, but it is above their direct control and that of the national courts.

His leadership often allowed him to translate this vision into reality through his extensive publication in the field since 1977 and active participation in various working groups and committees focused on the development of national and international arbitration rules and laws.

Recognizing that the success of international arbitration lies in its diversity and flexibility, Julian also established various initiatives in conjunction with the School of International Arbitration. The Annual Freshfields Arbitration Lecture and the ICC-SIA QMUL Annual Joint Symposium of Arbitrators are perhaps, two of the most prominent events which have built up a reputation of their own over the years. Although structured in different ways, the purpose of both events was essentially to create a space where the expression of new and different ideas was encouraged, the *status quo* was challenged, true intellectual and practical development was sought. Many more things can be said about Julian and his exceptional professional journey. But I will stop here and say one more thing only – Thank you, professor.

CHAPTER 41

Where Academic Scholarship and International Practice Converge

Eleanor Taylor

To dear Julian, I am honoured to be penning my first book chapter for your special 75th Birthday Liber Amicorum. When Stavros and Romesh first introduced the idea to me, and suggested including a contribution from Wolters Kluwer, I instantly accepted. At that point, without thought to what I would actually put down on paper, I knew if there was to be a special publication to honour you, and your contribution to the field of international arbitration, I wanted to be a part of it.

We have known each other since I started with Kluwer Law International in 2007, but your long-standing relationship with Wolters Kluwer significantly predates that. Your thesis on applicable law in international commercial arbitration[1] published with A.W. Sijthoff in 1978. It later become part of Wolters Kluwer's offering when Kluwer merged with Wolters Samsom circa 1987. And so, your relationship with Wolters Kluwer began. It was just the beginning of what would become a special and long-standing relationship and firmly establish you as a significant Wolters Kluwer author, thought leader and advocate.

It is quite incredible how the field of international arbitration, both practice and scholarship, has evolved during the years I have been with Wolters Kluwer. I fondly recall my first trip to the Willem C. Vis Moot in 2007, my first year at Kluwer Law International, a Wolters Kluwer company. At the time, Kluwer Law International were, I think, one of only two international arbitration publishers exhibiting in the top floor registration space of the Juridicum and, if I recall correctly, there were 100 or so moot teams competing. How times have changed!

Gwen (de Vries) first introduced us. I had only been at Kluwer Law International for a few weeks. Gwen flew over to London to introduce me to some of my important

1. Julian D.M. Lew, *Applicable Law in International Commercial Arbitration: A Study in Commercial Arbitration Awards* (Oceana Publications and Sijthoff & Noordhoff, 1978).

authors. As the series editor of the International Arbitration Law Library (IALL) series, we were going to be working closely together, but little did I know that, over the years, we would become friends too. What I then knew about international arbitration I could have written on a postage stamp. My knowledge, at that point, was very UK-centric from my previous publishing role. I was now the content person responsible for the prestigious Arbitration portfolio and, most importantly the much-acclaimed Kluwer Arbitration online service (that I was quickly becoming acquainted with).

Since 2007 we have drunk countless cups of tea together and wiled away countless hours speaking on the phone, discussing one arbitration-related topic, or another. When we met you were heading the International Arbitration Group at Herbert Smith, alongside your commitments at the School of International Arbitration, your writing projects, and arbitral appointments. However, as I think all will say throughout this publication, and all who know and work with you, you have always made time to speak with me. Now I'm not saying that I have never had to give you a friendly 'nudge' or had to reconvene our calls for a day when you had a bit more time, but never have you been too busy to give me, and any crazy arbitration ideas I have wanted to discuss, your full attention and consideration. Calls are never rushed, and there is always time to catch up on what family members are up to, both yours and mine. Margot and the girls, and now their own families, are at the fore of what you do. You talk of them with such pride and devotion, and it is lovely to hear.

As I recall, the IALL series, when I joined and took over the arbitration portfolio, consisted of approximately 15 titles, and was already an authoritative collection of comparative academic and practitioner titles. The IALL was very much your brain-child. Since the first volume published in 1993,[2] the series has published in-depth and analytical works on niche aspects of international arbitration, authored by specialists in the field. Not only did the books have to meet a high academic standard, you also ensured that the topics of the books were very relevant to practitioners. By keeping the bar high the series quickly got its authoritative reputation among both practitioners and academics.

The confluence of academic interest and practice is exactly why the IALL series, now in its 63rd Volume,[3] remains current today. And will continue to have value in an online age. The need for in-depth analysis will not disappear. By being an integral part of Kluwer Arbitration, the arbitration community will continue to have access to this incredible collection of topical and comparative commentaries.

The International Arbitration Law Library (IALL) series has gone from strength to strength. I remember having a discussion with you at some point about how we procure more PhD theses from universities outside of Europe. There was a conversation about writing letters to professors and introductions that we wanted to make, but neither were necessary. We started to receive a regular stream of thought-provoking

2. Moshe Hirsch, *The Arbitration Mechanism of the International Centre for the Settlement of Investment Disputes* (Wolters Kluwer, 1993).
3. Simon Foote, *The Bona Fide Investor: Corporate Nationality and Treaty Shopping in Investment Treaty Law* (Wolters Kluwer, 2021).

theses to review. Julian, that enviable arbitration library/bookshelf of yours must be very full indeed now.

Shortly before going on leave in 2019, we were preparing to celebrate our 50th IALL volume.[4] A wonderful achievement. We were in the exciting position of discussing how best we could celebrate the achievement – what to include on the book cover, the page in our eStore and exactly how we shout about this incredible milestone from the, metaphorical, rooftops.

Let us not forget Stavros' significant contribution. In 2018 we were delighted to welcome Stavros as co-General Editor of the series. It had become obvious that as the series was becoming larger and the amount of proposals we were receiving had increased significantly, that we required another pair of critical eyes to assist us. Stavros was the perfect choice, and I was thrilled he was able to join you as co-General Editor Julian.

In the meantime, Julian, you had retired from Herbert Smith and established yourself at Twenty Essex Street as a full-time arbitrator. And as seems the way in 'retirements' of this sort, you were becoming increasingly busier. I was becoming familiar with voices on reception at 20 Essex Street. But, as always, you made sure to call me back.

Julian, our working together has gone beyond the IALL series. I fondly remember working with you and the team, which you brought together, on *Arbitration in England*.[5] I knew at the time that something special was being created and that it would be a work that would be well received by the market, and inspire other works. It has done just that. I am proud to say that we now publish and include in Kluwer Arbitration, works on a broad range of jurisdictions including Sweden, Romania, India, Argentina, and Pakistan. Thank you, Julian, for your input and guidance on many of them.

Julian, you generously chaired my Kluwer Arbitration London Live event in 2018, the second live event Kluwer had hosted. I was delighted when you accepted. Being the busy international jet-setting arbitrator that you are, you asked me to check in with you two evenings prior to confirm that you were able to make it. I am very pleased you could – I had no back-up plan up my sleeve. And, as with all of the other projects we have worked on together, you did not let me down. Thank you. The session was a great success and the room was packed. In particular, I recall a really interesting panel discussion regarding academic publishing and the interplay between academia and practice – a topic very close to your heart.

I am smiling as I write this, and think back to Kluwer Arbitration London Live. I recall when I introduced one of your friends and co-authors to *Comparative International Commercial Arbitration*,[6] Stefan Kroll at the event. Stefan had kindly accepted a

4. Yulia Levashova, *The Right of States to Regulate in International Investment Law: The Search for Balance Between Public Interest and Fair and Equitable Treatment* (Wolters Kluwer, 2019).
5. Julian D.M. Lew, Harris Bor, Gregory Fullelove & Joanne Greenaway, *Arbitration in England with chapters on Scotland and Ireland* (Wolters Kluwer, 2013).
6. Julian D.M. Lew, Loukas Mistelis & Stefan Kroll, *Comparative International Commercial Arbitration* (Wolters Kluwer, 2003).

speaking spot and when I introduced him to the floor, I referred to him as being the co-author of *Comparative International Commercial Arbitration* and said that he was busily working on the second edition. Once the microphone was handed over to Stefan, and I was thanked for the introduction, he told me that the updating of the book was news to him! Julian, we still need to have that planning meeting about the second edition! I look forward to that.

Your input to scholarship in the field of international arbitration and in particular to Kluwer Arbitration is immense and it is incredible to think the impact the IALL series, with all of its 63 Volumes, has had on scholarship and international practice. When you published your thesis in 1978 international arbitration was not a distinct area of law/practice and yet now it is a topic taught by most universities and a busy practice area for major law firms.

Julian, over the years you have been a colleague, advisor and friend. You have generously given me your time, knowledge, expertise and warmth. When I returned from leave and resumed working on the IALL series again, I looked forward to speaking again and catching up on your news. I was thrilled to hear that you and Margot had become grandparents once again, and enjoying singing daily to your newest Australian-based family member.

Happy 75th Birthday Julian. I hope you enjoy your celebrations and I hope you enjoy reading this book that Stavros and Romesh have created for you. It has been a pleasure, and honour, to be involved in it.

Part III Personal Tributes

CHAPTER 42

Personal Tribute

Gloria Alvarez

I carry Julian's lessons everywhere I am. I met him in 2010, as my Professor of Comparative and International Commercial Arbitration. That privilege became very quickly an inspiration which transformed the rest of my professional life thereafter. I am an academic, because I want to display the same love and commitment that he shows to everyone in the classroom. I always wondered how after so many hours working in his chambers, he could always start a class with a good joke!

Of course, now, I keep asking my students what was first (chicken or egg?), and mostly in every conference I go to, I find the impact of his very seminal scholarship on autonomous arbitration. But, beyond that, Julian has taught me the one advice that only a real and generous mentor shares; which is to take pride in myself and my identity, and use my uniqueness to thrive as a female leader in arbitration.

I am not sure if words are enough to express all the respect and gratitude, I have for him. I know I will continue sharing his knowledge, take pride with me and of course try to share good jokes with students. Thank you, my dear Julian, for everything and feliz cumpleaños!

CHAPTER 43

Julian Lew: A Personal Tribute

Elizabeth Gloster

There are not many people whom I would classify as "inspirational" in my professional life, but Julian is firmly fixed in that small class of stars who have inspired me—as, I am sure, he has inspired many others. His invitation to me to deliver the annual Freshfields and Queen Mary University arbitration lecture opened the door for me to the exciting new world of arbitration. His generosity to me when, as a new recruit straight from the Bench, I started off down the arbitral path, was awesome. He not only gave me his time but also shared his vast experience with me. I have learnt so much from Julian—not just from his repertoire of scholarly writings, not just from the pleasure of sitting with him as an arbitrator, but from Julian, the person. I wish him all the very best for his 75th birthday.

CHAPTER 44

Personal Tribute

Doug Jones AO & Janet Walker CM

Julian's contribution to the practice and teaching of arbitration has been immense. As a senior counsel at Herbert Smith, he appeared in many significant arbitrations with renowned success; and later, as an arbitrator practising from 20 Essex, he was recognised by other arbitrators and by parties as one of the leading arbitrators. His teaching at Queen Mary University, London and his founding of the School of Arbitration represent iconic contributions to the field.

We have long been privileged to know Julian as a colleague and to count him among our dear friends. His warmth and generosity have made us feel all the more welcome in London in making it our second home; and his commitment to mentoring the next generation and to fostering in all of us an enduring spirit of inquiry have been an inspiration to us as practitioners and teachers of arbitration.

CHAPTER 45

Julian Lew: The Academic Teacher

Stefan Kröll

Julian has enjoyed a successful career in several fields. Beyond being a caring father he has been a partner in leading international litigation and arbitration firms, a world renown arbitrator in a prestigious barristers chamber and successful part-time academic which has influenced the careers of many of his former students, including mine.

I 'met' Julian for the first time in the library of the Institute for International Commercial law in Germany when doing research for a seminar, in form of his PhD-thesis and his book on the liability of arbitrators. Thus, it was clear that while doing my LLM in London I would drive out Monday evenings to Mile End to finally meet the author of the books in person.

Those lectures in the academic year 1992/1993 were the start of a relationship which lasted thirty years, included a jointly published treatise on Comparative International Commercial Arbitration and strongly influenced my own career as an academic in several respects.

First, being used to the German universities at the time, I was amazed how approachable Julian was for his students and how much he was interested in them. He took considerable time to discuss problems of my PhD-thesis with me, providing interesting and fascinating input from practice. In addition he also gave me access to his private library on arbitration which, at the time, was much better than the one at the British Institute of International and Comparative Law (BICL). I try to take the same approach to my students today, though I am by far not as entertaining as Julian in telling stories from practice to the next generation of arbitration students.

Second, at the time Julian drove me crazy with his style of lecturing. Instead of providing clear answers to the problems discussed he merely continued to ask questions and left many things open. In 1992 I still believed that there is a clear answer to every question ... only to drive my students mad today by asking more questions than providing answers. While there are probably still more answers than in Julian's lectures, I learned over the years not only to appreciate the values of the Socratic method cherished by Julian but also understood that the fact pattern encountered in arbitration are so diverse that they often prohibit simple answers.

Third, during the long discussions preceding the publication of our joint opus major on Comparative International Commercial Arbitration I learned from Julian that not every student in Vietnam speaks Latin (though I am still not entirely convinced as the sentence shows). Furthermore, Julian convinced me that sentences which go over several lines may be acceptable in German academic publishing but not for an international readership in a treatise on arbitration. And he even managed to convince me that there is rarely a clear right or wrong in international arbitration but only different arguments which may be weighed differently in different jurisdictions taking into account the particular circumstances of such jurisdictions. While that required at the time some mediation skills from Norah Gallagher and Loukas Mistelis, I am now largely subscribing to Julian's view.

Where we still disagree is as to the benefits of the concept of an entirely autonomous arbitration. But convincing a 'conservative' German on two out of three issues to change its view requires a very good teacher, i.e., someone like Julian.

I am certain that I am not the only one who has benefitted from his skills as a great teacher. Even if that were so: the School of International Arbitration as Julian's legacy to international arbitration will for many years still shape the knowledge and lives of future generations of students.

Ad multos annos!

CHAPTER 46
Personal Tribute

Mary Mitsi

Prof. Lew, the academic and teacher. When someone has the rare chance to be part of a socratic method of teaching, it becomes a memory to keep. Prof. Lew always started his first Comparative International Commercial Arbitration class with a question about the nature of international arbitration: Which came first, the chicken or the egg? This question was the beginning of a thought provoking dialogue with the students, as a way to encourage them to develop their arguments on the role of party autonomy in arbitration. In a concerted effort to explore their underlying beliefs, he shaped the student's views and encouraged an analytical and critical approach to arbitration.

Prof. Julian Lew, Head of the School of International Arbitration with a vision. He founded the school in 1985 when arbitration was considered part of procedural law and to see it as an autonomous field of law was a risky move at the time. In 2023, the School of International Arbitration counts more than 300 students that have embraced the allures of arbitration thanks to Julian's bravery to go beyond the procedure label. Students can choose from a number of modules including Investment Arbitration, Construction Arbitration and Energy arbitration proving that everything is a matter of perspective.

Prof. Julian D M Lew KC, the influential arbitrator. For a young lawyer and academic aspiring to practice in arbitration, having the chance to work with Julian is a blessing. He has the patience required to explain, clarify and repeat in a way that has shaped my understanding of how arbitration works in practice. The first lesson that will always stay with me is the respect with which he treats the parties emphasising that the arbitration belongs to them. The second lesson is that common sense plays a major role when acting as an arbitrator. Above all, he encouraged independent thinking and intellectual liberation being open to different views and approaches on every topic.

Julian, the mentor. Drawn into the world of a fascinating character is alone a source of inspiration. Coupled with kindness and always being there to offer support, Julian has shared a treasured insight in the complexity of (legal) life.

CHAPTER 47

Tribute to Julian Lew

William W. Park

Best wishes to Julian Lew.

Warmest congratulations to a great scholar, teacher, and colleague, on his 75th birthday.

From his friend, Rusty Park, Boston

CHAPTER 48
Personal Tribute

Stefan Riegler

While I had the privilege to be exposed to international arbitration fairly early in my career through the Willem C Vis Moot Court and my PhD thesis, it really was my time at Queen Mary's School of International Arbitration, London when I was taught about the fundamentals of what would later become the area of law I would be fortunate enough to practice. Back then, however, my expectation to be (simply and kindly) served with all the answers was – to my surprise – met with (almost Socratic) questioning by the head of the school, Professor Julian Lew. Julian did not waste time telling us what we could/should read for ourselves. Rather, by throwing questions, 'chicken and egg' dilemmas, etc. at us, Julian stimulated our thinking process so that we would first explore and then scrutinize, question and challenge the (perceived) basics of international arbitration.

The school has obviously become a tremendous success story, thanks to Julian. And his work as an academic, counsel and arbitrator is simply impressive.

A Liber Amicorum is well-deserved and was in fact long overdue.

Dear Julian, my sincere congratulations on your fabulous career.

CHAPTER 49

Personal Tribute

Sir Bernard Rix

It gives me the greatest possible pleasure to have the opportunity to record my sincere admiration for Julian Lew KC in this Liber Amicorum. I am grateful to count as one of his friends. I have known him for almost the whole of our professional lives. He has advised me with good humour and straightforward wisdom on the many gaps in my understanding of arbitration, even without me asking, and, when I asked, was always a fount of knowledge and good sense. I have heard him as a hugely impressive lecturer. I have enjoyed sitting in a room in chambers next to his, a great advantage for me. I regret not having had the chance of seeing him in action as a presider, but I can visualise him as an affable Solomon, for me the greatest compliment. I would have loved to have presented him with some accomplished chapter, but I feared I would not come up to his lofty standards. I send him my best of good wishes on this milestone, and look forward to sharing our wonderful profession for many more years to come.

CHAPTER 50

Dr Julian DM Lew KC and the Principles of Inclusion and Balance

Laurence Shore

There is little that Julian Lew has not accomplished in his professional and personal lives. In the international arbitration field, after he earned a doctorate in international law from the Catholic University of Louvain, Belgium, he built a career as a commercial arbitration practitioner and eventually created a vibrant practice group – facing more than a little resistance from national court litigators – at the Herbert Smith law firm (as it then was) in London. At the same time he was the prime mover in establishing the School of International Arbitration (SIA) in the Centre for Commercial Law Studies at Queen Mary University of London. The SIA remains a major force in arbitration scholarship and in furthering London's reputation as *the* global arbitration hub, attracting students, academics and practitioners from a multitude of jurisdictions. Julian then built yet another arbitration career, this time at the English bar, sitting as a full-time arbitration in investor-State as well as commercial arbitration cases. Along the way, he has been a teacher and mentor to hundreds of colleagues and a prolific lecturer and writer on arbitration topics.

While maintaining an incredibly busy career in arbitration, Julian has been a central figure in his community in London, and has enjoyed a wonderful family, which now features many grandchildren, and extends to Australia.

There are of course many reasons for Julian's professional and personal successes. Intelligence, hard work, kindness, and the highest ethical standards quickly come to mind. But I would like to focus on two principles that Julian has put into practice in his life in the law: inclusion and balance.

By inclusion, I mean Julian's practice of welcoming all those to the arbitration field, broadly defined, who wish to be part of an international community of practitioners and scholars. Simply put, Julian does not believe in barriers. He believes there is space for everyone. By way of example, perhaps some litigators wish to restrict advocacy opportunities in arbitration to trial lawyers and barristers; Julian believes that anyone can become an effective arbitration advocate and anyone who wishes to should be given the opportunity. Perhaps some construction specialists wish to restrict construction arbitration to those who allegedly hold that specialism; Julian believes that construction arbitration is, above all, arbitration. Perhaps some treaty specialists wish to restrict investor-State arbitration to public international law specialists; Julian believes that treaty arbitration is, above all, arbitration.

Julian's principle of inclusion has led him, from a very early stage of his leadership role in the profession, to lobby for bringing people from every jurisdiction into the field, paying particular attention to creating opportunities that are gender, race and age neutral. Discrimination of any type is repugnant to him. He has not had to 'adjust' to the push for diversity because he has always been a champion of diversity, whether as a law firm partner in developing the careers of associates or as an arbitrator in creating opportunities for younger practitioners to obtain their own arbitrator appointments. The principle of inclusion is a principal reason why Julian's work is known and appreciated worldwide. He loves his work, and this gives him the impetus to encourage younger lawyers to join the arbitral community.

But Julian also loves his family and his community. Unlike more than a few leaders in the field, Julian has achieved a remarkable 'work-life' balance *and* he wants all those with whom he works to achieve such balance. When his colleagues and mentees fall short in achieving the right balance, Julian does not hesitate to remind them that their responsibilities go well beyond the filing of an effective reply memorial or the issuance of a carefully designed procedural order; international arbitration does not, in his view, preclude – indeed, it must not preclude – devotion to family and community.

Julian is a greater respecter of certain traditions, but his adherence to the principles of inclusion and balance have also made him a modernist. His leadership in the field is therefore even more relevant in decades to come than in decades past. He truly deserves this book in his honour.

List of Publications

by Professor Julian D M Lew KC

Books

The Evolution and Future of International Arbitration, co-editor with Stavros Brekoulakis & Loukas Mistelis, Kluwer Law International, 2016

Arbitration in England with Chapters on Ireland and Scotland, co-editor with Harris Bor, Joanne Greenaway & Greg Fullelove, Kluwer Law International, 2013

Arbitration Insights – 20 Years of the Annual Lecture of the School of International Arbitration, co-editor with Loukas Mistelis, Kluwer Law International, 2007

Pervasive Problems in International Commercial Arbitration, co-editor with Loukas Mistelis, Kluwer Law International, 2006

Dossiers: Parallel State and State Arbitral Procedures in International Arbitration, co-editor with Bernardo M Cremades, ICC Institute of World Business Law, 2005

Comparative International Commercial Arbitration, joint author with Loukas Mistelis & Kröll, Kluwer Law International, 2003

Preface to 22nd edition of *Russell on Arbitration*, by David Sutton & Judith Gill, Sweet & Maxwell 2002

Enforcement of Foreign Judgements, co-edited with Louis Garb, Kluwer (loose-leaf)

Doing Business in Hungary, contributing author (for S J Berwin & Co), Confederation of British Industry, 1991

Doing Business in Czechoslovakia, contributing author (for S J Berwin & Co), Confederation of British Industry, 1991

The Immunity of Arbitrators, editor, School of International Arbitration and Lloyds of London Press, 1990

International Trade: Law and Practice, co-editor, 2nd edition, Euromoney, 1990

Contemporary Problems in International Commercial Arbitration, editor, Centre for Commercial Law Studies and Kluwer, 1986

International Trade, Law & Practice, co-editor, Euromoney, 1982

Selected Bibliography on International Commercial Arbitration, Oceana, 1979

Applicable Law in International Commercial Arbitration, Oceana, 1978

Selected Bibliography on East-West Trade, joint author with Clifford A. Rathkopf & Robert Starr, Oceana, 1976

English revision of: Istvan Szaszy, *Conflict of Laws in the Western, Socialist and Developing Countries*, Akademiai Kiado, 1974

Thesis

The Choice of the Application Law in International Commercial Arbitration, 3 vols, pp. 433, Index, Bibliography, Annexes, pp. 180 (Faculty of Laws, Université Catholique de Louvain)

Book Chapters

Forward in *Synergies of Legal Traditions in International Arbitration: Looking Beyond the Common and Civil Law Divide*, Stavros Brekoulakis and Nayla Comair-Obeid (eds), Kluwer Law International (2023)

Does Document Production add value in International Arbitration? forthcoming in Tribute to Professor Emmanuel Gaillard (Yas Banifatemi, ed. Forthcoming 2023)

'Cultures and the Taking of Evidence' (co-authored with Simona Valkova), in *Handbook of Evidence in International Commercial Arbitration: Key Concepts and Issues*, Franco Ferrari & Friedrich Jakob Rosenfeld (eds), Kluwer Law International, 2022, pp. 3-22

'Legal and Pragmatic Controls in International Arbitration', in *Reflections on International Arbitration – Essays in Honour of Professor George Bermann*, Julie Bedard & Patrick Pearsall (eds), Juris Publishing, 2022, pp. 307-321

'Procedural Efficiency: Prague Rules Applicable for the Particular Case', in *International Arbitration: When East Meets West – Liber Amicorum Michael Moser*, Neil Kaplan et al. (eds), Kluwer Law International, 2020, pp. 175-186

'Costs in International Arbitration: Can Costs Be Controlled?' in *Finances in International Arbitration: Liber Amicorum Patricia Shaughnessy*, Sherlin Tung et al. (eds), Kluwer Law International, 2019, pp. 291-298

Preface in *Rethinking Choice of Law in Cross-Border Sales*, Gustavo Moser, Eleven International Publishing, (2018)

'Practices, Arbitral Duties and Effects of Awards in Default Proceedings', in *Jurisdiction, Admissibility and Choice of Law in International Arbitration: Liber Amicorum Michael* Pryles, Neil Kaplan & Michael J. Moser (eds), Kluwer Law International, 2018, pp. 331-344

'Sulamérica and Arsanovia: English Law Governing Arbitration Agreements', in *Jurisdictional Choices in Times of Trouble, Dossiers of the ICC Institute of World Business Law*, Bachir Georges Affaki & Horacio Alberto Grigera Naón (eds), Volume 12, Kluwer Law International, ICC, 2015, pp. 136-144

Choice of Venue in International Arbitration (Foreword) in *Choice of Venue in International Arbitration*, Michael Ostrove et al. (eds), Oxford University Press, 2014, pp. v-vii

'The Tribunal's Rights and Duties: What do Parties and Arbitrators Bargain For?', in *Players' Interaction in International Arbitration: ICC Dossier IX*, Bernard Hanotiau & Alexis Mourre (eds), International Chamber of Commerce, 2013, pp. 47-64

'Development of the Arbitral System in England' (co-authored with Melissa Holm), in *Arbitration in England, with Chapters on Scotland and Ireland,* Julian D.M. Lew et al. (eds), Kluwer Law International, 2013, pp. 1-18

'Arbitrability' (co-authored with Oliver Marsden), in *Arbitration in England, with Chapters on Scotland and Ireland,* Julian D.M. Lew et al. (eds), Kluwer Law International, 2013, pp. 399-412

'Is There a Global Free-Standing Body of Substantive Arbitration Law?', in *International Arbitration: The Coming of a New Age? ICCA Congress Series No. 17,* Van den Berg, Albert Jan (ed.), Kluwer Law International, 2012, p 53-61

'Confidentiality in Arbitrations in England', in *Arbitration in England, with Chapters on Scotland and Ireland,* Julian D.M. Lew et al. (eds), Kluwer Law International, 2013, pp. 441-454

'The Basis for Applying Competition Law from and English Law Perspective', in *EU and US Antitrust Arbitration. A Handbook for Practitioners,* Gordon Blanke & Philip Landolt (eds), Kluwer Law International, 2011, pp. 785-809

'The Arbitrator and Confidentiality', in *Is Arbitration Only as Good as the Arbitrator? Status Powers and Role of the Arbitrator: ICC Dossier VIII,* Yves Derains & Laurent Lévy (eds), International Chamber of Commerce, 2011, pp. 105-129

'Document Disclosure, Evidentiary Value of Documents and Burden of Evidence,' in *Written Evidence and Discovery in International Arbitration, New Issues and Tendancies,* Teresa Giovannini & Alexis Mourre (eds), Kluwer Law International, ICC, 2009, pp. 11-27

'Competition Laws: Limits to Arbitrators' Authority', in *Arbitrability, International & Comparative Perspectives,* Loukas Mistelis & Stavros Brekoulakis (eds), Kluwer Law International, 2009, pp. 241-260

'LCIA Rules', in *Practitioners Handbook of International Commerical Arbitration* (2nd edn), Frank-Bernd Weigand (ed.), Oxford University Press, 2009, pp. 1616-1691

'Introduction: Fundamental Problems in International Arbitration', in Loukas A. Mistelis & Julian D.M. Lew (eds), *Pervasive Problems in International Arbitration,* International Arbitration Law Library, Volume 15, Kluwer Law International, 2006 pp. 1-8

'Foreword', in Ali Yesilirmak (ed.), *Provisional Measures in International Commercial Arbitration,* International Arbitration Law Library, Volume 12, Kluwer Law International, 2005, pp. v-vii

'Multi-Institutional Conciliation and the Reconciliation of Different Legal Cultures', in Albert Jan Van den Berg (ed.), *New Horizons in International Commercial Arbitration and Beyond,* ICCA Congress Series, Volume 12, ICCA & Kluwer Law International, 2005, pp. 421-429

'ICSID Arbitration: Special Features and Recent Developments', in Norbert Horn and Stefan Kroll, *Arbitrating Foreign Investment Disputes: Procedural and Substantive*

Legal Aspects, Studies in Transnational Economic Law, Volume 19, Kluwer Law International, 2004, pp. 267-282

'England as a Venue for International Commercial Arbitration', ICC Handbook 2002

'Arbitration and Other Dispute Settlement in Project Financing', in *Non-Judicial Dispute Settlement in International Financial Transactions*, Norbert Horn & Joseph L. Norton (eds), Kluwer Law International, 2000, p. 289

'Law Applicable to the Arbitration Clause', in *Improving the Efficiency of Arbitration Agreements and Awards: 40 Years of Application of the New York Convention*, Albert Jan van den Berg (gen. ed.), Kluwer Law International, 1999

'Relevance of Conflict of Law Rules in the Practice of Arbitration', in Albert Jan Van den Berg (ed.), *Planning Efficient Arbitration Proceedings: The Law Applicable in International Arbitration*, ICCA Congress Series, Volume 7, ICCA & Kluwer Law International, 1996, pp. 447-458

'The Case for Publication of Arbitration Awards', in *The Art of Arbitration: Essays on International Arbitration – Liber Amicorum Pieter Sander*s, Jan C. Schultsz and Albert Jan Van den Berg (eds.), Kluwer Law, 1982

Series Editor

International Arbitration Law Library (Kluwer)

Articles

'Law Governing the Arbitration Agreement' in *Arbitration and Beyond... une forme de vie - Liber Amicorum Pour Yves Derains*, Antonias Dimolitsa & Eduardo Silva Romero (eds), Pedone, 2021

Keynote Address: Transparency in International Arbitration: Practical Value or Voyeurism?, The American Review of International Arbitration, Vol. 31, No. 1, 2020

'Determining Relevancy of Facts in International Arbitration', in *Essays in Honour of Prof Dr Kaj Hober*, Eric Bylander, Anna Jonsson Corbek & Jakob Rangwaldh (eds), Iustus förlag, 2019, pp. 179-193

'International Commercial Arbitration: Harmonizing Cultural Differences' (co-authored with Laurence Shore), *Handbook on International Arbitration & ADR* (3rd edn), Juris Publishing, 2017, pp. 3-13

'Increasing Influence of Asia in International Arbitration', *Asian Dispute Review*, January 2014, pp. 4-9

'Panel 1: Decision-making and Deliberations: Steps and Issues', *Inside the Black Box: How Arbitral Tribunals Operate and Reach Their Decisions, ASA Special Series No 42*, Bernhard Berger & Michael E. Schneider (eds), 2014, pp. 13-14

'Serious Irregularity and Section 68 Applications to Court', in *Arbitrators' Insights: Essays in Honour of Neil Kaplan*, Bao, Chiann, & Felix Lautenschlager (eds), Thomson Reuters Hong Kong Ltd, 2013, pp. 217-230

'Fusion of Common Law and Civil Law Traditions in International Arbitration', in *The Practice of Arbitration: Essays in Honour of Hans van Houtte*, Wautelet, Patrick et al. (eds), Hart Publishing, 2012, pp. 1-12

'The Implications of the Dallah Case for International Commercial Arbitration', *Contemporary Issues in International Arbitration and Mediation, The Fordham Papers 2011*, Arthur W. Rovine, (ed.), BRILL, 2012, pp. 129-141

'International Commercial Arbitration: Harmonizing Cultural Differences', in *Handbook on International Arbitration & ADR* (2nd edn), AAA, Juris Publishing, 2012, p 3-13

'Iura Novit Curia and Due Process', in *Liber Amicorum en l'honneur de Serge Lazareff*, Laurent Levy and Yves Derains (eds), Editions A. Pedone, 2011, pp. 397-417

'Does National Court Involvement undermine the International Arbitration Process?', *American University Washington College of Law, Annual Lecture on International Commercial Arbitration*, 2007

'Achieving the Dream: Autonomous Arbitration?', in *Arbitration Insights: Twenty Years of the Annual Lecture of the School of International Arbitration*, Julian D.M. Lew and Loukas A. Mistelis (eds), Sponsored by Freshfields Bruckhaus Deringer, International Arbitration Law Library, Volume 16, Kluwer Law International, 2007, pp. 455-485

'When Should International Arbitrators Award Punitive Damages?', in *Contemporary Issues in International Arbitration and Mediation*, The Fordham Papers 2007, Arthur Rovine (ed.), BRILL, pp. 155-183

'Scope and Contents of the Request for Arbitration: A Comparative Perspective', in *Arbitral Procedure at the Dawn of the New Millenium*, Bruylant, 2005, pp. 29-40.

Session Two: The 'Fork in the Road' Revisited, TDM 4 (2005)

'Anti-suit Injunctions Issued by National Courts to Prevent Arbitration Proceedings', in *Anti-Suit Injunctions in International Arbitration*, Emmanuel Gaillard (ed.), Institute de l'arbitrage international, 2005, pp. 25-39.

'Panorama de Jurisprudence Anglaise', *Les Cahiers de L'Arbitrage*, No. 2003/2 - 2nde Partie, Gazette du Palais

'Panorama de Jurisprudence Anglaise', *Les Cahiers de L'Arbitrage*, No. 2003/1 - 1iere Partie, Gazette du Palais

'The UNIDROIT Principles on Lex Contractus Chosen by the Parties and Without an Explicit Choice of Law Clause: The Perspective of Counsel', in *UNIDROIT Principles of International Commercial Contracts – Reflections on their Use in International Arbitration*, 85, Special Supplement, ICC Bulletin (2002)

'Panorama de Jurisprudence Anglaise', *Les Cahiers de L'Arbitrage*, No. 2002/2 - 2nde Partie, Gazette du Palais

'Panorama de Jurisprudence Anglaise', *Les Cahiers de L'Arbitrage*, No. 2002/1 - 1iere Partie, Gazette du Palais

'Arbitrator's Control of Tactical and Procedural Issues in the 21st Century', *Foundations and Perspectives of International Trade Law*, Ian F. Fletcher, Loukas Mistelis & Marise Cremona (eds), Sweet & Maxwell, 2001, p. 247

'Dispute Settlement for Biotechnology Transactions' (with Andrew Rich). *Patent Law*, June/July 2001, 27

'International Dispute Settlement for Biotechnology Transactions'. *The Journal of Biolaw & Business*, Special Supplement, 2000, 56

'Multiparty Arbitrations', *Stockholm Arbitration Newsletter*, 2/2000
'Winning in the legal arena', *Financial Times*, 27 September 2000
'Commentary on Interim and Conservatory Measures in ICC Arbitration Cases', *The ICC International Court of Arbitration Bulletin*, Vol. 11, No. 1, Spring 2000, 23
'Proof of Applicable Law in International Commercial Arbitration', in *Festschrift für Otto Sandrock*, Klaus P Berger, Werner F. Ebke, Siegfried Elsing, Bernhard Grosfeld, Gunther Kuhne (eds), Verlag Recht und Wirtschaft GmbH, 2000, p. 601
'Achieving the Potential of Effective Arbitration', *Arbitration* (Millennium Issue), November 1999, 283
'Harmonizing Cultural Differences' (co-authored with Laurence Shore), *Dispute Resolution Journal*, Vol. 54, No. 3, 1999
'Arbitration in England and under English Law', in *Arbitragem Comercial Internacional*, Adriana Noemi Pucci (ed.), Editora LTR, 1998, 209
'Practical Developments in International Commercial Arbitration', in *Guide to the World's Leading Experts in Commercial Arbitration*, Euromoney, 1998
'Final Report on Intellectual Property Disputes and Arbitration', ICC Commission on International Arbitration, *The ICC International Court of Arbitration Bulletin*, Vol. 9, No. 1, May 1998, 37
'Contemporary International Law Issues: New Forms New Applications', in *Party Autonomy and the Application of Mandatory Public Law in Arbitration*, 1997 Hague Joint Conference of the American Society of International Law, T.M.C. Asser Instituut, The Hague, 1997, 176
'Determination of Applicable Substantive Law', *International Business Law*, Vol. 25, No. 4, April 1997, 157
'Interest on Money Awards in International Arbitration', in *Making Commercial Law – Essays in Honour of Roy Goode*, Ross Cranston (ed.), Clarendon Press, 1997, pp. 543-569
'New Act/New Look for English Arbitration', *ADR Currents* (Newsletter of Dispute Resolution and Practice), Summer 1996
'The Facts of Arbitration' *Financial Times*, 21 May 1996
'The 1995 Arbitration Bill', *International Commercial Litigation*, [1995], 45
'Dust Settles over Disputes', *Financial Times*, 15 August 1995
'Expert Report of Dr Julian D M Lew (in *Esso/BHP v Plowman*)' Confidentiality Issue, Arbitration International, Vol. (1995), 283
'A Question of Costs' *Financial Times*, 28 June 1994
'The Arbitration of Intellectual Property Disputes', *The American Review of International Arbitration*, Vol. 5, Nos 1-4, 1994
'ICC Working Party on Intellectual Property Disputes and Arbitration', in *Objective Arbitrability – Antitrust Disputes – Intellectual Property Disputes*: A Collection of Reports and Materials delivered at the ASA Conference held in Zurich on 19 November 1993 Report, ASA Special Series No. 6 [1994]
'Why Not Arbitrate Your IP Disputes?', in *Managing Intellectual Property* (June 1993), 19

'The Place of Arbitration and the Applicable Law in English Common', in *The Place of Arbitration*, M. Storme and F. de Lys (eds), Mys & Breesch, 1992, p. 77

'Privatisation and Joint Ventures in Czechoslovakia', in *Acquisition Monthly*, June 1991

'Happier to Settle out of Court', *The Times*, 2 October 1990

'International Licensing Contracts', *International Trade: Law and Practice*, Vol. I, 71

'Source of International Finance', *International Trade: Law and Practice*, Vol. II, 13

'Immunity of Arbitration under English Law', *The Immunity of Arbitrators*, 21

'The School of International Arbitration', *Journal of International Arbitration* Vol. 5 (1988), 127

'Determination of Arbitrators' Jurisdiction and the Public Policy Limitations on That Jurisdiction', *Contemporary Problems*, 73

'The Recognition and Enforcement of Arbitration Agreements and Awards in the Middle East', *Arbitration International* Vol. 1 (1985), 161

'Licensing Agreements and EEC Anti-Trust Law', *Swiss Review of Anti-Trust Law* (1984)

'Privacy and the Regulation of Data Banks' British Government Proposals', *Business Law Review* Vol. 3 (1982), 168

'Privacy and the Regulation of Data Banks', *Business Law Review* Vol. 3 (1982), 103

'The Case for the publication of Arbitration Awards' in the Art of Arbitration, *Essays on International Arbitration Liber Amicorum for Pieter Sander*, (1984), Jan C Schultsz and Albert Jan Van Den Berg (eds)

'Doing Business in Yugoslavia', *Business Law Review*, August, 1981

'Doing Business in Romania', *Business Law Review*, July, 1981

'Doing Business in Poland', *Business Law Review*, June, 1981

'The Iran-United States Arbitration' (The American Hostages Arbitration), *Business Law Review*, May, 1981

'EEC Law Restriction on Arbitration', Law Society Gazette 78, 18 March 1981, 299

'Doing Business in the German Democratic Republic', *Business Law Review*, January 1981

'Legal Aspects of Doing Business in Hungary', *Business Law Review*, January, 1981

'Legal Aspects of Doing Business in the GDR', *Business Law Review*, December 1980

'Legal Aspects of Doing Business in Czechoslovakia', *Business Law Review*, November 1980

'Legal Aspects of Doing Business in Bulgaria', *Business Law Review* October 1980

'Legal Aspects of Doing Business in the USSR', *Business Law Review*, Part I, April 1980; Part II, May 1980

'Doing Business in Britain', in CCH *Doing Business in Europe Reporter* (1980)

'Bona Fides in International Commercial Arbitration', in *the Hague-Zagreb Colloquium Essays 3, Carriage of goods by sea maritime collisions, maritime oil pollution, commercial arbitration*, Cornelis Carel Albert Voskuil and J.A.Wade (eds), T.M.C. Asser Institute the Hague (1980)

'Matrimonial Property, Private International and English Law', in *Le régime matrimonial et le droit international privé*'. Notariat Latin, Nêuchatel, Michel Verwilghen (eds) 1979

'The Structure and Role of Arbitration in Eastern Europe', *Arbitration Journal* (UK), Vol. 44 (1978), 210

'The Extra-Territorial Criminal Jurisdiction of the English Courts', *I.C.L.Q.*, Vol. 27 (1978), 160

'Commercial World', 127 *NLJ* 321, 31 March 1977. 127 *NLJ* 909, 15 September 1977

'Sovereign Immunity and International Law', 127 *NLJ* 732, 28 July 1977

'Recognition and Enforcement of Arbitration Awards in England', *International Lawyer* Vol. 10 (1976), 425

'Commercial World':

126 *NLJ* 72, 15 January 1976	126 *NLJ* 738, 22 July 1976
126 *NLJ* 195, 19 February 1976	126 *NLJ* 849, 19 August 1976
126 *NLJ* 296, 18 March 1976	126 *NLJ* 93-4, 16 September 1976
126 *NLJ* 408, 22 April 1976	126 *NLJ* 1049, 21 October 1976
126 *NLJ* 516, 20 May 1976	126 *NLJ* 1148, 18 November 1976
126 *NLJ* 610, 17 June 1976	126 *NLJ* 1248, 16 December 1976

'International Law: A Dismil Picture,' 126 *NLJ* 1872, 26 August 1976

'Jewish Law: Its Development and Co-existence in the Non-Jewish World,' *Rabels Zeitschrift fÜr Ausländisches und Internationales Privatrecht* Vol. 40 (1976), 101

'Economic Coercion, Economic Cooperation and International Law', *NLJ* Vol. 125 (27 November 1975), 1145

'EEC Draft Bankruptcy Convention', 125 *NLJ* 628, 26 June 1975

'The 5th International Arbitration Congress', New Delhi, January 1975, 125 *NLJ* 148, 13 February 1975

'The 56th International Law Association Conference', New Delhi, 1974, 125 *NLJ* 124, 6 February 1975

'Acquittals: Further Statistics', 125 *NLJ* 45, 9 January 1975

'The Arbitration Act 1975', *I.C.L.Q.* 24 (1975), 870

'La loi applicable aux contrats internationaux dans la jurisprudence des tribunaux internationaux', *Le contrat économique international*, Bruylant, 1975

Series of Articles entitled *'Legal Aspects of East West Trade'*:

(i) 'An Outline of the Problems of East-West Trade', Volume 124 *New Law Journal (NLJ)* 275, 21 March 1974;
(ii) 'Comecon' 124 *NLJ* 294 28 March 1974;
(iii) 'Structure of Foreign Trade Machinery', 124 *NLJ* 321, 4 April 1974;
(iv) 'Techniques of Doing Business', 124 *NLJ* 345, 11 April 1974;
(v) 'Promoting the Product', 124 *NLJ* 369, 18 April 1974;
(vi) 'Export Contracts', 124 *NLJ* 389, 25 April 1974;

(vii) 'UK Import and Export Controls', 124 *NLJ* 529, 6 June 1974;
(viii) 'Export Financing', 124 *NLJ* 553, 13 June 1974;
(ix) 'Bilateral Commercial Agreements', 124 *NLJ* 580, 20 June 1974;
(x) 'Co-operation Agreements' 124 *NLJ* 601, 27 June 1974;
(xi) 'Licence and Know-how Agreements', 124 *NLJ* 675, 18 July 1974;
(xii) 'East West Trade Arbitration', 124 *NLJ* 675, 18 July 1974;
(xiii) 'The Place of Comecon and the EEC in East West Trade Relations', 124 *NLJ* 697, 25 July 1974;
(xiv) 'Conclusion', 124 *NLJ* 724, 1 August 1974

Acquittals - A statistical Analysis'

123 *NLJ* 1104, 4 December 1973 (with co-author)

'Jewish Divorces - Limping Marriages'

123 *NLJ* 829, 11 September 1973

'Public Policy, Time and the Conflict of Laws'
Study presented to the Academy of International Law, Research Session, Summer 1971
'Shot-Down Aircraft - Legal Implications'

123 *New Law Journal NLJ* 480, 3 May 1973

'Law Applicable to International Contracts as Determined by Arbitration Tribunals in the Light of Disputes Before Them'
Paper delivered and published in Le Contrat Economique International, VIIe Journée d'Etudes Juridiques Jean Dabin, Louvain, Belgium. 1973, Vol.I, 1-A-5
'Commercial Arbitration in Yugoslavia - Procedural Rules and Regulations'

XIII *Rassegna dell 'Arbitrato* 97, (1973) (Italy)

'Commercial Arbitration Yugoslavia - Law applied to substantive disputes as illustrated by decisions of the Yugoslav Federal Arbitration Chamber'

28 *Arbitration Journal* 43, (1973) (USA)

Book Reviews

'Internationalisation of Arbitration'
'Arbitration Agreements: Form and Character', in *Essays on International Commercial Arbitration*, P. Sarcevic (ed.), Graham & Trotman/Martinus Nijhoff, 51
'Register of Laws of the Arabian Gulf', *Arbitration International* Vol. 5 (1989), 86
C. Schmitthoff, *Export Trade* (7th edn), Stevens, 1980, *Business Law Review* March 1981

L. Kos-Rabcewicz-Zubkowski, *Commercial and Civil Law Arbitration in Canada*, UOP, 1979, 30, *I.C.L.Q.*, 275 (1981)

Doing Business in Brazil, ed. Pinheiro, Neto & Cia, Oyez, 1979: *BLR*, January 1980

G. Wetter, *Arbitration in Sweden*: 28 I.C.L.Q. 535 (1979) R.M. Goode and K.R. Simmonds, eds., *Commercial Operations in Europe*: 28 *I.C.L.Q.* 783 (1979)

Ivan Szasz, *A Uniform Law of International Sales of Goods: The CMEA General Conditions*: 128 *NLJ* 30, 12 January 1978

A.C. Foustoucos, *L'arbitrage – interne et international – en droit privé hellénique*: 27 *I.C.L.Q.* 473 (1978)

J.-G. Castel, *Canadian Conflict of Laws and Cases, Notes and Materials on the Conflict of Laws*: 127 *NLJ* 933, 22 September 1977

P. Verrucoli, *Italian Company Law, European Commercial Law Liberty*, No. 5: 127 *NLJ* 1046, 27 October 1977

Bernardo Cremades, *Panoramica Espagnole del Arbitraja Comercial Internacional*: 43 *Arbitration Journal* (UK) 99 (1977)

Henri Motulski, *Ecrits, études et notes sur l,arbitrage:* 25 *I.C.L.Q.* 470 (1976)

Bernard Jackson, *Essays in Jewish and Comparative Legal History*: 25 *I.C.L.Q.* 707 (1976)

Avner Tomaschoff ed., *Contemporary Thinking in Israel: Halacha*: 5 Ha-Zvi 30 (1976)

Association Européenne d'Etudes Juridiques et Fiscal, *Product Liability in Europe:* 126 *NLJ* 451, 29 April 1976

Italian Arbitration Association, *Multilateral Conventions and Other Instruments on Arbitration*: 25 *I.C.L.Q.* 252 (1976)

Concordat Suisse sur l'arbitrage: 25 *I.C.L.Q.*, 253 (1976)

Sykes and Pryles, *A Casebook on International and Interstate Conflict of Laws:* 126 *NLJ* 121, 29 February 1976

Mathijson, *a Guide to European. Community Law:* 126 *NLJ* 20, 29 January 1976

Collins, *Europe Community Law in the United Kingdom*: 125 *NLJ* 1206, 11 December 1975

Lowndes & Rudolf, *The Law of General Average and the York-Antwerp Rules*: 125 *NLJ* 1125, 20 November 1975

Jacobs & Durand, *Reference to the European Court*: 125 *NLJ* 876, 4 September 1975

Gill, *Law of Arbitration*, 2nd ed. (Sweet & Maxwell, London 1975): 125 *NLJ* 631, 26 June 1975

Batiffol – Lagarde, *Traité de droit international .privé*, tôme 1, 6th edn (Dalloz, Paris 1974): 24 *I.C.L.Q.* 895 (1975)

Ficzere, *The Socialist State Enterprise*, Budapest, 1974: 24 *I.C.K.Q.* 596 (1975)

Blegvad, Bolding, Lando, *Arbitration as a Means of Solving Conflicts*, Copenhagen, 1973: 24 *I.C.K.Q.* 595 (1975)

Meznerics, *Law of Banking in East-West Trade*: 24 *I.C.L.Q.* 192 (1975)

Török, *The Socialist System of State Control*, Budapest, 1974: 24 *I.C.l.*

Reports of Conferences

International Commercial Arbitration: Report on the British Institute of International Comparative Law Conference, London October 3-6, 124 *NLJ* 976, 24 October 1974

Conference papers

'Internationalisation of Arbitration – The Answer to Unification' presented at the 5th International Arbitration Congress, New Delhi, January 1975

Julian D.M. Lew

Julian D M Lew KC

Resume

Professor Julian Lew was born in South Africa in 1948. He obtained a an LLB from the University of London in 1969 and a Doctorat Spécial en Droit International Prive from the Université Catholique de Louvain, Belgium in 1977. Julian became a Barrister at Law, Middle Temple, in 1970 before qualifying as a Solicitor of the Supreme Court of England & Wales in 1981 and then in 1985 an Attorney at Law, New York.

Julian's professional life has been dedicated to dispute resolution, particularly international arbitration, with a focus on public and private international law in practice and as an academic.

In 2003, Julian was appointed as Queen's Counsel (now King's Counsel) as a solicitor. Julian is proud to have practised as a partner and Head of International Arbitration at Herbert Smith LLP until 2005 when he became a full-time arbitrator at Twenty Essex. As an international arbitrator, Julian has accepted appointments in commercial and investor-state arbitrations under the rules of all major arbitral institutions and sits on the panel on many of the world's leading arbitral institutions.

He has been involved in the development of international arbitration including being Chairman of the Chartered Institute of Arbitrators Law Reform Committee (1991-1996), a Director of the LCIA (1984-2008), a member of the LCIA Court (2000-2008), UK member of the ICC International Court of Arbitration (2006-2018), member of the SIAC Court of Arbitration (2014-2016) and member of the HKIAC Advisory Board (since 2014). He was a member of the ICC Commission on International Arbitration (1990 -2018), Chairman of the ICC Commission Task Force on Intellectual Property Disputes and Arbitration (1992-1998), and Co-Chair of the ICC Task Force on Decisions as to Costs in International Arbitration (2012-2016). He was also a member of the Council of the ICC Institute of World Business Law.

Julian has always maintained his academic interests and accepted academic appointments commencing with Charge d'enseignment, Université De Namur, Belgium, 1976-1979 and Charge d'enseignment and Université Catholique de Louvain, Belgium, 1977-1979. Julian was a founder and has been a Professor and Head of School of International Arbitration, Centre for Commercial Law Studies, Queen Mary, University of London, since its establishment in 1985. In this period the School of International Arbitration has grown to become a home to seven academics, and over 4,000 students.

Index

D

E

F

G

T

U

V

www.ingramcontent.com/pod-product-compliance
Lightning Source LLC
LaVergne TN
LVHW010630300926
849162LV00001B/114